LQ
1977

MODERN CHRISTIAN THOUGHT

MODERN CHRISTIAN THOUGHT

From the Enlightenment to Vatican II

James C. Livingston

The Macmillan Company, New York
Collier-Macmillan Limited, London

The Macmillan Company
866 Third Avenue, New York, New York 10022

Collier-Macmillan Canada, Ltd., Toronto, Ontario

Library of Congress catalog card number: 76-121675

First Printing

CREDITS

Appreciation is expressed to the following authors, publishers, and organizations for permission to reprint excerpts from their publications:

Oxford University Press for excerpts from *An Essay Concerning Human Understanding* by John Locke, edited by A. S. Pringle-Pattison, 1956; *The Oxford Movement*, edited by Eugene R. Fairweather, 1964; and *God and Incarnation in Mid-Nineteenth Century German Theology*, edited by Claude Welch, 1965.

Stanford University Press and A. and C. Black Ltd. for excerpts reprinted from *The Reasonableness of Christianity* and *A Discourse of Miracles* by John Locke, edited by I. T. Ramsey, with the permission of the publishers, Stanford University Press. © 1958 by A. and C. Black Ltd.

Stanford University Press and A. and C. Black Ltd. for excerpts reprinted from *Lessing's Theological Writings* translated and edited by Henry Chadwick with the permission of the publishers, Stanford University Press. Copyright 1956 by A. and C. Black Ltd.

Cambridge University Press for excerpts from *Religious Thought in the Eighteenth Century* by Creed & Boys Smith, Cambridge University Press, 1934.

E. P. Dutton & Company and J. M. Dent & Sons for excerpts from *Emile: Or Education* by Jean Jacques Rousseau, translated by Barbara Foxley. Everyman's Library edition. Reprinted by permission of E. P. Dutton & Co., Inc. and J. M. Dent & Sons Ltd.

The Bobbs-Merrill Company and Thomas Nelson & Sons Ltd. for excerpts from David Hume: *Dialogues Concerning Natural Religion*, edited by Norman K. Smith, copyright © 1947 by Thomas Nelson & Sons Ltd., reprinted by permission of The Liberal Arts Press Division of The Bobbs-Merrill Company, Inc.

The Bobbs-Merrill Company for excerpts from David Hume: *An Inquiry Concerning Human Understanding*, edited by Charles W. Hendel, copyright © 1955 by The Liberal Arts Press Division of The Bobbs-Merrill Company, Inc.

Macmillan & Co. Ltd., The Macmillan Company of Canada, and St. Martin's Press, New York, for excerpts from Immanuel Kant, *Critique of Pure Reason*, translated by Norman K. Smith.

The Open Court Publishing Company, La Salle, Illinois, for excerpts from *Religion Within the Limits of Reason Alone* by Immanuel Kant (Torchbook edition, 1960).

Harper & Row, Publishers, for excerpts from *On Religion* by Friedrich Schleiermacher, translated by John Oman, 1958.

Stanford University Press and A. and C. Black Ltd. for excerpts reprinted from *Confessions of an Inquiring Spirit* by Samuel Taylor Coleridge, edited with an Introductory Note by H. St. J.

To My
Mother and Father
Nan and Deno

and to
Jackie
with Love

PREFACE

This book was born of a certain exigency. Teaching modern Christian thought for several years has convinced me of the need for a text covering the important intellectual developments in the history of modern Christianity. Older books in this genre are out of date and fail to deal adequately, if at all, with figures and movements now considered important, and with developments in this century. It is my intention and hope that this book can free the instructor from the necessity of lecturing on all the major developments in modern Christian thought, so that in the classroom he can pursue particular thinkers, movements, and problems in some detail and also concentrate on other matters not covered in this text.

The range of this work makes me painfully aware of the audacity of the enterprise I have undertaken. Few scholars could feel comfortable in attempting to do justice to so many thinkers and movements of the modern period. Some indication of the guiding principles and limits which I have set for myself will give the reader a clearer notion of the nature and purpose of the book. First of all, the book is not a history of modern Christian thought in the strict sense. There is no attempt to be comprehensive, and little attention is given to historical origins, developments, cultural influences, or the connections between the several movements. Such an effort would require several volumes and a historian of Promethean learning.

The book attempts a study of some of the major intellectual movements in modern Christian thought. Each chapter concerns itself with a separate movement and is relatively independent. The chapters follow essentially the same format: the historical setting of the movement is traced briefly, followed by a longer exposition of the distinctive ideas of the movement *as exemplified in the thought of a few major representative thinkers*. Selectivity, not comprehensiveness, has been the goal. I have made extensive use of quotations from primary works so that the reader can be engaged with a thinker's own ideas and then be assisted in understanding their meaning and import through further elucidation and analysis. In this I was guided by the masterful example of John Herman Randall's *The Making of the Modern Mind*.

The book focuses on developments in historical and philosophical theology, i.e., with the encounter between Christian thought and modern philosophy, history, and the natural sciences. It is not concerned with schools of theology or dogmatic developments *per se*, nor with the evolution of liturgical, ascetical, and moral theology or ecclesiastical structures. This, for example, is why the book gives special attention to such movements as Modernism and Neo-Thomism in the history of modern Roman Catholicism. This also explains the inclusion of such figures as Voltaire, Feuerbach, and Nietzsche. I agree with Berdyaev's claim that most of the great modern philosophers are "Christian" philosophers in the sense that without Christianity their philosophies would have been very different and, I might add, without whom Christian thought would not be exactly where it is today.

The book begins with the Enlightenment for two reasons, one substantive, the other practical. I have followed the lead of Ernst Troeltsch and others in the conviction that the real beginning of *modern* Christian thought is traceable to the scientific and philosophical revolutions of the seventeenth and eighteenth centuries and not to the Reformation, which was still largely Medieval in outlook. The practical reasons for beginning with the Enlightenment are that several excellent, up-to-date studies of the Reformation are available and that the attempt to deal adequately in one volume with developments in Christian thought since the sixteenth century invites superficiality.

There is also some indication that we are rapidly moving into a new postmodern era and that the Christianity that evolves will reveal thought forms and ways of doing theology that are radically different from the forms that we have come to identify with either the Medieval or Modern periods. Doubtless others see the history of the Modern period from quite another perspective, but I view it as a watershed in Christian history. It represents a series of severe crises marked by creative responses and advances. The last two hundred years have witnessed the most serious intellectual assaults against Christianity in its entire history—assaults that, nevertheless, have met with extraordinary resilience. Christianity today finds itself in a predominantly secular environment; nonetheless, it reveals considerable vitality.

Because the book is concerned with distinct movements of religious thought, I have not attempted a systematic study of

the historical development of certain key themes—e.g., God, Christology, the doctrine of man, and so on. Nevertheless, the reader will note that the author has concentrated on a few problems that have emerged again and again in the modern history of Christian theology. These include the problem of religious authority, whether it is to be concentrated in the individual reason, in the Church, or in the Bible; the question of the historical claims of Christianity, especially as they relate to the interpretation of the Bible and the problem of the historical Jesus; and the question of our knowledge of God and his relation to the world. These problems continue at the center of theological discussion today.

I have not attempted a moral appraisal of the historical development and direction of Christian thought since the eighteenth century. That accommodation to secularism has taken place on a wide scale and that this is largely irreversible is recognized and is not to be lamented. We are modern men, whether we like it or not. However, the notion, common in some circles, of the inevitable demise of Christianity through abject capitulation to modernity appears to me to be unwarranted on the basis of the evidence of the last two hundred turbulent years. Neither does it appear that Christian theologians will take to the ghetto and hold to entrenched positions in the teeth of change. The future will probably reveal a continuing series of challenges and creative responses. At least the modern history of Christianity leaves me rather hopeful for the future of Christian theology.

A word is perhaps in order on the book's treatment of twentieth-century movements. Most courses on the modern period get well into this century—at least to the demise of the older Liberalism and the emergence of Neo-Orthodoxy and Existentialism. These recent movements will no doubt be viewed from a quite different vantage in another generation or two. While this part of the book is the result of a certain inescapable myopia, I believe there is wide agreement on the choices I have made.

In writing a book of this scope one becomes especially aware of his indebtedness to others. My greatest debts are twofold. First, to my mentors at Kenyon College, Columbia University, and especially Union Theological Seminary in New York, who tutored me in the history of religious ideas; and, secondly, to the scholars, too numerous to mention, whose pioneering works serve as the indispensable foundation of this book. Specialists in the field will easily recognize my dependence. Partial acknowledgment is given to these scholars in the footnotes and bibliographies.

I also wish to take this opportunity to thank the President and Fellows of Clare Hall, Cambridge University, the Provost and Department of Religion of Southern Methodist University, and the College of William and Mary for making available funds and secretarial aid for the typing of the manuscript. Mrs. Mary Petty typed a good portion of the book in two drafts, usually under pressure of time. Her flawless work saved me hours of labor, for which I am very grateful. My wife, Jackie, assisted in numerous editorial tasks at every stage of the book's progress. She was especially helpful in stylistic matters and spared me many a gaffe. There is a limit, of course, to what even a wife can do, so I must take responsibility for the form of the book as it stands. Especially warm thanks are also owed my editors, Charles E. Smith and Joan Delaney, whose interest and considerateness have exceeded every expectation. A final word of appreciation is due those publishers who generously permitted their books to be quoted in the text and to Wendell S. Dietrich of Brown University who read the manuscript in its last stages and offered numerous helpful suggestions, several of which were adopted.

The College of William and Mary   J. C. L.

CONTENTS

CHAPTER ELEVEN
Neo-Orthodoxy 301

CHAPTER TWELVE
Christian Existentialism 345

CHAPTER THIRTEEN
Neo-Thomism 385

CHAPTER FOURTEEN
American Empirical and Naturalistic Theology 418

CHAPTER FIFTEEN
Christian Realism: Post-Liberal American Theology 446

H. R. Niebuhr / Faith in Gods and in God Inner and Outer History **Reinhold Niebuhr** / The Nature of Man The Dramas of History Love, Justice, and Power

CHAPTER SIXTEEN
Some Contemporary Trends 478

Radical Secular Theology / **Process Thought: A New Christian Natural Theology?** / **The Impact of Vatican II**

CHAPTER ONE

The Enlightenment
and Modern Christianity

Immanuel Kant

"Enlightenment," said Immanuel Kant, "is man's release from his self-incurred tutelage. Tutelage is man's inability to make use of his understanding without direction from another. . . . *Sapere aude!* ('Dare to know.') 'Have courage to use your own reason!'—that is the motto of the enlightenment."[1]

The term Enlightenment signifies that period of European history from the close of the Thirty Years War (1648) to the French Revolution. In the realm of ideas it is often designated as that era of modern thought from Francis Bacon's *Novum Organum* (1620) to Kant's *Critique of Pure*

Reason (1781). It is the age which brought together the humanistic spirit of the Renaissance and the scientific revolution of the seventeenth century and thereby ushered in what we call "the modern world." It was this period of roughly a century and a half that witnessed a general change in man's world-view of the most wide-ranging and deepest significance.

It is the conviction of many historians, and the contention of this study, that the *modern* history of Christian thought begins not with the Reformation of the sixteenth century but rather with that movement of the eighteenth century known as the

1

Enlightenment. All history is continuous, and the periodization of history into discrete epochs or world-views is never completely successful. Nevertheless, it is correct to say that there is more in common between the world views of the thirteenth and sixteenth centuries than between those of the sixteenth and nineteenth. Between the sixteenth and nineteenth centuries a revolution occurred in man's understanding of himself and his world which caused a sharp break with medieval civilization and ushered in the modern epoch.

A. C. McGiffert has expressed this change in the following way:

The whole world of thought and culture was transformed. . . . the dependence upon supernatural powers, the submission to external authority, the subordination of time to eternity, and of fact to symbol . . . the somber sense of the sin of man and the evil of the world, the static interpretation of reality, . . . the belief that amelioration can come only in another world beyond the grave—all of which characterize the Middle Ages—were widely overcome and men faced life with a new confidence in themselves, with a new recognition of human power and achievement, with a new appreciation of present values.[2]

What happened between the Reformation and the French Revolution were two revolutions of far-reaching importance. The first was the scientific transformation that came as a result of the work of Copernicus, Galileo, and Newton. What it did was to deprive man of his traditional place and value in the world, making him aware of both his "grandeur and misery" in a vast, mechanical universe. The second revolution was that of Descartes. What Descartes did was to make doubting the first principle of philosophy and the model for all the

sciences. Together these movements brought about a significant transformation of man's understanding of himself and his situation in the world.

What occurred in the seventeenth and eighteenth centuries was the development, imperceptible and yet pervasive, of a world-view strikingly different from either classical or medieval culture. From the point of view of Christianity this new modern epoch can be characterized as a culture emancipating itself from theological domination. The Enlightenment represents the loosening of the state and society from ecclesiastical control and the emergence of a culture largely secular in character. The theories and sanctions of modern social and political life are no longer derived from biblical revelation or Church authority but independently arrived at by natural reason and social experience. An essential feature of the Enlightenment and of our modern culture since the eighteenth century is the growing separation of Western civilization from the authority of Church and theological dogma.

Underlying this whole movement is a renewed awareness and trust in man's own capacities and appreciation of, interest in, and hope for human life on this earth. Reason supersedes revelation as the supreme court of appeal. As a result, theology faced a choice of either adjusting itself to the advances in modern science and philosophy and, in so doing, risking accommodation to secularization, or resisting all influences from culture and becoming largely reactionary and ineffectual in meeting the challenges of life in the modern world. The history of modern Christianity is thus frequently viewed as the history of the secularization of the West.[3]

The historian Carl Becker advises us

that if we are to understand the inner spirit of any age, we should look "for certain unobtrusive words." A brief look at some of the "unobtrusive" words common to the Enlightenment can give us a clearer picture of that age as well as a keener awareness of the spiritual heritage of the Enlightenment which remains a vital part of our own contemporary experience.

Autonomy

More than anything else the Enlightenment marks a revolt against authoritarianism and the emergence of individual reason and conscience as the primary arbiter of truth and action. While every age has produced remarkable individuals who have challenged the accepted authorities of their day by appeal to individual conscience, the Enlightenment is characterized by the spread of the spirit of autonomous reason far beyond the confines of the intellectual solons, especially among the burgeoning middle class.

The term autonomy (*autos* self + *nomos* law) means self-governed. It involves "man's release from his self-incurred tutelage"—from his inability to reason and to will without sanctions imposed from outside himself. John Locke describes the ideal of autonomy in his portrayal of the genuine lover of truth. Of such persons there is, remarks Locke, "one unerring mark, viz., the not entertaining of any proposition with greater assurance than the proofs it is built upon will warrant. Whoever goes beyond this measure of assent, it is plain . . . loves not truth for truth's sake, but for some other end."[4]

The ideal of the Enlightenment is the duty of not entertaining any belief that is not warranted by rational evidence, which means by the assent of autonomous reason rather than biblical or ecclesiastical authority. Autonomy, therefore, is that faculty which the reason and the will possess of being their own lawgiver. Opposed to autonomy is heteronomy (*heteros* = other) or the imposition of sanctions or authority on oneself from outside, which one would not impose on oneself if one were free, i.e., truly rational. Thus autonomy is the foundation of all true liberty. But autonomy does not mean freedom "to do as one pleases," for that could mean subjection of the will to what is merely particular and immediate. Rather, autonomy—and thus true liberty —is achieved only when the individual reason and will are in accord with universal laws of reason. One prominent form of heteronomy, or slavery, is evident in obedience to divine commands simply because some external authority, i.e., the Bible or the Church, demands obedience to such laws—laws which appear to the autonomous reason to be arbitrarily imposed. For the men of the Enlightenment, the will or law of God can only be followed autonomously— only when the divine commands can be transformed into general laws which can become universal, rational axioms of behavior. No longer, then, is authority simply imposed arbitrarily from without; authority now depends on its inherent ability to produce rational conviction.

Reason

The eighteenth century is rightly known as the Age of Reason. But the age was dominated by a peculiar kind of reason. It was not the reason of classical rationalism. The *philosophes*, it is true, looked to the rationalist Descartes as the one who had liberated the mind from blind authority. But Descartes' reason was too speculative and abstract. The model of reason in the Enlightenment was the empirical, experimental reason of Francis Bacon and John Locke. What was required was *an examination of the facts of experience*. Reason was now called upon to serve a critical function according to the model of contemporary natural science. As Cassirer points out, in the eighteenth century philosophic method came to be patterned after Newton's "Rules of Philosophizing" rather than Descartes' *Discourse on Method*—on analysis rather than pure deduction.[5] Thus Voltaire exhorted his contemporaries: "We must never make hypotheses; we must never say: Let us begin by inventing principles according to which we attempt to explain everything. We should say rather: Let us make an exact analysis of things. . . ."[6] Equipped with this new instrument of analysis, man could examine, weigh, sift, compare the facts again and again until he could discern the true from the false, the contingent and particular from the necessary and universal.

Reason was no longer a given heritage, an intellectual treasury. It was now conceived of as a vital, progressive force. Reason was no longer defined by its effects, a distinct body of truth, but by its function, by its ability to bind and loose, to separate fact from opinion. Ideas, beliefs, even our understanding of what constitutes facts change, but reason as a function is what remains immutable and universal. This was the great discovery and the source of the excitement and optimism of the age. Because misfortune and suffering arise very largely from ignorance, it was believed reason could cast its light into the darkness of superstition and deceit and bring man his long-anticipated enlightenment and happiness.

Nature

For the men of the Enlightenment what was "reasonable" was also "natural", grounded somehow in the very nature of things. The equation of the reasonable and the natural can be traced very largely to the new science of Newton. For Newton the laws of nature were orderly and uniform, always and everywhere the same. Likewise, what is reasonable in human affairs is what is natural, i.e., what is universal beneath the divergences of outward appearance. What was called for, then, was the excision of all the beliefs and practices that had taken hold as a result of man's deviation from nature. Man had become artificial, the victim of all kinds of heteronomous influences—the monarch, the church, the conventions of society—which had destroyed his freedom and corrupted his natural integrity. The *philosophes* felt like Alceste in Molière's *The Misanthrope*. They itched to "unmask" the hypocrisy and artificiality of the times and yearned to flee to what they believed to be the simplicities of nature—that state in which man existed before he was corrupted. This "state of nature" was very largely a cherished figment of the eighteenth-century imagination. Some thought they discerned it in earlier times, in a more rustic age in which men had simple needs which could be easily satisfied. Locke, Diderot, and others thought they perceived this natural state in far-off places such as China and America and Tahiti. The belief spread that in these distant lands there lived a society of "noble savages" who were superior to the European because they lived in accordance with Nature. Even the skeptical Voltaire thought of Confucius as exemplifying the simplicities of the natural man of reason. Little did he know what an artificial bourgeois *gentilhomme* Confucius really was!

The extent to which Nature and her rational laws were reverenced, even divinized, is evidenced in d'Holbach's paean, *Système de la Nature:* "O thou," cries Nature to man,

Dare to enfranchise yourself from the trammels of superstition.... denounce those empty theories which are usurpers of my privileges; return under the dominion of my laws.... It is in my empire alone that true liberty reigns.... Return, then, my child, to thy fostering mother's arms! Deserter, trace back thy wandering steps to Nature. She will console thee for thine evils; she will drive from thy heart those appalling fears which overwhelm thee. Return to nature, to humanity, to thyself.[7]

This could very well have served as a naturalistic surrogate for the Parable of the Prodigal Son.

Melioristic Optimism

Nature reflects not only great rational simplicity but also order and regularity. It was Newton who discerned the beautiful symmetry of nature—an order and harmony which is not always immediately apparent. Frequently what we regard as evil or out of joint from our immediate point of view is not so in the general order of things. What looks at a distance as indeed very gray may be a rosy pink on closer examination. Our vision is too limited to take in the complex whole. Alexander Pope thus reminded his age that

All are but parts of one stupendous Whole
Whose body Nature is, and God the soul ...
All Nature is but Art unknown to thee;
All chance, direction, which thou canst not
    see;
All discord, harmony not understood;
All partial evil, universal good;
And spite of Pride, in erring Reason's spite,
One truth is clear, Whatever is, is right.[8]

For Pope the world is like a vast canvas of Rembrandt, filled with shadows and eerie blackness. Yet, if we concentrate not only on these large patches of darkness but on the whole, we see that the shadows are indispensable to Rembrandt's art. The seeming evil or darkness is a kind of good in that it is a necessary constituent of the whole. Perhaps this is not the most perfect world conceivable, but it is in Leibnitz's terms "the best of all possible worlds."

Leibnitz's imposing argument for "all is well" was widely held, but not everyone in the eighteenth century was enamored of Leibnitz's optimism. Voltaire had been drawn to Leibnitz's theodicy, but news of the Lisbon earthquake in which thousands died on All Saints' Day, 1755, turned him against the cold abstractions of the German. In 1756 Voltaire composed a poem entitled, *The Lisbon Earthquake: An Inquiry into the Maxim "Whatever Is, Is Right."* In the preface to the poem Voltaire points out that, impressive as they are, views such as those of Leibnitz and Pope are a perverse justification of the *status quo.* Why, after all, should one seek to remove evil if this is actually the least evil of all possible worlds?

If this world, such as it is, be the best of systems possible, we have no room to hope for a happy future state. If the various evils by which man is overwhelmed end in general good, all civilized nations have been wrong in endeavoring to trace out the origin of moral and physical evil.[9]

In Voltaire's opinion, Leibnitz and Pope were apostles of hopelessness because they felt no need to change the human situation. Voltaire's hope lay not in the present but in the future:

All *may* be well; that hope can man sustain,
All *now* is well; 'tis an illusion vain.[10]

Voltaire's optimism was a melioristic optimism—a hope oriented, like that of most of the *philosophes*, in the future betterment of the human race.

Jean Jacques Rousseau was impressed by Voltaire's poem on the Lisbon disaster and had himself begun to approach the problem from a new perspective that has had far-reaching significance for Christian theology. Rousseau saw no need to explain away the present evil state of man; nor did he find it necessary to trace such an evil condition back to an original Fall of Adam. Rousseau introduced the distinction between "natural man" and "civilized man." Natural man is in a state of innocency in that he has not yet been tempted to subject others to his will. Rousseau believed it is the compulsions of human society that cause men to become egotistical and acquisitive and which lie at the root of man's misery and inhumanity to man. But for Rousseau, as later for Marx, such an acquisitive, heteronomous society was not man's inevitable fate. In the *Social Contract* he envisioned a community in which the individual will and the "general will" are one: i.e., an autonomous society in which individual liberty is in perfect accord with the common good.

Cassirer points out the significance of Rousseau's hope:

When the compulsory form of society, which has hitherto prevailed, falls and is replaced by a new form of political and ethical community—a community in which every member, instead of being subjected to the arbitrary will of others, obeys only the general will which he recognizes and acknowledges as his own—then the hour of deliverance has arrived. But it is futile to expect this deliverance from without. No God can bring it about for us; man must rather become his own deliverer and in the ethical sense his own creator. Society heretofore has inflicted the deepest wounds on mankind; yet it is society too which through a transformation and reformation can and should heal these wounds.[11]

The kind of melioristic hope in the future of the human race, which we find in Voltaire and Rousseau, lies at the heart of the modern doctrine of progress.

Progress

Chastened optimists like Voltaire and Rousseau held out a fervent hope for the advance of posterity to a condition in accord with nature and reason. Progress would not be easy, but for most of the *philosophes* it was inevitable.

Self-interest, ambition, vainglory, . . . inundate the earth with blood. Yet in the midst of their voyages manners are gradually softened, the human mind takes enlightenment, separate nations draw nearer to each other, commerce and policy connect at last all parts of the globe, and the total mass of the human race . . . marches always, although slowly, towards still higher perfection. . . .[12]

The feeling was widespread that the "new age" was in the imminent future, for signs pointed to the fact that the decisive battle in the age-old struggle between superstition and reason had been won. Signs of the victory were the advancements of science and the application of scientific method to politics and to social problems. There was, however, a tendency to join with a belief in inevitable progress the paradoxical idea that until the time of Bacon, Newton, and Locke men had lived for almost two thousand years in utter darkness. Many agreed with Condorcet who, in *The Progress of the Human Mind*, traced the persistence of superstition and error to the triumph of Christianity.

Contempt of human sciences was one of the first features of Christianity. It had to avenge itself for the outrages of philosophy; it feared that spirit of investigation and doubt, that confidence of man in his own reason, the pest alike of all religious creeds. . . . The triumph of Christianity was thus the signal for the entire decline of both the sciences and of philosophy.[13]

According to Condorcet, the seventeenth century had turned the tide, and the stage was now set for the new age, which he called the "tenth *époque*," in which the progress of the human mind was assured. With deep, religious feeling, Condorcet expressed his hopes in the inauguration of the "tenth *époque*."

How consoling for the philosopher . . . is this view of the human race, emancipated from its shackles, released from the empire of fate and from that of the enemies of its progress, advancing with a firm and sure step along the path of truth, virtue, and happiness! It is the contemplation of this prospect that rewards him for all his efforts. . . ."[14]

For men like Condorcet, hope for posterity became a kind of eschatological substitute for the traditional Christian hope in the Kingdom of God. "Posterity," said Diderot, "is for the philosopher what the other world is for the religious." Just as Rousseau had offered a secular answer to the Christian doctrine of the Fall and Redemption, so did Diderot and Condorcet provide a this-worldly hope in the future in place of an other-worldly expectation—in an earthly city in which there will be no more "mourning nor crying nor pain anymore, for the former things will have passed away." The end of human life now falls exclusively within the present world and its ideal transformation.[15]

Toleration

The concern for religious toleration in the eighteenth century was as much due to the exhaustion which set in after the Religious Wars of the two previous centuries and to the growing indifference to the dogmatic claims of revealed religion as to a sincere and broad-based interest in the establishment of civil liberties. Nevertheless, the late seventeenth century produced a number of treatises, including Roger Williams' *Bloudy Tenent of Persecution* (1644), Milton's *Areopagitica* (1644), Locke's *Letters on Toleration* (1689), and the writings of Pierre Bayle, all of which had considerable influence in shaping eighteenth-century sentiment.

For the men of the Enlightenment the great enemy was not religion but dogmatism and intolerance. Bayle had emphasized that "the obstacles to a good examination do not come so much from the fact that the mind is void of knowledge as it is full of prejudice." Following the model of science, in which "truth" is gradually discovered and ever-changing,

Bayle argued that there is no "truth" which is at any time so absolutely certain as to justify the suppression of contrary views by force. Even a belief that seems to be wrong must be tolerated because it might possibly prove to be right. Bayle's influence on the French Encyclopedists was considerable, and his views on toleration were frequently repeated by them. Following Bayle, Diderot writes:

The mind can only acquiesce in what it accepts as true. The heart can only love what seems good to it. Violence will turn man into a hypocrite if he is weak, into a martyr if he is strong. . . . Teaching, persuasion, and prayer, these are the only legitimate means of spreading the faith.[16]

Locke argued similarly. Once you allow that civil governments can enforce religious uniformity among their citizens, you have conceded the same right to London, Geneva, and Rome. But it is clear that these places hold different religions to be the true one, in which case it follows that you have conceded the right of forced uniformity to false religions as well as the true one. What makes such a position doubly ridiculous is that a man's eternal fate is solely dependent upon the place of his birth or residence rather than on the intrinsic or proven truth of his religious allegiance. It follows, in Locke's argument, that religious toleration will, in the long run, give the true religion the best chance of capturing the minds and hearts of a people. It is only false religion that has anything to fear from the tests of reason and experience. Because the truth of religion cannot be absolutely determined by purely theoretical criteria, such as the appeal to proofs of historical fact or logical argument, but is dependent upon internal conviction and moral suasion,

religious toleration is all the more imperative.

The view that toleration is required by the very fact that the truth claims of the historical religions cannot at present be indubitably proved is the moral of Lessing's famous fable of the three rings in his drama, *Nathan the Wise*. According to the fable, it was the custom in an ancient Eastern family for the father to bequeath to his son a ring which "possessed the secret power to make the owner loved of God and man." At last the ring came to the father of three sons, all of whom he loved alike. And so to each of the three he gave the ring, two being perfect imitations. The father died, and each of the sons considered the other two deceivers.

But all in vain, the veritable ring
Was not distinguishable—
Almost as indistinguishable as to us
Is now—the true religion.

The sons brought their case before a judge who, about to throw out the difficult case, recollects:

But stop; I've just been told that the right ring
Contains the wondrous gift to make its wearer
    loved,
Agreeable alike to God and man,
That must decide, for the false
Rings will not have this power.

The judge then gives the sons this sage advice:

But my advice is this:
You take the matter as it stands.
If each one had his ring straight from his
    father,
So let each believe his ring the true one.
'Tis possible your father would not longer tolerate
The tyranny of this one ring in his family,

And surely loved you all—and all alike,
And that he would not two oppress
By favoring the third.
Now then, let each one emulate in affection
Untouched by prejudice. *Let each one strive*
To gain the prize of proving by results
The virtue of his ring, and aid its power
With gentleness and heartiest friendliness,
With benevolence and true devotedness to
  God;
And if the virtue of the ring will then
Have proved itself among your children's
  children,
I summon them to appear again
Before this judgment seat,
After a thousand thousand years.
Here then will sit a judge more wise than I,
Who will pronounce.[17] (Italics added.)

Lessing was reminding his readers that they must be tolerant in religious matters for two quite different reasons. God, in his compassion, could not suffer the tyranny of one dispensation which would give special favor to one son, for God loves all his sons—and all alike. Lessing is, nevertheless, advocating religious toleration for another reason. One of the rings (religions) is in fact the genuine one, but the decision as to which one it is must wait until some future time when its truth can be made clear by its fruits, by "the proof of the spirit and the power." Meanwhile the practitioners of each religion should assume their faith to be the true one and seek to commend its truth through virtuous conduct.

Such were some of the "unobtrusive" convictions that permeated the thinking of the eighteenth-century Europe—convictions very largely secular in origin and character. The appeal to autonomous reason and conscience, the melioristic optimism with its attendant discontent with existing conditions of political and economic injustice, the undogmatic temper with its appeal to what is natural and universal and to tolerance in matters of belief, all of this reflects a break with both Medieval civilization and Protestant orthodoxy.

The Enlightenment was also to run its course, and its understanding of nature, man, and God required correction and supplementation. Today we are living in a quite different world, and yet the problems that Christianity continues to face today in the realms of historical and philosophical theology can, by and large, trace their beginnings to the intellectual effervescence of the eighteenth-century Enlightenment.

NOTES

1. I. Kant, "What Is Enlightenment?" tr. and ed. L. W. Beck (Chicago, 1955), p. 286.

2. *The Rise of Modern Religious Ideas* (New York, 1921).

3. See, for example, J. H. Nichols' *History of Christianity, 1650–1950* (New York, 1950).

4. *Essay Concerning Human Understanding*, ed. A. S. Pringle-Pattison (Oxford, 1934), Bk. IV, Chap. 19.

5. E. Cassirer, *The Philosophy of the Enlightenment* (Boston, 1960), p. 7.

6. Voltaire, *Traité de Metaphysique*, Chaps. III, V; quoted in Cassirer, op. cit., p. 12.

7. Baron d'Holbach, *Système de la Nature*, Part II, Chap. 14.

8. An Essay on Man, Epistle I, From *Poetical Works*, ed. H. F. Carey (London, 1872).

9. *The Works of Voltaire*, Vol. X, Part 2 (St. Hubert Guild Edition, 1901), pp. 5–7.

10. Ibid., p. 18.
11. Cassirer, op. cit., pp. 157–158.
12. A. R. J. Turgot, *Discourse at the Sorbonne*, The Life and Writings of Turgot, ed. W. Walker Stephens (London, 1895).
13. Quoted in C. Frankel, *The Faith of Reason* (New York, 1948), p. 134. Frankel should be read as a corrective to the views of C. Becker in his *The Heavenly City of the Eighteenth Century Philosophers*. Without denying that many of the *philosophes* were naïvely optimistic about the future, Frankel points up, correctly, that their concern to apply scientific method to social problems was a valuable and enduring contribution. See especially his defense of the much-maligned Condorcet, Chap. VII.
14. *Sketch for a Historical Picture of the Human Mind*, tr. June Barroclough (London, 1955).
15. For an excellent statement of this changed perspective, see Becker, op. cit., Chap. IV, "The Uses of Posterity," and R. R. Palmer, "Posterity and the Hereafter in Eighteenth Century French Thought," *Journal of Modern History* (June, 1937).
16. Diderot, in the article "Intolerance," *Encyclopedia: Selections*, ed. by T. Cassirer and N. Hoyt (New York, 1965), p. 148.
17. Tr. by Williams Jacks (Glasgow, 1894).

SUGGESTIONS FOR FURTHER READING

I

For detailed accounts of the history of the seventeenth and eighteenth centuries, including both political and intellectual developments, the reader should consult volumes by F. L. Nussbaum, J. B. Wolf, P. Roberts, W. L. Dorn, and L. Gershoy, in the series *The Rise of Modern Europe*, edited by W. L. Langer and published by *Harper Torch Books.

II

For general accounts of Church history and theological developments in the modern period, the student should first consult:

Cragg, G. R. *The Church and the Age of Reason, 1648–1789* (Baltimore: Penguin, 1961).

Nichols, J. H. *History of Christianity, 1650–1950* (New York: Ronald Press, 1950).

Vidler, A. R. *The Church in an Age of Revolution* (Baltimore: Penguin, 1961).

Walker, Williston. *A History of the Christian Church*, Rev. ed. (New York: Charles Scribner's Sons, 1950).

These volumes contain good bibliographies

* Indicates the book is published in a paperback edition.

of specialized studies in modern ecclesiastical and theological history.

III

Among the many books on the general history of ideas during the period of the Enlightenment, the following are highly recommended:

Becker, C. L. *The Heavenly City of the Eighteenth Century Philosophers* (New Haven: Yale University Press, 1962). A delightful, provocative, and controversial interpretation of the eighteenth-century thought. For an appraisal of Becker's view, see *Carl Becker's Heavenly City Revisited*, ed. R. O. Rockwood (Ithaca, N.Y.: Cornell University Press, 1958).

Brinton, C. *The Age of Reason Reader* (New York: The Viking Press, 1956). A good selection of brief texts exemplifying the thought and manners of the seventeenth and eighteenth centuries.

Cassirer, E. *The Philosophy of the Enlightenment* (Boston: The Beacon Press, 1960). Perhaps the profoundest philosophical interpretation of the Enlightenment. Very readable but requires some background knowledge.

Gay, Peter. *The Enlightenment: An Interpretation* (New York: Alfred Knopf, 1966). Written by one of the leading authorities on the thought of the eighteenth century, this book is subtitled *The Rise of Modern Paganism* and deals primarily with the intellectual origins of the Enlightenment.

Hazard, Paul. *The European Mind, 1680–1715* (New Haven: Yale University Press, 1953).

———. *European Thought in the Eighteenth Century* (New Haven: Yale University Press, 1954). Hazard's studies are a literary achievement in addition to being authoritative and stimulating. Not for the beginner.

Willey, Basil. *The Seventeenth-Century Background* (New York: Columbia University Press, 1942).

———. *The Eighteenth Century Background* (New York: Columbia University Press, 1941). These studies are illuminating and eminently readable.

CHAPTER TWO

The Religion of Reason

John Locke

The eighteenth century inaugurated the modern epoch. We are, whether we like it or not, children of the Enlightenment, imbued with its spirit, dedicated to many of its ideals. We are modern, and not medieval, men whose religious faith has passed through the analytical fires of the age of reason. We have passed through it and have become something else, but we are its children and we cannot deny our inheritance. The Reformation was still largely medieval, not modern. The movements which followed in the late sixteenth and early seventeenth centuries— the Catholic Counter Reformation, Calvinism, and Lutheranism—tended to emphasize, to an even greater extent than the medieval period, insistence on doctrinal orthodoxy and ecclesiastical authority. The seventeenth century was a period of Protestant "scholasticism"—a time not of evangelical enthusiasm, but of defining and systematizing sound doctrine. The Reformation had sought to return to what it thought to be the purity of the Christian faith, but the great reformers were in many respects negative and iconoclastic in their attacks upon the Catholic tradition. It was left to the next generations of theologians, men like Melancthon, to define, systematize, and conserve the purity of doctrine rediscovered by Luther and Calvin. To allow error to continue was to fail to carry out the very intention of the Reformation. The difficulty was, of course, to agree upon what the Reformers meant by their teaching and what constituted purity of doctrine.

The late sixteenth and most of the seventeenth century is a history of long and bitter theological controversies on the Continent and in England. Today we can better appreciate some of the issues that were the cause of such contention and divisiveness. Nevertheless, A. C. McGiffert is basically correct when he says that seventeenth-century theology

in spite of many differences in detail, was very largely that of the Middle Ages. . . . The reigning philosophy was that of Aristotle, as understood by the medieval schoolmen, and the supernatural realm was conceived in the same objective and realistic fashion. Compared with that of the Middle Ages, Protestant scholasticism was much more barren and at the same time narrower and more oppressive. . . . Of the new science and philosophy that were making headway in the world outside they took no account.[1]

Although it appears to be true that Protestant scholasticism was taking little account of the revolutionary movements in science and philosophy, these movements were having their effect on the consciousness of the age. The Cartesian reconstruction of philosophy was largely an inversion of medieval philosophy, and post-Copernican science radically modified the medieval view of the world and man's relation to it. These intellectual changes were bound to have their effect on man's religious ideas.

There were, however, two aspects of Protestant scholasticism that helped usher in the religion of reason in the eighteenth century. First, seventeenth-century scholasticism was already highly rationalistic in spirit and practice. Theological truth was arrived at not through religious experience but, rather, by logical deduction from certain first principles. The test of truth was that of rational consistency. The question became not whether Christianity was to be judged by rational standards, but, rather, what was to constitute a rational standard by which religion should be tested. Karl Barth has correctly remarked that in many respects the seventeenth-century orthodox rationalists and the eighteenth-century heterodox modernists were really bedfellows at heart! As we shall see, the move from orthodox supernaturalism to Deism was not as difficult as it might appear.

The second feature of seventeenth-century orthodoxy, instrumental in setting the stage for eighteenth-century Deism, was its divisiveness. Europe was worn out from a century of religious wars and persecutions, frequently based on theological issues of concern to only a very few. The theological conflicts in England ended with the Act of Toleration of 1689. There was now a desire to find some common religious foundation upon which all rational men of faith could agree, despite their differences. Reasonable men of all Christian sects could agree that the Scriptures were to be honored. But here the agreement ended, for these reasonable men could not agree on the interpretation and application of the Bible. Was it possible to bring the revealed principles of the Bible wholly within the sphere of reason itself? Thus began the long and involved modern history of the problem of reason and revelation, philosophy and the Bible.

An important attempt at answering this question was that of Edward Lord Herbert of Cherbury (1583–1648) as early as 1624. In that year Lord Herbert, who in the eighteenth century came to be known as the "Father of Deism," published *De Veritate* in which he argued for a natural religion which could be agreed upon by all men regardless of the positive (historical) differences among their many faiths. Lord Herbert believed there existed in all men certain innate principles (*notitiae communes*) distinguished by such marks as universality, practical necessity, and immediate cogency. Ideas to which these marks belong have, according to Lord Herbert, been imprinted by God on the mind of man for all time. They are axioms which neither require nor admit proof. In the area of man's religious beliefs there are five such innate principles:

1. That God exists.
2. That God ought to be worshipped.
3. That the practice of virtue is the chief part of the worship of God.
4. That men have always had an abhorrence of crime and are under the obligation to repent of their sins.
5. That there will be rewards and punishments after death.

Lord Herbert believed that natural religion, based on such principles and shared by all men, would lead to religious harmony or at least to toleration rather than the dissension wrought by the positive tenets of the several historical faiths.

In England in the seventeenth century there were a number of influential writers who, like Lord Herbert, sought to find a common platform on which all men of faith (or at least all Protestants!) could agree. Chillingworth's *Religion of Protestants, A Sure Way of Salvation* (1637), although written as a defense of Protestantism, nevertheless sought to make the Bible alone the sole guide of faith and to minimize all beliefs and practices not defined by the Scriptures.

Take away this persecuting, burning, cursing, damning of men for not subscribing to the words of men as the words of God. . . . I say take away tyranny and restore Christians to the first and full liberty of captivating their understandings to Scripture only; and as rivers when they have a free passage run only to the ocean, so it may well be hoped, by God's blessing, that universal liberty, thus moderated may quickly reduce Christendom to truth and liberty.[2]

Chillingworth assumed the authority of the Bible as a matter upon which all Christians were agreed. As long as no one questioned that tenet, all was well. But the fact was that the several sects could not agree upon the interpretation of Scripture. Was it not necessary to go back even further for a principle other than Scripture that was common to all Christians? The issue was joined. By the end of the seventeenth century most of the ablest religious thinkers were divided into two camps. The orthodox or rational supernaturalists insisted on the unique role of revelation and on the distinction between what could and what could not be rationally *established*. The more radical thinkers, who came to be known as Deists, rejected the necessity of revelation and insisted on the sufficiency of the unaided natural reason in religion. The development of this controversy is an interesting one, and the outcome of the battle was truly "epoch-making," for it led directly to the skepticism of David Hume and eventually, in France, to a more militant atheism. Many of the issues raised by the Deist controversy are still with us, in slightly different guise, in the second half of the twentieth century.

Rational Supernaturalism

John Tillotson. Chillingworth found a very able successor in John Tillotson, Archbishop of Canterbury. Tillotson (1630–1694) was the most famous preacher of his day, and his sermons and other writings were widely read and admired in the eighteenth century. The Archbishop was a leader in the controversy over the claims of the Roman church, and his attack upon Roman beliefs was avowedly rationalist. In fact, Hume was later to found his essay "Of Miracles" on Tillotson's favorite argument against Catholic Transubstantiation—namely, that the doctrine is contrary to the testimony of all our senses. "Nothing," says Tillotson, "ought to be received as a revelation from God which plainly contradicts the principles of natural religion."[3] No argument will prove a doctrine to be divine "which is not clearer and stronger than the difficulties and objections against it."[4] Religious beliefs are to be tested like any other propositions—by rational evidence.

According to Tillotson, the function and end of religion is found in the fact that it provides divine sanctions for morality. These sanctions are found in natural religion which teaches us (*a*) that there is a God, (*b*) that He requires that man live virtuously, and (*c*) that God will reward the righteous and punish the wicked. If Tillotson could reduce religion to so few principles of natural religion, why is he included among the rational supernaturalists? Part of the answer is that Tillotson did not believe that natural religion alone proved effective. It re-

quired the supplementation of revelation. Revelation clarifies the truths discerned by natural reason and makes for their more effective reception. "Natural religion is the foundation of all revealed religion and revelation is designed simply to establish its duties."[5] According to Tillotson, we can know an alleged revelation is genuine by the fact that it does not contradict the principles of natural religion and, secondly, that the reasons for supposing it a revelation are stronger than those reasons that can be brought against it.

Tillotson's rational supernaturalism is also evident in his defense of Christianity on the basis of the argument from miracle. In his sermon on "The Miracles Wrought in Confirmation of Christianity" the Archbishop asks: "In what circumstances and with what limitations are miracles a sufficient testimony to the truth and divinity of any doctrine?" His answer is that

there are two things [that] must concur to give the mind of man full satisfaction that any religion is from God. First, if the person that declares this religion give testimony of his divine authority, that is, that he is sent and commissioned by God for that purpose. And secondly if the religion which he declares contain nothing in it that is plainly repugnant to the nature of God. . . . *For though a doctrine be never so reasonable in itself, this is no certain argument that it is from God if no testimony from heaven be given to it; because it may be the result and issue of human reason and discourse; and though a doctrine be attested by miracles, yet the matter of it may be so unreasonable and absurd . . . that no miracles can be sufficient to give confirmation to it . . . .*[6] (Italics added.)

If, then, there is a concurrence of the "testimony of divine authority" and "nothing in it [the miracle] that is repugnant to the nature of God," then the miracle is "the principal external proof and confirmation of a doctrine."[7]

Today Tillotson's proof of Christianity from miracle would be regarded with astonishment because he is arguing that the proof of the faith lies in the miracles which attended its beginnings and were accomplished specifically to confirm its unique claims. More than that, he is saying that even though a thing be reasonably proved good and true, there is the additional need of the evidence of a miracle to insure that it is truly of God! To the modern believer there is something wooden about such an external, miraculous proof and something very wrong in Tillotson's conception of the function and purpose of the miracle stories in the Gospels. Yet Tillotson combined in his rational supernaturalism those characteristics which exemplified much of the orthodox rationalist thinking of his day: the conviction that nothing is to be accepted that does not commend itself to man's natural reason, and the belief that miracles are entirely reasonable and often can be adduced as certain proof of divine revelation. These characteristics are best seen in the writings of the foremost rational supernaturalist, the philosopher John Locke.

John Locke. John Locke (1632–1704), regarded by many as the most important of the English philosophers, thought of himself as a devout and orthodox Christian. He accepted the authority of both reason and the Bible and never saw any serious difficulty in serving both masters. In the Introduction to his great work, *An Essay Concerning Human Understanding* (1690), Locke says that his purpose was "to enquire into the original certainty and extent of human knowl-

edge, together with the grounds and degrees of belief, opinion and assent ...."[8] Toward the very end of this long but lucid work, Locke turns to the question of the nature and extent of our genuine knowledge of religion. In Book IV, Chapter 17, Locke makes an important distinction between what is "above, contrary and according to reason."

1. *According to reason* are such propositions whose truth we can discover by examining and tracing those ideas we have from sensation and reflection, and by natural deduction find to be true or probable.

2. *Above reason* are such propositions whose truth or probability we cannot by reason derive from those principles.

3. *Contrary to reason* are such propositions as are inconsistent with or irreconcilable to our clear and distinct ideas. Thus the existence of God is according to reason; the existence of more than one God is contrary to reason; the resurrection of the dead above reason.[9]

Genuine religious knowledge can be discovered by natural reason and in those propositions that are above but not contrary to reason. Assent to propositions that are "above" reason is the assent of faith to truths of revelation. Locke makes the following distinction between reason and faith:

Reason, as contradistinguished from faith, I take to be the discovery of the certainty or probability of such propositions or truths, which the mind arrives at by deductions made from such ideas which it has got by the use of its natural faculties, viz. by sensation or reflection.

Faith, on the other side, is the assent to any proposition, not thus made out by the deductions of reason, but upon the credit of the proposer, as coming from God in some extraordinary way of communication. This way of discovering truths to men we call *revelation*.[10]

Locke says that revelation may give a man genuine knowledge which is also discoverable by man's natural reason.

I say, that *the same truths may be discovered and conveyed down from revelation which are discoverable to us by reason* . . . . So God might, by revelation, discover the truth of any proposition in Euclid. In all things of this kind there is little need or use of revelation, God having furnished us with natural and surer means to arrive at the knowledge of them. For the knowledge we have that this revelation came at first from God, can never be so sure as the knowledge we have from the clear and distinct perception of the agreement or disagreement of our own ideas.[11]

Revelation may, however, give us knowledge that is above reason,

there being many things wherein we have very imperfect notions, or none at all; and other things, of whose past, present or future existence, by the natural use of our faculties, we can have no knowledge at all: these being beyond the discovery of our natural faculties and above reason, are, when revealed, *the proper matter of faith*. Thus that part of the angels rebelled against God, and thereby lost their first happy state: and that the dead shall rise and live again: these, and the like, being beyond the discovery of reason, are purely matters of faith, with which reason has, directly, nothing to do.[12]

Although such revelatory knowledge may be "above reason," revelation can never be admitted which is "contrary to reason."

Whatever God hath revealed is certainly true; no doubt can be made of it. This is the proper object of faith: but whether it be a divine revelation or no, reason must judge; which can never permit the mind to reject a great evidence to embrace what is less evident, nor allow it to entertain probability in opposition to knowledge and certainty. There can be no evidence that any traditional revelation is of divine original, in the words we receive it, so clear and so certain as that of the principles of reason. And therefore *nothing that is contrary to, and inconsistent with, the clear and self-evident dictates of reason, has a right to be urged or assented to, as a matter of faith wherein reason hath nothing to do*.[13]

The question which remains to be answered is, How do we know that propositions given in revelation ("above reason") are to be given our assent? That is, what reason have we for accepting "the credit of the proposer" who claims that certain truths were given him by revelation? Locke deals with this problem in Chapter 19 of Book IV, entitled "Of Enthusiasm." Locke sees "enthusiasm" as a third, though fallacious, "ground of assent," along with reason and revelation. It is that ground of assent which in effect "takes away both reason and revelation, and substitutes . . . the ungrounded fancies of a man's own brain . . . ."[14] The enthusiasts are those who "cannot be mistaken in what they feel . . . . they are sure because they are sure, and their persuasions are right, only because they are strong in them."[15] "But," says Locke,

to examine a little soberly this internal light and this feeling on which they build so much: the question here is, How do I know that God is the revealer of this to me; that this impression is made upon my mind by his Holy Spirit and that therefore I ought to obey it?[16]

The enthusiasts are caught in a vicious circle, for they claim the veracity of a revelation because they firmly believe it and they believe it because it is a revelation!

Locke's answer to the "enthusiast" is the following:

Light, true light in the mind is or can be nothing else but the evidence of the truth of any proposition; and if it is not a self-evident proposition, all the light it has, or can have, is from the clearness and validity of those proofs upon which it is received. . . . God, when he makes the prophet does not unmake the man. He leaves all his faculties in their natural state, to enable him to judge of his inspirations, whether they be of divine original or no . . . . If he [God] would have us assent to the truth of any proposition, he either evidences that truth by the usual methods of natural reason, or else makes it known to be a truth which he would have us assent to by his authority, and convinces us that it is from him, by some marks which reason cannot be mistaken in . . . . Every conceit that thoroughly warms our fancies must pass for an inspiration, if there be nothing but the strength of our persuasions, whereby to judge of our persuasions. If reason must not examine their truth by something extrinsical to the persuasions themselves, inspirations and delusions, truth and falsehood, will have the same measure, and will not be possible to be distinguished. Thus we see, the holy men of old, who had revelations from God, had something else besides that internal light of assurance in their own minds to testify to them that it was from God. They were not left to their own persuasions alone, that those persuasions were from God, but had outward signs to convince them of the Author of those revelations.[17]

What the holy men of old had that convinced them of the veracity of their revelations were "outward signs." For Locke the reasonableness of revelation depends, then, upon "outward signs," i.e., upon the external evidence of prophecy fulfillment and miracle. The sole purpose of such miracles is to give assurance that a person is a messenger of

God and thereby to confirm the divine origin of his revelation.

It is to be considered, that divine revelation receives testimony from no other miracles, but such as are wrought to witness his mission from God who delivers the revelation. All other miracles that are done in the world, how many or great soever, revelation is not concerned in.[18]

In 1695 Locke published *The Reasonableness of Christianity* in which the general principles of the *Essay* are applied directly to the Christian faith. In this little book Locke examines the Bible both to discover the essence of Christianity as revealed by Christ and to prove the reasonableness of Christ's credentials as a messenger of God. Locke's study of Scripture leads him to reject much of traditional Christian belief which he finds contrary to reason, but also to the discovery that Christ and his apostles taught only two things necessary for salvation: (a) belief that Jesus is the Messiah sent from God for our redemption and (b) the necessity of repentance and the bringing forth of the fruits of repentance by following a righteous life. What, asks Locke, could be more reasonable than this? The reasonableness of these truths revealed by Christ are clearly proved by two "external signs": (a) the fulfillment of the Messianic prophecies and (b) the performance of miracles.

For Locke the proof of prophecy is apparently determined by the successful fulfillment of the prediction. Jesus simply fits the label. I. T. Ramsey contends that Locke actually presents a form of intuitive proof from prophecy fulfillment.

May not Locke . . . have implied that in bringing alongside the person of Jesus the Messiah label, there strikes us an aptness and appropriateness of the kind which strikes us when, for example, we see at long last the island corresponding to the map we have pondered for years, or the lost piece in the jigsaw which is just what we had been told to expect. In other words, though Locke never says so, is it not possible that even in thinking of the Messiah as a descriptive label which fitted Jesus, Locke was appealing to some kind of disclosure situation . . . to something he called "intuition" . . . . ? May not intuition play the same part for propositions which are "above reason" as demonstration does in the case of propositions which are "according to reason"? In this case the broad reasonableness of Christian assent would lie in its intuitive character.[19]

In the light of modern biblical research the idea of Jesus' "fitting" the Messianic label is an especially difficult ground for proof for the simple reason that Jesus did not fit the Messianic labels in circulation. Locke's model of the "disclosure situation" is too simple to fit the facts. However, Locke's evidence from prophecy fulfillment might still be reasonable if the concept of "disclosure situation" is broadened.

It must now be an intuition which arises when a number of different labels are seen to fit an object to which none of these alone are adequate, such as is the case when we become intuitively aware of a cone by seeing various projections of it, or of a mountain by seeing various single aspects of it. Our previous map and jigsaw examples are too simple.[20]

That Locke was not involved in a crude empirical proof from prophecy and miracle is even clearer in his remarks concerning miracle. Miracles are credentials which, being plainly observable events, make reasonable the propositions of their performer. Locke appears at times to argue that if two people utter propositions which call for our assent, the more

reasonable assent simply depends upon the size or marvel of the miraculous act. This, however, is not Locke's view. In the *Third Letter on Toleration*, Locke compares the assenting power of a miracle with that of civil power and argues that the power of miracle is of quite a distinct kind. Again commenting on Locke's view, I. T. Ramsey says that for Locke

the power of a miracle is not measurable power, it is not power according to law. This means, I suggest, that a miracle must be given the same compelling power as belongs to an intuition, for this is all Locke has in his journeyman's bag beside idea particulars. Then Locke can justly say (as he does) that to distinguish between a pretended revelation and that which is truly divine "we need but open our eyes to see and be sure which came from [God]."[21]

Ramsey rightly indicates that for Locke the compelling power of divine miracle is intuitively disclosed and never adequately assessed in terms of "idea particulars" alone. Unlike his successors, the Deists, Locke appears to have desired to preserve not only reasonableness but also mystery as an irreducible component of the Christian faith.

The Reasonableness of Christianity was concerned to separate the essential articles of faith from the plethora of dogmas and rites with which "writers and wranglers in religion have filled it" and to indicate the reasonableness of Christ's credentials as the instrument of God's revelation. Having accomplished this, Locke turns, at the conclusion of the work, to certain objections that were yet to be met. The first difficulty had to do with those who lived before the time of Jesus Christ. If men are justified by God for believing Jesus to be the Messiah "what shall become of all mankind, who lived before

Our Saviour's time; who never heard of his name and consequently could not believe in him?"[22] The answer, says Locke, is "obvious and natural."

Nobody was or can be required to believe what was never proposed to him to believe .... All then that was required before his [Messiah's] appearing in the world was to believe what God had revealed, and to rely with a full assurance on God for the performance of his promise ....[23]

The greater difficulty has to do with those "who, having never heard of the promise or news of a Saviour, have had no thought or belief concerning him." Locke's answer is that those who were never in a position either to accept or to reject Christ's revelation, would be illuminated by that natural reason which is God's gift to all his children.

God had, by the light of reason, revealed to all mankind, who would make use of that light, that he was good and merciful. The same spark of the divine nature and knowledge of man, which making him a man, showed him the law he was under as a man; showed him also the way of atoning the merciful, kind, compassionate Author and Father of him and his being, when he had transgressed that law. He that made use of this candle of the Lord, so far as to find what was his duty, could not miss to find also the way to reconciliation and forgiveness, when he had failed his duty.[24]

Having admitted this much concerning the sufficiency of the religion of natural reason, Locke is required to answer why there needs be a revelation at all. Locke concludes *The Reasonableness of Christianity* with five arguments for revelation. All five are variations on the single theme that in human history revelation has proved practically useful and even necessary.

The rational supernaturalists Tillotson and Locke were agreed that natural religion is good as far as it goes, but that, practically, it has always needed to be supplemented by revelation. Christian revelation makes man's natural piety and duties plain, and the glory of Christian revelation lies in the fact that, while it serves to clarify and empower, it does so without contradicting or altering the findings of natural reason. The Rational Supernaturalists were also one in their insistence that the essentials of Christian revelation could be reduced to a very few doctrines and that these doctrines provided the divine sanctions for morality.

The second stage in the development of eighteenth-century theology was entered when those contemporaries of Locke, who came later to be called Deists, challenged the claim that the divine sanction for morality necessitated a special revelation—i.e., that a true natural religion necessitated the particular teachings of Christianity.

Deism in England

John Locke had maintained a place for those things that, while not contrary to reason, were, nevertheless, "above reason." Locke appears to have desired to preserve mystery as a genuine element in Christian faith. Locke's successors were eager, however, to exclude all mystery from revelation. This is evident in the work of John Toland, a man who considered himself a disciple of Locke.

John Toland. John Toland (1670–1722) was a graduate of Edinburgh and studied at Leyden and at Oxford where he was supported financially by a group of Protestant dissenters. While at Oxford he wrote his first and most important book, *Christianity Not Mysterious* (1696). In this book Toland follows a position similar to that of Locke's *Essay*, except that, unlike Locke, he does not allow for revelatory truths which are "above reason." Toland narrows Locke's three classes of natural religion, superstition, and revelation to two, for "according to reason" (natural religion) and "above reason" (revelation) are, for Toland, essentially of the same class. Thus, Toland rejects the possibility of the revelation of truths which, in themselves, are beyond the compass of reason. Toland admits that no one in his day would hold that reason and revelation are contradictory, but, perhaps with Locke specifically in mind, he continues,

very many affirm that though the doctrines of the latter cannot in themselves be contradictory to the principles of the former, as proceeding both from God; yet, that according to our conceptions of them, *they may seem directly to clash:* And that though we cannot reconcile them by reason of our corrupt and limited understandings; yet from the authority of Divine Revelation, we are bound to believe and acquiesce in them; or as the Fathers taught them to speak, *to adore what we cannot comprehend.*[25]

Toland's sharp reply to this view is that such a "famous and admirable doctrine is the undoubted source of all the *Absurdities* that ever were seriously vented among Christians. Without the pretence of it, we should never hear of Transubstantiation and other ridiculous Fables . . . ."[26]

But if we are never to assent by faith to what is "above reason," are we not saying that faith is no longer faith but knowledge? Toland answers that if by knowledge is meant understanding what is believed, then faith is, indeed, a form of knowledge. Does not then such a notion of faith as knowledge render revelation useless? Toland answers:

But pray, how so? for the question is not whether we could discover all the objects of our *Faith* by Ratiocination: I have proved on the contrary that no matter of fact can be known without *Revelation*. But I assert, that *what is once revealed we must as well understand as any other matter in the world, Revelation being only of use to enform us while the evidence of its subject persuades us.* Then reply they, *Reason* is of more dignity than Revelation. I answer, just as much as a *Greek Grammar* is superior to the *New Testament*; for we make use of Grammar to understand the language and of Reason to understand the sense of that book. But, in a word, I see no need of Comparisons in this case, for *Reason* is not less from God than *Revelation*; 'tis the Candle, the Guide, the Judge he has lodged within every man that cometh into this world.[27]

Toland argues that reasonable facts or truths may be discovered by us for ourselves or may be made known to us by the testimony of others which may be given by revelation. But in either case *revelation is never mysterious or incomprehensible once it is known.* Revelation is perfectly rational but concerns events that otherwise have not fallen under our observation or within our experience.

Most of the Deists of the late seventeenth and early eighteenth centuries sought to show that God's perfection demands a way of salvation open to all men and that positive (historical) revelation, being limited to special times and peoples, lacks universality. The true religion must be equally accessible to the natural reason of man at all times and places. The most complete exposition of this Deistic view was made in Matthew Tindal's *Christianity as Old as the Creation*, a book regarded as the culmination of the constructive phase of English Deism and referred to as "the Deist's Bible."

Matthew Tindal. Matthew Tindal's life (1655–1733), as a Fellow of All Souls College, Oxford, was peaceful and respectable in comparison with the tumultuous and bohemian life of Toland. In 1730, at the advanced age of seventy-three, Tindal published the first volume of *Christianity as Old as the Creation*. At his death three years later he left the manuscript of a second volume which was quietly destroyed by a bishop, fearful of its probable influence. The bishop's action, revealing an all-too-common intellectual timidity on the part of ecclesiastics, was not justified, however. The first volume elicited one hundred and fifty replies, including William Law's *The Case of Reason* (1731), Bishop Berkeley's *Alciphron* (1732), and, most important, Bishop Butler's *Analogy of Religion* (1736).

Tindal's book begins with two a priori principles on which his whole case is built. First, God is eternally the same, infinitely wise and good. What originates with a perfect, all-wise God must itself be perfect. Thus an absolutely perfect religion cannot be altered or increased or decreased. Secondly, human nature is always the same and unalterable in itself. Hence, God's perfect religion must dispense its truth equally to all men at all times. Historical revelation can add nothing to a religion that is absolutely perfect, universal, and unchanging.

If all own that God, at no time, could have any motive to give laws to mankind but for their good; and that he is at all times equally good, and at all times acts upon the same motives, must they not own with me, except they are inconsistent with themselves, that his Laws at all times must be the same?[28]

God in his infinite goodness desired that every man should come to a knowledge of true religion. If we assume that Christianity is the only true and perfect religion, then it must have been created for all of mankind from the beginning. The name "Christianity" may be of more recent origin, but the essentials of the Christian religion must have existed from the very beginning. Christianity is as old as the creation. From the beginning God has given all men the means to know and practice Christianity, the "means" being reason, that faculty that separates man from the beasts. God has created us rational creatures, that through this capacity we might know what constitutes the very law and will of Divine Reason. According to Tindal, what is offered to us as God's will must be reasonable and what is reasonable must itself be judged by reason. Nothing then can be admitted into Christianity except what our reason tells us is worthy of God.

The Holy Ghost can't deal with men as rational creatures, but by proposing arguments to convince their understandings, and influence their wills, in the same manner as if proposed by other agents; for to go beyond this would be making impressions on men, as a seal does on wax; to the confounding of their reason, and their liberty in choosing; and the man would then be merely passive, and the action would be the action of another Being acting upon him; for which he could be in no way accountable: but if the Holy Ghost does not act thus, and Revelation itself be not arbitrary; must it not be founded on the Reason of Things? And consequently, be a *Republication*, or Restoration of the Religion of Nature?[29]

Since Tindal holds that God has provided men at all times with the means of knowing what he requires of them, then natural religion and true, revealed religion cannot differ in substance but only in the manner in which each becomes known.

I think too great a stress can't be laid on Natural Religion, which, as I take it, differs not from Revealed but in the manner of its being communicated. The one being the internal, as the other the external Revelation of the same unchangeable will of a Being, who is alike at all times infinitely wise and good.[30]

According to Tindal, since God must have dealt equally with all men, it follows that doctrines not revealed to all cannot be doctrines imposed by God. With this principle in hand, Tindal makes a clean sweep of all those doctrines and practices of the church that cannot stand up to the scrutiny of natural reason. With shrewd and bitter sarcasm, Tindal jests at the "superstitions" of the Bible and the Roman Church. What right, he asks, has a Papist who rubs a dying man with oil to laugh at the Indian who thinks it will conduce to his future happiness to die with a cow's tail in his hands?[31] Like his French counterpart, Voltaire, Tindal discloses a completely uncritical admiration for the Chinese while jeering unmercifully at the beliefs and practices of the Jews and Christians.

For Tindal all beliefs and practices must be judged not only by natural reason but by their ability to promote human happiness. God's purpose in creation was not for His own glory or advantage, but the happiness of his creatures. God thus demands of man only what will contribute to his perfection and happiness.

Whoever so regulates his natural appetites as will conduce most to the exercise of his reason, the health of his body and the pleasures of his senses taken and considered together (since herein his happiness consists) may be certain he can never offend his Maker; who, as he governs all things according to their natures, can't but expect his rational creatures should act according to their natures.[32]

The end of religion, then, is morality, for true religion consists "in a constant disposition of mind to do all the good we can, and thereby render ourselves acceptable to God in answering the end of our creation."[33] The only difference between morality and religion is that morality is "acting according to the reason of things considered in themselves," while religion is "acting according to the same reason of things considered as the rule of God."[34] Anything in religion that is not required of man's moral life should be removed, for the more man "is taken up with the observation of things which are not of a moral nature, the less he will be able to attend those that are."[35]

Tindal is willing to call everything in religion superstitious and dangerous which is not directly conducive to morality.

As long as men believe the good of society is the supreme law, they will think it their duty to be governed by that law; and believing God requires nothing of them but what is the good of mankind *will place the whole of their religion in benevolent actions* . . . but if they are made to believe there are things which have no relation to this good, necessary to salvation, they must suppose it their duty to use such means as will most effectually serve this purpose, and that God, in requiring the end requires all those means as will best secure and propagate it. And 'tis to this principle we owe the most cruel persecutions, inquisitions, crusades and massacres.[36]

With Tindal, Christianity is reduced to the practice of virtue. Religion becomes the recognition of our moral duties as divine commands. Here Tindal arrives at a conception of religion and of Christianity that Immanuel Kant will adopt in his book on *Religion Within the Limits of Reason Alone*. With Tindal the center of focus has shifted from the religion of the older rationalism to the religion of practical reason. The rational supernaturalists had conceded too much, and it was left for Tindal to discredit their appeal to a special revelation. Tindal's shift to a theism based on practical reason was perhaps unconsciously due to the inherent weakness of the rational basis of the Deists' position itself. In any case, Tindal's own book reflects both the shaky foundation of rationalistic theism and, at the same time, the beginnings of a move in a quite new direction. In remarking on the change that occurred between Locke and David Hume, Leslie Stephen points to the pivotal role of Matthew Tindal in the decline of rational supernaturalism.

It was in vain that, after exhausting their eloquence to prove the competence of human reason and the absolute clearness and simplicity of religious truth, writers of that school laboured to establish some narrow standing-ground for revelation. They had, in their own opinion, raised such immovable pillars for the support of morality, that the old-fashioned props became first superfluous and then offensive. When their necessity was no longer felt in practice, men had leisure to remark upon their antiquated and grotesque design, and to observe how inadequate they were for the task imposed upon them. So far Tindal's victory was undeniable; though his own flank was equally liable to be turned, and his antagonists were not slow to perceive their advantage. So long as the controversy was confined within

the prescribed limits, nothing could run more easily than Tindal's logic.[37]

As long as the issues were kept within the prescribed limits, Deism won the day. However, in their slashing offensive against the orthodox, the Deists failed to examine their own fortifications. It was not long after the appearance of *Christianity as Old as the Creation* that Deism itself faced devastating attacks on two fronts. On the one hand, there were the defenders of orthodoxy, such as Bishop Butler, who sought to demonstrate the difficulties in belief in natural religion, thereby enhancing belief in revelation; on the other flank there emerged the great skeptic David Hume. But before examining at length the critique of the religion of reason, we must take a brief look at Deism in France and Germany.

Deism in France: Voltaire

There is a certain truth in the statement that the religion of reason had its origins in England but was made popular in France. The French *philosophes* were not formal philosophers but were, by and large, literary men, zealous popularizers and disseminators of the new knowledge which they believed would emancipate society from ignorance and fanaticism.

French Deism was much less theoretical and constructive than English Deism, although the former drew heavily from the latter for its weapons. The situations of the two countries explain in part, the differences in the development of rational religion. In England, religious toleration allowed for freedom of expression which even encouraged dialogue between the Deists and the representatives of orthodoxy and the established Church. In France these conditions did not exist.

The Catholic Church opposed free thinkers uncompromisingly and could call upon the State for assistance in repressing religious heterodoxy. The *philosophes* felt they were an embattled minority, standing against the forces of darkness: intolerance, fear, and superstition. The constant threat of persecution and repression gave to French Deism a militant, scurrilous, and yet devious quality that is predominantly negative in character. In speaking of Voltaire, G. R. Cragg describes well the tone and tactics of French Deism in general as follows:

This lurking threat of persecution explains a certain oblique disingenuousness in Voltaire, a readiness to hide behind the authority of others and to imply that he accepted more than he really did. He was sometimes abusive, sometimes cringing. He used abuse when he felt brave; he resorted to lies when he felt timid. But it also accounts for the violence, even the extravagance, into which the champions of reason and common sense allowed themselves to fall. When it was safe to do so, they attacked the strongholds of superstition with volcanic energy. Nothing was so sacred as to escape their ribald criticism, nothing so mysterious as to defy their constant analysis.[38]

The French *philosophes* popularized the views of the English Deists by reducing the often-tedious verbiage of the English dissertations to clear, crisp, and often witty pronouncements that were immediately grasped with a self-evident authority. The man who best exemplifies the phenomenon of French Deism is François Marie Arouet, who is known to us by his adopted name, Voltaire.

Voltaire (1694–1778) was for over half a century one of the most important influences on European thought and life. He was not a philosopher but a poet and dramatist turned critic and sage, whose pen changed the life and institutions of his native France.

Voltaire's religious beliefs have long occupied scholars.[39] Alfred Noyes, among others, has argued that Voltaire was a good Roman Catholic![40] Others have claimed Voltaire for Protestantism and for atheism. By picking and choosing from his writings, which span half a century, Voltaire can be made to champion everything from militant atheism to orthodox Catholicism. This is due not only to his long and active life but to the fact that he felt, with Emerson, that "consistency is the hobgoblin of small minds." He had a tough, pragmatic mind and, like most great men, the courage to change. Voltaire's writings have been aptly described as a "chaos of clarities." Nevertheless, most Voltaire scholars hold that the French sage was, through his mature life, a vague, mystical, and even emotional Deist.

Voltaire's early Deism is a simple natural religion, skeptical of speculation, but firmly convinced that the Newtonian universe justifies rational belief in the existence of a divine intelligence behind it. This is evident in his first attempt at a summation of his philosophic beliefs, the *Traité de Métaphysique*, written about 1734. In this essay Voltaire offers two arguments for the existence of God—the argument from design and the argument from the necessity of a final cause. In offering his argument from design, Voltaire uses the analogy between God and the watchmaker, an analogy which William Paley would later make famous in his *Natural Theology* (1802). The marvelous adaptation of means to particular ends, says Voltaire, argues for a designer.

When I see a watch whose hands mark the

hours, I conclude that an intelligent being has arranged the springs of this machine so that its hands will mark the hours. Thus, when I see the springs of the human body, I conclude that an intelligent being has arranged these organs to be received and nourished for nine months in the womb; that the eyes are given for seeing, the hands to seizing, etc., but from this sole argument I cannot conclude anything further than that it is probable that an intelligent and superior being has skillfully prepared and fashioned the matter.[41]

In typical rationalist fashion Voltaire offers his second argument for the existence of God, the argument from the necessity of a final cause.

I exist, hence something exists. If something exists, then something must have existed from all eternity; for whatever is, either exists through itself or has received its being from something else. If through itself, it exists of necessity, it has always existed of necessity, it is God; if it has received its being from something else, and that something from a third, that from which the last has received its being must of necessity be God . . . . Intelligence is not essential to matter, for a rock or grain do not think. Whence then have the particles of matter which think and feel received sensation and thought? It cannot be from themselves since they think in spite of themselves; it cannot be from matter in general, since thought and sensation do not belong to the essence of matter: hence they must have received these gifts from the hands of a Supreme Being, intelligent, infinite, and the original cause of all beings.[42]

Voltaire's conclusion in *Traité de Métaphysique* is that "In the opinion that there is a God there are difficulties; but in the contrary opinion there are absurdities."[43] In an article entitled *Théiste* in the *Dictionaire Philosophique*, Voltaire sums up his religious faith in a single page

that could well serve as the Confession of Faith of Deism:

The theist is a man firmly persuaded of the existence of a Supreme Being equally good and powerful, who has formed all . . . existences; who perpetuates their species, who punishes crimes without cruelty, and rewards virtuous actions with kindness.

The theist does not know how God punishes, how He rewards, how He pardons; for he is not presumptuous enough to flatter himself that he understands how God acts; but he knows that God does act and that He is just. The difficulties opposed to a providence do not stagger him in his faith, because they are only great difficulties, not proofs; he submits himself to that providence, although he only perceives some of its effects and some appearances; and judging of the things he does not see from those he does see, he thinks that this providence pervades all places and all ages.

United in this principle with the rest of the universe, he does not join any of the sects, who all contradict themselves. His religion is the most ancient and the most extended, for the simple adoration of a God preceded all the systems in the world . . . . He believes that religion consists neither in the opinions of incomprehensible metaphysics, nor in vain decorations, but in adoration and justice. To do good—that is his worship; to submit oneself to God—that is his doctrine. The Mohammedan cries out to him: "Take care of yourself, if you do not make the pilgrimage to Mecca." "Woe be to thee," says a Franciscan, "if thou dost not make a journey to our Lady of Loretta." He laughs at Loretta and Mecca; but he succours the poor and defends the oppressed.[44]

Until 1751 Voltaire refrained from any public attack upon Christianity. Here and there he would jab and mock at the foibles and fanaticism of the Church, but most of his religious writings consisted of praises of natural religion and pleas for mutual tolerance and understanding.

However, for over twenty years after 1751 Voltaire published a torrent of pamphlets and essays, scathing in their denunciation of Christianity. The causes of this declaration of war are not all known; three events in the decade following 1751 are certainly important. These events were the suppression of the *Encyclopédie*, for which Voltaire had written several articles; the facile theological explanations of the Lisbon earthquake of 1755, and the execution of Jean Calas, the Huguenot (Calvinist Protestant), in 1762, unjustly condemned on the charge of having killed his son to prevent his conversion to Catholicism.

Ecrasez l'infâme—"Crush the infamous thing"—was the battle cry from Ferney heard throughout Europe. Voltaire became so intoxicated with the slogan he even used it, in abbreviated form, as a signature: "Ecr. linf." What did Voltaire mean by *l'infâme* that required to be crushed? Four possibilities have been argued with some plausibility: fanaticism, Catholicism, Christianity, and religion. It is clear, however, that to the end of his life Voltaire expressed genuine, deep religious convictions. It is also evident that the object of his attack went beyond fanaticism in general and was primarily an assault on the doctrines and practices shared by Catholics and Protestants alike. *L'infâme* was quite certainly Christianity in any of its orthodox, institutional forms, whether found in Geneva or Rome.

Voltaire's declaration of war was the *Sermon of the Fifty*, written at the court at Potsdam. The *Sermon* and other writings of this period are vehement and cynical tracts whose critical insights now appear quaint but nevertheless reveal that Voltaire was *au courant* of the most advanced biblical criticism of his age. He pokes fun at the outmoded science and primitive morals of the ancient Hebrews, relating story after story of the lies, murders, and fornications of the noble Jewish patriarchs.

> What will you say of the holy King David, the king who found favour in the eyes of the God of the Jews, and merited to be an ancestor of the Messiah? This good king is at first a brigand, capturing and pillaging all he finds. Among others, he despoils a rich man named Nabal, marries his wife and flies to King Achish. During the night he descends upon the villages of King Achish, his benefactor, with fire and sword. He slaughters men, women, and children . . . . When he is made King he ravishes the wife of Uriah and has the husband put to death; and it is from this adulterous homicide that the Messiah—God himself—descends![45]

Voltaire delights in pointing out the incongruities and contradictions in the Bible. Here are just a few examples:

Adam and Eve:

> On the sixth day God makes man and woman; but the author, forgetting that woman has been made already, afterwards derives her from one of Adam's ribs. Adam and Eve are put in the garden from which four rivers issue; and of these rivers there are two, the Euphrates and the Nile, which have their sources a thousand miles from each other.

Noah and the Flood:

> [God] wished to save Noah and ordered him to make a vessel of poplar wood, three hundred cubits in length. Into this vessel were brought seven pairs of all clean and two pairs of the unclean. . . . You can imagine what would be needed to feed fourteen elephants, fourteen camels, fourteen buffaloes, and as many horses, asses, deer, serpents, ostriches . . . !

Jesus:

In the first place, Jesus is described as a descendant of Abraham and David, and the writer of Matthew counts forty-two generations. . . . Luke also gives a genealogy, but he assigns forty-nine generations after Abraham and they are entirely different generations. To complete the absurdity, these generations belong to Joseph and the evangelists assure us that Jesus was not the son of Joseph. Would one be received in a German chapter on such proofs of nobility?[46]

Voltaire ends the *Sermon* by imploring:

May the great God who hears me—a God who certainly could not be born of a girl, nor die on a gibbet, nor be eaten in a morsel of paste, nor have inspired this book with its contradictions, follies, and horrors—may this God have pity on the sect of Christians who blaspheme him![47]

Voltaire's attack on *l'infâme* never varied. The illustrations changed, but the sermon remained the same. Often the long explications of biblical passages are tedious and tendentious, but here and there they are lightened by brilliant and outrageous humor. What drove Voltaire to such feverish polemics was his conviction that organized Christianity supported irrational superstitions whose vulnerability led only to fanaticism. With psychological perception Voltaire recognized that fanaticism was usually the reaction of weakness covering up its seething uncertainty with acts of suppression. "If you were fully persuaded you would not be intolerant. You are intolerant only because deep in your heart you feel that you are being deceived."[48] The only way to reduce the evils of fanaticism was to unmask superstition, thus freeing men from the

source of their spiritual malaise: "In a word, less superstition, less fanaticism; and the less fanaticism, less misery."[49] Voltaire regarded most of the doctrines of the Christian tradition—the Incarnation, the Atonement, the Trinity, the Eucharist—as superstitious folly and the principal source of persecution and suffering. His comments on the Trinity will suffice.

Here is an incomprehensible question which for over sixteen hundred years has exercized curiosity, sophistical subtlety, bitterness, the spirit of cabal, the rage to dominate, the rage to persecute, blind and bloodthirsty fanaticism, barbaric credulity, and which has produced more horrors than the ambition of princes, which indeed has produced enough. Is Jesus Word? If he is Word, did he emanate from God, is he coeternal and consubstantial with him, or is he of similar substance? Is he distinct from him, or not? Is he created or engendered? Can he engender in turn? Has he paternity or productive virtue without paternity? Is the Holy Ghost created or engendered, or produced? Does he proceed from the Father, or from the Son, or from both? Can he engender, can he produce? Is his hypostasis consubstantial with the hypostasis of the Father and the Son? and why, having precisely the same nature, the same essence as the Father and the Son, can he not do the same things as these two persons who are himself? I certainly do not understand any of this; nobody has ever understood any of this, and this is the reason for which people have slaughtered one another![50]

Voltaire wanted to purify religion of *l'infâme*, of Christianity. He felt that health could be restored to society only when the infection of fanaticism was eliminated. Yet Voltaire was aware of the dangers of depriving the masses of their inherited religion, for it was the foundation of their moral sanctions and restraints.

Though cognizant of the social utility of an unquestioned religious tradition,[51] Voltaire was willing to take the chance that the untutored masses could be enlightened: "We know that our enemies have been crying for centuries that one must deceive the people; but we believe that the lowest people are capable of knowing the truth."[52] Christianity could not be exterminated immediately, however.

Such is the miserable condition of man that the true is not always the advantageous.... It would doubtless be desirable to overthrow the idol, and to offer God purer homage, but the people is not yet worthy of it. For the present it is enough to contain the Church in its limits. The more laymen are enlightened, the less harm priests will be able to do. Let us try to enlighten even them, to make them blush for their errors, to lead them gradually to becoming citizens.[53]

In the place of Christianity, Voltaire envisioned a new religion: a rather vague, popular form of Deism. Doctrine would be reduced to belief in one just God, whose service was the practice of virtue. Worship would be simple and would consist primarily in praise and adoration and lessons in morality. To the end of his life Voltaire held to his rational faith in God, despite the fact that his atheist supporters in Paris were now to turn on him in scorn and dismiss the old man with: "*Il est un bigot, c'est un déiste!*" In these last years Voltaire attacked the materialism of d'Holbach and in *We Must Take Sides* (1772) offered rational arguments for God reminiscent of the *Traité de la Métaphysique*.

The character of Voltaire's rational faith, which remained with him throughout his mature years, is nicely indicated in an incident that took place in his eightieth year. One morning in May 1774, Voltaire awakened before dawn and with a visitor climbed a hill near Ferney to see the sunrise. Reaching the top exhausted and overcome by the beauty of the glorious morning scene, Voltaire took off his hat, knelt down, and exclaimed, "I believe, I believe in you, Powerful God, I believe!" And then, getting to his feet, he told the visitor drily: "As for monsieur the Son and madame His Mother, that is a different story!"[54]

The Religion of Reason in Germany

The German *Aufklärung* was in several ways quite different from the comparable movements in England and France. For one thing, the philosophical roots of the German Enlightenment were in the Leibnitz-Wolff tradition of rationalism rather than the Anglo-French empiricism of John Locke. By the middle of the eighteenth century the Leibnitz-Wolff philosophy had taken on the proportions of a universal program for bringing all human thought and activity before the bar of reason—a deductive model of reason, ruled by the formal principles of noncontradiction and sufficient reason.

English and French influences in Germany were not lacking, however, and were especially significant in the religious sphere. Frederick the Great of Prussia (1712–1786) was particularly drawn to French and English thought. This free-thinking and skeptical monarch was for several years friend and patron of several philosophers, including Voltaire who lived at the court at Potsdam where, as we have seen, he wrote his anti-Christian *Sermon of the Fifty*. Locke was a favorite philosopher of the Prussian monarch, and he encouraged the study of the English-man's works. The effect of English and French thought in Germany was especi-ally important in the development of German Deism. At the beginning of the eighteenth century John Toland had traveled through Germany, visiting the courts of Hanover and Berlin. In 1741 Tindal's *Christianity as Old as the Creation* appeared in German.

H. S. Reimarus. The most promi-nent of the German Deists was Hermann Samuel Reimarus (1694–1768), a Pro-fessor of Oriental Languages in Hamburg. Only three of his works appeared during his lifetime, the most important being an essay entitled "The Leading Truths of Natural Religion." At his death he left a four-thousand-page manuscript on which he had labored for twenty years. The work was so controversial that it re-mained unpublished until the philosopher Lessing obtained permission from Rei-marus' daughter to issue it on the con-dition that the author's name not be divulged. The manuscript was originally entitled *An Apology for the Rational Worshippers of God*, but Lessing pub-lished only seven portions of it as the *Wolffenbüttel Fragments*, claiming that he had found the anonymous fragments at Wolffenbüttel where he was serving as librarian.

Armed with rationalist assumptions, Reimarus' *Apology* subjects the whole biblical history, and thus Christianity, to critical analysis. The third fragment, entitled "The Passage of the Israelites Through the Red Sea", is a witty, Voltairean exposé of the account of the Exodus from Egypt. If the biblical narrative is correct, Reimarus calculates that three million Israelites passed through the Red Sea (one warrior to every four

others). This would mean that if the Israelites moved in a column ten deep, the length of the column would have been one hundred and eighty miles, and would have taken nine days to cross at a minimum!

In the fifth fragment, "On the Resur-rection Narrative," the inconsistencies in the Gospel narratives are analyzed with the conclusion that the conflicting accounts point to the fact that the miracle itself is an imposture. In the last fragment, "On the Aim of Jesus and His Disciples," Reimarus not only rejects the miracles and the Resurrection but pictures Jesus as a Jewish apocalyptical fanatic who, on the Cross, cries out, "My God, my God, why hast Thou forsaken me?" as a con-fession of his error and bitter defeat.[55]

Reimarus was a man held in high honor among his contemporaries and during his lifetime remained a practicing churchman. Few, outside the inner circle of friends and family, were aware of the radicalness of his ideas or the passionate feeling and even hatred that flamed in his breast. He died a seemingly serene and certainly peace-loving professor, prefer-ring that his thoughts remain concealed rather than cause controversy and unrest. The editor and publisher of the fragments of his *Apology*, G. E. Lessing, was a man of different temperament who soon found himself in a heated controversy.

G. E. Lessing. Gotthold Ephraim Lessing (1729–1781) is perhaps the most representative and influential figure in the German Enlightenment. He is best known as a dramatist and art critic but, as recent studies have shown, his influence on modern theology has been very great. Lessing was the son of an orthodox Lutheran pastor. At seventeen he was sent to the University of Leipzig to study theology but soon gave up theology for his real passion—the theater. In 1769 Lessing was offered the post of librarian at the Duke of Brunswick's library at Wolffenbüttel, and in 1773 he began publishing a series of *Contributions to Literature and History* from the Ducal Library. Among these *Contributions* were the fragments from the *Apology* of Reimarus. Their publication stirred a controversy that consumed the last five years of Lessing's life. Lessing's own attitude toward the *Fragments* was ambivalent. He rejected the strict rationalist proofs of religion offered by Reimarus and did not hold Reimarus' scornful view of the positive, historical religions. However, he believed Reimarus had rendered a very important service to religion in freeing Christianity from its false supports. At the end of the *Fragments*, Lessing appended his own "Editor's Counterpropositions" in which he expressed his own attitude to such destructive criticisms.

And now enough of these fragments. Any of my readers who would prefer me to have spared them altogether is surely more timid than well instructed . . . .

For how much could be said in reply to all these objections and difficulties! And even if absolutely no answer were forthcoming, what then? The learned theologian might in the last resort be embarrassed, but certainly not the Christian. To the former it might at most cause confusion to see the supports with which he would uphold religion shattered in this way, to find the buttresses cast down by which, God willing, he would have made it safe and sound. But how do this man's hypotheses, explanations, and proofs affect the Christian? For him it is simply a fact—the Christianity which he feels to be true and in which he feels blessed. . . .

In short, the letter is not the spirit and the Bible not religion. Consequently, objections to the letter and to the Bible are not also objections to the spirit and to religion . . . . Moreover, religion was there before a Bible existed. Christianity was there before the evangelists and apostles wrote. A long period elapsed before the first of them wrote, and a very considerable time before the entire canon was complete . . . . The religion is not true because the evangelists and apostles taught it; but they taught it because it is true. The written traditions must be interpreted by their inward truth and no written traditions can give the religion any inward truth if it has none.[56]

The publication of the *Fragments* brought about a series of replies from the orthodox, especially from the Hamburg pastor, Johann Goeze. Goeze justly felt that the Reimarus fragments would upset the simple believers, but he recognized the "Counterpropositions" of Lessing as an even greater danger to the faith. Goeze's attack provoked a series of eleven violent articles from Lessing, entitled *Anti-Goeze*. These articles reveal Lessing's brilliant invective but little of his own religious thought. Lessing's most important reply to his orthodox critics was "On the Proof of the Spirit and of Power," addressed to J. D. Schumann of Hanover, who had sought to counter the Reimarus *Fragments* with traditional arguments from miracle and prophecy.

"On the Proof of the Spirit and of Power" is a critique of the proof of Christianity from the historical testimony of miracles and fulfilled prophecy. The assumptions underlying Lessing's argument reflect his own rationalist bent in that he accepts, at least provisionally, Leibnitz's distinction between the necessary truths of reason and the contingent truths of sensory experience. The truths of reason, which are assumed to be of a higher order, express relations that obtain among ideas that are always and everywhere the same. "Truths of reason," said Leibnitz, "are necessary and their opposite is impossible; those of fact are contingent and their opposite is possible."[57] Truths of reason are a priori and absolutely certain. Truths of fact are dubitable and therefore cannot serve as proof. To Lessing this is exactly the point. The orthodox theologians have been arguing for the indubitability of Christianity on the basis of miracle and prophecy, both of which are dependent upon historical testimony. But unqualified certainty, if not possible even for one who has personally experienced the alleged events, clearly is not indubitable when dependent on the testimony of others' experience. Lessing's argument is as follows:

Fulfilled prophecies, which I myself experience, are one thing; fulfilled prophecies, of which I know only from history that others say they have experienced them, are another.

Miracles, which I see with my own eyes, and which I have the opportunity to verify for myself, are one thing; miracles of which I know only from history that others say they have seen them and verified them, are another.

If I had lived at the time of Christ, then of course the prophecies fulfilled in his person would have made me pay great attention to him. If I had actually seen him do miracles . . . I would willingly have submitted my intellect to his, and I would have believed him in all things in which equally indisputable experiences did not tell against him.

Or: if I even now experienced that prophecies referring to Christ or the Christian religion . . . were fulfilled in a manner admitting no dispute; if even now miracles were done by believing Christians which I had to recognize as true miracles: what could prevent me from accepting this proof of the spirit and of power?

But . . . I live in the eighteenth century, in which miracles no longer happen . . . . The problem is that this proof of the spirit and of power no longer has any spirit or power, but has sunk to the level of human testimonies of spirit and power.

If then this proof of the proof (the contemporary reality of miracle) has now entirely lapsed . . . how is it expected of me that the same inconceivable truths which sixteen to eighteen hundred years ago people believed on the strongest inducement, should be believed by men to be equally valid on an infinitely lesser inducement?[58]

Lessing anticipates the answer, namely, that we believe on the basis of the testimony of reputable historians. But

what is asserted is only that the reports which we have of these prophecies and miracles are as reliable as historical truths ever can be. And then it is added that historical truths cannot be demonstrated: nevertheless we must believe them as firmly as truths that have been demonstrated.

To this I answer: who will deny (not I) that the reports of these miracles and prophecies are as reliable as historical truths ever can be? But if they are only as reliable as this, why are they treated as if they were infinitely more reliable?

And in what way? In this way, that something quite different and much greater is founded upon them than it is legitimate to found upon truths historically proved.

If no historical truth can be demonstrated, then nothing can be demonstrated by means of historical truths.

That is: *accidental truths of history can never become the proof of necessary truths of reason.*[59]

What the orthodox theologians had done was not only to prove, for example, the resurrection of Christ on the basis of historical testimony, but, worse, had "jumped" from this dubitable historical fact to a completely different class of truths.

If on historical grounds I have no objection to the statement that Christ raised to life a dead man; must I therefore accept it as true that God has a Son who is of the same essence as himself? . . . To jump with that historical truth to a quite different class of truths, and to demand of me that I should form all my metaphysical and moral ideas accordingly . . . if that is not a "transformation to another kind," then I do not know what Aristotle meant by this phrase . . . . *That, then, is the ugly broad ditch which I cannot get across, however often and however earnestly I have tried to make the leap.* If anyone can help me over it, let him do it, I beg him, I adjure him. He will deserve a divine reward from me.[60] (Italics added.)

It is widely acknowledged that Lessing's argument in "The Proof of the Spirit and of Power" is confused and open to serious question. Demonstrating Lessing's faulty reasoning is not our concern here; it is rather to see Lessing's own positive solution to the problem he posed.

What, then, binds Lessing to the teachings of Christ, if not the proof of his authority through miracle and prophecy? Simply the teachings themselves. The teachings are not authoritative because they are found in a sacred book; the book is sacred because it speaks an inward truth that existed long before the Bible. "Is the situation such that 'I should hold a geometrical theorem to be true not because it can be demonstrated, but because it can be found in Euclid'?"[61] No, of course not. "When the paralytic feels the beneficial shocks of the electric spark, does it worry him whether Nollet or Franklin or neither of them is right?"[62] Again, no.

These fruits I may see before me ripe and ripened, and may I not be satisfied with that? The old pious legend that the hand which scatters the seed must wash in snail's blood seven times for each throw, I do not doubt, but merely ignore it. What does it matter to me whether the legend is false or true? The fruits are excellent.[63]

If there be any "proof" of religion, it must be "the proof of the spirit and of power," i.e., of personal experience. And history serves a vital role in experience for it is the rough husk in which the kernel of truth is given to us to be appropriated. History is the necessary vehicle of the truth which, because it is always and everywhere the same, must also be then and there, here and now, i.e., locatable in the particular, contingent events of history. Lessing then, does not hold that the "necessary truths of reason" are evident without regard to time and space. Rather he makes an implicit distinction between "accidental truths of history" and "truths of history." Accidental truths of history, which cannot become proofs of necessary truths of reason, are, as Karl Barth has rightly suggested, "to be understood as such particular, concretely unique historical truths, about which I am merely informed by others. I have not myself encountered them, I have not myself experienced them as true."[64] On the other hand, "truths of history can become proof for me of necessary truths of reason, but only when they are not merely 'accidental' historical truths, but have become necessary to me."[65] When experienced as "necessary to me," such historical truths have "the proof of the spirit and of power." The proof of religion rests not in the historical events as such but through the personal experience of the inner truth mediated through these concrete historical events.

Is this inner truth of religion confined to the events of the biblical record? No, for "religion was there before a Bible existed.... It must be possible that everything the evangelists and apostles wrote could have been lost, and yet that the religion which they taught would have continued."[66] Because there is this primordial foundation of religious truth which is before and after the Bible, the kinds of radical doubts raised by Reimarus concerning the veracity of the biblical narratives are really irrelevant. Thus Lessing can conclude the essay by saying: "My wish is: May all who are divided by the Gospel of John be reunited by the Testament of John. Admittedly, it is apocryphal, this testament. But it is not on that account any the less divine."[67]

In *The Education of the Human Race*, published in 1777, Lessing reveals both his appreciation of historical revelation, which was so unlike the Deism of his time, and his rational faith that the positive religions will ultimately be superseded by the true gospel of reason. In fact, for Lessing revelation means the progressive education of the human race. The positive religions are simply stages in the advance of humanity from infancy to maturity. What education is to the individual, revelation is to the whole of the human race. Just as education gives man nothing which he does not already have within him, but brings it to light more quickly and easily, so does revelation give nothing to the human race which it could not itself arrive at on its own, but only the more important things more quickly.[68] Just as in education not everything can be imparted at once, so God has maintained a certain order in his revelation. Lessing then proceeds to detail God's educative process.

According to Lessing, the first man was endowed with the conception of one God. However, this idea did not retain its original purity, and man fell into idolatry and polytheism. Such beliefs might have continued for millions of years if God had not selected an individual people for his special education. This was the Hebrew people. Yet a race in its infancy is capable of receiving only an infant's instruction.

Every primer is only for a certain age.... A better instructor must come and tear the exhausted primer from the child's hands— Christ came!... That portion of the human race, which God had wished to embrace in one plan of education, was ripe for the second great step.[69]

For seventeen hundred years the New Testament has served as the second, better primer for the race of man. Some of the cleverer youths are even now growing impatient with it but, Lessing warns, those who are impatient should "take care that you do not let your weaker classmates notice what you are beginning to scent, or even see!"[70] The fact is that the New Testament cannot continue for ever; it, too, will serve its turn. Newer and better conceptions of the divine Being and of our own nature will come. "It will assuredly come! the time of a new eternal gospel, which is promised us in the primers of the New Covenant itself!"[71] This new eternal gospel is, conceivably, the *third age* prophesied by the apocalyptical enthusiasts of the thirteenth and fourteenth centuries and heralded in secular form by the likes of Condorcet. Perchance they only erred in that they predicted its too early arrival!

Go thine inscrutable way, Eternal Providence! Only let me not despair of thee because of this inscrutableness. Let me not despair of thee, even if thy steps appear to me to be going backward. It is not true that the shortest line is always straight.[72]

Such was Lessing's vision of the spiritual education of the human race. True to the Deism of his age, he believed that the positive revelation given in the Judeo-Christian Scriptures was only a temporary vehicle in God's educative program. The Jewish-Christian revelation would be superseded by a purer religion of reason. Yet Lessing was not an ordinary rationalistic Deist, for he was unwilling to accept the radical disjunction between the truths of natural religion and those of the positive revealed religions. In commenting upon the significance of Lessing, Cassirer suggests that

In his *Education of Humanity* Lessing created a new synthesis of the historical and the rational. The historical is no longer opposed to the rational; it is rather the way to the realization of the rational and the real, indeed the only possible place of its fulfillment. The elements, which Leibnitz's analytical mind had separated with such incomparable precision and clarity, now tend toward reconciliation. For religion, according to Lessing, belongs neither to the sphere of the necessary and eternal nor to that of the merely accidental and temporal. It is both in one; it is the manifestation of the infinite in the finite, of the eternal and rational in the temporal process of becoming. With this thought . . . Lessing has reached the turning point of the real philosophy of the Enlightenment.[73]

Lessing can be interpreted as a transitional figure—a true apostle of reason, an unflinching *Aufklärer*, but with a difference. In many ways he revealed tendencies that would become dominant in the nineteenth century, seen, for example, in his ideas of historical inevitability and progressive revelation and his distinction between historical fact and existential

truth. But to the end he remained a devoted disciple of natural religion, holding that even the best revealed religion is the one that contains the fewest additions to natural religion, and least hinders the good effects of natural religion. With his fellow Deists he died the implacable enemy of the dogmatic claims of special revelation and authoritarian creed. The story is told that when Lessing heard that Voltaire had received on his sickbed the rites of the priest of Saint Sulpice, he replied: "When you see me dying call for the notary; I will declare to him that I die in none of the positive religions."[74]

Conclusion

Despite the differences that did exist among the apostles of the religion of reason, there were many things they held in common which set them apart from those who came before and after. First of all, they believed religion was essentially a simple matter. There was a general desire, even among the supernaturalists, to reduce religion and Christianity to a very few doctrines and even fewer practices. Sacraments and rituals were regarded as useless, even dangerous, mumbo jumbo. Locke argued for Christian revelation on the grounds that it did away with the "pompous, cumbersome ceremonies" of the Jews and the priests. The eighteenth century was anticlerical and antiecclesiastical. Institutional Christianity was considered the instrument of wily priests. As Voltaire expressed it, "the first divine was the first rogue who met the first fool."

It was generally agreed that Christianity was simple and that its essence lay in providing divine sanctions for morality. Religion was very largely confined to the performing of one's moral duties conceived of as divine commands. Endowed with a free will, man could, it was presumed, choose the good and avoid evil. Nature and man were thus taken from the Fall. It was assumed that the natural man could come to the truths of religion by reason, and, discerning these truths, he would naturally pursue the good. Future rewards and punishments would be determined solely by one's conduct on earth. Implied in such a view was the attitude that religion was solely a matter between the individual and God and therefore a highly individualistic affair. Consequently, the Church was thought of as a voluntary association.

There emerged in the eighteenth century several distinct views of the historical role of the Christian religion which have had a continuing significance in the modern quest for the nature and essence of Christianity.[75] Out of the debates of the eighteenth century there emerged the central question: What is Christianity? What constitutes its essence? Does it include the whole heritage of the centuries, or the teachings of Jesus, or the apostolic teachings? A number of views were expressed. There was first the view that Christianity was a corruption of true religion and, therefore, an evil to be opposed and eradicated. This was the view taken by most of the French *philosophes* and by the historian Gibbon. Christianity's influence was seen as largely pernicious and the positive doctrines as fraudulent superstitions. Culture and society would be far better off without this nefarious influence. *Ecrasez l'infâme!*

A second view identified Christianity with the religion of nature. Christianity, when purified of many of its historical accretions, was seen as a *republication* of the original religion of nature, which is open to all men by the light of their natural reason. This was the view of constructive Deism, of men like Toland and Tindal, and later the view taken by Kant. The essence of Christianity is none other than that of the religion of reason, but couched in the more or less imperfect form of an historical tradition. Beneath the historical illustration lies the essential and universal truth which is evident to all men of reason. According to this view, historic revelation is a mere convenience or concession to human weakness.

A third view distinguishes historic Christianity from natural religion by conceiving of the former as a necessary supplement or higher type. This was the view of the theologians of the Middle Ages but is restated in the Enlightenment by the rational supernaturalists such as John Locke. Natural religion is excellent and legitimate as far as it goes but, for one reason or another, is not sufficient. It needs the supplementation of certain supernatural doctrines which are found only in special revelation in Scripture. For Locke such special revelation is evidenced in the outward signs or divine warrants for the claim that Jesus is the Messiah. Only in Scripture are these supernatural warrants given—hence the need for special revelation "above" but not "contrary" to natural reason.

Finally, there was the attempt to conceive of Christianity as one historic stage in the progress toward a perfect, universal religion which lies in the future. This view is represented in Lessing's "Education of the Human Race" and was to become a popular view in the nineteenth century. Here Christ or Christianity is not seen as the historic republication of the original religion of nature or as the full and complete revelation of divine truth. Christianity has led mankind one step further in humanity's pilgrimage toward that "new eternal Gospel which is promised . . . in the New Testament itself." Christianity is neither the original nor final religion for it, too, will give place to the universal religion of the future.

All four of these views of Christianity will continue to find exponents in the nineteenth century. Underlying all of them—even though imperceptibly—is a new concern for history, for establishing the originality, the warrants, or the relative and transitory character of Christianity by an appeal to history. The Enlightenment was, it is true, an age of reason but its empirical spirit did not allow it to remain in a world of rational abstractions. There is the emergence of an historical consciousness which does not come into the full light of day until the nineteenth century. But before we consider the beginnings of the new spirit of the nineteenth century, we must give some attention to the final breakdown of the religion of reason.

NOTES

1. A. C. McGiffert, *Protestant Thought Before Kant* (New York, 1962).
2. W. Chillingworth, *Religion of Protestants* (1638), p. 198.
3. J. Tillotson, *Sermons*, Vol. 1, p. 225; quoted in L. Stephen, *English Thought in the Eighteenth Century*, Vol. 1, p. 78.
4. Ibid.
5. Tillotson, *Works* (London, 1857), II, 333.
6. *Works*, III, 493 ff., quoted in McGiffert, op. cit., p. 197 ff.
7. Ibid.
8. J. Locke, *An Essay Concerning Human Understanding*, ed. A. S. Pringle-Pattison (Oxford, 1956), p. 9.
9. Ibid., p. 354.
10. Ibid., p. 355.
11. Ibid., p. 356.
12. Ibid., p. 357.
13. Ibid., p. 357–358.
14. Ibid., p. 360.
15. Ibid., p. 361.
16. Ibid.
17. Ibid., pp. 362–363.
18. J. Locke, *A Discourse of Miracles*, in Stanford edition of *The Reasonableness of Christianity*, ed. I. T. Ramsey, p. 80.
19. Introduction, *The Reasonableness of Christianity* (Stanford, 1958), p. 13.
20. Ibid., p. 14.
21. Ibid., p. 15.
22. Ibid., p. 52.
23. Ibid., pp. 52–53.
24. Ibid., p. 55.
25. *Christianity Not Mysterious*; quoted in Creed and Boys Smith, *Religious Thought in the 18th Century*, p. 17.
26. Ibid.
27. Ibid., p. 20.
28. *Christianity as Old as the Creation*, quoted in Creed and Boys Smith, op. cit., p. 34.
29. Ibid., pp. 33–34.
30. Ibid., p. 32.
31. Tindal, op. cit., p. 111; cited in L. Stephen, *English Thought in the Eighteenth Century*, I, 140.
32. Tindal, op. cit., p. 14.
33. Ibid., p. 18.
34. Ibid., p. 270.
35. Ibid., p. 125
36. Ibid., p. 134.
37. L. Stephen, op. cit., pp. 144–145.
38. G. R. Cragg, *The Church in the Age of Reason: 1648–1789* (New York, 1961), p. 240.
39. A survey of the various positions that have been argued is found in René Pomeau's *La religion de Voltaire*. See also Peter Gay, *Voltaire's Politics*, pp. 389–391.
40. Alfred Noyes, *Voltaire*, 1936. On March

31, 1769, before witnesses, Voltaire did sign an affirmation that he wished to die in the Roman Catholic religion.

41. Voltaire, *Works*, XXI, 239.
42. Ibid., pp. 240–241.
43. Cited in J. H. Randall, Jr., *The Making of the Modern Mind* (New York, 1926), p. 296.
44. Voltaire, *Works*, VII, 82–83.
45. *Sermon*, in J. McCabe, ed., *Toleration and Other Essays by Voltaire*, p. 168.
46. Ibid., pp. 170, 177. Voltaire proceeds similarly in *The Questions of Zapata* written in 1767. The essay pretends to be a series of questions put to a committee of theologians by a professor of theology at the University of Salamanca.
47. Ibid., p. 182.
48. Voltaire, *Notebooks*, p. 452; quoted in P. Gay, op. cit., p. 251.
49. *Philosophical Dictionary*, article "Superstition," H. I. Wolff, ed. (New York, 1924), p. 298.
50. *Philosophical Dictionary*, article "Arius"; quoted in P. Gay, op. cit., p. 253.
51. On numerous occasions Voltaire wrote of the social utility of religion. A story about Voltaire reveals both his humor and practicality. D'Alembert and Condorcet were dining at Ferney and during the course of the dinner were making antireligious remarks. Voltaire stopped them, sent the servants out of the room, and said, "Now, messieurs, you may continue. I was only afraid of having my throat cut tonight . . . ." Cited in P. Gay, op. cit., pp. 262–263.
52. Cited in P. Gay, op. cit., p. 263.
53. Ibid., p. 271.
54. Ibid., p. 241.
55. Reimarus is the first modern critical scholar to hold the "consistent eschatology" position now made famous by Albert Schweitzer. This position within New Testament criticism contends that Jesus held views consistent with radical Jewish apocalypticism and that the failure of these apocalyptic hopes led to the development of Church dogma. Here is Schweitzer's estimate of Reimarus' historical role:
It is time that Reimarus came into his own, and that we should recognize a historical performance of no mean order in this piece of Deistic polemics. His work is perhaps the most splendid achievement in the whole course of the historical investigation of the life of Jesus, for he was the first to grasp the fact that the world of thought in which Jesus moved was essentially eschatological. (*The Quest of the Historical Jesus* [New York, 1964], pp. 22–23.)
56. *Lessing's Theological Writings*, ed. Henry Chadwick (Stanford, 1957), pp. 17–18.
57. *Monadology* (Everyman ed.), p. 9.
58. Lessing, op. cit., pp. 51–53.
59. Ibid., p. 53.
60. Ibid., pp. 54–55.
61. *Theological Writings*, III, 127; quoted in K. Barth, *From Rousseau to Ritschl*, p. 136.
62. Lessing, op. cit., pp. 17–18.
63. Ibid., p. 55.
64. K. Barth, op. cit., p. 137.
65. Ibid., pp. 137–138.
66. Lessing, op. cit., p. 18.
67. Ibid., p. 56.
68. Ibid., p. 83.
69. Ibid., p. 91.
70. Ibid., p. 93.
71. Ibid., p. 96.
72. Ibid., p. 97.
73. E. Cassirer, *The Philosophy of the Enlightenment*, p. 194.
74. Lessing, op. cit., pp. 44–45.
75. The author is dependent on the analysis of William A. Brown in *The Essence of Christianity*.

SUGGESTIONS FOR FURTHER READING

For general accounts of the Religion of Reason in the eighteenth century, the following are especially recommended:

Cragg, G. R. *Reason and Authority in the Eighteenth Century* (Cambridge: Cambridge University Press, 1964). An excellent survey of English theology in the Age of Reason —from Locke through the Deists, Butler, Hume, Wesley, and others.

Creed, J. M. and Boys Smith, J. S. *Religious Thought in the 18th Century* (Cambridge: Cambridge University Press, 1934). A good collection of brief texts illustrating the religious thought of the period. Helpful since many of the texts are difficult to come by.

McGiffert, A. C. *Protestant Thought before Kant* (New York: Harper Torchbooks, 1962). Chapter X of this book contains an excellent survey of eighteenth-century theological Rationalism.

Mossner, E. C. *Bishop Butler and the Age of Reason* (New York: The Macmillan Company, 1936). Mossner places Butler in the context of the religious thought from Locke to Hume, especially in relation to the Deist controversy.

Pattison, Mark, "Tendencies of Religious Thought in England 1688–1750," *Essays and Reviews* (1860). A not very accessible but, nevertheless, important essay on the subject.

Randall, J. H., Jr. *Making of the Modern Mind* (New York: Houghton Mifflin Co., 1926). In Chapter XII Randall gives an interesting, brief account of the Religion of Reason.

Stephen, Leslie. *English Thought in the Eighteenth Century*, Vol. I (New York: G. P. Putnam's Sons, 1927). This is the fullest and ablest account of eighteenth-century English theology available.

Waring, E. Graham. *Deism and Natural Religion* (New York: Ungar, 1967). A good collection of Deist writings.

Useful works in English on French and German religious thought in the eighteenth century are rare. For Voltaire see the excellent Chapter V of Peter Gay's *Voltaire's Politics* (Princeton, 1959). Also two works by Norman L. Torrey: *The Spirit of Voltaire* (New York, 1938) and *Voltaire and the English Deists* (New Haven, 1930). Chapter I of Franklin Baumer's *Religion and the Rise of Scepticism* is a lively account of French skepticism in the Age of Reason.

For Lessing see E. Cassirer, *The Philosophy of the Enlightenment* and Karl Barth's essay in *From Rousseau to Ritschl* (New York, 1959). Also, the "Introduction" to *Lessing's Theological Writings*, ed. Henry Chadwick (Stanford, 1957). A brief survey of German theological rationalism is given in A. L. Drummond, *German Protestantism Since Luther* (London, 1951).

CHAPTER THREE

The Breakdown of the Religion of Reason

David Hume

Like the Temple of Reason in Notre Dame de Paris, the cult of reason was relatively short-lived. This was because reason has a way of turning upon itself. The Enlightenment proved, finally, to be as much the critic as disciple of rationalism. Philosophers such as Rousseau, Joseph Butler, Hume, and Kant, all of whom remained true children of the eighteenth century, were led in quite different ways to question the very foundations of the rationalist credo. The religion of reason was in a sense consumed in the fires of its own analysis.

The failure of the religion of reason was occasioned by a number of factors. First of all, it was unable to attract the masses. It was too abstract, too intellectual in spite of its claim to simplicity. It also lacked feeling and the aesthetic sense which, even though unarticulated, is required of any religious faith that expects a wide appeal. Deism also lacked unity. The radical demands of autonomy were liberating but did not contribute to *fraternité*, to a sense of a common bond of faith and worship. The chief reason, however, for the decline of Deism is that it was dismantled by its own analytical tools. In this chapter we shall examine some of the major developments in the breakdown of the eighteenth-century religion of reason.

Jean Jacques Rousseau

The historic significance of Jean Jacques Rousseau (1712–1778) lies, in part, in the fact that he was largely responsible for shifting the discussion of nature, man, and God to a new plane by freeing reason from its isolation from feeling and willing. In this Rousseau was a precursor of Romanticism. The discovery of feeling, will, and the affections as indispensable ingredients in man's rational life forced Rousseau to disassociate himself from many of his rationalist contemporaries, particularly from those *philosophes* who identified themselves with the materialism of d'Holbach. The passion and melancholy of Rousseau's own life is symptomatic of his break with the rationalist spirit of his age. Lytton Strachey testified accurately to the historic uniqueness of Rousseau when he said that Rousseau

possessed one quality which cut him off from his contemporaries, which set an immense gulf betwixt him and them . . . . he belonged to another world—the new world of self-consciousness, and doubt, and hesitation, of mysterious melancholy, and quiet intimate delights, of long reflexion amid the solitudes of Nature, of infinite introspections amid the solitudes of the heart.[1]

In short, Rousseau imbued the rationalist temper with the powerful force of feeling. In this he contributed to the demise of the older rationalist credo and to the construction of a religious faith grounded in man's moral sentiments.

Rousseau's own religious pilgrimage was a stormy one. Born in Geneva into a family of Calvinists, Rousseau had early aspirations toward being a preacher. His Protestant, Genevan childhood was of unusually significant import in the development of his mind and character in maturity. Yet at sixteen he ran away to Savoy where, seemingly without difficulty, he was converted to Catholicism. He was then sent to Madame de Warens of Annecy, an attractive young woman who combined zeal for the Catholic religion with a notable lack of restraint in affairs romantic. Through Madame de Warens' insistence, Rousseau found himself at the monastery at Turin where he was baptized and received into the Roman Church. During his stay at Turin, Rousseau gained the friendship of several priests, including the Abbé Gaime, whose piety so impressed him that he later served as one of the models for Rousseau's Savoyard Vicar. Rousseau lived with Madame de Warens for the better part of a decade, during which time she served him as both mother and mistress. In 1845 at the age of thirty-three, Rousseau moved to Paris, a fervent though heterodox Catholic. There his faith was tested in the long struggles with the atheists and materialists. He came out of the ordeal a Deist, but with the flame of religious sentiment still burning. He now felt that reason was incapable of substantiating most of the traditional dogmas of Christianity, but he was equally certain, against the d'Holbach circle, that reason gave evidence of a providential deity.

In 1754 Rousseau once again visited Geneva and returned to the Protestantism of his childhood. In these years Rousseau was troubled continuously with religious questions and sought out a Genevan cleric, Pastor Vernes, as a confidant to whom he could unburden his mind. This, too, failed when Vernes proved to be unbending in his biblical orthodoxy. During this period of lonely, spiritual searching,

Rousseau vowed he would find a faith that would be satisfying. The product of that resolve was "The Profession of Faith of the Savoyard Vicar" (1762), regarded by some as the masterpiece of his pen.

The "Profession of Faith" is inserted into the fourth book of Rousseau's longer work *Emile*, his novel on the principles of a natural education. The inclusion of the religious profession in *Emile* was no accident, either of form or substance. The novel form allowed Rousseau a more concrete, personal way of expressing his own religious creed while calling upon the reader to test the author's own deeply felt sentiments with his own religious experience. The substance of Rousseau's religious profession is also entirely consistent with the educational doctrine he sets forth in the earlier books of *Emile*. Rousseau insists that all genuine knowledge or insight must be acquired by the pupil for himself. It cannot be achieved through a detached, mechanical process of rote book learning. In every field of knowledge true understanding comes only through personal experience. We learn, Rousseau insisted, by doing. And so it is in our religious understanding. Religious faith is sterile and perfunctory unless it is grounded in personal experience. Religious conviction is nothing but a certainty arrived at by the individual self in its encounter with the world.

The "Profession" opens with the kindly, unorthodox Vicar of Savoy speaking to a young boy who has fled from Geneva to Rome and, having changed religions, is filled with uncertainty and distress. The Vicar assures the boy that he does not want to argue with him or even convince him. "It is enough for me to show you, in all simplicity of heart, what I really think. Consult your own heart as I speak; that is all I ask."[2]

In many respects the Savoyard Vicar's profession is similar to that of other eighteenth-century Deists. For example, Rousseau includes a discussion on revelation and Scripture in which the difficulties encountered in the evidential claims of all special revelations are made abundantly clear. The boy, perplexed by the conflicting claims of rival positive religions, asks the vicar for guidance in this matter. The Vicar replies that since we are offered so many revelations, each claiming for itself the truth, one of two things must obtain.

Either all religions are good and pleasing to God or if there is one which he prescribes for men, if they will be punished for despising it, he will have distinguished it by plain and certain signs . . . alike in every time and place, equally plain to all men, great or small . . . .[3]

But, in fact, neither condition obtains. None of the positive religions admit the truth of their rival's claims. One religion must then be true. But how do I find out? God has spoken? To whom has he spoken? To men. Why, then, have I heard nothing? He has instructed others to make himself known to you. But I would rather have heard from God himself; then I should be secure from fraud. For what other men tell me is so contradictory. But God protects you from fraud by showing that his messengers come from him. How so? By miracles. Where are these miracles? In books. And who wrote the books? Men. And who saw the miracles? The men who bear witness to them. What! Nothing but human testimony. Nothing but men to tell me what other men have told them![4] This, says the Vicar, is the answer that the positive religions are always giving. Since this is the situation, one has no choice but to test all the religions!

Consider, my friend [says the Vicar] the terrible controversy in which I am now engaged; what vast learning is required to go back to the remotest antiquity, to examine, weigh, confront prophecies, revelations, facts .... What exactness of critical judgement is needed to distinguish genuine documents from forgeries, translations with their originals; to decide as to the impartiality of witnesses ... that nothing has been added, altered or falsified.[5]

And when a person has managed to surmount all these obstacles and has come to regard certain miracles as genuine, he faces a greater question: how does one know such genuine miracles are of God, since the Bible convinces us that the devil is a miracle worker, too? The answer given is that those miracles are genuinely of God which the message certifies. "So when we have proved our doctrine by means of miracles, we must prove our miracles by means of doctrine .... What think you of this dilemma?"[6]

The Vicar's conclusion concerning the claims and counterclaims of the historical religions is that he finds in them objections and contradictions which he cannot overcome and therefore must maintain "an attitude of reverent doubt."

I call to witness the God of Peace whom I adore, and whom I proclaim to you, that my inquiries were honestly made; but when I discovered that they were and always would be unsuccessful, and that I embarked upon a boundless ocean, I turned back, and restricted my faith within the limits of my primitive ideas .... I closed all my books. *There is one book which is open to every one—the book of nature. In this good and great volume I learn to serve and adore its Author.* If I use my reason, if I cultivate it, if I employ rightly the innate faculties which God bestows upon me, *I shall learn by myself to know and love him*, to love his works, to will what he wills and to fulfil all

my duties upon earth .... What more can all human learning teach me?[7] (Italics added.)

Rousseau, like his beloved Vicar, was forced back to what he came to regard as the only reliable book, the book of nature, by which he means his own natural self. Reduced, like Descartes, to doubting all, he learned to restrict all inquiries to what concerned himself,

to admit as self-evident all that I could not honestly refuse to believe, and to admit as true all that seemed to follow directly from this; all the rest I determined to leave undecided, neither accepting nor rejecting it, nor yet troubling myself to clear up difficulties which did not lead to any practical ends.[8]

Beginning then with only those truths which compel consent, Rousseau's Vicar goes on to establish certain principles of belief that, like his critique of the positive religions, is reminiscent of the then-reigning Deism. First, beginning with reflections on his own existence, he arrives at the conviction that just as in man there is the principle of free judgment which is the origin of our spontaneous actions, so in the world at large one must go back to some first, spontaneous, willful cause. "I think that a will moves the universe and animates nature. That is my first article of faith." The second article of belief arises out of the order and harmony of nature which points to an *intelligent* first cause: "If the movement of matter reveals to me a will, the movement of matter according to certain laws reveals to me an intelligence; that is my second article of faith." The third article has to do not with God but with the uniqueness of man in the order of nature. Reflecting on the conflict in man between reason and the passions, the Vicar concludes that the intelligent faculty in man is free and independent of the body. "Man is free in his actions and as such is animated by an immaterial substance; this is my third article of faith."

From these three convictions the Vicar goes on to deduce other religious convictions, such as the explanation of evil in God's world and the immortality of the soul. All this sounds very much like the natural theology of the age, which it is. And yet Rousseau infuses his religious apology with a new *sensibilité* that is foreign to most of the rationalism of his time. It is this new religious sentiment that is important and needs closer examination.

In the "Profession of Faith" Rousseau seeks to found religion on what he sometimes calls the "inner light" or "feeling" or "conscience." The apparent vagueness of these terms has led some scholars to dismiss Rousseau's philosophy of religion with such epithets as "romantic enthusiasm" and "emotional Deism." More recently Rousseau's theory of religion has been interpreted much more favorably, and the importance of his philosophy of religion in the general history of ideas has been accurately assessed.[9] What Rousseau means by sentiment and feeling has nothing to do with sentimentality or effusive emotion. It is closer to an intuitive disclosure or innate moral sense. Rousseau was convinced that the questions of theism, such as the existence and nature of God and the immortality of the soul, could not be answered if the intellect was called upon without the guidance of our inner sentiments and moral experience. Like Augustine and Pascal before him and Newman after him, Rousseau recognized that religious certitude comes not from abstract reasoning alone but from what Newman was to call the "illative sense"—from a con-

vergence of rational evidences, religious intuition, and moral conviction. Reason cannot produce assent to religious beliefs until it is in harmony with man's affections and conscience. This is made clear in what appears to be Rousseau's appeal to the rational arguments for God from the necessity of a first, voluntary cause and from the order of nature. Rousseau calls upon his reader to "compare the special ends, the means, the ordered relations of every kind," but then he adds,

then let us listen to the inner voice of feeling; what healthy mind can reject its evidence? Unless the eyes are blinded by prejudice can they fail to see that the visible order of the universe proclaims a supreme intelligence?[10]

Not, says Rousseau, if the eyes of the rational mind are in harmony with the inner voice of feeling.

For Rousseau there are two requisites for any affirmation of religion. The first is that religious ideas, doctrines, or convictions be related to and a reflection upon our personal experience.

I see God everywhere in his works; I feel him within myself; I behold him all around me; but if I try to find out where he is, what he is, what is his substance, he escapes me and my troubled spirit finds nothing. Convinced of my unfitness, I shall never argue about the nature of God unless I am driven to it by the feeling of his relations with myself.[11]

God is known only as he is known *pro me*, only as he is known through my religious feeling. The second requirement of religious doctrine is that it be related to my moral sentiments. Other concerns are idle speculation.

I believe that the world is governed by a wise and powerful will; I see it or rather I feel it, and it is a great thing to know this. But has this same world always existed, or has it been created? Is there one source of all things?... I know not; and what concern is it of mine? When these things become of importance to me I will try to learn them; till then I abjure these idle speculations, which may trouble my peace but cannot affect my conduct....[12]

Theology, as Rousseau sees it, is moral theology. What does not affect our action we can respect in silence or regard with humble skepticism, "but," says Rousseau, "this skepticism is in no way painful to me, for it does not extend to matters of practice.... I only seek to know what affects my conduct."[13]

The Savoyard Vicar's final advice to the youth epitomizes Rousseau's own faith.

My son, keep your soul in such a state that you always desire that there should be a God and you will never doubt it. Moreover, whatever decision you come to, remember that the real duties of religion are independent of human institutions; that a righteous heart is the true temple of the Godhead; ... remember there is no religion which absolves us from our moral duties; that these alone are really essential....[14]

For Rousseau, man's moral conscience is a natural sentiment, a feeling of the heart, not an acquired idea.

The decrees of conscience are not judgements but feelings: Although all our ideas come to us from without, the feelings by which they are weighed are within us.... To know the good is not to love it; this knowledge is not innate in man; but as soon as his reason leads him to perceive it, his conscience impels him to love it; it is this feeling that is innate.[15]

Conscience is, then, our true guide, for to obey conscience is to obey that which is innately part of our very nature. These moral sentiments of the heart cannot lead to emotional anarchy because the conscience isn't the mere product of our bodily passions. And this moral sense in man, according to Rousseau, has been essentially the same irrespective of time and place. Like the love of our own good, which is prior to all knowledge in us, there are in the depth of the soul innate sentiments of justice and virtue, native to man long before he has any knowledge of good and evil.

This innate sentiment of conscience is, for Rousseau, the true image of God in man. It is the sole link between this ambiguous human creature and the holy God.

Conscience! Conscience! Divine instinct, immortal voice from heaven; sure guide for a creature ignorant and finite indeed, yet intelligent and free; infallible judge of good and evil, making man like God! In thee consists the excellence of man's nature and the morality of his actions; apart from thee, I find nothing in myself to raise me above the beast....[16]

To interpret Rousseau's doctrine of religion as a sentimental nature mysticism is to misunderstand his concept of nature. Rousseau did not deify the natural world. It is true that he speaks passionately about nature, and nature serves him, as it did Wordsworth, as the occasion for eliciting religious feeling. But the foundation of Rousseau's religious faith is the natural conscience, and the fruition of that faith is moral action. The traditional proofs of natural theology are cold abstractions, lacking in conviction when divorced from our moral sentiments. As Kant was to show with much greater clarity a few decades later, man cannot bridge the chasm between nature and God by pure reason alone. Moral conscience, not nature, is the only mediator between God and man.

Rousseau brings to complete realization the religious autonomy of the Enlightenment. But, as is evident, in so doing he also points ahead to those movements of the nineteenth century in which religious doctrine is grounded not in abstract, rational demonstration, but in personal experience. A twentieth-century philosopher evaluates Rousseau's contribution to the philosophy of religion as follows:

> The significance of Rousseau's philosophy of religion for cultural history can be described in a single phrase: he eliminated from the foundation of religion the doctrine of *fides implicita*.* No one can believe for another and with the help of another; in religion everyone must stand on his own .... Neither Calvinism nor Lutheranism had ever radically overcome the doctrine of the *fides implicita*; they had only shifted its center by replacing faith in tradition with faith in the Word of the Bible. But for Rousseau there existed no kind of inspiration outside the sphere of personal experience.[17]

That Cassirer has focused on the crux of Rousseau's view of religion is evidenced in a letter Rousseau sent to Jacob Vernes, the young minister in Geneva who had questioned Rousseau's unorthodox attitude toward Scripture. Rousseau replied:

> I have told you many times: no man in the world respects the Gospel more than I. It is to my taste the most sublime of all books. . . . But in the end, it is just a book. . . . No, my good friend, it is not on a few scattered pages one ought to go seek the law of God, but in

* *Fides implicita* refers to assent to the truths taught by the Church even though one has no knowledge of what these teachings are about or the evidence of their truth.

the heart of man, where His hand has deigned to write: "O man, whatsoever man thou art, enter into thyself, learn to consult thy conscience and thy natural faculties, thou wilt then be just, good, virtuous, thou wilt incline thyself before thy master, and thou wilt participate in his heaven in an eternal blessedness."[18]

The significance of Rousseau for the modern history of religion lies in the fact that he strove for a conception of reason more consonant with human experience than the narrow rationalism of the critical Deists. His contribution to the development of a more adequate basis of religious conviction is very great, as we shall see when we come to Kant and to the romantic movement.

The rationalist pretensions of critical Deism were not only opposed by Rousseau but also came under severe attack in England in the middle decades of the eighteenth century. William Law, in *The Case of Reason* (1731), and Bishop Berkeley, in *Alciphron* (1732), raised serious questions about the model of abstract reason by which Deists like Tindal dictated what could and could not serve as warrants of belief. Law pointed out that Tindal's conception of a perfect natural reason, by which men can test all truth claims, is an a priori assumption which has no grounds in actual experience.

> An enquiry about the light, and strength, and sufficiency of reason to guide and preserve men in the knowledge and practice of true religion is a question as *solely* to be resolved by *fact and experience*, as is the enquiry about the shape of a man's body or the number of his senses. And to talk of a light and strength of reason, natural to man, which fact and experience have not yet proved, is egregious nonsense ... so their cause ought to be looked

upon to be vain and romantic, as if they had asserted that men have senses naturally fitted to hear sounds and see objects at all distances though fact and experience has proved quite the contrary.[19]

The most effective of these critiques of natural religion came from the pen of Bishop Butler, who in 1736 published his *Analogy of Religion, Natural and Revealed.* Butler's book proved so devastating in its exposure of the weaknesses of the Deist doctrine that no one of the opposition attempted a reply. Butler's *Analogy*, more than any other writing, brought to a close the debate between Deism and traditional Christianity. But the good Bishop's *Analogy of Religion* had an unexpected and ironic influence. Meant to restore confidence in the truths of Christian revelation, its somber, unblinking reminders of the defects of nature proved to be only more fuel for the fires of skepticism. For the likes of David Hume, the difficulties of belief in natural religion were easily convertible into an attack upon the claims of Christian theology as well. As we shall see, Butler's negative method of arguing, by seeking to establish the probabilities of revelation by stressing the difficulties in natural religion, appeared to less pious minds to lead to general skepticism concerning all rational arguments for theism. It would be left to Immanuel Kant to construct out of the skepticism of Hume and the moral philosophy of Rousseau a new basis of religious faith.

Joseph Butler

Joseph Butler (1692–1752) was raised a Presbyterian but, before entering Oxford, joined the Church of England. He was a precocious youth and corresponded with the elder Samuel Clarke on metaphysical problems while he was still a schoolboy. At Oxford Butler found the "frivolous lectures and unintelligible disputations" unsuitable and was persuaded to take holy orders. In 1719 he was appointed preacher at Rolls Chapel in London. The product of this assignment was *Fifteen Sermons Preached at Rolls Chapel*, published in 1726 and generally acknowledged as establishing Butler as one of the preeminent English moralists. The *Sermons* also insured the success of Butler's ecclesiastical career. In 1736, he became Clerk of the Closet to Queen Caroline and that same year published *The Analogy of Religion*. Although he published nothing more, his ecclesiastical position steadily improved. He was successively Bishop of Bristol, Dean of St. Paul's, Clerk of the Royal Closet to George II, and Bishop of Durham. He died in 1752, at the age of sixty, having lived a life of exemplary moral and intellectual integrity. He was, in Leslie Stephen's words, a man "honest enough to admit the existence of doubts, and brave enough not to be paralysed by their existence."

In the Advertisement to *The Analogy of Religion* Butler acknowledged that it has come to be taken for granted that Christianity is "discovered to be fictitious" and "a principal subject of mirth and ridicule." Butler's purpose was to show that such was not the case and that there were good grounds for not doubting the truths of Christianity.

The *Analogy* was addressed to those Deists who would readily concede the existence of God as a moral governor of the world but were skeptical of the particular claims of Christianity. Butler's procedure was to show that the Deist belief in God, the author of nature, when coupled with consideration of the facts of our experience of the natural world, would lead one to acknowledge that perhaps belief in revelation is no more difficult than belief in the claims of natural religion. That is, if the Deist is going to appeal to the evidences of nature, he must in honesty appeal to the whole of nature—and that means warts and all!

The Deists' chronic complaint was that if God had revealed himself in the Scriptures, he would not have allowed for such ambiguities and contradictions. He would have spoken plainly and not left us in such perplexity. But, says Butler, look at nature without your rose-tinted glasses! There you will observe just as many ambiguities and defects in proving God as you will find in the Bible, for both are full of difficulties and, when examined, these difficulties prove to be of the same kind. Neither nature nor the Bible gives us indubitable proof of the claims of theism. Both are baffling to our limited minds. And so for us finite beings, "probability is the very guide of life." Like William James, Butler holds that religious claims cannot rise above the level of probability, so

if the result of examination be, that there appears **on the whole,** any the lowest presumption on one side, and none on the other, or a greater presumption on one side, though in the lowest degree greater; this determines the question; . . . and in matters of practice, will lay us under an absolute and formal obligation, in point of prudence and of interest, to act upon that presumption or low probability, though it be so low as to leave the mind in a very great doubt which is the truth.[20]

Having shown that the evidences of nature, too, are only probable, Butler sums up his analogical method by quoting from Origen that "*he, who believes the Scripture to have proceeded from him who is the Author of nature, may well expect to find the same sort of difficulties in it, as are found in the constitution of nature.*"[21] The whole design of Butler's argument is therefore

to show that the several parts principally objected against in this moral and Christian dispensation . . . are analogous to what is experienced in the constitution and course of nature . . . that the chief objections which are alleged against the former are no other than what may be alleged with like justice against the latter, where in fact they are found to be inconclusive; and that the argument from analogy is in general unanswerable, and undoubtedly of weight on the side of religion.[22]

What, then, are these analogies that Butler finds unanswerable and which will weigh the probabilities in favor of the traditional religious claims? We cannot survey all of the analogies drawn by Butler in this long and carefully argued book; indication of a few will suffice for our purposes.

Butler begins with the question of a future life, a subject of which we know very little. But consider for a moment nature and the several changes which it undergoes without being destroyed, and see what analogy here might be drawn with our own death and whether it is probable that we survive such a change in our condition. We would all concede that it is a general law of nature that the same creatures exist in degrees of life and experience, in one period of their being greatly different from other periods: "The states of life in which we ourselves existed formerly in the womb and in our infancy, are almost as different from our present in mature age as it is possible to conceive any two states or degrees of life can be."[23] Butler goes on then to suggest that because we have powers of enjoying pleasure and suffering pain before birth, it is *sufficiently probable* that we shall retain these powers after death, especially since no one actually knows what death is. But is there not a difference in these two states, for does not death bring to an end the physical organism? A living agent is not, contends Butler, to be confused with its physical effects. The organs of our body, such as the eye or the limbs, are only instruments which the living agent makes use of to perceive and move. But there is no evidence that the dissolution of these organs is the destruction of the perceiving or moving agent. From this Butler infers (illicitly surely)

that the destruction of several of the organs and instruments of perception and of motion . . . is not their (the agents') destruction shows demonstratively that there is no ground to think that the dissolution of any other matter will be the dissolution or destruction of living agents.[24]

If we follow the analogy of nature, we may look upon our death as in some respects like our birth "which is not a suspension of the faculties which we had before it, or a total change of the state of life in which we existed when in the womb, but a continuation of both, with such and such great alterations." So, similarly, "death may immediately . . . put us into a higher and more enlarged state of life as our birth does; a state in which our capacities and sphere of perception and of action may be much greater than at present."[25]

Butler argues that we can also know something of the nature of the government of the future life from our observation of the government of our natural lives. We observe that our present life is governed by moral justice. Pleasure and pain are the natural effects of our actions.

Intemperance will bring disease, temperance health. Our civil life is analogous. Civic happiness and misery are dependent on our moral conduct. By analogy this life can also be seen as a period of probation for the next. Just as infancy, childhood, and youth are a necessary discipline for maturity, so the present life is a state of moral discipline for the next:

The fact of our case, which we find by experience, is that [God] exercises dominion or government over us at present, by rewarding and punishing us for our actions. . . . And thus the whole analogy of nature . . . most fully shows that there is nothing incredible in the general doctrine of religion, that God will reward and punish men for their actions hereafter.[26]

To the objection that the moral government of this life seems to be fairly obscure, Butler humbly acknowledges that both nature and revelation are shrouded in mystery. But assuming, with the Deists, that God does exercise a moral government over this world, we can be assured, on the basis of strong probability, of a similar government in the future life, but equally "beyond our comprehension."

But what about the biblical miracles? Had not the Deists mounted a concerted attack on the evidential value of miracles as contrary to natural law? Yes, but implied in the Deist argument is the inference that while revelation is contingent and mysterious, nature is uniform and transparent in its intelligibility. This, according to Butler, is where the Deists deceive themselves, i.e., in assuming that we know nature. What we experience in nature is but a mere point when compared with the whole plan reaching throughout eternity past and future. Yet the fact that things be beyond our experience, "is no sort of presumption against the truth and reality of them" for there are innumerable things in the constitution of the universe "which are beyond the natural reach of our faculties."[27] We should not, then, presume against miracles of Scripture on account of their being unlike the known course of nature, "for there is no presumption at all from analogy that the *whole* course of things, naturally unknown to us, and *everything* in it, is like to anything in that which is known."[28] Nature teems with puzzles. We know some of her laws, "but we know in a manner nothing by what laws, storms and tempests, earthquakes, famine, pestilence, become the instruments of destruction to mankind."[29] These laws are so unknown to us that "we call the events which come to pass by them, accidental." It is only from our experience of a portion of nature as exhibiting general laws that we conclude the same for the mysterious remainder. If this be our inference concerning our knowledge of nature, then, Butler argues, it

is sufficient for answering objections that God's miraculous interpositions may have been, all along in like manner, by *general* laws of wisdom. . . . These laws are unknown indeed to us; but no more unknown than the laws from whence it is that some die as soon as they are born, and others live to extreme old age . . . .[30]

Butler thus concludes:

Upon the whole then: The appearance of deficiencies and irregularities in nature is owing to its being a scheme but in part made known . . . . Now we see no more reason why the frame and course of nature should be such a scheme, than why Christianity should . . . . And from all this it is credible that there might be the like appearance of deficiencies and irregularities in Christianity, as in nature . . . .

And these objections are answered by these observations concerning Christianity; as the like objections against the frame of nature are answered by the like observations concerning the frame of nature.[31]

Butler uses the same method of analogy to defend the particularity of Christian revelation. To attack Christianity because revelation is not given equally to all men everywhere at all times is sophistical. God's providential wisdom recognizes that his self-revelation needs be different for different peoples and changing circumstances. Nature demonstrates that a system such as this world implies great variety and change. Even if relevation were universal, it would not result in uniformity for

from men's different capacities of understanding . . . their different educations and other external circumstances . . . their religious situations would be widely different and the disadvantage of some in comparison of others, perhaps, altogether as much as at present.[32]

It is just because man's condition is so varied and his knowledge so imperfect that he is in need of special revelation. Christianity does not contradict the religion of nature; rather it is a "republication" of natural religion "adapted to the present circumstances of mankind" and "containing an account of a dispensation of things not discoverable by reason."[33] It is true, then, that much found in revelation is not readily apparent to our reason—which explains just why revelation is needed. But to complain of the mysteries of revelation is not to distinguish it from natural religion for nature, as we have seen, is full of dark irrationalities and melancholy uncertainties. Such is the good Bishop's conclusion.

The value of Butler's *Analogy* lay in the fact that he demonstrated with powerful consistency that natural religion had no privileged position over Christian revelation because of the former's perfect rationality. The perfection of nature was no more obvious than the perfection of biblical revelation. Belief in God, the author of nature, required the same convergence of probabilities as belief in the God of Christian revelation. As Butler would say, taken *on the whole* there is no more reason to doubt the testimony of Scripture than the testimony of natural reason.

The weakness of Butler's apology lay in the fact that he assumed that his contemporaries' faith in natural religion was so strong as to be unshakable in the face of his negative method of argument. Butler failed to see that his method was a two-edged sword—that it is not the most promising argument for revelation to say that because nature is a mess of riddles, we cannot expect revelation to be any clearer! This may equalize the difficulties in the rational warrants that are offered in defense of Deism and of Christianity but on the other hand, it might lead those with slightly different sentiments to the conclusion that both Christianity and natural religion are irrational. The convictions of many Deists were so attenuated as to need very little to turn them into skeptics. "It seems not to have occurred to the good Bishop," remarks Leslie Stephen, "that if natural religion were, rationally considered, on no firmer a foundation than revelation, there might be some men willing to reject them both."[34]

Butler's *Apology*, though printed in several editions in his own lifetime, had a mixed reception due to the dangerous ambiguity of its argument. The year after its publication the Deist Thomas Chubb used Butler's theory of probability and analogy to show that it could be used to justify all forms of belief. He pointed out that Butler's use of analogy might

possibly prove a very dangerous experiment because perhaps the same kind of reasoning may answer the same purpose to every scheme of religion.... For what difficulty is there that attends either the popish or Mahometan, or the pagan religion, but artful and inquisitive men may find out something or other in nature which they can call a difficulty and represent as analogous to it? And perhaps the application may be as just as in the former case.[35]

A few years later a remarkable pamphlet was issued by Henry Dodwell the Younger, entitled *Christianity Not Founded on Argument* (1742). Dodwell's book maintained in effect that religious faith has nothing to do with reason but is an appeal to authority and internal illumination by the Holy Spirit. He claimed that rational theology actually produced infidelity rather than conviction and, like Anthony Collins before him, suggested that no one ever thought of doubting the existence of God before reading Samuel Clarke's rationalistic defense of theism in the Boyle Lectures. If religion were a matter of rational proof, says Dodwell,

the excellent *Analogy of Reason and Revelation** lately communicated might induce me yet more powerfully to acknowledge at least a very great and specious appearance of truth in its traced connections and inferences.... But when I consider all these enlightening lucubrations as proofs actually insisted upon ... as that which any part of the evidence of Christianity is to stand upon or depend for its

---

* An obvious reference to Butler's *Analogy*.

support . . . I cannot but draw to myself very different consequences. . . . They suggest strongly to me that a position can never be a *necessary truth* which stands in need of any such farfetched apologies and labored accounts to reconcile and explain it.[36]

So it was that, contrary to his intentions, Butler's labored apology for Christianity served the cause of skepticism, religious irrationalism, and fideism. It was but a short way to David Hume, who knew Butler's work as early as 1736, and whose writings in the next few decades were to prove to be the final death blow to the religion of reason. But it was Law, Dodwell, and especially Bishop Butler who served as significant links between the Deism of Tindal and its downfall at the hands of Hume.

David Hume

The writings of David Hume (1711–1776) stand with the works of Kant as a watershed in the history of philosophical theology. Although some of his writings did not have as wide an influence on theology during his own lifetime as he himself expected, all subsequent philosophical theology, that dares to call itself by that name, has had to take Hume's inquiries into account. Hume was raised in the strict Calvinist environment of eighteenth-century Scotland, but at an early age shed the Calvinist influences of his home. His later reputation as a charitable and virtuous man of unusual excellence appears to owe nothing to a personal religious faith. He never experienced the soul-searching *angst* and spiritual uncertainties that mark what William James called the "twice born" man.

In his maturity Hume not only found religion personally unnecessary but his-

torically, in the main, a malignant influence. At the end of his essay on *The Natural History of Religion* he concluded that if you examine the religious principles which have prevailed in the world "you will scarcely be persuaded that they are anything but sick men's dreams."[37]

Hume was not, however, an atheist. In fact, the agnostic Scotsman was shocked and amused at the dogmatic atheism of the Parisian *philosophes*.[38] Yet Hume had no belief in a personal providence or special revelation or in any specifically religious duties. What he called religion was "little more than a repudiation of all superstition," and knowledge of God was for him reducible to "one simple, though somewhat ambiguous, at least undefined proposition: that the cause or causes of order in the universe probably bear some remote analogy to human intelligence."[39]

A vivid depiction of Hume's "natural irreligion" is given in James Boswell's account of his last interview with the dying philosopher. The subject of immortality was broached. Hume indicated that he had no belief in an after-life, for it was "a most unreasonable fancy." The prospect of annihilation gave him no uneasiness, for he did not wish to be immortal. The reason, Hume drolly replied, was "that he was very well in this state of being and that the chances were very much against his being so well in another state." Boswell concludes his reminiscence by saying that

Mr. Hume's pleasantry was such that there was no solemnity in the scene; and death for the time did not seem dismal. It surprised me to find him talking of different matters with a tranquility of mind which few men possess at any time. . . . I left him with impressions which disturbed me for some time.[40]

Hume's writings were to prove to be as unsettling as his personal presence.

The fact is, however, that Hume did not relish controversy and had no desire to be a Scottish Voltaire dedicated to crushing *l'infâme*. As early as 1737, Hume "castrated" his *Treatise of Human Nature* by excising all theological controversy from the book in order that "it shall give as little offence as possible."* However, a decade later Hume resolved to include theological considerations in his *An Inquiry Concerning Human Understanding* (1748), for these matters lay at the very heart of his philosophical doctrine.[41]

Eighteenth-century apologetics concentrated on two basic theistic proofs: the argument from miracle and prophecy and the argument from design.[42] It is not coincidental that Hume includes an extensive discussion of both of these "proofs" in Sections X and XI of the *Inquiry*. The essay "Of Miracles" (X) had its precursor in the original "Reasonings Concerning Miracles" which had been left out of the *Treatise* in deference to Dr. Butler. Hume apparently still felt that he must proceed prudently, for he begins the essay with the *imprimatur* of the Archbishop of Canterbury by referring to John Tillotson's "concise and elegant" argument against the *real presence* in the Eucharist as the model for his own reflections.

Hume begins the essay by reasserting the premise of his whole "experimental method," namely, that experience be our only guide in reasoning concerning matters of fact. Experience admittedly is not infallible; there are all imaginable degrees of assurance from the highest certainty to the lowest possible proba-

bility. "The wise man, therefore, proportions his belief to the evidence." The wise man must weigh the evidence, and here he can proceed with assurance but there with doubt and hesitation. All reasonable judgments, however, are made on evidence which does not exceed probability.

Having established the ground rules, Hume proceeds to apply these principles to the issue at hand: reasoning based on the testimony of others. "Evidence derived from witnesses and human testimony," says Hume,

is regarded either as a *proof* or a *probability*, according as the conjunction between any particular kind of report and any kind of object has been found to be constant or variable. There are a number of circumstances to be taken into consideration ... and the ultimate standard by which we determine all disputes that may arise concerning them is always derived from experience and observation.[43]

If the fact which the historical testimony endeavors to establish is "extraordinary and marvelous," the evidence will admit of a diminution "greater or less in proportion as the fact is more or less unusual." But if the fact which the witnesses affirm, instead of being marvelous, is actually miraculous and "the testimony, considered apart and in itself, amounts to an entire proof—in that case there is proof against proof, of which the strongest must prevail."[44] That is, according to Hume, a miracle is by definition a violation of the laws of nature, "and as a firm and unalterable experience has established these laws, the proof against a miracle, from the very nature of the fact, is as entire as any argument from experience can possibly be imagined."[45] For example, if a man in seeming good

---

* Hume was especially concerned not to give offense to the esteemed Dr. Butler.

health should suddenly die, it would not be considered miraculous since, though unusual, such events are rather frequently observed. But if a dead man should come to life, it would be miraculous, for it has not been previously observed.

There must, therefore, be a uniform experience against every miraculous act, otherwise the event would not merit that appellation. And as a uniform experience amounts to a proof, there is here a direct and full *proof*, from the nature of the fact, against the existence of any miracle.[46]

The plain consequence which Hume draws from the above is that "no testimony is sufficient to establish a miracle unless the testimony be of such a kind that its falsehood would be more miraculous than the fact which it endeavors to establish."[47] That fact is, then, that it appears that no testimony for any kind of miracle has ever amounted to a probability, much less a proof, "and therefore we may establish it as a maxim that no human testimony can have such force as to prove a miracle and make it a just foundation for any such system of religion."[48]

Hume wishes to make it clear that he has only established that "a miracle can never be proved so as to be the foundation of a system of religion." He does not categorically deny the possibility of miracles or violations of the *usual course* of nature. In cases of strong and general testimony concerning unusual events, one should be disposed not to doubt such occurrences in an unreasonable manner but rather to search out the causes of such prodigies.

Suppose that all the historians who treat of England should agree that on the first of January 1600, Queen Elizabeth died; that both

before and after her death she was seen by her physicians and the whole court . . . and that, after being interred for a month, she appeared again, resumed the throne and governed England for three years—I must confess that I should be surprised at the concurrence of so many odd circumstances but should not have the least inclination to believe so miraculous an event. I should not doubt her pretended death and of those other public circumstances that followed it. I should only assert it to have been pretended, and that it neither was, nor possibly could be, real . . . . I would still reply that the knavery and folly of men are such common phenomena that I should rather believe the most extraordinary events to arise from their concurrence than admit of so signal a violation of the laws of nature.[49]

Hume is arguing that unless one can assume a complete knowledge of the possibilities of natural occurrence so as to exclude from any event every possible natural cause, it is not possible to prove any particular event a miracle. Inexplicable as it may appear, it is always more reasonable to seek out some natural explanation of the phenomenon. Hume's conclusion is that the rational proof of religion from the testimony of miracle is entirely specious. In fact, religion is founded on faith, not reason. "I am the better pleased," concludes Hume,

with the method of reasoning here delivered, as I think it may serve to confound those dangerous friends or disguised enemies of the *Christian religion* who have undertaken to defend it by the principles of human reason. Our most holy religion is founded on *faith*, not on reason; and it is a sure method of exposing it to put it to such a trial as it is by no means fitted to endure.[50]

How is this to be understood? Was Hume involved in a *volte-face* as A. E. Taylor claims,[51] or is this an example of Hume's derisive mockery? That Hume was being sardonic there is little doubt. Yet there is no reason why we should not take Hume's words here in a straightforward manner. Hume has shown that miracles are no proof of the Christian religion and will later demonstrate that reason is not able to prove the claims of Christianity. Yet Hume was well aware that for the faithful belief itself was a divinely conferred miracle. And so his concluding words, though not without scornful irony, are stating what in fact was believed by many to be the case:

Upon the whole we may conclude that the Christian religion . . . at this day cannot be believed by a reasonable person without [a miracle]. Mere reason is insufficient to convince us of its veracity. And whoever is moved by *faith* to assent to it is conscious of a continued miracle in his own person which subverts all the principles of his understanding and gives him a determination to believe what is most contrary to custom and experience.[52]

It must be remembered, however, that Hume is saying not only that reason is impotent to convince us of the claims of faith, but also that the rational man, who proportions his belief to the evidence, cannot take the way of faith. Here is the religious cul-de-sac that Hume alone appears to have grasped.

Section XI of the *Inquiry*, "Of a Providence and a Future State", was intended by Hume to be taken together with the section "Of Miracles." The latter, as we have seen, was to serve as a refutation of the proof from miracles; the former is an attempt to show that on the basis of the traditional argument from design, it is not possible to establish the kind of Deity that belief in a particular providence and a future state presuppose. The subjects of the title of Section XI are

hardly touched on, the focus of Hume's analysis being the argument from design.[53] That Hume was aware of the explosive implications of this essay is evident in the fact that he resorts to a dialogue form by which his own views can be disguised in the words of an Epicurean friend "who loves skeptical paradoxes." Nevertheless, Hume is no longer willing to defer to the revered Bishop Butler who had confidently pronounced that "to an unprejudiced mind ten thousand instances of design cannot but prove a designer." Hume is now determined to attack the very citadel of rational theology.

Hume's "friend" observes that religious philosophers, rather than being satisfied with their traditions, indulge in rash curiosity in trying to prove religion by rational argument. "They paint in the most magnificent colors the order, beauty, and wise arrangement of the universe," claiming that such evidence points to a wise and benevolent Creator. They contend that the chief argument for a divine existence is found in the very order of nature. The "friend" continues:

You allow that this is an argument drawn from effects to causes. From the order of the work you infer that there must have been project and forethought in the workman. If you cannot make out this point, you allow that your conclusion fails, and you pretend not to establish the conclusion in a greater latitude than the phenomena of nature will justify. These are your concessions. I desire you to mark the consequences.[54]

The consequences are twofold. First,

when we infer any particular cause from an effect, we must proportion the one to the other and can never be allowed to ascribe to the cause any qualities but what are exactly sufficient to produce the effect. A body of ten ounces raised in any scale may serve as a proof that the counterbalancing weight exceeds ten ounces, but can never afford a reason that it exceeds a hundred.[55]

Secondly, it is not permissible to begin with an inferred cause and infer other effects than those already known.

We can never be allowed to mount up from the universe, the effect, to Jupiter, the cause, and then descend downward to infer any new effect from that cause, as if the present effects alone were not entirely worthy of the glorious attributes which we ascribe to that deity.[56]

This was precisely Butler's procedure in the *Analogy*. From consideration of justice in our natural life, Butler infers a higher but analogous justice in some future state. He concludes from observation of this life that it is but a passage to something further—"a porch which leads to a greater and vastly different building." But let's take Butler's example of justice:

Are there any marks of distributive justice in the world? If you answer in the affirmative, I conclude that, since justice here exerts itself, it is satisfied. If you reply in the negative, I conclude that you have then no reason to ascribe justice, in our sense of it, to the gods. If you hold a medium between affirmation and negation, by saying that the justice of the gods at present exerts itself in part, but not in full extent, I answer that you have no reason to give it any particular extent, but only as far as you see it, *at present*, exert itself.[57]

At this point Hume asks his "friend" a question. If you observed a half finished building, surrounded by bricks and mortar, could you not properly infer that was a work of design and would it not be reasonable to infer that in time the building would be finished? Why, then, do you refuse to admit the same inferences with regard to the order of nature? The "friend's" answer is that the infinite difference of the subjects precludes such an analogy. In the case of human art we can advance from effect to cause and then make new inferences concerning the effect because we already possess considerable knowledge concerning the capacities and practices of men. The case is not the same with our reasoning concerning the works of nature.

The Deity is known to us only by his productions, and is a single being in the universe, *not comprehended under any species or genus*, from whose experienced attributes or qualities we can, by analogy, infer any attribute or quality in him. As the universe . . . shows a particular degree of perfections, we infer a particular degree of them, precisely adapted to the effect which we examine. But further attributes or further degrees of the same attributes, we can never be authorized to infer.[58] (Italics added.)

The supposition of further divine attributes is mere speculation. This is, Hume contends, exactly what occurs with the "religious hypothesis." But such ascribing of attributes to the Supreme Being "savors more of flattery and panegyric than of just reasoning." For "no new fact can ever be inferred from the religious hypothesis, no event foreseen or foretold, no reward or punishment expected or dreaded, beyond what is already known by practice and observation."[59]

The practical result of natural theology is, then, very slight. Certainly no reasonable inferences can be drawn from nature concerning such cornerstones of Christian belief as a wise and benevolent creator, a special providence, or future rewards and punishments. Epicurus' conclusion is that the religious inferences drawn from our experience of nature are "uncertain and useless." Uncertain because we cannot legitimately draw any inferences from nature beyond what we already know; useless because we cannot make any additions to our common experience of nature from which we would derive principles of moral conduct. Despite Hume's opening disavowal, he ends convinced by Epicurus that the argument from design is religiously worthless.

The Dialogues Concerning Natural Religion. The fact that Hume recognized the argument from design to be the foundation of the rational theology of his day is evident in the central place he gives to analyzing it in his masterpiece, *The Dialogues Concerning Natural Religion.* *The Dialogues* were written during 1751–1757, Hume's most productive period; they were revised in 1761, and remained his chief preoccupation during the last months of his life. Hume was persuaded by friends, among them Adam Smith, not to publish the work during his lifetime, but he left definite instructions that if the *Dialogues* did not appear within two and a half years of his death, his nephew and heir should see to their publication. This request was carried out, without any revision of the text, in 1779.

The *Dialogues* are modeled after and are, in many ways, dependent on Cicero's *De Natura Deorum.* Hume presents his analysis of theology through the mouths of three protagonists. Like Butler, Cleanthes is the model of the eighteenth-century Christian rationalist. Demea represents most often traditional orthodox fideism, but, on occasion, the older a priori rationalism. Philo plays the gadfly and skeptic. Earlier studies of the *Dialogues,* taking Hume's words at their face value, claimed that Hume identified

himself with Cleanthes. Such a verdict is based principally on the final words of the *Dialogues* where Hume concludes that "upon serious review of the whole, I cannot but think, that Philo's principles are more probable than Demea's; but that those of Cleanthes approach still nearer the truth." The identification of Hume with Cleanthes fails, however, to consider the import of Hume's whole argument in the *Inquiry* as well as the *Dialogues,* his use of irony and even ridicule, and his academical skepticism which caused him on occasion to concede ample place to historical convention and psychological need. Hume also desired to leave his readers free to judge for themselves rather than impose a dogmatical conclusion onto his analysis. The "bow" to Cleanthes leaves Hume's own view more ambiguous than would otherwise be the case.

More recently scholars have agreed with Kemp Smith's interpretation that Hume's own teaching is developed in and through the argument as a whole and that something of his own beliefs are put in the mouths of all three protagonists. Nevertheless,

Philo, from start to finish represents Hume; Cleanthes can be regarded as Hume's mouthpiece only in those passages in which he is explicitly agreeing with Philo or ... while refuting Demea, he is also being used to prepare the way for one or other of Philo's independent conclusions.[60]

The above view is correct, except that it does not give enough place to the very important agreements between Philo and Demea against the rationalist Cleanthes.

The central issue of the *Dialogues* is not *the existence* but *the nature* of God. Nevertheless, Hume's conclusions, which suggest that the *nature* of God is inaccessible to reason, raises the question as to what such an unknown God could possibly mean for religious faith. No summary of the argument of the *Dialogues* can begin to do justice to the richness and subtlety of the dialectical movement of the discussion. An account of the major arguments must, however, be attempted if we are to understand the nature and force of Hume's contribution.

The conversation turns on our knowledge of the nature of God. Demea affirms that due to our human weakness God remains unknown to our reason; further, that it is impious to seek to pry into his essence. Rather, as "finite, weak and blind creatures, we ought to humble ourselves in his august presence and . . . adore in silence his infinite perfections."[61] Philo concurs: "Our ideas," he affirms,

reach no farther than our experience. We have no experience of divine attributes and operations. I need not conclude my syllogism. . . . And it is a pleasure to me that just reasoning and sound piety here concur in the same conclusion, and both of them establish the adorably mysterious and incomprehensible nature of the Supreme Being.[62]

Cleanthes conceives the matter differently. He finds that the curious adapting of means to ends in nature resembles human art and that since these effects resemble each other, "we are led to infer, by all the rules of analogy, that the causes also resemble, and that the Author of nature is somewhat similar to the mind of man."[63] The issue is thus drawn. Philo now proceeds in his series of arguments with an Olympian calm. Cleanthes' views are countered one after another, and yet Hume maintains the dramatic interest by leading the reader to believe that Cleanthes is withholding the heavier

weapons of his arsenal for the final engagements.

Philo first opposes Cleanthes with the argument offered previously in the *Inquiry*, namely, that Cleanthes is assuming that the universe may be taken as of the same species with houses and ships and furniture.

Is a part of nature a rule for another part very wide of the former? Is it a rule for the whole? Is a very small part a rule for the universe . . . ? And will any man tell me with a serious countenance that an orderly universe must arise from some thought and art like the human because we have experience of it? To ascertain this reasoning it were requisite that we had experience of the origin of worlds.[64]

Cleanthes does not reply to Philo's criticism but merely persists in his belief that the similarity of the works of art and of nature are "self-evident."

Philo's second major line of argument concerns Cleanthes' analogy between the human and divine minds. To claim that the plan of nature is derived from the mind of God as a building can be traced to a plan in the mind of an architect is to solve nothing. Whether we are considering a human or divine mind, there is no reason in considering questions of cause and effect to stop with ideas or mental causes, for "a mental world or universe of ideas requires a cause as much as does a material world or universe of objects."[65] That is,

have we not the same reason to trace that ideal world into another ideal world or new intelligent principle? But if we stop and go no farther, why go so far? Why not stop with the material world? How can we satisfy ourselves without going on *ad infinitum* . . . ? If the material world rests upon a similar ideal world, this ideal world must rest on some other, and so on without end. It were better, therefore, never to look beyond the present material world. By supposing it to contain the principle of its order within itself, we really assert it to be God; and the sooner we arrive at that divine Being, so much the better.[66]

That is, if we claim that it is some *rational faculty* in the mind of the Creator that produces the order of the material world, we are merely making *an assertion*, and a similar claim could be as easily made for "the nature of material objects, and that they are all originally possessed of a *faculty* of order and proportion." Philo's conclusion is that neither hypothesis has any advantage over the other since "an ideal system, arranged of itself . . . is not a whit more explicable than a material one which attains its order in a like manner."[67]

The crux of Philo's argument comes in Part V of the *Dialogues*. Cleanthes persists in maintaining his analogy between the human and divine minds. Pressed by Philo, Cleanthes affirms that when considering the analogy between the divine and human minds, "the liker, the better." With an air of triumph Philo now calls upon Cleanthes to mark the consequences.

First, . . . you renounce all claim to infinity in any of the attributes of the Deity. For as the cause ought only to be proportioned to the effect, and the effect, so far as it falls under our cognisance, is not infinite; what pretensions have we . . . to ascribe that attribute to the divine Being . . . ? *Secondly*, you have no reason, on your theory, for ascribing perfection to the Deity, or for supposing him free from every error . . . . At least you must acknowledge that it is impossible for us to tell, from our limited views, whether the system contains any great faults or deserves any considerable praise if compared to other possible and even real systems. . . . Many worlds might

have been botched and bungled throughout an eternity, ere this system was struck out . . . . And what shadow of an argument, continued Philo, can you produce from your hypothesis to prove the unity of the Deity? A great number of men join in building a house or ship, in rearing a city, in framing a commonwealth; why may not several deities combine in contriving and framing a world?[68]

If Cleanthes insists, in arguing by analogy, that the cause must be proportioned to the effect, then we have no grounds for ascribing to God such attributes as infinity, perfection, and unity.

To this point Cleanthes has maintained that a rational mind is needed to explain order in nature. He has continuously argued this point from the analogy of human art. Philo now questions Cleanthes' use of this particular analogy. If we look around us, we must acknowledge that the natural world bears a greater resemblance to "an animal or vegetable than it does a watch." The cause of the world, it is more probable, resembles the cause of the former rather than the latter. We know that the cause of animal or vegetable is generation or vegetation. Therefore, it is no "less intelligible or less conformable to experience to say that the world arose by vegetation, from a seed shed by another world, than to say that it arose from a divine reason or contrivance, according to the sense in which Cleanthes understands it."[69]

Here Demea raises an objection to Philo's speculation concerning the vegetative origin of the world by asking, "How can order spring from anything which perceives not that order which it bestows?"[70] Does not order presuppose the conscious mind of an orderer? To this Philo replies that our ordinary experience would lead to no such conclusion for "a tree bestows order and organization on that tree which springs from it, without knowing the order; an animal in the same manner on its offspring."[71] To hold that all order in nature proceeds ultimately from design, one would be required to prove a priori, "both that order is, from its nature, inseparably attached to thought and that it can never of itself or from unknown principles belong to matter."[72] *Experience alone* affords no justification for Cleanthes' view that mind is the only source of order. "Judging by our limited and imperfect experience, generation has some privileges above reason; for we see every day the latter arise from the former, never the former from the latter."[73]

At this point in the dialogue Hume allows for a digression from Philo's relentless pursuance of the argument from design, in order to consider briefly the cogency of the a priori argument for the existence of God. The argument, put into the mouth of Demea, is a combination of the cosmological and ontological arguments used by Samuel Clarke in his *Discourse Concerning the Being and Attributes of God* (1704). The argument proceeds as follows. Whatever exists has a cause which precedes it. In going from effects to causes we must proceed in an infinite regression or have recourse to some cause that is *necessarily existent*. The question of why this particular succession of causes existed from eternity and not nothing requires reasonable explanation, since there is nothing absurd in *nothing* having existed from eternity. What was it, then, that determined *something* to exist rather than nothing? It could not be some *external cause*, for that would simply open the way for an infinite regress.

Chance is a word without meaning. Was it *nothing*? But that can never produce anything. We must, therefore, have recourse to a

necessarily existent Being who carries the *reason* of his existence in himself, and who cannot be supposed not to exist without express contradiction. There is, consequently, such a Being.[74]

Philo and Cleanthes agree that Demea's a priori demonstration has no force for the reason that matters of empirical fact cannot be proved by a priori arguments. Here is Cleanthes' refutation:

Nothing is demonstrable unless the contrary implies a contradiction. Nothing that is distinctly conceivable implies a contradiction. Whatever we conceive as existent, we can also conceive as non-existent. *There is no Being, therefore, whose non-existence implies a contradiction. Consequently there is no Being whose existence is demonstrable.* . . . . The words, therefore, *necessary existence* have no meaning or, which is the same thing, none that is consistent.[75] (Italics added.)

Unable to answer Cleanthes' refutation, Demea shifts the discussion to the subject of evil—a topic more in line with his original position. He now declares that it is from "a consciousness of imbecility and misery rather than from any reasoning" that man is led to belief in a Being on whom all nature is dependent.

The whole earth, believe me, Philo, is cursed and polluted. A perpetual war is kindled amongst all living creatures. Necessity, hunger, want, stimulate the strong and courageous: Fear, anxiety, terror agitate the weak and infirm.[76]

Philo agrees, but points out that man is not exempt from these evils which plague the lower animals: "Man is the greatest enemy of man. Oppression, injustice, contempt, contumely, violence, sedition, war, calumny, treachery, fraud; by these they mutually torment each other."[77] Having catalogued the sorrows and miseries of human life, Philo asks:

And is it possible, Cleanthes, . . . that after all these reflections . . . you still persevere in your anthropomorphism, and assert the moral attributes of the Deity, his justice, benevolence, mercy, and rectitude, to be of the same nature with these virtues in human creatures? His power, we allow, is infinite; whatever he wills is executed; but neither man nor any animal is happy; therefore he does not will their happiness. His wisdom is infinite; he is never mistaken in choosing the means to any end; but the course of nature tends not to human or animal felicity; therefore, it is not established for that purpose. Through the whole compass of human knowledge there are no inferences more certain and infallible than these. In what respect, then, do his benevolence and mercy resemble the benevolence and mercy of men?[78]

Demea intervenes at this point to offer the "probation" or "porch" theory used earlier by Bishop Butler. This life of hardship is but a testing ground for the future life in eternity. At this point it is Cleanthes who counters Demea's argument, since, being committed to argument a posteriori, he cannot accept any inferences which are not consistent with the facts of actual experience. The only legitimate method of argument is, according to Cleanthes, to show that *in this life* "health is more common than sickness; pleasure than pain." To this Philo replies that Cleanthes has established the warrants for religion on a very frail base. For the belief that human health and happiness in this life exceeds pain and misery is contrary to much human experience, and it is not possible,

to compute, estimate, and compare all the pains and all the pleasures in the lives of all men and of all animals; and thus, by your resting the whole system of religion on a point which, from its very nature, must ever be uncertain, you tacitly confess that that system is equally uncertain. . . . Here, Cleanthes, I find myself at ease in my argument. Here I triumph.[79]

Cleanthes makes one last attempt to shore up the argument from analogy. To abandon all human analogy is unthinkable, for to do so is to abandon rationality in religion. But perhaps we can preserve the human analogy and conceive of "the Author of nature to be *finitely* perfect, though far exceeding mankind." Philo does not attempt here to present objections to Cleanthes' hypothesis of a finite God, for that is not the point at issue. The question is whether the ambiguous mixture of good and evil in the world justifies inferring to a God, *whether finite or infinite*, such moral attributes as justice and benevolence. If a person were brought into this world without any antecedent conviction concerning a supreme and benevolent intelligence but were

left to gather such a belief from the appearances of things—this entirely alters the case, nor will he ever find any reason for such a conclusion. He may be fully convinced of the narrow limits of his understanding, but this will not help him in forming an inference concerning the goodness of superior powers, *since he must form that inference from what he knows*, not from what he is ignorant of.[80] (Italics added.)

As long as the goodness of the Deity cannot be established a priori and because such moral qualities must be inferred from experience, there can be no grounds for such inferences while the world is so full of evil.

Look round this universe. What an immense profusion of beings. You admire this prodigious variety and fecundity. But inspect a little more narrowly these living existences . . . . How hostile and destructive to each other . . . . The whole presents nothing but the idea of a blind nature, impregnated by a great vivifying principle, and pouring forth from her lap, without discernment or parental care, her maimed and abortive children.[81]

Our experience, says Philo, would indicate that the first cause of things is benignly indifferent to our human judgments of good and evil.

With this Philo's refutation of Cleanthes' argument from design comes to a conclusion. The force of the entire argument, as it reaches its climax in the depiction of man in a blindly indifferent universe, appears irrefutable. Hume has not only countered the theistic proofs but has left us with a feeling of existential abandonment. His concluding comment is that "to be a philosophical skeptic is, in a man of letters, the first and most essential step towards being a sound, believing Christian."[82] Hume was here again expressing his sardonic attitude toward popular faith. There is, however, more in this and other similar statements than mere mordant irony. There is a very modern ring to these words, for in the almost two centuries since Hume, metaphysical skepticism and religious faith have often joined in a strange alliance. Hume's counsel certainly has been used to endorse Demea's views and to give philosophical support to many contemporary fideists of skeptical temperament. In this sense Hume anticipates several movements of the nineteenth and twentieth centuries.

It seems clear that Hume himself recognized the practical impossibility of Philo's skepticism and that he was sympathetic to Cleanthes' strictures against persisting in "total skepticism" and "philosophical melancholy." He certainly recognized that for the majority of mankind the skeptics' calm and leisurely negations are child's play in face of life's practical needs. Where Hume joins with all the fideists of the modern period is in their common conviction that reason is impotent to either establish or falsify religious *beliefs*. This is one source of Hume's modernity and continuing importance in theological work. Hume, like many analytical philosophers and theologians in the twentieth century, did not consider religious beliefs as factual assertions about the empirical world. For Hume religious convictions, like certain philosophical ideas, are what can be called *natural beliefs*. By this is meant beliefs that are not themselves factual inferences but instinctive and practical attitudes toward the world. Hume held that "there is a great difference between such opinions as we form after a calm and profound reflection, and such as we embrace by a kind of instinct or natural impulse on account of their suitability and conformity to the mind."[83] Among men's "natural beliefs" are the existence of the external world, the identity of the self, and such religious convictions as a particular providence and a future life. Hume thus held that there are these natural beliefs which are neither proven nor falsified by the experimental method, for the reason that such convictions are not to be confused with empirical assertions. Since religious belief does not involve factual assertions, the ground is cut from under the empirical skeptic. The price of such a victory for the theologian is very high, however, viz., the acknowledgment that religion does not claim to make metaphysical assertions about the world.

As we shall see, this issue posed by Hume is one of the most basic in the history of modern theology.[84]

Hume's modernity is also traceable to his candidly realistic view of human nature and history. There is in Hume's depiction of nature's "maimed and abortive children" a nihilism more chilling than that of any twentieth-century atheistic existentialist. Hume is no Dostoevskian "underground man," but the germ of a more militant skepticism is certainly present in the *Dialogues*. Strangely enough, Hume is even more modern than the strident nihilists of the nineteenth century. In spite of his skeptical pessimism, Hume is completely above the romantic storm and stress. He is able to descend into the skeptical abyss with Olympian calm. His indifference to the "religious hypothesis" is more typical of the healthy agnosticism of the modern secular man "come of age" described by Dietrich Bonhoeffer in his *Letters and Papers from Prison*. Hume is the modern secular man par excellence.

Immanuel Kant

Hume's importance in the history of theology has been essentially negative. He concluded his *Enquiry Concerning Human Understanding* by throwing down the following gauntlet:

If we take in our hand any volume of divinity or school metaphysics, let us ask, *Does it contain any abstract reasoning concerning quantity or number?* No. *Does it contain any experimental reasoning concerning matter of fact and existence?* No. Commit it then to the flames for it can contain nothing but sophistry and illusion.[85]

This has remained to the present a direct challenge to all philosophical theologians who wish to establish rational warrants for religious belief. It was Kant's own reading of Hume's critical analysis of the older metaphysics that first interrupted his "dogmatic slumber."[86] Kant came to recognize that the human mind finds itself in the peculiar situation of being burdened by certain metaphysical questions which it is unable to ignore but which also appear to transcend the mind's power to answer. Kant's importance for modern theology lies in the fact that he both extended Hume's critique of traditional natural theology *and* laid the theoretical groundwork for an entirely new approach to theology. Kant remarks in the Preface to *The Critique of Pure Reason* that he had "found it necessary to deny knowledge in order to make room for *faith*."[87] This sounds exactly like Hume in its denial of any relationship between religion and matters of empirical knowledge; but this is as far as the similarity goes. It is important to note that Kant is contrasting *faith* with empirical *knowledge*, not faith and reason. Kant believed that there was a reasonable form of faith which the rational man would recognize as *implied* in an analysis of experience. Religious faith and knowledge are not radically opposed in Kant as in Hume for they are two quite different, though equally necessary, aspects of reason. Kant's pivotal role in modern theology lies in the fact that he freed theology from the corrosion of classical empiricism while maintaining the rationality of religious belief.

Immanuel Kant (1724–1804) was born in Königsberg in East Prussia. Both his parents were devout Pietists and Kant was nurtured in this form of Protestant piety, both at home and at the Collegium Fredericianum, where he studied from

1732 to 1740. Pietism placed great emphasis on ardent, personal religious experience and on strict moral integrity. The latter influence remained with Kant throughout life and is basic to understanding his character and philosophy. Nevertheless, while Kant always remained respectful of the good qualities of Pietism, the emotional fervor and hypocrisy which he encountered at the Collegium gave him a lifelong abhorrence of such "emotional" exercises as hymn singing and prayer.*

Kant lived his entire life in Königsberg where, as one writer noted, his life was like the most regular of regular verbs. He attended the University of Königsberg, became a tutor to a private family, and in 1755 returned to the University where he remained for the rest of his life. Despite his outwardly uneventful life, Kant was known to his students and friends as an eloquent, popular lecturer and charming host.

Kant began his career as a convinced disciple of the Leibnizian-Wolffian rationalism that reigned in the German universities. However, in the period between 1770 and 1781 he began to reject the Leibnitz-Wolff system and to work out his own philosophy. In 1781 *The Critique of Pure Reason* appeared and ushered in the Kantian "Copernican Revolution" in philosophy and theology. Once the first *Critique* appeared, a dozen or more additional works followed in quick succession for almost a quarter of a century, until his death in 1804. Kant's philosophical output after his fifty-seventh year is an unparalleled accomplishment.

What was Kant's "Copernican Revolution"? Among the British empiricists, from Locke to Hume, there was general agreement that the mind functions in a passive role. According to the empiricists, there are no innate ideas in the mind; rather, the mind at its beginning is an empty vessel, a *tabula rasa* receiving "impressions" from the exterior world. From these single impressions the mind somehow "collects" ideas, and thus all ideas come from empirical experience. Hume carried British empiricism to a skeptical blind alley by contending that belief in the simplicity or identity of the self or objects in the external world was simply the result of habit, since identity "is nothing really belonging to these different perceptions and uniting them together; but it is merely a quality which we attribute to them because of the union of their ideas in the imagination."

Kant came to believe that it was the empiricists' passive and dualistic view of cognition, which conceived of the mind as simply a receptor of particular external sense impressions, that was inadequate and which led to Hume's skepticism. Kant suggested another hypothesis concerning the mind.

Hitherto it has been assumed that all our knowledge must conform to objects. But all attempts to extend our knowledge of objects by establishing something in regard to them *a priori*, by means of concepts, have, on this assumption, ended in failure. We must therefore make trial whether we may not have more success in the tasks of metaphysics, if we suppose that objects must conform to our knowledge. This would agree better with what is desired, namely, that it should be possible to have knowledge of objects *a priori*,

---

* As an adult Kant attended church services only rarely and only to fulfill official responsibilities. It is told that when Kant became rector of the University, he duly led the academic procession to the cathedral for the customary service, but deserted it at the door.

determining something in regard to them prior to their being given.[88]

Kant wished to begin with a new hypothesis: that the mind is active. That is, instead of beginning with the object as something already given to which the mind must conform, Kant reverses the order and conceives of the object as in some respects constituted by the a priori contributions of the knower. The mind imposes upon the material of experience its own forms of cognition, determined by the very structure of the human understanding. The raw material of experience is thus molded and shaped along certain definite lines according to the cognitive forms within the mind itself. These forms of the mind are the way we "put things together." All experience presupposes these a priori categories which are not themselves observable.

It is important to notice that Kant meant that the cognitive forms of experience determine the possibility of objects of *knowledge*. That is, the categories of experience determine our knowledge of *phenomena*. If the word object were taken to refer to *things-in-themselves*, things apart from any relation to a knowing subject, then we could not say they are *known by the human mind*. We cannot, then, according to Kant, *know noumena* or things-in-themselves, i.e., supersensible objects, for we lack the necessary cognitive organ. The categories of human understanding are limited to the domain of empirical experience, of phenomena, and although the mind can conceive of a supersensible object, the mind cannot produce knowledge of such a transcendent being.

The Critique of Metaphysics. Such was Kant's "Copernican Revolution."

The implications of Kant's hypothesis are twofold. First of all, Kant has established the possibility of objective knowledge of the phenomenal world, since the synthetic function of the mind's a priori categories serves as a kind of universal law or structure of all possible experience and thereby makes a pure science of nature possible. To rehabilitate empiricism and establish the possibility of a pure science of nature was, however, only half of Kant's purpose. He also wished to show that such objective knowledge is thwarted when it is applied to a sphere which transcends that of space, time, and perception. That is, such metaphysical concepts as God's existence are not matters of experience and, if known at all, must be known in some other way.

In the section of the first *Critique* entitled the "Transcendental Analytic", Kant had sought to prove the validity of scientific knowledge. In the next section called the "Transcendental Dialectic," Kant seeks to extend Hume's refutation of rationalistic metaphysics. Because of its importance for philosophical theology we must give some attention to the critique of theology as developed in the "Dialectic." Kant considers three areas of rationalistic speculation—the self, being in general, and God. We will limit our discussion to Kant's critique of speculative knowledge of God.

There are, Kant held, three possible ways of proving the existence of God by means of pure reason—the *ontological*, the *cosmological*, and the *physico-theological* (or argument from design). The ontological proof which was originally conceived by Anselm in the eleventh century was revived in the seventeenth century by Descartes and Leibnitz. The ontological argument proceeds from the very definition of God as a perfect being. A perfect being must possess all perfections, for otherwise it would not be perfect. In the concept of a most perfect being existence must be included for if it were not, the concept would not be that of a most perfect being. Therefore, by definition such a being must necessarily exist.

Kant refutes the argument by demonstrating that "existence" is not a predicate and therefore cannot be a predicate of even a most perfect being. There is, he acknowledges, no difficulty in giving a verbal definition such as that there is something the nonexistence of which is impossible. But such a definition is

taken from *judgements*, not from *things* and their existence. But the unconditional necessity of judgements is not the same as an absolute necessity of things. . . . The [mathematical] proposition does not declare that three angles are absolutely necessary, but that, under the condition that there is a triangle [that is, that a triangle is given], three angles will necessarily be found in it . . . .

If in an identical proposition, I reject the predicate while retaining the subject, contradiction results; and I therefore say that the former belongs necessarily to the latter. But if we reject subject and predicate alike, there is no contradiction; for nothing is left that can be contradicted. To posit a triangle and yet to reject its three angles is self-contradictory; but there is no contradiction in rejecting the triangle together with its three angles. The same holds true of the concept of an absolutely necessary being. If its existence is rejected, we reject the thing itself with all its predicates; and no question of contradiction can then arise . . . .

If we admit, as every reasonable person must, that all existential propositions are synthetic how can we profess to maintain that the predicate of existence cannot be rejected without contradiction? This is a feature that is found only in analytic propositions, and is precisely what constitutes their analytic character . . . .

Being is obviously not a real predicate; that is, it is not a concept of something that could be added to the concept of a thing . . . . The proposition "God is omnipotent" contains two concepts, each of which has its object—God and omnipotence. The small word "is" adds no new predicate *in its relation* to the subject. If, now, we take the subject [God] with all its predicates, and say "God is," we attach no new predicate to the concept of God, but only posit the subject in itself with all its predicates. . . . A hundred real thalers do not contain the least coin more than hundred possible thalers. For as the latter signify the concept, and the former the object and the positing of the object, should the former contain more than the latter, my concept would not, in that case, express the whole object, and would not therefore be an adequate concept of it. My financial position is, however, affected very differently by a hundred real thalers than it is by the mere concept of them . . .; yet the conceived hundred thalers are not themselves in the least increased through thus acquiring existence outside my concept.[89]

Kant's conclusion is that the attempt to establish the existence of God by means of the ontological argument is futile for "we can no more extend our stock of [theoretical] insight by mere ideas than a merchant can better his position by adding a few noughts to his cash account."[90] Since existence is not a predicate, if I deny God's existence, I am not denying a predicate of a subject, hence no logical contradiction is involved as the proponents of the argument contend.

From the ontological argument Kant turns to the two arguments which claim to be based on the facts of experience. The first of these is the cosmological proof. The argument runs thus:

If anything exists, an absolutely necessary being must also exist. Now I, at least, exist. Therefore an absolutely necessary being exists.

The minor premise contains an experience, the major premise the inference from there being any experience at all to the existence of the necessary.[91]

Kant finds at least two difficulties in this proof. First, this proof claims to take its stand on experience, but, says Kant,

the cosmological proof uses this experience only for a single step in the argument, namely, to conclude the existence of a necessary being. What properties this being may have, the empirical premise cannot tell us. Reason therefore abandons experience altogether, and endeavours to discover by mere concepts what properties an absolutely necessary being must have . . . . Thus the so-called cosmological proof really owes any cogency which it may have to the ontological proof from mere concepts.[92]

The second difficulty with the cosmological proof is that the major premise ("an absolutely necessary being exists") rests on a "transcendent" use of the principle of causality, that is, a use of the principle of causality beyond the realm of sense experience when it cannot be legitimately used to transcend the world given in sense experience. Says Kant:

The principle of causality has no meaning and no criterion for its application save only in the sensible world. But in the cosmological proof it is precisely in order to enable us to advance beyond the sensible world that it is employed.[93]

Kant considered the physico-theological proof (from design) to be "the oldest, the clearest and the most accordant with the common reason of mankind" and yet, Kant adds, "we cannot approve the claims which this mode of argument would fain advance." Like Hume before him, Kant found the argument from design logically inadequate.

Since Kant's refutation resembles Hume's, we need not detail it here. Let it suffice to say that Kant concludes that the utmost the argument from design can prove

is an *architect* of the world who is always very much hampered by the adaptability of the material in which he works, not a *creator* of the world to whose idea everything is subject. This, however, is altogether inadequate to the lofty purpose which we have before our eyes, namely, the proof of an all-sufficient primordial being. To prove the contingency of matter itself, we should have resort to a transcendental argument, and this is precisely what we have here set out to avoid.[94]

Kant defined natural theology as inferring "the properties and the existence of an Author of the world from the constitution, the order and unity, exhibited in the world."[95] For Kant the attempt of such a natural theology to prove the existence and attributes of God is completely fruitless. It must be noted, however, that Kant is carefully delimiting what he means by natural theology and that implied in his critique of metaphysics is not only the claim that God's existence cannot be theoretically proven, but also that by pure reason alone neither can God's nonexistence be demonstrated. Kant's criticism of natural theology thus leaves the possibility open for another approach to and use of metaphysical concepts, or what Kant called "transcendental ideas."

Unlike Hume, Kant did not believe that such metaphysical concepts as self, world, and God were vain illusions. Kant had a deep respect for these persistent metaphysical impulses in man and believed that, while we are mistaken in conceiving of such transcendental ideas as the self, the world, and God as *objects* of knowledge, they are natural to reason and do have an important *regulative* use. That is, these ideas or concepts function as regulative maxims in guiding our scientific inquiry. Take, for example, the concept of a highest intelligence.

Thus I say that the concept of a highest intelligence is a mere idea, not to be taken as consisting in its referring directly to an object . . . . It is only a schema . . . which serves only to secure the greatest possible systematic unity in the empirical employment of our reason. . . . We declare, for instance, that the things of the world must be viewed *as if* they received their existence from a highest intelligence. The idea is thus really only a heuristic, not an ostensive concept. It does not show us how an object is constituted, but how, under its guidance, we should *seek* to determine the constitution and connection of the objects of experience.[96]

The use of these regulative ideas is not, then, for the extension of our knowledge to objects beyond our normal experience but as a principle of systematization and unity. The idea of God as a supreme intelligence and cause of the world leads us to conceive of nature as a systematic, teleological whole, under the guidance of causal laws. Such a conception of the unity of nature is a spur to scientific investigation. The regulative use of the idea of God is thus both necessary and beneficial.

Here Kant is steering a kind of middle path between skepticism and dogmatism. He denies any knowledge of the attributes of God in himself and yet finds a legitimate function in the idea of a God of perfect intelligence, goodness, and justice "for us," that is, in the interests of furthering our knowledge of nature and its laws.

Kant's defense of a rational theism did not rest finally on his conception of the

regulative use of the transcendental idea of God. The important problems raised by the third section of *The Critique of Pure Reason* were the prolegomena to Kant's fundamental concern, i.e., ethics and the primacy of moral faith. It is only in this context that we can understand Kant's statement that he "found it necessary to deny *knowledge* in order to make room for *faith*." The first *Critique* paved the way for *The Critique of Practical Reason* (1788). It is in this latter work that Kant establishes theistic belief as a postulate of pure practical reason. In order to understand Kant's reconstruction of rational faith in God we must understand something of the purpose and theory of this second great work.[97]

The Moral Foundation of Rational Faith. In the second *Critique* Kant sought to show that man's relation to the world is not limited to scientific knowledge (fact) for the world is a stage upon which we must *act*—a realm of moral value. Kant's task in the second *Critique* was to demonstrate that there are not only a priori categories of our pure or scientific reason, by which scientific knowledge can be assured, but that the very limits of our empirical knowledge point to a pure reason operative in our practical life. That is, there are certain a priori propositions which constitute the moral order or realm of value. The most needful principles of our practical, moral life are, then, completely independent of our empirical experience and the principles of pure reason. Thus, according to Kant, we do not need to wait until the scientists determine the nature of the empirical world before we can know what we ought to do. Our knowledge of what we ought to do is prior to and more certain than any scientific findings.

Kant accepted as axiomatic that we are living in a moral world. Men experience different moral obligations, but the experience of "oughtness" is universal. According to Kant, to act morally is not to act from inclination or even prudence but from a sense of duty. And dutiful action derives its warrant not from its consequences but from the conformity of such actions with some general law which can serve the will as a principle of action. Such a moral law is a "fact of reason" since it is not an empirical fact but announces itself as originally legislative. This originally legislative principle is the categorical imperative, namely, that one should, "act only on that maxim whereby thou canst at the same time will that it should become a universal law."⁹⁸

Kant held that we respect the moral law because it is a law which we as rational beings legislate for ourselves. The moral law is not something imposed from without but that which we voluntarily obey. This is what Kant calls moral autonomy. Moral commands are not, then, derived from some source outside the self, such as the Bible or the Church. Kant thus denies any theological foundation for his ethical theory. Morality is not based on knowledge of God. Quite the contrary—knowledge of God is, for Kant, a postulate of moral reason. Whereas traditionally morals were grounded in theology, Kant reverses this order and attempts to demonstrate that the fundamental beliefs of religion are in need of the support of our moral reason. Thus Kant can say that "it is reason, by means of its moral principles, that can first produce the concept of God." This is Kant's "Copernican Revolution" in theology! Here Kant reveals his kinship with, and perhaps his dependence upon, Rousseau. Kant, like Rousseau, rejects

speculative theology based on metaphysical proofs. For him the only way to knowledge of God is through the moral conscience, the only genuine theology is ethical theology.

How is it that our moral conscience produces religious convictions? Kant's way of putting it is that our moral nature *demands* the reality of the objects of religious belief. They are moral *postulates*, that is, logically required by our acknowledgment of the implications of the moral law which is a "fact of reason." To deny them would lead to the overthrowing of the concept of moral law. They are, then, a "work of reason" or "a pure moral need." Religion is, for Kant, "trust in the promise of the moral law."

The way Kant establishes the religious postulates is as follows. What kind of world is required, Kant asks, if we are to make sense of the fact of the moral law? The only finally good thing is a good will, or virtue, what Kant called the supreme good (*supremum bonum*). Kant realized, however, that although virtue is an unconditional good, it does not follow that it is the perfect good (*summum bonum*), for the complete good includes both virtue and happiness, that is, "the distribution of happiness in exact proportion to morality." The perfect accordance of the will with the moral law is the supreme good, and perfection would include an exact proportion of happiness. This state of affairs, our moral reason tell us, *ought* to obtain and "the ought implies the *can*." Nevertheless, in spite of this moral demand, it is abundantly clear that no rational being is capable of attaining this supreme good within this allocated span of life. Yet

since it is required as practically necessary (i.e., it is a state that ought to exist), it can only be found in a *progress in infinitum* towards that perfect accordance.... Now this endless progress is only possible on the supposition of an *endless* duration of the *existence* and personality of the same rational being.... [99]

Thus, Kant postulates the immortality of the soul.

Pursuing this same line of argument, Kant holds that our experience teaches us that in this life the morally virtuous people are not always the happiest. The possibility of a *summum bonum*, which our moral reason demands, leads to the supposition of a cause adequate to this effect; in other words, the postulate of a Supreme Being. Here is Kant's way of stating the proof:

The *summum bonum* is possible in the world only on the supposition of a Supreme Being having a causality corresponding to moral character. Now a being that is capable of acting on the conception of laws is an *intelligence* (a rational being), and the causality of such a being according to this conception of laws is his *will*; therefore the supreme cause of nature, which must be presupposed as a condition of the *summum bonum* is a being which is the cause of nature by *intelligence* and *will*, consequently its author, that is God .... Now it was seen to be a duty for us to promote the *summum bonum*; consequently it is not merely allowable, but it is a necessity connected with duty as a requisite, that we should presuppose the possibility of this *summum bonum*; and as it is possible only on condition of the existence of God, it inseparably connects the supposition of this with duty; that is, it is morally necessary to assume the existence of God. [100]

This is Kant's demonstration that "morality inevitably leads to religion" and that religion is founded on man's moral faith. It is important to recognize that for Kant this moral necessity of theism is *subjective*, that is, a *want*, and not

objective, that is, a duty, for there can be no moral duty to believe in the existence of anything. That concerns only the empirical employment of reason. Nevertheless, these theological beliefs are *rational postulates* and, being based on the requirements of practical reason, can best be considered as objects of pure *rational faith*.

Reason is compelled to admit such a supersensible object as God but "only so far as it is defined by such predicates as are necessarily connected with the pure practical purpose." We cannot know God as he exists in himself, only as he exists *for me*. Luther had maintained, similarly, that God could be known only "in his benefits." Luther had said that faith and God must be held together for "whatever thy heart clings to and relies upon, that is properly thy god." Kant, likewise, holds that knowledge of God is dependent upon faith, but in Kant's case it is a strictly moral faith. For Kant true religious faith is synonymous with "the recognition of all our duties as divine commands."

Kant's treatment of theology in the two *Critiques* reveals both his break and continuity with the Enlightenment. Like Rousseau and Lessing, he was one of the great transitional figures between the Age of Reason and the nineteenth century. His critique of the metaphysical proofs of theism constituted an epochal break with the rationalistic theological pretensions of the eighteenth century. On the other hand, his conception of theology as a moral theology was certainly in keeping with the conception of religion in the Enlightenment. For Kant worshiping God was synonymous with obeying the moral law, and "everything which, apart from a moral way of life, man believes himself capable of doing to please God" was for Kant "mere religious delusion."

Rational Faith and Christianity. Of all the positive religions, Kant believed that Christianity, despite its historical imperfections, came closest to approaching the idea of a pure, rational, moral faith. Five years after the publication of *The Critique of Practical Reason*, Kant published his *Religion Within the Limits of Reason Alone* (1793). His desire to write a book on Christianity was no doubt partly motivated by his Pietist upbringing but, more important, because certain "hard" facts of human experience forced him to pursue ethical issues left unresolved in the earlier works.

In *The Critique of Practical Reason* Kant had acknowledged that freedom includes not only moral autonomy but also absolute spontaneity, involving the capacity to reject the moral law. Thus Kant faced the ethical problem of the power of free persons to misuse their freedom. It was largely this issue which led Kant to a philosophical analysis of the Christian faith in the *Religion*. The real fact of sin and evil, so central to the Christian conception of man, was, Kant recognized, at odds with his whole ethical doctrine. Yet Kant could not ignore the fact of evil; he considered it an incontestable element within experience and, therefore, made the fact of evil the starting-point for his analysis of Christianity.

The *Religion* sets out to demonstrate two things: (a) how the free will, though radically evil, can regenerate itself and (b) how Christianity, rationally interpreted, exemplifies this process of moral regeneration. The *Religion* opens, then, with a discussion of the radical evil in human nature. Kant rejects both the

optimistic view of the *Aufklärung*, that mankind is naturally free from any evil propensity, and the opposite view of total depravity. Neither view accords with human experience. Man must be good. The propensity to evil could not be imputed to us if we did not conceive of some state of goodness from which we have fallen. At the same time we cannot ascribe our penchant for evil to a *natural* defect such as man's finitude, for that would destroy moral responsibility. Nor can we conceive of our radical evil as an *inheritance*, such as an inherited disease (medicine), debt (law), or sin (theology). All these remove the responsibility of it from ourselves and place it on our progenitors. The source of every actual sin is to be sought in intelligible acts of freedom, which Kant, like the biblical writers, does not attempt further to explain. The propensity to evil is of inscrutable origin. Kant does, however, find the usual motive of evil actions in self-love.

The question, then, is how this evil disposition can be converted to a good one—that is, how the moral imperative ("the ought") implies the ability ("the can") to overcome freely the evil propensity. Kant answers that such a recovery is not to be conceived of as a gradual reformation but a fundamental revolution of man's habits, a conversion tantamount to a new birth. "But," Kant asks, "if a man is corrupt in the very ground of his maxims, how can he possibly bring about this revolution by his own powers and of himself become a good man? Yet duty bids us do this and duty demands nothing of us which we cannot do."[101]

Here is the crux of Kant's problem. The *ought* implies the *can*, and yet the *radical* corruption of the will raises the question of how such an imperative is

possible. Kant hints that divine cooperation is necessary.

For despite the fall, the injunction that we
ought to become better men resounds un-
abatedly in our souls; hence this must be
within our power . . . *even though what we are
able to do is in itself inadequate and though we
thereby only render ourselves susceptible of higher
and for us inscrutable assistance.*[102] (Italics added.)

Yet a few sentences earlier Kant had
asserted that, granted the need for supernatural cooperation,

man must first make himself worthy to receive
it . . . that is, he must adopt this positive increase of power into his maxim, for only thus
can good be imputed to him and he be known
as good.[103]

Kant is saying that our radically evil
disposition requires supernatural aid to
overcome it and yet that it must be in our
power to deserve such aid. Here Kant
founders on the religious concept of
grace. Redemption from evil involves an
antinomy, for redemption includes the two
paradoxical realities of grace and freedom. It involves an enabling grace which
is not within our power and the ability to
make ourselves worthy of such supernatural aid which is within our power.
The difficulty is that while these are
meant to be conjoined, we cannot conceive of them experientially except under
the form of succession. Either grace begets
a moral life or man freely makes himself
worthy of enabling grace.

Kant recognized that this religious
problem could not be resolved *theoretically*. The work of grace, like the means of
grace (the sacraments, etc.) are parergon,
i.e., subordinate or accessory works of
religion within the limits of reason alone.
Reason does not dispute the possibility of
such operations, but it cannot include
them within the province of knowledge
since our use of the concept of cause and
effect cannot be extended beyond matters
of natural experience. When, however,
we give *practical* consideration to this
paradoxical matter, and for Kant this is
the principal issue, the resolution is clear:

But practically the question arises . . . where
shall we start, i.e., with a faith in what God
has done on our behalf, or with what we are
to do to become worthy of God's assistance?
In answering this question we cannot hesitate
in deciding for the second alternative . . . we
can certainly hope to partake in the appropriation of another's atoning merit, and so of
salvation, only by qualifying for it through
our own efforts to fulfill every human duty—
and this obedience must be the effect of our
own action and not, once again, of a foreign
influence in the presence of whom we are
passive.[104]

For Kant the moral individual makes
himself into whatever he becomes. Moral
character must be determined by the
exercise of individual free will. No man
can be good for another. Each man must
bear the responsibility for his own actions.
Kant thus faced a dilemma. He recognized the incompatibility of the imputation of forgiveness and autonomous
freedom, and yet he was aware of man's
radical evil and inescapable guilt. He
sought to resolve this difficulty by insisting that grace implies that man has done
all that he can. But here Kant's solution
breaks down, and either autonomous
freedom or radical evil must be denied.
For if the individual has done what is
required to deserve grace, he does not
really need grace, for it is in the initial
break with radical evil that enabling
grace is needed. If grace is not operative
until it is earned, it is useless, for the will

has within its own power the ability to choose the good. In this case evil must be thought of as only superficial, not radical. It is clear that Kant prefers to give up his conception of grace and radical evil than deny his conception of moral autonomy.

Book One of the *Religion*, on the radical evil in human nature, is the most original and courageous of the whole treatise, in spite of the fact that Kant fails to resolve the antinomy of grace and freedom. Books Two through Four deal principally with Kant's conception of Christ and the Church. Both conceptions proved to be of considerable importance in subsequent developments in the nineteenth century. Nevertheless, in both cases Kant reveals a much closer kinship with the Enlightenment than is true in his wrestling with the problem of evil.

Kant begins Book Two by asserting that "Mankind in its complete moral perfection is that which alone can render a world the object of a divine decree and the end of creation."[105] According to Kant, the idea of Man in his moral perfection eternally exists in God, essential to his nature, as his only-begotten Son, "and only in him and through the adoption of his disposition can we hope 'to become the sons of God'."[106] "Now," says Kant,

it is our universal duty as men to *elevate* ourselves to this ideal of moral perfection, that is, to the *archetype* of the moral disposition in all its purity—for this idea itself, which reason presents to us for our zealous emulation, can give us power. But just because we are not the authors of this idea, and because it has established itself in man without our comprehending how human nature could have been capable of receiving it, it is more appropriate to say that this archetype has *come down* to us from heaven and has assumed our humanity. . . . Such union with us may therefore be re-

garded as a state of *humiliation* of the Son of God . . . . For man can frame to himself no concept of the degree and strength of a force like that of a moral disposition except by picturing it as encompassed by obstacles, and yet, in the face of the fiercest onslaughts, victorious.[107]

Despite the fact that, due to our sinful disposition, we must conceive of the Son of God as a heavenly ideal *come down* to earth, rather than as an earthly man become heavenly, every

man may then hope to become acceptable to God (and so be saved) through *a practical faith in this Son of God*. . . . In other words, he, and he alone, is entitled to look upon himself as an object not unworthy of divine approval who is conscious of such a moral disposition as enables him to have a well-grounded confidence in himself and to *believe* that under like temptations and afflictions, . . . he would be loyal unswervingly to the archetype of humanity and by faithful imitation, remain true to his exemplar.[108]

The important point here is Kant's emphasis on awakening the minds of men to the ideal of moral perfection, by which they can become the sons of God for which they were created. For this purpose a historical exemplar (such as Jesus) may be very effectual, for a person "in actual possession of this eminence . . . must attune our hearts to admiration, love and gratitude." Nevertheless, Kant insists that we need no historical example as our pattern.

From the practical point of view this idea is completely real in its own right, for it resides in our morally-legislative reason. We *ought* to conform to it; consequently we must *be able* to do so. . . . We need, therefore, no empirical example to make the idea of a person well-pleasing to God our archetype; this idea as an archetype is already present in our reason . . . . According to the law, each man ought really to furnish an example of this idea in his own person; to this end does the archetype reside always in the reason: and this, just because no example in outer experience is adequate to it; for outer experience does not disclose the inner nature of the disposition but merely allows of an inference about it though not of strict certainty.[109]

Kant shares the eighteenth century disregard of, and even disdain for, history. Therefore, the question which has so exercised theologians since the nineteenth century, i.e., whether the Gospel traditions give us the real, historical Jesus, was of no concern to Kant. The historical question neither can nor need be answered, for the real object of faith is the ideal of the Son of God well-pleasing to God. Whoever lets this ideal govern his actions may believe that he is justified in the sight of God; for the rightness of one's moral disposition covers or atones for the imperfection of one's previous evil deeds. This is how Kant conceives of the atoning *work* of the Son of God.

Kant felt as strongly as had Anselm that man must make satisfaction for the guilt incurred before his conversion. He therefore took seriously the conception of Christ's vicarious atonement as a satisfaction for sinners. However, inasmuch as an actual substitution cannot take place between two persons without setting aside the moral law, the conception must be taken symbolically as a process within the heart of the individual believer, whereby in the daily discipline of obedience the new moral or *noumenal* man in us suffers vicariously for the old, *phenomenal* man.

The coming forth from the corrupted into the good disposition is, in itself (as "the death

of the old man," "the crucifying of the flesh"), a sacrifice and an entrance upon a long train of life's ills. These the new man undertakes in the disposition of the Son of God, that is, merely for the good, though really they are due as punishments to another, namely, the old man (for indeed the old man is *morally* another).[110] (Italics added.)

The new man *in us* is our Redeemer who accepts the punishment of the old man's sins as a vicarious punishment.

Kant did think of Jesus Christ as the historical exemplification of the archetype of humanity well-pleasing to God, and no more. Living faith in this archetype is *in itself* a moral idea of reason and, therefore, not dependent upon the archetype in its phenomenal (historical) appearance. Hence, belief in Christ is, for Kant, nothing more than belief in a moral example whereby one places in oneself confidence that one will "under like temptations and afflictions . . . be loyal to the archetype of humanity and, by faithful imitation, remain true to his exemplar."[111]

While Kant conceived of salvation as an inward experience of the individual, unlike many a fellow *Aufklärer* Kant gave considerable place to the Church. He recognized that the rule of the good principle can only be assured by the upbuilding and maintaining of a society which makes the moral kingdom its end. Kant defined the Church as "an ethical commonwealth whose supreme lawgiver is God." The Church is distinguished from a civil theocracy by the fact that the Church's laws are "purely inward." The *invisible* Church is not an object of possible experience but, like the postulates, an ideal of moral reason. The *visible* Church is the actual union of men into a whole which harmonizes with that ideal. The true, visible Church is, then, that society which exhibits the moral kingdom of God on earth so far as it can be brought to pass by men. Such a Church would be characterized by universality, purity, freedom, and unchangeableness, since it would be guided by universal principles of pure moral reason, accessible to every rational man.

Kant was confident that the empirical Church-faith, though falling far short of the ideal archetype, nevertheless must and would be brought under the guidance of the principles of natural religion. The gradual transition from the statutory Church-faith to the faith of pure rational religion would constitute "the approach of the Kingdom of God." Kant emphasized that God alone is the founder of his Kingdom but that men have a moral obligation to fit themselves to be citizens of this Commonwealth. And because the only divine service is the discharge of our moral duties, the only proper service in the visible Church will be directed toward the active dissolution of the visible, statutory, institutional Church through loyalty to the pure religion within reason alone.

All "false worship" is, for Kant, that which puts the ecclesiastical, and statutory in place of the pure, moral service of God. Kant acknowledged that originally special acts of ceremonial and special statutory regulations may have been useful in promoting a purer, moral faith but that these had now largely become hindrances to moral progress. Therefore, all that man thinks he can do, outside his moral duty, to become well-pleasing to God, is "mere illusion and false worship." For Kant a "spirit of prayer" should pervade man's whole life, and yet special acts of prayer are unnecessary. So-called "means of grace" such as attending church services and partaking of the sacraments are usually followed, Kant believed, in order to evade the only true "means of grace," i.e., a good life. Therefore, such ceremonials have value only insofar as they promote a good, moral disposition, and Kant acknowledged that such practices did frequently serve such a moral end.

We can recognize throughout Kant's discussion of the Church a sublime moral seriousness which is, nevertheless, almost totally lacking in appreciation of the place of emotion in the religious life. For Kant moral reason remains supreme over all historical revelation and practice, and Kant remained true to the spirit of the Enlightenment in his confidence that the consummation of such a rational faith was insured.

We have good reason to say that "the Kingdom of God is come unto us" once the principle of the gradual transition of ecclesiastical faith to the universal religion of reason . . . has become general and has gained somewhere a *public* foothold . . . . For since this principle contains the basis for a continual approach toward such a consummation, there lies in it (invisibly), as in a seed that is self-developing and in due time self-fertilizing, the whole, which one day is to illumine and rule the world.[112]

When we look at Kant's philosophical theology as a whole and from the vantage point of the mid-twentieth century, it is true to say that Kant's contribution to modern theology lies primarily in the far-reaching influence and use of his ideas rather than in the intrinsic worth of his own theological doctrine. Kant's influence on modern religious thought is immeasurable. No one, with the possible exception of Schleiermacher, has had a greater influence. What Kant did was to sow the seeds of many tendencies of religious thought in the nineteenth century, tendencies which often took widely different directions. Kant's importance, then, lies in the wealth and suggestiveness of his ideas. *The Critique of Pure Reason* helped sow the seeds of modern religious agnosticism. Religious "illusionism" and "subjectivism" are often traced to Kant's "regulative" use of such ideas as God in Chapter III of the "Transcendental Dialectic." Religious pragmatism has also been discerned in Kant's moral postulates for God and immortality. Kant's view of the a priori categories in the first *Critique* influenced Schleiermacher, and later others, in the search for the religious a priori, that is, for the uniquely religious category independent of both science and ethics. On the other hand, a number of important theologians, principally Albrecht Ritschl and his successors, took their lead from Kant's second *Critique* and, on the basis of Kant's separation of knowledge and moral faith, sought to construct an ethical theism. The catalogue of Kant's influence on subsequent theology could be extended. However, we must turn our attention now to those thinkers who, though dependent on Kant, nevertheless found his rationalistic, moralistic, and unhistorical interpretation of religion unacceptable. These thinkers constitute the cultural movement known as Romanticism.

NOTES

1. Lytton Strachey, *Books and Characters* (1922), p. 174.
2. *The Creed of a Priest of Savoy*, tr. B. Foxley; in Everyman edition of Jean Jacques Rousseau's *Emile* (London, 1961), p. 228.
3. Ibid., p. 260.
4. Ibid., p. 261.
5. Ibid., pp. 261–262.
6. Ibid., p. 263.
7. Ibid., pp. 270–271.
8. Ibid., p. 232.
9. See the work of E. H. Wright, *The Meaning of Rousseau* (New York, 1963); also E. Cassirer, "Kant and Rousseau," in *Rousseau-Kant-Goethe* (Princeton, 1947), and *The Question of Jean-Jacques Rousseau* (New York, 1954); also C. Hendel, *Jean-Jacques Rousseau: Moralist* (New York, 1934).
10. *Emile*, op. cit., p. 237.
11. Ibid., p. 239.
12. Ibid.
13. Ibid., p. 272.
14. Ibid., pp. 275–276.
15. Ibid., p. 253.
16. Ibid., p. 254.
17. Cassirer, *The Question of Jean-Jacques Rousseau*, pp. 117–118.
18. *Correspondance générale de J. J. Rousseau*, Vol. III, No. 490, as cited in C. Hendel, op. cit., pp. 39–40.
19. William Law, *The Case of Reason*, Chap. IV; quoted in J. M. Creed and J. S. Boys Smith, *Religious Thought in the 18th Century* (Cambridge, 1934), pp. 94–95.
20. Butler, Works, Vol. I, p. 6. References to Butler are to the W. E. Gladstone edition of 1896 unless otherwise cited. Volume I contains the *Analogy*.
21. Ibid., p. 9.
22. Ibid., p. 18.
23. Ibid., p. 22.
24. Ibid., p. 36. Butler simply overlooks the inordinate difference between the loss of an organ or limb and the loss of the brain and nervous system.
25. Ibid., pp. 42–43.
26. Ibid., pp. 54–55.
27. Ibid., p. 212.
28. Ibid.
29. Ibid., p. 247.

30. Ibid., pp. 247–248.
31. Ibid., pp. 248–249.
32. Ibid., p. 284.
33. Ibid., p. 188.
34. J. H. Randall, Jr., *Making of the Modern Mind* (1926), p. 299.
35. *Equity and Reasonableness of the Divine Conduct in Pardoning Sinners upon Their Repentance Exemplified . . . Occasioned by Dr. Butler's Late Book, Entitled The Analogy of Religion*, p. 35; quoted in E. C. Mossner, *Bishop Butler and the Age of Reason* (New York, 1936), p. 101.
36. *Christianity Not Founded on Argument*, pp. 20–21; quoted in Mossner, op. cit., p. 143.
37. *The Natural History of Religion* (H. E. Root edition; Stanford, 1957), p. 75.
38. E. C. Mossner, *The Life of David Hume* (1954), p. 485. For information on Hume's life and religious beliefs, the student should consult the excellent studies by Mossner and N. K. Smith's "Introduction" to the Library of Liberal Arts edition of the *Dialogues Concerning Natural Religion*.
39. N. K. Smith, op. cit., p. 21.
40. *Private Papers of James Boswell*, Vol. XII (1931), pp. 227–232; quoted in Smith, op. cit., p. 76 ff.
41. For a thorough study of the centrality of the theological essays to the argument of the *Enquiry* and to Hume's philosophy as a whole and rejection of the contention that they are irrelevant insertions, see A. Flew, *Hume's Philosophy of Belief* (London, 1961).
42. Butler explicitly states this in the *Analogy*, op. cit., pp. 302–303.
43. *An Inquiry Concerning Human Understanding* (C. H. Hendel edition; New York, 1955), p. 120.
44. Ibid., p. 122.
45. Ibid.
46. Ibid., pp. 122–123.
47. Ibid., p. 123.
48. Ibid., p. 137.
49. Ibid., p. 138.
50. Ibid., pp. 139–140.

51. "David Hume and the Miraculous" in *Philosophical Studies* (London, 1934), p. 143.
52. *Inquiry*, op. cit., pp. 140–141. N. K. Smith points out that Hume's conclusion, though mordant, "was the declared teaching of the Reformed Churches that Faith is impossible save with the aid of divinely conferred grace." Smith, op. cit., p. 47. A twentieth-century follower of the teachings of Karl Barth would find Hume's conclusion very congenial.
53. Hume's first choice for a title of this section was "Of the Practical Consequences of Natural Theology," which would have been a much more accurate indication of its content and intention.
54. *Inquiry*, op. cit., p. 145.
55. Ibid., pp. 145–146.
56. Ibid., pp. 146–147.
57. Ibid., pp. 150–151.
58. Ibid., p. 153.
59. Ibid., p. 155.
60. N. K. Smith, op. cit., p. 59.
61. *Dialogues* (N. K. Smith, 2nd edition), p. 141. All references to the *Dialogues* are to the Kemp Smith edition in The Library of Liberal Arts.
62. Ibid., pp. 142–143.
63. Ibid., p. 143.
64. Ibid., pp. 149–150.
65. Ibid., p. 160.
66. Ibid., pp. 161–162.
67. Ibid., p. 164.
68. Ibid., pp. 166–167.
69. Ibid., p. 178.
70. Ibid., p. 179.
71. Ibid.
72. Ibid.
73. Ibid., pp. 179–180.
74. Ibid., p. 189.
75. Ibid., pp. 189–190.
76. Ibid., p. 194.
77. Ibid., p. 195.
78. Ibid., p. 198.
79. Ibid., p. 201.
80. Ibid., p. 204.
81. Ibid., p. 211.

82. Ibid., p. 228.
83. *A Treatise of Human Nature*, ed. T. H. Green and T. H. Grose, Vol. I, p. 501.
84. Recently, several British analytical philosophers have defended Christianity by conceding that religious beliefs do not claim to be *assertions* and therefore are neither verifiable or falsifiable. According to these philosophers, religious statements are "bliks" or "feelings" similar to Hume's "natural beliefs." See the essays by R. M. Hare and T. McPherson, in Flew and MacIntyre, *New Essays in Philosophical Theology* (New York, 1955).
85. *Inquiry*, op. cit., p. 173.
86. See Kant's comments on Hume's role in the development of his own critical philosophy in the *Prolegomena to Any Future Metaphysics* (New York, Liberal Arts Press), p. 5 ff.
87. *Critique of Pure Reason*, tr. N. K. Smith, 2nd edition (London, 1958), p. 29.
88. Ibid., p. 22.
89. Ibid., pp. 501–505.
90. Ibid., p. 507. Some scholars contend that Kant's argument that "existence is not a predicate" misses the whole point of the ontological argument, the point being that on rational analysis existence is a predicate which belongs *necessarily* to the most perfect Being. Kant's insistence that existence is not a property of anything has also been extensively debated in philosophy. For the important texts and discussion of the ontological argument both before and since Kant,

see A. Plantinga, ed., *The Ontological Argument* (New York, 1965).
91. Ibid., p. 508.
92. Ibid., pp. 509–510. For a criticism of Kant's contention that the cosmological proof necessarily relapses into the ontological argument, see F. Copleston, *History of Philosophy*, Vol. VI (London, 1960), pp. 298–299.
93. Ibid., p. 511.
94. Ibid., p. 522.
95. Ibid., p. 526.
96. Ibid., p. 550.
97. We cannot attempt an examination of Kant's ethical theory but will sketch its important features as they relate to his philosophy of religion.
98. *Fundamental Principles of the Metaphysic of Morals*, in T. K. Abbott, *Kant's Theory of Ethics*, p. 38.
99. *The Critique of Practical Reason*, in Abbott, op. cit., p. 218.
100. Ibid., pp. 221–222.
101. *Religion Within the Limits of Reason Alone* (New York, 1960), p. 43.
102. Ibid., pp. 40–41.
103. Ibid., p. 40.
104. Ibid., pp. 108–109.
105. Ibid., p. 54.
106. Ibid.
107. Ibid., pp. 54–55.
108. Ibid., p. 55.
109. Ibid., pp. 55–57.
110. Ibid., p. 68.
111. Ibid., p. 55.
112. Ibid., p. 113.

SUGGESTIONS FOR FURTHER READING

The works of Cragg, Mossner, Stephen, and Creed and Boys Smith cited in the bibliography for Chapter Two deal with the breakdown of the Religion of Reason.

For a very interesting analysis of the breakdown of rationalism in the modern period, see G. Clive, *The Romantic Enlightenment* (New York: World Publishing Co., 1960).

A. C. McGiffert's *The Rise of Modern Reli-*

gious Ideas (New York: The Macmillan Co., 1921) traces the disintegration of the older rationalism and the rise of the new religious spirit in the nineteenth century.

Among the specialized studies the following are recommended:

ROUSSEAU

Cassirer, Ernst. *The Question of Jean-Jacques*

Rousseau, tr. and ed. Peter Gay (New York: Columbia University Press, 1954).

————. "Kant and Rousseau" in *Rousseau-Kant-Goethe* (Princeton: Princeton University Press, 1947).

Hendel, C. *Jean-Jacques Rousseau, Moralist* (New York: Oxford University Press, 1934). Especially Chap. XVII on "The Profession of Faith."

Wright, E. H. *The Meaning of Rousseau* (London: Oxford University Press, 1929). Especially Chap. IV on "The Natural Religion."

JOSEPH BUTLER

Mossner, E. C. *Bishop Butler and the Age of Reason* (New York: The Macmillan Co., 1936).

Norton, W. J., Jr. *Bishop Butler, Moralist and Divine* (New Brunswick, N.J.: Rutgers University Press, 1940).

DAVID HUME

Flew, Antony. *Hume's Philosophy of Belief* (London: Routledge and Kegan Paul, 1961). Chaps. VIII and IX are particularly important for Hume's contribution to philosophical theology. Contains an excellent bibliography of books and articles on Hume's philosophy of belief.

Smith, N. K. "Introduction" to David Hume, **Dialogues Concerning Natural Religion* (Indianapolis: Bobbs-Merrill, Library of Liberal Arts, n.d.). Smith's introduction is the most thorough analysis available of Hume's personal views regarding religion, his general critique of religion, and the argument of the *Dialogues*.

IMMANUEL KANT

Green, T. M., and Silber, J. "Introduction," **Religion Within the Limits of Reason Alone* (New York: Harper, 1960). Green traces Kant's early religious training and the development of his philosophy of religion, and analyzes the *Religion Within the Limits of Reason Alone*.

Jones, W. T. *A History of Philosophy* (New York: Harcourt, Brace, 1952). Chaps. 30 and 31 contain an excellent, brief analysis of Kant's philosophy as a whole. For another brief study, see S. Körner, *Kant* (Penguin Books, 1955).

Kroner, R. *Kant's Weltanschauung*, tr. J. E. Smith (Chicago: University of Chicago Press, 1956). Attempts to set forth in brief compass the basic perspective of Kant's philosophy. Kroner interprets Kant's philosophy as focusing on the primacy of moral faith and action over all speculation.

Webb, C. C. J. *Kant's Philosophy of Religion* (Oxford: Clarendon Press, 1926). Traces the development of Kant's philosophy of religion and gives considerable attention to his treatment of Christianity in *Religion Within the Limits of Reason Alone*.

CHAPTER FOUR

Christianity and Romanticism

Friedrich Schleiermacher

In Chapter Three we have seen that eighteenth-century rational theology came under severe attack by men who were themselves committed to the ideals and scientific methods of the Age of Reason. This is especially evident in the work of Hume and Kant. Toward the close of the eighteenth century in Europe there came to prominence a generation of artists and thinkers who, though in many ways strikingly different, can nevertheless be grouped together as a single movement because of a spiritual kinship which clearly sets them apart from the ideals of eighteenth-century Classicism and Deism.

The men of this generation have been called Romanticists, and the revolution which they brought about is called the Romantic Movement. The first and purest phase of the Romantic Movement ran from 1780 to about 1830. During these fifty years Byron, Blake, Wordsworth, Coleridge, Beethoven, Chopin, Balzac, Goethe, Hölderlin, Novalis, and the theologian Schleiermacher, among many others, poured forth the fruits of their genius and died. Though of widely different temperament and holding quite divergent convictions, these men reflect certain beliefs and sympathies which make them spiritually akin and distinguish them from the spirit of the Enlightenment. It would be quite wrong, however, to envision the Romantic Movement as simply a repudiation of the Age of Reason. Rather, the Romanticists strove to enlarge the vision of the eighteenth century and to return to a wider, more richly diversified tradition.

Romanticism did not merely oppose or overthrow the neoclassic "Reason" of the Age of Enlightenment but sought to enlarge its vision and fill out its lacks by a return to a wider tradition—national, popular, medieval, and primitive as well as modern, civilized and rational. At its fullest, Romanticism cherishes both experience and tradition, both emotion and reason, both the Greco-Roman and Medieval heritage, both religion and science, both formal strictness and the claims of substance, both the real and the ideal, both the individual and the group, both order and freedom, both man and nature.[1]

The aim of Romanticism was *inclusiveness*, and for that reason the romantic spirit is difficult to define simply. However, there are certain convictions and values widely held by the Romanticists which set the movement off as a transition from the age of Newton to the world in which we live today. First of all, the Romanticists were unwilling to reduce experience either to rationalism or a narrow, scientific empiricism. Experience involved much that eluded both analytical reasoning and scientific experiment, including the power of imagination, feeling, and intuition.

It was an emphasis on the less rational side of human nature, on everything that differentiates man from the coldly calculating thinking machine; and correspondingly a revolt against viewing the world as nothing but a vast mechanical order. It was the voicing of the conviction that life is broader than intelligence, and that the world is more than what

physics can find in it . . . . Experience, in its infinite richness and color and warmth and complexity, is something greater than any intelligible formulation of it . . . .[2]

Wearied of the kind of rationalistic proofs put forward, for example, by William Paley in *Evidences of Christianity* (1794), the Romanticist was unashamed to declare: "My experience is my proof!" Warrant for belief was now focused on the intensity of *personal experience* rather than on what was common to all. Individuality and free self-expression were given primacy over rules and conventions and rational demonstrability.

The Romantic appeal to personal experience was dependent in part on Kant's conception of the transcendental ego, interpreted, however, as a gloriously unlimited, creative personality which each individual must seek to develop and enjoy. Coupled with this emphasis on personal experience and expression was a new concern for the rich diversity of human life and the cultivation of a feeling for, or imaginative insight into, points of view, tastes, and values of others—even those experiences and tastes that might appear eccentric and even monstrous.[3]

The appeal to diversity was also expressive of a new and revolutionary conception of Nature and Nature's God. Nature was no longer conceived after the model of a great, cosmic machine (the purpose of which, as Spinoza suggested, being "to make men uniform, as children of a common mother,") but, rather, as an insatiably creative process of increasing diversification. The God of this creative process was conceived of, once again, as the Platonic Demiurge, the creative Eros who makes for the actualization of all creative potentials and who values creative diversity above all else. Life and art should, in turn, be a copy of Nature's insatiate creativity and the God who is the very soul of Nature's pulsing, multiform life. The Romanticists were, in most instances, advocates of an unrestrained catholicity.

The Eternal Spirit knows that each man speaks the language which he has provided for him, that everyone expresses what is within him as he can and should . . . . [God] looks with satisfaction upon each and all, and rejoices in the variety of the mixture . . . . To him the Gothic church is as well-pleasing as the Grecian temple; and the rude war music of the savage is a sound as dear to him as religious anthems and choruses composed with richest art. Yet when I turn my gaze back from the Infinite to earth, and look about at my brothers—ah! how loudly must I lament that they so little strive to become like their great model in Heaven.[4]

To appeal to what is universally standard, uniform, and immutable is, as Schleiermacher remarked, to be guilty of "a radical lack of feeling for the fundamental characteristic of living Nature, which everywhere aims at diversity and individuality."[5]

This diversity is found not only in nature and art but in religion. The Deist search for a universal creed is pernicious, for variety is the very essence of religious experience. Schleiermacher calls upon the rationalists to

abandon the vain and foolish wish that there should be only one religion; you must lay aside all repugnance to its multiplicity; as candidly as possible, you must approach everything that has ever, in the changing forms of humanity, been developed in its advancing career from the ever fruitful bosom of the spiritual life . . . . You are wrong therefore, with your universal religion that is to be natural to all; for no one will have his own true and right religion if it is the same for all . . . .[6]

The Romanticists, while stressing individuality and variety, nevertheless shared a profound mystical sense of the elemental unity of Nature's dissimilitude. Man and nature are not irreparably split into a Cartesian dualism of thought and extension. Man and nature are fundamentally akin, for they are but variant manifestations of one infinite Whole. This sense of Nature's organic unity was experienced as an aesthetic wholeness— felt or intuited rather than comprehended rationally. Many Romanticists found in man's communion with Nature an artless wisdom which touches the very core of reality and which alone can give to the human spirit the understanding and repose which passes knowledge. Wordsworth expressed this feeling as simply and directly as any:

Books! 'tis a dull and endless strife:
Come, hear the woodland linnet,
How sweet his music! on my life,
There's more of wisdom in it.

And hark! how blithe the throstle sings!
He, too, is no mean preacher:
Come forth into the light of things,
Let Nature be your Teacher . . . .

One impulse from a vernal wood
May teach you more of man,
Of moral evil and of good,
Than all the sages can . . . .

Enough of Science and of Art;
Close up those barren leaves;
Come forth and bring with you a heart
That watches and receives.[7]

Common to the Romanticists was the feeling that behind Nature some Spirit or Vital Force was at work. This Spirit in Nature, call it God if you will, was not

the Deist watchmaker God, dispassion-
ately transcendent over his creation, but
the vital Spirit immanent in all things, the
creative Eros in which everything moves
and has its being. The feeling for and
longing to be in communion with this
Infinite Spirit gave to Romanticism a
distinctly religious sensibility. The Romanticist felt himself a part of a larger,
spiritual reality, and in this the Romanticist exemplifies the quintessence of the
homo religiosus.

The Romanticist feeling for the Whole,
though often acknowledged as a uniquely
religious sentiment, was not always
equated with Christian belief. For many,
including Friedrich Schlegel, all human
striving for the infinite belongs to a
peculiarly religious intuition. Typical of
this rather vague and often deeply
emotional feeling is Faust's response to
Marguerite's question whether he believes in God:

Sweet one! my meaning do not misconceive!
Him who dare name
And who proclaim,
Him I believe?
Who that can feel,
His heart can steel,
To say: I believe him not?
The All-embracer,
All-sustainer,
Holds and sustains he not
Thee, me, himself?
Lifts not the Heaven its dome above?
Doth not the firm-set earth beneath us lie?
And beaming tenderly with looks of love,
Climb not the everlasting stars on high?
Do I not gaze into thine eyes?
Nature's impenetrable agencies,
Are they not thronging on my heart and
   brain,
Viewless, or visible to mortal ken,
Around thee weaving their mysterious chain?
Fill thence thy heart, how large soe'er it be;
And in the feeling when thou utterly art blest,

Then call it, what thou wilt, —
Call it Bliss! Heart! Love! God!
I have no name for it!
'Tis feeling all;
Name is but sound and smoke
Shrouding the glow of heaven.[8] (Italics added.)

The feeling for the rich wholeness and
infinite possibilities of life also expressed
itself in a new enthusiasm for the past
and especially for those periods which
appeared superstitious and barbaric to the
philosophes. The Middle Ages were
admired because they represented chival-
ric romance and the Christian ideal of the
unity of faith and culture. The new interest in the past, however, was not confined to the Middle Ages. It represented a
more universal historical consciousness,
the beginnings of which we have already
seen in Lessing's *Education of the Human
Race.* Attacking the past now appeared
childish, since every age, every culture
has its own unique individuality and
contribution to make to the richness and
progress of humanity. This new interest
in and appeal to history which flowered
in the Romantic era proved later to be a
two-edged sword for theology. It was
responsible for a new appreciation of
ancient tradition and led, for example, to
renewed historical arguments for Catholic Christianity in the writings of Lamennais in France and John Henry Newman
in England. At the same time, appeal to
the genetic, historical method ushered in
a period of intensive investigation of the
origins and development of Christianity,
the results of which have not even yet
been fully felt or assessed.

In short, the Romanticists did nothing
less than inaugurate a revolution in
Western consciousness which, among
other things, launched a new era in
theology.

Romantic Traditionalism and Fideism

The Romantic protest against the narrow rationalism of the eighteenth century and the renewed interest in the historical past brought forth a new and vigorous expression of Traditionalism and Fideism in theological writing. In the minds of many, Rationalism had sown the seeds of skepticism and individualism, the fruits of which were the horrors of the French Revolution. Many Romanticists, Wordsworth and Coleridge for example, began their careers as fervent liberals, but, recoiling from the excesses of the French Revolution, became conservatives in their later years. Unbridled rationalism, it was thought, had proved socially contentious and divisive. What was needed was the authority and cohesive strength of the wisdom of the past handed down in the form of a great tradition. Traditionalism stood for the lessons of historical experience as a surer guide for man and society than autonomous reason. Among the most ancient and sublime of traditions was, of course, the collective experience of the Catholic Church. Here many found a tradition that was both authoritative and unitive in a revolutionary world cut loose from its historic moorings.

The political reaction to the French Revolution, which we identify with the age of Metternich, had its counterpart in a religious reaction, especially in France. There the Napoleonic era ushered in a Catholic revival that was closely allied with the spirit of Romanticism. In 1802 François René, Vicomte de Chateaubriand (1768–1848), published *Génie du Christianisme*, a sentimental but skillful and widely influential apology for Catholic Christianity. Like Schleiermacher, whose *Speeches on Religion* appeared three years earlier, Chateaubriand sought to defend Christianity on new grounds, by shifting the discussion from rationalist argument to aesthetic feeling. By appealing to history, Chateaubriand argued that the arts and civilization find their main source and support in the Christian tradition. For Chateaubriand the sublime truth and divine authority of Christianity lies in its unexcelled beauty. In good Romantic fashion, Chateaubriand saw Catholic Christianity as the universal symbolization of all human aspiration.

Another traditionalist, at least in his early career, was Félicité Robert de Lamennais (1782–1854). In 1817 he published his *Essai sur l'Indifférence en Matière de Religion*, of which 40 000 copies were sold within a few weeks and which led to many conversions to the Roman Catholic Church. In this and subsequent volumes, Lamennais argued, like Pascal, that men long for belief in order to avoid the nagging emptiness of skepticism. But certitude can never be reached by individual reason, which is always tentative and dissentious. Certitude, and hence peace, can only come from the general reason, the universal consent, or *sens commune* of mankind. Certitude, then, is not produced by rational argument but by the authority of the concensus of the race. Thus certitude is a matter of faith in the testimony of others, and the Catholic religion is the tradition with the largest number of witnesses. Therefore, Lamennais argues that only in the Catholic Church can one experience the embodiment of universal reason, the *sens commune*, which alone can bestow intellectual and spiritual repose.

Perhaps the greatest of the romantic

traditionalists was Joseph Marie Comte de Maistre (1753–1821). The Revolution of 1789 turned de Maistre against the rationalism and liberalism of the eighteenth century, and he found in the Catholic Church a safeguard against both intellectual and political instability. He condemned the new theories of liberty and equality and of popular sovereignty and, in his book *Du Pape* (1819), argued that the only foundation of society lay in authority, which he found best exemplified in monarchy and the papacy. De Maistre argued, however, for the supremacy of papal authority over even the national monarchy and insisted that since the Pope is universal sovereign, his decisions are not subject to appeal and, even more, are infallible. De Maistre became one of the leading theorists of Ultramontanism, the advocacy of centralization of authority in the papal Curia, the position which finally triumphed in 1870.

Traditionalism held that reason alone was an uncertain guide, the fruits of individual reason being atheism and political anarchy. The traditionalists appealed rather to faith in a great tradition, a *sens commune* or consensus. Hence traditionalism and fideism often went hand in hand—but not always. In Catholic countries, such as France, romantic protests against rationalism and the appeal to other kinds of evidences seldom meant a total repudiation of reason in matters of theological knowledge. For such a denial was contrary to the official teachings of the Church. When the Abbé Bautain (1796–1867), a priest and professor of theology at Strasbourg, insisted that faith in divine revelation was man's only source of knowledge of God, he was obliged to sign a recantation.

Radical fideism was more the product of German Romanticism and the heritage of Protestant Lutheranism and Pietism. There appeared in Germany at the close of the eighteenth century several thinkers who not only opposed the rationalism of the Enlightenment but also the theological implications of the new Kantian reconstruction. These men reexamined the role of faith in human experience and found this dimension of man's life sorely misunderstood and ignored by the rationalists, including Kant. Prominent among these fideists were Johann Hamann and Friedrich Jacobi.

Johann Georg Hamann (1730–1788) is best known as a minor figure in the *Sturm und Drang* movement in German literature and as a friend but critic of Kant. More recently Hamann's influence on Kierkegaard has become apparent; indeed, in Hamann one can discern many Kierkegaardian themes in embryonic form. Prominent among these is a profound rediscovery of the meaning of faith. To call Hamann a fideist requires qualification, however, for while he attacked rationalism, he also developed a subtle understanding of the relationship between faith and reason.[9]

Nevertheless, the center and starting point for Hamann was faith. Faith meant, first of all, a kind of Socratic ignorance. Like Hume, who influenced him deeply, Hamann believed that reason has a way of dissolving our common-sense view of the self and the world. Reason brings us to the limits of human understanding, to ignorance. In a letter to Kant, Hamann writes:

Reason is not given to you in order that you may become wise, but that you may know your folly and ignorance; as the Mosaic law was not given to the Jews to make them righteous, but to make their sins more sinful to them.[10]

But, unlike Hume, who resignedly counseled a return to habitual belief, Hamann
saw such ignorance as the positive departure from faith. Consciousness of the
limits of reason engages the whole person
in a new awareness of his existential
situation and thereby opens the way for
genuine faith. Faith, then, is not pre-
rational or antirational but *beyond* reason,
in that faith recognizes that real existence
is not merely an affair of *ratio*. Faith for
Hamann is a positive recognition and
acceptance of the givenness of existence
in its wholeness, seen as the creative gift
of God.

Hamann attacked the reduction of faith
to the limits of what is rationally demonstrable for, like Hume, he held that "our
own being and the existence of all things
outside us must be believed, and cannot
be established in any other way."[11] Thus
he could write that "what one believes
has no need to be proved . . . . Faith is not
a work of reason and therefore cannot
succumb to any attack by reason; because
believing happens as little by means of
reason as tasting and seeing."[12] For
Hamann, faith and reason are dialectically
related in such a way that faith needs
reason as reason needs faith. Yet what is
especially significant for Hamann is the
fact that the ground of religion lies in the
wholeness of man's existential encounter
with the world which lies beyond the
simple determinations of discursive
reason.

While Hamann's thoughts on faith
were given unsystematized in brilliant
aphorisms and striking flashes of insight,
a more systematic *Glaubensphilosophie*, or
philosophy of faith, was developed by
Hamann's contemporary, Friedrich Hein-
rich Jacobi (1743–1819). Jacobi was profoundly influenced by the critical work
of Kant and Hume. With Kant, Jacobi

agreed that scientific reason is limited to
the phenomenal world and cannot prove
the existence of supersensible realities. But
if we are confined to the world of
phenomena, then we can, Jacobi believed,
only pass from the conditioned to the
conditioned, the result being a naturalistic
determinism and monism such as Spinoza's, whose system Jacobi regarded as
the perfect exemplification of demonstrative reason.

Jacobi considered determinism and
monism intolerable, for he believed they
led to moral nihilism and atheism.
Though Jacobi acknowledged that human
freedom and God's existence are rationally undemonstrable, he felt both were
confirmed in experience. Hume had
rightly contended that even though we
cannot prove the existence of an external
world, we accept its reality as a "natural
belief." Likewise, so Jacobi contended,
we have an intuitive feeling or faith in
the certainty of supersensible realities.
Jacobi held that just as we are endowed
with sense perception, we are also invested with a "higher reason," a spiritual
faculty which is natural to every man. At
first Jacobi designated this spiritual
faculty as *Glaube* or Faith. Later, to indicate that he was not referring to formal or
positive beliefs, he called his higher
reason *Vernunft* or "Reason," which
comes from the German *vernehmen* and
means "to apprehend." *Vernunft* he contrasted with *Verstand*, or "Understanding," which he identified with scientific
reason.

Jacobi thus gave to reason a wholly
new meaning. Reason is now conceived
as that faculty which makes immediately
present to us supersensible realities such
as God—as immediately present as nature
is to our sensory faculties. Like Kant,
Jacobi divides reality into the noumenal

and phenomenal, but, unlike Kant, he assumed a faculty by which noumenal realities can be immediately perceived. Both *Vernunft* and *Verstand* give us certain knowledge—but of quite different kinds.

As the reality which reveals itself to our outer senses needs no guarantor, inasmuch as it is itself the strongest witness to its truth, so the reality which reveals itself to that inner sense, which we call reason, needs no guarantor. It, too, is itself and alone the strongest witness of its truth. Man necessarily believes his senses and necessarily believes his reason, and there is no higher certainty than the certainty of such belief.[13]

What is most significant about these new philosophies of faith is that they point to the fact that a whole generation of thinkers were now in search of a richer and more inclusive conception of experience and knowledge which would go beyond the limits of scientific demonstration. They were in quest of a reason which would include feeling, imagination, and intuition. Theologically, it involved the attempt to find a more adequate basis for the religious life than the rationalism and moralism of the eighteenth century. In this search there emerged two intellectual giants who have left their mark on British and European, as well as American, theology. In England there appeared Samuel Taylor Coleridge; in Germany, Friedrich Schleiermacher. Both men were leaders in the Romantic movements in their respective countries and both men sought to establish religious belief and life on a new foundation, based on a new conception of experience.

Samuel Taylor Coleridge

Samuel Taylor Coleridge (1772–1834) represents better than any other figure in England the Romantic protest against Rationalism in the early decades of the nineteenth century. Coleridge was a poet, philosopher, literary critic, and theologian who directed all his energies against what he believed to be the deadening effect of a "mechanical philosophy" upon human life and culture. J. S. Mill, writing in 1838, saw in Jeremy Bentham and Coleridge the two seminal minds of his age in England. In Bentham, Mill saw the empirical and scientific heritage of the eighteenth century sustained. On the other hand, Coleridge's doctrine expressed to him the revolt of the human mind against the philosophy of the eighteenth century. Coleridge's doctrine was ontological because the eighteenth century was experimental; "conservative, because that was innovative; religious, because so much of that was infidel; concrete and historical, because that was abstract and metaphysical; poetical, because that was matter-of-fact and prosaic."[14]

More than any other individual, Coleridge was responsible for the rebirth of a vital English theology out of the cold and spare remains of late eighteenth-century orthodoxy and rationalism. Coleridge's own mind was catholic, and his influence on British theology in the decades after 1830 was not limited to any one school or party. John Henry Newman recognized Coleridge as one of the few men responsible for breathing new life into England's spiritual torpor, thereby giving impetus to the Catholic revival. Coleridge's influence on F. D. Maurice, perhaps the most influential English theologian of the nineteenth century, is also well attested to in the Dedication of Maurice's *The Kingdom of Christ*.[15]

Coleridge did not begin his intellectual

career as a critic of eighteenth-century rationalism and republicanism. As a student at Cambridge he was an ardent supporter of Unitarian and republican views. For a while he even envisioned setting up, with the poet Robert Southey, a Utopian community modeled after the radical social theories of William Godwin. But Coleridge's social and religious liberalism was not deeply grounded, and by the time he left Cambridge he had already repudiated "Godwinism."

One of the major events of Coleridge's life was his meeting with the poet Wordsworth in 1795. Three years later, the two friends jointly published *Lyrical Ballads* and then traveled together to Germany. While Wordsworth explored the countryside, Coleridge studied the German language, attended philosophical lectures, and purchased a considerable number of German philosophical works which he brought back with him to England. It is to a considerable extent through Coleridge that German Romantic and Idealistic philosophy was introduced into British intellectual life.

The maturing of Coleridge's own spiritual philosophy was largely the product of his discovery of the aesthetic principle of the Imagination in the poetry of his friend Wordsworth and the new conception of mind and experience which he found in his reading of Kant and German transcendental philosophy. The coincidence of what he found in Wordsworth and Kant with what he had been working out in his own mind served to confirm his ideas and set him on the way to articulating his own doctrine. A brief analysis of these influences will be helpful in understanding Coleridge's unique contribution to religion.

In his *Biographia Literaria* Coleridge relates how the reading of Wordsworth's poetry freed him from the narrow sensationalism that had dominated British thought since the time of Locke. What struck Coleridge in reading the poetry of Wordsworth was "the union of deep feeling with profound thought: the fine balance of truth in observing, with the imaginative faculty in modifying the objects observed." Coleridge contrasted this "imaginative faculty" with what he called "fancy." Fancy is the mere juxtaposition of images in a deliberate and even contrived fashion. According to Coleridge, inferior poetry is the product of "fancy." Truly great poetry, such as Wordsworth's, is not a contrivance but a genuine creation. Such creation requires imagination, for a poem is not an assemblage but a new whole, a spiritual unity. Artistic creation, then, is the fusion of mind and materials, or subject and object, into a spiritual unity through the faculty of Imagination.

The philosophical importance of Coleridge's discovery of the faculty of Imagition lies in the fact that he now conceives of the mind as active and not merely as a passive receptacle of sensations: "If the mind is not *passive*, if it be indeed made in God's Image, and that, too, in the sublimest sense, the Image of the Creator, there is ground for suspicion that any system built on the passiveness of the mind must be false, as a system."[16]

Coleridge's discovery of the Imaginative faculty was confirmed in his reading of Kant. What Kant confirmed in Coleridge's mind was the belief that "the highest truths are those which lie beyond the limits of experience." Kant had affirmed that all our metaphysical truths are postulates of our practical reason— that is, of our *experience as moral beings*, not of our empirical or sensory knowledge. Like Kant, Coleridge taught that such metaphysical postulates as God, freedom, moral conscience, and immortality are derived from our moral convictions. "My metaphysics," he says, "are merely the referring of the mind to its own consciousness for truths indispensable to its own happiness."[17]

Reason, Understanding, and Faith.

The creative activity of the mind, which Coleridge discovered in the faculty of Imagination and which was confirmed in his reading of Kant, served as the basis of his attack upon the sensationalism and mechanical philosophy of the eighteenth century. Coleridge found a counterpart for the aesthetic faculty of Imagination which he believed would save religion and morality from the fatal malady of materialism. That faculty he called Reason.

For Coleridge, Reason is the complement of Imagination. It is the "organ of the supersensuous." On the other hand, Fancy finds its counterpart in what Coleridge calls Understanding. Understanding is the "faculty of judging according to sense." Understanding is, then, the passive, receptive faculty, "the *vis receptiva* or recipient property of the soul, from the original constitution of which we perceive and imagine all things under the forms of space and time."[18] It is the empirical, synthetic faculty of Kant.

According to Coleridge, Europe was presently living under "the dynasty of the Understanding," the result being materialism, atheism, utilitarianism. This "imperialism" of the Understanding stood for everything Coleridge regarded as a threat to the human spirit. Reason implied everything that defined the unique spirituality of humanity. Basil Willey

sums up Coleridge's distinction in this striking way:

Understanding is the faculty by which we generalize and arrange the phenomena of perception. Reason is "the knowledge of the laws of the whole considered as one"; Understanding is the "science of phenomena." Reason seeks ultimate ends; Understanding studies means. Reason is "the source and substance of truths above sense"; Understanding is the faculty which judges "according to sense." Reason is the eye of the spirit, the faculty whereby spiritual reality is spiritually discerned; Understanding is the mind of the flesh.[19]

Coleridge did not deny the value of the Understanding. In its own province he deemed it useful, even necessary. Yet the most important of truths—God, freedom, moral conscience—lie beyond its scope. Reason alone is concerned with moral and religious truth, for Reason alone is the instrument of spiritual apprehension, of those "truths above sense."

Coleridge never defined his conception of Reason systematically. Yet from his innumerable references to it we can discern much of what he meant by the term. First, Reason is unique to man. Other creatures may possess the faculty of Understanding, if only in the form of instinct, but man alone is a rational animal. Secondly, Reason is a moral imperative, what Kant would call a "want of reason."

We (that is the human race) *live by faith.* Whatever we do or know that in kind is different from the brute creation has its origin in a determination of the reason to have faith and trust in itself. This, its first act of faith, is scarcely less than identical with its own being . . . . It is itself therefore the realizing principle, the spiritual *substratum* of the whole complex body of truths.[20]

Thirdly, Reason should be thought of not as a separate faculty but, rather, as a *power*, an intuitive apprehension by which the total personality—senses, will, and emotions—act as a whole. Apprehension of such supersensuous truth is the fruit of feeling and will in unity with sense and intellect; the heart acting upon and in union with the head. Reason, therefore, is that power by which the faculties are united and are enabled to experience an intuitive apprehension of the truth.

Whereas for Kant the ideas of the practical reason are merely regulative ideas, for Coleridge the ideas intuited by Reason are the objects of knowledge; they have real ontological status. Here Coleridge parts with Kant and reveals his dependence upon the Platonism of the seventeenth-century English divines. Human Reason serves as the unitive power by which all disparate experiences and truths are bound together and apprehended as a spiritual Whole, because Reason is grounded in the one Being (God) who "is the ground of all relations."

It is the office, and as it were, the instinct of the reason, to bring a unity into all our conceptions and several knowledges. On this all system depends; and without this we could reflect connectedly neither on nature nor our own minds. *Now this is possible only on the assumption or hypothesis of a One as the ground and cause of the universe, and which, in all succession and through all changes, is the subject neither of time nor change* . . . .[21] (Italics added.)

Coleridge was especially fond of quoting the opening verse of the Gospel of John: "In the beginning was the Logos [Reason] and the Logos was with God and the Logos was God." Spiritual truths which transcend our sensory experience are real objects of knowledge because our human Reason is grounded in and is the image of the one infinite, eternal Reason—God.[22]

Especially significant in understanding Coleridge's concept of Reason is the importance he placed on the relation of Reason and Will. It is the Will which defines man as a free, self-determining being rather than simply as a link in the natural chain of cause and effect. It is the Will which separates man from Nature's necessity and the conditionedness of time and space. In *Aids to Reflection* (1825) Coleridge developed his concept of the Will in some detail, opposing his doctrine to that of the materialists and determinists. Coleridge sums up the distinction as follows:

Nature is a line in constant and continuous evolution. Its beginning is lost in the supernatural: and for our understanding therefore it must appear as a continuous line without beginning or end. But where there is no discontinuity there can be no origination, and every appearance of origination in nature is but a shadow of our own casting. It is a reflection from our own will or spirit. Herein, indeed, the will consists. This is the essential character by which Will is opposed to Nature, as spirit, and raised above nature as self-determining spirit—this namely, that it is a power of originating an act or state.[23]

For Coleridge, metaphysical truths are never discerned by the speculative or discursive reason alone but by the whole man, which includes deep feeling and willing.[24] The apprehension of spiritual truth involves the emancipation of the soul from the "debasing slavery to the outward senses" and the awakening of the mind "to the true *criteria* of reality, namely, permanence, power, *will mani-*

fested in act, and *truth operating as life.*"[25] Thus Coleridge looked with particular horror on the many books purporting to "prove" Christianity by discursive reason alone.

I more than fear the prevailing taste for books of natural theology, physico-theology, demonstrations of God from Nature, evidences of Christianity, and the like. *Evidences of Chrsitianity!* I am *weary of the word. Make a man feel the want of it; rouse him, if you can, to the self-knowledge of his need of it; and you may safely trust it to its own evidence* [italics added] remembering only the express declaration of Christ himself: *No man cometh to me, unless the Father leadeth him.*[26]

In Coleridge's view, Christianity is not principally a set of doctrines but a way of life. The proper approach to the honest doubter, then, is not to seek to resolve his speculative difficulties but to call upon him to "Try it!"[27] The proof is found in the practice. In fact, for Coleridge theological dogmas are beyond apprehension unless grasped by the practical reason. This is where Coleridge leaves orthodoxy and, with Schleiermacher, founds modern theological apologetics on a new basis, i.e., human experience. According to orthodoxy and rationalism, theological dogmas were true without reference to any subjective judgment. Dogma was either evidenced positively in an authoritative book or was the product of rational demonstration. With Coleridge this conception of religious doctrine is left behind. Christian doctrines are vital, living truths of experience or they are incomprehensible. Theologians have too long failed to realize this fact.

Too soon did the Doctors of the Church forget that the *heart,* the moral nature, was the beginning and the end; and that truth, knowledge, and insight were comprehended in its expansion. This was the true and first apostasy —when in council and synod the divine humanities of the Gospel gave way to speculative systems, and religion became a science of shadows under the name of theology . . . without life or interest, alike inaccessible and unintelligible to the majority of Christians.[28]

Dogmas accepted by intellect or authority alone, and not evidenced by being lived in practice, are the very opposite of spiritual truths, for such truths are inextricably related to the moral Will. Coleridge thus makes an important distinction between objects of *faith* and objects of sight and demonstrative assent. Objects of religious faith are "the assurance of things hoped for, the conviction of things not seen," and are confirmed not by sight or logical persuasion but by experience and moral suasion. Coleridge thus advises initiates in the faith to

translate the theological terms into their moral equivalents; saying to themselves—This may not be *all* that was meant, but it *is* meant, and it is that portion of the meaning, which belongs to *me* in the present stage of my progress.[29]

Thus in speaking of the thorny doctrine of election, Coleridge commends the view of Leighton who "avoids all metaphysical views of Election, relatively to God, and confines himself to the doctrine in its relation to man."[30] He then adds:

The following may, I think, be taken as a safe and useful rule in religious inquiries. Ideas, that derive their origin and substance from the moral being, and to the reception of which as true objectively (that is, as corresponding to a reality out of the human mind) we are determined by a practical interest exclusively, may not, like theoretical positions, be pressed onward into all their logical consequences. The law of conscience, and not the canons of discursive reasoning, must decide in such cases. At least, the latter have no validity, which the single *veto* of the former is not sufficient to nullify. The most pious conclusion is here the most legitimate.[31]

Coleridge was so convinced of this rule in matters of spiritual truth that he could say, concerning the doctrine of God:

It could not be intellectually more evident without becoming morally less effective; without counteracting its own end by sacrificing the *life* of faith to the cold mechanism of a worthless, because compulsory, assent.[32]

For Coleridge, faith and reason could not possibly be considered separately as two distinct modes of spiritual knowledge, since spiritual truth is apprehended only by the moral being, i.e., the individual conscience which is the union of Reason and Will. Coleridge, in fact, defines faith as *the act of conscience*, i.e., the act "by which we take upon ourselves an allegiance, and consequently the obligation of fealty." Here is Coleridge's fullest description of faith:

Faith subsists in the synthesis of the reason and the individual will. By virtue of the latter therefore it must be an energy, and inasmuch as it relates to the whole moral man, it must be exerted in each and all of his constituents or incidents, faculties and tendencies; . . . it must be a total, not a partial; a continuous, not a desultory or occasional energy. And by virtue of the former, that is, reason, faith must be a light, a form of knowing, a beholding of truth. In the incomparable words of the Evangelist, therefore—*faith must be a light originating in the Logos, or the substantial reason, which is coeternal and one with the Holy Will, and which light is at the same time the life of men.* Now as life is here the sum or collective of all

moral and spiritual acts . . . so is faith the source and sum, the energy and principle of the fidelity of man to God, by the subordination of his human will, in all provinces of his nature to his reason, as the sum of spiritual truth, representing and manifesting the will Divine.[33]

Experience and the Interpretation of Scripture. Coleridge's conception of the moral and experiential apprehension of spiritual doctrine or truth is most thoroughly worked out in his thoughts on the interpretation of Scripture, which appeared in *Confessions of an Inquiring Spirit*, published posthumously in 1840. In the *Confessions* Coleridge finds himself opposed to both the orthodox view of scriptural inerrancy and the skeptical conclusions of the rationalists. Coleridge is among the first of that new breed of nineteenth- and twentieth-century Christian who desires to preserve the truths of orthodoxy while remaining committed to the findings of historical-critical research.

During the early decades of the nineteenth century, English theology was dominated by what Coleridge called *Bibliolatry*, i.e., the belief in the literal inerrancy of Scripture. The English divines had little knowledge of the critical scholarship on the Bible that had long been underway in Germany. Coleridge had been introduced to this new critical movement during his year on the Continent—especially through his reading of Lessing whose influence is evident in the *Confessions*. Coleridge recognized that the doctrine of biblical inerrancy was simply playing into the hands of the infidel skeptics, the likes of Tom Paine, who were having a field-day demonstrating the contraditions and incongruities in the biblical texts. More than that, the inerrancy doctrine was forcing Christians to use all kinds of tortured and intellectually deceitful stratagems to seek to prove the Bible's infallibility. It was in this context that Coleridge wrote his *Letters on the Inspiration of the Scriptures* (published as the *Confessions*). The seven letters are addressed to a friend on the subject of whether it is "necessary, or expedient to insist on the belief of the divine origin and authority of all, and every part of the Canonical Books as the condition, or first principle, of Christian Faith?"[34] How, Coleridge asks, is it possible to accept biblical errancy and fallibility without at the same time falling into the "negative dogmatism" of those who regard the biblical texts as simply profane? How does one approach the Bible when one views it as neither inerrant nor merely profane?

Coleridge's answer is that the Bible should be taken up like "any other work" and that if it contains spiritual truth, those truths will "find me"—that is, the Bible will "bear witness for itself that it has proceeded from a Holy Spirit." What Coleridge means when he says that the Bible should be read like any other book is indicated in the analogy he draws with the reading of Shakespeare.

In the course of my Lectures on Dramatic Poetry, I, in half a score instances, referred my auditors to the precious volume before me—Shakespeare—and spoke enthusiastically both in general and with detail of particular beauties, of the plays of Shakespeare, as in all their kinds, and in relation to the purposes of the writer, excellent. Would it have been fair, or according to the common usage and understanding of men, to have inferred an intention on my part to decide the question respecting Titus Andronicus, or the larger portion of the three parts of Henry VI? *Would not every genial mind understand by Shakespeare that unity*

or total impression comprising, and resulting from, the thousand-fold several and particular emotions of delight, admiration, gratitude excited by his works?[35] (Italics added.)

The answer, of course, is that certainly this is what we mean by Shakespeare and that the appreciation of Shakespeare's incomparable literary merit is not called into question simply because his work includes Titus Andronicus. And so it is, says Coleridge, when we consider the Bible.

The reason for Coleridge's complaint is the faulty reasoning which holds that the spiritual truth of the Bible is dependent on its total and complete inerrancy. Coleridge argues that it is only in the *real humanity* of the biblical texts that its spiritual truth and power can be discerned. The Bible "finds me," says Coleridge, *only when it speaks to my human condition.*

But let me once be persuaded that all these heart-awakening utterances of human hearts —of men of like faculties and passions with myself, mourning, rejoicing, suffering, triumphing—are but as a *Divina Commedia* of a superhuman—oh bear with me, if I say— Ventriloquist . . . that this *sweet Psalmist of Israel* was himself as mere an instrument as his harp, an *automaton* poet, mourner, and suppliant; all is gone—all sympathy, at least, and all example. I listen in awe and fear but likewise in perplexity and confusion of spirit.[36]

The doctrine of biblical inerrancy transforms the real-life persons of the Bible, with their "pathetic appeals," "their piercing outcries," "their hollow truisms," into the dead automatons of an infallible Intelligence! What has happened is that biblical authority has been logically confused with biblical infallibility, a doctrine *about* the Bible has been substituted for the inherent authority contained *within the spiritual experiences* of the biblical personalities—a confusion which "has the effect of substituting a barren acquiescence in the letter for the lively *faith that cometh by hearing.*"[37]

The proof of the Bible's spiritual authority, according to Coleridge, lies "in its fitness to our nature and our needs." He calls upon us to be only

as orthodox a believer *as you would have abundant reason to be*, though from some accident of birth, country, or education the precious boon of the Bible, with its additional evidence, had up to this moment been concealed from you; —and then read its contents with only the same piety which you freely accord on other occasions to the writings of men, considered the best and wisest of their several ages! *What you find therein coincident with your preestablished convictions, you will of course recognize as the revealed Word*, while as you read the recorded workings of the Word and the Spirit in the minds, lives, and hearts of spiritual men, the influence of the same Spirit on your own being, and the conflicts of grace and infirmity in your own soul, will enable you to discern and to know in and by what spirit they spoke and acted—as far at least as shall be needful for you, and in the times of your need.[38] (Italics added.)

That the spiritual power and authority of the experience of the men of the Bible will "find you" in the depths of your own spiritual experience is no mere pious hope. It is historical fact.

In every generation, and wherever the light of Revelation has shone, men of all ranks, conditions, and states of mind have found [the Bible] . . . a spiritual World—spiritual, and yet at the same time outward and common to all. You in one place, I in another, all men somewhere or at some time, meet with an assurance that the hopes and fears, the thoughts and yearnings are not dreams or fleeting singularities [for] . . . the hungry have found food, the thirsty a living spring, the feeble a staff . . . and as long as each man asks on account of his wants, and asks what he wants, no man will discover aught amiss or deficient in this vast and many-chambered storehouse . . . . Good and holy men, and the best and wisest of mankind . . . have borne witness to its influences, have declared it to be beyond compare the most perfect instrument, the only adequate organ, of Humanity.[39]

Are we to say, in the light of our own experience and that of "the best and wisest of mankind," that these experiences are to lose their value and warrant because, in the case of the Bible, "a few parts may be discovered of less costly materials and of meaner workmanship?" Certainly not. Because contradictions, errors of judgment, moral weakness are found in the Bible, are we to say that

the Apostle's and Nicene Creed is not credible, the Ten Commandments not to be obeyed, the clauses of the Lord's Prayer not to be desired, or the Sermon on the Mount not to be practised?—See how the logic would look. David cruelly tortured the inhabitants of Rabbah (2 Sam. XII, 31; Chron. XX, 3), and in several of the Psalms he invokes the bitterest curses on his enemies; *therefore* it is not to be believed that *the love of God toward us was manifested in sending his only begotten Son into the world, that we might live through Him* (I John IV, 9).[40]

The logic, of course, is foolish. It is based on the specious conjunction of two very different statements. To say that "the Bible contains the religion revealed by God" is not the same as saying, "Whatever is contained in the Bible is religion, and was revealed by God." One can hold to the former while rejecting the latter. According to Coleridge, the Bible contains all that is necessary for faith and for practice; it is "the appointed conservatory, an indispensable criterion, and a continual source and support of true belief. *But that the Bible is the sole source; that it not only contains but constitutes the Christian Religion,*"[41] [italics added] is a doctrine that cannot be found in the Bible itself nor is it one that Christendom has widely held.

Coleridge advances the hermeneutical principle that the Bible can become "the living Word of God" only when it is read "in faith." By this he means that what in the Bible constitutes the indispensable kernel of the Christian faith requires some interpretive "master key." For Coleridge this key includes all that constitutes the Christian tradition—the confessions and doctrinal standards of the Church, the continued succession of the ministry, the spiritual experience of the whole communion of saints:

Friend, it is my conviction that in all ordinary cases *the knowledge and belief of the Christian Religion should precede the study of the Hebrew Canon. Indeed, with regard to both Testaments, I consider oral and catechismal instruction as the preparative provided by Christ himself in the establishment of a visible Church.*[42] (Italics added.)

Thus Coleridge counsels that it is only where one sees a desire to believe, "a beginning of love of Christ" that one should then say

there are likewise sacred Writings, which taken in connection with the institution and perpetuity of a visible Church, all believers revere as the most precious boon of God, next to Christianity itself . . . . In them you will find all the revealed truths which have been set forth and offered to you . . . in addition to

these, examples of obedience and disobedience . . . the lives and actions of men eminent under each dispensation, their sentiments, maxims, hymns, prayers—their affections, emotions, conflicts; in all of which you will recognize the influence of the Holy Spirit, *with a conviction increasing with the growth of your own faith and spiritual experience.*[43] (Italics added.)

Unless one comes to the Bible "in faith" and instructed in the Christian religion, one will be prone to lay hold of an isolated text here or there and say, "of what spiritual use is this," which only proves "that nothing can be so trifling as to supply an evil heart with a pretext for unbelief."

Coleridge's biblical hermeneutic was clearly directed against the orthodox and rationalist view of the Bible and Christian belief as something objectively given and "wholly external, and like the objects of sense, common to all alike." It is sometimes charged that the Romanticists, in abhorrence of rationalist objectivity, fell into the opposite error of subsuming the whole of faith within the receptive or subjective pole—thus reducing Christianity to subjective feeling or will. Such a charge certainly cannot be leveled at Coleridge. In several places he makes it clear that divine revelation is neither a wholly objective or subjective reality but requires both poles—objective fact and existential appropriation.

I comprise and conclude the sum of my convictions in this one sentence. Revealed Religion is in its highest contemplation the unity, the identity or coinherence, of Subjective and Objective. It is in itself, at once inward Life and Truth, and outward Fact and Luminary . . . no man, I say, can recognize his own inward experiences in such writings [the Scriptures], and not find an objectiveness, a confirming and assuring outwardness, and all the main characters of reality reflected therefrom on the spirit . . . . The unsubstantial, insulated Self passes away as a stream; but these are the shadows and reflections of the Rock of Ages, and of the Tree of Life.

On the other hand, as much of reality, as much of objective truth, as the Scriptures communicate to the subjective experiences of the Believer, so much of present life, of living and effective import, do these experiences give to the letter of Scriptures.[44]

Coleridge does not subsume the objective side, the givenness of revelation, within the receptive pole of experience. Where he does part with the orthodox and the rationalists is in his awareness of the role of subjective experience in the discernment of spiritual truth. *Revelation occurs only at the convergence of objective reality and the subjective judgment of lived experience and need.* Spiritual truth is, then, partly dependent upon the subjective mode of experience—i.e., upon the imagination, will, and emotion—as well as the understanding.

Coleridge's principles of biblical interpretation had considerable influence, especially in certain university circles, during the mid-nineteenth century in Britain. The effect of the *Confessions* on the authors of *Essays and Reviews** (1860) was very great, although acknowledged in only one or two instances. It is safe to say that had Coleridge's *Confessions* had a wider reading, much of the furor and misunderstanding in the Victorian era over the interpretation of Scripture could have been avoided. Nevertheless, Coleridge, the man of catholic mind and romantic sensibility, had considerable effect on the renewal of Christian theology in Britain, both in the Anglo-Catholic and Broad

* See Chapter Eight.

Church movements. Among the Romanticists there is perhaps only one man who surpasses Coleridge in establishing a new religious sensibility and in refashioning the whole conception of what constitutes Christian faith—that man is Friedrich Schleiermacher.

Friedrich Schleiermacher

Friedrich Schleiermacher (1768–1834) is generally considered the dominant Protestant theologian between John Calvin and Karl Barth. He carried out a "Copernican revolution" in theology as consequential as Kant's revolution in philosophy. Schleiermacher's conception of religion and the Christian faith has wide influence and appeal even today, which may be explained partly by the fact that we are still living in a later phase of that Romantic movement inaugurated by Schleiermacher and his circle at the beginning of the nineteenth century.

Schleiermacher's theology is rightly acknowledged as the most forceful and systematic statement of the Romantic and liberal understanding of the Christian religion. For some this is enough to damn him without further notice. In our own century Schleiermacher became the *bête noire* of the early Neo-Orthodox movement led by Karl Barth and Emil Brunner. The "dead end" reached by liberal Protestant theology in the years just prior to World War I is traced by the Neo-Orthodox to what they consider the "false start" inaugurated by Schleiermacher one hundred years earlier. Whether he is right or wrong in his interpretation of the man's thought, Barth is certainly correct in seeing Schleiermacher as *the* watershed of modern theology.

Schleiermacher's thoughts on religion

emerge naturally out of his own personal history. He was born Friedrich Daniel Ernst Schleiermacher into the family of a Prussian army chaplain. In his teens he attended Moravian schools noted for their fervent pietism. Although he later found the intellectual atmosphere of these schools too narrow, the experience of these early years was lasting. Later in life he could write:

It was here that I awoke for the first time to the consciousness of the relation of man to a higher world .... Here it was that that mystic tendency developed itself, which has been of so much importance to me, and has supported and carried me through all the storms of skepticism. Then it was only germinating; now it has attained its full development, and I may say that after all I have passed through I have become a Moravian again, only of a higher order.[45]

In 1787 Schleiermacher entered the University of Halle—despite his father's protestations. Here he read Kant and Spinoza and in the next few years his imagination was opened upon a whole new world completely foreign to the parochial Moravian piety. Schleiermacher's imaginative powers did not fully emerge, however, until he went to Berlin in 1796 and soon attached himself to a new literary society that included many writers who were soon to become the leaders of the German Romantic movement. Chief among these persons was Friedrich Schlegel. Schlegel and Henrietta Herz, whose salon Schleiermacher attended almost daily, recognized Schleiermacher's brilliance, tutored him in literature and the arts, and encouraged him to write. Schlegel's prodding and Schleiermacher's own religious unrest led to his first literary effort in 1799. In that

year he published *On Religion: Speeches Addressed to Its Cultured Despisers*. It served as both an apology for his own religious views and vocation and as a critique of his cultured friends' conception of the religious life. The success of the book led to the publication of *The Soliloquies* the following year (1800). *The Soliloquies* is Schleiermacher's "Confession" and represents the quintessence of the Romantic spirit. In this book Schleiermacher calls upon every man to accept his unique place in the sphere of humanity and to develop his own individual spirit to the full.

The early Berlin years ended, nevertheless, in anguish when Schleiermacher fell in love with Eleanor Grunow, wife of a Berlin clergyman. A strong sense of duty made Eleanor stay with the husband she did not love and renounce Schleiermacher forever. In 1804 he left Berlin and became a professor of theology at the University of Halle. For the next few years he poured his energies into lectures and writing—on almost every subject in the theological curriculum. In 1809 he was called back to Berlin as preacher at the Holy Trinity Church. That same year, at the age of forty, he married Henriette von Willich, the widow of an old friend.

In 1811 Schleiermacher was offered the chair of theology at the University of Berlin. This marked a new era in his life. He now began to give proof of his creative and organizing power as a theologian. The crowning achievement of these years was his theological masterpiece, *The Christian Faith*, appearing in two parts in 1821 and 1822 and in a revised second edition in 1830. His other lectures and prospective books were not published before his death in February, 1834. Later, students and friends compiled his literary remains which today comprise over thirty volumes of books, lectures, sermons, and letters.

Schleiermacher's contribution to modern theology and his own theological development is best seen in his two greatest books, *On Religion*, the product of his youthful, Romantic period, and *The Christian Faith*, the crown of his maturity. In both of these works Schleiermacher developed revolutionary interpretations—in the first work, a new conception of religion; in the second, a new interpretation of Christian theology.

The Speeches on Religion. Perhaps the foremost contribution of Romanticism to modern religious thought is its attempt to establish the nature and warrants of religious belief on an entirely new foundation. Chief among these attempts at reconstruction was that of Schleiermacher in his speeches *On Religion*. Schleiermacher wished to show the educated, the cultured, of his own time that what they despised and rejected in religion wasn't the essence of religion at all. What they considered religion was, for Schleiermacher, the mere external and dispensable husk concealing the real essence of religion. The "externals" of religion are the product of what Coleridge and Schleiermacher would call "the handiwork of the calculating understanding." As Wordsworth was to complain, "our meddling intellect / Misshapes the beauteous forms of things;— / We murder to dissect." This dissected corpse, this work of our "meddling intellect," is what we mistakenly identify as religion. Schleiermacher calls upon his fellows to turn away from such an external, intellectual view.

What else can they be, these systems of theology, these theories of the origin and the

end of the world, these analyses of the nature of an incomprehensible Being, wherein everything runs to cold argufying . . . this is certainly not the character of religion. If you have only given attention to these dogmas and opinions, therefore, you do not yet know religion itself, and what you despise is not it. Why have you not penetrated deeper to find the kernel of this shell?[46]

Schleiermacher is astonished at the easy ignorance by which true religion is obscured because of the failure to penetrate beneath externals.

Why do you not regard the religious life itself, the first of those pious exaltations of the mind in which all other known activities are set aside or almost suppressed and the whole soul is dissolved *in the immediate feeling of the Infinite and Eternal*? In such moments the disposition you pretend to despise reveals itself in primordial and visible form. He only who has studied and truly known man in these emotions can rediscover religion in those outward manifestations.[47] (Italics added.)

Schleiermacher also wishes to reject all attempts to define or defend religion on utilitarian or hedonistic grounds.

Yet you need not fear that I shall betake myself in the end to that common device of representing how necessary religion is for maintaining justice and order in the world. Nor shall I remind you of an all-seeing eye, nor of the unspeakable short-sightedness of human management, nor the narrow bounds of human power to render help. Nor shall I say how religion is a faithful friend and useful stay of morality, how it makes the struggle with self and the perfecting of goodness much easier for weak men . . . . To recommend religion by such means would only increase the contempt to which it is at present exposed.[48]

If religion cannot justify itself in terms

of its own inherent value, then it is not worth bothering about, for "what is loved and honoured only on account of some extraneous advantage may be needful, but it is not in itself necessary."[49] But this is not Schleiermacher's view of the matter, for he contends that religion or piety is both a unique faculty and, in and of itself, of indispensable worth to the spirit of man.

Having set the stage for his defense, Schleiermacher turns in the second Speech to define what he conceives to be the true nature of religion. Customarily we think of religion as either "a way of thinking, a faith, a peculiar way of contemplating the world" or as "a way of acting, a peculiar desire and love, a special kind of conduct and character." That is, we tend to think of religion from either the theoretical (metaphysical) or practical (ethical) point of view. The orthodox rationalists and Hegel, Schleiermacher's more famous colleague at Berlin, identified religion with theoretical knowledge; the Deists and Kant equated religion with morality. But this is to reduce religion to something else and therefore to make religion itself unnecessary. Religion "must be something different from a mixture of opinions about God and the world, and of precepts for one life or two." "*Piety*," Schleiermacher retorts sharply, "*cannot be an instinct craving for a mass of metaphysical and ethical crumbs*."[50] (Italics added.) Religion resigns at once all claims on anything that belongs either to theoretical science or morality. Take, for example, our scientific knowledge.

However high you go; though you pass from the laws to the Universal Lawgiver, in whom is the unity of all things; though you allege that nature cannot be comprehended without God, *I would still maintain that religion has nothing to do with this knowledge, and that quite apart from it, its nature can be known. Quantity of knowledge is not quality of piety. Piety can gloriously display itself, both with originality and individuality, in those to whom this kind of knowledge is not original.*[51] (Italics added.)

If religion were really the highest knowledge, then reason or the scientific method would be the appropriate organ for its attainment. Religion or piety would be acquired by study and the most knowledgeable would also be the most pious. Therefore, says Schleiermacher, "I cannot hold religion to be the highest knowledge, or indeed, knowledge at all."

Neither is religion to be confused with morality. In fact,

religion by itself does not urge men to activity at all. If you could imagine it implanted in a man quite alone . . . the man, according to what we have said, would not act, *he would only feel.*[52] (Italics added.)

According to Schleiermacher, psychology teaches us that there are three essential elements in all mental life: perception, feeling, and activity. Perception issues in knowledge; activity in the conduct of the moral life; feeling is the peculiar faculty of the religious life. Hence, says Schleiermacher, "only when piety takes its place alongside of science and practice, as a necessary, an indispensable third, as their natural counterpart . . . will the common field be altogether occupied and human nature . . . complete."[53]

For Schleiermacher, feeling is the unique element of the religious life; religion is essentially *feeling*. What Schleiermacher means by feeling is not entirely clear, especially as he uses the term in his earlier writings. It is certain, however, that he is not speaking of feeling as a purely psychological emotion. As Paul Tillich has said in reference to Schleiermacher, feeling may be subjective, but it is also the impact of the universe upon us and the universe is not subjective! Schleiermacher states that feeling is, first of all, an *"immediate self-consciousness."* This phrase bears some analysis.

By *immediate* Schleiermacher means that religious feeling is not derived, not the product of ratiocination—it is an immediate *intuition*. But it is also a special kind of intuition—that of the self present to the self as a unique, underived unity or identity. The feeling or intuition of immediate self-consciousness which issues in the uniquely *religious feeling* is, furthermore, "the immediate consciousness of the universal existence of all finite things, *in and through the Infinite, and of all temporal things in and through the Eternal . . . . It is to have life and to know life in immediate feeling, only as such an existence in the Infinite and Eternal."* [54] (Italics added.)

Schleiermacher, then, does not mean that all feeling is religious as such. It is the intuition of the self "in and through the Infinite"—as mysteriously posited and dependent: "The sum total of religion is to feel that, in its highest unity, all that moves us in feeling is one . . . to feel, that is to say, that our being and living is a being and living in and through God." [55] This does not mean that God must be present as a distinct concept or object. All healthy feelings are pious insofar as they are the result of the operation of God on us "by means of the operation of the world upon us." It is also important to keep in mind that by such a "feeling for the Infinite" Schleiermacher is not advocating a state of mystical absorption.

The "Infinite," as Schleiermacher uses the term, simply means feeling the infinity of existence in the concrete world "upon us" and in relation to us. This feeling for the infinite through our experience of the world is the primordial means of God's operation upon us— whether or not this feeling issues in thought or action. It was only later, in *The Christian Faith*, that Schleiermacher was able to give greater clarity to his definition of religion by speaking of it as the feeling of absolute dependence.

The common element in all diverse expressions of piety, by which these are conjointly distinguished from all other feelings, or in other words, the self-identical essence of piety is this: the consciousness of absolute dependence, or, which is the same thing, of being in relation with God. [56]

Having defined the essence of religion, Schleiermacher then turns to a discussion of how it is to be discovered and cultivated. First, one can discover and cultivate the peculiar feeling for the Infinite in nature "which is to many the first and only temple of the Godhead . . . the inmost sanctuary of religion." But emotions evoked by nature are ambiguous. Schleiermacher is not unmindful that nature is also, in Bertrand Russell's words, "the trampling march of unconscious power." The sense of the whole must then "be found chiefly within our own minds, and from thence transferred to corporeal nature." [57]

One thing is clear—and that is that no man is religious as a result of acquiring knowledge of doctrine and principles of action. Such men "have memory and imitation," but they do not have religion. "They have no ideas of their own from which formulas might be known, so they must learn them by rote, and the feelings which they would have accompanying them are copies."[58] True piety can issue only from one's own original, indubitable feelings and not from the pale descriptions of the feelings of others.

If this is the true character and source of religion, whence come then those dogmas and doctrines that are so widely considered the essence of religion? "They are," Schleiermacher replies,

the result of the contemplation of feeling. . . . The conceptions that underlie these propositions are nothing but general expressions for definite feelings . . . . They are not necessary for religion itself, scarcely even for communicating religion . . . but when feeling is made the subject of reflection and comparison they are absolutely unavoidable.[59]

Doctrines are the product of reflection on feelings, but just because a man holds certain religious *ideas* does not necessarily make him a religious person. Take, for example, the belief in an inspired sacred book such as the Bible.

Every sacred writing is in itself a glorious production, a speaking monument from the heroic time of religion, but, through a servile reverence, it would become merely a mausoleum, a monument that a great spirit once was there, but is now no more . . . . Not every person has religion who believes in a sacred writing, but only the man who has a lively and immediate understanding of it, *and who, therefore, so far as he himself is concerned, could most easily do without it.*[60] (Italics added.)

The same is true of those first articles of any religious belief—God and immortality. The ideas of God or immortality may, in the case of any man, be badly or vaguely conceived. Some conceive of God in grossly anthropomorphic fashion,

while those who seek to avoid such a conception often tend toward a vague pantheism.

Nothing seems to me less fitting than for the adherents of the former view [the anthropomorphists] to charge with godlessness those who, in dread of this anthropomorphism, take refuge in the other, or for the adherents of this latter view [the pantheists] to make the humanness of the idea of God a ground for charging the adherents of the former with idolatry, or, for declaring their piety void.[61]

It doesn't matter what conceptions a man adheres to, for his piety may be, nay *is*, better than his ideas. Ideas are never the sign of a perfect or imperfect religion. It is "the manner in which the Deity is present to a man in feeling [that] is decisive of the worth of his religion, not the manner, always inadequate, in which it is copied in idea."[62]

A corollary of all this is that because religion has to do with the manner of a person's innermost feelings, it cannot be taught.

All that the activity and art of one man can do for another is to communicate conceptions to be the basis of thoughts . . . . Our opinions and doctrines we can indeed communicate, if we have words and our hearers have the comprehending power of the understanding. But we know very well that these things are only shadows of our religious emotions, and if our pupils do not share our emotions, even though they do understand the thought, they have no possession that can truly repay their toil. This retreat into oneself, there to perceive oneself, cannot be taught.[63]

Man's engagement in the everyday world of getting and spending, Coleridge's world of the understanding, does not allow one the calm moments needed for "retreat into oneself" for undisturbed contemplation. But it is only in such moments of repose that the religious feelings can be cultivated.

A religious man must be reflective, his sense must be occupied in the contemplation of himself. Being occupied with the profoundest depths, he abandons meanwhile all external things, intellectual as well as physical, leaving them to be the great aim of the researches of the people of understanding . . . . Hence it comes that, from of old, all truly religious characters have had a mystical trait, and that all imaginative natures . . . have at least some stirrings of piety.[64]

Here Schleiermacher touches the profoundly mystical and imaginative tendencies in Romanticism. Like Rousseau before him, Schleiermacher encourages each man to give full rein to the development of his own individuality, to his own imagination and feeling. And yet, like his fellow Romanticists, Schleiermacher emphasizes the social nature of man. Deeply felt *individual* experience issues in a sense of common bond with all men. Schleiermacher would concur with Wordsworth's sentiments, expressed in "Lines upon a seat . . . ,"

> that he who feels contempt
> For any living thing, hath faculties
> Which he has never used; that thought with him
> Is in its infancy. The man whose eye
> Is ever on himself doth look on one,
> The least of Nature's works, one who might move
> The wise man to that scorn which wisdom holds
> Unlawful ever. O be wiser, thou!
> Instructed that true knowledge leads to love.[65]

For Schleiermacher, the deeper our personal life, the more we will "endeavor to become conscious of and to

exhibit the true relation of our own life to the common nature of man."[66] Religion begins in the innermost recesses of the individual, but it is essentially social "for that is the nature of man." Each individual's deeply-felt religious sentiments cry out to be shared.

Schleiermacher recommends, however, that the cultivation of religion in association with others not be attempted within too wide circles but quickened in "the more familiar conversation of friendship or the dialogue of love, where glance and action are clearer than words."[67] There is, nevertheless, a place for the common worship of God where all peoples of like spirit can assemble. Schleiermacher depicts such a communion in language that reflects his own Moravian piety:

Would that I could depict to you the rich, the superabundant life in this city of God, when the citizens assemble, each full of native force seeking liberty of utterance and full at the same time of holy desire to apprehend and appropriate what others offer. When one stands out before the others he is neither justified by office nor by compact . . . . It is the free impulse of his spirit, the feeling of heartfelt unanimity and completest equality . . . . He comes forward to present to the sympathetic contemplation of others his own heart as stirred by God, and, by leading them into the region of religion where he is at home, would infect them with his own feeling.[68]

In such a society the usual distinction between priest and layman is transcended, for each man is equally capable of expressing some rich experience of that religious feeling which is boundless in its individuality. For this very reason a communion of kindred spirits will always reflect diversity, but it will be a manifoldness within an organic whole. No individual or group, however, would seek to bring all others into some single, definite *form* of religion—none would adhere to that "awful watchword, 'No salvation save with us.'" There is, then, no proselytizing.

The society of the pious . . . is occupied purely with mutual communication, and subsists only among persons already having religion of some kind. How can it be their business to change the minds of those who already profess to have a definite religion . . . . The religion of this society as such is simply the collective religion of all the pious. As each one sees it in others it is infinite and no single person can fully grasp it . . . . If any man, therefore, has any share in religion, it matters not what, would it not be a mad proceeding for the society to rend from him that which suits his nature? And how would they cultivate persons to whom religion generally is still strange?[69]

Schleiermacher is quite aware that the Church he is describing is the ideal Church, the Church triumphant. Nevertheless, it is the Church as it was meant to be and is whenever it is true to its real nature. The empirical and militant Church fails to be a true Church for many reasons. Chief among them, of course, is the fact that the Church does not reveal the "free inspiration that is proper to religion" but a "school-mastering, mechanical nature" which employs "creeds which are naturally last in religious communication, to stimulate what should properly precede them."[70] A further reason for the failure of the Church is its union with, and subservience to, the state. "As soon as a prince declared a church to be a community with special privileges, a distinguished member of the civil world, the corruption of that church was begun and almost irrevocably decided."[71] The state pollutes the pure spiritual fellowship of the Church by introducing its own special interests into the spiritual society.

Schleiermacher called upon the Church to preserve its uniquely spiritual calling. He believed this could be done if it gave only a secondary role to creedal subscription, if it minimized the distinction between priest and laity, if it did not confuse unity with uniformity, and if it remained free of all external interests, which would be impossible in any union with the civil state.

In the final Speech Schleiermacher turns from a consideration of the Church as a pure spiritual fellowship to the question of the plurality of religions. Here he reveals himself once again as a true Romanticist and a vigorous opponent of the rationalist conception of religion. He begins by affirming that, contrary to rationalist doctrine, the multiplicity of the positive religions is based upon the very nature of religion.

The whole of religion is nothing but the sum of all relations of man to God, apprehended in all the possible ways in which any man can be immediately conscious in his life. In this sense there is but one religion . . . . Yet all men will not by any means apprehend them in the same way, but quite differently. Now this difference alone is felt and alone can be exhibited . . . . As long as we occupy a place there must be in these relations of man to the whole a nearer and a farther, which will necessarily determine each feeling differently in each life. Again, as long as we are individuals, every man has greater receptiveness for some religious experiences and feelings than for others.[72]

Religion always exhibits itself in some definite shape. There is no such thing as religion in general. Here Schleiermacher is critical of the abstract and unhistorical conception of religion held by the rationalists. Such a natural religion "is usually so much refined away, and has such metaphysical and moral graces, that little of the peculiar character of religion appears."[73] Religion is by its very nature concrete and particular and only those who "pitch their camp in some such positive form, have any fixed abode and . . . any well-earned right of citizenship in the religious world."

Schleiermacher does not mean that every religious person must affiliate himself with one of the existing sects or forms of religion. "It is only necessary that his religion be developed in himself characteristically and definitely"—that is, that it concretely reflect a religious sense suitable to the individual's own nature. However, most religious revelations reflect a feeling that is "great and common" and not merely idiosyncratic and personal. Thus "most men, following their nature, will belong to an existing form, and there will be only a few whom none suffices."

Those who advocate a universal natural religion and inveigh against the demands of the positive religions that their adherents abide by a certain sectarian uniformity have, in fact, a uniformity of their own—"the uniformity of indefiniteness." Schleiermacher observes that the resistance to "the positive and arbitrary" is nothing but resistance to "the definite and real."

If a definite religion may not begin with an original fact, it cannot begin at all. There must be a common ground for selecting some one religious element and placing it at the center, and this ground can only be a fact. And if a religion is not to be definite, it is not a religion at all, for religion is not a name to be applied to loose, unconnected impulses.[74]

Schleiermacher counsels his readers:

Go back, then, if you are in earnest about beholding religion in its definiteness, from this enlightened natural religion to those despised positive religions. There everything appears active, strong, and secure.[75]

At the conclusion of his discussion of the religions, Schleiermacher raises the question of Christianity and its place in relation to the other positive religions. He considers Christianity to be a deeper, more sublime and universal religion than those positive religions which have preceded and followed it. The sublimity and power of Christianity is, for Schleiermacher, manifest in the peculiar role of its Founder. He sees the truly divine element in Jesus Christ neither in "the purity of his moral teachings," nor in "the individuality of his character," but in the glorious clearness with which the great idea of mediation between God and man came to expression in his person. Schleiermacher does not develop his conception of Christ's mediatorial role in any detail in this fifth Speech, but what he does make clear is that there is no evidence that Jesus conceived of himself as the sole mediator between God and man. What is central to the Gospels is not the uniqueness of Jesus' person but Jesus' profound *idea* of mediation:

He [Jesus] never maintained He was the only mediator, the only one in whom His idea actualized itself. All who attach themselves to him and form His Church should also be mediators with Him and through Him. And He never made His school equivalent to His religion, as if His idea were to be accepted on account of His person, and not His person on account of His idea.[76]

A time may come when there is no

need of a mediator, when God shall be all in all, but Schleiermacher believes that such a condition lies beyond this changing, corruptible existence. New mediators from God will be required in every new epoch. And even if there are always Christians, Christianity will never claim to be

the sole type of religion, to rule alone in humanity. *It scorns this autocracy* . . . . As nothing is more irreligious than to demand general uniformity in mankind, so *nothing is more unchristian than to seek uniformity in relgion* . . . . Varied types of religion are possible, both in proximity and in combination, and if it is necessary that every type be actualized at one time or another, it is to be desired that, at all times, there should be a dim sense of many religions.[77] (Italics added.)

Schleiermacher concludes the *Speeches* with an appeal to all who experience the first traces of the religious feeling "to enter at once into the one indivisible fellowship of the saints, which embraces all religions and in which alone any can prosper."[78]

The historical significance of the *Speeches* lies principally in the fact that Schleiermacher reversed the traditional method of proceeding theologically. Religion, according to Schleiermacher, does not emerge out of certain given institutions and doctrines. Rather, doctrines and institutions are the creations of a prior self-consciousness that is natural to human existence. Religion is a unique a priori form of self-consciousness that should not be confused with either moral or scientific knowledge. Related to this discovery of the religious feeling prior to all thought is Schleiermacher's sense of religion as a historical, social phenomenon which can best be described in terms of an empirical or experiential analysis of a

community's self-consciousness at a given time. Such an experiential and historical conception of religion was something relatively new, and Schleiermacher sought to apply this approach systematically in his description of the Christian religion in his great work, *The Christian Faith*.

The Christian Religious Affections. Dogmatics, or the explication of "the Christian religious affections as set forth in speech," can never, according to Schleiermacher, be speculative and abstract. *Dogmatics is the formulation in language of the prior Christian feelings.* Hence it presupposes the Christian community, the Church, and is only meant for that Christian community which shares these common religious affections. Theology is thus conceived of as essentially confessional, not apologetic. It is principally an exercise in self-analysis on the part of the Christian community at a given time.

As we have learned, Schleiermacher believes religion should be distinguished from all other human feelings by the consciousness of absolute dependence— and that the several religions have historically developed their consciousness in different ways. Schleiermacher defines the unique character of the Christian faith in the following way:

Christianity is a monotheistic faith belonging to the teleological [moral] type of religion, and is essentially distinguished from other such faiths by the fact that in it everything is related to the redemption accomplished by Jesus of Nazareth.[79]

All Christian doctrines are determined by reference to the consciousness of redemption accomplished by Jesus. Thus, it is impossible for Christian theology to begin with natural reason or a speculative metaphysics, since it must begin with the Christian experience of redemption in Jesus. Schleiermacher's theology then is fundamentally Christo-centric in that the Christian's God-consciousness always comes to realization in the person of Jesus Christ as the Redeemer—as *Christus pro nobis.*

According to Schleiermacher, we can never know God as He is in Himself—but only as He is known in relation to us. God cannot possibly be known as an independent object, out there somewhere, but only in relation to our own self-consciousness. However, this is not to confuse self-consciousness and God, but only to say that

any proclamation of God which is to be operative *upon and within us can only express God in His relation to us*; and this is not an infra-human ignorance concerning God, but the essence of human limitedness in relation to Him.[80] (Italics added.)

All the attributes of God discussed in a Christian dogmatics will be those which express the various ways in which the Christian feeling of absolute dependence is referred to God.

When we consider the ways in which we feel our dependence on God, there are two primary modes of apprehending this dependence: First, God's being as felt in our experience of the totality of the world or nature, and, secondly, the divine attributes as related to our consciousness of sin and redemption. In the first instance, we can speak of God's Eternity as "the absolutely timeless causality of God, which conditions not only all that is temporal, but time itself as well."[81] Likewise, the Omnipresence of God is understood as "the absolutely spaceless causality of God, which conditions not only all that is spatial but space itself."[82] In similar fashion Schleiermacher deals with such traditional attributes of God as Omnipotence and Omniscience.

The Christian does not become conscious of the divine causality only, or primarily, in the apprehension of the natural world but principally in his sense of dependence on God in the experience of sin and redemption. The fact that the Christian traces the annulment of sin by redemption to the divine causality is a fact that we may premise as given universally in the Christian consciousness.[83] The primary attributes of God which we relate to our consciousness of sin are God's holiness and justice. To speak of God as holy and just is to speak of that aspect of the divine causality which involves the activity of man's conscience. Conscience simply apprehends God's relation to the world as morally legislative.

It is not possible to outline here Schleiermacher's whole systematic treatment of the Christian doctrine of God. Suffice it to say that each attribute is related to a feeling that is integral to the Christian experience of dependence. For this reason, Schleiermacher did not include any consideration of the doctrine of the Trinity in the main body of *The Christian Faith* but discussed it in an appendix as an addendum to the doctrine of God. The reason for this is that he did not consider the Trinity as immediately given in the Christian consciousness. This is not to say that he thought the doctrine unimportant. Schleiermacher recognized that behind the metaphysical abstraction lay a profound religious truth—namely, that the whole of Christianity is dependent upon the reality of the union of the divine with the human, both in the person of Jesus Christ and in the union of the divine Spirit and the Church. Nevertheless, the Trinity is not immediately given in the Christian consciousness of dependence, hence is not of *primary* concern to faith.

At the center of Schleiermacher's reconception of the Christian faith is his understanding of human sin and the redemptive work of Jesus Christ. Therefore, some analysis of his conception of these matters is necessary. Knowledge of sin, according to Schleiermacher, is not derived from a reading of Scripture but is intimately bound up with our consciousness. Specifically, we have consciousness of sin whenever our God-consciousness "determines our self-consciousness as pain." Sin is the experience of our innate God-consciousness being hindered by the conflict between our fleshy, sensuous nature and our higher spiritual nature.

If in any particular moment under examination God has formed part of our self-consciousness, but this God-consciousness has not been able to permeate the other active elements therein . . . then sin and the consciousness of sin are simultaneous, and the sensuous self-consciousness by reason of its having been gratified is affected with pleasure, but the higher, owing to the impotence of the God-consciousness, with pain.[84]

Here Schleiermacher conceives of sin, much as does Augustine, as a disorder and confusion of man's loves, whereby man places his love in that which is temporal and worldly rather than in God and the eternal.

Sin then is an arrestment of the God-consciousness due to the preponderance of the "flesh" over the "spirit" and is accompanied by a sense of discontent and instability for which the Christian feels himself responsible. Man is free to sin, and this very freedom implies responsibility, guilt, and misery. However, man is not free and able to overcome his sin. In fact, for Schleiermacher, it is Christ as Second Adam, as the true norm or archetype of human nature who convicts us of our sin and makes us sensitive to how, through our sensuousness, we have obscured our God-consciousness.

The other side of the coin is that consciousness of sin, which comes into sharpest relief in the light of Christ, the true man, has its antithesis in the grace and blessedness which proceeds from the person and work of this same Jesus Christ. Sin must always be seen, then, in relation to its antithesis, grace, for sin is nothing but the privation of true blessedness.

Though Schleiermacher stressed the point that man must always come to a personal consciousness of sin through individual experience, he was not unmindful of the social character of sin. Man is a communal being, and his life is intimately bound up with the life of the community and race. Sin is always in a social matrix, being caused by the sins of others and in turn causing others to sin. However, Schleiermacher refuses to accept the ancient conception of man's sin as due to the curse placed upon the first man, Adam, because of his disobedience, and which has been transmitted through Adam to the generations of his progeny. Such a conception is unacceptable because, first of all, it would require that we conceive of human nature as very different before and after Adam's fall, a belief which destroys the unity of the race and its religious consciousness. Secondly, for Schleiermacher, it is unthinkable to hold that the action of a *single* individual could so completely change the whole human race.

In place of the old myth of Adam, Schleiermacher pictures the human race from the creation as possessing a sinful propensity. Man's original perfection was not a static state of innocence; rather it was the latent potentiality or predisposition in all men to develop a full God-consciousness. However, concomitant with this latent perfection is the universal propensity of human nature to sin and thereby to fail to bring this God-consciousness to fruition. Man's latent perfection and disposition to sin are both equally "original." But the very fact that man's original latent perfection and predisposition to sin are equal means, in Schleiermacher's view, that righteousness cannot *by itself* triumph, for

from the concomitance and development of the two there could issue no active righteousness properly so called, but at best a vacillation between vitiated spiritual efforts and increasing and fully matured sin.[85]

Having discarded the mythical conception of an actual first Adam, Schleiermacher is faced with the question of how men come to an acknowledgement of their sinful fallenness. Schleiermacher's answer is that the power to recognize our sin comes not from Adam but from Jesus Christ. As R. R. Niebuhr has commented,

If we adhere in our reasoning to the logic of *The Christian Faith*, we not only *may* dispense with this mythical Adam as the mirror of true righteousness, but we *must* do so, for while each man's self-consciousness belongs indefeasibly to himself, the power which raises it toward the equilibrium of blessedness comes not from the storehouse of the imagination alone but from the ever renewed historical

communication of the life and light that originates in the preaching of Jesus of Nazareth.[86]

The work of redemption comes only from outside man, issuing from the person of Jesus Christ by means of his self-communication to man of his unique God-consciousness. Consistent with his method, Schleiermacher holds that Christ is known only through his benefits (his work) and that his effect upon us is the impress of the special dignity of his person, his unique God-consciousness. Christ's God-consciousness was perfectly realized in that, along with the growth of his natural powers, his God-consciousness gained perfect control of his entire person. In this sense we can speak of Jesus' perfection and sinlessness.

The only explanation of this historical realization of God-consciousness is that it was a *miraculous manifestation* of the ideal of man as the subject of a perfect God-consciousness. Hence, Jesus Christ is best understood as the full historical realization of archetypal humanity, the second or true Adam. He embodies concretely the new race of men and thus becomes for us the exemplar of God's will for us. Jesus Christ, therefore, is the mirror in which we see our true image and measure. But more than that, for Christ is not principally an example to be followed; he is the redeemer who gives a new impetus and power to man "in the flesh." It is wrong, therefore, to contend, as some have, that Schleiermacher's understanding of the work of Christ is reducible to a conception of Jesus as moral example. Such a conception was unacceptable to Schleiermacher because it implied (*a*) the possibility that man could of himself establish such a conception of absolute perfection and (*b*) that man has the power to deliver himself from the control of his sensuous affections.

Schleiermacher believed that the religious self-consciousness infected by sin could not of itself produce the exemplar of perfected humanity as it is given to us in the person of Jesus Christ. Here Schleiermacher takes exception to Kant's notion of the exemplary role of Christ set forth in *Religion Within the Limits of Reason Alone*. Schleiermacher wished to stress that man does not posit his own exemplar and yet that the Redeemer is exemplary (*Vorbildlichkeit*) in that he stands in a continuum with the rest of the human race—i.e., in solidarity with them, without which there could be no communication of redemption. Christ is the exemplar of perfect human nature in that he is the *medium* for the communication of God's redemptive power. However, the power itself lies beyond human nature and can be appropriated only as a gift. Christ, therefore, is both exemplar and Redeemer. R. R. Niebuhr sums up Schleiermacher's view of the person and work of Christ as exemplar and Redeemer in the following way:

It is neither the naked power of God that Christ communicates, nor is it merely himself as teacher of a new doctrine about God that Christ proffers to others. What he gives are the power of God in the embodiment of his own ideal humanity and himself as the source from which men may receive that same power. These two aspects of Jesus, which Schleiermacher calls his *Urbildlichkeit* (ideality) and his *Vorbildlichkeit* (exemplarity), cannot be separated. By virtue of the former he is the redeemer; by virtue of the latter he communicates redemption. Therefore, while the *Vorbildlichkeit* or exemplary status of Jesus does not signify his life-giving power as the redeemer appointed eternally by God, it does signify his solidarity with the human race,

apart from which there could be no communication of redemption.[87]

The work of Christ in redemption consists in the implanting of the God-consciousness as the dominant principle of life, thereby gaining the victory over the sensuous impulses and ordering man's consciousness in such a way that pain and melancholy give way to a new sense of equilibrium and joy, a new attunement of the soul in its relation to God and the world.

For Schleiermacher it was quite natural that the power of Jesus' God-consciousness should result in the formation of a community around him. The Church is that community of persons whose person-hood has been formed by the mind of Christ and whose vocation it is to communicate that unique Christian consciousness to those who come in contact with this community. If Schleiermacher's earlier writings reflect at times a too individualistic conception of the religious life, the writings of his maturity reflect a profound awareness of the place of community in the formation of self-consciousness. For Schleiermacher, a person's religious consciousness emerges out of the community life one shares, and therefore the Church is the historical medium of Christ's redemptive work.

It was Schleiermacher's awareness of the mediational role of the community that caused him to reject what he called a "magical" conception of redemption. A magical view is one which denies the necessary mediation of Christ's redemption through an empirical community. It is magical because it posits Jesus' influence as not presently mediated through anything historical and natural. Schleiermacher was responsible for producing a new awareness of the role of the Church in a Protestantism that had become highly individualistic and anti-ecclesiastical. He also gave new meaning to doctrines and practices, not by defending or reviving old institutional forms, but by showing that forms and doctrines are the natural fruit of a community's experience and life together.

Schleiermacher can justly be called the Kant of modern theology, both because of the new beginning which his work marks in the history of theology and because the issues which his theological reconstruction posed are issues which are still at the very center of theological discussion today. As was indicated earlier, the Neo-Orthodox theologians who came to prominence between the 1920's and 1940's believed that Protestant theology had reached a cul-de-sac due, in large measure, to the fact that it had followed the path mapped out by Schleiermacher in *The Christian Faith*. Karl Barth sees the distinctive character of Schleiermacher's work and its subsequent influence as grounded in Schleiermacher's desire to be both a Christian *and* a modern man and that inevitably this led Schleiermacher to take a position *above* Christianity. In other words, Schleiermacher approached his task in the serene confidence that he knew what Christianity was and that neither the Bible nor Church dogma could set any bounds to his sense of confidence and unrestricted freedom in the work of reconstruction.

There is considerable truth in what Barth says here. With Schleiermacher, theology undergoes a radical transformation in its notion of theological authority. It is erroneous to say that for Schleiermacher the Bible and the Church no longer are theologically normative, for we know that Schleiermacher conceived of doctrine as the true expression of the

Christian consciousness *in the Church* at a given time, and that such a consciousness must be a genuine expression of that piety which appears in the New Testament. Nevertheless, for Schleiermacher the real locus of authority does lie in the religious experience, for the religious man has his own consciousness as the ultimate court of appeal. All external evidences and authorities are finally of no account if they are not confirmed experientially in the religious consciousness of the individual. In the last analysis, theology is the descriptive setting force of the contents of the religious consciousness. Religious authority, therefore, can never be something external, nonexperiential, and imposed from without. Therefore, is Barth not right that man's own consciousness becomes the master of Christianity and final arbiter of its truth? Does the reality of Christianity not become imprisoned in a colossal self-consciousness? Schleiermacher has been charged by others besides Barth with fathering a form of religious subjectivism that finds its inevitable working-out in the psychological reduction of all religious beliefs— for example, in the writings of Ludwig Feuerbach. That is to say, Schleiermacher's method results in a view of religion no longer concerned with metaphysical claims about objective reality but rather with the study of man's own subjective aspirations, fears, and ideals as they become objectified in theological ideas and institutions.

Related to the charge of subjectivism is the further levy of agnosticism. Schleiermacher held that God is apprehended only in feeling and that we can never know God as he is *in himself*. Thus feeling serves Schleiermacher much the same way that the practical reason served Kant. All attempts at knowing God in himself by means of scientific or metaphysical analysis are doomed to failure. God is known only through a subjective "moral want" or, in the case of Schleiermacher, a feeling of absolute dependence—i.e., God in relation to our needs and feelings. Schleiermacher's awareness of the limits of our knowledge of God, like Kant's no doubt played its part in the growth of a more thoroughgoing agnosticism later in the century, but it is quite misleading to refer to Schleiermacher as agnostic. That he denied access to knowledge of God as he is *in himself* is quite true, but he was, if anything, excessively confident that one could come to a knowledge of God and his attributes in one's own experience.

Schleiermacher's so-called subjectivism also needs careful qualification. For him the importance of the Christian Community in the forming of self-consciousness has already been mentioned. For Schleiermacher there never was person-formation in a vacuum. It was always in the context of a community, through the mediation of other men. Self-consciousness, then, is never entirely subjective, for it is always formed through the encounter with others who can serve both to illuminate and to check our own experience. One does sense, all the same, that Schleiermacher gave too large a place to religious experience in his reconstruction of Christian doctrine, to the point of disregarding such other sources as biblical exegesis and doctrinal tradition.

That Schleiermacher's reconstruction of Christian faith left serious questions concerning the doctrine of God, sin, Christ, and redemption was widely acknowledged in his own time as well as today. What is more significant, however, is that Schleiermacher saw the necessity of theological reconstruction

and had the courage and systematic power to carry it through. At the center of his reconstruction is the concentration on experience as the starting point for theology. After Schleiermacher, theology no longer felt obliged to vindicate itself at the court of science or even Kant's practical reason. Theology now had a new sense of its own self-authentication in experience for, while it could no longer claim to be scientifically verified, its truth was now to be found in the symbolic rendering of the experiences of the life of feelings. Here Schleiermacher established a method followed to the present day by the liberal schools of "empirical" and "experiential" theology.

This radical change in the fundamental conception of theology and its foundation led to a more open and critical attitude toward the Bible and the creeds. It resulted in a deeper historical and psychological understanding of both Scripture and tradition but, at the same time, led to a purging of all doctrine and practice that failed to find any place in the Christian experience of redemption—e.g., the virgin birth, the Trinity, the second coming of Christ. Schleiermacher's psychological and historical conception of religion also gave considerable impetus to the comparative study of religions and to the scientific analysis and classification of religious phenomena—for example, in the work of the twentieth-century historians of religion, Ernst Troeltsch and Rudolf Otto.

Finally, Schleiermacher and his fellow Romanticists played a significant role in the demise of the eighteenth-century deistical conception of God and in overcoming the sharp bifurcation between the natural and supernatural that was common to the eighteenth century. It was the Romanticists' rediscovery of the immanence of God in the world of nature and history that made possible once again a more deeply felt personal experience of God. God was no longer banished from the world, remote and inaccessible, but was experienced as present in the most common, prosaic events of everyday life. All nature was once again revelatory of the divine, for

Earth's crammed with heaven,
And every common bush afire with God . . . .

(Elizabeth Barrett Browning)

The development of the conception of divine immanence and its significance for a reinterpretation of traditional Christianity was, however, to be carried out much more rigorously and systematically by a colleague of Schleiermacher at Berlin—G. W. F. Hegel. It is to Hegel and the school of Christian Idealism that we will turn after examining a movement of considerable importance in the English-speaking world—the Oxford Movement and Anglo-Catholicism.

NOTES

1. Jacques Barzun, *Berlioz and the Romantic Century* (Boston, 1950), I, 379.
2. J. H. Randall, Jr., *The Making of the Modern Mind* (New York, 1926), p. 395.
3. For an excellent account of the new discovery in Romanticism of the value of diversity, see A. O. Lovejoy's essay, "Romanticism and Plenitude," in *The Great Chain of Being* (Cambridge, 1936).
4. Wackenroder, *Herzensergiessungen* (1797), as cited in Lovejoy, op. cit., p. 305.
5. F. Schleiermacher, *On Religion*, tr. John Oman (New York, 1958).
6. Ibid., pp. 214, 217.
7. "The Tables Turned," in *The Complete Poetical Works of William Wordsworth* (London, 1928), p. 85.
8. J. W. von Goethe, *Faust*, tr. Anna Swanwick (New York, n.d.).
9. For an excellent discussion of Hamann's understanding of faith and reason, which rejects the conception of Hamann as a prophet of irrationalism, see R. G. Smith, *J. G. Hamann, A Study in Christian Existence* (London, 1960).
10. *Hamanns Schriften*, ed. F. Roth, X, 429 ff.; cited in R. G. Smith, op. cit., p. 50.
11. F. Roth, op. cit., II, 35; Smith, op. cit., p. 57.
12. F. Roth, op. cit., II, 36; Smith, op. cit., pp. 55–56.
13. F. H. Jacobi, *David Hume über den Glauben*, *Sämmtliche Werke*, II, 107 f.; cited in A. C. McGiffert, *The Rise of Modern Religious Ideas*, pp. 119–120.
14. J. S. Mill, *Dissertations and Discussions* (London, 1867), I, 403.
15. Maurice says: "I am sure that I should not have had courage to differ from them or him [Coleridge] if he had not assisted me to believe that truth is above both, most of all above myself and my own petty notions and apprehensions, that it is worthy to be sought after and loved above all things, and that he who is truth, is ready, if we will obey him, to guide us into it." *The Kingdom of Christ* (London, 1958), II, 364.
16. S. T. Coleridge, *Letters*, ed. E. H. Coleridge (1895), I, 352.
17. *The Friend* (Bohn ed.), p. 67.
18. *The Friend* (Shedd ed.), II, 164n.
19. *Nineteenth Century Studies* (New York, 1966), p. 29.
20. *The Statesman's Manual* (Shedd ed.), I, 430.
21. *Aids to Reflection* (Shedd ed., 1853), I, 210–211.
22. Coleridge's philosophical handling of the doctrine of God has often been considered "pantheistic." That Coleridge sought to

avoid pantheism is very evident; whether he entirely succeeded is still debated. See J. D. Boulger, *Coleridge as Religious Thinker* (Yale, 1961), Chap. IV.

23. *Aids to Reflection*, p. 272.

24. Coleridge wrote in one letter: "And this I believe not because I understand it; but because I *feel* that is not only suitable to, but needful for my nature, and because I find it clearly revealed." *Unpublished Letters*, ed. E. L. Griggs, I, 203.

25. *Aids to Reflection*, p. 363.

26. Ibid. Elsewhere Coleridge wrote that spiritual truths were "substantiated for us by their correspondence to the wants, cravings, and interests of the moral being . . . . For some of the faithful these truths have, I doubt not, an evidence of reason; but for the whole household of faith their certainty is in their working." *Literary Remains*, p. 366.

27. *Aids to Reflection*, p. 233.

28. Ibid., p. 226.

29. Ibid., p. 150.

30. Ibid., p. 209.

31. Ibid., pp. 209–210.

32. *Biographia Literaria* (Showcross ed.), I, 135–136.

33. *Essay on Faith* (Shedd ed.), V, 565.

34. S. T. Coleridge, *Confessions of an Inquiring Spirit*, ed. H. St. J. Hart (Stanford, 1956), p. 38.

35. Ibid., p. 49. Again: "I demand for the Bible only the justice which you grant other books of grave authority, and to other proved and acknowledged benefactors of mankind. Will you deny a spirit of wisdom in Lord Bacon, because in particular facts he did not possess perfect science . . . ?" *Confessions*, p. 62.

36. Ibid., p. 53.

37. Ibid., p. 66.

38. Ibid., pp. 64–65.

39. Ibid., pp. 68–70.

40. Ibid., p. 74.

41. Ibid., p. 60.

42. Ibid., pp. 65–66.

43. Ibid., p. 67.

44. Ibid., pp. 79–80.

45. *Aus Schleiermachers Leben in Briefen*, ed. W. Dilthey, I, 308; *Letters*, tr. F. Rowan (London, 1860), I, 283.

46. *On Religion: Speeches to Its Cultured Despisers*, tr. John Oman (New York, 1958), p. 15.

47. Ibid., pp. 15–16.

48. Ibid., pp. 18–19.

49. Ibid., p. 21.

50. Ibid., p. 31.

51. Ibid., p. 35.

52. Ibid., p. 57.

53. Ibid., pp. 37–38.

54. Ibid., p. 36.

55. Ibid., pp. 49–50.

56. *The Christian Faith*, ed. H. R. Mackintosh and J. S. Stewart (Edinburgh, 1948), p. 12.

57. *On Religion*. p. 71.

58. Ibid., p. 48.

59. Ibid., pp. 87–88.

60. Ibid., p. 91.

61. Ibid., p. 95.

62. Ibid., p. 97.

63. Ibid., p. 122.

64. Ibid., pp. 132–133.

65. William Wordsworth, op. cit., p. 34.

66. *On Religion*, p. 149.

67. Ibid., p. 150.

68. Ibid., p. 151.

69. Ibid., p. 155.

70. Ibid., p. 161.

71. Ibid., p. 167.

72. Ibid., pp. 217–218.

73. Ibid., p. 214.

74. Ibid., p. 234.

75. Ibid.

76. Ibid., p. 248.

77. Ibid., pp. 251–252.

78. Ibid., p. 253.

79. *The Christian Faith*, op. cit., p. 52.

80. Ibid.

81. Ibid., p. 203. See the whole of Schleiermacher's discussion of the Eternity of God in §52, p. 203 ff.

82. Ibid., p. 206. See §53.

83. Ibid., p. 325.

84. Ibid., p. 271.

85. Ibid., p. 303.

86. *Schleiermacher on Christ and Religion* (New York, 1964), p. 208. The account given in this chapter of Schleiermacher's understanding of sin and the work of Christ

draws heavily on Niebuhr's excellent analysis in Chaps. IV–V of the above book.

87. Ibid., p. 226.

SUGGESTIONS FOR FURTHER READING

ROMANTICISM

Barzun, Jacques. *Classic, Romantic, and Modern* (New York: Doubleday Anchor Book, 1961). An excellent study of Romantic art and life and the phases of Romanticism by a foremost cultural historian.

Lovejoy, A. O. "Romanticism and the Principle of Plentitude," *The Great Chain of Being* (Cambridge: Harvard University Press, 1936).

Randall, J. H., Jr. *The Making of the Modern Mind*, Chap. XVI (New York: Houghton Mifflin Co., 1926). A brief analysis of Romanticism as a protest against the Age of Reason.

SAMUEL TAYLOR COLERIDGE

There are numerous excellent studies of Coleridge the poet and critic. The following are the best studies of Coleridge the religious thinker:

Barth, J. R. *Coleridge and Christian Doctrine* (Cambridge: Harvard University Press, 1969).

Boulger, James D. *Coleridge as Religious Thinker* (New Haven: Yale University Press, 1961).

Muirhead, J. H. *Coleridge as Philosopher* (New York: The Macmillan Co., 1930).

Sanders, Charles R. *Coleridge and the Broad Church Movement* (Durham: Duke University Press, 1942).

Willey, Basil. *Nineteenth Century Studies*, Chap. I (New York: Harper Torchbook, 1966). An excellent brief study of Coleridge as religious thinker.

FRIEDRICH SCHLEIERMACHER

Many of the best studies of Schleiermacher are in German. The following studies in English are recommended:

Barth, Karl. *Protestant Thought from Rousseau to Ritschl* (New York: Harper & Brothers, 1959). Barth's essay on Schleiermacher is provocative but must be read critically.

Brandt, Richard R. *The Philosophy of Schleiermacher* (New York: Harper & Brothers, 1941).

Niebuhr, Richard R. *Schleiermacher on Christ and Religion* (New York: Charles Scribner's Sons, 1964). An up-to-date study and reinterpretation of certain themes in Schleiermacher's thought.

Selbie, W. B. *Schleiermacher* (New York: E. P. Dutton and Co., 1913). A somewhat dated yet still helpful survey of Schleiermacher's philosophy of religion and theology.

Spiegler, Gerhard. *The Eternal Covenant: Schleiermacher's Experiment in Cultural Theology* (New York: Harper and Row, 1967).

CHAPTER FIVE

The Oxford Movement and Anglo-Catholicism

John Henry Newman

Viewed from the vantage point of over one hundred years' distance, the Oxford Movement can be seen as a part of that larger spiritual and cultural movement which reacted against the Age of Reason and is known as Romanticism. The men of the Oxford or Tractarian Movement* reflect much that characterized the Romantic poets and novelists. They abhorred what they considered the presumptuous usurpation by "reason alone"

* Also referred to as the Anglo-Catholic Revival, the Anglican "Counter Reformation" and, by contemporaries of the movement, as "Puseyism," after Dr. E. B. Pusey, one of the Oxford leaders.

of all claims to truth. They looked upon "private judgment" as evidence of a shallow sense of history and as politically and religiously divisive. They possessed a deep but often uncritical admiration of ancient ways, looking to the glory of unified Christendom in the Middle Ages or the ascetic purity of the primitive martyrs with a certain sentimental wistfulness. They loved mystery, sometimes reveling in their paradoxes to the point of unintelligibility—and thereby closing themselves off from those outside their party. They possessed a deep mystical feeling and were essentially poetic spirits

115

concerned to restore a sense of humble obedience before the holy mysteries—in a church shorn of the *mysterium tremendum*.

The Oxford Movement was not only, nor even principally, a movement of religious *thought*. First of all, it was a movement of religious devotion and discipline. However, the revival of a more Catholic piety was accompanied by historical and theological investigations of ancient thought and practice, and these studies gave theological warrant for the Church's religious renewal. The writings of the Tractarians—Keble, Newman, Pusey—lacked, for the most part, the originality of the German theologians. By their learning and prolific writing, however, the Oxford men were able to make not only the Church of England but much of non-Roman Christendom aware of the riches of her pre-Reformation heritage. This effect was not immediate. Resistance to the Oxford revival was very great within the Anglican Church itself and no more so than among her bishops. Nevertheless, the Oxford Movement has had a slow and almost imperceptible influence on European and American Christianity in the last century. Outwardly that influence can easily be seen in the areas of spiritual discipline and liturgy but, in turn, this revival of the religious life and worship has had a significant, though less observable, influence on theology, on the renewal of mission, on social thought, and on ecumenism.

The Beginnings of the Anglo-Catholic Revival

Before turning to the characteristic *thought* of the Oxford Tractarians, something must be said of the beginnings and

development of the movement itself. Much can be learned about the character of the Oxford Movement by looking closely at the political and social situation existing in Europe in the first decades of the nineteenth-century. Both on the Continent and in England there was a reaction against the excesses of the French Revolution and the Terror. Originally drawn to the Revolution by its heroic denunciation of despotism, many Romantics—Coleridge among them—found the outcome of radical republicanism, in the likes of Tom Paine, horrifying. As we have seen, in France the reaction took a strongly political turn in the Catholic traditionalism of de Bonald and de Maistre, who combined royalism and papalism. In England the distrust of the new liberalism was epitomized in Edmund Burke's *Reflections on the French Revolution* (1790).

French radicalism helped to effect a conservative reaction in England to such a degree that, in the words of the historian Froude, it "frightened all classes out of advanced ways of thinking, and society in town and country [became] Tory in politics, and determined to allow no innovations upon the inherited faith."[1] In the early decades of the nineteenth century the Tory party had become increasingly reactionary but, under the pressure of dissent, had been required in 1828 to repeal the old Test and Corporation Acts which had excluded Dissenters from Parliament and other public office. A year later came Catholic Emancipation. The old High Church Anglican ideal of the union of Church and State was in jeopardy. Then, in 1830 the Whigs came to power, and in two years the famous Reform Bill was passed. The alliance of Whigs, Dissenters, and emancipated Catholics marked evil days ahead for the

Established Church. Thomas Arnold wrote at the time that "the Church, as it now stands, no human power can save."

In 1833 the Whig administration introduced the Church Temporalities Bill into Parliament. The measure sought to reform the Irish Church by reducing the number of bishoprics and redistributing the rich, ecclesiastical incomes. The Irish Church had long needed reorganization, but the conservative bishops were quite opposed to change. The Whig Irish Church Temporalities Bill of 1833 was in fact a moderate and reasonable measure. Nevertheless, after the victories of the Reform Bill, it was interpreted as one more defeat for the Church in its struggle with the growing tide of secular power. The High Church party saw a growing Erastianism slowly weakening the hold of the Church of England over the lives of the people and, moreover, transforming the Church into a dutiful servant of the secular state. The Oxford Movement, can, in part, be seen as a *political* reaction to the growth of this political liberalism. One historian has recently stressed this particular factor. "The Tractarian Movement," writes J. H. Nichols, "was the English equivalent of the French traditionalism of de Maistre, de Bonold and Lamennais . . . conservative reactions to the reforming tendencies of liberalism in Church and State."[2] There is truth in this view, but it doesn't get at the essence of the Oxford counter-revolution. Erastianism was but a symptom of a much greater danger, i.e., the pretensions of reason and science to solve all of man's difficulties, thus calling into question the need for any supernatural religion at all. The real enemy of the Tractarians was Benthamism and the growing scientific positivism. E. R. Fairweather states it well:

The Oxford Movement was unquestionably an affirmation of the Church's God-given authority and inherent power, but this affirmation was part of an attempted renewal of the Church in the interests of supernatural religion. Over against the aridities of empiricist philosophy and Utilitarian ethics, the Tractarians sought a renewed awareness of transcendent mystery and a renewed sense of human life as guided by a transcendent power to a transcendent goal. If they insisted on the authority of the Church they did so because they saw in the Church an indispensable witness to the grace and truth that came by Jesus Christ—not because they looked to it as one more bulwark of a threatened social order.[3]

According to its own leaders, the Oxford Movement began with a sermon preached by John Keble before His Majesty's Judges of Assize at Oxford on July 14, 1833.* The immediate cause of the sermon was the Church Temporalities Bill and the suppression of the ten Irish bishoprics, in defiance of the Church's opinion. What alarmed Keble and others was the fact that the state had taken upon itself, without the Church's consent, to determine episcopal authority, even episcopal existence! Keble entitled his sermon "National Apostasy." In the Advertisement to the First Edition he wrote:

The legislature of England and Ireland (*the members of which are not even bound to profess belief in the atonement*), this body has virtually usurped the commission of those whom our Saviour entrusted with *at least one voice* in making ecclesiastical laws, on matters wholly or partly spiritual. The same legislature has also ratified, to its full extent, this principle— that the apostolical Church in this realm is henceforth only to stand, in the eye of the state

* Years later J. H. Newman wrote: "I have ever considered and kept the day as the start of the religious Movement of 1833."

as *one sect among many*, depending, for any preeminence she may still appear to retain, merely upon the accident of her having a strong party in the country.[4]

Keble counted such action a "profane intrusion" into the realm of divine authority. He called upon churchmen to treat such an intrusion as they would treat any other "tyranny"; "deprecate and adjure it." The cause of this situation was the growing indifference of people toward the supernatural realities of religion, disguised in the garb of toleration. Keble called such a condition *Apostasy:*

Under the guise of charity and toleration we are come almost to this that no difference, in matters of faith, is to disqualify for our approbation and confidence, whether in public or domestic life. Can we conceal it from ourselves, that every year the practice is becoming more common, of trusting men unreservedly in the most delicate and important matters, without serious inquiry, whether they do not hold principles which make it impossible for them to be loyal to their Creator, Redeemer and Sanctifier?... The point really to be considered is, whether, according to the coolest estimate, the fashionable liberality of this generation be not ascribable, in a great measure, to the same temper which led the Jews voluntarily to set about degrading themselves to a level with the idolatrous Gentiles. And, if it be true anywhere, that such enactments are forced on the legislature by public opinion, is APOSTASY too hard a word to describe the temper of that nation?[5]

Keble's sermon summed up the sentiments of many of the younger churchmen who were distressed and angered by the Church's acquiescence to secularism. The sermon served as a call to action. Between the 25th and 29th of July, 1833, a small meeting was held in Hugh James Rose's rectory at Hadleigh to consider what might be done. Those joining Rose were Hurrell Froude, Arthur Perceval, and William Palmer, all of Oxford. John Henry Newman and John Keble did not attend but were kept informed of the plans. It was agreed that an Association of Friends of the Church should be formed and that certain petitions and addresses to the Archbishop of Canterbury and others should be drawn up. Not a great deal came of these plans, but they did prepare the way for the famous *Tracts for the Times* which contained the fundamental principles of the Movement.

The series of Tracts began to appear in the early autumn of 1833. The first one, only four pages in length, was written by Newman. It was entitled *Thoughts on the Ministerial Commission Respectfully Addressed to the Clergy.* Its urgency and confidence served as a keynote for the series. Its theme was *apostolic succession* since it was this, and this alone, Newman argued, to which the clergy must look for their authority. If the state were to deprive the Church of its temporal benefits, on what, Newman asked the clergy, would they establish their office?

Should the government and the country so far forget their God as to cast off the Church, to deprive it of its temporal honours and substance, *on what* will you rest the claim of respect and attention which you make upon your flocks? Hitherto you have been upheld by your birth, your education, your wealth, your connexions; should these secular advantages cease, on what must Christ's ministers depend . . . *on what* are we to rest our authority when the state deserts us?

Christ has not left his Church without claim of its own upon the attention of men. Surely not. Hard Master he cannot be, to bid us oppose the world, yet give us no credentials for so doing. There are some who rest their divine mission on their own unsupported assertion; others, who rest it on their popularity; others on their success; and others, who rest it upon their temporal distinctions. This last case has, perhaps, been too much our own; I fear we have neglected the real ground on which our authority is built—OUR APOSTOLICAL DESCENT.

We have been born not of blood, nor of the will of the flesh, nor of the will of man, but of God (Jn. 1:13). The Lord Jesus Christ gave his Spirit to his apostles (cf. Jn. 20:22); they in turn laid their hands on those who should succeed them; and these again on others; and so the sacred gift has been handed down to our present bishops, who have appointed us as their assistants, and in some sense representatives.[6]

The notion had gone abroad that the State could deprive the clergy of their power by confiscating the Church's property. A confusion had been made between the divine commission of the priestly office and the temporal power of the Church. Newman concludes Tract I with an appeal to the clergy to enlighten their flocks on this matter, and with the following challenge:

If you will not adopt my view of the subject, which I offer to you, not doubtingly, yet (I hope) respectfully, at all events, CHOOSE YOUR SIDE. To remain neutral much longer will be itself to take a part. *Choose* your side; since side you shortly must, with one or other party, even though you do nothing. Fear to be of those whose line is decided for them by chance circumstances, and who may perchance find themselves with the enemies of Christ, while they think but to remove themselves from worldly politics. Such abstinence is impossible in troublous times. HE THAT IS NOT WITH ME IS AGAINST ME, AND HE THAT GATHERETH NOT WITH ME SCATTERETH ABROAD (Mt. 12:30).[7]

The early tracts and Newman's sermons at St. Mary's Church, Oxford, incited a movement, and soon new recruits were joining the cause—among them the young statesman Gladstone. The most important of these new adherents was Edward B. Pusey, Regius Professor of Hebrew at Oxford and a man of vast influence in the University and in the world outside clerical Oxford. Pusey's accession to the Movement was signaled by the appearance of Tract 18 on Fasting, which appeared over his initials in 1837. The next year he published three Tracts (67, 68, 69) on Baptism which grew into a treatise of four hundred pages. It was a learned work, summing up the theology and spirit of the Anglo-Catholic party. It also proved to be a turning point in the Movement's history, in that it gave to it a theological erudition and responsibility which it had not yet entirely achieved. Looking back at the Movement years later, Newman commented on the significance of Pusey's entrance into the cause.

Dr. Pusey's influence was felt at once. He saw that there ought to be more sobriety, more gravity, more careful pains, more sense of responsibility in the Tracts and in the whole Movement. It was through him that the character of the Tracts was changed . . . I suspect it was Dr. Pusey's influence and example which set me, and made me set others, on the larger and more careful works in defence of the principles of the Movement which followed in a course of years.[8]

By 1835 the Movement was a power to be reckoned with. It continued to grow in numbers and influence for the next several years. There were some setbacks, however. In 1836 Hurrell Froude died, and his letters and papers were published by Newman and Keble two years later. The anti-Protestant sentiments expressed in Froude's journals incensed many and scared others away.* In 1839 the suspicions raised by Froude's papers were deepened by the publication of Tract 80, written by Isaac Williams and titled *On Reserve in Communicating Religious Knowledge*. Williams objected to the Evangelicals' careless use of sacred language and appealed to the whole tradition of the Church as a corrective to the Evangelical practice of focusing almost exclusively on the doctrine of the Atonement. Nevertheless, it was attacked widely as exemplifying the worst evils of Romanism.

The word "Reserve" was enough. It meant that the Tract-writers avowed the principle of keeping back part of the counsel of God. It meant, further, that the real spirit of the party was disclosed; its love of secret and crooked methods . . . its deliberate concealments, its holding doctrines and its pursuit of aims which it dared not avow, its *disciplina arcani*, its conspiracies, its Jesuitical spirit.[9]

Such was the state of mind in which Tract 80 was received by the opponents of the Revival—a suspiciousness which was never again allayed.

Despite these and other reversals, the Movement reached its zenith between 1836 and 1838. In the latter year over 60,000 Tracts were sold, Newman's published sermons were widely read, and the *British Critic*, the organ of the party edited by Newman, was flourishing. However, outward appearances were deceptive. Between 1840 and 1845 the Movement was about to move into a second phase, which was marked by doubts and divisions, caused partly by

the influx of new, often extreme men whose tendency was clearly Romanward. The breakup of the Oxford Movement and its dispersion during these years can be observed in a series of events, especially in John Henry Newman's own changing course. First of all, there was a series of defeats and humiliations for the Tractarians at the hands of their Oxford opponents. In August of 1838 the Bishop of Oxford, in a charge to his clergy, had accused the Tractarians of Romanish practices. This was especially bitter for Newman because of his deep sense of obedience to his episcopal superior. During the same year a proposal was introduced for the raising of a subscription for an Oxford memorial to the Reformation martyrs Cranmer, Ridley, and Latimer. This was clearly a move directed against the High Church party. Newman and Keble would have nothing to do with it, but the subscription was a success, and the Martyrs' Memorial was built.

In 1841 a proposal was made, and accepted by men in high authority, for the establishment of an Anglo-Prussian Protestant Bishop of Jerusalem. The bishop was to be nominated alternately by England and Prussia and consecrated by English Bishops for jurisdiction over English and German Protestants in Palestine. The idea that the English Church, which was out of communion with both the Roman and the Eastern Church, could enter lightly into communion with Protestant heretics was against all that the Oxford party was fighting for. Newman protested bitterly and later acknowledged that this was one of the blows that led to his final disillusionment with the *Via Media* of the English Church.

During the same period a controversy

---

* Froude had written such things as: "Really I hate the Reformation and the Reformers more and more," and "The Reformation was a limb badly set; it must be broken again to be righted."

over the Poetry Professorship at Oxford increased the rift between the parties. Isaac Williams, a loyal Tractarian and fine poet, was thought to be the natural choice for the Chair, but because of his Tractarian affiliation he was opposed and defeated. In the next years the Tractarians suffered two additional humiliations which, while revealing the fear and even panic of their Oxford opponents, also made clear the serious differences between the Catholic party and the majority within the English Church. In 1844, Dr. Pusey was suspended for two years from preaching in the University. The suspension was the result of a sermon Pusey had preached on "The Holy Eucharist, a Comfort to the Penitent." He was accused of teaching transubstantiation and other heretical doctrines and, without a hearing or trial, he was found guilty by a board of six professors, all of whom opposed "Puseyism."

A year later William G. Ward, a zealous newcomer to the Catholic cause, was censured and stripped of his University degrees for statements published in a book entitled *The Ideal of a Christian Church*. The book actually does reveal how Romanized the Movement had become, at least among some of the younger leaders. Ward could find nothing excellent in the English Church. At the same time he looked uncritically to the Roman Communion as the historical exhibition of his "Ideal." He also exulted in the fact that he found "the whole cycle of Roman doctrine gradually possessing numbers of English Churchmen" and boasted that he still retained his Oxford Fellowship after having publicly stated "that in subscribing the Articles I renounce not one Roman doctrine." It is no wonder that his book was condemned, but the punishment of reducing

Ward to the status of an undergraduate was a ridiculous act, only making plain the bitter strife of the time.

All of these events had their effects in demoralizing and dividing the Movement during the early '40's, but none was as important in the Movement's decline as the unsettlement of Newman's own mind and his final secession from the Church of England. Newman's religious pilgrimage during these years cannot be detailed here; only a few of the most important factors can be sketched. *

While becoming increasingly assured that the Anglican Church, though differing from Rome, should on the whole be more like it, up to the summer of 1839 Newman did not question his claim that the Church of England represented the Church's genuine antiquity. Then in the summer of that year his confidence was first shaken. He had been absorbed in reading about the Monophysite heresy of the fifth century A.D. and saw in this fifth century controversy an analogy to his own times. The English Church was like the Monophysites, a small, unsteady island broken away from the firm, majestic mainland. At this very moment of uncertainty Newman records that he received "the first real hit from Romanism." A friend had put into his hands an article written by the English Roman Catholic Bishop, Nicholas Wiseman. The article compared the isolation of the Anglican *Via Media* with the Donatist sect which had seceded from Rome in the fourth century. What struck Newman was not the parallel between the Donatists and the English

---

* This is a fascinating history and can be found in Newman's own spiritual autobiography, *Apologia Pro Vita Sua*. Also, there is a lively account of these years in Geoffrey Faber's *Oxford Apostles*.

Church but Wiseman's citation of a phrase from St. Augustine—*securus judicat orbis terrarum*—against the Donatists. The phrase, "the wide world is secure in its judgment," made Newman conscious that the English Church, like the heretical sects of the fourth and fifth centuries, was a small, prideful communion, glorying in its separation from the great universal Church. Not only did the Anglican Church lack Catholicity; in Newman's eyes it no longer could appeal to Antiquity. The significance of this occasion is recorded by Newman:

What a light was hereby thrown upon every controversy in the Church! . . . *the deliberate judgement, in which the whole Church at length rests and acquiesces, is an infallible prescription and a final sentence against such portions of it as protest and secede . . . .* For a mere sentence, the words of St. Augustine, struck me with a power which I had never felt from any words before . . . . *Securus judicat orbis terrarum! By those great words of the ancient Father, the theory of the Via Media was absolutely pulverized.*[10] (Italics added.)

For Newman, as well as for Ward and other younger men, Rome now possessed the true marks of the Church. Yet Newman was not yet ready to give up his apologetic for the Church of England. If Rome possessed the notes of the true Church, it was necessary to show that Anglicanism was actually compatible with Rome. The stumbling-block, of course, was the Thirty-Nine Articles. Could it be shown that these Articles were compatible with the doctrine of the Old Church? In 1841 (in the famous Tract 90, entitled *Remarks on Certain Passages in the Thirty-Nine Articles*) Newman undertook to show that this was, indeed, possible. He put down as the

first principle of interpreting the Articles the following rule:

It is a duty which we owe both to the Catholic Church and to our own, to take our reformed confessions in the most Catholic sense they will admit: We have no duties towards their framers.[11]

This principle led many to claim, with considerable warrant, that Newman's allegiance was already to Rome. The tortured, ingenious, and often seemingly inconsistent arguments of the Tract also did not allow for any greater confidence, outside the Roman-ward party, in Newman's position. One example of his procedure will suffice. Article XXI states that forasmuch as General Councils are assemblies of men, "they may err and sometimes have erred in things pertaining to God. Wherefor things ordained of them as necessary to salvation have neither strength nor authority, unless it may be declared that they are taken out of Holy Scripture." Newman adds the gloss that "General Council, then, may err, *as such*—may err, *unless* in any case it is promised, as a matter of supernatural privilege, that they shall *not* err; a case which lies beyond the scope of this Article, or at any rate beside its determination."[12]

Newman's motives for writing Tract 90 will never be completely known. Was he simply hoping to remove the barrier of the Thirty-Nine Articles for those extreme Romanizers in the party, such as William G. Ward? Or, like Ward, was he wishing to put the final challenge to the Church of England? In any case, Tract 90 produced a storm of protest, and in March of 1841 the Heads of Houses at Oxford condemned the Tract, claiming it to be dishonest and incompatible with the University Statutes. Things grew steadily worse for the Catholic Party in Oxford; High Churchmen were discriminated against in numerous ways. In February of 1842 Newman retired to Littlemore. It was now only a matter of waiting for the ties with the past to be broken and the new conviction to gain assurance before he would be received into the Roman Church. In the evening of October 8, 1845, in the same year as the condemnation of Ward's *The Ideal of the Christian Church*, Newman fell on his knees before the Passionist Father Dominic and begged to be received "into the Church of Christ."

Newman's secession was a severe blow to the Anglo-Catholic movement. After Newman the Movement continued to influence the life of the Church, but it never again achieved the spiritual power, depth, and brilliance of the Movement of the 1830's and early 1840's. Some men like J. A. Froude and Mark Pattison were cast adrift by Newman's action and ended up as skeptics. Others like Ward, Faber, Manning, and Robert Wilberforce sooner or later joined Newman in the Roman Church. Others like Keble and Pusey remained in the English Church and continued their labors in the cause of Anglo-Catholicism. In 1855 Pusey published his book on *The Real Presence* and in 1857 Keble's *On Eucharistic Adoration* appeared. Both works were characteristic of the continuing work of the Anglo-Catholic party within the Anglican Communion. The leadership of the Movement soon passed into the hands of able, younger men such as H. P. Liddon and R. W. Church and, at the end of the century, was taken up by men of a more liberal Catholic mind, such as Scott Holland and Charles Gore, who were associated with *Lux Mundi*.* However,

what is most distinctive about the Movement between 1850 and 1890 is the revival of ritualism and ceremonial and the growth of monastic communities. Our chief concern remains the characteristic *thought* of the early Oxford Movement, and to that we now turn.

The Thought of the Oxford Movement: Keble, Newman, and Pusey

The Oxford Movement was a revival of Catholic piety, and the leaders, therefore, considered themselves restorers of the ancient faith and practice. They abhorred the idea of being *innovators* and distrusted novelty. Liberal change appeared to the Tractarians as nothing but apostasy. However, the Movement was not a mere repristination of the theology of the Fathers; it was, most clearly in the case of Newman, a creative restatement of the ancient verities. In this respect its role in the nineteenth century is, in some ways, similar to the movements of Neo-Orthodoxy and Neo-Thomism in the twentieth.†

To understand the thought of the Tractarians it is first necessary to grasp the peculiar spirituality of men like Keble, Newman, Pusey, and Isaac Williams. In their feeling for the fresh beauty of nature, for the mystery of medievalism and in the awe and thrill with which they approached the heritage of the past, they were men of the Romantic era. The unique piety which marks them all can, perhaps, best be seen in their genuine feeling for supernatural mystery, in their sense of humble reserve, and in the attention they gave to self-denying obedience. An understanding of these

* See Chapter Ten.
† See Chapters Eleven and Thirteen.

spiritual qualities is indispensable to an appreciation of Tractarian thought.

In an age of growing immanentism (Schleiermacher and Hegel), what is most striking about the Tractarians is their feeling for the actuality of the supernatural and the invisible heavenly world of angels and spirits. This is especially true of Newman and Pusey (referred to by Brilioth as the *doctor mysticus* of the Movement), for whom the visible world is but an appearance, at best symbolizing but more often veiling the reality of the invisible. Newman expresses this in his sermon on "The Invisible World."

Even when it [the earth] is gayest, with all its blossom on, and shows most touchingly what lies hid in it, yet it is not enough. We know much more lies hid in it than what we see. A world of Saints and Angels, a glorious world, the palace of God, the mountain of the Lord of Hosts, the Heavenly Jerusalem, the throne of God and Christ, all these wonders lie hid in what we see . . . . We know that what we see is as a screen hiding from us God and Christ, and his Saints and Angels. And we earnestly desire and pray for the dissolution of all that we see, from our longing after that which we do not see . . . .[13]

For the Tractarians our sense experience and our ideas are but pale expressions of the spiritual truths which they feebly attempt to approximate. But the Christian can let go his hold on these visible things, for he understands the transience of this world. Because the world is a veil hiding the vast mysteries of the invisible world, the Christian will not fear to believe what seems credulous in the eyes of the world, for the religious mind will always appear superstitious to the worldly-wise. But when one considers how baffling Nature is, is it any wonder that the supernatural should be

ineffably mysterious? "It would be strange indeed," says Newman, "if any doctrine concerning God's infinite and eternal Nature were not mysterious." It is understandable then that the Trinity and the Incarnation, being the highest mysteries of the faith, are not rationally explicable. They are to be approached in reverent awe:

No earthly images can come up to the awful and gracious truth, that God became the Son of Man—the Word became Flesh, and was born of a woman. This ineffable mystery surpasses human words.[14]

Think but for a moment of the awful mystery of the Passion:

Now I bid you consider that that Face, so ruthlessly smitten, was the Face of God Himself; the Brows bloody with the thorns, the Sacred Body exposed to view and lacerated with the scourge, the Hands nailed to the Cross . . . it was the Blood, and the Sacred Flesh, and the Hands and the Temples, and the Side, and the Feet of God Himself, which the frenzied multitude then gazed upon. This is so fearful a thought, that when the mind first masters it, surely it will be difficult to think of anything else; so that while we think of it, we must pray to God to temper it to us, and to give us strength to think of it lightly, lest it be too much for us.[15]

According to the Tractarians, religious truth is so sublime as to require that it be approached in wonder, fear, and reserve —in the spirit of the Greek *Cherubikon*: "Let all mortal flesh keep silence and with fear and trembling stand." It was, therefore, a first principle of the Tractarians that a man's soul must be spiritually prepared to receive and understand the mysteries of the faith. One feeds milk, not strong meat, to spiritual babes. The Tractarians found support for this view in the practice of the *disciplina arcana* in the ancient Fathers. This secret discipline taught that the Creed should be declared to the Catechumens only as they became morally and spiritually prepared to receive it and that the holy rites and mysteries should be kept from being profaned by unbelievers. The Tractarians considered Evangelical preaching irreverent for it exposed the most sacred mysteries to the indifference and mockery of the crowd.

This sense of reserve in communicating religious knowledge is especially evident in the personality and writings of John Keble and in the poems of Isaac Williams. In Williams' poem "The Cathedral" the church's choir screen serves as the symbol of the *disciplina arcana*, but the whole poem is expressive of this feeling.

When out of Sion God appear'd
    For perfect beauty fear'd,
The darkness was His Chariot,
    And clouds were all about.
Hiding His dread sublimity,
    When Jesus walked nigh,
He threw around His works of good
    A holier solitude,
Ris'n from the grave appear'd to view,
    But to a faithful few.

Alone e'en now, as then of old,
    The pure of heart behold
The soul-restoring miracles
    Wherein His mercy dwells;
New marvels unto them reveal'd,
    But from the whole concealed.
Then pause, and fear—when thus allowed
    We enter the dark cloud,
Lord, keep our hearts, that soul and eye
    Unharm'd may Thee descry.[16]

Spiritually akin to this reverential reserve before the supernatural is a certain self-abasement and quality of humble obedience. This is again expressed by Williams in his tract "On Reserve in Communicating Religious Knowledge," one of the most characteristic treatises of the Movement. In addressing himself to the danger of private judgment in religious matters, Williams writes:

Surely we know not what we do when we venture to make a scheme and system of our own respecting the revelations of God. His ways are so vast and mysterious that there may be some great presumption in our taking one truth, and forming around it a scheme from notions of our own . . . . The very idea of forming such a scheme arises from a want of a due sense of the depth and vastness of the divine counsels, as if we could comprehend them . . . . Religious doctrines and articles of faith can only be received according to certain dispositions of the heart; these dispositions can only be formed by a repetition of certain actions. And therefore a certain course of action can alone dispose us to receive certain doctrines . . . . For instance, charitable works alone will make a man charitable, and the more anyone does charitable works, the more charitable will he become; that is to say, the more will he love his neighbour and love God . . . . Or again, he only will be humble in heart who does humble actions, and no action is (morally speaking) an humble action but such as proceeds from the spirit of humility; and he who does humble actions most will be most humble; and he who is most humble will be most emptied of self-righteousness, and therefore will most of all value the Cross of Christ, being least of all sensible of his own good deeds: and the more he does these works, the more will the Holy Spirit dwell with him, according to the promises of Scripture, and the more fully will he come to the knowledge of that mystery which is hid in Christ.[17]

The Tractarians felt that only such a sense of awe before the holy mysteries of God could lead to a condition of humility. And only in humility are we able to cast ourselves on God, in obedience to whom alone lies a knowledge of His Truth. For the Tractarians a humble obedience was not only a sign of one's awareness of the vast mystery of God's dealings but also served as a check on personal pride and vanity. Obedience to the teachings of the Church provided a way of witnessing to both of these deeply felt sentiments.

Much might be said on that mode of witnessing Christ which consists in conforming to His Church. He who simply did what the Church bids him do (if he did no more) would witness a good confession to the world, and one which cannot be hid; and at the same time, with very little, if any, personal display. He does only what he is told to do; he takes no responsibility on himself. The Apostles and Martyrs who founded the Church, the saints in all ages who have adorned it, the Heads of it now alive, all these take from him the weight of his profession, and bear the blame (so to call it) of seeming ostentations. I do not say that irreligious men will not call such a one boastful, or austere, or a hypocrite; that is not the question. The question is, whether in God's judgement he deserves the censure; whether he is not as Christ would have him, really and truly (whatever the world may say) feigning humility to a bold outward profession; whether he is not, in thus acting, preaching Christ without hurting his own pureness, gentleness and modesty of character. If indeed a man stands forth on his own ground, declaring himself as an individual, a witness for Christ, then indeed he is grieving and disturbing the calm spirit given us by God. But God's merciful providence has saved us this temptation, and forbidden us to admit it. He bids us unite together in one, and to shelter our personal profession under the authority of the general body. Thus we show ourselves as lights to the world far more effectively . . . at the same time we do so with far greater secrecy and humility.[18]

The spiritual disposition just described —the awesome sense of divine mystery, the reserve and obedience—was a necessary climate for the development of the most fundamental of the Anglo-Catholic doctrines: the authority of the Church.

The Authority of the Church. The question of authority is the touchstone of any religious system or school. It is the first principle, implied or explicitly acknowledged, on which all else hangs. We have already seen which principles of final authority informed the doctrines of several earlier movements. For the Tractarians the seat of authority is to be found in the ancient traditions and corporate teachings of the Church.

The reasons why the Oxford men looked to *tradition* for their authority are many. The novels of Scott and others contributed to a romantic idealizing of the past. But far more important was the awareness that an unshakable breakwater was required against the inundation of liberal individualism. Yet, appeal could no longer be made to "Scripture alone" —the Bible was the cause, not the cure, of sectarian division. Hume and Bentham were enough to convince Newman of the corrosive, skeptical tendencies of reason. There was additional need of a firm base on which to take a stand against the secular State and Erastianism in the Church. All of these feelings and needs found their answer in an appeal to the ancient Church, and, more specifically, to the principle of Apostolic Succession. This is not to say that the Tractarians were desperately searching for such a foundation and happily fell upon this principle. The High Church party had always looked to the traditions of the Fathers as uniquely authoritative. Hooker, Lancelot Andrews, and, in the Tractarians' own age, John Jebb, had all stressed the importance of apostolic succession. It was what they considered the undeniable truth of the principle, and not its utility, that led the Oxford men to give such preeminence to the doctrine. In any case, it became the *first principle* of the Movement. The encouragement and calm hope and the romance which it gave to the Tractarians' cause in those early years is captured in one of Newman's sermons:

The royal dynasty of the Apostles is far older than all the kingly families which are now on the earth. Every Bishop of the Church whom we now behold is a lineal descendant of St. Peter and St. Paul after the order of a spiritual birth . . . . He, Christ, has continued the line of His apostles onwards through every age, and all troubles and perils of the world. Here then surely is somewhat of encouragement for us amid our loneliness and weakness. The presence of every Bishop suggests a long history of conflicts and trials, sufferings and victories, hopes and fears, through many centuries. His presence at this day is the fruit of them all. He is the living monument of those who are dead. He is the promise of a bold fight and a good confession and a cheerful martyrdom now, if needful, as was instanced in those of olden time. We see their figures on our walls, and their tombs are under our feet; and we trust, nay we are sure, that God will be to us in our day what He was to them.[19]

The theme of apostolic succession runs like a continuous thread through the early Tracts. The arguments are presented with great confidence. It was felt that history clearly demonstrated apostolic succession to be a fact which scarcely could be questioned. And does not our own experience as well as the testimony of Scripture argue strongly for such a succession as the base of authority?

Consider how *natural* is the doctrine of a Succession. When an individual comes to me, claiming to speak in the name of the Most High, it is natural to ask him for his authority. . . . In the case of the Catholic Church, the person referred to, *i.e.*, the Bishop, has received it from a predecessor, and he from another, and so on, till we arrive at the Apostles themselves, and thence Our Lord and Saviour. . . . Lastly, the *argument from Scripture* is surely quite clear to those who honestly wish direction from *practice*. Christ promised He should be with His Apostles always, as ministers of His religion, even unto the end of the world. In one sense the Apostles were to be alive till He came again; but they all died at the natural time. Does it not follow that there are those now alive who represent them? Now, who were the most probable representatives of them in the generation next their death?[20]

Succession did not constitute the only argument for the authority of the Church. In the sermons and later writings, a wider and deeper base is found for the Church's claims in the *tradition* of the ancient and undivided Church, particularly the teachings of the Fathers. Of course, the appeal to the ancient traditions of the Fathers was not new with the Tractarians. Those traditions had long been appealed to by the old High Church party, and among Roman Catholics they were basic to Gallican apologists like Jacques Bénigne Bossuet (1627–1704). The most important statement of the Tractarian position, vis-à-vis Protestantism and Rome, is found in Newman's *Lectures on the Prophetical Office of the Church, Viewed Relatively to Romanism and Popular Protestantism*, published in 1837. Newman's thesis is that both the Protestant appeal to the "Bible alone" and the Roman claim to infallibility are historically untenable. Newman did not deny that the Bible, as the Articles state, contains all things necessary to salvation but, rather, that the individual unaided reason is able to interpret the Bible properly. Private judgment concerning Scripture is no ground of authority; it is an invitation to chaos.

The Bible is a small book; anyone may possess it; and everyone, unless he is very humble, will think he is able to understand it. And therefore, I say, controversy is *easier* among Protestants, because anyone can controvert; easier but not shorter; because though all sects agree together as to the *standard* of faith, viz. the Bible, yet no two agree as to the *interpreter* of the Bible, but each person makes himself the interpreter, so that what seemed at first sight a means of peace, turns out to be a chief occasion or cause of discord .... Accordingly acute men among them see that the very elementary notion which they have adopted ... is a self-destructive principle.[21]

The Tractarians rightly observed that the Scriptures were not originally written as systematic essays on doctrine but were received by Christian communities which had already appropriated the common, unwritten faith of the Church. Newman did not deny the Protestant principle of responsible, personal judgment concerning the teachings of Scripture. Rather, the deeper question was what are the means which are to direct our choice of interpretations. In addition to the internal means such as natural experience and reason, there are external means of equal place: "The existing Church, Tradition, Catholicity, Learning, Antiquity, and the National Faith." According to Newman, since Scripture was not written "to instruct in doctrine," but

with intimations and implications of the faith, the qualifications for rightly apprehending it

are so rare and high, that a prudent man, to say nothing of piety, will not risk his salvation on the chance of his having them; but will read it with the aid of those subsidiary guides which have ever been supplied as if to meet our need. I would not deny as an abstract proposition that a Christian may gain the whole truth from the Scriptures, but would maintain that the chances are very seriously against a given individual. I would not deny but rather maintain, that a religious, wise and intellectually gifted man will succeed; but who answers to this description but the collective Church? There, indeed, such qualifications might be supposed to exist; what is wanting in one member being supplied by another, and the contrary errors of individuals eliminated by their combination. The Catholic Church may truly be said almost infallibly to interpret Scripture.[22]

All the Tractarians taught that the ancient tradition was the indispensable guide to interpreting Scripture. The Church prepares the mind of the individual for the proper reading of the Bible. In fact, it is clearly demonstrable that before the canon of the New Testament was established, the unwritten tradition actually served as a test for the apostles' own writings. Tradition was, in the words of Keble, "divinely appointed in the Church as the touchstone of canonical Scripture itself." The Tractarians agreed with the Romanists that authority rested in Scripture *and* the ancient traditions of the Church. But how, after all, is such a general concept as ancient tradition to be understood? Newman sums up the Tractarian view in *The Prophetical Office* as follows:

Let us understand what is meant by saying that antiquity is of authority in religious questions. Both Romanists and ourselves maintain as follows: That whatever doctrine the primitive ages unanimously attest, whether by consent of Fathers, or by Councils, or by the events of history, or by controversies, or in whatever way, whatever may fairly and reasonably be considered to be the universal belief of those ages is to be received as coming from the apostles.... The rule or canon which I have been explaining is best known as expressed in the words of Vincentius of Lérins in his celebrated treatise upon the tests of heresy and error; viz., that that is to be received as apostolic which has been taught "always, everywhere, and by all."* Catholicity, antiquity, and consent of the Fathers is the proper evidence of the fidelity or apostolicity of a professed tradition. Infant baptism, for instance, must have been appointed by the apostles or we should not find it received so early, so generally, with such a silence concerning its introduction.... The washing of feet enjoined in the thirteenth chapter of St. John is not a necessary rite or a sacrament because it has never been so observed—did Christ or his apostles intend otherwise, it would follow (which is surely impossible) that a new and erroneous view of our Lord's words arose even in the apostles' lifetime, and was from the first everywhere substituted for the true.... The sabbatical rest is changed from the Sabbath to the Lord's Day because it has never been otherwise since Christianity was a religion.[23]

The confidence with which the Tractarians asserted the canon of antiquity as the foundation of their doctrine of authority is somewhat astonishing to an age sensitive to the findings of modern historical-critical research. For the Tractarians there appears to be little problem concerning the purity or unity of the apostolic traditions. Part of their assurance was due to an inference drawn from a conviction agreed upon by all Christians alike—viz., that there was an original revelation which has not been

superseded and which was given as *the* means of salvation. If one believes in such a supernatural gift of God, can one easily doubt the truth of a belief or practice that has been held by God's Church from the beginning, everywhere, and at all times? William Palmer reflects the characteristic fervor and assurance with which this argument was proposed:

If any given doctrine was universally believed by those Christians who had been instructed by the apostles and the disciples of the apostles; if this doctrine was received by all succeeding generations as sacred and divine, and strictly conformable to those scriptures which were read and expounded in every church; this belief, one and uniform, received by all churches, delivered through the ages, triumphing over novel and contradictory doctrines which attempt to pollute it, guarded with jealous care ... and after a lapse of eighteen hundred years believed in firmly by the overwhelming mass of Christians among all nations as when it was first promulgated; *such a doctrine must be a truth of revelation. It rests on evidence not inferior to that which attests the truth of Christianity. Is it possible that the infinite majority of Christians in all ages can have mistaken or adulterated their own religion? ... If so, then they may have been equally deceived as to the authenticity of Scripture, as to the truth of the mission of our Saviour; and the whole fabric of revelation totters to its base. Hence I maintain that Christians cannot possibly admit that any doctrine established by universal tradition can be otherwise than DIVINELY, INFALLIBLY, TRUE.*[24] (Italics added.)

The Tractarians were certain that the unwritten, authoritative tradition of the apostolic Church could be established as *historical fact* with the same kind of tools of research one would apply to any historical question. If the testimony of the Fathers, the Councils, and the ancient customs are rejected as uncertain, then

* "quod semper, quod ubique, quod ab omnibus."

eo ipso all human testimony is uncertain, and there can be no facts of history. But, they believed, there is no good reason for such radical skepticism. The authentic documents give us clear evidence of the primitive tradition, and it is here that the Tractarians built their case against Rome. The question was naturally raised as to how in fact the Anglican doctrine of authority differed from that of Rome. Did they not both appeal to the ancient tradition as the true interpreter of Scripture and guide in faith and practice? Yes, but in the Roman system there is another canon which supersedes even that of Vincent of Lérins, namely:

They profess to appeal to primitive Christianity; we honestly take their ground, as holding it ourselves; but when the controversy grows animated, and descends into details, they suddenly leave it and desire to finish the dispute on some other field . . . . In truth there is a tenet in their theology which assumes quite a new position in relation to the rest, when we pass from the abstract and quiescent theory to the practical workings of the system. The infallibility of the existing Church is then found to be its first principle . . . . Whatever principles they profess in theory . . . yet when they come to particulars, when they have to prove this or that article of their creed, they supersede the appeal to Scripture and antiquity by the pretence of the infallibility of the Church, thus solving the whole question by a summary and final interpretation both of antiquity and of Scripture.[25]

Newman points out that the Vincentian canon, to which the Roman theologians frequently appealed, is altogether silent on the subject of the Church's infallibility, let alone the Pope's supreme authority. He challenges the Romanists to prove their doctrines apostolic. Newman asserts that they are not continuous with antiquity but "innovations," traditions of

men. For the Tractarians the departures of the post-Tridentine Roman Catholic Church brought it far from the pure stream of antiquity, the Church of England alone having preserved the true, apostolic marks of the undivided Church. Today when one reads the Tractarians on the authority of the Church, one senses a naïve smugness reflecting an extraordinarily insular view of the history of the Church. This is especially pronounced in Isaac Williams' "The Church in England," though the poem is not atypical of Tractarian apologetic.

When the infatuate Council named of Trent
Clogg'd up the Catholic course of the true
    Faith,
Troubling the stream of pure antiquity,
And the wide channel in its bosom took
Crude novelties, scarce known as that of old;
Then many a schism overleaped the banks,
Genevese, Lutheran, Scotch diversities.
Our Church, though straiten'd sore 'tween
    craggy walls,
Kept her true course, unchanging and the
    same,
Known by that ancient clearness, pure and
    free,
With which she sprung from neath the Throne
    of God.[26]

The Tractarian doctrine of authority was founded on an appeal to history. Yet, except for Newman, its view of the historical was primitivist and static, just at the time when Europe was beginning to think of history in organic and evolutionary categories. It was the period of Hegelian ascendancy on the Continent, but the Oxford men did not read the Hegelian theologians, not even the Catholic Möhler. Brilioth has rightly concluded that the Tractarian appeal to antiquity "was no result of a learned inquiry" but "a bold postulate," "profoundly unhistorical and doomed to failure." The reason was that the Oxford school never clearly defined what it meant by Christian antiquity, when it ended, or how the diverse developments of Christian experience in the early centuries represented a discernible unity of faith and practice. The Vincentian canon appealed to a standard that was, if not unreal, at least historically elusive. The strength of the Tractarian conception of the Church was in its appeal to apostolicity. Yet it was an appeal made with zeal and deep feeling but fraught with difficulties. More significantly, it was an appeal made at the expense of Catholicity and Unity. Newman came to realize this in the summer of 1839 while working on the history of the Monophysite controversy. It forced him to rethink not only his concept of the Church but also his view of history. The result was his essay on *The Development of Christian Doctrine*, the rejection of the static, Tractarian concept of history, and a bold new apologetic for an organic, evolutionary theory of doctrinal development. It also paved the way for his entrance into the Roman Catholic Church.

The Doctrine of Faith. *Faith and Reason.* As one would expect, there is a close relationship between the Tractarian doctrine of authority and its view of faith and reason. Behind both is the deep sense of the mystery of divine revelation, that this truth is a gift of grace and requires moral submission. In the Tractarian writings on faith there is a clear distrust of the traditional "evidences" of Christianity. Most of the Tractarians had a strong element of metaphysical skepticism in them. This was due in part to their own piety, which found the rational demonstrations of Paley arid and cold,

and to the influence of Bishop Butler and Coleridge.* Newman in particular has been called a philosophical skeptic, who, surrendering to the authority of the Church, was able to revel in the irrational and credulous. T. H. Huxley declared that if he were writing a primer of infidelity, he would draw generously from the writings of Newman! The skeptical element is there, but to refer to the Tractarians as such is inexcusably misleading. The Tractarian view of faith and reason, with Newman's doctrine representing its most subtle expression, was profound and influential.

It is important, first of all, to appreciate what the Tractarians meant by reason and its role in human life. By reason they meant "mere" reason, demonstration, or proof—what Coleridge called the Understanding or "the mind of the flesh." Such reason has its vital role in human life, but it is not the sole guide or rule; especially is it not the root or final warrant of faith, as maintained by the Rationalists. But such it had become; reason, since the Reformation, had been ascendant, encroaching on and judging all other provinces of life. In the eyes of the Tractarians it had become the sole arbiter of truth.

Newman addressed himself to this situation in an early sermon of 1831, entitled "The Usurpations of Reason." Newman's theme is that while reason is but one faculty of human life—moral sense, feeling, and imagination being others—it has been made unduly "judge of those truths which are subjected to

---

* Butler's influence on the Tractarians, especially on Newman, is pronounced. Coleridge influenced many of the Oxford men, although Newman did not read him until 1835. Nevertheless, Newman acknowledged that he found Coleridge's views congenial.

another part of our nature." The fact of the case is that reason alone is peculiarly unsuited to make such judgments in morality and religion, for example. It is clearly taught throughout Scripture "that there is no necessary connexion between the intellectual and moral principles of our nature; that on religious subjects we may prove anything or overthrow anything, and can arrive at truth but accidentally, if we merely investigate what is commonly called reason."[27] On this matter Scripture is supported by common experience. Why should Christians be desirous of disguising the fact that many men of intellectual brilliance are indifferent to revealed religion, unless Christians have been falsely led to believe that there is a necessary connection between reason and man's religious sense?

Yet is it not a fact . . . when the humblest village may show us that those persons who turn out badly—are commonly the very men who have received more than the ordinary share of intellectual gifts? . . . Thus much it seems to show us, that the powers of the intellect . . . do not necessarily lead us in the direction of our moral instincts, or confirm them; but if the agreement between the two be but a matter of accident, what testimony do we gain from the mere reason to the truths of religion?[28]

What Newman found repellent in theological rationalists like Paley was the attempt to prove Christianity independently of the grace of faith. Rationalistic apologetic is wrong because it

draws men away from the true view of Christianity and leads them to think that Faith is mainly the result of arguments, that religious Truth is a legitimate matter of disputation. . . . For is not this error, the common and fatal error, of the world, to think itself a

Judge of Religious Truth without preparation of heart?[29]

What disturbed Newman was the rationalist assumption that any men, mentally endowed, could rightfully discuss religion and enter into disputes about the most sacred mysteries "in a careless frame of mind, in their hours of recreation, over the wine cup." "Is it wonderful," Newman asks, "that they so frequently end in becoming Indifferentists?"

Not only do the rationalists fail to take account of faith as the necessary foundation of religious knowledge; they overlook the fact that the so-called natural "evidences" are compelling only to those who already believe—but "when men have not already recognized God's voice within them, ineffective." Indeed, says Newman, "It is a great question whether Atheism is not as philosophically consistent with the phenomena of the physical world, taken by themselves, as the doctrine of a creative and governing Power."[31]

According to Newman, religious faith and truth may on occasion be justified by reason, but reason can never *produce* faith. Religious knowledge arises from *moral obedience*, out of the hunger and thirst after righteousness. Faith is essentially a moral principle. Pusey states the Tractarian view as follows:

Scripture gives us but one rule, one test, one way of attaining the truth, *i.e.*, whether we are keeping God's commandments or not, whether we are conformed to this world, or whether we are, by the renewing of our minds, being transformed into His image . . . . The knowledge is not in our own power to attain. It is the gift of God, vouchsafed or withheld by Him, and each more or less according as man becomes conformed to the world and things earthly or to God and things divine . . . . It is in vain that people will even strive to retain a belief in high and holy things, while their life is wrong. They will strive to convince themselves, but it is in vain; they study but it is of no use . . . . As their thoughts are more and more occupied with the world, holy truth becomes fainter and fainter . . . .[32]

What distinguishes the evidences of reason from the assurances of faith is what today we would call the existential factor —what the Tractarians called the moral sense. The proofs of reason are impersonal. A man does not make the proofs; they exist independently of him and require but a hearing to elicit acceptance. There is no room for choice. But a man is responsible for his faith, because, as Newman asserts, "he is responsible for his likings and dislikings, his hopes and his opinions, on all of which his faith depends." In other words, faith has to do with those things which cannot be measured, demonstrated, proved but which require an act of moral judgment.

Faith is created in the mind, not so much by facts, as by probabilities; and since probabilities have no definite ascertained value, and are reducible to no scientific standard, what are such to each individual, depends on his moral temperament. A good man and a bad man will think very different things probable. In the judgement of a rightly disposed mind, objects are desirable and obtainable, which irreligious men will consider to be fancies.[33]

Newman acknowledges that faith does not require evidence as strong as is demanded by reason. Why?

For this reason, because it is swayed by antecedent considerations . . . . Faith is influenced by previous notices, prepossessions, and (in the good sense of the word) prejudices; but Reason, by direct and definite proof. The mind that believes is acted upon by its own

hopes, fears and existing opinions. . . . Faith is a principle of action, and action does not allow time for minute and finished investigations.[34]

The disparity between assent of faith and that of reason may not actually be as great as men might think. Newman had read Hume and did Hume not convince us that even our most assured empirical knowledge is grounded in habit and at best probable?

However full and however precise our producible grounds may be, however systematic our method, however clear and tangible our evidence, yet when our argument is traced down to its simple elements, there must be something assumed ultimately which is incapable of proof . . . . For instance, we trust our senses, and that in spite of their often deceiving us. They even contradict each other at times, yet we trust them. But even were they ever consistent, never unfaithful, yet their fidelity would not thereby be proved. We consider that there is so strong an antecedent probability that they are faithful, that we dispense with proof. We take the point for granted; or if we have grounds for it, these lie in our secret belief in the stability of nature, or in the preserving presence and uniformity of Divine Providence—which, again, are points assumed . . . so it need not be weakness or rashness, if upon a certain presentiment of mind we trust to the fidelity of testimony offered for a revelation . . . . Nothing, then, which Scripture says about Faith, however startling it may be at first sight, is inconsistent with the state in which we find ourselves by nature with reference to the acquisition of knowledge generally—a state in which we must assume something to prove anything, and can gain nothing without a venture.[35]

If the assent of reason is not free of assumptions, its probabilities are, nevertheless, based on a stricter and more exacting evidence than the rather vague and slender evidence of faith. Newman acknowledged this. What, then, is to safeguard faith from all manner of prejudice and bigotry, credulity, and superstition? "Antecedent probabilities may be equally available for what is true, and what pretends to be true, for a revelation and its counterfeit, for Paganism, or Mohametanism, or Christianity." Newman felt the difficulty, but he rejected the rationalists' ready answer, "Cultivate the reason." Reason alone is no safeguard of true faith; the true safeguard is love.

> The safeguard of Faith is a right state of heart. This it is that gives it birth; it also disciplines it. This is what protects it from bigotry, credulity and fanaticism. It is holiness or dutifulness, or the new creation, or the spiritual mind, however we word it, which is the quickening and illuminating principle of true Faith. . . . It is Love which forms it out of the rude chaos into an image of Christ; or in scholastic language, justifying Faith, whether in Pagan, Jew or Christian, is *fides formata charitate.*[36]

For the Tractarians, a faith which is safeguarded by a holy and obedient life is an intellectual act, a form of knowledge, justified as reasonable and open to the scrutiny of reason, though not solely dependent on reason. Newman summed up the Tractarian view as follows:

> Such, then, under all circumstances is real Faith; a presumption, yet not a mere chance conjecture—a reaching forward, yet not of excitement or of passion—a moving forward in the twilight, yet not without clue or direction; a movement from something known to something unknown, kept in the narrow path of truth by the Law of dutifulness which inhabits it, the Light of heaven which animates and guides it . . . . It is itself an intellectual act, and takes its character from the moral state of the agent. It is perfected not by mental

cultivation but by obedience. It does not change its nature or its function, when thus perfected. It remains what it is in itself, an initial principle of action; but it becomes changed in its quality, as being made spiritual. It is, as before, a presumption, but the presumption of a serious, sober, thoughtful, pure, affectionate and devout mind. It acts because it is Faith; but the direction, consistency, and precision of its acts, it gains from Love.[37]

Faith and Sanctification. The important place which the Tractarians gave to moral obedience as the ground of true Faith made them extremely suspicious of the Protestant doctrine of "justification by faith *alone.*" The Tractarians interpreted Luther as teaching that justification was simply a "declaring" righteous, a gift of grace which was to be understood as distinct from a holy or sanctified life itself. They believed such a doctrine contributed to an antinomian disregard of good works and was therefore a dangerous threat to the religious life. For the Tractarians, Justification and Sanctification are one, inseparable gift.

The Tractarian doctrine finds its definitive statement in Newman's *Lectures on Justification* of 1838. The lectures represent the best theological work of the Movement and are a classic example of the Anglican *Via Media.* Newman attempts to show that the Protestant emphasis on justification by faith alone and the Roman emphasis on justification by obedience are both defective. The issue had been put as follows:

> One side says that the righteousness in which God accepts us is *inherent*, wrought in us by the grace flowing from Christ's Atonement; the other says that it is *external*, reputed, nominal, being Christ's own sacred and most perfect obedience on earth, viewed by a merciful God *as if* it were ours. And issue is

joined on the following question, whether justification means in Scripture *counting* us righteous, or *making* us righteous.[38] (Italics added.)

For Newman, this way of putting the issue is mistaken. No one, he asserts, denies that justification is a free act of divine mercy, but neither is it possible to believe that God's grace leaves the soul in the unregenerate state in which it was found. It stands to reason that a soul that is justified is not in the same state as if it had not been justified. "Surely it is a strange paradox to say that . . . the glory of His pronouncing us righteous lies in His leaving us unrighteous." What, then, is the state of the justified man? It is not enough, Newman contends, to assert with Luther that "a state of justification consists in the foregiveness of sins, or in acceptance, or in adoption" for all these things are God's acts.

When faith is said to be the inward principle of acceptance, the question rises, what gives to faith its acceptableness? Why is faith more acceptable than unbelief? Cannot we give any reason at all for it, or can we conceive unbelief being appointed the instrument of justification? Surely not; faith is acceptable as having something in it which unbelief has not; that something, what is it? It must be God's grace if God's grace acts *in* the soul and not merely externally. . . . If it acts in us . . . then the having that grace or that presence, and not faith, which is its result, must be the real token, the real state of a justified man.[39]

In Newman's opinion, Justification is not only "counting" righteous but the actual "making" righteous, the imparting to the soul of a supernatural quality of grace. It is the actual indwelling of the divine: "I mean the *habitation* in us of God the Father and the Word Incar-

nate through the Holy Ghost . . . . *This is to be justified, to receive the divine presence within us and be made a temple of the Holy Ghost.*"[40] Salvation, therefore, does not consist only of being forgiven our sins but in a life of *holiness*. Newman can even say that if a man "is justified and accepted, *he has ceased to be a sinner*. The Gospel only knows of justified saints; if a saint sins, he ceases to be justified and becomes a *condemned* sinner."[41] Here we see that strain of moralism that many commentators have found at the very heart of Tractarian piety. A man cannot tell he has faith by feeling himself a sinner, or by consciousness of his dependence on God, or even by praising God and resolving to live according to His will. Why?

Because there is an immeasurable distance between feeling right and doing right. A man may have all these good thoughts and emotions, yet (if he has not yet hazarded them to the experiment of practice), he cannot promise himself that he has any sound and permanent principle at all. Though a man spoke like an angel, I would not believe him on the mere ground of his speaking . . . . Do fervent thoughts make faith *living*? St. James tells us otherwise. He tells us *works*, deeds of obedience, are the life of faith.[42]

The Tractarians believed that righteousness, being maintained and enlarged by the faithful use of God's grace in works of obedience, admits of more and less.

When we compare the various orders of just and acceptable beings with one another, we see that though they all are in God's favour, some may be more "pleasant," "acceptable," "righteous," than others, that is, may have more of the light of God's countenance shed on them; as a glorious saint is more acceptable than one still in the flesh. In this sense, then, *justification does admit of*

increase and of degree; and whether we say justi-
fication depends on faith or on obedience, in the
same degree that faith or obedience grows so does
justification. And again, if justification is conveyed peculiarly through the sacraments . . .
so must [they] be the instrument of a higher
justification. On the other hand, those who are
declining in their obedience, as they are
quenching the light within them, so are they
diminishing their justification.[43] (Italics added.)

Here we are at the center of the Tractarian doctrine. Justification/Sanctifica-
tion is an intrinsic quality or substance of
the soul whose presence is witnessed by a
holy and obedient life—the sacraments
being the special means of imparting this
very presence of Christ in the soul. True
faith, then, is the actual indwelling of
divine grace, confirmed in a life of good
works, especially through sacramental
obedience. What distinguishes the Tractarian doctrine of faith is its stress on the
objectivity of sanctifying grace transmitted through the outward and visible
sacraments and ordinances of the Church.
These sacramental means are efficacious in
their operation independent of subjective
feeling or moods. The Church is not a
voluntary fellowship of likeminded believers; it is *the* divinely appointed means
of grace.

The Sacramental Principle. The
Tractarians were not exceptional in looking to the Incarnation as the mysterious
foundation of redemption. They did,
however, give special attention to one
aspect of the doctrine. As the Incarnation
is the perfect indwelling of the divine in
the human, it is the precondition of the
divine nature being imparted to our
human nature. Christ, therefore, is the
firstborn of a new human creation:
deified man. Following St. Athanasius'
words, "He became man that we might

be made divine," Pusey writes that "He
came to Deify our nature by His own
indwelling in us."

For the Tractarians this sanctifying or
deifying of our fallen human nature is
most often spoken of in relation to the
ministration of the Sacraments. And they
are not averse to referring to the sacramental elements as "the Food of Immortality," since grace is conceived as the
infusion of an objective reality in the
most substantial sense. This high, mystical
doctrine of the sacramental imputation
and indwelling of the divine is especially
prominent in Pusey's sermons. Since
holiness is the actual presence of Christ's
virtues in the soul, Pusey can speak
of the Sacraments as "the channels
whereby . . . He conveys these Exceeding
Gifts to us. . . . All of which we have, we
have in Him, by being made members of
Him. And members of Him we are made
and preserved through His Sacraments."[44]

The essentiality and objectivity of the
Sacraments is exemplified in the Tractarian writings on Baptismal Regeneration, especially in Pusey's Tract Sixty-
seven, entitled "Scriptural Views of
Holy Baptism." Throughout the Tract
Pusey stresses the theme that Infant Baptism is a pledge that God's forgiveness
and regeneration do not depend on the
faith of the recipient, since the infant is
unable to respond in faith. The child
receives God's grace by virtue of the
Church's faith. And in no way other than
Baptism can there be a complete washing
away of sins.

We are not said, namely, to be born again *of*
faith, or love, or prayer, or any grace which
God worketh in us, but to be "born *of* water
and the Spirit (Jn. 3:5) . . . . Our life in Christ
is, throughout, represented as commencing
when we are by baptism made members of

Christ and Children of God. That life may through our negligence afterwards decay, or be choked, or smothered, or well-nigh extinguished ... but a *commencement* of life in Christ *after* baptism, a death unto sin and a new birth unto righteousness at any other period than at that one first introduction into God's covenant, is as little consonant with the general representations of Holy Scripture as a commencement of physical life long after our natural birth is with the order of his providence.[45]

Because the Tractarians held such a high conception of Baptism, it being the only means of losing the blight of original sin, they also took a very serious view of post-Baptismal sin. The reason was that receiving the gift of baptismal grace in no way in itself insured the recipient against losing it. As Robert Wilberforce was to comment, "it is sometimes forgotten that baptism does not determine what *shall be* men's future state, but what *is* their present position."[46] Every sin committed after Baptism, the Tractarians believed, weakens the effect of baptismal grace. This explains in part the Tractarian introspection and scrupulous concern for daily devotions, penitence, and good works— all of which were integral to its piety. It also partially explains the central place of the Sacrament of the Eucharist, for if Baptism gives the soul its spiritual birth, the Eucharist is the spiritual food which sustains the soul during its earthly pilgrimage, keeping it unstained from the world. It is *the* Sacrament through which the soul is continually renewed and maintained. The sacramental principle made it quite natural for the Tractarians to speak of the elements of the Eucharist as a "heavenly feast," a "spiritual food" and to equate failure in receiving the Sacrament with "the starvation and death of the soul." John Keble describes the

receiving of Christ in the Sacrament by just such an image.

Now the gift of the Holy Eucharist is Christ himself .... And how can we conceive even Power Almighty to bring it more closely and more directly home to each one of us, than when his Word commands and his Spirit enables us to receive him as it were spiritual meat and drink ? entering into and penetrating thoroughly the whole being of the renewed man, somewhat in the same way as the virtue of wholesome meat and drink diffuses itself through a healthful body ....[47]

This indwelling of Christ in which He becomes "one with us, and we with Him," is the literal infusion and presence of God's grace and power in the soul, the closest possible union of God and man. The Tractarians were one in affirming the *real presence* of Christ in the Eucharist— that we receive, really and spiritually, the flesh and blood of the Incarnate Son which are present beneath the natural elements of bread and wine. Yet their writings lack any precise definition as to what they meant by Christ's real presence. They clearly denied the Roman doctrine of transubstantiation and the Zwinglian conception of the elements as symbolic "memorials"— but they resisted any attempt to give a dogmatic or metaphysical explanation of what they felt was a most holy and supernatural mystery. Pusey's most explicit statement is typical in its vagueness.

The presence of which our Lord speaks has been termed sacramental, supernatural, mystical, ineffable, as opposed *not* to what is real, but to what is natural. The word has been chosen to express, not our knowledge, but our ignorance .... We know not the manner of his presence, save that it is not according to the natural presence of our Lord's human flesh. But it is a presence without us, not only within us . . . . It is not a presence simply in the soul of the receiver . . . . But while the consecrated elements remain in their natural substances, still, since the Lord says, "This is my body," "This is my blood," the Church of England believes that "under the form of bread and wine," so consecrated, we "receive the body and blood of our Saviour Christ."[48]

What was of point to the Tractarians was not the mode of the real presence but its *reality*. And because the Sacrament was conceived as the spiritual food, indispensable to the health of the soul, Tractarian sacramental piety was marked by frequent Communion. Since the Eucharist has as its end the infusion of Divine grace, "the cleansing of our sins, the refining of our corruptions, the repairing of our decays," is it any wonder, Pusey asks, that where the Eucharist is forgotten, "love should have waxed cold and corruptions abound?" Is it strange that "the Divine life becomes so rare, all higher instances of it so few and faint when 'the stay and staff,' the strength of that life is willingly forfeited? How should there be the fulness of the Divine life, amid all but a month-long fast from our 'daily Bread'?"[49]

According to the sacramental principle, the sacraments and ordinances of the Church are the divinely appointed means of growth in devotion and holiness. Frequent Communion not only sustains us but teaches us a deeper discipline and a reverence for the outward and visible signs through which the spiritual grace is made known. While the Tractarians were generally conservative as regards ritual and ceremonial, their high doctrine of the Sacraments led naturally to a greater appreciation of the forms of worship and their role in inciting a greater spirituality. According to the

sacramental principle, the whole of nature shows forth symbolically the glory of God. The things of sense—water, bread, color, movement—are to be used to make known and bear witness to the great acts of God's providence and mercy. Ritual, ceremonial, the adornment of churches, spiritual disciplines, the so-called "forms" of religion are not to be scorned; they serve as the natural vehicles "to make the beauty of holiness visible," thereby encouraging a more reverent worship and tutoring us in a deeper spirituality. The Tractarians realized that these symbols and forms could teach religious truths and mold Christian character unconsciously, as it were, where more prosaic, didactic methods fail. Faith must receive the assent of the whole man, not only his intellect.

These symbols have I gazed on long and oft,
Threading their morals and their mysteries,
And thence beguiled to deeper, holier,
    thoughts.
And surely heart-expanding Charity,
If ought she finds that ministers to good,
To others would like instruments supply.
For objects pleading through the usual sense
Are stronger than discourses to the ear
More powerfully they reach and move the
    soul.

The Church 'tis thought, is wakening through
    the land
And seeking vent for the o'erloaded hearts
Which she has kindled—pours her forth
    anew—
Breathes life in ancient worship—from their
    graves
Summons the slumbering Arts to wait on her,
Music, and Architecture, varied forms
Of Painting, Sculpture, and of Poetry;
These are allied to sense, but soul and sense
Must both alike find wing and rise to Heaven;
Both soul and body took the Son of man,
Both soul and body must in Him serve God.[50]

The sacramental principle not only encouraged the use of sacramental forms, thereby inculcating a profound devotion and a greater reverence for the Church, but required a view of the Church as itself the visible, divinely appointed channel of God's grace. It conceived of the Church as God's own earthly Tabernacle, the very Body of Christ. For does the Incarnation not teach that the Word became flesh? It therefore follows that "where His Flesh is, there He is, and we receiving It receive Him, and receiving Him, are joined on to Him through His Flesh to the Father, and He dwelling in us, dwell in Him, and with Him in God."[51] Through the Communion of the Sacrament, Christ and his Church are made One. "There is then One Man Christ, Head and Body. What is His Body? His Church, the Apostle saith, 'for we are Members of His Body.'"[52] As members of His Body, the Church possesses the very virtues of Christ's holiness because "she is His Body, indwelt by His Divinity . . . living by His Life, moved by His Will, informed by His Spirit, [It is] imperishable because as the Head forsaketh not the members, so neither He the Body He hath taken."[52]

Such a sacramental view of the Church as Christ's mystical Body prepared the way for a conception of the Church as *the extension of the Incarnation*.* One discovers at the heart of Tractarian faith an incarnational theology which joins inseparably the Incarnation, the Sacraments, the Church, and the holy life. As Professor Fairweather has remarked,

To their minds it was no less clearly a part of the Christian message that the saving person

and work of the Mediator were effectually "re-presented" in the Church by means of certain sacramental "extensions of the Incarnation." It was, they insisted, supremely fitting that the life-giving flesh and blood of God's Eternal Son who was made man should be communicated through fleshly signs wrought by human hands. Indeed, they were prepared to argue that the failure to recognize the "extensions of the Incarnation" stemmed from a feeble apprehension of the two-fold truth of the Incarnation itself—on the one hand, that man's salvation comes from God alone; on the other, that God's saving action really penetrates and transforms man's world and man's life.[54]

When viewed in its fullness and richness, the thought of the Oxford Movement is in essentials remarkably uniform and consistent. Their conception of the Christian life, their view of the sacraments, their concern for the integrity of the Church and its ministry, and their doctrine of authority are all strikingly interdependent—this despite the fact that the Tractarians were not systematic theologians.

The Movement which had its beginnings in Oxford in the 1830's came to an end by 1845, but by that time its influence was already felt throughout the English Church and beyond. The ideals and principles of the early Tractarians were carried on by Keble and Pusey and taken up by younger men, such as Church and Liddon. Anglo-Catholicism did not remain static but grew and changed. Yet these later developments cannot be understood without Keble, Newman, and Pusey. The long-term theological influence of the Oxford Movement is difficult to trace because many of its results are indirect and have been unconsciously appropriated in later years by very different traditions. It is true that a

* For an early development in this direction see, for example, Robert Wilberforce's important *The Doctrine of the Incarnation* (1848).

good many of the Tractarian doctrines and interpretations were repudiated or proven historically indefensible within a generation of their publication. Yet many influences are felt even today. The Tractarian view of faith as having its ground in moral judgment is perhaps the most significant contribution of the Movement to modern philosophy of religion. In the realm of biblical studies, no modern theologian can now overlook the role of tradition in the development of a hermeneutical theory or in considering the question of biblical authority. The Tractarians thus contributed in no small way to the rejection of a naïve doctrine of *sola Scriptura*. The Tractarian concern for apostolicity, catholicity, and unity compelled them to take with utmost seriousness the question of the One, Undivided Church. This concern contributed to the beginnings of the modern Ecumenical discussion and the search for reunion not only with Rome but with all Christians in one visible Church. All of these results are there but are not easy to trace out concretely.

The Tractarian influence on worship and religious discipline is much easier to document. The role of the Oxford revival in the introduction into services, not only Anglican but Reformed and Free Church as well, of such practices as regular Communion, liturgical music, and increased ceremonial is well attested. The Movement also had a lasting influence upon the devotional life of the Church, as reflected in the increase in daily services, Lenten observance, private confession, and in the opening of many communities for the "religious" in the English Church in the last half of the nineteenth century. In all this, the Movement contributed to a renewed and deepened awareness of the holy; to a vivid sense of the

awesome mystery of the divine, and the peace and joy that comes from obedient service.

If the more strictly theological doctrines of the Tractarians failed to have a wide or lasting influence, it was largely due to the fact that the Oxford men had insulated themselves from the new movements in science and history that were just appearing and would not be put down. The Tractarians and some of their followers of the next generation were not prepared to tackle the enormous questions that the new theories of Darwin and the German biblical critics were beginning to pose. As a result, many of their doctrines were merely anachronistic by 1860. Frederick Denison Maurice, a contemporary of the Movement, who was at first attracted and then repelled by its doctrine, aptly remarked that the tragic weakness of the Tractarians consisted "in opposing to the spirit of the present age the spirit of a former age, instead of the ever-living and active Spirit of God." It was not until the last years of the century that a group of Anglican theologians of Catholic mind were able to reconcile their Catholicism with the new science and the new criticism. Out of this convergence of tradition and criticism emerged the movement known as *Liberal Catholicism*. Only then was Tractarian theology again tenable, but only because it was developed and clothed in quite new modes of thought. Anglo-Catholicism at the turn of the century had, in the words of Professor Chadwick,

abandoned most of the positions characteristic of Dr. Pusey upon the authority of the Church. They had accepted a far looser idea of Biblical inspiration. They had rejected the belief that the ancient and undivided Church was inerrant. But in their sweeping revolution they sought to preserve what they believed to be of essential value in the position which Newman, Keble, and Pusey had taken up. . . . They [the Tractarians] provided for the liberal movement in England a ballast which helped it not to be swept along by the excesses of evolutionary theology and philosophy.[55]

Before examining the development of Liberal Catholicism, we must first turn to those tumultuous movements of religious thought in Germany and in mid-Victorian England. It was through those fires that theology was now to be tested.

NOTES

1. J. A. Froude, *Short Studies on Great Subjects* (1886), IV, 239.
2. *Romanticism in American Theology* (Chicago, 1961), p. 78.
3. *The Oxford Movement*, ed. Eugene R. Fairweather, Library of Protestant Thought (New York, 1964), p. 5.
4. Ibid., p. 48.
5. Ibid., pp. 41–42.
6. Ibid., pp. 55–56.
7. Ibid., p. 59.
8. John Henry Newman, *Apologia pro Vita Sua* (London, 1965), pp. 142–143.
9. R. W. Church, *The Oxford Movement 1833–1845* (London, 1892), pp. 264–265.
10. *Apologia*, op. cit., pp. 184–185.
11. Ibid., p. 197.
12. *The Oxford Movement*, op. cit., p. 153.
13. *Parochial Sermons* (London, 1839), Vol. IV, No. 13, p. 239.
14. Ibid., Vol. I, No. 16, p. 233 f.
15. Ibid., Vol. VI, No. 6, pp. 80–81.
16. Isaac Williams, *The Cathedral* (1838), pp. 210–211.
17. *The Oxford Movement*, op. cit., pp. 263–266.
18. *Parochial Sermons*, op. cit., Vol. I, No. 12, pp. 176 f.
19. Ibid., Vol. III, No. 17, p. 272 f.
20. *Tracts for the Times* (London, 1834), Vol. I, Tract Seven, "The Episcopal Church Apostolical," p. 3.
21. *The Oxford Movement*, op. cit., pp. 114–115.
22. *The Prophetical Office* (1838), p. 193.
23. Ibid., pp. 62–65. Cf. Keble in the sermon on "Primitive Tradition": "The paramount authority of the successors of the apostles in Church government; the three-fold order established from the beginning; the virtue of the blessed Eucharist as a commemorative sacrifice; infant baptism; and above all, the Catholic doctrine of the most Holy Trinity, as contained in the Nicene Creed. All these, however surely confirmed from Scripture, are yet ascertainable parts of the primitive, unwritten system, of which we yet enjoy the benefit. If anyone asks how we ascertain them, we answer, by application of the well-known rule, *Quod semper, quod ubique, quod ab omnibus*—Antiquity, Universality, Catholicity . . . ."
24. W. Palmer, *A Treatise on the Church of Christ* (3d edition, 1842), II, 35–36.
25. *Prophetical Office* (1838).
26. *Thoughts in Past Years* (Oxford, 1838), p. 263.
27. *The Oxford Movement*, op. cit., p. 22.
28. Ibid., p. 25.
29. *Sermons, Chiefly on the Theory of Religious Belief* (London, 1843), pp. 189–190.
30. Ibid., pp. 190–191.
31. *Fifteen Sermons Preached Before the University of Oxford* (London, 1872), p. 194.
32. E. B. Pusey, *Parochial Sermons* (1878), III, 202–203.
33. *Sermons, on the Theory of Religious Belief*, op. cit., pp. 182–183.
34. Ibid., p. 179.
35. Ibid., pp. 205–207.
36. Ibid., pp. 227–228. Many of Newman's contemporaries found this aspect of his argument as unconvincing as we do today.

37. Ibid., pp. 243–244.
38. *The Oxford Movement,* op. cit., p. 218.
39. Ibid., p. 222.
40. Ibid., p. 227.
41. *Parochial Sermons,* op. cit., V, 217.
42. Ibid., I, 197. Orthodox Lutherans would have found subjective feeling as the ground of justification as repellent as Newman found it.
43. *The Oxford Movement,* op. cit., p. 232.
44. E. B. Pusey, *Sermons During the Season from Advent to Whitsuntide* (Oxford, 1848), p. 220.
45. *The Oxford Movement,* op. cit., pp. 209–211.
46. Ibid., pp. 353–354.
47. Ibid., pp. 381–382.
48. Ibid., p. 374.
49. E. B. Pusey, *Sermons Preached Before the University of Oxford* (1879), pp. 28–29.
50. Isaac Williams, *The Baptistry* (1842–1844), pp. IX–X.
51. E. B. Pusey, *A Sermon Preached Before the University in the Cathedral Church of Christ* (Oxford, 1841), p. 14. This was the sermon that brought about the condemnation of Pusey in Oxford.
52. E. B. Pusey, *Sermons from Advent to Whitsuntide,* op. cit., p. 333.
53. Ibid., pp. 54–55.
54. *The Oxford Movement,* op. cit., p. 11.
55. *The Mind of the Oxford Movement* (Stanford, 1967), p. 60.

SUGGESTIONS FOR FURTHER READING

There are two excellent, recently published books of selections from the writings of the Tractarians:

Chadwick, Owen, ed. *The Mind of the Oxford Movement* (Stanford: Stanford University Press, 1967). A broad, judicious selection of short passages, with a fine introductory essay on the Oxford Movement.

Fairweather, Eugene R., ed. *The Oxford Movement,* Library of Protestant Thought (New York: Oxford University Press, 1964). An excellent selection of materials from most of the important Tractarian writings, with very helpful introductions. The book includes a good selected bibliography of primary and secondary sources on the Movement.

Among the numerous studies of the Oxford Movement, the following are especially recommended:

Brilioth, Yngve. *The Anglican Revival: Studies in the Oxford Movement* (London: Longmans, Green, 1925). This book is still regarded as the best comprehensive study of Tractarian piety and thought.

Church, R. W. *The Oxford Movement: Twelve Years, 1833–1845* (London: Macmillan and Co., 1892). A beautifully written, sympathetic, firsthand story of the Movement, still highly praised for its historical balance.

Faber, Geoffrey. *Oxford Apostles: A Character Study of the Oxford Movement* (Baltimore: Penguin Books, 1954). A lively, absorbing account of the Movement and the personalities connected with it. Especially interesting on Newman.

O'Connell, Marvin, R. *The Oxford Conspirators: A History of the Oxford Movement* (New York: The Macmillan Co., 1969). The most recent, up-to-date narrative history of the Movement.

The number of studies of J. H. Newman is staggering. The following are among the best:

Bouyer, L. *Newman: His Life and Spirituality* (London: Burns Oates, 1958).

Harrold, C. H. *John Henry Newman: An Expository and Critical Study of His Mind, Thought and Art* (New York: Longmans, Green and Co., 1945).

CHAPTER SIX

Christianity and Speculative Idealism

G. W. F. Hegel

Few periods in history have been as rich in intellectual activity as the years immediately preceding and following 1800 in Germany. During this time Kant, Goethe, Fichte, Schelling, Schleiermacher, and Hegel wrote some of their most important works. The works of Kant, Schleiermacher, and Hegel alone determined the course of theology for at least the next century and a half. We have examined the ways in which Kant and Schleiermacher sought to reconstruct Christianity; we must look now at the philosophy of Hegel which is perhaps the most audacious attempt yet devised to resolve the conflict between Christianity and philosophical speculation.

Hegel was consumed by the problem of the reconciliation of religion and culture from the very earliest period of his career, and his philosophic reinterpretation of Christianity had a very wide appeal in the universities and seminaries in the latter half of the nineteenth century, not only in Germany but in England and the United States as well. At Oxford, Hegelianism was the reigning philosophy from the 1870's to the turn of the century. In America, Emerson and the Transcendentalists were deeply indebted to German Idealism, and Josiah Royce "taught scores of Harvard students how to sublimate Calvinism into what Santayana called the 'genteel tradition' of religious Idealism . . . . Hegelianism was the philosophy introduced into the colleges during the 1890's to save the students' faith."[1]

With the discovery of Kierkegaard and the emergence of Neo-Orthodoxy in the 1920's, Idealism came under severe criticism, and the union of theology and philosophical speculation was widely repudiated. Nevertheless, Hegel was a dominant influence in Christian theology for almost a century. His rich influence is still present, though often unrecognized. We shall examine Hegel's own conception of Christianity, look at a few major examples of Hegelianism in later nineteenth-century theology, and then conclude with a brief assessment of the enduring influence and importance of Hegel for modern Christianity.

G. W. F. Hegel

Georg Wilhelm Friedrich Hegel (1770–1831) was the greatest of the German Idealists and one of the most fertile minds in the history of Western thought. He was born at the waning of the Enlightenment and came to maturity during the birth of Romanticism. He was influenced by both of these movements and yet was satisfied with neither. His philosophy was, in one sense, a bringing together of the insights of both into a grand synthesis.

In 1788 Hegel entered the Protestant theological seminary at Tübingen where he formed close friendships with the poet Hölderlin and the philosopher Schelling. The spirit at Tübingen was still that of enlightened rationalism, and such an atmosphere did not speak to the young Hegel who was beginning to discover the values of emotion and imagination espoused by the young Romanticists. When Hegel left the university in 1793, his academic record was unexceptional. He worked as a family tutor in Berne and Frankfurt between 1793 and 1800. These would appear to be uneventful years, but we now know that this was an extremely important period in Hegel's intellectual development. It was during this period that Hegel wrote his first essays on religion and Christianity.[2] These essays furnish important insights into Hegel's early theological speculation as well as into the beginnings of the dialectical method which so controls his later thought.

In 1801, Hegel was offered a teaching position at the University of Jena but was deprived of his job when the University was closed after the battle of Jena. For several years he served as rector of the Gymnasium at Nuremberg, during which time he produced his *Science of Logic* which inaugurated his mature period, that best known to English language scholars. In 1818 Hegel was invited to the chair of philosophy at the University of Berlin, a position he occupied until his death in 1831. During this Berlin period Hegel rose to unrivaled prominence in the philosophical world in Germany. His popularity among Berliners who attended his lectures had to be shared, nevertheless, with a colleague in the chair of theology by the name of Schleiermacher. The two men had little in common and never could appreciate one another's teaching. Hegel apparently felt only contempt for Schleiermacher's conception of religion as intuition and feeling and called the author of the *Speeches* a "virtuoso of edification and enthusiasm."

Hegel is said to have remarked that if the essence of religion consists in the feeling of an absolute dependence, "then the dog would be the best Christian." For the Hegel of the Berlin years religion is not principally a feeling of the divine presence or even a doing of God's will. Religion means to *know* God, and theology is, in its final phase, philosophic knowledge—a going beyond the images of positive religion to a knowledge of their universal conceptual significance.

Hegel's Early Theological Writings.

Hegel's early theological writings did not share this antipathy to Romanticism. In fact, the earliest fragments, collected by Nohl under the title *Volksreligion und Christentum*, reveal the profound influence of Greek culture on the young Hegel—as interpreted, nevertheless, through Romanticist eyes. At this time Hegel made a sharp distinction between an objective religion of the understanding and a subjective religion of the heart.

Objective religion can be arranged in one's head, can be brought into a system, set forth in a book.... subjective religion expresses itself only in attitudes and actions. When I say of a man that he is religious I do not mean that he has a knowledge of it, but that his heart feels the activity, the awe and presence of the Godhead...he bows before Him, utters thanks and praise.[3]

What the young Hegel found lacking in Christianity was that, unlike the *Volksreligion* of the Greeks, it did not reflect the spirit and genius of a people. Christianity appeared to the young Hegel as something imposed and alien, lacking a sense of beauty and joy. In these earliest fragments one can already see the

beginnings of the Hegelian theme of estrangement—what Hegel was later to call the "contrite consciousness."

It was during his stay in Berne in 1794 that Hegel undertook an intensive re-examination of Kant's moral philosophy. The writings of 1794–1796 are inspired almost entirely by Kant's *Religion Within the Limits of Reason Alone*. Kant had suggested in that book that it was necessary to attempt to harmonize the teachings of Jesus with the dictates of reason. Hegel set himself this task in 1795 by writing a *Life of Jesus*—again not for publication but principally to clarify his own thinking.[4] In this essay Hegel simply interpreted the life and teachings of Jesus in the spirit and, indeed, even the letter of Kant. He has Jesus advise men to "act on the maxim which you can at the same time will to be a universal law among men." According to Hegel, Jesus was forced to emphasize the uniqueness of his mission only because the Jews were accustomed to thinking of all truth as coming from a special revelation given by a messenger of God.

Hegel recognized that while there is a unity between Kant's rational ethics and Jesus' teachings, there is also a wide gulf between Kant's ethics and the later ecclesiology and dogma of the Church. How is it that the teachings of Jesus, so much in agreement with Kant's principles of moral reason, could develop into the objective law of the Church—what Kant had called "statutory religion," which is not rational but "positive" and imposed from without? Hegel sought to answer this question in *The Positivity of the Christian Religion* (1795–1796). He found the displacement of the Greek autonomous religion, which developed neither dogma nor ecclesiastical institutions, by a Christian positive religion largely in the social and political changes which brought the ancient world to a close.

The Greek and Roman religion was a religion only for a free people and with the loss of their freedom, the meaning, the power and the suitability of their religion must also have been lost. The prime reason for this loss of freedom is economic and political; wars and the increase of wealth and luxury lead to aristocracy and to inner decay. Loyalty and freedom, the joyous participation in a common life all disappeared . . . . All activity, all purposes were now referred to individuals; no more was there an activity for the sake of a totality, for an Idea.[5]

The center of gravity of man's life was no longer found in the Polis: "Cato turned to Plato's *Phaedo* only after what had been for him the supreme order of things, his world, his republic was destroyed; then he took refuge in another world."[6]

Positive Christianity won out, according to Hegel, because it was adapted to the exigencies of the time since its ideal, its center of gravity, was the remote, the transcendent. The world was estranged from itself, and this explains the reception of the Christian conception of God as a transcendent being.

The despotism of the Roman emperors had driven the spirit of man from the earth, the loss of freedom compelled him to rescue his eternal, his absolute, by taking refuge in the deity; and the spread of misery forced him to seek and expect blessedness in heaven. The objectification of the deity went hand in hand with the slavery of man.[7]

Hegel believed that Jesus was thus compelled by circumstances to describe his message as the will of God, as if its sanction consisted in its derivation from some foreign, supernatural authority. So

destitute of genuine moral autonomy were Jesus' followers that in no other way could they be made to listen to his message. As a result, the "Christians have come to just the place where the Jews were—slaves under the law."[8]

Hegel's break with Kant is clearly evidenced in the series of writings completed during the last two years of the decade. These essays have been grouped together by Nohl under the title, *The Spirit of Christianity and Its Fate*. Once again Hegel tried to develop a conception of the true religion—this time, however, not against the background of the "positivity" of Christianity, but in reaction to the "estrangement" he had come to find epitomized in Hebrew religion and Kant's moral philosophy.

The Hebrew religion is interpreted by Hegel as the religion of a people in conflict with themselves and with nature, of a people not at home in their universe. The first recorded act of Abraham was an act of estrangement, the leaving of his fatherland.

The first act which made Abraham the progenitor of a nation is a disseverance which snaps the bonds of communal life and love. The entirety of the relationship in which he had hitherto lived with men and nature . . . he spurned. Cadmus, Danaus, etc., had forsaken their fatherland too, but they forsook it in battle; they went in quest of a soil where they would be free and they sought it that they might love. Abraham wanted *not* to love, wanted to be free by not loving . . . while the others by their gentle arts and manners won over the less civilized aborigines and intermingled with them to form a happy and gregarious people.[9]

Even the one love Abraham had, love for his son, he was willing to sacrifice.

The whole world Abraham regarded as his opposite; if he did not take it to be a nullity, he looked on it as sustained by the God who was alien to it. Nothing in nature was supposed to have any part in God; everything was simply under God's mastery.[10]

The successive misfortunes of the Jewish people are simply the consequence of their complete estrangement from nature and their slavish dependence upon their alien God. It is quite clear that here Hegel is teaching us by parable. The Hebrews are his symbol of the estranged and contrite human consciousness.

Hegel's dissatisfaction with Kant is now also evident in his new portrayal of Jesus. Jesus is now pictured as having "made undetermined subjectivity, character, a totally different sphere, one which was to have nothing in common with the punctilious following of objective [rational] commands."[11] The spirit of Jesus is a spirit raised above morality.

The Sermon does not teach reverence for the laws; on the contrary, it exhibits that which fulfils the law but annuls it as law and so is something higher than obedience to law and makes law superfluous. Since the commands of duty presuppose a cleavage [between reason and inclination] and since the domination of the concept declares itself in a "thou shalt," that which is raised above this cleavage is by contrast an "is," a modification of life.[12]

This modification of life is a quality of life in which reason and inclination are in harmony. Kant had reduced the command "love God first and then your neighbor" to the categorical imperative, unmindful that the whole point of Jesus' message is that love cannot be commanded, that it is beyond the law and respresents an "is" rather than an "ought," that it is a synthesis of law

[reason] and inclination. This "is," which is the confluence, the mutual sharing of the universal and the particular, of law and inclination, is difficult to conceptualize, but Hegel calls it Life (*Leben*). The dynamic relationship of different elements in life (*Leben*) is Love. Hegel characterizes love as a feeling for the whole—a unity of self and world.

Hegel now turns to the question of how an Abraham, estranged from the wholeness of Life, might once again be reconciled to Life. He finds that in the concept of Fate such a reconciliation can be effected. When punishment comes as the act of Fate and not as the retribution of an alien Law, it does not stand forever above and against the individual. Since all Life is one and is a totality, the wrong-doer comes to see that through his wrong he has really injured his own life and not merely violated an external law. He has introduced a separation within his own real life. Hegel develops his idea of reconciliation in an important passage which we will quote at length:

The wrong-doer supposed that it was but an external foreign thing that his sin affected; really he has but torn asunder his own life. For no life is separate from Life, because all life is divine and of God. The wrong-doer has in his wantonness, to be sure, done damage—but it is the friendliness of Life which he has injured; he has made it an enemy . . . . Thus his punishment, regarded as his fate, is the return of his own deed, a force which he himself has set in motion, an enemy of his own making . . . . It seems far more hopeless to expect a reconciliation with this Fate, than with the Law; for in order to become reconciled with Fate, it would appear necessary that the injury itself should disappear. But Fate has the advantage over an external Law, because with Fate, the entire process goes on within *Leben*. A wrong-doing in the Kantian realm of law is in the realm of irreconcilable opposites, both of which are fixed realities. There is no possibility here of transcending the punishment or of allowing the consciousness of having done wrong disappear. The law is a power, to which all *Leben* is a slave, and to which there is nothing superior, for God himself is but the giver of the law . . . . *Leben* can heal its wounds, can bring back to itself that sundered, hostile life which the wrong-doing caused to split-off; can atone for and sublate the bungling work of the wrong-doer, the law and the punishment. From just the moment when the wrong-doer feels the wounding of his own life [suffers punishment] or is conscious of his own life as sundered and bruised [in remorse], then the working of Fate has commenced and the consciousness of the wounded life must also be a longing for its restoration. The lost life is now appreciated as his own, as that which should now be his but which is not. This gap, this void, is not a mere nothing, but is actively known and felt as the lack of life . . . . Opposition is the possibility of reunification, and the extent to which in affliction life is felt as an opposite is also the extent of the possibility of resuming it again . . . . This sensing of life, a sensing which finds itself again, is love, and in love fate is reconciled.[13]

Hegel identifies this healing of fate through love with the teaching of Jesus. It is necessary, however, to understand what he means by love, for it is not the meaning which has traditionally been given to Christian love. For Hegel, love means wholeness—a union of reason, sense, feeling, and will. It is a harmony in which reason and inclinations are no longer at war with one another.

Love itself pronounces no imperative. It is no universal opposed to the particular . . . . To love God is to feel oneself in the "all" of life, with no restrictions . . . . In this feeling of *harmony* there is no universality, since in

harmony the particular is not in discord but in concord.[14]

Professor Kroner[15] has called this period of Hegel's philosophy a "Pantheism of Love." Jesus is depicted as restoring man's estranged existence to its original unity through the love which heals the split between duty and inclination. In *The Spirit of Christianity* one can discern many themes that Hegel was later to develop with great logical power. One sees, for example, his opposition to a one-sided rationalism but also his revulsion to excessive emotionalism and his concern to reconcile dialectically the opposites of experience into a higher unity. Nevertheless, *The Spirit of Christianity* proved a failure for Hegel. He came to recognize that love is a kind of "holy innocence," an unconscious, undeveloped unity—only one [the subjective] side of mature consciousness. Hegel realized that if estrangement is the emergence of intellect from the level of natural immediacy to the consciousness of one's particular selfhood, then reconciliation cannot be thought of in terms of a simple return to immediacy. Hegel now sees the necessity of a third stage—a synthesis of subjective immediacy and objective form in what he calls *religion*.

Love is a divine spirit but it falls short of religion. To become religion, it must manifest itself in an objective form. A feeling, something subjective, it must be fused with the universal, with something represented in idea . . . . The need to unite subject with object, to unite feeling and feeling's demand for objects, with the intellect, to unite them in something beautiful, in a god, by means of fancy, is the supreme need of the human spirit and the urge to religion.[16]

Hegel was certain, in any case, that

Christianity failed to embody this religious synthesis of subjective feeling and objective form. The fate of Christianity is to extract the spirit of unitive love from the contents of its consciousness and submit to that which is positive and intellectualistic. His conclusion is that it is the fate of Christianity "that church and state, worship and life, piety and virtue, spiritual and worldly action, can never dissolve into one."[17]

As is evidenced in these early essays, the young Hegel was consumed by the problem of finding a thought form that could encompass the dynamic polarities of experience. From his obsession with religion and Christianity it would appear that he was convinced that religious experience, as expressed in such concepts as estrangement, incarnation, love, and reconciliation, could afford him a clue to such a form of thought. However, the early theological writings did not satisfy Hegel's search. The closest he came was the following statement from *The Spirit of Christianity*: "What is religious is the pleroma ['fulfillment'] of love; it is reflection and love united, bound together in thought."[18]

The writings of the 1790's indicate that Hegel was convinced that the dynamic polarities of experience, subject and object, finite and infinite, the one and the many, could not be united by conceptual thought. Thought tends either to deny the distinction or to dissect reality into discrete parts. Christianity also failed to achieve such a stage of synthesis, for it remained hopelessly positive. The search for a *religious stage* which would be capable of restoring man to his wholeness was thus given up after 1800.

The years between 1800 and 1807 mark Hegel's effort to find a *philosophical form* which could express his ideal synthesis of

emotion and intellect, life and thought— that is a new form of logic which could conceptualize the unity of reality without denying multiplicity and individuality. The years 1800 to 1807 reveal Hegel's metamorphosis from a theologian, or antitheologian, to a logician and philosopher. However, his attitude toward Christianity is no longer negative, satirical, and shrill. It is as if Hegel's wrestling with Christianity and rejection of its traditional form freed him to see it in a new way. In terms of his new dialectic, Hegel's conception of Christianity had to be *aufgehoben*.* This new attitude toward the Christianity he had scathingly denounced is indicated as early as 1800 in comments he makes about his plans for rewriting "The Positivity of Christianity." He writes that

The following essay does not have the purpose of inquiring whether there are positive doctrines and commandments in the Christian religion . . . . The horrible blabbering in this vein with its endless extent and inward emptiness has become too boring and has altogether lost interest . . . . *Rather, one would have to deduce this now repudiated dogmatics out of what we now consider the needs of human nature and thus show its naturalness and its necessity. Such an attempt would presuppose the faith that the convictions of many centuries—that which the millions, who during these centuries lived by them and died for them, considered their duty and holy truth—were not bare nonsense or immorality.*[19] (Italics added.)

Hegel recognized that his earlier view of Christianity was too narrow and negative and needed to be transcended. Hegel now developed a more historical

---

* The German verb *aufheben* conveys the double meaning of having "done away with" and at the same time "preserved" on a higher level.

orientation to philosophy and recognized that the faith held by millions for centuries could not simply be dismissed as "bare nonsense." The positive, historical, dogmatic medium of Christianity needed to be *aufgehoben* so that its truth could be more adequately seen and attested to in philosophy. Historical Christianity had grasped the truth in representational form, but philosophy grasps this same truth in its rational necessity. Nevertheless, truth is now not something abstract and ahistorical for Hegel. "The universal must pass into actuality through the particular" and only then can it be seen in its rational necessity. The truth of Christianity, therefore, is not to be reduced to certain abstract principles but seen in the historical actualization of the unity of the divine and human and the coming into being of the Absolute Spirit. This is what it means to say that God has revealed himself in history:

In the Christian religion God has revealed himself, *i.e.*, he has given men to understand what he is, so that he is no longer a concealment, a secret. This possibility to know God lays upon us the duty to do so; and the development of thinking Spirit which has proceeded from this basis, from the revelation of the divine Being, must finally proceed *to grasp in thought that which has at first been exhibited to Spirit in feeling and representation*. Whether the time has come to comprehend depends upon whether that which is the final purpose of the world has at last passed into actuality in a universally valid and conscious way.

Now what distinguishes the Christian religion is that with it this time has come; this constitutes the *absolute epoch* in world history. . . . So we know as Christians what God is; now God is no longer unknown: if we still say that, we are not Christians. The Christian religion demands the humility . . . to apprehend God, not on its own terms, but on the terms of God's own knowledge and appre-

hension. Christians are initiated into the mysteries of God and so the key to world history is also given to us. Here is given a definite apprehension of providence and its plan.[20] (Italics added.)

In the historical events of Christianity's origin "the final purpose of the world" has been actualized, or has made explicit what was only implicit before. What is now called for is that what has been mediated through historical representation (revelation) now be "grasped in thought."

Hegel's Conception of Christianity. *The Fall of Man.* According to Hegel, man's actual history on this earth is a chronicle of misery and suffering. This condition is largely attributable to man's self-alienation and his longing for a reconciliation of the ceaseless contradictions between spirit and flesh, between infinite, free selfhood and slavish finitude. This conflict and estrangement within self-consciousness is what Hegel calls the "Unhappy Consciousness," [21]history being the sorry panorama of the successive forms of this human self-alienation. Hegel finds the world historical importance of Israel in the fact that it was the Jewish people who brought this sense of alienation to absolute self-consciousness. This feeling

we find expressed most purely and beautifully in the Psalms of David, and in the Prophets; the chief burden of whose utterances is the thirst of the soul after God, its profound sorrow for its transgressions, and the desire for righteousness and holiness.[22]

Man's contrite or unhappy consciousness is, of course, most powerfully depicted in mythopoetic form in the biblical story of the Fall of Adam. Hegel finds this poetic representation of man's estrangement rich in significance and totally lost to the narrow rationalism of the Enlightenment. When grasped in thought, the story of the Fall of Adam expresses the conceptual truth of our human condition.

Man, created in the image of God, lost, it is said, his state of absolute contentment, by eating of the Tree of the Knowledge of Good and Evil. Sin consists here only in Knowledge: this is the sinful element, and by it man is stated to have trifled away his Natural happiness. *This is a deep truth, that evil lies in consciousness: for the brutes are neither evil nor good* [italics added]; the merely Natural Man quite as little. Consciousness occasions the separation of the Ego, in its boundless freedom as arbitrary choice, from the pure essence of the Will—*i.e.*, from the Good. Knowledge, as the disannulling of the unity of mere Nature, is the "Fall," which is no casual conception, but the eternal history of Spirit. For the state of innocence, the paradisaical condition, is that of the brute. Paradise is a park, where only brutes, not men can remain. For the brute is one with God only *implicitly* (not consciously). Only Man's Spirit has a self-cognizant existence. This existence for self, this consciousness, is at the same time separation from the Universal and Divine Spirit. If I hold to *my* abstract Freedom, in contraposition to the Good, I adopt the standpoint of Evil. The Fall is therefore the Mythus of Man—in fact, the very transition by which he becomes man. Persistence in this standpoint is, however, Evil, and the feeling of pain at such a condition and of longing to transcend it, we find in David, when he says: "Lord create for me a pure heart, a new *steadfast* Spirit." This feeling we observe even in the account of the Fall; though an announcement of Reconciliation is not made there, but rather one of continuance in misery. Yet we have in this narrative the *prediction* of reconciliation ... profoundly expressed where it is stated that when God saw that Adam had eaten of that tree he said, "Behold Adam is become as one of us, knowing Good and Evil." God confirms the words of the Serpent.[23]

It is evident that in Hegel's view the Fall of man is to be interpreted in a quite different manner from the traditional exegesis. He believes the Fall is a necessary movement from innocence to self-consciousness. If we speak of it as a "fall," we must remember that it is a "necessary" and fortunate movement toward making *explicit* man's *implicit* unity with God. The estrangement that results from the Fall is evil, of course, but it is also a positive advance beyond innocence. To Hegel, life in Paradise is a "dreaming innocence" which is lacking in the knowledge of good and evil, lacking in self-consciousness and deliberate choice. "Innocence implies the absence of will, the absence of evil, and consequently the absence of goodness."[24] It is just this sinless state of innocence that Hegel believes must be "judged and condemned," for it is knowledge that makes man conscious of his independent being and which separates man from the animals and plants.

Nevertheless, knowledge is evil since it leads to separation and estrangement.

In this connection it may accordingly be remarked that as a matter of fact it is knowledge which is the source of all evil, for knowledge or consciousness is just the act by which separation, the negative element, judgement, division in the more definite specific form of independent existence or Being-for-self in general, comes into existence. Man's nature is not as it ought to be; it is knowledge which reveals this to him, and brings to light that condition of Being in which he ought not to be [the Unhappy Consciousness] ... and the fact that he is not what he should be originates first of all in the sense of separation or alienation, and from a comparison between what he is and what he is in his essential nature . . . .

It is therefore not the case that reflection stands in an external relation to evil, but on the contrary, reflection itself is evil. This is the condition of contrast to which Man, because he is Spirit, must advance . . . . It is in this disunion that independent Being or Being-for-self originates, and it is in it that evil has its seat; here is the source of the evil, but here also the point which is the ultimate source of reconciliation.[25]

The Fall, the movement from innocence to knowledge, is evil because it implies alienation, but it is also the necessary step toward reconciliation. Adam and Eve, in yielding to the temptations of the Devil, are in reality making the necessary move toward realizing the highest nature of the Spirit.

The serpent says that Man by the act of eating would become equal to God, and by speaking thus he made an appeal to Man's pride. God says to Himself, Adam is become as one of us. The serpent had thus not lied, for God confirms what he said.[26]

Much confusion has resulted from this biblical declaration by God that "Adam is become as one of us." Some have given these words an ironical interpretation, but "the truer explanation," Hegel declares, "is that the Adam referred to is to be understood as representing the second Adam, namely Christ."[27] The knowledge which comes with the Fall, then, is not only the source of alienation but "supplies also the principle of man's divineness . . . or, in other words, it involves the promise and certainty of attaining once more the state in which Man is the image of God."[28]

Fallen man is historical man—no longer innocent and yet estranged and painfully cognizant of his separation from God. But this disunion is not permanent; man's yearning for "a new steadfast Spirit" will be answered "in the fullness of time." This *kairos*, or right time, was heralded by the Jewish people. In Israel the opposition between God and man, subject and object, finite and infinite, comes to consciousness; the time is now ripe for reconciliation:

From that unrest of infinite sorrow—in which the two sides of the antithesis stand related to each other—is developed the unity of God with Reality . . . . The recognition of the identity of the Subject and God was introduced into the World when *the fulness of Time was come:* the consciousness of this identity is the recognition of God in his true essence . . . . The nature of God as pure *Spirit* is manifested to man *in the Christian Religion.*[29]

The Incarnation. The *implicit* unity of God and man is made *explicit* in Christianity in that the foundation of Christianity is laid on *the historical fact* of the Incarnation. In Jesus Christ the God-man unity is realized in a concrete temporal event. Hegel maintains that Christ is divine because he is the embodiment of the Truth, the incarnation of God in himself (*an sich*), God manifest in the world. As speculative idea, the God-man unity is only implicit. Hence Christ's uniqueness lies not principally in his teachings but in the fact that he *is* God manifest in the world. Nevertheless, this fact cannot be established by historical-critical research.

Considered only in respect of his talents, character and morality—as a Teacher and so forth—we place him [Jesus] in the same category with Socrates and others . . . . But excellence of character, morality, etc.—all this is not the *ne plus ultra* in the requirements of Spirit . . . . If Christ is to be looked upon only as an excellent, even impeccable individual, and nothing more, the conception of . . . Absolute Truth is ignored. But this is the desideratum, the point from which we have to start. Make of Christ what you will, exegetically, critically, historically—demonstrate as you please, how the doctrines of the Church were established by Councils, attained currency as the result of this or that episcopal interest or passion—let all such circumstances have been what they might—the only concerning question is: What is the Idea or the Truth in and for itself?[30]

Christ's unique God-manhood, Hegel believes, is posited upon the speculative Idea, upon Hegel's conception of Absolute Truth. This very Idea demands that the implicit truth be historically manifest.

This implicit unity exists in the first place only for the thinking speculative consciousness; but it must also exist for the sensuous, representative consciousness—it must become an object for the World—it *must appear*, and that in the sensuous form appropriate to Spirit which is the human. *Christ has appeared*—a Man who is God—God who is Man; and thereby peace and reconciliation have accrued to the World . . . . The appearance of the Christian God involves further its being *unique* in its kind; it can occur only once, for God is realized as Subject, and as manifested Subjectivity is exclusively One individual.[31]

The Idea demands the unique historical appearance of the God-man union in human form but, as has been indicated, such an historical occurrence is immune to any historical-critical test.[32] It is clear, as many critics of Hegel have shown, that Hegel is more interested in the symbolic truth in the doctrine of the divine–human union in Christ than in the historical life of Jesus of Nazareth. Nevertheless, Hegel does emphasize the historical reality and uniqueness of the Incarnation, the con-

crete actualization of the universal in a particular historical individual. Christ is not simply symbolic of the divine presence in every man, *for with Jesus Christ the history of both God and man has actually changed*. God has passed from abstract idea into historical individuality and *only in so doing attains full reality*. The history of Jesus Christ is the history of *both* God and man.

Central to the Incarnation, of course, is the passion and death of the Christ. For Hegel the conceptual truth of the crucifixion is to be found in the fact that when Spirit becomes united with the finite, it must take on radical finitude, which includes estrangement and death. Otherwise, God is not fully manifested in finite existence. The highest peak of finitude is death, for in death our temporality is fully revealed.

Christ's death primarily means that Christ was the God-man, the God who had at the same time human nature, even unto death. It is the lot of finite humanity to die; death is the most complete proof of humanity, and Christ in fact died the aggravated death of the evildoer . . . in Him humanity was carried to its furthest point.[33]

The death of Christ symbolizes the destruction of finitude, so that in the crucifixion we see in sensible form the yielding up of "all that is peculiar to the individual, all those interests and personal ends with which the natural will can occupy itself, all that is great and counted as of value in the world."[34] Absolute Spirit must, in other words, lose its life before it can fully realize itself. Understood conceptually, Spirit must not only undergo the negation of its finitude. *Spirit or God must die!* But what God's death on the cross symbolizes is that God's finitude is only a transitional moment in the emergence of Absolute Spirit. What dies is the existence of God as an individual standing over against us; the personal transcendent God of traditional theism. "Death then ceases to signify what it means directly—the nonexistence of *this* individual [God]—and becomes transfigured into the universality of spirit which lives in its own communion."[35]

The death of the God-man, however, is only one aspect of a single event. The cross is followed by the resurrection and ascension. The conceptual understanding of this event does not, then, terminate with God's death, for God maintains himself in this process. Hence God's death is really the death of death, the negation of finite negativity. The resurrection and ascension into Heaven is the pictorial representation of the truth that Spirit sacrifices its particular embodiment and thereby initiates the advent of Absolute Spirit, the coming of the Holy or Universal Spirit. In this history of the Christ, therefore, we have the representation

of the process of what constitutes Man or Spirit . . . . It is the consciousness of the Spiritual Community, which thus makes the transition from man pure and simply to a God-man, and to a perception, a consciousness, a certainty of the unity and union of the Divine and human natures, that the Church or Spiritual Community begins, and it is this consciousness which constitutes the truth upon which the Spiritual Community is founded.[36]

For Hegel, consciousness of the spiritual significance of Christ's death as including his resurrection and ascension is consciousness of the fact that God's death is merely the transitional stage in the emergence of true Spirit or the Spiritual Community.

The sensuous existence in which Spirit is embodied is only a transitional phase. Christ dies; only as dead is he exalted to Heaven and sits at the right hand of God; only thus is he Spirit. He himself says: "When I am no longer with you, the Spirit will guide you into all truth." Not till the Feast of Pentecost were the Apostles filled with the Holy Ghost. To the Apostles, Christ as living was not that which he was to them subsequently as the Spirit of the Church, in which he became to them for the first time an object for their truly spiritual consciousness.[37]

The inauguration of the Kingdom of the Spirit represents the universal reconciliation of the divine and human that was implicit from the beginning. As Christ overcame sin and death, so we, as heirs of the Spirit, must strip ourselves of our finite point of view.

It has already been remarked that only after the death of Christ could the Spirit come upon his friends; that only then they were able to conceive the true idea of God, viz., that in Christ man is redeemed and reconciled; for in him the idea of eternal truth is recognized, *the essence of man acknowledged to be Spirit, and the fact proclaimed that only by stripping himself of his finiteness and surrendering himself to pure self-consciousness does he attain the truth.* Christ—man as man—in whom the unity of God and man has appeared, has in his death, and his history generally, himself presented the eternal history of Spirit—*a history which every man has to accomplish in himself, in order to exist as Spirit, or to become a child of God,* a citizen of his kingdom. The followers of Christ, who combine on this principle and live in the spiritual life as their aim, form the Church, which is the Kingdom of God.[38] (Italics added.)

The reconciliation accomplished in

Christ is passed on to his followers for their appropriation. However, Christ's atonement is not to be conceived of as simply a moral influence, for in Christ *alone* has the divine-human union been made fully explicit. In the singular events of Christ's history, the relationship of God and man has actually been changed. We are, then, the heirs of his benefits in that we can appropriate the reconciliation which he alone accomplished on our behalf.

The Kingdom of the Spirit and Christianity as the Absolute Religion. The Kingdom of the Spirit, as Hegel understands it, is the goal of the entire process of history and is that moment which inaugurates the Absolute Religion. Christianity is the Absolute Religion, for in Christianity alone do we see the actual dialectical process by which Spirit (God) works itself out to full expression in history. God is Spirit, but to Hegel this means something very different from what most Christians mean by the term. For him Spirit is *the process of life itself,* "it is life, movement" whose nature it is "to differentiate itself, to give itself a definite character, to determine itself."[39]

According to Hegel, Spirit develops and realizes itself according to a dialectical process that must be comprehended under three determinations. It is for this reason that universal Spirit has found its adequate sensuous representation "in the Christian religion under the name of the Holy Trinity, and this is God Himself, the eternal Triune God."[40] The divine Trinity, as Hegel sees it, is the sensuous representation of the dialectical process of the Absolute Spirit, and in the Kingdom of the Spirit (the Synthesis of the Logic) the truths contained in the Kingdoms of the Father and the Son are reconciled and

overcome. It can be said, then, that for Hegel God only comes to *full historical actualization* in the Kingdom of the Spirit. The Holy Spirit is the only member of the Trinity in which the *reality* of God is fully manifest. This is why Christianity is rightly called *the* "revealed" religion, for in the Kingdom of the Spirit God is no longer an object "out there" or "back then" but is a God who has not only revealed Himself but has Himself come to consciousness in and through the finite world. Thus, for Hegel, without the world God is not God.[41] When God is regarded as Spirit but "is not present in His Church as a living Spirit, [He] is Himself characterized in a merely one-sided way as object."[42]

The Kingdom of the Spirit *is* the Church or "the Spiritual Community" (*Die Gemeinde*). God, as fully actualized Spirit, is realizable only in a community of finite human minds for, as Hegel maintains, Spirit achieves consciousness only through finite particularization or concretion. Since it is only through finite consciousness in its manifold forms that Absolute Spirit realizes itself, God as Father and as Son does not enjoy such perfection of consciousness. And if it is the case that God comes to full realization in and through the Spiritual Community of finite consciousness, then the naïve conception of God as *a person* must be left behind. Spirit actualized in a community of finite minds may have the unity of a personality but certainly cannot be *a person.*[43]

Christianity, according to Hegel, must give up its traditional theistic view, for such a view still conceives of God as a personal, transcendent Being "out there." It has not yet made the dialectical move from the Kingdom of the Son to that of Absolute Spirit; it still persists in retaining the theistic gulf between man and God and fails to realize that "pure knowledge . . . is not merely intuition of God Himself" in finite consciousness. In other words, the absolute religion is the one in which

man knows God only insofar as God knows Himself in man. This knowledge is God's self-consciousness but also God's knowledge of man. God's knowledge of man is also man's knowledge of God. *The spirit of man which is to know God is only the spirit of God Himself.*[44] (Italics added.)

Christianity's Aufhebung *into Philosophy.* Christianity, *the* Revealed Religion, is the Absolute Religion in that for the first time religion realizes the *notion* of religion—i.e., of being the self-revelation of Absolute Spirit. And yet, for Hegel, Christianity has not yet risen to the level of speculative truth, to Absolute Knowledge in its scientific form. Religion, even the Absolute Religion, apparently never can rise above the external and objective mode of imaginative, pictorial presentation to pure conceptual thought. The spiritual content of religion is not itself to be confused with pure truth, for it is only the presentation of truth in the form of art, which is that of "feeling" (*Gefühl*), and "representation" (*Vorstellung*).[45] Therefore, religion, or spiritual content in the form of sensuous representation, is a kind of exoteric metaphysics for Hegel which is needful for those who cannot rise to pure conceptual universality. Nevertheless, such religious representations must finally be *aufgehoben* into the forms of pure thought (*Begriffe*), for there clings to such *Vorstellungen* something of the historically accidental and contingent and, therefore, leaves

them open to rational attack. The transcending of the point of view of religious representation into forms of pure thought does not mean moving to the level of formal abstraction. It means, rather, that the truth represented in finite experience is raised to the level of rational universality without sacrificing its concreteness. Spirit achieves its concrete fulfillment only in conceptual thought, for only in this moment does it overcome both individuality and abstraction by becoming the concrete universal—the perfect union of content and form. Contrary to general opinion, the transformation of religion into philosophy does not, according to Hegel, destroy the content of religion; rather it elevates it from the level of imagination to that of conceptual universality.

For Hegel it was the very "translation" of Christianity into philosophy which *justified* the Christian religion. It is quite clear in Hegel's mind that refusal to carry out such an *aufhebung* would result in a rational and historical critique of Christianity that would culminate in its dissolution. Christianity finds its only justification in its philosophical conceptualization. Many post-Hegelian thinkers believed, of course, that Hegel's claim that Christianity is justified only in its conceptual transformation led him to substitute a "philosophical surrogate for Christianity, a figurative way of using dogmatic terms to express his own systematic concepts."[46]

It would appear, however, that Hegel's own attitude toward Christianity was ambiguous, and this very ambiguity led his contemporaries and later thinkers to see in him both the archcritic of Christianity and its modern philosophic savior. The historical significance of Hegel's attempted justification of Christianity in philosophy is well stated by Karl Löwith:

The distinction, and the consequent exaltation, of religion out of the form of feeling and imagination into that of the notion, are the means by which Hegel accomplishes his positive justification of the Christian religion, and at the same time his criticism of it. The ambiguity of this distinction forms the background for all post-Hegelian criticism of religion; it even produced the breakdown of the Hegelian school into a left and right wing . . . . Ecclesiastical orthodoxy declared Hegel's translation to be non-Christian because it destroyed the positive content of the faith; the Young Hegelians, on the contrary, were offended by Hegel's retention of dogmatic Christianity even in the *form* of his concept.[47]

The division of the Hegelian school into a right and a left wing is one of the most interesting and important intellectual developments in the nineteenth century. There were many philosophers and theologians in the latter decades of the nineteenth century who found in Hegel's philosophy the most adequate scientific tool for reconstructing Christianity in terms acceptable to modern experience. Those theologians in Germany who used Hegel, entirely or in part, in their reconstruction of Christianity were known generally as the Right-Wing Hegelians. In Britain they were called the Neo-Hegelians. The Right-Wing movement in Germany included such important theologians as Philipp Marheineke (1780–1846), Karl Daub (1765–1836), and A. E. Biedermann (1819–1885). In Britain, Hegelian categories dominated the theological writings and reinterpretation of Christianity in John and Edward Caird.

From our present position in the latter third of the twentieth century, the more important of the Hegelian movements appears to be the radical or Left-Wing Hegelian school. These "Young Hegelians," as they were also known, were in most cases not interested in using Hegel's ideas as a bulwark for preserving Christianity. On the contrary, the more radical members of the group saw in Hegel's philosophy the possibility of canceling and overcoming the Christian tradition. Among these "Young Hegelians" were D. F. Strauss, Bruno Bauer, Ludwig Feuerbach, and Karl Marx. Their critique of the Christian religion was so radical and historically so significant for an understanding of Christianity in the last century that we will postpone our account of this movement to the next chapter.

However, before leaving Hegel, some indication of his constructive influence will give a more balanced view of his immense contribution to nineteenth-century religious thought. It will also set the stage for the radical critique which follows. A single example of later German and English Hegelianism will suffice for our purposes.

A. E. Biedermann

One of the last important representatives of German Hegelian theology was Alois Biedermann who was a student of Marheineke and served as professor of dogmatics at Zurich from 1860 to his death in 1885. Biedermann was not dependent solely on Hegel for his philosophical ideas—he drew also from Kant and Schleiermacher—but the dominant influence on his thought and language in his *Christliche Dogmatik* is that of Hegel. Biedermann's importance lies, in part, in his attempt to answer the negative critique of theology of D. F. Strauss and the other radical "Young Hegelians" by offering a speculative reconstruction of theology through the use of categories which were essentially Hegelian. He also corrects certain difficulties in Hegel's own reconstruction of Christianity, especially the latter's Christology, and therefore represents an Hegelian theology more consistent with the Church's creedal traditions.[48]

Biedermann was convinced that the Left-Wing Hegelian critique of Christianity was often correct as far as it went but that it did not go beyond a negative criticism of historical representation to the purification of the historical in conceptual thought. But for Biedermann this did not mean a final disinterest in the representational form of religion as it did for Hegel and some of his followers. For Biedermann the natural language of religion is the sensuous or representational, and the conceptual form is not so much an *aufhebung* of the historical as it is the clarification of the real meaning of the representational form.

Biedermann's handling of the difficult question of the "personality" of God illustrates his general interest in preserving the representational form of religion while clarifying its conceptual meaning. He argues that "personality" is actually the definition of *finite* spirit. When we speak of a personal subject, we think not only of a spirit but a *finite* spirit, "spirit with a sensuous, natural presupposition in itself," a natural, individual corporeality. But when we *think* of God or Absolute Spirit as having a personality, we run into difficulties:

When we identify absolute spirit with absolute personality, we either actually think it as personality—but then not as truly absolute or we think it as only absolute—but then personality is present only as an image. We *think* absolute spirit; we have an absolute personality only in *representation*, *i.e.*, we view the purely spiritual in an abstract sensuous way, but this sensuousness we have abstracted from human personality, to the essence of which it belongs . . . .[49]

Does this mean that the personality of God is an illicit conception? Not at all, if it is properly understood.

Permission to *represent* God as personality, and to speak of him in expressions that are taken from human personality, remains. Now for the first time . . . it finds its psychological foundation and therein its justification. We can only think absolute spirit, and only represent absolute personality. And the two indeed coincide: absolute spirit as conception and absolute personality as representation . . . [But only] in thinking of God as absolute do we know that, and why, we must also represent him to ourselves as personality. Yes—if we would represent him to ourselves at all! But that is already sufficiently cared for by the psychological nature of our spirit. All our thinking is first thinking in representations, and our thinking as pure thinking is only scientific reworking of our representations. It is only the unspeakably wooden ineptitude with which most people deal with the basic psychological concepts, when they suppose because thinking is an abrogation and absorption of representation in ideas, that he who ventures to do this therefore ceases to lead his conscious life in the form of representation and becomes an abstract thinking machine. However scientifically concerned for pure thought, we lead our conscious life, before as after, in representation, we seek only to make ourselves aware, intellectually certain, of the truth of our representations, when we abrogate and absorb representations in their conceptions and no longer forthwith identify our subjective representational form with the objective truth dwelling in the representation . . . . Only man as finite spirit is personality; God as absolute spirit is not. Yet the religious intercourse is always a personal one, and indeed not merely in subjective representation but in objective truth, because it goes on between the infinite and finite spirit within the finite human spiritual life and thus must take place throughout in the form of the latter.[50]

Biedermann's concern to show the conceptual content appropriate to the ecclesiastical, representational form is best seen in his discussion of Christology. What is basic to all the traditional Christological formulae is what Biedermann calls "the Christian principle" and how this principle is related to the historical person of Jesus. According to Biedermann, Hegel was quite right in his emphasis on the principle or *Idée* of the Incarnation; but where Hegel failed, in part, and Strauss certainly failed, was in relating the principle adequately to the person of Jesus.

First of all, Biedermann holds that it is quite wrong to conceive of the "Christian principle" as an abstraction, "a kind of subjective idea first generated by our thought or abstracted from actuality," as did some of the Young Hegelians. The Christian principle

first entered the actuality of history, in the actual event of Jesus' religious self-consciousness and of faith in him. The definition of its content is therefore not to be understood as if the content has also been realized *eo ipso* in human history before and apart from that fact.[51]

Having said this, however, it is important not to confuse the "idea newly appearing in human history in his [Jesus'] person" with "a personal definition of the single person Jesus."

The principle shows itself as the actualiza-tion of the true relation between God and man, and thereby as the principle of salvation for the natural humanity which through sin stands in contradiction to God and its own divine destiny. Its content must therefore still be identified as intrinsically contained in the full actualization of what is contained therein.[52]

If this latter conception is not taken with utter seriousness, "then the Christian principle is not understood as truly human and as the truly human religious principle, but as something supernatural in the bad supernaturalistic sense of the word."[53] The "Christian principle" first entered into history factually in the person of Jesus, "but *intrinsically* it is eternally contained in the essence of God and man as their true religious relationship."[54] Whereas the Church's dogma personified the principle and identified it immediately with the person bearing the revelation of the principle—hence calling him the God-man—the proper designation should be God-manhood which in Jesus became a religious actuality in human spiritual life. What the Church represented in mythological form as the God-man is in actuality the definition of the true relation between God and man, the absolute and the finite spirit, or what Biedermann calls the "absolute religious self-consciousness." This is the new principle of religious consciousness which entered history with Jesus and which can be appropriated in faith. What Jesus actualized in human history is intrinsically immanent in human spiritual life. Biedermann's way of stating this reveals his indebtedness to Hegel.

Thus wherever a human ego achieves the actualization of its true being as man, *viz.* as finite spirit, there the being of God, of absolute spirit, is revealed in it and proved in it to be the active power of its subjective spirituality

. . . . Now if that which accordingly is intrinsically immanent in every human spiritual life as the active principle lying at its basis, *i.e.*, the absoluteness of spirit as such in its pure being-in-self, is actualized in a human person as the actual content of its own subjective spiritual life—which actualization is objectively the self-verification of absolute spirit in creaturely finite spirit, and subjectively is this finite ego's self-consciousness of its being elevated by God from its natural determination outside of God into spiritual fellowship with God in the *actus purus* of its own self-elevation into free being-in-self—then this humanly personal self-consciousness of the absoluteness of spirit is the factual union of the divine and the human essences as the unity of personal spiritual life, or thus the entrance of the principle of God-manhood (which is intrinsically immanent in man as finite spirit) into the actuality of the life of humanity.[55]

God-manhood, which is intrinsically immanent in finite human spirit, has first been historically actualized in Jesus. However, the question of *the actual historical form* of this source of Christianity is the subject of historical research and not dogmatics. Dogmatics is concerned "to bring the essence of this religious self-consciousness (historically primitive in Jesus) to its pure conceptual expression."[56] Nevertheless, Biedermann is concerned that the relation between the historical Jesus and the Christian principle not be considered as "external and accidental" as it was considered by Strauss and other Left-Wing Hegelians:

It would be accidental and external either if that principle had merely consisted in a doctrine newly delivered by Jesus or if its emergence in history had merely indirectly received impetus from the person of Jesus. But Jesus' personal religious life was the first self-actualization of that principle as a world-historical figure, and it is the source and

efficacy of this principle in history: Jesus is the historical redeemer as the historical revelation of the principle of salvation.[57]

The purpose of dogmatics, for Biedermann, is to bring to conceptual expression the essence of Jesus' religious self-consciousness. The creedal definitions point to conceptual truths but, as such, "wear themselves out in pure contradictions." Dogmatics, then, must trace out the intention which came to expression in representational, creedal form. Only then can its historical legitimacy be shown. What happened historically was that the original relation of the man Jesus to God "was elevated by the believing consciousness, as it sought to give account of the essentially new therein, into the view of a metaphysical relation of the preexistent ego of Christ to God."[58] This was the necessary and "correct expression of the fundamental truth that it is not the historical person as such but a principle entering human life in this person which is the actual ground of the new religious relation of divine childhood disclosed to humanity in this person."[59]

In the latter part of the *Dogmatik*, in a section entitled "The Rational Nucleus of the Christian Faith," Biedermann sets forth the conceptual bases of the Christological formulae. Here is a brief sampling of his conceptual understanding of the Church's positive dogma:

§820. That the metaphysical divine sonship was pressed to the full homoousia ["of one substance"] was the necessary expression of the truth that the absoluteness of spirit that discloses itself in the self-consciousness of divine childhood [Jesus] is the revelation of the essence of absolute spirit itself.

§821. That the church's doctrine also demanded time and full humanity for its God-man was the expression of the truth that the absolute religious self-consciousness of divine childhood is at the same time nothing other than the true and full actualization of the human essence, in which the sensuous natural presupposition in man also achieves the fulfillment of its destiny as the medium for man's absolute destiny.

§822. The Chalcedonian definition of the equally inseparable and unmixed unity of the two natures in the God-man was the necessary expression in the Church's doctrine of the truth that in the absolute religious self-consciousness the absoluteness of spirit and the creaturely finitude of the ego constitute the two elements, surely logically to be distinguished but in actuality undivided, of the *one* personal life-process of this self-consciousness.

§825. The pre-worldly eternal being of the Son with the Father is the representational and therefore mythologizing expression of the truth that in the essence of absolute spirit its self-revelation in finite spirit is already co-posited in itself.[60]

Like Hegel, Biedermann found in the Christian dogma of the Trinity the representational form in which the truth of Absolute Spirit has come to historical expression. The Trinity is the highest and most sublime of all representations of God:

If the true concept of God is the concept of absolute spirit and that of the Christian principle is the absoluteness of spirit in the religious self-consciousness of finite spirit, then the core of the doctrine of the Trinity, or the Christian trinitarian concept of God, is this: The absoluteness of spirit which proves itself in finite spirit to be the power of annulling finite spirit's self-contradiction and discord, is an element of the *actus purus* of absolute spirit itself; and what is more, in the actual entrance of this principle into history God is first actually manifest in humanity as absolute spirit.[61]

Biedermann, like a number of other

mid-nineteenth-century speculative and mediating theologians, sought a middle way between the old supernaturalism and the new naturalism and materialism of the radical Hegelians. Like Schleiermacher, he regarded the religious self-consciousness as something intrinsic and enduring which could never be replaced by any higher form of knowledge, such as philosophy. Philosophy can purify our religious modes of conceiving reality, but it can never replace religious faith itself. Thus Biedermann rejected Hegel's *aufhebung* of Christianity into a philosophy. Nevertheless, Biedermann held that the old supernaturalism was quite unable to explain the proper relation between God and the world, and he found in Hegel a conceptual framework which would delineate this relationship in a way more consonant with experience and philosophical reflection—and which would, at the same time, point to the real intention behind the church's creedal representations.

John and Edward Caird

Neo-Hegelianism in theology became dominant in Britain in the last decades of the nineteenth century primarily through the writings of the Scottish brothers Caird. Both Cairds possessed rare gifts as writers and public speakers and thus exercised considerable influence on a generation of university students. Edward Caird (1835–1908) was successively Fellow of Merton College, Oxford, Professor of Moral Philosophy at the University of Glasgow (1866–1893), and Master of Balliol College, Oxford. He wrote important studies of Kant and Hegel, and in 1893 his Gifford Lectures, entitled *The Evolution of Religion*, were published in two volumes.

John Caird (1820–1898) was a Presbyterian clergyman and was appointed to an academic post, as Professor of Theology at Glasgow, only in his middle years. From 1873 until his death in 1898, he served as Principal of Glasgow University. His two important works on religion, *Introduction to the Philosophy of Religion* (1880) and his Gifford Lectures, published posthumously in 1899 as *The Fundamental Ideas of Christianity*, show the indelible stamp of Hegel. Yet neither Caird was a slavish disciple of their German master, but took from him the general lines of the Hegelian system and adapted it, especially in the case of John Caird, to a form of piety and theological style unique to Scottish divines.

In his book *The Evolution of Religion*, Edward Caird approaches both the doctrine of God and the history of man's religions from the perspective of the Hegelian dialectic. According to Caird, it is man's natural religious consciousness which drives him to seek an underlying unity and ground of self and world or subject and object. Man's uniqueness lies in the fact that his experience of the finite causes him to seek after the Infinite. If we consider the general nature of man's conscious life, we find that that life is circumscribed by *three ideas* which are indissolubly connected:

These are the idea of the object or not-self, the idea of the subject or self, and the idea of the unity which is presupposed in the difference of the self and the not-self and within which they act and react on each other: in other words the idea of God .... The *object* is the general name under which we include the external world and all the things and beings in it, all that we know and all that we act on, the whole environment, which conditions the activity of the ego .... There is only one thing which stands over against this complex whole of existence and refuses to be regarded *simply* as part of the system; and that is the ego, the self, the *subject* for which it exists. For the primary condition of the existence of this subject is that it should distinguish itself from the object as such .... All our life, then, moves between these two terms which are essentially distinct from, and opposed to, each other.[62]

Our consciousness recognizes that these two ideas are indivisible but also necessarily opposed, else the one could be subsumed within the other as a mere phase. Such an awareness forces us

to seek the secret of their being in *a higher principle, of whose unity they in their action and reaction are the manifestation, which they presuppose as their beginning and to which they point as their end* .... To put it more directly, the idea of an absolute unity, which transcends all the oppositions of finitude, and especially the last opposition which includes all others—the opposition of subject and object—*is the ultimate presupposition of our consciousness* .... Every creature who is capable of the consciousness of an objective world and of the consciousness of a self, is capable also of the consciousness of God. Or, to sum up the whole matter in one word, *every rational being as such is a religious being*.[63] (Italics added.)

For Caird, apart from God nothing can be known, for God is the unitary ground of all being and knowing. This does not mean that all men are aware of God as this unitary ground. In fact, the history of religion is the history of the successive stages of man's developing rational consciousness—or, put another way, "history is just religion progressively *defining itself*." If we study the history of man's religious (rational) consciousness, Caird believes that we will note that it has passed through three distinct stages in which each of the three ideas predominates.

Hence we can distinguish three stages in the development of man, in which the form of his consciousness is successively determined by the ideas of the object, of the subject and of God as the principle of unity in both; and each of these stages brings with it a special modification of the religious consciousness.[64]

Caird describes the first or objective stage of religious consciousness in much the way Hegel described Greco-Roman religion.

The earliest life of man is one in which the objective consciousness rules and determines all his thoughts, or that in this stage both his consciousness of himself and his consciousness of God are forced to take an objective form. Man at first looks outward and not inward: he can form no idea of anything to which he cannot give a "local habitation and name," which he cannot body forth as an existence in space and time . . . . God necessarily at this time must be represented as an object among other objects.[65]

The second stage of religious consciousness is that in which the subjective element predominates. This is best exemplified in the inner, prophetic religion of later Judaism, which prepared the way for the third stage, Christianity. The second period is one in which

the *form of self-consciousness* prevails and determines both the consciousness of objects and that of God. In such a period, the interest of life becomes predominantly moral, or at least subjective and the outward world loses its power over the human spirit. . . . . His mind, his inner life, is now "his kingdom" . . . . He is freed from the superstitious dread of outward things . . . the poetic halo vanishes from nature. A glory has passed away from the earth, and "great Pan is dead" . . . . The manifestation of the divine is no longer found in nature but in man. . . . Man alone is supposed to be made in the image of God . . . .[66]

The third stage, or synthesis, which is exemplified in Christianity, is that in which

the object and the self appear, each in its proper form, as distinct yet in essential relation, and, therefore, as subordinated to the consciousness of God, which is recognized as at once the presupposition and as the end of both. Here, for the first time the religious consciousness takes its true place in relation to the secular consciousness, and God is known in the *true form of His idea* . . . . This is the only form which religion can take for the modern world. It is impossible for any one who has breathed the spirit of modern science . . . to believe in a purely objective God: to worship any power of nature or even any individualized outward image such as those of Apollo or Athene . . . . Again, though our own religion is developed out of Judaism, it is impossible for moderns to recall the attitude of the pure Monotheist, to whom God was only a subject among other subjects, though lifted high above all the rest. We cannot think of the infinite Being as a will which is external to that which it has made. We cannot, indeed, think of Him as external to anything, least of all to the spiritual beings who, as such, "live and move and have their being in Him." This idea of the immanence of God underlies the Christian conception; and . . . we can see that it is an idea involved in all modern philosophy and theology.[67]

Edward Caird, like most Hegelian theologians, conceived of Christianity as the final or absolute religion in that it was the historial synthesis of the philosophically antithetical objective and subjective consciousness—the absolute religion in which God is known not as external object or highest subject but as the immanent unitary ground of all knowing and being, of subject and object.

John Caird took up the task where his brother's *The Evolution of Religion* left off, namely, with Christianity established as the absolute religion. In his *Fundamental Ideas of Christianity*, John Caird proceeds, like Hegel, to attempt to demonstrate that the seeming contradictions of positive Christian revelation are transcended when advanced to the level of speculative idea and that the Chrisian *idea* is congruent with the highest philosophical analysis of experience. Take, for example, the difficult question of God's relation to the world. Caird, like Hegel, finds in the Christian conception of God's revelation and Incarnation, a representational expression of the truth of the God-world relationship. Neither Pantheism nor Deism has been able to give an adequate view of the relation of God to the world, "Pantheism by the annulling of the finite world or its absorption in the Infinite, Deism by reducing God to a finite anthropomorphic personality." The human mind cannot rest, according to John Caird, in the idea of a God who is all only by obliterating the finite world.

The pantheistic notion of the unreality and illusoriness of the finite world involves a self-contradiction. For even *as* a mere semblance or illusion it needs to be accounted for; and that it is more than an illusion the capacity to detect its illusoriness is the unconscious witness. The mind that can look on the world from the point of view of the Infinite virtually asserts for itself something more than a negative relation to the Infinite. The contradiction thus involved in its thought forces it onwards in quest of an Infinite which contains and accounts for the finite instead of annulling it.[68]

Likewise, Deism is not rationally satisfying.

In finding a place for the finite in the presence of the Infinite, Desim satisfies the consciousness of freedom, but it does so only by rending in twain the system of the universe. It lends a false elevation to its anthropomorphic God, by placing Him in hard, transcendent opposition to the world, and it leaves in nature, and still more in the finite spirit, elements which are in no inner and essential relation to Him. The gulf between the infinite and the finite remains unbridged.[69]

Caird finds in the Christian idea of God an understanding of God's relation to the world which neither Pantheism nor Deism can satisfy. The Christian doctrine of God as Infinite, Self-revealing Spirit or Mind contains all the elements necessary for an adequate theology. It shows:

1. That it is Infinite Mind or Intelligence which constitutes the reality of the world, not simply as its external Creator, but as the inward Spirit in and through which all things live and move and have their being;

2. That by its very nature, Infinite Mind or Spirit has in it a principle of self-revelation —a necessity of self-manifestation to and in a world of finite beings; and

3. That the infinitude of God, conceived of as Infinite Spirit, so far from involving the negation or suppression of the finite world, is rather the principle of the individuality and independence of nature and man.[70]

Theology had long conceived of God as the first cause and creative source or ground of the world. What is new in Hegel and, in turn, in Caird is the idea that God's being and the world are interdependent and that this insight is rooted in the Christian doctrine of God's triune nature. Caird develops a doctrine of God similar in ways to that of twentieth-century Panentheism. *

* Contemporary Panentheists, as distinguished from Pantheists and Deists, hold that God and the world are interdependent. While

Not only is it true that the finite world can be understood only in the light of the idea of God, but there is a sense in which that idea [God] involves the existence of a finite world. In the nature of God as self-revealing Spirit, there is contained, so to speak, the necessity of His self-manifestation in and to a world of finite beings, and especially in and to a world of finite intelligences made in His own image. If it be true that without the idea of God, nature and man would be unintelligible, there is a sense in which it is also true that without nature and man God would be unintelligible.[71]

For Caird, as for Hegel, God fulfills and realizes His own nature in the temporal existence of the world, and above all in the spiritual life of man:

When we say that the plant is related to the root or germ, not arbitrarily, but by an inward and essential necessity of nature, so that the former could not be what it is without the latter, we imply conversely that the root or germ has in it something which seeks its realization in the plant, and without the latter would remain unfulfilled and incomplete. So, when we say that, in its whole spiritual nature—its intelligence, its moral and religious life, the finite spirit rests on and is rooted in the Infinite, what we imply is that in the Infinite there is that which involves the existence of the finite spirit. If there be a divine element in man, *there must be a human element in God, of which the whole spiritual life and history of the world is the manifestation.*[72] (Italics added.)

For Caird, the idea of the self-mani-

festation of Spirit, or God, in the history of the world is formulated in the language of Scripture in the expression that man is "made in the image of God." That is, human nature, though in one view only a finite existence, is nevertheless differentiated from all other existences in that it is in a special sense a manifestation of the Infinite. Part of the difficulty with such a conception lies, Caird believes, in a mistaken reading of the biblical text. Theologians have suffered from the mistaken notion that only what is perfect can have come from the hand of God or constitute God's self-manifestation. Hence theologians have indulged in imaginary pictures of the original, paradisaical perfection of man, picturing

the first representatives of mankind . . . [as] full-fledged specimens of humanity, equipped with the wisdom of the sage, the exalted virtue of the hero, the piety and holiness of the saint.[73]

This is to fail to realize that what the *imago Dei* "points to is not the *initial* or *original*, but the *ideal* perfection of man's nature . . . what it is capable of becoming."[74] Caird's reading of the biblical teaching concerning the image of God in man is essentially Hegelian.

It is not to man as originally created that likeness to God is exclusively ascribed in the Old and New Testament Scriptures. However we are to conceive of the paradisaical state, it is represented as prior to that "knowledge of good and evil," without which moral action cannot really exist and goodness can, at most, be only the unconscious innocence of childhood. Though, again, the act of disobedience by which this knowledge comes is depicted as a retrogression, it is, on the other hand, described as an advance; though it loses one kind of likeness to God, it marks the rise of another: *"Ye shall be as*

God does not limit the real freedom of the world, nor the world exhaust God's being and creativity, nevertheless, the one is unthinkable without the other. God influences the world, and the world influences God. Since there is real freedom, the future is open both for the world and God. Hence, God is, in some sense, temporal. This view is most systematically developed by A. N. Whitehead and Charles Hartshorne.

gods, knowing good and evil." And finally, the highest form of Godlikeness, according to the Scripture representation, is neither man's primitive state nor the restoration of that state. A return to forfeited innocence, a recovery of the unconscious harmony of nature which sin has broken up is impossible . . . . But the discord which sin has introduced is but the transition step to a more glorious harmony. Out of the death of nature rises a higher and nobler life. On the soul that has passed through the terrible experience of evil and, through the redemptive power of the Christian faith, has triumphed over it, there begins to be impressed a likeness to God far surpassing in spiritual beauty the lost image of Paradise . . . . It is of the very essence of a spiritual nature that its ideal perfection cannot be an immediate gift of nature, but must be wrought out by its own conscious activity.[75]

John Caird's Christology is much more orthodox than Hegel's, but even here his Hegelianism is ever present. This is especially the case in his attitude toward the historical Jesus where his Idealism is pronounced. Speaking of Christ, Caird remarks that

it is not the facts of His individual history, but the ideas that underlie it, that constitute the true value of his life. A true idea is true independently of the facts and events that first suggested it. There are many universal ideas which are their own evidence, apart from the superficial phenomena or the historic events that were the particular occasion of their discovery. The latter—the empirical, historic, element—may be disputed, may be difficult to ascertain, may even turn out to be more or less fictitious . . . . The principle remains true, whatever becomes of the facts. The life of Christ has been the source of ideas concerning God and man, and relations of human nature to the divine, transcending in originality and importance the contributions made to our knowledge of spiritual things by all other teachers. But, even if many of the details of Christ's life and teaching should fail to stand the test of scientific criticism . . . still the ideas and doctrines . . . which had their historic origin in that life, would be recognized as true in themselves, and as having an indestructible evidence in the reason and conscience of man.[76]

Because it is the *idea* which Christ represents rather than the historical occasion of Jesus as the Christ which is paramount for Caird, he can, with Hegel, give greater place to the Kingdom of the Spirit than the Kingdom of the Son. Thus, according to Caird, those who were in direct, personal contact with Jesus could only form vague and imperfect conceptions of his spiritual greatness. It was St. Paul, with his *idea* of the organic unity of all believers in Christ as their living Spirit or Head, who first saw the true import of the Christological idea. According to Caird's interpretation of Paul, no division is possible between Christ and the Church; both must be seen as a living, interdependent organism. Hence, for Caird, Christ is not fully actualized when considered in isolation from the community of believers.

And if the members live and fulfil themselves only in union with the universal principle, so, on the other hand, *does it fulfil or realize itself in them*. Apart from its members or organs, the principle of life is only an abstraction. It is, at most, not a reality, but only an unrealized possibility. . . . As an individual person He [Christ] has long passed away from the world; but He lives forever, as the everpresent, ever-active principle of its highest life.[77]

The dispensation of the Spirit is depicted pictorially in the New Testament in a variety of ways—in terms of Christ's ascension, his exaltation, the sending of the Holy Spirit at Pentecost—but underlying all these pictorial representations is the *idea* that

the divine principle which manifested itself in the human person and life of Christ, never did or can pass away from the world; and that, now and forever, it manifests itself in the life of every individual believer and in the universal or corporate life of the Church, in which "dwelleth all the fulness of the Godhead bodily."[78]

Life in the Kingdom of Absolute Spirit is described by Caird in language at once authentically Christian and markedly Hegelian:

What this absolute principle . . . demands of every human spirit is the sacrifice, the surrender, the abnegation of our private, particular self—its limited ends and interests; that we cease to think our own thoughts, to gratify our own desires, to do our own will, but rejoice to let this absolute, all-comprehending will reign in us and over us.

Yet, on the other hand, it is also the experience of the religious life that, in thus losing and abnegating, we truly gain ourselves: that our true will is not the will of this particular and private self, but a will that is in harmony with the absolute will . . . when we lose all sense of anything that divides our own self-consciousness from the consciousness of God.[79]

The Hegelianism of men like John and Edward Caird can be viewed as a kind of "third force" in the nineteenth-century defense of Christianity. First of all, there were the Kantians and especially the followers of Albrecht Ritschl (of whom we have yet to speak in Chapter Nine) and the Romanticists. Of the three major movements, Hegelianism is in certain respects the most important, although Hegel's own direct influence was shortest lived. Hegelian theology suffered the

general fate of German Idealism around the turn of the century—that is, it was abandoned as the result of philosophical analysis. Kant and Schleiermacher continue to have a pronounced influence on theological discussion, Hegel hardly any at all. Yet the seeming abandonment of Hegelian categories and ideas is deceptive; his influence lives on indirectly. Many of the issues at the center of contemporary theology find their origin in Hegel.

Part of the difficulty in assessing the present significance of Hegel lies in the ambiguity of his own position, which led to the wide-ranging interpretation of his thought by his disciples. In many ways it is easier to trace the more radical and negative influences of Hegel on theological speculation—for example, his influence on Strauss' Christ-myth theory, on Feuerbach's reduction of theology to anthropology, on Marx, and on recent theologies of the "death of God." Of all this we shall have more to say in the next chapter.

Hegel's most enduring influence on Christian thought, that which has outlived the disintegration of his own system, is his conception of nature, history, and God as fundamentally in process. For Hegel, time and history are no longer accidents of nature but the very essence of reality. The key to the structure of reality, for Hegel, is evolutionary process. The importance of such a revolution in man's comprehension of his world is still impossible to assess fully. But it is the case that today truth and reality are no longer conceived as timeless, immutable, finished. Rather, for Hegel, as for most moderns, truth is continually developing and in a process of at least becoming more fully explicit. The impact of such an idea on the study of the history of Christian dogma and tradition has been extensive both within Protestantism and Catholicism. Due largely to Hegel, a new appreciation of the totality of human spiritual life has become a part of our historical consciousness. Hegel saw the human race passing through successive stages, each reflecting a necessary moment in the development of human consciousness and each adding to a fuller comprehension of the truth. Hegel's vision of the phenomenology of the human spirit is one of the determinative influences on the historical and phenomenological study of religion in currency today.

Hegel's theistic speculation has been interpreted as leading either to "atheism," in which case God is merged with the world in such a way that divine spirit is absorbed into human spirit, or to "acosmism," in which case the world, including human spirit, is absorbed into God, who is the sole reality. Whatever may be the truth about Hegel's speculation, it is clear that Hegel and many of his disciples, like John Caird, were committed to offering a theistic position that would seek to transcend the unsatisfactory position of both pantheism and deism. In this they contributed, along with evolution, to contemporary panentheistic doctrines as developed by Samuel Alexander, Whitehead, Edgar Brightman, and Hartshorne, in which God, subject to becoming, is in some sense finite and temporal.

Hegel's system is now almost universally repudiated, and it is doubtful if his form of speculative Idealism will ever be revived. The greatness of Hegel, however, lies in the very fact that his germinal ideas have long outlived his system and continue to illumine our spiritual experience today.

NOTES

1. John H. Randall, Jr., *The Career of Philosophy*, II, 343.
2. The essays written between 1793 and 1800 were published for the first time in 1907 by Herman Nohl who entitled the collection *Hegel's Early Theological Writings*. Because Hegel scholarship went into eclipse in the English-speaking world about the time these essays were published, Hegel's early religious writings have not been widely considered in English studies of his thought. Acknowledging the great importance of Hegel's early writings, Walter Kaufmann (*Philosophical Review*, Jan. 1954) nevertheless finds Nohl's title misleading. Kaufmann considers these writings antitheological. Kaufmann is right if we mean by *theological* that which is creedal or orthodox. But a deep religious interest and conviction runs through all these writings.

3. Nohl, *Hegels theologische Jugendschriften* (Tübingen, 1907), p. 6.
4. There is considerable disagreement as to just what were Hegel's intentions in writing *Das Leben Jesu*. Kroner ("Introduction," *Hegel's Early Theological Writings*, ed. T. M. Knox, Harper, 1961) and Kaufmann (*Hegel*, Doubleday, 1965) agree that Hegel did not intend it for publication. Kroner, however, believes Hegel did not commit himself to the book's interpretation, whereas Kaufmann holds that it "is plainly Hegel's attempt to write a scripture for such a folk religion as he had envisaged" and that "it may have been at least partly the grotesqueness of this effort that persuaded him once and for all that man could *not* be restored in his totality and harmony by religion." T. M. Knox ("Hegel's Attitude Toward Kant's Ethics," *Kant-Studien*, Vol. 49, No. 1)

contends that Hegel was seriously under the influence of Kant at this time and discharged his duty of writing a life of Jesus in harmony with his master's spirit, but that this very duty "eventually helped to convince him that there was something wrong with the enterprise."

5. Nohl, pp. 221–223.

6. Ibid., p. 222.

7. Ibid., p. 227. The similarity of this statement to those made by the later Left-Wing Hegelian critics of Christianity, such as Feuerbach and Marx, is striking.

8. Ibid., p. 208.

9. "The Spirit of Christianity . . .", in T. M. Knox, ed., *Hegel's Early Theological Writings*, p. 185.

10. Ibid., p. 187.

11. Ibid., p. 209.

12. Ibid., p. 212.

13. Nohl, op. cit., pp. 280–283.

14. "The Spirit of Christianity," op. cit., p. 247.

15. Ibid., p. 11.

16. Ibid., p. 289.

17. Ibid., p. 301.

18. Ibid., p. 253.

19. Nohl, op. cit., as cited in Kaufmann, op. cit., pp. 65–66.

20. Hegel, *Vorlesungen über die Philosophie der Weltgeschichte*, I, 45. Ed., Hoffmeister (Hamburg, 1955); cited by Stephen Crites, "The Gospel According to Hegel," *The Journal of Religion*, XLVI (April, 1966), 248. Crites' article is an excellent, brief summary of the mature Hegel's understanding of Christianity and was of considerable help to this writer in grasping an overview of Hegel's interpretation of Christianity.

21. Hegel deals with the "Unhappy Consciousness" at considerable length in *The Phenomenology of Spirit*, where he identifies it especially with the religious life of the Middle Ages under the dominion of the Roman Catholic Church and Feudalism.

22. *The Philosophy of History*, tr. J. Sibree (New York, 1944), p. 321.

23. Ibid., pp. 321–322. Hegel was fond of explicating the text from Genesis concerning Adam's Fall and discussions of it can be found, in addition to the above, in *History of Philosophy*, tr. Haldane, III, 8–10; *The Philosophy of Religion*, tr. Speirs and Sanderson, II, 200–204, III, 46–59; and, in an earlier form, in *The Phenomenology of Spirit*, tr. Baillie, pp. 770–772.

24. *Philosophy of Religion*, tr. Speirs and Sanderson, III, 48.

25. Ibid., pp. 52–53.

26. Ibid., p. 54.

27. Ibid.

28. Ibid.

29. *Philosophy of History*, op. cit., p. 323.

30. Ibid., pp. 325–326.

31. Ibid., pp. 324–325.

32. Here Hegel's Christology has much in common with the views of Paul Tillich. See this writer's "Tillich's Christology and Historical Research" in *Religion in Life* (Winter, 1966).

33. *Philosophy of Religion*, op. cit., p. 89.

34. Ibid.

35. *Phenomenology of Spirit*, op. cit., p. 780.

36. *Philosophy of Religion*, op. cit., p. 99.

37. *Philosophy of History*, op. cit., p. 325.

38. Ibid., p. 328.

39. *Philosophy of Religion*, op. cit., p. 10.

40. Ibid., p. 11.

41. Ibid., I, p. 100.

42. *Philosophy of Religion*, op. cit., II, 334.

43. See J. M. E. McTaggart's comments on the personality of God in Hegel's theology in *Studies in Hegelian Cosmology* (Cambridge, 1918), pp. 205 f.

44. *Philosophy of Religion*, op. cit., III. Cf. *The Encyclopedia*, ¶564.

45. For Hegel's discussion of religious *Vorstellungen*, see *Philosophy of Religion*, I, 142 f.

46. James Collins, *God in Modern Philosophy* (Chicago, 1959), p. 235. For a different view of Hegel's demand that Christianity be *aufgehoben* into philosophy, see the article by Stephen Crites, op. cit.

47. Karl Löwith, *From Hegel to Nietzsche* (New York, 1964), p. 333.

48. It is interesting to note that Karl Barth has some very positive things to say about Biedermann's program: "The task of free theological study [for Biedermann] was just to study Christian doctrine, as it developed in accordance with its inner necessity, and illuminate it by considering the question of its real meaning . . . in other words, to raise it from the level of intuition to that of pure concept . . . . It was, in the sense in which he [Biedermann] understood it, a good programme, and a most promising legacy. And if I were a liberal theologian I should ask myself if it might not be salutary, even at the cost of having to go a good way along with Hegel, to take it up fresh in its entirety." (*The Hibbert Journal*, LIX [April, 1961], p. 215).

49. A. E. Biedermann, *Christian Dogmatics*, §716, n. 6, as translated in Claude Welch, ed., *God and Incarnation in Mid-Nineteenth Century German Theology* (New York, 1965), p. 363.

50. Ibid., pp. 363–364.

51. Ibid., p. 367.

52. Ibid.

53. Ibid.

54. Ibid.

55. Ibid., pp. 368–369.

56. Ibid., p. 374.

57. Ibid., p. 375.

58. Ibid., pp. 375–376.

59. Ibid., p. 376.

60. Ibid., pp. 376–379.

61. Ibid., p. 381.

62. Edward Caird, *The Evolution of Religion* (New York, 1893), I, 64–65.

63. Ibid., pp. 67–68.

64. Ibid., pp. 188–189.

65. Ibid., p. 189.

66. Ibid., pp. 191–192.

67. Ibid., pp. 195–196.

68. John Caird, *The Fundamental Ideas of Christianity* (Glasgow, 1915), I, 140–141.

69. Ibid., p. 142.

70. Ibid., pp. 143–144.

71. Ibid., p. 154.

72. Ibid., pp. 155–156.

73. Ibid., pp. 170–171.

74. Ibid., p. 169.

75. Ibid., pp. 171–172.

76. Ibid., II, 241–242.

77. Ibid., pp. 245–246.

78. Ibid., p. 247.

79. Ibid., pp. 249–250.

SUGGESTIONS FOR FURTHER READING

INTRODUCTIONS TO HEGEL'S PHILOSOPHY

Caird, Edward. *Hegel* (Philadelphia: J. P. Lippincott Co., 1883). Still regarded as the best brief outline.

Findley, J. N. *Hegel: A Re-Examination* (New York: The Macmillan Co., 1958). A suggestive, sympathetic account, minimizing the metaphysical aspects of Hegel.

Kaufmann, W. *Hegel* (New York: Doubleday Anchor Book, 1965). A recent re-evaluation of Hegel the man, the philosopher. Takes into account the important early years and writings. Excellent bibliography.

Mure, G. R. G. *The Philosophy of Hegel* (New York: Oxford University Press, 1965). Good beginning introduction for the general reader.

Stace, W. T. *The Philosophy of Hegel* (New York: Dover Publications, 1955). A detailed summary of Hegel's mature system, but ignores the early Hegel.

HEGEL'S EARLY THEOLOGICAL WRITINGS

Kaufmann, W. *Hegel, op. cit.*, and "The Young Hegel and Religion" in *From Shakespeare to Existentialism* (New York: Doubleday Anchor Books, 1960). Kaufmann interprets the young Hegel differently than does Kroner.

Kroner, Richard. "Introduction," *On Christianity: Early Theological Writings*, ed. T. M.

Knox (New York: Harper Torchbook, 1961). This volume contains the most important of Hegel's early theological writings with an excellent introduction by Kroner.

HEGEL'S MATURE PHILOSOPHY OF RELIGION

Crites, Stephen. "The Gospel According to Hegel," *The Journal of Religion*, XLVI (April, 1966). An excellent brief account.

Fackenheim, Emil. *The Religious Dimensions of Hegel's Thought* (Bloomington: Indiana University Press, 1967).

McTaggart, J. M. E. *Studies in Hegelian Cosmology* (Cambridge: Cambridge University Press, 1918). Brilliant analysis of some of Hegel's religious concepts, including his interpretation of Christianity.

CHAPTER SEVEN

The Post-Hegelian Critique of Christianity in Germany

Ludwig Feuerbach

Each in his own way, Kant, Schleiermacher, and Hegel had attempted to reestablish the positive Christian tradition on a new philosophical basis. Beginning in the 1830's, these grand syntheses began breaking down. From Hegel to Nietzsche, German thought was characterized in one respect by its relentless philosophical criticism of Christianity. The 1830's and 1840's were dominated philosophically by the students of Hegel, whose system had left considerable room for dispute.

This was especially true of two fundamental issues of the time: theism and social philosophy. These issues divided the Hegelians into two parties, the Right and Left Wing. The Right Wing, made up of men like K. Daub, P. Marheineke, and A. Biedermann, believed that Hegel's speculative idealism was the perfect instrument for interpreting the truths of historic Christianity. The Left Wing, or "Young Hegelians," were convinced that Hegel's *Aufhebungen* represented a dissolution of historical Christianity and the emergence of a new religion of man.

Among the radical "Young Hegelians" were David Friedrich Strauss, Ludwig Feuerbach, Bruno Bauer, and Karl Marx. These men reveal much in common. All were radical Hegelians; all were activists, and their writings were characterized by a polemical, programmatic spirit; all were ruthlessly logical and honest and, as a result of their writings, were outcasts who suffered from the loss of teaching positions and withdrawal from society. Each contributed to the most far-reaching historical and metaphysical critique Christianity has yet had to face. An understanding of the writings of these men will therefore illuminate considerably the issues which dominate much of later nineteenth- and twentieth-century theology.

David Friedrich Strauss (1808–1874)

Karl Barth has said that D. F. Strauss signifies the bad conscience of modern theology, for he "confronted theology with a series of questions upon which it has not, right down to the present day, perhaps, adequately declared itself."[1] The questions which Strauss raised in a radical way were the historical questions concerning Christianity's origins—questions which, as Barth suggests, more recent theologians have "simply by-passed." Strauss is not read any more, and his influence on academic theology was not as considerable as one might expect, even in his own day. However, there probably was no theologian of the nineteenth century who was better known and had a greater influence on intellectual circles outside the Church in

both Germany and England than D. F. Strauss.*

D. F. Strauss was born at Ludwigsburg in Germany and from 1821 to 1825 attended the theological seminary at Blaubeuren where he was a student of the historian F. C. Baur. In 1825 he went to Tübingen where he came under the influence of the writings of Hegel. He served briefly as an assistant pastor at Klein-Ingersheim near Ludwigsburg and then, in 1831, went to Berlin to attend the lectures of Schleiermacher and Hegel. A few months after his arrival Hegel died of cholera, and Strauss soon lost sympathy with Schleiermacher's teachings. In the spring of 1832 Strauss returned to Tübingen to take up the position of assistant lecturer in the theological college. This offered him an opportunity to lecture on philosophy, and he did so as a zealous disciple of Hegel. At this point in his career he could write:

In my theology philosophy occupies such a predominant position that my theological views can only be worked out to completeness by means of a more thorough study of philosophy, and this course of study I am now going to prosecute uninterruptedly and without concerning myself whether it leads me back to theology or not.[2]

Strauss had already come to realize that his theological views were an offense to his colleagues, so he refused to deliver lectures on theology. Nevertheless, it was during this period that he wrote his *Leben Jesu, kritische bearbeitet* (*Life of Jesus, a Critical Treatment*) which was first published in two volumes in 1835. This book propelled Strauss into the limelight and

---

* The influence of Strauss on mid-Victorian English religious thought will be indicated in the next chapter.

made him at once the most controversial theologian in Germany. It also destroyed any opportunities for further advancement in either the university or Church. Steudel, the conservative president of the theological college, succeeded in having Strauss removed from his post as lecturer.

Strauss' academic career thus came to an abrupt end. He returned to Stuttgart where he lived for many years and busied himself with writing to his critics and preparing new editions of the *Leben Jesu*. For reasons not entirely known, Strauss issued a third edition of the book in 1838–1839 which was irenical in spirit and conceded many points to his critics. That same year he published a series of monologues entitled "Transient and Permanent Elements in Christianity" which was reissued the following year as "Leaves of Peace." It appeared that these actions might bring about Strauss' reinstatement in the academic world, and in January of 1839 he was appointed professor of dogmatics at Zurich. However, conservative opposition prevailed; the government revoked the appointment and Strauss was pensioned off. This, and his own coming into financial independence at the death of his father, gave Strauss a new sense of freedom and turned him, once and for all, against all attempts at compromise.

In 1840–1841 he published *Die christliche Glaubenslehre* (*The Christian Doctrine of Faith*) in which he sought to show how Christian doctrine grew out of its ancient environment and became harmonized with later philosophical speculation. The book concludes by advocating the dissolution of traditional supernaturalism, replacing it with a purely secular, Hegelian theology of Absolute Spirit.

From the early 1840's to 1864 Strauss removed himself from theological debate.

During this time he served as a journalist, wrote biographies of Ulrich von Hutten and H. S. Reimarus, and entered politics. Strauss reentered the theological arena once again in 1864 with his second life of Jesus, this one entitled *A Life of Jesus for the German People*. It is totally different from the first *Leben Jesu*. Whereas the first book called into question the very possibility of reconstructing a life of Jesus, the book of 1864 is hardly a notch better than the common, garden-variety lives of Jesus that became so popular in the latter decades of the nineteenth century. Strauss tried to write a life of Jesus for the German people as Ernst Renan had done for his fellow Frenchmen. Whereas Renan succeeded in presenting a portrait of Jesus which was, though fanciful, full of life and popular appeal, Strauss failed. The new life of Jesus was stiff and sober, devoid of movement and feeling.

Strauss' last book, *The Old Faith and the New*, appeared in 1872. This last work reveals no Promethean anti-Christ but, rather, the ideals of an intellectual bourgeoisie without, as Barth remarks, "the slightest notion of all the true heights and depths of life, the bourgeoisie quality in its specific national German form at the sunset hour of the age of Goethe."[3]

Indeed, the Strauss of the *Leben Jesu* of 1864 and of *The Old Faith and the New* is a pale, almost unrecognizable reflection of the author of the first *Leben Jesu*. Although these later books went through several editions, they were scorned by the theologians who now declared Strauss intellectually bankrupt. Strauss suffered all his life from rebuffs but never so painfully as in these last years. Not a year after the publication of *The Old Faith and the New*, Strauss was stricken with an internal ulcer which he suffered from for several months until his death in February of 1874. The great enemy of Christianity was now dead—dead but not overcome, for the questions which he raised in the *Leben Jesu* of 1835 continue to rise up before us even today. It is, therefore, to the *Leben Jesu* of 1835 that we must turn to learn of the real challenge put to Christian theology by D. F. Strauss.

The *Leben Jesu* of 1835. Albert Schweitzer says of Strauss' first *Life of Jesus* that it "is one of the most perfect things in the whole range of learned literature." The book is provocative and programmatic. Strauss was convinced that the study of the New Testament was impaled on "the antiquated systems of supranaturalism and naturalism" and that the new hermeneutical key to the New Testament, and especially to the study of the Gospel accounts of Jesus, was the *mythical*.

Strauss acknowledged that this interpretive key was not new but that it had never to his own time been applied to the New Testament in a radically consistent manner. Biblical interpretation had from ancient times been either *supernaturalist* or *rationalist*.

The exegesis of the ancient church set out from the double presupposition: first, that the gospels contain a history, and secondly, that this history was a supernatural one. Rationalism rejected the latter of these presuppositions, but only to cling the more tenaciously to the former, maintaining that these books present unadulterated, though only natural history. Science cannot rest satisfied with this half measure: the other presupposition must also be relinquished, and the inquiry must first be made whether in fact, and to what extent, the ground on which we stand in the gospels is historical.[4]

This is Strauss' program: to test *the historical claims* of the New Testament concerning Jesus. Strauss felt that most theologians of his day were lacking in the one requirement needed for the pursuit of this task, "namely, the internal liberation of the feelings and intellect from certain religious and dogmatical presuppositions,"[5] the freedom which Strauss had achieved by means of his philosophical studies. Strauss, the disciple of Hegel, concludes his Preface to the first edition with the following claim that could only amaze and shock theologians and historians standing outside the Idealist camp:

The author is aware that the essence of the Christian faith is perfectly independent of his criticism. The supernatural birth of Christ, his miracles, his resurrection and ascension, remain eternal truths, whatever doubts may be cast on their reality as historical facts ... that the dogmatic significance of the life of Jesus remains inviolate: in the meantime let the calmness and insensibility with which, in the course of it, criticism undertakes apparently dangerous operations, be explained solely by the security of the author's conviction that no injury is threatened to the Christian faith.[6]

The long introduction to the book consists of an analysis of the development of biblical interpretation to Strauss' own time, the threshold of the mythical point of view, and a consideration as to the reasons why the mythical viewpoint was so long opposed. The basic reasons why the concept of myth was not readily adapted to the study of the New Testament was the long association of the term with the study of pagan religion and the false idea that myth was found principally in primitive cultures in which written records of events were not common. Strauss points out that since the investigations of Bauer, Gabler, and Eichhorn it is clear that, while the New Testament history is by no means altogether mythical, the history is woven through with mythical materials.

Another reason why theologians failed to apply the concept of myth to the New Testament was the supposition that the Gospel events were written by eye-witnesses.

But this alleged ocular testimony, or proximity in point of time of the sacred historians to the events recorded, is mere assumption, an assumption originating from the titles which the biblical books bear in the Canon .... But that little reliance can be placed on the headings of ancient manuscripts, and of sacred records more especially, is evident, and in reference to biblical books has long since been proved .... It is an incontrovertible position of modern criticism that the titles of the biblical books represent nothing more than the design of their author or the opinion of Jewish or Christian antiquity respecting their origin.[7]

The fact was that by Strauss' time historians seriously questioned the notion that the Gospel writers were eye-witnesses, and even if only a single generation separated Jesus from these writers, that was more than enough time to allow for mythical elaboration.

Finally, some brave souls had conceded that myth can be found in the traditions concerning the origin and final destiny of Jesus, the birth and ascension traditions, but extended their application of the mythical theory no further.

Thus the two extremities were cut off by the pruning knife of criticism, whilst the essential body of the history, the period from the baptism to the resurrection, remained as yet unassailed: the entrance to the gospel history was through the decorated portal of mythus and the exit was similar to it, whilst the intermediate space was traversed by the crooked and toilsome paths of natural interpretation.[8]

Strauss finds no scientific justification for such a limited application of myth as an interpretive key.

The proceedings of these Eclectics is most arbitrary, since they decide respecting what belongs to the history and to the mythus almost entirely upon subjective grounds. Such distinctions are equally foreign to the evangelists, to logical reasoning and to historical criticism. In consistency with these opinions, this writer applies the notion of the mythus to the entire history of the life of Jesus; recognizes mythi or mythical embellishments in every portion, and ranges under the category of mythus not merely the miraculous occurrences during the infancy of Jesus, but those also of his public life; not merely miracles operated on Jesus, but those wrought by him.[9]

That Strauss overestimates the place of mythical material in the Gospels is generally acknowledged today. However, this should not obscure the significance of Strauss' *historical* discovery, namely that the supernaturalists and rationalists were reading their own presuppositions into the thought forms of primitive Christianity. Quite aware that the Palestinian Jews of Jesus' day lacked an historical consciousness, Strauss assumes, in part rightly, that they thought in mythopoetic terms.

To be unable to conceive of the Jews of Jesus' day thinking mythically is indicative of the failure of the theologians to think historically. Myth, for Strauss, is the natural mode of perception in the prescientific, prehistorical mind. Unmindful of this, or refusing to accept such a view, the supernaturalists are forced to exempt the events of biblical history from the laws of general experience, whereas the rationalists are forced to admit that the witnesses misinterpreted what they saw or that the writers were misinformed. In any case, unconscious or conscious deception was at work. For Strauss no such tortured arguments are required. Myth is the natural language of religion.

If religion be defined as the perception of truth, not in the form of an idea, which is the philosophic perception, but invested with imagery, it is easy to see that the mythical element can be wanting only when religion either falls short of it, or goes beyond its peculiar province, and that in the proper religious sphere it must necessarily exist.[10]

According to Strauss, the Gospel writers were generally not guilty of fraudulent intention. The myths with which Jesus' life and works were invested were not inventions but simply lay at hand in the Jewish expectations of a coming Messiah.

The expectation of a Messiah had grown up amongst the Israelitish people long before the time of Jesus and just then had ripened to full maturity . . . thus many of the legends respecting him (Jesus) had not to be newly invented; they already existed in the popular hope of the Messiah . . . and had merely to be transferred to Jesus and accommodated to his character and doctrines. In no case could it be easier for the person who first added any new feature to the description of Jesus, to believe himself its genuineness, since his argument would be: Such and such things must have happened to the Messiah; Jesus was the Messiah; therefore such and such things happened to him.[11]

Thus it was that very few new myths were actually formed by the early Christian community; there remained only

the necessity of transferring to Jesus the living Messianic legends, already formed, with very few alterations.

Having shown the possible existence of myth as a natural phenomenon in the New Testament, Strauss turns next to the question of how, in particular cases, the presence of myth can be determined— i.e., the criteria for distinguishing the mythical and the historical in the Gospels. Strauss recognizes both negative and positive criteria for determining the presence of mythical material. One can be relatively certain that an event could not have taken place as described, i.e., could not be historical, if the following conditions are present:

I. *Negative. First.* When the narration is irreconcilable with the known and universal laws which govern the course of events. Now according to these laws, agreeing with all just philosophical conceptions and all credible experience, the absolute cause never disturbs the chain of secondary causes by single, arbitrary acts of interposition, but rather manifests itself in the production of the aggregate of finite causalities, and their reciprocal action. When therefore we meet with an account of certain phenomena or events of which it is either expressly stated or implied that they were produced immediately by God himself (divine apparitions—voices from heaven and the like), or by human beings possessed of supernatural powers (miracles, prophecies), such an account is *in so far* to be considered as not historical.

Another law which controls the course of events is the law of succession, in accordance with which all occurrences, not excepting the most violent convulsions and the most rapid changes, follow in a certain order of sequence of increase and decrease. If therefore we are told of a celebrated individual that he attracted already at his birth and during his childhood that attention which he excited in his manhood; that his followers at a single glance recognized him as being all that he actually was; if the transition from the deepest despondency to the most ardent enthusiasm after his death is represented as the work of a single hour; we must feel more than doubtful whether it is a real history which lies before us. Lastly, all those psychological laws, which render it improbable that a human being should feel, think and act in a manner directly opposed to his own habitual mode and that of men in general, must be taken into consideration. As for example, when the Jewish Sanhedrin are represented as believing the declaration of the watch at the grave that Jesus was risen, and instead of accusing them of having suffered the body to be stolen away whilst they were asleep, bribing them to give currency to such a report. By the same rule it is contrary to all the laws belonging to the human faculty of memory that long discourses, such as those of Jesus given in the fourth Gospel, could have been faithfully recollected and reproduced . . . .

Secondly. An account which shall be regarded as historically valid must neither be inconsistent with itself, nor in contradiction with other accounts. The most decided case falling under this rule, amounting to a positive contradiction, is when one account affirms what another denies. Thus, one gospel represents the first appearance of Jesus in Galilee as subsequent to the imprisonment of John the Baptist, whilst another Gospel remarks, long after Jesus had preached both in Galilee and in Judea, that 'John was not yet cast into prison . . . .'

Sometimes an occurrence is represented in two or more ways, of which only one can be consistent with reality; as when in one account Jesus calls his first disciples from their nets while fishing on the sea of Galilee, and in the other meets them in Judea on his way to Galilee. We may class under the same head instances where events or discourses are represented as having occurred on two distinct occasions, whilst they are so similar that it is impossible to resist the conclusion that both the narratives refer to the same event or discourse.

II. *Positive.* The positive characters of legend and fiction are to be recognized sometimes in the form, sometimes in the substance of a narrative.

If the *form* be poetical, if the actors converse in hymns, and in a more diffuse and elevated strain than might be expected from their training and situations, such discourses, at all events, are not to be regarded as historical. The absence of these marks of the unhistorical do not however prove the historical validity of the narration, since the mythus often wears the most simple and apparently historical form; in which case the proof lies in the substance.

If the *contents* of a narrative strikingly accord with certain ideas existing and prevailing within the circle from which the narrative proceeded, which ideas themselves seem to be the product of preconceived opinions rather than of practical experience, it is more or less probable . . . that such a narrative is of mythical origin. The knowledge of the fact that the Jews were fond of representing their great men as the children of parents who had long been childless, cannot but make us doubtful of the historical truth of the statement that this was the case with John the Baptist; knowing also that the Jews saw predictions everywhere in the writings of the prophets and poets, and discovered types of Messiah in all the lives of holy men recorded in their Scriptures; when we find details of the life of Jesus evidently sketched after the pattern of these prophecies and prototypes, we cannot but suspect that they are rather mythical than historical.[12]

Equipped with these rules of historical criticism, Strauss turned to the Gospel accounts of the life of Jesus and painstakingly examined each separate pericope. Each incident is carefully considered, first as it was traditionally explained according to supernaturalism and then according to the accounts of rationalism. Strauss plays the one type of interpretation off against the other, thus opening up the possibility of a mythical explanation of many of the events and discourses of Jesus' career. However, it would be quite wrong to say, as has been done, that Strauss dissolved the life of Jesus into myth. Because of his systematic application of the mythical theory and his isolated approach to each pericope, it is true that Strauss saw far less historical material in the New Testament than most critical historians working on the Gospel traditions today. Nevertheless, he acknowledged that many incidents have an historical core—including, for example, Jesus' baptism, the cleansing of the Temple and even Jesus' Messianic consciousness. Strauss also makes it clear that the real facts of the case often cannot be determined and wishes especially to guard himself, in those instances where he declares "he knows not what happened, from the imputation of asserting that he knows that nothing happened."[13]

Despite the fact that Strauss saw more myth in the Gospels than is warranted, his work on the life of Jesus, in Schweitzer's words, "marked out the ground which is now occupied by modern critical study."[14] We can be fairly certain that those who are still confident of reconstructing the life of Jesus without taking into consideration the considerable amount of mythical tradition in the Gospels have either not taken the trouble to read Strauss or fear to do so. Some indication of the assumptions concerning life-of-Jesus research before Strauss will make clearer the historical significance of his critical work. Until the appearance of Strauss' *Leben Jesu* it was widely assumed that the Gospel traditions were historical sources for the life of Jesus in the very same sense that Roman histories of Livy could be used as sources for the life of the Emperors; also, that the historical Jesus could be easily distinguished

from the sources themselves, as the kernel can be extracted from its husk; even more, that Jesus as an historical personality, including his development and his own self-consciousness, were accessible to historical research.

Strauss called all of these assumptions into question. He did not deny that many of the sources had an historical core but emphasized instead that these traditions are fundamentally mythical-religious ideas couched in poetic imagery. Peel away the mythical material, and there is some history, here and there, but exceedingly little—certainly not enough to reconstruct a life of the man Jesus so that he might become accessible as a human personality. For Strauss, the only Jesus who is accessible in the sources, i.e., the apostolic testimonies, is the superhuman God-man, the mythical Messianic figure prophesied in the Jewish literature.

It was Strauss who first raised, in such a radical way, the question of the historical accessibility of Jesus, and whether it was possible to separate the Jesus of history from the Christ of faith. And Strauss' importance as a theologian is assured if for no other reason than for raising this historical question, for it has remained at the center of theological discussion to the present day.

Strauss put the *historical* warrants for Christian faith on a very uncertain foundation, and all those who take Christianity seriously as an historical religion have had to come to terms with Strauss' questions. If Strauss remains, as Barth claims, the bad conscience of modern theology, it is because too many theologians since his time have avoided and bypassed his challenge. Chief among these "avoiders" of Strauss, as we shall see later, are Karl Barth himself and the theologians of the Neo-Orthodox movement. It is significant that Barth, who claims to love the questions which Strauss raised, has at the same time said that "proper theology begins just at the point where the difficulties disclosed by Strauss are seen *and then laughed at*"! (Italics added.) It will, however, take considerably more than laughter to silence D. F. Strauss.

Strauss' work, it was soon shown, had many serious faults.[15] Like many innovators, he carried his discovery too far. The historical material in the New Testament is more extensive than Strauss was wont to admit, and his rather narrow concern with the question of "What really happened" blinded him to other important historical questions such as the *meaning* of the mythical narratives.[16] Nevertheless, these limitations do not detract seriously from Strauss' real significance, which was to demonstrate that as an historical religion Christianity could not escape the scrutiny of historical-critical research and that this very inquiry raised the vexing question of whether and just how the claims of theology and the findings of critical historical research could be held together.

As if this were not enough, having confronted the historical question in Strauss, Christian theology soon faced an attack of equally serious proportions on its metaphysical flank in the person of Ludwig Feuerbach.

Ludwig Feuerbach (1804–1872)

Unlike Strauss, Ludwig Feuerbach was not only a follower of Hegel but studied for two years under the master in Berlin. Son of a Bavarian lawyer, Feuerbach began his academic career in theology at Heidelberg as a student of the rationalist Paulus (who was criticized by Strauss in

his *Leben Jesu*) and the Hegelian, Karl Daub. Feuerbach was as little impressed by Paulus as was Strauss, calling the former's teachings "a spider web of sophistries." Feuerbach moved to Berlin in 1824 to hear Schleiermacher, Marheineke, and Neander but was drawn to Hegel and soon devoted himself entirely to philosophy. He concluded his studies under Hegel with a dissertation in 1828 and was appointed a Privatdozent in philosophy at Erlangen. There he gave a controversial lecture, "Thoughts on Death and Immortality," which destroyed his chances for any further academic advancement. As a result, Feuerbach gave up his academic career and became a private scholar, living for some time in a small Bavarian village. There he wrote a *History of Modern Philosophy* as far as Spinoza, studies on Leibniz and Pierre Bayle, and, in 1839, a critique of Hegel's philosophy. Between 1841 and 1848 Feuerbach produced three of his most important works on philosophy and religion, *The Essence of Christianity* (1841), *The Philosophy of the Future* (1843), and *The Essence of Religion*, delivered as lectures in Heidelberg in 1848, but not published until 1851. At the time of his death in 1872 he was living as a private scholar near Nuremberg.

The Critique of Hegel. Although Feuerbach was deeply influenced by Hegel, even as a student he was resolved not to become simply a Hegelian. His dissertation revealed an early move away from Hegel's Idealism toward a more sensuous and materialistic dialectic. In fact, Feuerbach has been referred to as "Hegel's fate," in that his thought represents the complete antithesis of Hegel's, while at the same time having required and been prepared for by the Hegelian system.

Feuerbach found Hegel's philosophy especially deficient in its understanding of the role of sense-experience in knowledge. Feuerbach agreed with Hegel that philosophy starts with Being, but for Feuerbach Being is not to be equated with Thought, but with Nature; and Nature is the ground of all human consciousness and thought, not the reverse. For Feuerbach philosophy must not begin with abstract thought but with the many determinate things which are immediately given to us in sensory experience. According to Feuerbach, philosophers since Descartes have disregarded sense experience and have been like men "who have torn their eyes out of their heads in order to think more clearly." This is due in part to the fact that modern philosophy has been in bondage to theology. This is especially true of Hegel. Idealism is, in fact, nothing but a new form of Neoplatonism and, for Feuerbach, Hegel is the last of a long line of Christian apologists.

Hegelian philosophy is the last refuge, the last rationalistic support of theology. Just as once the Catholic theologians became *de facto* Aristotelians in order to combat Protestantism, so now the Protestant theologians must become *de jure* Hegelians in order to combat atheism . . . . Hegelian philosophy is the last ambitious attempt to reestablish lost, defeated Christianity by means of philosophy, by following the universal modern procedure and identifying the negation of Christianity with Christianity itself. The much lauded speculative identity of spirit and material, infinite and finite, divine and human, is nothing more than the accursed paradox of the modern age: the identity of belief and unbelief, theology and philosophy, religion and atheism, Christianity and paganism, at the very summit, the summit of metaphysics. Hegel conceals this contradiction by making of atheism, the negation, an objective component of God—God as a process, and atheism as one component of this process.[17]

Feuerbach rejects such speculative theology and the various surrogates for God that philosophy has devised. He calls for the first principle of philosophy to be "a *real* being, the true *Ens realissimum—man.*"[18] If one looks deeply within the Hegelian speculative theology, one can discern this true *Ens realissimum*, for Hegel's metaphysics is, Feuerbach contends, in truth "an esoteric psychology." If one pierces behind the outward form of Hegel's metaphysical nonsense, one discovers profound psychological and anthropological truths. What Hegel's religious speculations reveal essentially is the psychological fact of man's own self-alienation reflected in his religious consciousness of God. Hegel has unconsciously brought to light the fact that religion is the revelation of a self-alienated humanity.

For Hegel man was conceived as God in his self-alienation; for Feuerbach the exact opposite is the truth, i.e., *God is man in his self-alienation.* Thus to understand the truth of Hegel, one must carry out what Feuerbach calls "transformational criticism."

It suffices to put the predicate in place of the subject everywhere, i.e., *to turn speculative theology upside down*, and we arrive at the truth in its unconcealed, pure, manifest form.[19]

Hegel would state his doctrine of God as follows:

Man is the revealed God: in man divine essence first realizes itself and unfolds itself. In the creation of Nature God goes outside of himself, he has relation to what is other than himself, but in man he returns into himself:—man knows God, because in him God finds and knows himself, feels himself as God.[20]

For Feuerbach this is the truth turned on its head; God is the revealed man:

If it is only in human feelings and wants that the divine "nothing" becomes something, obtains qualities, then the being of man is alone the real being of God—man is the real God. And if in the consciousness which man has of God first arises the self-consciousness of God, then the human consciousness is, *per se*, the divine consciousness. Why then dost thou alienate man's consciousness from him, and make it the self-consciousness of a being distinct from man, of that which is an object to him? . . . The true statement is this: man's knowledge of God is man's knowledge of himself, of his own nature . . . . Where the consciousness of God is, there is the being of God—in man, therefore; in the being of God it is only thy own being which is an object to thee, and what presents itself *before* thy consciousness is simply what lies *behind* it. If the divine qualities are human, the human qualities are divine.[21]

Turned upside down, Hegel's "speculative theology" gives us the key to the secret about man, for the secret of theology is anthropology. In theology man projects his own being into objectivity (God) and hence man's religion is man's own self and activity externalized and objectified. "God is, *per se*, his (man's) relinquished self."[22]

The Reduction of Christianity to Anthropology. Feuerbach originally intended to entitle *The Essence of Christianity*, "Know Thyself," for the essence of religion was man's own alienated self. Feuerbach conceived of himself as a

second Luther, for just as Luther had given birth to a new form of Christianity out of the old, so Feuerbach saw himself bringing to birth a new religion of man; to label him an atheist is to fail to appreciate the deeply religious motivation of his work. His religion of man was, he claimed, badly misunderstood when simply labeled "atheism."

He who says no more of me than that I am an atheist, says and knows *nothing* of me. The question as to the existence or non-existence of God, the opposition between theism and atheism, belongs to the sixteenth and seventeenth centuries but not to the nineteenth. I deny God. But that means for me that I deny the negation of man . . . The question concerning the existence or non-existence of God is for me nothing but the question concerning the existence or non-existence of man.[23]

According to Feuerbach, his critics could rightly accuse him neither of negative motives nor of wishing to destroy religion.

The reproach that according to my book religion is an absurdity, a nullity, a pure illusion, would be well-founded only if, according to it, that into which I resolve religion, which I prove to be its true object and substance, namely, *man—anthropology*, were an absurdity, a nullity, a pure illusion . . . . I, on the contrary, while reducing theology to anthropology, exalt anthropology into theology, very much as Christianity, while lowering God into man, made man into God . . . .[24]

Feuerbach proceeds to examine Christianity, as the perfect paradigm of religion, according to a strict anthropological method. That is, traced genetically to their human source, Christian beliefs and practices reveal man's own deepest self-consciousness—his needs, his fears, and his fondest hopes. "Religion," says

Feuerbach, "is the dream of the human mind." But he adds,

even in dreams we do not find ourselves in emptiness or in heaven, but on earth, in the realm of reality; we only see things in the entrancing splendour of imagination and caprice.[25]

What needs to be done, then, is to "change the object as it is in the imagination into the object as it is in reality."

Religion is actually the revelation of man's uniqueness. Only man is a *homo religiosus*, for only in man is religion identical with self-consciousness, with the consciousness that man has of his own unique nature.

Religion, expressed generally, is consciousness of the infinite; thus it is and can be nothing else than the consciousness which man has of his own—not finite and limited, but infinite nature. A really finite being has not even the faintest adumbration, still less consciousness, of an infinite being, for the limit of the nature is also the limit of the consciousness. The consciousness of the caterpillar, whose life is confined to a particular species of plant, does not extend itself beyond this narrow domain . . . . A consciousness so limited we do not call consciousness, but instinct. Consciousness, in the strict or proper sense, is identical with consciousness of the infinite; a limited consciousness is no consciousness; consciousness is essentially infinite in its nature. The consciousness of the infinite is nothing else than the consciousness of the infinity of the consciousness; or, in the consciousness of the infinite, the conscious subject has for his object the infinity of his own nature.[26]

In Feuerbach's opinion, God is the projection of mankind's own infinite self-consciousness. Man is always projecting great models for emulation, but these models or objects are nothing else but the subject's own, although objectified, nature. Religious consciousness of an object is synonymous with self-consciousness.

The object of any subject is nothing else than the subject's own nature taken objectively. Such as are a man's thought and dispositions, such is his God; so much worth as a man has, so much and no more has his God. Consciousness of God is self-consciousness, knowledge of God is self-knowledge. By his God thou knowest the man, and by the man his God; the two are identical. Whatever is God to a man, that is his heart and soul; and conversely, God is the manifested inward nature, the expressed self of a man—religion the solemn unveiling of a man's hidden treasures, the revelation of his intimate thoughts. . . .[27]

God is "nothing else than the human being, or, rather, the human nature purified, freed from the limits of the individual man, made objective—*i.e.*, contemplated and revered as another, a distinct being."[28]

This projection of idealized man as a distinct divine being to be revered and worshipped is an unconscious process. Ignorance of it is fundamental to the religious consciousness. Religious consciousness is, in fact, the historical sign of man's unconscious self-estrangement. Here Feuerbach develops an idea of far-reaching significance, viz., that religion is the principal sign of man's self-alienation. In religion we see man as a divided self. On the one hand, unconsciously he is his own projected perfection objectified as a deity; on the other hand, he sees himself, in comparison with his projected self, an imperfect, contemptible being. Feuerbach thus says that

Religion is the disuniting of man from himself; he sets God before him as the antithesis of himself. God is not what man is—man is not what God is. God is the infinite, man the finite being; God is perfect, man imperfect; God eternal, man temporal; God almighty, man weak: God holy, man sinful. God and man are extremes: God is the absolutely positive, the sum of all realities; man the absolute negative, comprehending all negations.[29]

The specific nature of the self-alienation and repression is revealed in the nature of the deity revered and worshiped. Feuerbach contends that in those religions where the differences between God and man are great, or where the identity of the divine and human is denied, human nature is especially depreciated. "To enrich God, man must become poor; that God may be all, man must be nothing."[30]

Man's depreciation of himself is not a loss of the self but only a sign of the self's alienation and repression. What one denies oneself, one enjoys vicariously in God. In a passage which augurs of Freud, Feuerbach explains the psychological process at work.

> He desires to be nothing in himself, because what he takes from himself is not lost to him, since it is preserved in God. Man has his being in God; why then should he have it in himself? . . . What man withdraws from himself, what he renounces in himself, he only enjoys in an incomparably higher and fuller measure in God.
>
> The monks made a vow of chastity to God; they mortified the sexual passion in themselves, but therefore they had in heaven, in the Virgin Mary, the image of woman—an image of love. They could all the more easily dispense with real women in proportion as an ideal woman was an object of love to them. The greater the importance they attached to the denial of sensuality, the greater the im-

portance of the heavenly virgin for them: she was to them in the place of Christ, in the stead of God. The more the sensual tendencies are renounced, the more sensual is the God to whom they are sacrificed.[31]

Man's projection of his desires and ideal self in God is not only a sign of man's self-alienation but also of the fact that this alienated consciousness is what Hegel would call the unhappy or "contrite consciousness." God is the ideal which man recognizes he *ought* to be. The very disparity between man's empirical and latent self leads to a condition of self-depreciation and suffering. Such a condition could not exist, however, if there were not a genuine identity between the two divided selves.

> The inherent necessity of this proof is at once apparent from this—that if the divine nature . . . were really different from the nature of man, a division, a disunion could not take place. If God is really a different being from myself, why should his perfection trouble me?[32]

Man's self-alienation reflects man's disposition to *project* his own being into God to the extent that his real life is bereft of value and meaning. However, man also uses this contemplation of himself in God as a *compensation* for the poverty of his own empirical life. Here Feuerbach reminds us not only of Freud but of Marx. Man's vision of God becomes a surrogate (or opiate) for a real life on earth.

Feuerbach's analysis of the ways in which man's own self-alienation finds compensation in his religious consciousness is exhaustive and had considerable influence on Marx and later Marxist theories of human alienation. A particularly striking example of a

Feuerbachian idea that was a forerunner of Marxist theory is the notion of man's alienation from his own creative activity.

The idea of activity, of making, of creation, is in itself a divine idea; it is therefore unhesitatingly applied to God. In activity man feels himself free, unlimited, happy; in passivity, limited, oppressed, unhappy. Activity is the positive side of one's personality . . . . And the happiest, the most blissful activity is that which is productive . . . . Hence this attribute of the species—productive activity—is assigned to God; that is, realized and made objective as divine activity.[33]

In projecting creativity in God, man fails to live up to his own productive potential. Man simply experiences creativity vicariously in his imaginative vision of God as Eternal Creator. Such is the nature of man's self-alienation. However, to recognize that religion is at the root of man's problem does not mean that the beliefs and practices of religion must be rooted out and destroyed. Rather, it means that what, in the childhood of the race, was thought to be objective must now be recognized as subjective; "what was formerly contemplated and worshipped as God is now perceived to be something *human.*" From an objective point of view the Christian doctrines and sacraments are nothing but fantasy and illusion but, understood subjectively, are expressions of profound human truths. Thus Feuerbach proceeds to examine each Christian doctrine—Incarnation, Trinity, Holy Spirit, Prayer, Baptism, the Lord's Supper—to demonstrate how they reflect natural human hopes and ideals, these being the true, anthropological essence of religion. Two examples of Feuerbach's analysis—the Resurrec-

tion, and the Trinity—will make plain his psychogenetic method.

What lies at the basis of the Christian belief in the mystery of Christ's resurrection? According to Feuerbach's method, the answer should not be hard to determine as follows:

Man, at least in a state of ordinary well-being, has the wish not to die. This wish is originally identical with the instinct of self-preservation. Whatever lives seeks to maintain itself, to continue alive, and consequently not to die. Subsequently, when reflection and feeling are developed under the urgency of life, especially of social and political life, this primary negative wish becomes the positive wish for a life, and that a better life, after death. But this wish involves the further wish for the certainty of its fulfillment. Reason can afford no such certainty. It has therefore been said that all proofs of immortality are insufficient, and even that unassisted reason is not capable of apprehending it, still less of proving it . . . . Such a certainty requires an immediate personal assurance, a practical demonstration. This can only be given me by the fact of a dead person, whose death has been previously certified, rising again from the grave; and he must be no indifferent person, but, on the contrary, the type and representative of all others, so that his resurrection also may be the type, the guarantee of theirs. The resurrection of Christ is therefore the satisfied desire of man for an immediate certainty of his personal existence after death—personal immortality as a sensible, indubitable fact.[34]

Such is Feuerbach's analysis of the "true or anthropological" explanation of belief in the resurrection of Jesus. This belief has something naturally human about it, whereas the Greek concept of the immortality of the soul is far too abstract and bloodless. According to Feuerbach, a belief in bodily resurrection could alone fully gratify the feelings of men, and, therefore, the resurrection of the body "is the highest triumph of Christianity" over the "sublime but abstract spirituality of the ancients."

The paradoxical mystery of the Trinity is, likewise, just an objective or alienated reflection of a beautiful human truth. Man can only be satisfied with himself as a whole man, not as disunited and limited. Thus "man's consciousness of himself in his totality is the consciousness of the Trinity."[35] And the reason for this is that man's self-consciousness is never an empty, solitary consciousness; it is always a consciousness of self and other, of *I and thou* in separation and participation. So it must be, therefore, with God. Full self-consciousness in God is consciousness of unity in participation.

From a solitary God the essential need of duality, of love, of community, of the real, completed self-consciousness, of the *alter ego*, is excluded. This want is therefore satisfied by religion thus: in the still solitude of the Divine Being is placed another, a second, different from God as to personality, but identical with him in essence—God the Son, in distinction from God the Father. God the Father is *I*, God the Son *Thou* . . . . Participated life is alone, true, self-satisfying, divine life—this simple thought, this truth, natural, immanent in man, is the secret, the supernatural mystery of the Trinity. But religion expresses this truth as it does every other, in an indirect manner, *i.e.*, inversely, for it here makes a general truth into a particular one, the true subject into a predicate when it says: God is a participated life, a life of love and friendship. The third Person of the Trinity expresses nothing further than the love of the two divine Persons toward each other, the unity of the Son and the Father, the idea of community . . . .[36]

What Christians have done is to substitute for the natural love and real bond

of family life this purely religious idea of love and unity. Thus, in compensation for a lost or rejected human love and family fellowship, the Christians have a Father and Son in God. And so the Trinity continues to be an object of wonder and reverence "because here the satisfaction of those profoundest human wants which in reality, in life, they denied, became to them an object of contemplation in God."[37]

When man recognizes the "latent" truth in Christian belief, he no longer needs to objectify these beliefs in a being outside man but can perceive them as fully human. Only then can man achieve authentic self-realization or what Feuerbach would call "realized Christianity." Such a humanized religion has at its core the love of neighbor; not the love of an illusory God but of a real human being. Authentic religion is found only in true human communion.

The being of man is given only in communion, in the unity of man with man, a unity resting on the reality of the distinction between the I and the Thou . . . . Man for himself is man in the ordinary sense; man in communion with man, the unity of the I and Thou, is God.[38]

According to Feuerbach, a social unity based on such a religion of love can alone effect true community, for political unity is always a unity of force or power. Not only is love the basis of true community, but it is also the root of a purposeful life. The real atheist, the man devoid of genuine religious sensibility, is the man who has no goal in life.

Every man must place before himself a God, *i.e.*, an aim, a purpose. The aim is the conscious, voluntary, essential impulse of life . . . .

He who has no aim, has no home, no sanctuary; aimlessness is the greatest unhappiness . . . . He who has an aim, an aim which is in itself true and essential, has, *eo ipso*, a religion, if not in the narrow sense of common pietism, yet—and this is the only point to be considered —in the sense of reason, in the sense of the universal, the only true love.[39]

Here, as Professor Randall has pointed out,[40] Feuerbach identifies religion with the current existentialist theme of an "ultimate concern" which alone can overcome the threat of meaninglessness.

Feuerbach closes *The Essence of Christianity* with a call for making sacred the most profane of everyday activities. Eating and drinking should be approached, for example, as religious acts.

Think, therefore, with every morsel of bread which relieves thee from the pain of hunger, with every draught of wine that cheers thy heart, of the God who confers these beneficent gifts upon thee—think of man! But in thy gratitude toward man forget not gratitude toward holy Nature! . . . Forget not the gratitude which thou owest to the natural qualities of bread and wine! . . . Hunger and thirst destroy not only the physical but also the mental and moral powers of man; they rob him of his humanity . . . . It needs only that the ordinary course of things be interrupted in order to vindicate to common things an uncommon significance, *to life, as such, a religious import.* Therefore let bread be sacred for us, let wine be sacred, and also let water be sacred! Amen.[41]

Such, in brief, was Feuerbach's psychogenetic critique of Christianity and his own humanistic philosophy of religion. Feuerbach's influence on modern thought far exceeds that of thinkers of much greater reputation and popularity. Many themes in Feuerbach foreshadow ideas now commonplace in Existentialism. Kierkegaard, Nietzsche, Heidegger, and Sartre are all deeply influenced by Feuerbach's work. Contemporary social psychology, especially the work of Freud and Erich Fromm on religion, is difficult to conceive without Feuerbach, and Martin Buber's philosophy of I-Thou is profoundly indebted to Feuerbach's view of man in community. But most significant of all is Feuerbach's role in the development of the social theories of Karl Marx and Friedrich Engels. Early Marxism is unthinkable without Feuerbach, and Marx's mature thought was, of course, built on the foundation of his early writings. Feuerbach, therefore, served as *the* bridge between Hegel and Marxism. It was Feuerbach's *The Essence of Christianity* which both liberated the young Marx from Hegel and also made him aware of the profound truth latent in Hegel's thought. Marx's first reaction to the appearance of *The Essence of Christianity* was to advise all speculative theologians that "there is no other road to truth and freedom for you than through the 'brook of fire' (Feuerbach). Feuerbach is the *purgatory* of our time."[42] Friedrich Engels was also to write later about the "liberating effect" that Feuerbach's book had on the Young Hegelians and how they "all became disciples overnight."

Feuerbach's influence on Marx and Engels is especially important for our purposes for, while his effect on these men was far-ranging, it was of particular significance in the development of their critique of Christianity—a critique that prevails in large parts of the world today. The Hegelian critique of Christianity finds its historical consummation in the socioeconomic theories of Karl Marx and his later disciples.

Karl Marx (1818–1883)

Karl Marx was born into the family of a Westphalian lawyer. His father, Herschel Marx, was of Jewish descent, politically liberal and philosophically rationalist, being an admirer of Voltaire and Kant. Herschel Marx, nevertheless, was baptized a Protestant Christian in 1816, although his new religious confession apparently was lukewarm and motivated largely by prudential considerations. Young Karl was baptized in 1824. At seventeen Karl entered the University of Bonn to study law but transferred the next year to Berlin. At Berlin he joined the circle of Young Hegelians called the Doctors Club. Here Marx came under the influence of Strauss, Bauer, and Feuerbach. However, Berlin proved too conservative for this radical new Hegelian, and he moved on to the University of Jena where he received his doctor's degree in 1841. The following year Marx began his long and stormy career as a journalist. He joined the staff of the newly founded *Rheinische Zeitung*, a daily paper of which he soon became editor-in-chief. In 1843 the Prussian government suppressed the paper, and Marx went to Paris where he joined a group of fellow radicals, including Arnold Ruge, in the publication of the *Deutsch-Französische Jahrbücher*. In the first and only issue that appeared, Marx wrote an article entitled "Introduction to the Criticism of the Hegelian Philosophy." In this article Marx set forth his first critical thoughts on religion. As we shall see, at this point Marx still reflects the dominant influence of Feuerbach.

It was during this Paris period that Marx met his future friend and collaborator, Friedrich Engels. Engels was the son of a wealthy industrialist but had come under the influence of both the radical Hegelians in Germany and the English socialists. He had just come to Paris from Manchester where, while working for his father's firm, he had written a study of the situation of the working classes in England.

Early in 1845, Marx and his collaborators were expelled from France. He moved to Brussels, and there he wrote eleven "Theses on Feuerbach," which were discovered and published by Engels forty years later. The "Theses" and "The German Ideology," written with Engels in 1845–1846, signal Marx's break with Feuerbach and the emergence of his own socioeconomic critique of religion.

In 1847 Marx joined the International Communist League and was commissioned with Engels to write a declaration of aims for the League's Congress held in London. The result was *The Communist Manifesto*.

In 1864 Marx founded the International Working Men's Association, or First International, and in 1867 the first volume of *Das Kapital*, "the Bible of the working class" as it was called, was published in Hamburg. The second and third volumes were published only posthumously by Engels in 1885 and 1894.

Marx's naturalistic critique of religion is found in the earliest of his writings. In the preface to his doctoral dissertation he wrote:

Philosophy makes no secret of it. Prometheus' admission: 'In sooth all gods I hate' is its own admission, its own motto against all gods, heavenly and earthly, who do not acknowledge the consciousness of man as the supreme divinity.[43]

What Marx had early received from

Feuerbach was a naturalistic humanism freed from the abstruse speculations of Hegelian theology. Between 1841 and 1844 Marx remained a true Feuerbachian, and his comments on religion during this period reflect Feuerbach's influence. Read carefully, however, they indicate the beginning of a movement away from Feuerbach's rather abstract discussion of man's self-alienation in religion to a more concrete analysis of the historical factors producing such an alienated consciousness. In the Introduction to *The Critique of Hegel's Philosophy of Right* of 1844, Marx says, in Feuerbachian fashion, that man has searched for a superman in some heavenly realm but has found nothing but his own alienated reflection. The basis of all criticism of religion must, therefore, be that

Man makes religion, religion does not make man. In other words, religion is the self-consciousness and self-feeling of man who has either not yet found himself or has already lost himself. But *man* is no abstract being squatting outside the world. Man is *the world of man*, the state, society. This state, this society, produce religion, *a reversed world-consciousness* because they are *a reversed world*. [Religion] is ... *the fantastic realization* of the human essence because the *human essence* has no true reality. The struggle against religion is therefore mediately the fight against *the other world*, of which religion is the spiritual *aroma* .... Religion is only the illusory sun which revolves round man as long as he does not revolve round himself.[44]

Marx goes on, however, to indicate more exactly than Feuerbach the sociopolitical source of man's distress.

Religious distress is at the same time the *expression* of real distress and the *protest* against real distress. Religion is the sigh of the oppressed creature, the heart of a heartless world. ... It is the opium of the people .... The abolition of religion as the *illusory* happiness of the people is required for their *real* happiness. The demand to give up the illusions about its condition is the *demand to give up a condition which needs illusions*. ... Thus the criticism of heaven turns into the criticism of the earth ... the *criticism of theology* into the *criticism of politics*.[45]

The criticism of religion does not end, then, with a general psychogenetic analysis of alienation; it proceeds to an analysis *and* overthrow of all social and economic relations that so debase and enslave man that he requires the solace of religious illusions. Take away the social conditions that produce illusions about another world, and the religious need for such otherwordly illusions will wither away. Here is the revolutionary imperative in Marx which was lacking in Feuerbach's humanism. It is stated with classic succinctness by Marx in his eleventh thesis on Feuerbach: "The philosophers," says Marx, "have only *interpreted* the world, in various ways; the point, however, is to *change* it."[46]

Marx's break with Feuerbach and the development of an historically "realized" humanism is indicated in the "Theses on Feuerbach" written a year after the critique of Hegel but not published until 1886. Feuerbach's theory of religious self-alienation is inadequate, according to Marx, because it fails to explain concretely what historical conditions produced certain kinds of illusory beliefs. Feuerbach's theory is deficient, therefore, in its exclusive concentration on individual psychology. For Marx, the real source of alienation is rooted in man's social life and not in personal alienation from some abstract essence. This is expressed as follows in Marx's fourth thesis:

Feuerbach starts out from the fact of religious self-alienation, the duplication of the world into a religious, imaginary world and a real one. His work consists in the dissolution of the religious world into its secular basis. He overlooks the fact that after this work is completed the chief thing still remains to be done. For the fact that the secular foundation detaches itself from itself and establishes itself in the clouds as an independent realm is really only to be explained by the self-cleavage and self-contradictoriness of this secular basis. The latter must itself, therefore, first be understood in its contradiction, and then revolutionized in practice by the removal of the contradiction. Thus, for instance, once the earthly family is discovered to be the secret of the holy family, the former must then itself be criticized in theory and revolutionized in practice.[47]

Self-alienation is not found by turning inward on the self but outward on the realities of the social life of men.

Feuerbach resolves the religious essence into the *human* essence. But human essence is no abstraction inherent in each single individual. In its reality it is the ensemble of the social relations . . . . Feuerbach, consequently, does not see that the "religious sentiment" is itself a *social product*, and that the abstract individual whom he analyzes belongs in reality to a particular form of society.[48]

For Marx the nature of a religion can be learned by examining the concrete social conditions that produced it. Therefore, there is no single essence of religion such as Schleiermacher's reduction of religion to the feeling of absolute dependence. Religion is always a cultural product, and thus each religion reflects the unique social conflicts of its particular culture. Remove the social conflicts, and you remove the religious illusions required by the conflicts.

In his work *The German Ideology*, written with Engels in 1845–1846, Marx developed for the first time his theory of the relationship between religion and "ideology." In this work, Marx contends that consciousness, including man's religious ideas, is the product of society. Man's primordial consciousness was rather limited, consisting principally of a consciousness of his immediate sensuous surroundings. But as man's social life evolved, his consciousness became more and more determined by other, social factors, principally by the division of labor and attendant economic changes. This was, of course, evident to other sensitive observers during the "Iron Age" of the Industrial Revolution—the period during which Marx wrote. However, for Marx the *determinative* shapers of man's consciousness were the economic conditions which separated men into classes and which perpetuated social conditions by means of a "ruling class" ideology. Ideology, according to Marx, was any social idea—legal, philosophic, religious—which was used by the class in political and economic power to maintain its own class interests. Marx remarked that "the ruling ideas of each age have always been the ideas of its ruling class."[49] It therefore follows that the religion of a particular culture not only reflects the conflicts inherent in that culture's social structure but also reveals the religious ideology or system which perpetuates the interests of the ruling class. However, we should not think that every ruling class ideology is a cynical form of brainwashing. Most often it is an unconscious and sublimated product of the material conditions producing the particular socioeconomic structure. But that such ideological consciousness is the product of material life-processes is unquestionable. In *The Communist Manifesto* written in 1847–1848, two years after *The German Ideology*, Marx asks:

Does it require deep intuition to comprehend that man's ideas, views and conceptions, in one word, man's consciousness, changes with every change in the conditions of his material existence, in his social relations and in his social life? What else does the history of ideas prove, than that intellectual production changes its character in proportion as material production is changed? ... When people speak of ideas that revolutionize society, they do but express the fact that within the old society the elements of a new one have been created, and that the dissolution of the old ideas keeps even pace with the dissolution of the old conditions of existence.[50]

During the early 1840's both Marx and Engels came under the influence of another Left-wing Hegelian named Moses Hess. Hess had transformed Feuerbach's conception of religious self-alienation into a theory of economic alienation. According to Hess, man's essential attribute is his creativity or productive activity. However, this original creativity has been perverted by egoistical men who exploit human productivity for their own selfish gain. They exploit human labor in order to amass private property or money. Hence, for Hess, money was the symbol of man's alienation from man, "Money," says Hess, "is the product of mutually alienated men; *it is externalized man*."[51] He saw an analogy between Feuerbach's interpretation of man's self-alienation in Christianity and the social alienation in capitalist societies. In fact, he interpreted both Christianity and capitalism as different expressions of the same egoistic religious phenomenon. Money and God are both forms of externalized man and *human* alienation. In the one case man externalizes himself psychologically in God; in the other he externalizes himself materially in money. Hess thus contended that the "essence of the modern world of exchange, of money, is the realized essence of Christianity. The commercial state ... is the promised kingdom of heaven, as, conversely, God is only idealized capital."[52] Hess called upon men to give up their worship of both God and worldly acquisitions.

You have been told that you cannot serve two masters at once—God and Mammon. But we tell you that you cannot serve either one of them, if you think and feel like a *human* being. Love one another, unite in spirit, and your hearts will be filled with that blessedness which you have so vainly sought for outside of yourselves, in God. *Organize*, unite in the real world, and by your deeds and works you will possess all wealth, which you have so vainly sought in *money*.[53]

Marx was profoundly influenced by Hess' economic transformation of Feuerbach's doctrine of alienation, and one can observe in the writings of the mid-1840's and later Marx's joining together the themes of economic alienation and religious ideology. The influence of Hess is most pronounced in a concluding section of Marx's essay "On the Jewish Question." Following Hess, Marx saw a parallel between the alienation produced by the capitalist religion of money-worship and the self-alienation produced by Christianity. However, Marx called this practical religion of money "Judaism," probably because the word in German (*Judentum*) connoted "commerce," as well as the religion of the

Jewish people. For Marx, "Judaism" is the worship of money:

What is the world cult of the Jew? *Huckstering.* Who is his worldly god? *Money* .... Money is the jealous one God of Israel, beside which no other God may stand. Money dethrones all the gods of man and turns them into a commodity. Money is the universal, independently constituted value of all things. It has, therefore, deprived the whole world, both the world of man and nature, of its own value. Money is the alienated essence of man's work and his being. This alienated being rules over him and he worships it.[54]

In Marx's view, Christianity and "Judaism" (capitalism) are the theoretical and practical forms of man's egoistic alienation. Marx believed that historical evidence showed that Christianity served as a theoretical or "ideological" superstructure and justification for capitalism. Just as belief in God is a surrogate for a genuine personal life, so a man's work in capitalist society is no longer his own, but belongs to another. In *Capital* Marx indicates that Christianity and capitalism go hand in hand.

The religious world is but the reflex of the real world. And for a society based upon the production of commodities, in which the producers in general enter into social relations with one another by treating their products as commodities and values, whereby they reduce their individual private labour to the standard of homogeneous human labour—for such a society, Christianity with its *cultus* of abstract man ... is the most fitting form of religion.[55]

Marx, of course, did not contend that Christianity is the *cause* of man's alienation. Christianity is merely one of the evil, attendant effects of the socioeconomic system. Thus Marx was not basically concerned with attacking religion,* for he was confident that a revolutionary change in the socioeconomic order which made such a religion possible would lead to the withering away of Christianity. Where the conditions of alienation no longer exist, there will be no need for the religious hypothesis— religion will be "transcended." Marx prophesied that such a stage of human history would come with the proletarian revolution and the abolition of private property, the source of human alienation. Communism would, therefore, be the *definitive* resolution of the conflict between man and man. It is, Marx said, "the solution of the riddle of history."

The question of whether Marx's "solution" to the riddle of history, as set forth in *Capital*, should be viewed as in the tradition of empirical science or imaginative vision is much debated. One can legitimately view Marx's writings as a great mythical drama of secular redemption or as a vast apocalyptical prophecy.[56] Marx has his own concept of the *imago Dei* in man's creativity or productivity; he has his fall and expulsion from Paradise, occasioned by man's egoistic greed and resulting in man's estrangement from himself and his fellow-man. Marx also has his Anti-Christ (the Capitalists), his Armageddon and Last Judgment (the Proletarian Revolution

* Neither did Marx make a careful study of the origins of any of the world's great religions on the basis of dialectical materialism, as Freud did with his discovery of the Oedipus complex and infantile projection. However, later Marxists, including Engels, did apply Marxist principles to the interpretation of movements in the history of Christianity. Engels wrote a Marxist interpretation of Early Christianity and of the Peasants Revolt at the time of the Reformation. For a classic example of the application of Marxist principles to the study of the origins of Christianity, see Karl Kautsky, *Foundations of Christianity* (New York, 1953).

and defeat of the Capitalists), and his New Jerusalem (the classless society). Louis Halle, for example, sees Marx as a messianic herald of a new religion for our secular, industrial age.

We understand Marx best as a visionary who was overcome by a great dramatic vision . . . . We understand him best as the maker of a myth . . . . He was a man of vast literary imagination who had a mythic vision that, in the circumstances of the industrial revolution, was destined to move men with the power of a new religion. At a time when factories were mushrooming in England and on the Continent, when millions of people were losing their ancient independence and becoming wage-slaves to the owners of the new machines—at such a time, what could have greater appeal than this drama in which the oppressed proletarian, suddenly in the last act, overthrows the capitalist tyrant, bringing into being the Kingdom of Heaven on Earth? Jesus had spoken to shepherds in pastoral terms, not to factory workers in the terms of industrial society . . . . Marxism met the city man's need for a new body of belief. It met the need for a religion of the industrial age.[57]

It is not difficult to point out the serious limitations in Marx's critique of Christianity and the simplicity of his own religious vision of the overthrow of the capitalists and the emergence of the classless paradise. It takes some credulity to believe that a change in economic systems will bring about a race of selfless, peaceful, and just men. Marx's prophetic attack on the dehumanizing structures of nineteenth-century industrial society lacked any sense of prophetic self-criticism of communist society itself. As Paul Tillich has pointed out, one of the tragedies of Marxism is the fact that the victorious Communist party has not been able to apply criticism against itself.[58]

Marx's contention that religious be-liefs and sentiments would wither away with a change in man's socioeconomic condition also lacks historical and empirical support. Social science has demonstrated, nevertheless, that there is a close relationship between socioeconomic class and the *form* of religious belief and practice *and* that socioeconomic structures are frequently supported by religious ideologies. Marx's recognition of the relationship between religious belief and social ideology is a genuinely positive contribution to the study of religion, and contemporary sociologists of religion are greatly in his debt.

The world-historical influence of Marx's ideas are epochal, of course, and it is not predictable what the final effect of Marxist materialism will have on Christianity. Its effect on the institutional Church in Russia, China, and parts of Europe and Africa has been immense, though Christianity has by no means been stamped out in these Communist dominated countries. However, there is no doubt that because of its historical consequences, Marx's critique of Christianity has been the most devastating attack the latter has yet suffered in the modern world.

Our account of the post-Hegelian critique of Christianity in Germany would not be complete without consideration of another prophetic figure who is less easily located historically than Strauss, Feuerbach, and Marx. That person is Friedrich Nietzsche. Nietzsche came at the end of the nineteenth-century tradition and, like Kierkegaard, stands closer to twentieth-century developments in many ways. Nevertheless, unlike Kierkegaard, Nietzsche was not ignored in the last years of the century and is the last great nineteenth-century herald of the "death of God," of the demise of Christian civilization, and of a new humanity of "free spirits."

Nietzsche's critique of Christianity is also quite different from those we have just examined. Strauss attacked Christianity on historical grounds, Feuerbach used psychogenetic criticism, and Marx used the tools of sociology and economics. Nietzsche's attack was *moral*, but it was a moral criticism quite different from that of the eighteenth-century *philosophes*.

Friedrich Nietzsche (1844–1900)

Of all the critics of Christianity in the modern period, Nietzsche's relation to Christianity is perhaps the most difficult to assess. He has most frequently been attacked as its archenemy, but he has also been interpreted as the restorer of primitive Christianity[59] and as a man who "knew and admitted the Christian basis of his real motivating forces."[60] Nietzsche could say that he was honored "to come from a breed which was in earnest about its Christianity" and, at the same time, call "Christianity the one great curse . . . the one immortal blemish of mankind." It will be our task to attempt to describe the true nature of Nietzsche's attack on Christianity, which is interpreted by many as the most merciless yet waged on the Christian faith.

Friedrich Nietzsche was the child of a Lutheran parsonage. Not only his father, but his mother's father and grandfather, were Lutheran pastors. Nietzsche's father died when he was only five years old, and he was brought up in Naumberg in an excessively feminine environment with his mother, sister, grandmother, and two aunts. We are told that young Nietzsche was serious and introspective and was known by his companions as "the little pastor."

During his early school years Nietzsche's lifelong admiration of Greek culture was aroused, and his alienation from Christianity was begun. At eighteen his religious doubts were already matured. This is evident in an essay entitled *Fate and History*, where he admits that, regarded with an impartial eye, many conclusions would have to be drawn concerning Christianity that would conflict with commonly held opinions. He then adds that an attempt at such a free, impartial inquiry

is the work, not of a few weeks, but of a lifetime. To dare to launch out on the sea of doubt without compass or steersman is death and destruction for undeveloped heads; most are struck down by storms, very few discover new countries. From the midst of this immeasurable ocean of ideas one will often long to be back on firm land . . . .[61]

In 1864 Nietzsche entered the University of Bonn but the following year moved to Leipzig to continue his philological studies under his mentor, Friedrich Ritschl. While in Leipzig, Nietzsche first read Schopenhauer's *World as Will and Idea*. The book's theme of blind Will and its atheism were appealing to the young classicist whose break with Christianity was by now complete.

In 1869, on the recommendation of Ritschl, Nietzsche was appointed to the Chair of Philology at the University of Basel without yet having completed his doctorate! It was during these early years in Basel that Nietzsche became a close friend of the composer Richard Wagner, whose villa on Lake Lucerne Nietzsche visited frequently. Nietzsche's attachment to Wagner at this time is reflected in his first important work, *The Birth of Tragedy*, published in 1871. During these years of teaching, Nietzsche also published *Thoughts Out of Season*, which consisted of attacks on D. F. Strauss as the "philistine of culture," and on historical learning, and essays extolling Schopenhauer and Wagner. Nietzsche resigned his chair at Basel in 1879, for reasons of persistent ill health and a growing dissatisfaction with what he considered academic pedantry. For the next ten years he led the life of a wanderer, seeking a cure for his physical ailments at various places in Switzerland and Germany. During the early years of this period he produced *Human—All Too Human*, *The Dawn of Day*, and *Joyful Wisdom*, all of which reflect a new phase of his career. Now begins his attack on metaphysics, traditional morality, self-renunciation, and on Christianity which, for Nietzsche, represented the amalgam of all these evils.

Nietzsche's most famous work, *Thus Spake Zarathustra*, appeared in four parts between 1883 and 1885. In this visionary and poetical work he presents two of his most significant ideas: the transvaluation of values and the *Übermensch*.* *Zarathustra* was followed by *Beyond Good and Evil* (1886) and *A Genealogy of Morals* (1887). *Beyond Good and Evil* was meant to be a prologue to Nietzsche's greatest work, one on which he was already at work, but which he never completed. The notes for this *magnum opus* were published posthumously as *The Will to Power*.

During this period Nietzsche found himself more and more alienated from old friends and isolated by his failure to communicate his innermost thoughts. He wrote to his sister: "A profound man needs friends, unless indeed he has a God. And I have neither God nor friend!" He came to see himself as an exception, one given the unique vocation of heralding the coming of the superior man. But the conflict between his deep emotional desire for companions and disciples and his growing isolation, coupled with his feverish mental activity, brought him to the brink of exhaustion. The writings of 1888, *Nietzsche contra Wagner*, *The Twilight of the Idols*, *The Antichrist*, and *Ecce Homo*, are the work of a hostile, frenzied but brilliant and powerful mind—a mind pushed to the extreme of mental tension. The extravagant self-exaltation of *Ecce Homo* borders on madness.

In January of 1889 Professors Burckhardt and Overbeck of Basel received bizarre letters from Nietzsche who was then living in Italy. Overbeck rushed to Turin where he found his friend in a state of insanity. Nietzsche never recovered. He lived the remaining years under the care of his mother and then his sister and died in Weimar on August 25, 1900.

The "Death of God" and the Revaluation. Nietzsche viewed the modern world in a state of cultural decline—in what he called a condition of nihilism. Like Matthew Arnold, Nietzsche saw himself "between two worlds, one dead, the other powerless to be born." Speculative philosophy was spent, but its place was taken by an effete liberalism and a crude, acquisitive materialism. A complacent, philistine optimism was rife. Nietzsche expressed this condition of cultural nihilism in a powerful parable of "the Madman," cited here in its entirety.

---

* Since the term Superman may connote something supernatural and has come to be identified with Nazi racial theories and with a comic book character, it is preferable to translate Nietzsche's term *Übermensch* as "Overman" or superior man.

The Madman

Have you not heard of that madman who lit a lantern in the bright morning hours, ran to the market place, and cried incessantly, "I seek God! I seek God!" As many of those who do not believe in God were standing around just then, he provoked much laughter. Why, did he get lost? said one. Did he lose his way like a child? said another. Or is he hiding? Is he afraid of us? Has he gone on a voyage? or emigrated? Thus they yelled and laughed. The madman jumped into their midst and pierced them with his glances.

"Whither is God?" he cried. "I shall tell you. *We have killed him*—you and I. All of us are his murderers. But how have we done this? How were we able to drink up the sea? Who gave us the sponge to wipe away the entire horizon? What did we do when we unchained this earth from its sun? Whither is it moving now? Whither are we moving now? Away from all suns? Are we not plunging continually? Backward, sideward, forward, in all directions? Is there any up or down left? Are we not straying as through an infinite nothing? Do we not feel the breath of empty space? Has it not become colder? Is not night and more night coming on all the while? Must not lanterns be lit in the morning? Do we not hear anything yet of the noise of the gravediggers who are burying God? Do we not smell anything yet of God's decomposition? Gods too decompose. God is dead. God remains dead. And we have killed him. How shall we, the murderers of all murderers, comfort ourselves? What was holiest and most powerful of all that the world has yet owned has bled to death under our knives. Who will wipe this blood off us? What water is there for us to clean ourselves? What festivals of atonement, what sacred games shall we have to invent? Is not the greatness of this deed too great for us? Must not we ourselves become gods simply to seem worthy of it? There has never been a greater deed; and whoever will be born after us—for the sake of this deed he will be part of a higher history than all history hitherto."

Here the madman fell silent and looked again at his listeners; and they too were silent and stared at him in astonishment. At last he threw his lantern on the ground, and it broke and went out. "I come too early," he said then; "my time has not come yet. This tremendous event is still on its way, still wandering—it has not yet reached the ears of man. Lightning and thunder require time, the light of the stars requires time, deeds require time even after they are done, before they can be seen and heard. This deed is still more distant from them than the most distant stars— *and yet they have done it themselves.*"

It has been related further that on that same day the madman entered divers churches and there sang his *requiem aeternam deo*. Led out and called to account, he is said to have replied each time, "What are these churches now if they are not the tombs and sepulchers of God?"[62]

For Nietzsche the "death of God" is not the result of philosophical investigation but a cultural fact, the consequences of which have not yet been fully revealed to Western man's consciousness. Yet we are living in the shadow of the dead God and, when we awaken to the fact that God is truly dead, madness will erupt. For the death of God means the death of the ultimate ground and support of all traditional values.[63] For over two thousand years men have derived their "thou shalt" and "thou shalt not" from God, but that is now coming to an end. Man will be thrown back upon himself where "there is no one to command, no one to obey, no one to transgress." Man will be caught in a terrifying dilemma: to proclaim the death of God will be to deny everything its ultimate meaning and value, but to believe in the existence of God will be to live in a world of fictions, to embrace nihilism. For, according to Nietzsche, it is Christianity which destroyed truth, the truth of life proclaimed by the early Greeks, and substituted the fictional supports of God, moral universals, grace, and immortality. This problem of nihilism is "far too great, too distant, too far from the comprehension of the many," but it is on its way and must be faced. The alternatives, then, are a return to decadence, to the nihilism of Christianity, or a courageous "transvaluation of values" in which man must decide for himself what is good and evil, true and beautiful.

Nietzsche believed that men had come to see through the dogmas created by Christianity but that they hadn't the courage to face the consequences of being thrown back on their own resources. At this point Nietzsche develops the interesting idea that it was the truth-seeking which was encouraged by Christianity which led to its own death. Nietzsche admits that "even we students of today, who are atheists and anti-metaphysicians, light our torches at the flame of a millennial faith: the Christian faith, that God is truth, and truth divine."[64] Atheism is, then, the last evolutionary phase of that Christian ideal of divine truth.

It is the catastrophe, inspiring of respect, of a discipline in truth that has lasted for two millennia and which now prohibits the lie implicit in monotheistic belief.... Thus Christianity as dogma perished by its own ethics, and in the same way Christianity as ethics must perish; we are standing on the threshold of this event. After drawing a whole series of conclusions, Christian truthfulness must now draw its strongest conclusion, the one by which it shall do away with itself. This will be accomplished by Christianity's asking itself: "What does all will to truth signify?" .... It is by this dawning self-consciousness of the will to truth that ethics must now perish. This is the great spectacle of a hundred acts that will occupy Europe for the next two centuries, the most terrible and problematical but also the most hopeful of spectacles....[65]

The Critique of Christianity.
From what has been said, it is clear that for Nietzsche atheism is not based primarily on rational skepticism concerning God's existence but on the belief that the God of the Christian tradition is no longer worthy of support.

That we find no God—either in history or in nature or behind nature—is not what differentiates *us*, but that we experience what has been revered as God, not as "godlike" but as miserable, as absurd, as harmful, not merely as an error, but as a *crime against life*. We deny God as God. If one were to *prove* this God of the Christians to us, we should be even less able to believe in him.[66]

For Nietzsche, the Christian God is a degenerate conception, representing the very contradiction of life, "the declaration of war against life, against nature, against the will to live!... the deification of nothingness, the will to nothingness pronounced holy!"[67] Like Marx, Nietzsche hit upon a theory of rationalization which he believed explained the persistence of the alienated and otherworldly consciousness of Christian civilization. Christian belief and practice is the unconscious product of *ressentiment*—of the *resentment* of the weak masses against their aristocratic superiors. Nietzsche believed that Christianity, being the quintessential expression of resentment, was the root of Western decadence.

Strange as it may seem, resentment is actually a form of power. The source and motivation of all human behavior is, according to Nietzsche, a vital force or energy which he called the *will to power*, similar to what Freud was later to call the *libido*. This will to power expresses itself in a great variety of ways, e.g., in monastic asceticism as well as in Titanic physical prowess. The fact is that the will to power is often channeled in ways which disguise its true character. The principal manifestation of this disguised will to power is *resentment*, the exact opposite of genuine sublimation of Dionysian power.

Related to the concept of resentment is Nietzsche's theory of morality. According to Nietzsche, there are two types of morality—"master-morality" and "slave-morality." Slave-morality has its origins in Judaism and its fruition in Christianity. In both cases this form of morality is the result of the frustration and resentment of a weak, priestly class in revolt against its aristocratic masters, the Romans. The Jews started the slave revolt in morals, for it was the Jews who first succeeded in avenging themselves on their enemies by radically inverting the cultural values of their masters. Their weapon was their own impotence! "It is their impotence," says Nietzsche, "which makes their hate so violent and sinister, so cerebral and poisonous." The Jews avenged themselves by an act of the most spiritual vengeance, "a strategy entirely appropriate to a priestly people in whom vindictiveness had gone most deeply underground."

It was the Jew who, with frightening consistency, dared to invert the aristocratic value equations good/noble/powerful/beautiful/happy/favoured-of-the-gods and maintain, with the furious hatred of the underprivileged and impotent, that "only the poor, the powerless, are good; only the suffering, sick and ugly, truly blessed." But you noble and mighty ones of the earth will be, to all eternity, the evil, the cruel, the avaricious, the godless, and thus the cursed and the damned.[68]

The slave revolt in morals had its beginnings in a resentment turned malevolently creative. Resenting the power of the strong, the Jews and Christians, perhaps unconsciously, condemned the morally strong, their own morals of pity, mercy, self-denial being but shrewd compensation for their own weakness. Resentment is therefore at the heart of all herd-morality, for the herd is made up of those who "love one another" because of fear of their superiors. All the values of the master are thus condemned as "evil" because these are the very traits that are lacking in and therefore feared by the weak.

For Nietzsche, Christian love is not the manifestation of a strong self-discipline but the product of resentment.

From the tree trunk of Jewish vengeance and hatred ... grew a branch that was equally unique: a new love, the deepest and sublimest of loves. From what other trunk could this branch have sprung? But let no one surmise that this love represented a denial of the thirst for vengeance, that it contravened the Jewish hatred. Exactly the opposite is true. Love grew out of hatred as the tree's crown, spreading triumphantly in the purest sunlight, yet having in its high and sunny realm, the same aims—victory, aggrandizement, temptation—Jesus of Nazareth, the gospel of love made flesh, the "redeemer," who brought blessing and victory to the poor, the sick, the sinners—what was he but temptation in its most sinister and irresistible form, bringing men by a roundabout way to precisely those Jewish values and renovations of the ideal?[69]

Jesus and the Christian Church have merely universalized the Jewish transvaluation of values. "Everything," says Nietzsche, "is rapidly becoming Judaized or Christianized, or mobized.... The progress of this poison throughout the body of mankind cannot be stayed."[70]

Nietzsche's attitude toward Jesus and his repudiation of Christ is rather complex and deserves special attention.

Nietzsche attacks both the historical Jesus and the Christ of Church dogma but, while he despises the latter, he respects the former for his integrity. There was, in truth, "only *one* Christian," Nietzsche asserts, "and he died on the cross. The 'evangel' *died* on the cross. What has been called 'evangel' from that moment was actually the opposite of that which *he* had lived: '*ill*-tidings,' a *dysangel*."[71]

Nietzsche interprets Jesus as being the paradigm of a particular human psychological type—one who realized in his own inner life a serene sense of redemption from the cares of the world, a sense of blessedness which allowed him to pass through the world without anxiety or care. What Jesus exemplifies is the Eastern achievement of an otherworldly serenity which the trampling power of external events can never disturb. This is perfectly manifest in Jesus' life of love and non-resistance, a love that is nonprudential and unconditional. It is perfectly summed up in Jesus' attitude toward death:

This "bringer of glad tidings" died as he had lived, as he had taught—*not* to "redeem men" but to show how one must live. This practice is his legacy to mankind: his behavior before the judges, before the catchpoles, before the accusers and all kinds of slander and scorn—his behavior on the *cross*. He does not resist, he does not defend his right, he takes no step which might ward off the worst; on the contrary he *provokes* it. And he begs, he suffers, he loves *with* those, *in* those, who do him evil. *Not* to resist, *not* to be angry, *not* to hold responsible—but to resist not even the evil one—to *love* him.[72]

Nietzsche scorns the attempts of liberal historians, such as Ernst Renan, to picture Jesus as a "genius" and "hero."

M. Renan, that buffoon *in psychologicis*, has introduced the two most inappropriate concepts possible into his explanation of the Jesus type: the concept of *genius* and the concept of the *hero*. But if anything is unevangelical it is the concept of the hero. Just the opposite of all wrestling, of all feeling-oneself-in-a-struggle, has here become instinct: the incapacity for resistence becomes morality here ("resist not evil"—the most profound word of the Gospels, their key in a certain sense), blessedness in peace, in gentleness, in not *being able* to be an enemy .... To make a *hero* of Jesus! And even more, what a misunderstanding is the word "genius"! ... Spoken with the precision of a physiologist, even an entirely different word would still be more nearly fitting here—the word *idiot**.[73]

Jesus is seen by Nietzsche after the image of Dostoevsky's "Idiot," for he represents all the childlike qualities.

The "glad tidings" are precisely that there are no longer any opposites; the kingdom of heaven belongs to the *children* .... it is, as it were, an infantilism that has receded into the spiritual. The case of puberty being retarded and not developing in the organism as a consequence of degeneration ....[74]

Earlier Nietzsche had proclaimed through Zarathustra that Jesus "died too early; he himself would have recanted his teaching had he reached my age. Noble enough was he to recant."[75]

Nietzsche admired Jesus' noble integrity, the fact that he lived his doctrine to the end. Yet he rejects Jesus, for Jesus exemplifies the psychological type set on rejecting the world—one possessed of an instinctive will to nothingness!† If such

---

* It would appear that Nietzsche is using the word "idiot" in the sense in which Dostoevsky, in his novel *The Idiot*, calls Prince Myshkin by that term. It is not certain, however, that Nietzsche read *The Idiot*.

† Again, Nietzsche's interpretation of the Jesus of the Gospels is widely repudiated, even by those critics most sympathetic to Nietzsche.

a way of life were to be universally followed, it would lead to nihilism, to the
extirpation of all the higher values of
culture and the destruction of man.

Nietzsche's critique of Christianity
was not principally directed against Jesus,
however. His most violent attack was
aimed at the Church's transformation of
the "good tidings" of Jesus into the
doctrine of faith in Christ. Nietzsche believed that Christianity constituted the
complete distortion of Jesus' life and
teaching. Walter Kaufmann has shown
that Nietzsche's critique of the Church's
faith in Christ was twofold: a criticism of
faith versus action and of *faith versus
reason.*[76]

The whole transformation of Jesus'
"glad tidings" began with his death on
the cross. This unexpected, disgraceful
event confronted the disciples with several
questions:

Who was this? What was this? Their profoundly upset and insulted feelings, and their
suspicion that such a death might represent the
refutation of their cause .... this state is only
too easy to understand. Here everything *had*
to be necessary, had to have meaning, reason
.... Only now the cleft opened up: "*Who*
killed him? *Who* was his natural enemy?"
This question leaped forth like lightning.
Answer: *ruling* Jewry, its highest class. From
this moment one felt oneself in rebellion
against the existing order, and in retrospect
one understood Jesus to have been *in rebellion
against the existing order.* Until then this war-
like, this No-saying, No-doing trait had been
lacking in his image; even more, he had been
its opposite.[77]

_____

See Kaufmann's *Nietzsche*, Chap. 12. To
Nietzsche, the strong, apocalyptical Jesus is the
product of the Gospel editors and totally foreign
to Jesus' own consciousness. Was Nietzsche the
victim of the nineteenth-century liberal lives of
Jesus after all?

What now gripped the disciples was
a most unevangelical feeling, the desire
for *revenge*. "Once more the popular
expectation of a Messiah came to the
foreground; a historic moment was
envisaged: the 'kingdom of God' comes
as a judgement over his enemies."[78] A
second question emerged:

How *could* God permit this? To this the
deranged reason of a small community found
an altogether horribly absurd answer: God
gave his son for the remission of sins, as a
sacrifice. In one stroke, it was all over with the
evangel! ... Jesus had abolished the very
concept of "guilt"—he had denied the
cleavage between God and man; he *lived* this
unity of God and man as his "glad tidings"
.... From now on there enters into the type
of the Redeemer, step by step, the doctrine of
judgement and return, the doctrine of death
as a sacrificial death, the doctrine of the
resurrection with which the whole concept of
"blessedness" ... is conjured away—in favor
of a state *after* death.[79]

For Nietzsche, it was the apostle Paul
who was most responsible for transforming the gospel into a doctrine of revenge
and decadence.

In Paul was embodied the opposite type to
that of the "bringer of glad tidings": the
genius in hatred .... How *much* this dys-
angelist* sacrificed to hatred![80]

According to Nietzsche, Paul "invented
his own history of Christianity" and at
the center of his nihilistic doctrine was
erected the belief in "justification by
faith." It was this, more than anything
else, that denied Jesus' emphasis on practice. Faith now became *the* substitute for
action. The doctrine of justification by
faith was but a shrewd *rationalization* for

_____

* "Bringer of ill tidings."

Paul's, and later for Luther's, own weakness and failure to live out the radical demands of Jesus:

'Faith' was at all times, for example, in Luther, only a cloak, a pretext, a *screen* behind which the instincts played their game.... 'Faith'... the characteristic Christian *shrewdness*—one always *spoke* of faith, but one always *acted* from instinct alone.[81]

Not only did the doctrine of faith serve the Christian community as a rationalization for their failure in practice, it justified a *sacrificium intellectus* and the maintenance of a double standard of truth. "Faith," says Nietzsche, "is the *veto* against science."[82] Faith divides the world into two spheres, one known by reason, the other based on belief or conviction. This allows the Christian a double standard by which to judge matters which others must judge by reason alone. Nietzsche was especially incensed by the double standard used by Christian scholars in his own field of philology.

The philology of Christianity

How little Christianity educates the sense of honesty and justice can be seen pretty well from the writings of its scholars: they advance their conjectures as blandly as dogmas and are hardly ever honestly perplexed by the exegesis of a Biblical verse. Again and again they say, "I am right, for it is written," and the interpretation that follows is of such impudent arbitrariness that a philologist is stopped in his tracks, torn between anger and laughter, and keeps asking himself: Is it possible? Is it honest? Is it even decent?[83]

At the conclusion of a note in *The Will to Power*, Nietzsche adds the remark: "A very popular error: having the courage of one's convictions; rather it is a matter of having the courage for an *attack* on one's convictions!!"[84] No man has the

"right" to believe something, even if reason cannot decide the issue. Neither happiness nor utility is a proper criterion for judging matters of truth. Nietzsche found a theological pragmatism abhorrent:

How many people still make the inference: "one could not stand life if there were no God... consequently there *must* be a God (or an ethical significance of existence)!... what presumption to decree that all that is necessary for my preservation must also really *be there*! As if my preservation were anything necessary!"[85]

Nietzsche was so opposed to utilitarian and pragmatic proofs that he believed appeals to pleasure and utility were in fact, "counter-proofs" against any truth claims that might be advanced. There is no necessary correlation between truth and pleasure.

The experience of all severe, of all profoundly inclined spirits teaches the *opposite*. At every step one has to wrestle for truth; one has had to surrender for it almost everything to which the heart, to which our love, our trust in life, cling otherwise. That requires greatness of soul; the service of truth is the hardest service. What does it mean after all to have *integrity* in matters of the spirit? That one is severe against one's heart, that one despises "beautiful sentiments," that one makes of every Yes and No a matter of conscience. Faith makes blessed: consequently it lies![86]

Faith, for Nietzsche, is a sure sign that not even a beginning has been made in the discipline of truth-seeking. Moreover, it is the sign of a "need born of *weakness*. The man of faith, the 'believer' of every kind, is necessarily a dependent man— one who cannot posit *himself* as an end. ... The 'believer' does not belong to *himself*. . . . Every kind of faith is itself an expression of self-abnegation, of self-alienation."[87] Strength and freedom are born only of a fearless openness to truth. All "great spirits," Nietzsche says, "are skeptics." And yet the great mass of men prefer the martyrs and fanatics, the sick spirits, for "the fanatics are picturesque; mankind prefers to see gestures rather than to hear *reasons*."[88]

We are back, once again, to Nietzsche's original critique: Christian faith is the manifestation of a weakness which supports an escape from, and contempt for, all strong and honest instincts and values. Nietzsche thus concludes the *Antichrist* with this thunderous denunciation:

> I *condemn* Christianity. I raise against the Christian church the most terrible of all accusations that any accuser ever uttered. It is to me the highest of all conceivable corruptions . . . . Parasitism is the *only* practice of the church; with its ideal of anemia, of "holiness," draining all blood, all love, all hope for life; the beyond as the will to negate every reality; the cross as the mark of recognition for the most subterranean conspiracy that ever existed—against health, beauty, whatever has turned out well, courage, spirit, *graciousness* of the soul, *against life itself* . . . . I call Christianity the one great curse . . . the one great instinct of revenge . . . . I call it the one immortal blemish of mankind.[89]

The *Übermensch*. The *Antichrist* closes with Nietzsche's call for a new reckoning of time. We have until now calculated time from the first day the "calamity" of Christianity began. "*Why not*," he asks, "*rather after its last day? After today?* Revaluation of all values!"[90] Nietzsche looked to the coming of a new type of human existence in which there would be a transvaluation of all values. The new values would be embodied in

the new man, the *Übermensch* or superior man, who would emerge after the death of nihilism. However, Nietzsche did not believe that the superior man was inevitable. "Progress," he said, "is a merely modern idea . . . . further development is altogether *not* according to any necessity in the direction of elevation, enhancement, or strength."[91] The higher type of man, Nietzsche believed, could be discovered in widely different times and cultures and "such fortunate accidents of great success . . . *will* perhaps always be possible."[92] And yet, despite Christianity's war to death against this higher type of man, Nietzsche prophesied that such a man would emerge after the madness brought on by the consciousness of the "death of God" had been fully vented.

The *Übermensch* will be "God's successor".

> Once one said God when one looked upon distant seas; but now I have taught you to say: overman. God is a conjecture; but I desire that your conjectures should not reach beyond your creative will. Could you *create* a god? Then do not speak to me of any gods. But you *could* create the overman . . . . Away from God and gods this will has lured me; what could one create if gods existed? . . . But my fervent will to create impels me even again toward man . . . . The beauty of the overman came to me as a shadow. O my brothers, what are the gods to me now?[93]

The *Übermensch* succeeds God, but he will also supersede man. "Man is something that should be overcome," and the man who has overcome himself has become an overman. What Nietzsche means by man overcoming himself is highly significant and should make clear that Nietzsche's superior man was the antithesis of the cruel, tyrannical Nazi,

with whom he has frequently been identified. The overcoming of man has, once
again, to do with the will to power. As
we have learned, all creatures, without
exception, are possessed of the will to
power, but what sets man apart from the
animals is the fact that he can channel his
will to power toward *self-mastery*. In fact,
that which requires the greatest exercise
of power is the overcoming or mastery
of oneself. The overman demands just
such self-discipline and hardness toward
himself. The *Übermensch*, in the words of
Walter Kaufmann,

has overcome his animal nature, organized
the chaos of his passions, sublimated his impulses, and given style to his character—or, as
Nietzsche said of Goethe: "... he disciplined
himself into wholeness, he *created* himself"
and became "the man of tolerance, not from
weakness, but from strength, a spirit who has
become free."[94]

The key to the superior man is, first of
all, self-discipline.

The most spiritual men, as the *strongest*, find
their happiness where others would find their
destruction: in the labyrinth, in hardness
against themselves and others, in experiments;
their joy is self-conquest; asceticism becomes
in them nature, need, instinct. Difficult tasks
are a privilege to them; to play with burdens
that crush others, a recreation .... They are
the most venerable kind of man; that does not
preclude their being the most cheerful and
the kindliest.[95]

Hardness toward oneself and achievement of self-conquest does not result in
the superior man's lording it over others.
It is only the weaklings who think
"themselves good because they have no
claws"; the superior man has claws but
does not use them. "When the exceptional human being treats the mediocre

more tenderly than himself and his peers,
this is not mere politeness of heart—it is
simply his *duty*."[96] In the superior man
alone is graciousness a sign of strength
and not weakness. Most of the powerful
heroes of history—e.g., Cesar Borgia
and Napoleon—lack the virtues of the
superior man, especially the realization
of self-mastery through sublimation of
power. Julius Caesar came close to it, but
the ideal would be the Roman Caesar
with Christ's soul.

The *overman's* life is just that: over-
abundant, overjoyed. It is the Dionysian
life, possessed of the yea-saying instinct.
It is just this affirmation of the moment
that gives joy to the superior man's life
despite the loss of all belief in an ultimate
meaning to history, in human progress,
or in any supramundane redemption or
existence. The *Übermensch* alone can
embrace and exult in Zarathustra's teaching of the eternal recurrence of all things:
suffering and joy, good and evil, pain
and pleasure. He alone can will that every
moment of life recur eternally. The
overman has passed beyond the need to
justify the ways of the world. His song
is "Once More"; his motto, *Amor fati*.
He not only bears necessity, he loves it.
He has become what Nietzsche longed to
become—only an affirmer, a yea-sayer
(*Ja-sager*).

Like Marx, Nietzsche offered to what
he considered a resentful and repressed
humanity a new naturalistic religious
vision. It is his substitute for a Christianity
which he felt to be inherently self-
alienating. In place of God, Nietzsche
envisions the *Übermensch*. Healing will
come not by supernatural grace but by a
superhuman will to power—power sublimated into a form of perfect self-
mastery. In place of eternal life, Nietzsche
offers the ecstatic joy of eternal return.

Nietzsche was among those visionary prophets of the nineteenth century who, like Dostoevsky and Kierkegaard, sensed the decadence and death ingenerate in modern bourgeois culture. Nietzsche believed this nihilism was rooted in the soil of Christian values. His equation of Christianity and the sickness of nineteenth-century European culture was in part true but was one-sided and myopic. As Santayana has remarked, Nietzsche was "living in the light of the ideal," and in that light popular Christianity could appear only weak, resigned, hypocritical. He could not appreciate the simple virtues of the unsung life of countless Christians, virtues expressive of a noble sublimation of power; nor, apparently, could he understand the freedom and life-affirming joy that was at the center of genuine Christian faith.

Nietzsche was, nevertheless, quite right in his rejection of much in European culture which, through the influence of Christianity, had become the source of weakness, self-deprecation, and suffering. There is an element of "world-weariness" in Christianity, traceable to the very beginnings of the Christian movement, which has been the cause of much pessimism, apathy, and failure to will a more complete and better life. There is also a tradition of radical asceticism in Christianity which, psychologically, is often but the outward manifestation of self-hatred and a morbid, perverted attitude toward the body and sexuality. And Nietzsche was correct in his observation that Christian love had degenerated into a sentimentalized emotion of pity—and that pity is degrading and condescending and the hidden source of self-gratification. In attacking this weak, exploitative form of love, Nietzsche served the Christian faith well. In fact, one of Nietzsche's greatest contributions to Christianity and to the modern world was his insight into the concealed and perverse motivations of many of our "virtuous" deeds and the role of the egoistic "will to power" in even our most altruistic actions.

Nietzsche's significance for Christian thought, however, lies principally in his parable of the "death of God." For Nietzsche the death of God was a cultural fact which had not yet fully reached the consciousness of men. But it symbolized the fact that for men God, or the Ultimate, and the moral sanctions imposed by the Ultimate were no longer real. Hence God could not for long continue to be the bearer of a system of values. Man would be thrown back upon himself. Nietzsche believed that men were not yet aware of this fact and thus were still living off those standards and values rooted in the soil of Christian belief. But, once uprooted, the flowers of Christian civilization, such as democracy, would wither and die and men would find themselves, as J. S. Mill said of Victorian England, "destitute of faith, but terrified at skepticism." The tension brought on by the breakdown of belief, Nietzsche prophesied, would usher in a period of active nihilism which would lead to violence and "wars such as there have never been on earth before." Nietzsche believed that this period of nihilism, though inevitable, would nevertheless, be followed by the emergence of the superior man. And although thrown into a godless world both tragic and absurd, the *Übermensch* would yet retain his integrity in the face of nothingness. In our own day Albert Camus' Sisyphus is just such an *Übermensch* for he, too, "teaches the higher fidelity that negates the gods" and instructs us that "the struggle itself toward the heights is enough to fill a man's heart." It is this legacy of Nietzsche in twentieth-century atheistic Existentialism which stands today as one of Christianity's most powerful challenges.

NOTES

1. Karl Barth, *From Rousseau to Ritschl* (New York, 1959), p. 386.
2. *Deutsche Revue*, June 1905, pp. 343 ff.; quoted in Albert Schweitzer, *The Quest of the Historical Jesus* (New York, 1961), pp. 70–71.
3. Barth, op. cit., p. 370.
4. D. F. Strauss, *The Life of Jesus Critically Examined*, tr. from 4th German ed. by George Eliot (London, 1906), p. xxix.
5. Ibid., p. xxx.
6. Ibid.
7. Ibid., p. 70.
8. Ibid., p. 64.
9. Ibid., pp. 64–65.
10. Ibid., p. 80.
11. Ibid., pp. 83–84.
12. Ibid., pp. 87–89.
13. Ibid., p. 92.
14. Schweitzer, op. cit., p. 84.
15. Strauss' own contemporary F. C. Baur, while recognizing the genuine importance of the *Leben Jesu*, offered some trenchant criticisms of Strauss' handling of the Gospel sources and his extreme negativity toward some of the New Testament data. See P. Hodgson, *The Formation of Historical Theology: A Study of Ferdinand Christian Baur* (New York, 1966), pp. 73–84.
16. On this point see the criticism of Van A. Harvey, "D. F. Strauss' *Life of Jesus* Revisited," *Church History*, Vol. 30 (June 1961), pp. 191 ff.
17. L. Feuerbach, "Zur Kritik der Hegelschen Philosophie," *Sämtliche Werke*, II (Jodl edition, 1959), p. 277.
18. L. Feuerbach, *The Essence of Christianity*, tr. George Eliot (New York, 1959), p. xxxv.
19. L. Feuerbach, *Kleine Philosophische Schriften*, ed. Max Gustav Lange (Leipzig, 1950), p. 56.
20. *Essence of Christianity*, op. cit., p. 228.
21. Ibid., p. 230.
22. Ibid., p. 31.
23. *Sämtliche Werke*, 1846, I, xiv–xv; cited in Sidney Hook, *From Hegel to Marx* (New York, 1950), pp. 222–223.
24. *Essence of Christianity*, op. cit., p. xxxviii.
25. Ibid., p. xxxix.
26. Ibid., pp. 2–3.
27. Ibid., pp. 12–13.
28. Ibid., p. 14.
29. Ibid., p. 33.
30. Ibid., p. 26. Again: "The more empty life is, the fuller, the more concrete is God. The impoverishing of the real world and the enriching of God is one act. Only the poor man has a rich God" (p. 73).
31. Ibid., p. 26.
32. Ibid., p. 33.
33. Ibid., pp. 217–218. For this reference and its significance for Marx, as elsewhere in this chapter, the author is dependent on Robert Tucker's excellent discussion of Feuerbach and Marx in chapters five and six of *Philosophy and Myth in Karl Marx* (Cambridge, 1961).
34. Ibid., p. 135.
35. Ibid., p. 65.
36. Ibid., p. 67.
37. Ibid., p. 70.
38. *Kleine Philosophische Schriften*, p. 169; cited in Tucker, op. cit., p. 91.
39. *Essence of Christianity*, p. 64.
40. J. H. Randall, Jr., *The Career of Philosophy*, II, p. 374.
41. *Essence of Christianity*, pp. 277–278.
42. K. Marx and F. Engels, *Historische-Kritische Gesamtausgabe, erste Abteilung*, I, 1, p. 175; cited in Tucker, op. cit., p. 81.
43. Karl Marx, *On Religion* (Moscow, n.d.), p. 15.

44. Ibid., p. 41–42.
45. Ibid., p. 42.
46. Ibid., p. 72.
47. Ibid., p. 70.
48. Ibid., p. 71; Theses VI and VII.
49. Ibid., p. 88.
50. Ibid.
51. Hess, *Sozialistische Aufsätze*, p. 167; cited in Tucker, op. cit., p. 110.
52. Ibid., p. 170; Tucker, p. 110.
53. Ibid., p. 149; cited in Hook, op. cit., p. 198.
54. *Historische-Kritische Gesamtausgabe*, I, 1, pp. 601, 603; cited in Tucker, op. cit., p. 111.
55. Marx, *On Religion*, p. 135.
56. The "anti-religious" religion of Marx has often been commented on. Reinhold Niebuhr, Robert Tucker, Louis Halle (see bibliography), and many others have interpreted Marx as a secular religious visionary and mythmaker.
57. Louis J. Halle, "Marx's Religious Drama," *Encounter* (October 1965), p. 37.
58. Tillich, *Perspectives on 19th and 20th Century Protestant Theology*, p. 191.
59. Ernst Benz, in "Nietzsches Ideen zur Geschichte des Christentums," *Zeitschrift für Kirchengeschichte*, Vol. 56 (1937), suggests that Nietzsche's concept of Jesus is "a positive contribution to the realization of a new form of Christian life and thought."
60. Karl Jaspers, in *Nietzsche and Christianity* (1961), seeks to demonstrate the Christian basis of Nietzsche's view of history and of his moral and scientific integrity.
61. Cited in R. J. Hollingdale, *Nietzsche* (London, 1965), p. 30.
62. *The Gay Science*, in *The Portable Nietzsche*, tr. and ed. W. Kaufmann (New York, 1960), pp. 95–96.
63. Martin Heidegger interprets Nietzsche's words "God is dead" as the pronouncement that metaphysics can no longer concern itself with the "beyond" or with a supersensory, transcendent ground of Being but returns us to the pre-Socratic concern with things-that-are-within-this-

world. See "Nietzsches Wort, 'Gott ist tot,'" in *Holzwege* (Frankfurt, 1950).
64. *The Genealogy of Morals*, tr. Francis Golffing (New York, 1956), p. 288. This and other passages give support to Jaspers' contention that Christian faith constitutes the basis of Nietzsche's radical truthfulness and his uncompromising approach to reality.
65. Ibid., pp. 296–298.
66. *Antichrist*, 47; Kaufmann, op. cit., p. 627.
67. *Antichrist*, 18; Kaufmann, op. cit., pp. 585–586.
68. *Genealogy of Morals*, op. cit., pp. 167–168.
69. Ibid., pp. 168–169. It is widely agreed that Nietzsche was not attacking genuine Christian love but a sentimentalized conception of love as pity. Erich Fromm calls this a "symbiotic love," based on weakness and unconscious exploitation.
70. Ibid., p. 170.
71. *Antichrist*, 39; Kaufmann, op. cit., p. 612.
72. Ibid., 35; pp. 608–609.
73. Ibid., 29; pp. 600–601.
74. Ibid., 32; p. 604.
75. Kaufmann, op. cit., p. 185.
76. We will follow Kaufmann's analysis at this point. Our account of Nietzsche's portrayal of Jesus is also dependent, in part, on Kaufmann's interpretation. See Walter Kaufmann, *Nietzsche* (New York, 1959), Chap. 12.
77. *Antichrist*, 40; Kaufmann, *Portable*, op. cit., pp. 614–615.
78. Ibid., p. 615.
79. Ibid., 41; p. 616.
80. Ibid., 42; p. 617.
81. Ibid., 39; p. 613.
82. Ibid., 47; p. 627.
83. *The Dawn*, 84; Kaufmann, op. cit., p. 80.
84. Kaufmann, *Nietzsche*, op. cit., p. 303.
85. Ibid., p. 305.
86. *Antichrist*, 50; Kaufmann, *Portable*, op. cit., p. 632.
87. Ibid., 54; pp. 638–639.
88. Ibid., 54; p. 639.
89. Ibid., 62; pp. 655–656.
90. Ibid., 62; p. 656.
91. Ibid., 4; p. 571.

92. Ibid.
93. *Zarathustra*, Kaufmann, *Portable*, op. cit., pp. 197–200.
94. *Nietzsche*, op. cit., p. 274.

95. *Antichrist*, 57; Kaufmann, *Portable*, op. cit., pp. 645–646.
96. Ibid., p. 647.

SUGGESTIONS FOR FURTHER READING

THE POST-HEGELIAN CRITIQUE OF CHRISTIANITY IN GENERAL

Hook, Sydney. *From Hegel to Marx* (Ann Arbor: University of Michigan Press, 1962).

Löwith, Karl. *From Hegel to Nietzsche* (New York: Holt, Rinehart and Winston, 1964).

Marcuse, Herbert. *Reason and Revolution: Hegel and the Rise of Social Theory*, 2d ed. (Boston: Beacon Press, 1960).

Tillich, Paul. *Perspectives on 19th and 20th Century Protestant Theology* (New York: Harper, 1967).

DAVID FRIEDRICH STRAUSS

Barth, Karl. *From Rousseau to Ritschl* (New York: Harper, 1959). An interesting appraisal of Strauss and his significance.

Harvey, Van A. "D. F. Strauss' *Life of Jesus* Revisited," *Church History*, Vol. 30 (June, 1961). A fine analysis of the strengths and weaknesses of Strauss' historical work.

Schweitzer, Albert. *The Quest of the Historical Jesus* (New York: The Macmillan Co., 1961). Remains the best treatment of Strauss in English.

LUDWIG FEUERBACH

The works of Barth, Hook, Löwith, Marcuse, and Tillich cited above all contain interesting accounts of Feuerbach's philosophy and critique of Christianity. In addition, the following studies are recommended:

Barth, Karl. "Introduction," Ludwig Feuerbach. *The Essence of Christianity* (New York: Harper Torchbook, 1958).

Chamberlin, W. B. *Heaven Wasn't His Destination: The Philosophy of Ludwig Feuerbach* (London, 1941).

Tucker, Robert C. *Philosophy and Myth in Karl Marx* (Cambridge: Cambridge University Press, 1961). Chapters V and VI of this book give an excellent analysis of Feuerbach's philosophy and his influence on Marx.

KARL MARX

The works of Hook, Löwith, Marcuse, Tillich, and Tucker, cited above, all contain worthwhile accounts of Marx's critique of religion. Especially recommended is R. C. Tucker's book which makes clear both Marx's critique of religion and the religious and mythic character of his own thought. The following studies are also recommended:

Fromm, Erich. *Marx's Concept of Man* (New York: Frederick Ungar, 1961). A sympathetic account of the humanism of Marx's early writings.

Halle, Louis J. "Marx's Religious Drama," *Encounter* (October, 1965).

Popper, Karl. *The Open Society and Its Enemies*, Vol. II: *The High Tide of Prophecy: Hegel, Marx and the Aftermath* (New York: Harper Torchbook, 1963). A formidable criticism of Marx's philosophical and historical doctrines.

Among the biographies of Marx, those of Isaiah Berlin, E. H. Carr, and Franz Mehning are highly recommended. Edmund Wilson gives an excellent intellectual portrait of Marx in *To the Finland Station*.

THE CONTEMPORARY MARXIST-CHRISTIAN DIALOGUE

Garaudy, Roger. *From Anathema to Dialogue: A Marxist Challenge to the Christian Churches* (New York: Herder and Herder, 1966). A leading Marxist theoretician analyzes the fundamental differences between Christianity and Marxism but calls for a new openness on common concerns.

Moltmann, Jürgen. *The Theology of Hope* (New York: Harper and Row, 1967). Although this is not a specific dialogue with Marxism, Moltmann makes extensive use of the Marxist categories of Ernst Bloch in developing his own future-oriented theology.

Ogletree, Thomas, ed. *Openings for Marxist-Christian Dialogue* (Nashville: Abingdon Press, 1969). Essays by theologians expressive of the new openness to Marxist humanism.

West, Charles. **Communism and the Theologians* (New York: Macmillan, 1963). An excellent study of five types of Christian response to Marxism in the pre-1960 period. Includes bibliographical reference to the relevant works of Brunner, Tillich, Niebuhr, Barth, and Hromadka on Marxism.

Friedrich Nietzsche

In addition to the discussions of Nietzsche in the works of Löwith and Tillich, cited above, the following studies are recommended:

Hollingdale, R. J. *Nietzsche: The Man and His Philosophy* (Baton Rouge: Louisiana State University Press, 1965). An excellent attempt to combine an account of Nietzsche's life and thought, taking into account the most recent Nietzsche scholarship.

Jaspers, Karl. *Nietzsche,* tr. C. F. Wallroff and F. J. Schmitz (Tucson: University of Arizona Press, 1965). One of the major studies of Nietzsche by a world-renowned philosopher. Not for the beginner.

———. **Nietzsche and Christianity* (Chicago: Henry Regnery, 1961). An interesting analysis of Nietzsche's interpretation of and dependence on Christianity.

Kaufmann, Walter. **Nietzsche: Philosopher, Psychologist, Antichrist* (New York: World Publishing Co., 1968). Regarded by many as the best study of Nietzsche to date. It includes a very interesting discussion of Nietzsche and Christianity.

CHAPTER EIGHT

The Conflict Between Science and Theology: Biblical Criticism and Darwinism

Charles Darwin

If English thought was out of touch with intellectual movements on the Continent in the early decades of the nineteenth century, the isolation could not last long. The Oxford Movement certainly delayed the full airing of critical questions in the Church; and its failure to see anything but "Infidelity" in the work of scientific criticism was, in part, responsible for the uncertainty and the loss of faith that gripped so many of the ablest young minds in England during the 1840s and 1850s. Keble's advice to Thomas Arnold "to pause in his inquiries and to pray earnestly for help and light from above," sincere as it was, did not meet the challenge of persistent intellectual questioning which sensitive young men were unable to put aside. Liberal views were beginning to have a wider exposure in the universities. In 1846 George Eliot's translation of Strauss' *Life of Jesus* was published and had a very large sale. Strauss' critical principles and mythical theories were also introduced to the public by his English disciple, Charles Hennell, whose *Inquiry Concerning the Origin of Christianity* appeared in 1838. This was at a time when, in spite of Coleridge, the verbal inerrancy of Scripture was still the popular view in England, and scholars like Pusey still held a rather crude precritical view of biblical inspiration. Not only did the new biblical criticism create uneasiness; the growing interest in the new discoveries and theories of natural science also caused religious unrest. In the period between 1830 and 1860, England saw a rapid rise of popular interest in science and the appearance of numerous popular books on natural history. Especially significant was Robert Chambers' *Vestiges of the Natural History of Creation*, a book that acquainted the English public with the idea of evolution. This flood of new ideas, complex and not easily assimilated, brought on a variety of response and ushered in an age of doubt and perplexity.* Some responded to the new knowledge by ignoring it or, like Pusey, by convincing themselves that it would eventually be proven wrong. Others, like Frederick Harrison, hastily and often uncritically accepted the new science and became apostles of August

Comte and Positivism. For most, however, there was no easy victory but a long and often indecisive battle between the recognition of the undeniable findings of science and the deep convictions of a sensitive religious spirit.* Many hoped against hope that the old religious views could be preserved but, as the great New Testament scholar B. F. Westcott observed at the time, "The broad stream of events could not be stayed." The question was whether theology could be "guided along fertilizing channels" or whether it would be allowed to follow a reactionary course.

The conflicts between theology and the new sciences is a major chapter in the intellectual history of the second half of the nineteenth century. Not all of the controversies can be chronicled here. However, two of them—occurring almost simultaneously in the 1860's—stand out as especially significant, both in their effects and because they raised the most fundamental issues theology has yet found itself faced with in an age of unprecedented scientific advance. The one controversy had to do with the historical criticism of the Bible and was provoked by the publication of a book entitled *Essays and Reviews* (1860). The other focused on Darwin's *The Origin of Species* (1859) which appeared to destroy the biblical doctrine of creation and providence and, with them, the uniqueness of man as a special creature of God. In the case of each dispute, an attempt will be made to clarify what the real issues were by giving a brief account of

---

* Many factors were responsible for the Victorian crisis of belief and the growth of skepticism and agnosticism. Biblical criticism and science were major causes, but the apparent cruelty implied in such Christian doctrines as predestination and eternal damnation was also a significant factor in turning sensitive spirits like Francis Newman and J. A. Froude away from orthodoxy. See H. R. Murphy, "The Ethical Revolt Against Christian Orthodoxy in Early Victorian England," *American Historical Review* (LX, 1955).

* The spiritual conflicts and pilgrimages of many of the eminent Victorians is a fascinating and moving story. For an introductory account of Victorian belief and unbelief, see Basil Willey, *More Nineteenth Century Studies: A Group of Honest Doubters* and A. O. J. Cockshut, *The Unbelievers.*

the conflict itself. Then it can be illustrated how a few representative theologians responded to the scientific challenge and something of the present significance of this chapter of Victorian history.

Essays and Reviews

In February of 1860 a collection of seven essays was published under the title *Essays and Reviews*. At first the book was taken little account of but soon became the center of one of the most bitter religious controversies of the century. The significance of *Essays and Reviews* was twofold. Scientifically, it was a landmark in the acceptance of a historical-critical study of the Bible in the English-speaking world. Popularly, it helped to introduce theological issues to the educated public and to make for a more liberal attitude toward differences of religious conviction. Of this latter effect the historian Lecky has written:

No change in English life during the latter half of the nineteenth century is more conspicuous than the great enlargement of the range of permissible opinions on religious subjects. Opinions and arguments which not many years ago were confined to small circles and would have drawn down grave social penalties, have become the common-place of the drawingroom and the boudoir. The first very marked change in this respect followed, I think, the publication in 1860 of the "Essays and Reviews."[1]

The publication of such a book of essays was first proposed by Henry Bristow Wilson (1803–1888), a country vicar and graduate of St. John's College, Oxford. Wilson had long been a champion of theological freedom and was one of the liberal opponents of the Trac-

tarians. He asked Benjamin Jowett, then Regius Professor of Greek at Oxford, to contribute an essay to the volume. The invitation appealed to Jowett, since it offered him the opportunity of publishing an article on the critical study of Scripture on which he had been at work for a decade. Jowett's essay proved to be the most important, if not the most controversial, of the seven that were printed. All of the essays were concerned with theological freedom; three had to do specifically with freedom to examine Scripture in the light of current discoveries in the historical and natural sciences. What was especially significant, and shocking to some, was the fact that all but one of the essayists were ordained clergymen. Three (Jowett, Frederick Temple, and Mark Pattison) were also distinguished educators and Oxford men of high reputation.

What all of the essayists felt deeply was that because of its fear of scholarly criticism, Christianity was losing the best minds of the generation. As Jowett remarked: "In a few years there will be no religion in Oxford among intellectual young men, unless religion is shown to be consistent with criticism."[2] Many recognized this and yet feared that an open statement of the problems facing Christian belief would be too negative and might upset or even destroy the faith of the less mature. Jowett was sensitive to this possibility but felt the situation made silence morally reprehensible.

We do not wish to do anything rash or irritating to the public or the University, but we are determined not to submit to this abominable system of terrorism, which prevents the statement of the plainest facts, and makes true theology or theological education impossible. . . .[3]

Most of what the essayists wrote would be considered fairly commonplace today. One or two of the essays were slightly contentious and, in retrospect, needlessly provocative. Professor Baden Powell's "On the Study of the Evidences of Christianity" smacks of a too-confident rationalism and some statements of Temple and Jowett cause us to smile at their optimism and Victorian moralism. Nevertheless, the significant critical principles for which these men sought recognition are considered indispensable today to the serious biblical scholar.

What concerned most of the essayists were the dogmatic constraints which had been placed upon the interpretation of the Bible—especially the concept of inspiration which conceived of divine revelation as coextensive with the written Scripture itself. The term "Word of God" was particularly mischievous for it is

a phrase which begs many questions when applied to the canonised books of the Old and New Testaments, a phrase which is never applied to them by any of the Scriptural authors, and which, according to Protestant principles, never could be applied to them by any of sufficient authority from without. In that which may be considered the pivot Article of the Church this expression does not occur, but only "Holy Scripture," "Canonised Books," "Old and New Testaments." It contains no declaration of the Bible being throughout supernaturally suggested, nor any intimation as to which portions of it were owing to a special divine illumination, nor the slightest attempts at defining inspiration. . . . nor the least hint of the relation between the divine and human elements in the composition of the biblical books. . . .[4]

The essayists wished to free theology of a crude biblicism which was making it increasingly difficult to be both a Christian and a thinking man. What was needed was an openness to the findings of modern science and a widening of the ideas of inspiration and revelation. In Rowland Williams' essay on "Bunsen's Biblical Researches," a concern to acknowledge the results of the literary and historical study of the Bible is the predominant theme, while in C. W. Goodwin's "On the Mosaic Cosmogony" the desperate attempt to salvage the scientific veracity of Genesis is shown to be doomed to failure. The two essays reflect the two major threats to the old biblicism: critical historiography and natural science.

The Essays of Williams and Goodwin. Williams' essay is an enthusiastic review of the biblical researches of Baron von Bunsen, a learned Prussian diplomat whose popular works on the Bible showed the influence of the most critical German scholarship. Williams uses his review of Bunsen as a means of commending the methods and findings of historical criticism and to suggest a more acceptable view of revelation. He begins with the hermeneutical principle affirmed by most of the essayists: the Bible must be read like any other book. "We cannot," Williams contends, "encourage a remorseless criticism of Gentile histories and escape its contagion when we approach Hebrew annals; nor acknowledge a Providence in Jewry without owning that it may have comprehended sanctities elsewhere."[5] If the Bible is studied like other texts, much that was taken before as only fantastic can now be seen in its natural light.

Our deluge takes its place among geological phenomena, no longer a disturbance of law from which science shrinks, but a prolonged play of the forces of fire and water, rendering the primeval regions of North Asia uninhabitable, and urging the nations to new abodes.[6]

Nor should the critic blink at what the science of literary analysis tells us about many cherished Christian beliefs concerning prophecy.

Fresh from the services of Christmas, he may sincerely exclaim, *Unto us a Child is born;* but he knows that the Hebrew translated *Mighty God,* is at least disputable, that perhaps it means only Strong and Mighty One, Father of an Age; and he can never listen to anyone who pretends that the Maiden's Child of Isaiah VII, 16, was not to be born in the reign of Ahaz, as a sign against the Kings Pekah and Rezin.[7]

To recognize the natural and therefore fallible character of the biblical writings does not require the denial of the spiritual preeminence of Scripture; it does, however, demand that we change our way of reading the Bible. It is childish to think that "apart from omniscience belonging to the Jews, the proper conclusion of reason is atheism." Revelation does not require inerrancy.

It is not inconsistent with the idea that Almighty God has been pleased to educate men and nations, employing imagination no less than conscience, and suffering His lessons to play freely within the limits of humanity and its shortcomings.[8]

According to Williams, the critical approach to the Bible requires a wider conception of revelation which, while recognizing God's hand in the history of Jewry, also sees God's spirit as a perpetual presence in human history. Like Coleridge, Williams holds that the Bible is inspired only as, through the Spirit, it

"finds" him. It was such a view that brought charges against Williams in the ecclesiastical courts. He had been bold to say that "If such a Spirit did not dwell in the Church the Bible would not be inspired, for the Bible is, before all things, the written voice of the congregation."[9] Williams contended that such a conception of inspiration was held by the early Church and was the only one which the facts of Scripture would allow:

The Sacred Writers acknowledge themselves men of like passions with ourselves, and we are promised illumination from the Spirit which dwelt in them. . . . Instead of objecting that everyone of us is infallible, we should define inspiration consistently with the facts of Scripture, and of human nature. These would neither exclude the idea of fallibility among Israelites of old, nor teach us to quench the Spirit in true hearts for ever.[10]

Williams' criticism of the static, inerrant view of inspiration is forceful. However, he was ambiguous on whether there was to be any distinction between biblical inspiration and the inspiration of a Milton and, if so, just what was the difference. The question of general and special revelation is not discussed. It is clear, however, that Williams does not wish to maintain any radical distinction between natural and revealed religion.

Williams emphasized, as Coleridge did before and Matthew Arnold did after him, the importance of distinguishing the language of image and metaphor from the language of science. What the biblical authors often meant as metaphors or poetic vision has been misread as literal fact. We must not, Williams urged, be forced into a position which demands that we equate the truths of Scripture with a scientific literalism.

Literalism is a modern aberration which has turned "symbol and poetry into materialism."

Williams' own "demythologizing" of Scripture is often ingenious and rationalistic. What does stand, however, is his appeal for freedom of criticism and his recognition that Christian faith could not long survive when blatant falsehoods continued to be taught concerning the foundation of the faith.

Charles Goodwin says much the same concerning the relations between theology and natural science in his essay "On the Mosaic Cosmogony." The difficulties in which theology finds itself are due not only to its rejection of science but to its pathetic attempts to harmonize the Bible with the new science. It is a losing battle that, after each new defeat, only makes Christian belief less tenable in the minds of thinking persons.

Goodwin saw the situation in the nineteenth century as similar to that of the sixteenth century. As the earlier period was shaken by Copernicus, so now was belief challenged by geology. The school books now taught that the earth moves but still assured the child that it is less than six thousand years old—at a time when geologists of firm religious faith were agreed that the earth had existed for millions of years. This situation had forced the theologians to attempt once again to reconcile the Mosaic narrative with the new scientific facts. Goodwin viewed this attempt as disastrous for scientific honesty and for a true reading of Scripture. His thesis is that if the value of the Bible is to be maintained,

it must not be striving to prove it scientifically exact, at the expense of every sound principle of interpretation, and in defiance of common sense, but by a frank recognition of the erroneous views of nature which it contains.[11]

Goodwin skillfully demonstrates that the popular attempts to harmonize Genesis and geology cancel one another out and in each case do violence to the clear meaning of the Hebrew text. There were at the time two principal approaches to the reconciliation of the Mosaic narrative and geology. The one was best represented by Dr. Buckland in his *Bridgewater Treatise*. It held that most geological ages evolved between "the beginning" and the "first day":

It is nowhere affirmed that God created the heaven and the earth in the *first day*, but in the *beginning*; this beginning may have been an epoch at an unmeasured distance. . . . No information is given to events which may have occurred upon this earth, unconnected with its history of man, between the creation of its component matter recorded in the first verse, and the era at which its history is resumed in the second verse; nor is any limit fixed to the time during which these intermediate events may have been going on: millions of millions of years may have occupied the interval between the beginning in which God created the heaven and the earth and the evening or commencement of the first day of the Mosaic narrative.[12]

For Buckland it was not necessary to maintain that "the substance of the sun and moon was first called into existence on the fourth day," for otherwise how could life be maintained? "The fact of their creation had been stated before in the first verse."[13] Nevertheless, this did require that Buckland account for the narrative of the fourth day. This he did by describing the primeval darkness of the first day as

a temporary darkness, produced by an accumulation of dense vapours upon the face of the deep. . . . An incipient dispersion of these vapours may have readmitted light to the earth, upon the first day, while the existing cause of light was obscured; and the further purification of the atmosphere upon the fourth day may have caused the sun and the moon and the stars to reappear in the firmament of heaven. . . .[14]

Goodwin's caustic reply to Buckland's theory is typical of his refutation:

The violence done to the great and simple words of the Hebrew writer must strike every mind. "And God said Let there be light—and there was light—and God saw the light that it was good. And God divided the light from the darkness, and God called the light day, and the darkness called he night; and the evening and the morning were the fourth day." Can anyone sensible of the words suppose that nothing more is here described, or intended to be described, than the partial clearing away of fog? Can such a manifestation of light be dignified by the appellation of day?[15]

It is clear that Buckland's zeal has forced him to torture a meaning out of the text that is quite foreign to its intention.

A second approach to the conciliation of Genesis and geology is typified in the works of the famous Scottish naturalist, Hugh Miller. Miller refuted Buckland's hypothesis of a great geological age between "the beginning" and the "first day" and the latter's view of the six subsequent days as natural days of twenty-four hours. Miller held to the biblical order of creation but considered each of the six days to be vast periods of time. Goodwin finds two principal difficulties in Miller's view. They concern the biblical order of creation and Miller's use of the concept "day." To be sure, there is a certain vague resemblance between the Hebrew poet's order of Creation and the findings of geology. But, when pressed very far, the resemblance vanishes.

The agreement is far from exact, as according to geological evidence, reptiles would appear to have existed ages before birds and mammals, whereas here the creation of birds is attributed to the fifth day, that of reptiles to the sixth. There remains, moreover, the insuperable difficulty of the plants and trees being represented as made on the third day—that is, more than an age before fishes and birds, which is clearly not the case.[16]

Likewise there are problems in the use of the word "day":

It is evident that the bare theory that a "day" means an age of immense geological period might be made to yield some strange results. What becomes of the evening and the morning of which day is said to have consisted? Was each geologic age divided into two long intervals, one all darkness, and the other all light? And if so what becomes of the plants and trees created in the third day or period, when the evening of the fourth day (the evenings, be it observed, precede the mornings) set in? They must have passed through half a seculum of total darkness, not even cheered by that dim light which the sun, not yet completely manifested, supplied on the morning of the third day. Such an ordeal would have completely destroyed the whole vegetable creation, and yet we find it survived. . . .[17]

Such labored isogesis of the biblical texts would be unnecessary if only the theologians would admit that the Mosaic cosmogony is not science but Hebrew poetry. "The spectacle," writes Goodwin, "of able, and we doubt not, conscientious writers engaged in attempting the impossible is painful and humiliating." It was not the object of the divine revelation to instruct mankind in physical science, for man was given natural facilities for such knowledge. If we admit that physical science is not what the

Hebrew writers profess to convey, "Why," Goodwin asks, "should we hesitate to recognize their fallibility on this head?"[18]

Jowett's "On the Interpretation of Scripture." Jowett's long essay appeared last in the book and was a fitting conclusion to the whole. Though the essay discusses issues touched on earlier, Jowett gives to the problems of biblical interpretation his own scholarly experience and moral earnestness. The essay rounds out the volume with a moving paean of praise to the life of scholarship and the love of truth.

Distinguished scholars had long called for silence on the difficulties of scriptural interpretation on two grounds: one, that the problems were of an esoteric sort, having no real impact on the ordinary layman and, secondly, that the issues were still indecisive, making any statement premature. Jowett contends that the difficulties referred to are very well known; "they force themselves on the attention of every intelligent reader of the New Testament." But because no one dares break through the veil of silence, there is abroad "a sort of smoldering scepticism." Nor is it possible any longer to ignore the results of criticism. "The Christian religion is in a false position when all the tendencies of knowledge are opposed to it."[19] A terrible mischief has come upon the Church when intelligent criticisms are automatically ascribed to atheism! "It would be a strange and almost incredible thing," Jowett muses, "that the Gospel, which at first made war only on the vices of mankind, should now be opposed to one of the highest and rarest of human virtues, the love of truth."[20]

The fundamental cause of this mischief lies in the fact that the Bible is not read like any other book. It is overladen with a priori notions concerning its origin and nature. The reasons for this are several. There is a natural conservatism in the religious community which dislikes challenging the critical canons of former ages. Chief among those canons is the rather modern identification of the written Scriptures with the inerrant "Word of God." The result is that the blatant discrepancies in the books of Kings and Chronicles, for example, must be considered as somehow only apparent. There is also the desire to adapt the words of Scripture to the doctrines of the Church's Creeds and, especially among modern apologists, to conform the statements of the Bible to the language and practice of the present age. An example of the former procedure is seen in the way St. Paul is made to agree with the abstract formulas of the Nicene and Athanasian Creeds:

Absorbed as St. Paul was in the person of Christ with an intensity of faith and love . . . high as he raised the dignity of his Lord above all things in heaven and earth—looking to Him as the Creator of all things . . . he does not speak of Him as "equal to the Father" or "of one substance with the Father."[21]

A priori notions are not, however, the possession only of the orthodox. The liberals also have their rules of faith by which they distort the natural sense of biblical texts. All parties are guilty of extracting selected verses from the Bible which are then "eagerly appealed to and made too much use of," being "forced into the service of received opinion and beliefs," while other texts "have been either unnoticed or explained away." Our "favorite verses shine like stars, while the rest of the page is thrown into the shade."22

So much for the mischievous principles that guide the interpretation of most divines. Against this Jowett set his own critical canons of interpretation. Most people considered them outrageous at the time. They were and are open to serious criticism but stand, nevertheless, as a kind of charter for critical biblical scholarship even today.

Jowett's basic principle was what most shocked his contemporaries. His hermeneutics was but an expansion of one canon: "*Interpret the Scripture like any other book.*" For Jowett this meant that the biblical scholar was to bring no special notions to the study of Scripture that he would not also expect to apply to the texts of Plato or Shakespeare. The purpose of the author—the meaning of the text—remains as it was first produced. It is not the function of the critic to find other meanings.

The book itself remains as at the first unchanged amid the changing interpretations of it. The office of the interpreter is not to add another, but to recover the original one: the meaning, that is, of the words as they struck on the ears or flashed before the eyes of those who first heard and read them. He has to transfer himself to another age to imagine that he is a disciple of Christ or Paul; to disengage himself from all that follows. The history of Christendom is nothing to him. . . . All the after thoughts of theology are nothing to him. . . . The greater part of his learning is a knowledge of the text itself; he has no delight in the voluminous literature which has overgrown it.23

The science of hermeneutics must be an inductive one, based on the thoughts and narratives of the writers themselves. The critic begins with only a few commonsense rules of thumb. The first, as we have seen, is that Scripture has one meaning. To reconstruct the inner and outer life of Jesus and His contemporaries is no easy task. But the alternative is not to intrude into this problem certain a priori solutions. This means that the scholar will often have to choose the more inconclusive or difficult interpretation "and refuse the one more in agreement with received opinions." This will not increase the scholar's popularity. To the charge that he is merely making the reading of the Bible "difficult and perplexing," the scholar can only answer: "that may very well be—it is a fact." One thing is clear: admitting the problems of interpretation does not mean that the scholar is "willing to admit to hidden or mysterious meaning."

In the same way we recognize the wonders and complexity of the laws of nature to be far beyond what eye has seen or knowledge reached, yet it is not therefore to be supposed that we acknowledge the existence of some other laws different in kind from those we know which are incapable of philosophical analysis. In like manner we have no reason to attribute to the Prophet or Evangelist any second or hidden sense different from that which appears on the surface.24

Jowett's second precept is an application of the general rule, "Interpret Scripture from itself." This simply means that, since little other contemporary literature survives, one passage of Scripture must be interpreted in the light of other similar passages. This must, of course, be done with great care, since all parts of the Bible are not to be regarded as "an indistinguishable mass." The Old Testament is not to be identified with the New, nor the Gospels with the Epistles. It is therefore necessary that this rule should be confined to the writings of the same age and the same authors, except where the writings of different ages or persons offer obvious similarities. It may be said further that illustrations should be chiefly derived not only from the same author, but from the same writing, or from one of the same period of his life.[25]

What Jowett found especially pernicious was the common practice of indiscriminately using seemingly parallel passages from one part of Scripture and applying them to other very different biblical texts.

Jowett goes on to contend that a critical hermeneutics would also require a quite different view of inspiration than was current in his day. It would demand, first of all, that the supernatural doctrine of inerrant inspiration be refuted. The critical canons enunciated by Jowett would not allow that there is any foundation for such a doctrine in the New Testament writings themselves.

There is no appearance in their writings that the Evangelists or Apostles had any inward gift, or were subject to any power external to them different from that of preaching or teaching . . . nor do they anywhere lead us to suppose that they were free from error or infirmity. St. Paul . . . exhibits all the emotions and vicissitudes of human feeling, speaking, indeed, with authority, but hesitating in difficult cases and more than once correcting himself, corrected, too, by the course of events in his expectation of the coming of Christ.[26]

In Jowett's opinion the nature of inspiration can be known only from a study of Scripture itself. "To the question, 'What is Scripture?' the first answer is 'The idea of Scripture which we gather from a knowledge of it.'" If we examine the Bible we must acknowledge that it is a book embracing beliefs and practices

of a widely different nature—a mixture of the monstrous and the sublime, the true and the false. And such should be expected, unless we come to the Bible with some preconceived ideas as to what it must contain. A study of the Bible leads us, Jowett argues, to some conception of *progressive revelation* or progressive inspiration.

For what is progressive is necessarily imperfect in its earlier stages, and even erring to those who come after . . . . Scripture itself points the way to answer the moral objections to Scripture.[27]

Such a principle is of value to the interpreter, since it allows him to be faithful to the whole of Scripture while free to distinguish clearly the several parts.

It leaves him room enough to admit all the facts of the case. No longer is he required to defend, or to explain away, David's imprecations against his enemies . . . . Still, the sense of "the increasing purpose which through the ages ran" is present to him, nowhere else continuously discernible or ending in divine perfection.[28]

Jowett nowhere reflects the mid-Victorian *Zeitgeist* more than in his conception of progressive revelation. Like Lessing, he compares the history of God's people to a kind of progress from childhood to manhood.

In the child there is an anticipation of truth; his reason is latent in the form of feeling. . . . he is led by temporal promises, believing that it is good to be happy always; he is pleased by marvels and has vague terrors. . . . he imagines God to be like a human father only greater and more awful. . . . As he grows older he mixes more with others. . . . At length the world opens upon him; another work of education begins; and he learns to discern more truly the meaning of things. . . . And as he arrives at manhood he reflects on his former years . . . and he now understands that all this was but a preparation for another state of being. And . . . looking back on the entire past, which he reads anew, perceiving "that the events of life had a purpose or result which was not seen all the time."[29]

If a critical study of Scripture requires some such concept of progressive revelation, it also demands another rule disapproved of and neglected by most writers.

It is this—that any true Doctrine of inspiration must conform to all well-ascertained facts of history or of science. The same fact cannot be true and untrue any more than the same words can have two opposite meanings. The same fact cannot be true in religion . . . and untrue in science when looked at through the medium of evidence or experiment.[30]

Jowett felt that there was no need to reconcile religion with science; "they reconcile themselves the moment any scientific truth is distinctly ascertained." If this canon appears now to be rather oversimple and Jowett too zealous in embracing the "certainties" of science, we must keep in mind the times in which he wrote as well as the many reckless and dishonest efforts to discount the advances in scientific knowledge.

Jowett did not fear the scientific study of the Bible because he possessed deep assurance that while the Bible is like any other book, it is also unique. When examined with the canons of criticism

the Bible will still remain unlike any other book; its beauty will be freshly seen, as of a picture that has been restored after many ages to its original state; it will create a new interest and make for itself a new kind of authority by the life that was in it.[31]

The "life" that Jowett found afresh in the Bible was essentially the life patterned after the moral example of Christ. It was this which became for him the hermeneutical key to the Bible. Late in life Jowett wrote down his musings on the future of Christian belief. He asked himself "What is the possible limit of changes in the Christian religion?" He acknowledged that belief in miracles might be abandoned, that the personality of God might be given up, and that "doctrines may become unmeaning words." Yet the essence of religion would remain. And for Jowett that meant the life and death of Christ—i.e.,

the life and death of Christ in the soul, the imitation of Christ—the inspiration of Christ—the sacrifice of self—the being in the world and not of it, the union with God and the will of God such as Christ had.[32]

The Book's Reception. At first *Essays and Reviews* received little notice. The storm broke after the appearance of an article in the *Westminster Review* by Frederick Harrison entitled "Neo-Christianity." Harrison had been a High Church Anglican who had lost his faith through exposure to the new science and had become a disciple of Auguste Comte. Harrison took pleasure in pointing out the unorthodox notions of the essayists and the fact that these leading churchmen were now agreed with many of the findings of the Positivists.

Harrison's article provoked another response from Bishop Samuel Wilberforce, the famous and attractive evangelical leader who had recently entered the lists against Darwinism. Wilberforce's denunciation of *Essays and Reviews* produced alarm and panic among orthodox churchmen of both the High Church and Evangelical parties and united them against their new common enemy. Petitions and protests against the book urged the bishops to do something. They met and, under the leadership of Wilberforce, issued a letter expressing their horror that such opinions could be held by clergymen of the Church and promising that the question of condemnation of the book was under consideration. The book was now widely attacked by prelates and village curates who never even took the time to read it. The seven authors were labeled *Septum Contra Christum*, the seven against Christ!

The book was discussed in both Houses of Convocation, resulting in a decision of the bishops to prosecute in the church courts. As it happened, only Williams and Wilson could be tried in this way. Their cases were brought before the Court of Arches, and they were condemned on five of thirty-two charges, the principal accusation being a denial of the inspiration of Scripture. The two men appealed to the Privy Council which overruled the previous decisions on the grounds that the Thirty-Nine Articles simply did not define inspiration. The orthodox parties found the decision demoralizing, for once again the Church courts allowed the silence of the Articles to condone views that they believed stood contrary to the long traditions of the Church.

But the storm was not over. Dr. Pusey, in alliance with the Evangelicals, circulated a petition which was signed by 11,000 clergymen and 137,000 laymen protesting the Privy Council's decision and declaring their

firm belief that the Church of England and Ireland, in common with the whole Catholic Church, maintains without reserve or quali-

fication, the Inspiration and the Divine Authority of the whole Canonical Scriptures, as not only containing but being the Word of God. . . .[33]

When the Convocation of Canterbury met in April, 1864, Wilberforce moved that the bishops condemn the book. After a few months of heated debate and committee study, Wilberforce prevailed and the book was condemned by a large majority in both Houses of Bishops.

The essayists, of course, should not only be condemned; they must be refuted. Each of the orthodox parties produced a volume of essays in 1861 countering the opinions of the "seven against Christ." *Replies to Essays and Reviews* was edited by Bishop Wilberforce who, in his preface, frankly admitted that he had never read *Essays and Reviews*! Excepting one or two essays, the *Replies* make plain the rather poor state of orthodox apologetics. Christopher Wordsworth, later Bishop of Lincoln, and J. W. Burgon, Dean of Chichester, both attacked Jowett's view of inspiration by defending the infallibility of the biblical text.

The essays in *Aids to Faith* were, on the whole, more balanced and reasonable. Yet even the more liberal of these defenses were marred by claims and evidences that would not stand up to historical-critical scrutiny. The literal account of creation in Genesis, the Mosaic authorship of the Pentateuch, and the predictive gift of prophecy were all defended. The essay on "Inspiration" by Harold Browne, the Norrisian Professor of Divinity at Cambridge, was the most advanced and irenic. Unlike most of his collaborators, Browne acknowledged that the Church cannot claim that the Bible is inerrant in matters of history and science. He recognized the real human element in Scripture and that it is just this element that makes any theory of biblical inspiration extremely difficult. Nevertheless, Browne rejects a view such as Coleridge's as hopelessly subjective and falls back upon a rather wooden assurance that what we have is "*an infallible* depository of religious truth."[34] This, he argues, follows from our assurance that God did appoint special messengers to communicate His will to mankind and that "it is surely proof enough that they would never be permitted to mislead us in questions of faith."[35]

The replies to *Essays and Reviews* reveal that both ignorance and fear of the advances in science were to be found in the highest places in the Church. The whole effort was based on precritical assumptions. It is regrettable that men dedicated to critical standards, and yet of a more orthodox faith, did not come forth with a modifying position somewhere between Pusey and Jowett. The authors of *Essays and Reviews*, correct as they were in their defense of the critical method and results, were not possessed of profound theological minds. They were men of vast learning whose conception of religion was largely rationalistic and moral. "What is wanted," Bishop Tait wrote at the time, "is a deeply religious liberal party, and almost all who might have formed it have, in the alarm deserted. . . . The great evil is that the liberals are deficient in religion and the religious are deficient in liberality."[36]

Among those "deeply religious" liberals who might have served as a mediating force, and whose work later did perform this function, were the Cambridge New Testament scholars Lightfoot, Westcott, and Hort. Hort had originally been invited to contribute to *Essays and Reviews*. In declining he expressed his agreement with the essayists "in maintaining absolute freedom of criticism" but wrote that he had

a deeply-rooted agreement with High-Churchmen as to the Church, Ministry, Sacraments and, above all, Creeds, though by no means acquiescing in their unhistorical and unphilosophical treatment of theology.[37]

After the appearance of *Essays and Reviews*, Hort expressed even greater sympathy with the aims of the contributors. When his friend Westcott, concerned about the injury the book might cause, suggested the preparation of a volume of mediating essays, Hort demurred. However, the fact that *Essays and Reviews* was causing some to give up their faith and forcing others into uncritical traditionalism finally induced Hort to agree to such a volume.[38] As it turned out, the project came to nothing when Lightfoot declined the proposal because of the press of other work. Nevertheless, in the next decade the important commentaries, critical studies, and textual work of Lightfoot, Westcott, and Hort did seriously challenge the more radical theories of the liberal critics and gave warrant, on critical grounds, for the historical reliability of portions of the New Testament previously dismissed. However, in the 1860's and 1870's there was little to choose from between the traditionalists and the modernists.

Though their work appeared largely negative, the authors of *Essays and Reviews* made an invaluable contribution to the progress of Christian thought in an age of scientific revolution. They played the commanding role in the renewal of scholarly freedom in the church at a time when that freedom had suffered an eclipse. If their work was too destructive, it can be argued that such weapons were required to shatter the false foundations on which the faith had been lately constructed. It would be left to others to build anew in time on "deeper foundations." Speaking in general of the contribution of nineteenth-century biblical scholars, Leonard Hodgson states well Christianity's debt to the authors of *Essays and Reviews*:

> When in the nineteenth century that way of accepting the Bible was challenged by the progress of scientific and historical enquiries, the challenge had to be met, and the only honest way in which the Church could meet it was by encouraging its theologians themselves to subject the Bible to the most rigorous criticism. This had to be done, and we today owe a debt of gratitude to those of our forefathers who had faith enough to do it. . . . We should think of those scholars as men upon whom the circumstance of their time laid the intolerable strain of finding that what they had taken to be the foundation of their faith was full of quick sands, as men who had faith and courage enough to dig and sift until they reached the solid ground on which they could and we can stand. For the time being this digging and sifting was a whole time job. If they could not be expounding the Bible as the Word of God, that was because they were occupied in making it possible for us to do so.[39]

The Darwinian Controversy

The Situation Before Darwin. The change in world view that occurred in England in the less than sixty years between Paley's *Natural Theology* (1802) and Darwin's *Origin of Species* (1859) is a fascinating chapter in the history of ideas.[40] Paley's book represented the

eighteenth-century argument from design in its quintessential form. "There cannot be design without a designer," Paley wrote. "Arrangement, disposition of parts, subserviency of means to an end, relation of instruments to a use, imply the presence of intelligence and mind."[41] The world is like a great machine, made of infinitely complex parts, each working for the well-being of the whole. And such a vast design requires the existence of an eternal omniscient Designer for, according to Paley, such a magnificent world could not have been the result of blind, unthinking chance. It is in the very intricate choices and adaptations of small organisms that the proof of a creative, providential Intelligence is most clearly demonstrated.

Paley's world is still Newtonian, based on a static mechanical model of nature. It was a world of design, not development, concerned with the order of nature, not the history of nature. The Newtonian world was especially suitable for a natural theology, for this theology was itself traceable to the static, immutable categories of Greek metaphysics. In the eighteenth century, science was the handmaid, not the enemy, of theology. This alliance between theology and natural science continued well into the nineteenth century in England. Darwin read Paley while at Cambridge and had commented that he had "hardly ever admired a book more than Paley's Natural Theology."[42] And yet, after the discovery of natural selection not many years later, Darwin considered Paleyism overthrown, the belief in a Providential design in nature inadmissible on the evidence.

The change in world view that occurred within those decades is illustrated by comparing Paley's perception of nature with Tennyson's very different view in *In Memoriam*. In 1802 Paley wrote:

It is a happy world after all. The air, the earth, the water, teem with delighted existence. In a spring noon or a summer evening, on whichever side I turn my eyes, myriads of happy beings crowd upon my view. "The insect youth are on the wing." Swarms of new-born flies are trying their pinions in the air. Their sportive motions, testify their joy and the exultation which they feel in their lately discovered faculties.[43]

Tennyson, in 1850, had a quite different perception of nature. It was a "Nature red in tooth and claw."

LV

Are God and Nature then at strife,
That Nature lends such evil dreams?
So careful of the type she seems,
So careless of the single life;

That I, considering, everywhere
Her secret meaning in her deeds,
And finding that of fifty seeds
She often brings but one to bear,

I falter where I firmly trod. . . .

LVI

So careful of the type? but no.
From scorped cliff and quarried stone
She cries, "A thousand types are gone:
I care for nothing, all shall go."

Tennyson's grimly pessimistic view of nature was due in large part to the fact that he looked at the natural world through the eyes of contemporary science. He had read Charles Lyell's *Principles of Geology* (1830–1833), Robert Chambers' *The Vestiges of Creation* (1844) and other scientific works of the time. He no longer saw nature proclaiming the glory of God but witnessing to a blind, inexorable development, heedless of human values, destroying everything that could not compete in the unending struggle for life. This change in world view is very largely attributable to the evolutionary theories current in the first half of the century.

In the eighteenth century there had been little challenge from the natural scientist concerning the biblical account of creation. Among the first works to raise doubts about Genesis was James Hutton's *Theory of the Earth* (1795). Hutton never mentioned Genesis, nor did he attempt to give any account of the earth's origin. He confined his attention to what he was able to observe and deduce from the present condition of the earth. Nevertheless, his findings forced him to conclude that the earth had existed for an indefinitely long time. This, of course, challenged a literal reading of the biblical account of creation which, if accepted, required that the earth has existed for only 6,000 years.

Most geologists at the time of Hutton were Neptunists, a theory which held that the earth had undergone a sequence of periodic revolutions which explained its geological strata. The Neptunist theory could rather easily be reconciled with the six days of Genesis since the theory's time-scheme was vague and did imply that the forces which had produced the periodic changes were no longer at work. The Neptunists believed that the earth had now achieved its divine design, a rather stable place for man's habitation. Variations on the Neptunist theory later came to be known as Catastrophism. Recognizing the age of the earth to be vastly more than 6,000 years old, the Catastrophic theorists postulated a series of creations divided by periodic geologic upheavals. Often these creations or epochs were represented as the six days of Genesis which were now to be read not as literal days but as periods of indefinite length. It is clear that Neptunism and Catastrophism were compromises between religious tradition and scientific advance. They recognized periodic change but not continuity of development. Among those advocating one or another form of this theory was Adam Sedgwick, Darwin's teacher.

Opposing Catastrophism were the advocates of "Uniformitarianism," a theory not widely accepted until Charles Lyell published his *Principles of Geology*. Lyell convinced the scientific world of Uniformitarianism by amassing an immense amount of evidence to discount the need for a theory of world catastrophies. Lyell challenged the Catastrophists by asserting that

when we are unable to explain the moments of past change, it is always more probable that the difference arises from our ignorance of all the existing agents, or all their possible effects in an indefinite lapse of time, than that some cause was formerly in operation which has ceased to operate.[44]

Lyell further maintained that the natural history of the earth can be understood only when it is accepted

that all former changes of the organic and inorganic creation are referrable to one uninterrupted succession of physical events governed by the laws now in operation.[45]

When Lyell wrote *Principles of Geology* he was not an evolutionist but, as G. S. Carter has remarked,

the result of his book was to establish a picture of the history of the world which gave a possible background in geology for evolution if on other grounds it was shown to have occurred. Indeed, more than this can be said. If the living world was not destroyed by a

catastrophe at the end of each epoch, it must have given rise to the life of the next epoch which could be shown by study of the fossils to be different. Change of form, and therefore evolution, must have taken place.[46]

While Lyell paved the way for acceptance of evolution among the scientists, the appearance of *The Vestiges of the Natural History of Creation* in 1844 did much to prepare the public for Darwin's theories. *The Vestiges* was published anonymously but later was shown to be the work of Robert Chambers, an amateur naturalist and prolific writer on a wide range of subjects. The book was an immediate success and went through eleven editions by 1860. It represents the last of Paleyism and a decisive step toward the thoroughgoing naturalism of Darwin. Chambers saw in the uniform law of natural development the very expression of God's mind and plan.

We have seen powerful evidence that the construction of this globe and its associates ... was the result, not of any immediate or personal exertions on the part of the Deity, but of natural laws which are the expression of His will. What is to hinder our supposing that the organic creation is also a result of natural laws, which are in like manner an expression of His will?[47]

Chambers connected the idea of creation according to natural law with the idea of continuous evolutionary development.

The idea which I form (of the progress of organic life) is, *that the simplest and most primitive types, under a law to which that of like production is subordinate, gave birth to the type superior to it . . . that this again produced the next higher, and so on to the highest, the advance being in all cases small.*[48]

He saw dimly some of the theories which would soon be established on a sound scientific basis by Darwin. Chambers spoke, for instance, of organic structures modifying in accordance with external circumstances such as food and habitat, thus foreshadowing Darwin's theory of adaptation. He also saw man as a species continuous with the whole organic creation and recognized the fact that the individual finds himself thrown into the great, amoral struggle for existence. Chambers wrote:

It is clear from the whole scope of the natural laws, that the individual, as far as the present sphere of being is concerned, is to the Author of Nature a consideration of inferior moment. Everywhere we see the arrangements for the species perfect; the individual is left, as it were, to take his chance amidst the melee of the various laws affecting him.[49]

Chambers even foresaw the possible emergence of a higher species than the present type of humanity.

It is startling to find an appearance of imperfection in the circle to which man belongs, and the ideas which rise in consequence are no less startling. Is our race but the initial of the grand crowning type? Are there yet to be species superior to us in organization, purer in feeling, more powerful in device and act who shall take a rule over us?[50]

If Chambers presaged much that was to be established by Darwin, *The Vestiges* was not a book of scientific distinction. It was soon demolished by the professional naturalists. Nevertheless, it did influence popular opinion and helped prepare the way for 1859. Darwin wrote that in his opinion the book had "done excellent service in calling in this country attention to the subject, and in removing prejudice."[51] It must be kept in mind, however, that the *Vestiges of Creation* was accepted by the public despite the book's advocacy of evolution only because Chambers saw himself as serving the cause of religion.

When all is seen as the result of law, the idea of the Almighty Author becomes irresistible, for the creation of a law for an endless series of phenomena—an act of intelligence above all else that we can conceive—could have no other imaginable source.[52]

Astute minds recognized that Chambers' evolutionary Uniformitarianism was, in fact, a grave threat to the idea of a providential control of nature. A special Providence appeared to find its last sure ground in the immutability of species, and it was this that Chambers was willing to give up. Chambers was simply saying that Providence is what is. In such a view, Providence was nothing more than a name for order. But why, then, appeal to some extranatural agency to explain the orderly process of nature? Only because the creation of new species remained unaccountable on natural grounds? If so, then one only need find a natural explanation, and the belief in a governing Providence would no longer be required.

Such an explanation was discovered by Darwin in natural selection. Darwin agreed that natural selection provides a more reasonable account of the evolutionary process than the idea of an intervening Providence, for a continuous Providence is not intelligible in light of our knowledge of variations in species. Darwin expressed this view in a letter to his friend Lyell who, at the time, continued to believe in a Providential control over the course of natural evolution.

If you say that God ordained that at some time and place a dozen slight variations should arise, and that one of them alone should be preserved in the struggle for life and the other eleven should perish in the first or few generations, then the saying seems to me to be verbiage. It comes to merely saying that everything that is, is ordained. . . . Why should you or I speak of variation as having been ordained and guided, more than does an astronomer in discussing the fall of a meteoric stone? . . . Would you have him say that its fall at some particular place and time was "ordained and guided without doubt by an intelligent cause on a preconceived and definite plan"? Would you not call this theological pedantry or display?[53]

With the discovery of natural selection, the last support of Paleyism seemed to Darwin to be removed.

The old argument of design in nature, as given by Paley, which formerly seemed to me so conclusive, fails now that the law of natural selection has been discovered. We can no longer argue that, for instance, the beautiful hinge of a bivalve shell must have been made by an intelligent being, like the hinge of a door by man. There seems to be no more design in the variability of organic beings, and in the action of natural selection, than in the course which the wind blows.[54]

Darwin's theory did not deny the possibility of an original Creator, but his conception of nature did exclude the idea of a superintending Providence. If there is a God, at best he is a radically remote and impersonal deity.

Darwin's Theory. The traditional theory had held that each species was created directly by God. This insured the distinctiveness of each species and agreed with the account of Genesis. Neptunist and Catastrophic theories of the earth's history gave additional support for a theory of discontinuous organic change. As we have seen, Lyell and the Uniformitarians challenged this traditional theory. Darwin accepted the Uniformitarian view of natural development but was unable to give an adequate natural explanation of the continuous development of species from one or a few descendants, from the lower to the higher animals.

In 1838 Darwin read Malthus' *Essay on Population* "for amusement." Malthus had put forward the thesis that because "population increases in a geometrical, food in an arithmetical ratio," population will inevitably outrun the food supply unless other factors are introduced to check the population explosion. It was Malthus' essay that suggested to Darwin the idea of natural selection as an explanation of the origin of species.

Being well prepared to appreciate the struggle for existence which everywhere goes on from long-continued observation of the habits of animals and plants, it at once struck me that under these circumstances favorable variations would tend to be preserved, and unfavorable ones to be destroyed. The result of this would be the formulation of new species.[55]

For the next twenty years Darwin amassed an astounding amount of evidence in support of this theory. He was planning to write a multivolume defense of his thesis when, in the summer of 1858, he received an essay from the biologist A. R. Wallace. The essay expressed ideas about natural selection very similar to Darwin's own. Darwin was shaken and sought the counsel of his friends Lyell and Hooker. They persuaded him to allow a summary of his views, given in an unpublished essay of 1844, to be read before the Linnaean

Society and to be published with Wallace's essay in the Society's *Journal*. Darwin was now stirred to action. He gave up the idea of a massive work and, late in 1859, published *On the Origin of Species by Means of Natural Selection, or the Preservation of Favored Races in the Struggle for Life*. The essentials of Darwin's theory in the *Origin*, which he defended with a wealth of evidence, is summarized in a single passage:

It is interesting to contemplate a tangled bank, clothed with many plants of many kinds, with birds singing on the bushes, with various insects flitting about, and with worms crawling through the damp earth, and to reflect that these elaborately constructed forms, so different from each other, and dependent upon each other in so complex a manner, have all been produced by laws acting around us. These laws, taken in the largest sense, being Growth and Reproduction; Inheritance which is almost implied by reproduction; Variability from the indirect and direct action of the conditions of life, and from use and disuse; a Ratio of Increase so high as to lead to a struggle for life, and as a consequence to Natural Selection, entailing Divergence of Character and Extinction of less-improved forms. Thus from the war of nature, from famine and death, the most exalted object which we are capable of conceiving, namely the production of higher animals, directly follows.[56]

What disturbed Darwin's contemporaries was the inference, not elaborated in the *Origin*, that man was not different in kind from other members of the animal class. Even biologists like Wallace, who accepted the theory of natural selection in general, held that man's unique qualities could not be fully explained by this law. Darwin feared that just such arguments for man's unique moral and intellectual faculties would ultimately undermine the theory of natural selection itself. Darwin did not deny the extraordinary difference between man and the brutes but, from his long and intimate study of animal behavior, was convinced that the differences were of degree, not kind, and that such differences could be explained as the result of evolution over a long course of time. As J. C. Greene has written:

He (Darwin) who had seen the naked Fuegians gathering limpets and mussels in the cold rain or squatting in their wretched shelters "conversing" in hoarse grunts, he who had seen one of their chiefs dash his own child against the rocks for dropping a basket of sea urchins, would not be inclined to exaggerate the difference between the lowest man and the highest animals or reject as preposterous the suggestion that both might be descended from common ancestors.[57]

Darwin determined to write *The Descent of Man* specifically to make plain his views on the place of man in natural history. The book appeared in 1871. As most people feared, Darwin traced man's descent back through the Old World monkeys and their progenitors.

In the class of mammals the steps are not difficult to conceive which led from the ancient Mono-tremata to the ancient Marsupials; and from these to the early progenitors of the placental mammals. We may thus ascend to the Lemuridae; and from these to the Simiadae. The Simiadae then branched off into two great stems, the New World and the Old World monkeys; and from the latter, at a remote period, Man the wonder and glory of the Universe proceeded.

Thus *we have given to man a pedigree of prodigious length, but not, it may be said, of noble quality*. The world, it has often been remarked, appears as if it had long been preparing for the advent of man: and this in one sense is strictly true, for he owes his birth to a long line of progenitors. *If any single link in this chain had never existed, man would not have been exactly what he is now.* Unless we willfully close our eyes, we may, with our present knowledge, approximately recognize our patronage; nor need we feel ashamed of it. The most humble organism is something much higher than the inorganic dust under our feet; and no one with an unbiased mind can study any living creature, however humble, without being struck with enthusiasm at its marvelous structure and properties.[58] (Italics added.)

Darwin's last sentence in the above was small comfort to his contemporaries, for what stuck in their minds were the sentences we have set off in italics as well as others which were written with such apparent serenity. Those sentences challenged the very foundations of Christian belief. Darwin's interpretation of nature was infinitely more damaging to a Christian vision of the world than the revolutions of either Copernicus or Newton. If the theories of these earlier scientists forced certain readjustments in the Christian's conception of man's and God's place in nature, they did not essentially threaten the Christian drama of Creation, Fall, and Redemption. Darwinism challenged the entire biblical account of man's unique creation, fall, and need for redemption. The doctrine that man was the product of a long evolutionary process from lower to higher species was simply incompatible with the traditional interpretation of the Fall in Genesis. In Darwin's opinion man had risen from a species of dumb animal, not fallen from a state of angelic perfection. How could one impute a sinful fall to a creature so superior to his brutish ancestors in intellect and morals? And if man is the *chance* product of natural variation, what sense does it make to say that man

is the crown of God's plan, created in the very image of his Creator?

Darwin came at the end of a long development in which the classical metaphysics, which had persisted since Aristotle, was giving way to a new world view which stressed the qualities of process, change, and diversity. The static, hierarchical "block universe" of Greek metaphysics was breaking up. *The Origin of Species* provoked a violent response because, coming when it did, it symbolized the final death blow to orthodox metaphysics. More particularly, it destroyed the argument from design by showing that the creation of species, including man, required no rational plan but originated by chance, fortuitous events.* This demise of the older metaphysics had one crucial result for theology: it appeared to remove God's providential hand from the whole of natural history. Evolutionism

appeared to many as another step by which God was being pushed out of the created order. In the Newtonian world it was still possible to relate God the Creator to the world machine. . . . In the geological and biological theories which followed there was no apparent need for the God hypothesis. It was not that he could be excluded. No one could prove that. But for all practical purposes, He seemed unnecessary; and that was most damaging. Moreover it was difficult to relate God to a process of such endless duration and such apparently chaotic and unstructured development. . . . Every need for God as a necessary source of explanation had disappeared.[59]

The Reception of Darwin's Theories: Aubrey Moore, Charles Hodge, and Lyman Abbott. Considering the

* For a brilliant analysis of the effect of the new ideas of evolution and process on classical metaphysics, see the latter chapters of Arthur Lovejoy's *The Great Chain of Being.*

revolution in man's understanding of himself and his world wrought by evolution, it is little wonder that it caused such a heated response. The enormity of the issues ought to make us rather more sympathetic toward those who now appear to have reacted so unreasonably. We must also keep in mind that it was not simply a battle between the scientists and the theologians. Most of the biologists of the time opposed *The Origin of Species*. T. H. Huxley wrote that, besides himself, only two or three noted biologists accepted Darwin's view of evolution immediately after the publication of *The Origin of Species*. The theologians were clearly encouraged in their opposition by the support of eminent natural scientists. It is known, for example, that Sir Richard Owen, England's leading anatomist, assisted Bishop Samuel Wilberforce in his critical review of Darwin's book, which appeared in the *Quarterly Review*. It should be further remarked that it was not only the religionists who reacted in ignorance and with violence. A scientist has recently reminded us that "It is perhaps through the spirit of the age that we remember the arrogance of conservative theologians rather than of revolutionary Darwinists."[60]

The beginning of the conflict is now traditionally associated with Bishop Wilberforce's attack upon Darwin's theories at a meeting of the British Association held at Oxford in June, 1860. No careful record of the meeting was kept, but those in attendance reported that the Bishop's attack was flippant and unscientific. The climax apparently was the Bishop's now-famous question to Huxley, appealing to the sentimental Victorian idealization of women: "If anyone were willing to trace his descent through an ape as his grandfather, would he be willing to

trace his descent similarly on the side of his *grandmother*?" It is claimed that T. H. Huxley, then a young anatomist who was later to be known as Darwin's "Bulldog" because of his zealous propagation of Darwin's theories, whispered to his neighbor, "The Lord hath delivered him into my hands." Huxley then rose, gave a forthright, scientific defense of Darwin's theories and, addressing himself to Wilberforce's question, concluded with this *coup*:

I asserted—and I repeat—that a man has no reason to be ashamed of having an ape for a grandfather. If there were an ancestor whom I should feel shame in recalling, it would rather be a *man*, a man of restless and versatile intellect who, not content with an equivocal success in his own sphere of activity, plunges into scientific questions with which he has no real acquaintance, only to obscure them by an aimless rhetoric, and distract the attention of his hearers from the real point at issue by eloquent digressions and skilled appeals to religious prejudice.[61]

Most of the scientists opposed to Darwin were motivated by strongly scientific questions, especially concerning the theory of natural selection. Some of the theories set forth in *The Origin of Species* have now been rejected; others have been modified and extended, while the answers to some of those original questions continue unresolved to this day. Nevertheless, the main lines of Darwin's theories concerning evolution and its mechanism (natural selection) are now generally agreed upon by natural scientists. There were scientists, on the other hand, with deeply felt religious convictions who did oppose Darwin largely on moral and religious grounds. Darwin's views did not accord with their religious beliefs. The story of these men—the naturalist Philip Gosse, for example—is often painful and pathetic. Gosse held that the world was created in six days, as Genesis records, and was only a few thousand years old. In order that his knowledge of geology might conform to these religious beliefs, Gosse theorized about a pre-Creation world which was fashioned into the present biblical one, with certain species fully evolved and even extinct. In this ingenious way he explained the existence of fossils in rocks!*

A number of scientists attacked Darwinism because of its denial of a divine teleology. For example, Adam Sedgwick, upon receiving a copy of *The Origin of Species*, expressed indignation at learning of his former pupil's denial of supernatural design.

> Tis the crown and glory of organic science that it *does*, through *final cause*, link material to moral. . . . You (Darwin) have ignored this link; and, if I do not mistake your meaning, you have done your best . . . to break it. Were it possible (which, thank God, it is not) to break it, humanity, in my mind, would suffer a damage that might brutalize it, and sink the human race into a lower grade of degradation than any into which it has fallen since its written records tell us of its history.[62]

Even Asa Gray, the American botanist and Darwin's friend and defender, was disturbed by the Englishman's rejection of design. Writing on the import of the theory of natural selection, Gray asked:

> Will such a mind, under such circumstances, infer the existence of the designer—

God—when he can, at the same time, satisfactorily account for the thing produced, by the operation of this natural selection? It seems to me perfectly evident that the substitution of natural selection, by necessity, for design in the formation of the organic world, is a step decidedly atheistical.[63]

These scientists and the conservative theologians were agreed in their conviction that, at present, there was little alternative between a literal biblicism and a rather vague, theistic teleology. Philip Gosse remained committed to a biblical fundamentalism, while Asa Gray and other scientists developed a spiritual conception of evolution that had very little in common with traditional Christianity.

The reaction to Darwin outside the scientific community was extremely varied. There were those whose religious beliefs continued as in the past, blissfully free from any intellectual problems. There were others who claimed to have lost their faith as a result of reading Darwin. In most of these instances, as in the case of the agnostic Leslie Stephen, their faith had already been weakened through a gradual process of doubt. A third group sought to exorcize the Darwin specter by scorn or by ignoring it. Such was the response of Carlyle, Samuel Butler, and George Bernard Shaw. Carlyle replied that if Darwin's theory was true, "it was nothing to be proud of, but rather a humiliating discovery, and the less said about it the better."[64] There were still others who responded by dividing science and faith into two radically different spheres, advancements in science being considered quite irrelevant to the truths of faith. This, as we shall see, was the response of the Ritschlian theologians.

While the challenge of Darwinism to

---

* For a moving account of this Victorian scientist's pathetic attempt to combine a fundamentalist's religion and the new science, and to force his son to accept similar views, see Edmund W. Gosse, *Father and Son: A Study of Two Temperaments* (London, 1964).

faith should not be exaggerated, there were many thoughtful laymen and theologians who saw the revolutionary implications of Darwinism and knew that these problems had to be faced. It is this direct response to Darwin's ideas and the attempts to come to some resolution of the real issues between evolution and the theological tradition which will occupy us for the remainder of this chapter.

First of all, there were a number of theologians who, while holding orthodox beliefs, acknowledged the force of Darwin's conclusions. In England many of these men were of the Broad Church party or of the Cambridge school. In 1860, Hort wrote to Westcott: "Have you read Darwin? . . . In spite of the difficulties, I am inclined to think it unanswerable."[65] Charles Kingsley sent sympathetic letters to both Darwin and Huxley. He informed Darwin that he had now come to reject the permanence of species and the idea that a Christian doctrine of God required belief in His special acts of creation. Kingsley wrote:

I have gradually learnt to see that it is just as noble a conception of Deity to believe that He created primal forms capable of self-development into all forms needful *pro tempore* and *pro loco*, as to believe that He required a fresh act of intervention to supply the *lacunas* which He Himself had made.[66]

Even John Henry Newman recognized the weight of Darwin's findings and entered the following in a private notebook in 1863:

It is strange that monkeys should be so like man with no historical connection between them. . . . I will either go the whole hog with Darwin or, dispensing with time and history altogether, hold not only the theory of distinct species but also of the creation of fossil-bearing rocks.[67]

The openness of many orthodox theologians toward Darwinism is perhaps best exemplified in the writings of Aubrey Moore, a theological tutor at Oxford and a contributor to *Lux Mundi*. Moore was disturbed by the apologetics of his time for, while accepting the general idea of evolution, most theologians continued to place great stock in the argument from design and for special creations, particularly in contending for the unique status of man. Moore perceived that these arguments were essentially deistical and contrary to the Christian understanding of God's relation to the world. Moore even found this deistical tendency in Frederick Temple's very progressive Bampton lectures on *The Relations Between Religion and Science* (1884). Temple had rejected the idea of special creation but, in defending a wider conception of teleology, had written:

God did not make the things we may say; no, but He made them make themselves. And surely this rather adds than withdraws force from the great argument. It seems in itself something more than majestic, something more befitting Him . . . thus to impress His will *once for all* on His Creation, and provide for all its countless variety by His *one original impress*, than by special acts of creation to be perpetually modifying what He had previously made.[68]

Moore saw in Temple's argument the influence of Hume which, he remarks,

might be none the worse for that if it were not that, in the words we have italicized, Hume's Deism reappears. It is one thing to speak of God as 'declaring the end from the beginning,' it is another to use language which seems to imply . . . that God withdraws Himself from His Creation and leaves it evolve itself.[69]

Moore had to agree with Darwin that he had "done good service in overthrowing the dogma of separate creations." Separate creation implies gaps in nature and a primitive conception of an absentee God who intervenes supernaturally in the natural world from time to time. Moore found such a conception neither in the Bible, nor the Fathers, nor the Schoolmen. It had its origin, Moore believed, in Milton's *Paradise Lost*. For Moore, the doctrine of "special creation" was not only opposed to the scientific evidence but was theologically indefensible. Evolution,

as a theory is infinitely more Christian than the theory of "Special Creation." For it implies the immanence of God in nature, and the omnipresence of his creative power. Those who opposed the doctrine of evolution in defense of "a continued intervention" of God seem to have failed to notice that *a theory of occasional intervention implies as its correlative a theory of ordinary absence*. . . . Anything more opposed to the language of the Bible and the Fathers can hardly be imagined. . . . Cataclysmal geology and special creation are the scientific analogue of Deism. Order, development, law, are the analogue of the Christian view of God.[70]

Moore also considered the argument from design poor apologetic. He believed that for Christian theism the argument had received its death blow by Kant. The old *couleur de rose* view of nature was no longer possible. "Destruction is the rule; life is the exception." The Christian now, as in Paley's day, trusts that God is omnipotent and loving and that there is design and purpose everywhere.

But he is not bound to know, or to say that he knows what that purpose is, or to show that marks of beneficence are everywhere apparent. Still less is he bound to assert, as the old teleology did, that he can demonstrate the wisdom and goodness of God from nature alone.[71]

The man of science and the Christian both start with certain "acts of faith," one being "that everything is rational, even that which is at present irreducible to law" and the other "that God is good," despite the obvious suffering in the world.

The attempt of the Christian apologists to insure a unique place for man in nature also produced some strange heresies. The theory of A. R. Wallace is a good example. Wallace accepted Darwin's theory of natural selection but only as it applied to subhuman life. He held that natural selection would have given man a brain a little superior to that of an ape and since man is greatly superior, a "higher intelligence" must have supervened and *used* the law of natural selection to produce man. Wallace called his theory his scientific "heresy." To this Moore responded:

Whether, from the scientific side, this is rightly called a "heresy" or not, it is not necessary to decide; but certainly from the religious side, it has a strangely unorthodox look. If, as a Christian believes, the "higher intelligence" who used these laws for the creation of man was the same God who works in and by these same laws in creating the lower forms of life, Mr. Wallace's distinction as a distinction of cause disappears; and if it was not the same God, we contradict the first article of the Creed. Whatever be the line which Christianity draws between man and the rest of the visible creation, it certainly does not claim man as "the work of God," and leave the rest to "unaided nature."[72]

What disturbed many Christians was Darwin's low view of man. They called Darwinism a "gospel of dirt." As a label of rebuke Moore found it peculiarly inappropriate coming from the mouths of Christians.

If such a charge had come from a representative of those nations which held the descent of man from gods or demigods, it would have been intelligible enough, but it sounds strange in the mouth of those who believe that "the Lord God formed man of the dust of the ground."[73]

Far from degrading man, Darwinism traces his rise from the lowest of origins to his place as vicegerent over the earth, having dominion over all other species. But what of the soul? Is the soul also a product of evolution, or did it require a "special creation"? Moore contends that, like original creation, the origin of the soul lies in the realm of mystery. Nevertheless, two things can be said. First, science must remain silent on the subject of the soul, since it lies outside its province. Theologically we can say that "the soul cannot be a 'special' creation whether in Adam or his children" for "there is no species of soul. We may call it, if we will, an 'individual' creation but is not all creation 'individual' creation from the religious point of view?"[74]

Moore takes the position that the Christian theologian is not bound to any theory of the origin of the soul. What the theologian is alone required to uphold is "the *fact* that, by God's creative act, man's relation to Himself is unique among created beings, and that this unique relationship of man to God is . . . represented invariably as a relation of likeness."[75] Moore perceived that Chris-

tians were guilty of the "genetic fallacy" of judging a thing by its origin. What Christians have to contend for is the present reality of man's moral and spiritual life. What man came from and how are not the important issues and in no way determine the present stature of man.

When Darwin, in all the wealth of his scientific experience, and all the strength of his disciplined reason, gives us his matured judgement on the processes of nature, who would dream of saying "How can I trust the conclusions of a man who was once a baby?" We trust him for what he *is*, not what he *was*. And man is man, whatever he came from.[76]

Moore was confident that two fundamental doctrines of Christianity considered vulnerable to Darwinism in fact remained untouched by it. For that reason, Christians had nothing to fear from a completely open attitude toward evolution.

The original creation of the world by God, as against any theory of emanation, is a matter of faith! The existence of the soul—i.e., the conscious relation of man with God—lies at the root of all religion. Guard those two points—and they are both strictly beyond the range of inductive science—and for the rest, we are bound to concede to those who are spending their lives in reading for us God's revelation of Himself in nature, absolute freedom in the search, knowing that truth is mighty and must in the end prevail.[77]

There were many theologians, not only of orthodox but of conservative views, whose response to Darwinism was very different from Moore's. They saw evolution as a serious threat to Christian belief and approached Darwinism defensively and negatively. Their principal weapons were the lacunae and contradictions in the scientific evidence then available, which they compiled with great energy and care. The most learned and indomitable of these conservatives was the American Presbyterian Charles Hodge (1797–1878), Professor of Theology at Princeton Theological Seminary. Unlike his contemporary, Albrecht Ritschl, Hodge would not separate science and theology into two different spheres of fact and value. For Hodge science and the Bible were reconcilable. Conflicts could only be apparent and would be shown to be so when either the facts were better known or the truth of the Bible more clearly discerned. As a conservative Hodge was naturally cautious in accepting new theories. Yet it is apparent that his defense of the Bible against Darwinism consisted almost entirely of citations of bits and pieces of scientific information which appeared to contradict evolutionary theories. Reading Hodge today makes one aware of how desperate and dangerous is a theological apologetic based on the "gaps" in scientific knowledge.

Hodge's critique of Darwinism is given in both his monumental three-volume *Systematic Theology* (1872) (which is still used in some conservative Protestant seminaries) and in a more popular book entitled *What is Darwinism?* (1874). Hodge's basic criticism of Darwinism is that it is a fantastic hypothesis lacking full factual evidence. In addition, it must be rejected theologically because of its unjustified denial of both the uniqueness of man and the design of creation.

The first objection to the theory is its *prima facie* incredibility. . . . Darwin wants us to believe that all living things, from the lowly violet to the giant redwoods of California,

from the microscopic animalcule to the Mastodon, the Dinatherium—monsters the very description of which fill us with horror . . . came one and all from the same primordial germ.[78]

It is, Hodge insists, an incredible hypothesis and can claim to be no more. Hodge makes much of Darwin's own candor in admitting the tentativeness of his own theories. "There is," Hodge writes, "no pretence that the theory can be proved. Mr. Darwin does not pretend to prove it. . . . All he claims for the theory is that it is possible. . . ."[79] Yet the facts can be accounted for in other ways. Darwinists have generally failed to make important distinctions between facts and theories deduced from them and have expected theologians to swallow some rather far-fetched interpretations.

No sound-minded man disputes any scientific fact. Religious men believe with Agassiz that facts are sacred. They are revelations from God. Christians sacrifice to them, when duly authenticated, their most cherished convictions. . . . Religious men admit all the facts connected with our solar system; all the facts of geology, and of comparative anatomy and of biology. Ought not this to satisfy scientific men? Must we also admit their explanations and influences? If we admit that the human embryo passes through various phases, must we admit that man was once a fish, then a bird, then a dog, then an ape, and finally what he is now? . . . It is to be remembered that the facts are from God, the explanations from men; and the two are often as far apart as Heaven and its antipode.[80]

Hodge was, of course, only partly correct in his distinction between fact and interpretation. Facts and interpretations are interdependent. When the facts are few or vague, honesty should demand very tentative interpretations. More and clearer facts eliminate some theories and make others more or less probable. Hodge could emphasize the distinction because at the time when he wrote the evidence in support of Darwin's theories was, in important instances, imprecise and partial. Hodge thus based his critique on what he considered the paucity of the facts and that they did not appear to support uniformly any single explanation. But the facts in support of Darwin's hypothesis were neither as scarce nor as ambiguous as Hodge made them out to be, and as time passed new facts gave greater weight to Darwin's theories. However, Hodge could justifiably claim at the time that Darwin himself had acknowledged "many facts for which his theory will not account."[81]

Hodge did his homework well. He was able to marshal a considerable amount of information which appeared to argue, for example, against the antiquity of man and the modification of species. Yet, much of this ammunition consists of citations of overhasty conclusions drawn by geologists and archaeologists concerning human antiquity. A piece of pottery discovered at the mouth of the Nile was claimed to have come from the prehistoric period—until it was proved that it came from the Roman period! Lake-dwellings discovered in Switzerland and dated in the stone age later revealed bones of species of living, domesticated animals, and so on. Fossil remains of creatures mixed together, though of widely different periods, are explained by open fissures in the earth into which the more recent species had fallen. Human bones found deeply buried and mingled with extinct animals are accounted for by "sudden catastrophies" such as earthquakes.[82] And so Hodge's argument proceeds. It is not

even necessary, he concedes, to accept Archbishop Usher's calculation that the world was created only four thousand years before Christ. Usher adopted the Hebrew text as his guide and assumed that in the genealogical tables each name marked but one generation. But most biblical scholars adopt the Septuagint chronology "so that instead of four thousand years from the creation to the birth of Christ we have nearly six thousand years." And considering the fact that probably more than one generation was designated by each name the facts of science and history might "make it necessary to admit that eight or ten thousand years have elapsed since the creation of man."[83] Nothing in the Bible, Hodge grants, would stand in the way of such a concession!

What Hodge could not concede was natural selection and the evolution of new species, for these theories conflicted with the clear teaching of Scripture. According to Hodge's reading of the Bible,

each species was specially created, not *ex nihilo*, nor without the intervention of secondary causes, but nevertheless originally, or not derived, evolved, or developed from pre-existing species. These distinct species... separately originated, are permanent. They never pass from one into the other.... if at any time since the original creation new species have appeared on the earth, they owe their existence to the immediate intervention of God.[84]

Hodge's arguments for the fixity of species were plausible at the time, but the study of members of single species geographically separated over long periods, as well as advances in genetics, prove Hodge's arguments empty today. Hodge argued, for example, that members of species geographically separated remain fixed in their original forms and therefore would be able to breed successfully if reunited. Evidence now shows that this is not true and that, because the hybrid offspring of such unions are at a disadvantage, natural selection will favor the development of barriers to such breeding and in time, through separation, the two forms will evolve into different species.[85]

Fundamental, of course, to Hodge's doctrine of the fixity of species was his protest against the view that man was a developed ape. This ran counter to belief in the *special* creation of man in a state of original perfection. When Hodge wrote, the oldest known human skull was the "Engis" found in Belgium. One scientist had commented at the time that it was comparable to the skull of an American Indian which, according to Hodge, only went "to show that the earliest men were better developed than any extant races."[86] Again, Hodge cannot be faulted for having written this before the discovery of *Pithecanthropus erectus*, but the precariousness of his method, of picking an isolated statement from a scientist here and appealing to a scientific "gap" there, is evident enough.

In one form or another the teleological argument has remained, up to the present, the basic argument in the arsenal of natural theology. Hodge was aware, from statements of Darwin and Huxley and others, that the Darwinian denial of design implied atheism, though did not demand it. The focus of Hodge's critique of Darwin was directed toward exposing this implication. For Hodge the peculiar character and danger of Darwinism was neither in its advocacy of evolution, or even natural selection, but in its rejection of teleology.

The conclusion of the whole matter is that the denial of design in nature is virtually the denial of God. Mr. Darwin's theory does deny all design in nature, therefore his theory is virtually atheistical; his theory, not he himself. He believes in a Creator. But when that Creator, millions on millions of ages ago, did something—called matter and living germ into existence,—and then abandoned the universe to itself to be controlled by chance and necessity, without any purpose on his part as to the result, or any intervention or guidance, then He is virtually consigned, so far as we are concerned, to non-existence. . . . Mr. Darwin's admirers adopt and laud his theory, for the special reason that it banishes God from the world.[87]

Hodge was convinced that, despite some inadequacies, the argument from design was compelling. For example, he thought preposterous Darwin's suggestion that the eye was the product of the unintended action of blind physical forces: "To any ordinarily constituted mind, it is absolutely impossible to believe that it is not the work of design."[88] Nevertheless, Hodge did not appeal to the teleological argument, as did Asa Gray and other evolutionary theists. The reason was that Hodge rightly discerned that, as far as a Christian vision of things was concerned, a vague theistic doctrine was not much of an improvement on atheism. Except for belief in a Creator, most orthodox Christian doctrines were irrelevant to an evolutionary theistic teleology. Such a theism is frequently nothing but deism.

The second method of accounting for contrivances in nature admits that they are foreseen and purposed by God, and that he endowed matter with forces which He foresaw and intended should produce such results. But here his agency stops. He never interferes to guide the operation of physical causes. He does nothing to control the course of nature or the events of history. . . .[89]

Hodge considered this banishing of God from the world intolerable. Such a God is sub-Christian, is utterly different from the God revealed in the Scriptures and would render such Christian practices as prayer irrational.

Hodge considered Darwinism to be atheism; he saw no middle ground between it and a Christianity based on the infallible teaching of the Bible. Hodge sensed better than the liberals of his day the real threat of Darwinism, and his refusal to recast Christian belief in the form of a general evolutionary theism was salutary. Where Hodge, and most conservatives like him, failed in meeting the challenge of evolution was in the attempt to deny the factual evidence for the antiquity of man, the mutability of species, and other scientific theories by rather desperate appeals to a few scraps of evidence which could be read in other ingenious ways. It was a hazardous apologetic, since it rested on the slender hope that more definite evidence would not be forthcoming. It was based on the belief that science would never close the "gap" on such questions as the creation of life and the link between the higher apes and rational man. Since Hodge's position was that Scriptural teaching never conflicted with scientific fact, he demanded that one respond to new evidence by either denying its validity or defending the infallibility of Scripture by more tortured and ingenious methods of interpretation. This has been the policy of Fundamentalism to the present day.

Hodge represented the conservative response to Darwin. At the other pole were the theological liberals whose accommodation to evolutionary theories frequently represented a severe reduction in the substance of Christian belief. Some of these men began as orthodox and evangelical believers but, largely through the influence of evolution, became liberal —even humanistic—in their religious views. In England the accommodation of theology to evolutionary views is best represented in the writings of Henry Drummond (1851–1897). Drummond was a scientist and amateur theologian whose own piety was strongly evangelical. He remained a close friend of conservative theologians and evangelists all his life. Yet his interpretation of Christianity was far from orthodox. It was an optimistic, evolutionary theism that ignored the profound enigmas and paradoxes of Christian faith.

The liberal Christian accommodation to evolution was more sweeping in America than in England or on the Continent. Among the earliest and most important of the American reconcilers of evolution and theism was John Fiske (1842–1901). His views were formulated in *Outlines of Cosmic Philosophy* (1874). Fiske's religious speculations had very little relation to Christian theology, but he did exert a strong influence on Unitarian and liberal Trinitarian theologians. Another influential work was *Evolution and its Relation to Religious Thought* (1888) by Joseph LeConte. The first prominent American preacher to join the evolutionists was Henry Ward Beecher (1813–1887) who, in *Evolution and Religion* (1885), declared that science was "the deciphering of God's thought as revealed in the structure of the world."

One of the most thoroughgoing and influential Christian evolutionists was Lyman Abbott (1835–1922), the successor to Beecher in the pulpit of the Plymouth Church in Brooklyn. Abbott was not an original thinker, but few men exerted a greater influence on the American people between 1865 and 1920 than Lyman Abbott. He was a popularizer of new ideas and, at the time of his death, was something of a national patriarch.[90] Once converted to an evolutionary view, Abbott saw in it the intellectual framework within which Christianity could again be made meaningful to thinking persons. Abbott spoke of himself as an evolutionist and not a Darwinist, for he identified the latter with the struggle for existence and survival of the fittest—i.e., with laissez-faire social Darwinism, which he considered unchristian. He adopted LeConte's definition of evolution ("continuous progressive change, according to certain laws and by means of resident forces") as his own and gave it a theological interpretation.

> God's work, we evolutionists believe, is the work of progressive change—a change from a lower to a higher condition; from a simpler to a more complex condition. It is a change wrought according to certain laws which are capable of study. It is never arbitrary. Finally the process of growth is produced by forces that lie within the phenomena themselves. . . . God dwells in nature fashioning it according to His will by vital processes from within, not by mechanical processes from without.[91]

For Abbott the evolutionary laws discovered from a study of nature were identical with the laws of the spiritual life, and he came to believe that the latter were only adequately understood when viewed as analogous to the former. This meant that the older theology, based on a hierarchical feudal model, had to be set aside. It assumed a God apart from the Universe, ruling over it like a Roman emperor and governing His domain by a series of interventions. The New Theology, as Abbott called it, conceived of God's relation to the world in immanentist and evolutionary categories. It taught that

> God has but one way of doing things . . . the way of growth or development, or evolution; that He resides in the world of nature and in the world of men; that there are no laws of nature which are not the laws of God's own being; that there are no forces of nature, that there is only one divine infinite force, always proceeding from, always subject to the will of God; that there are not occasional or exceptional theophanies, but that all nature and all life is one great theophany; that there are not occasional interventions in the order of life which bear witness to the presence of God, but that life is itself a perpetual witness to His presence.[92]

Abbott used a few basic evolutionary categories to interpret anew the beliefs and institutions of Christianity. Everything is now seen in terms of change, development, progress. In the Bible we do not see a complete and perfect revelation but "men gradually receiving God's revelation of Himself." The Bible is the "history of the growth of man's consciousness of God."[93] Abbott even spoke of the development of Semitic religion as witnessed to in the Bible as a "process of natural selection."[94]

Abbott's firm belief in historical progress demanded that he reject the traditional view of man as having fallen from a state of original perfection. He faced the issue squarely.

> The doctrine of the Fall and of redemption (as traditionally stated) is inconsistent with the doctrine of evolution. It is impossible to reconcile the two. Evolution declares that all life begins at a lower stage and issues through gradual development into a higher.[95]

This means that mankind has progressed from a bestial position to a higher and higher spiritual condition. Sin, for Abbott, is thus described as a relapse caused by the persistence of those depraved elements that lie in the older nature. Sin is the ever-present human experience of partial retrogression. Abbott's definition is similar to Schleiermacher's.

(The) fall is not an historic act of disobedience by the parents of our race in some prehistoric age, through which a sinful nature has descended. . . . It is the conscious and deliberate descent of the individual soul from the vantage ground of a higher life to the life of the animal from which he had been uplifted.[96]

Spiritual progress is not easy, but Abbott saw too many evidences of man's moral growth to doubt that it was an historical fact. Society has progressed naturally, or providentially if you prefer, under the impetus of that one "resident force," God. The goal of spiritual evolution was, for Abbott, the full incarnating of Christ in humanity. Christ came not only to exhibit divinity to us "but to evolve the latent divinity which he has implanted in us." Christ is to be seen as "the type and pattern of that which will be wrought in universal humanity when spiritual evolution is consummated."[97]

Abbott envisioned human history as the progressive evolving of divinity out of humanity, and his use of the categories of process and immanent spiritual law led him to stress the continuity and likeness between divinity and humanity. He wrote that "the difference between God and man is a difference not in essential nature," and argued that the Bible taught that "in their essential nature they are the same."[98] An evolutionist, Abbott

maintained, could view the divinity of Christ as different only in degree from that of every other man.

There are differences in degree so great that they became equivalent to a difference in kind; but, with this qualification, I answer unreservedly, the difference is in degree and not in kind. There are not two kinds of divinity. . . . The divinity of man is not different in kind from the divinity of Christ, because it is not different in kind from the divinity of God.[99]

Abbott surveyed human history and saw in it a continuous progressive change from animal instinct to moral virtue, moving according to certain spiritual laws and by means of the force of God. He did not see this process as a grim and ultimately futile struggle for existence but, rather, as a slow but certain victory of Christian love, freedom, and fraternal democracy over selfish individualism and paternalism. History, as Abbott saw it, was the story of a spiritual pilgrimage depicting "the life of God in the soul of man, recreating the individual; through the individual constituting a church; and by the church transforming human society into a kingdom of God."[100]

Abbott's optimistic theology was hailed by liberals as the best restatement of Christianity yet made in the United States. Conservatives attacked him severely for his views on the Bible and for robbing Christ of a unique divinity. It is fairly obvious that Abbott's adjustment of Christianity to evolution was paid for at the price of Christian substance. Abbott played fast and loose with the biblical texts. His talk about the evolutionary unfolding of man's latent divinity finds no biblical support. His view of sin was superficial and his doctrine of redemption naïvely voluntaristic. The weakness of Abbott's evolutionary theism lay in the fact that he lacked a profound knowledge of theology and knew very little about the technical aspects of evolution. His correlation, therefore, was lax and superficial, plumbing the depths of neither doctrine.

Yet Abbott hit upon certain aspects raised by evolution which today continue to find a place at the center of philosophical theology. For example, Abbott was concerned with the question of how God was related to the natural order and whether He is the chief metaphysical exemplification of that order, or whether God is to be thought of as apart from and foreign to the world. He was concerned to restate the divine-human natures of Christ in such a way as to make sense of the continuity of Christ's humanity with our own. These are issues presently at the forefront of discussion by process theologians, using the organic and evolutionary categories of A. N. Whitehead. Abbott's theism may be different from that of Whitehead, but it is clear that the language and categories of both men are traceable to the evolutionary ideas current since Darwin.

Because of the public utterances of men like Aubrey Moore and Charles Kingsley in England and Beecher and Abbott in the United States, it was frequently reported in the press during the 1880's and 1890's that the quarrel between Darwinism and theology had passed. For men like Abbott this was true. But the conservatives continued to fight on. In the United States the Darwinian controversy did not reach its most bitter and notorious stage until the famous Scopes "Monkey" trial in Tennessee in 1920. In America, Darwinism was always close to the center of the Fundamentalist-Modernist battle throughout

the first third of the present century. Impervious to the evidence as were the conservatives and the fundamentalists, they did realize the depths of the challenge of Darwinism of which the liberals were too frequently unaware. The liberal compromises with the theological tradition were indeed great. Huxley expressed the annoyance of conservatives and skeptics alike when he protested: "There must be some position from which the reconcilers of science and Genesis will not retreat."[101]

It was true that Darwinism did not exclude theism from its view, but it did require a more radical reconception of the doctrine of God than statements like "Evolution is God's way of doing things" appeared to require. Assuming Darwin's doctrines, God appeared to many thoughtful people to be either a rather remote First Cause or a God not assuredly in control. "They asked how an omniscient mind which knows precisely what is wanted can set Nature *groping* her way forward as if she were blind to find the path of least resistance."[102] Darwinism did not settle the theistic issue by dressing it in evolutionary terms, as Abbott and others had hoped. What Darwinism did was to set the theistic question in an entirely new context. Accepting evolution meant a change in world-view, hence a new understanding of God and His relation to the world. Would, then, the old attributes of God still apply? For instance, is God's omnipotence and omniscience believable in Darwin's radically fortuitous world of natural selection? These questions could no longer be settled by appeal to a pre-Darwinian metaphysics.

The conservative theologians also recognized Darwin's challenge to traditional Christian anthropology. They saw how fatal to human values was natural selection and the survival of the fittest. Again, Abbott's rosy vision of progress simply ignored this whole dimension of Darwinism. For Darwin, survival was a brute fact. In no way did it imply the victory of moral values. Survival of the fittest was not equivalent to the survival of goodness or beauty. Huxley understood this better than most evolutionists. "Let us understand once and for all," he wrote, "that the ethical progress of society depends, not on imitating the cosmic process, still less in running away from it, but in combating it."[103] The biblical picture of man was perhaps true after all, despite its deception. Is not man that unique creature found at the crossroads of nature and spirit, a creature of evolution who at the same time finds himself reluctant master of the evolutionary process itself?

The profound moral ambiguities of human nature and history, made more rather than less acute by Darwinism, were seldom plumbed by the liberal theologians. The times, of course, lent support to a progressive, optimistic vision of human history. Events of the twentieth century would prove grim reminders of other dimensions of the human spirit. Neo-Orthodox and Existentialist theology would find much in Darwin, as in Freud, which would support the Bible's realistic portrayal of man. They would also find in the Bible dimensions of human existence and spiritual resources ignored by positivism and naturalism.

The contribution of Darwinism to Christian thought was very great. It called into question age-old interpretations of the Bible, it challenged traditional conceptions of God and man and forced theology to reconceive its doctrines in new metaphysical categories. If the immediate threat was frequently traumatic, the long-term effect has been salutary. Christian thought was forced to give up much that was untenable and which stood in the way of an honest profession of faith. If some Christian substance was lost in the process of accommodation, more recent history has shown that the fundamental substance of Christian belief has survived. But, contrary to common opinion, the conflict between Darwinism and Christianity is far from over. Certain issues are now agreed upon, others are still under debate, but the world-views of Darwinism and Christianity are, on a few fundamental issues, irreconcilable. The discussion continues and, as we shall see, the problems raised for Christian theism by evolution have elicited creative new responses in recent years from Process philosophers like Whitehead and Charles Hartshorne and from the scientist-theologian Père Teilhard de Chardin.

NOTES

1. *Democracy and Liberty* (1896), Vol. 7, pp. 424–425; as cited in E. Abbott and L. Campbell, *The Life and Letters of Benjamin Jowett* (London, 1897), Vol. I, p. 196.

2. *Life and Letters of Benjamin Jowett*, E. A. Abbott and Lewis Campbell (1897), Vol. I, p. 345.

3. Ibid., pp. 275–276.

4. H. B. Wilson, "The National Church," in *Essays and Reviews*, 10th ed. (London, 1862), pp. 209–210. Unless otherwise

indicated, future citations will be taken from this edition.

5. Ibid., p. 60.
6. Ibid., p. 66.
7. Ibid., p. 82.
8. Ibid., p. 92.
9. Ibid.
10. Ibid., pp. 92–93.
11. "On the Mosaic Cosmogony," *Essays and Reviews*, op. cit., p. 254.
12. Ibid., pp. 270–271.
13. Ibid., p. 272.
14. Ibid., pp. 273–274.
15. Ibid., p. 274.
16. Ibid., p. 288.
17. Ibid., p. 289.
18. Ibid., pp. 301–302.
19. "On the Interpretation of Scripture," *Essays and Reviews*, op. cit., p. 454.
20. Ibid., p. 453.
21. Ibid., p. 429.
22. Ibid., pp. 434, 444.
23. Ibid., pp. 408–409.
24. Ibid., p. 461.
25. Ibid., p. 464.
26. Ibid., p. 418.
27. Ibid., p. 420.
28. Ibid., pp. 469–470.
29. Ibid., pp. 470–471.
30. Ibid.
31. Abbott and Campbell, op. cit., Vol. II, p. 273.
32. Ibid.
33. Geoffrey Faber, *Jowett* (London, 1957), p. 278.
34. *Aids to Faith*, ed. W. Thomson (London, 1861), p. 318.
35. Ibid., p. 314.
36. As cited in G. Faber, *Jowett*, p. 288.
37. *Life and Letters of F. J. A. Hort*, ed. A. F. Hort (London, 1896), pp. 399–400.
38. Ibid., pp. 428, 440, 442.
39. *Biblical Theology and the Sovereignty of God* (Cambridge, 1947), pp. 16–17. I am indebted to Basil Willey's *Nineteenth Century Studies* for this reference.
40. For an account of this period, see Charles C. Gillespie, *Genesis and Geology: A Study in the Relations of Scientific Thought,*

Natural Theology, and Social Opinion in Great Britain, 1790–1850.
41. *The Works of William Paley*, ed. G. W. Meadley (Boston, 1810), Vol. I, p. 16.
42. Francis Darwin, *Life and Letters of Charles Darwin* (London, 1887), II, p. 219.
43. Paley, op. cit., p. 311. I am indebted to David Lack's *Evolutionary Theory and Christian Belief* (London, 1957) for this striking comparison.
44. *Principles of Geology* (London, 1830–1833), I, p. 164.
45. Ibid., p. 144.
46. *A Hundred Years of Evolution* (London, 1957), p. 22.
47. *Vestiges of the Natural History of Creation,* 4th ed. (London, 1844).
48. Ibid., p. 232.
49. Ibid.
50. Ibid.
51. *On the Origin of the Species*, 4th ed. (London, 1866), XVIII.
52. *Vestiges*, op. cit., p. 158.
53. *More Letters*, I, p. 194, cited in John C. Greene, *The Death of Adam* (Ames, Iowa, 1959), p. 302.
54. *The Autobiography of Charles Darwin*, ed. Nora Barlow (London, 1958), p. 87.
55. *Life and Letters*, op. cit., I, p. 83.
56. *Origin of Species*, op. cit., p. 577.
57. *The Death of Adam*, op. cit.
58. *The Descent of Man* (New York, 1962), p. 528.
59. John Dillenberger, *Protestant Thought and Natural Science* (London, 1961), pp. 217–218.
60. David Lack, op. cit., p. 18.
61. This is the account of J. R. Green (*Letters*, p. 45); except for the use of the word "equivocal", Huxley was satisfied with the statement's accuracy.
62. Clark and Hughes, *Life of Sedgwick*, II, 357–358; cited in C. Gillespie, op. cit., p. 217.
63. Asa Gray, *Darwiniana* (New York, 1876), p. 69. Gray tried unsuccessfully to convert Darwin to a modified theistic teleology. Darwin vacillated in his own attitude toward teleology. At times he

acknowledged a teleology but rejected most of the teleological speculation of his scientific contemporaries. His own view is probably best expressed in a letter to Gray, in which he wrote: "I cannot think that the world as we see it is the result of chance; and yet I cannot look at each separate thing as the result of design. . . . I am, and shall ever remain, in a hopeless muddle." (*Life and Letters*, II).

64. D. A. Wilson and D. W. MacArthur, *Carlyle in Old Age* (London, 1834).

65. *Life and Letters of F. J. A. Hort*, op. cit., I, p. 474.

66. *Life and Memories of Charles Kingsley*, ed. Mrs. Kingsley (London, 1877), II, p. 288.

67. Cited in D. Lack, op. cit., p. 19.

68. F. Temple, *The Relations Between Religion and Science* (London, 1884), p. 115.

69. Aubrey Moore, *Science and the Faith* (London, 1889).

70. Ibid., pp. 184–185.

71. Ibid., p. 199.

72. Ibid., pp. 202–203.

73. Ibid., p. 204.

74. Ibid., p. 208.

75. Ibid., p. 210.

76. Ibid., p. 212.

77. Ibid., pp. 230–231.

78. C. Hodge, *What is Darwinism?* (New York, 1874), pp. 142–143.

79. Ibid., pp. 144–145.

80. Ibid., pp. 131–132.

81. C. Hodge, *Systematic Theology*, II (New York, 1872), p. 19.

82. Ibid., pp. 29–47.

83. Ibid., pp. 40–47.

84. Ibid., p. 26.

85. D. Lack, op. cit., pp. 24–25.

86. *What is Darwinism?* op, cit., p. 158.

87. Ibid., pp. 173–174.

88. Ibid., p. 60.

89. Ibid., p. 44.

90. Ira V. Brown, *Lyman Abbott* (Cambridge, 1953), p. 2.

91. Lyman Abbott, *The Theology of an Evolutionist* (London, 1897), p. 21.

92. Ibid., pp. 9–10.

93. L. Abbott, *The Evolution of Christianity* (London, 1892), p. 66.

94. Abbott, *Christianity*, op. cit., p. 249.

95. Ibid., p. 206.

96. Ibid., p. 227.

97. Ibid., pp. 250–251.

98. Abbott, *Theology*, op. cit., pp. 188–189.

99. Ibid., p. 73.

100. Abbott, *Christianity*, op. cit., p. 258.

101. T. H. Huxley, *Essays on some Controverted Questions*, p. 89; cited in G. Himmelfarb, *Darwin and the Darwinian Revolution* (London, 1959), p. 328.

102. R. H. Hutton, *Aspects of Religious and Scientific Thought*, p. 48; cited in Himmelfarb, op. cit., p. 328.

103. Thomas Huxley, *Evolution and Ethics and Other Essays* (New York, 1896), p. 83.

SUGGESTIONS FOR FURTHER READING

"Essays and Reviews"

There is no recent full-length study of the conflicts brought about by biblical criticism in mid-Victorian England. The most interesting accounts of this period are found in the "Life and Letters" of those involved—i.e., Jowett, Stanley, Hort, and others. Among the numerous brief accounts the following are especially recommended:

Faber, Geoffrey. *Jowett* (London: Faber and Faber, 1957).

Willey, Basil. *More Nineteenth Century Studies* (New York: Harper Torchbook, 1966).

The Darwinian Controversy

The literature on Darwinism and its impact on religious beliefs is immense. The following books are recommended for being both scholarly and enjoyable reading.

Evolution before Darwin, Darwin's theories and their reception:

Eisely, Loren. *Darwin's Century* (New York: Doubleday Anchor Book, 1958).

Gillespie, Charles C. *Genesis and Geology* (New York: Harper Torchbook, 1959).

Greene, John. *The Death of Adam* (New York: Mentor Books, 1961).

———. *Darwin and the Modern World View* (New York: Mentor Books, n.d.).

Himmelfarb, Gertrude. *Darwin and the Darwinian Revolution* (London: Chatto and Windus, 1959).

The impact of Darwinism on American social and religious thought:

Furniss, N. F. *The Fundamentalist Controversy* (New Haven: Yale University Press, 1954).

Hofstadter, Richard. *Social Darwinism in American Thought* (New York: G. Braziller, 1959).

Persons, Stow, ed. *Evolutionary Thought in America* (New Haven: Yale University Press, 1950).

The current status of the discussion between evolutionary theory and Christian theology:

Birch, L. Charles. *Nature and God* (London: SCM Press, 1967).

Lack, David. *Evolutionary Theory and Christian Belief* (London: Methuen, 1957).

CHAPTER NINE

The Ritschlian Theology and Protestant Liberalism

Albrecht Ritschl

In the last decades of the nineteenth century in Germany, Hegelian Idealism was in sharp decline. The time was ripe for a new effort to bring Christianity into a creative relationship with the intellectual *Zeitgeist*. The closing decades of the century witnessed a rather widespread repudiation of speculative idealism and a revival of the critical idealism of Kant. It was also a time of advance in the application of the methods of historical-critical research to the biblical texts and the history of dogma. The intellectual climate was therefore one of metaphysical agnosticism and historical positivism. Kant's critical epistemology had shown that knowledge is limited to the experience of phenomena. For Kant, the only access to God, the only route out of our finitude was by way of the practical reason. With the demise of Hegelianism the German Neo-Kantians returned to this position of Kant.

The rejection of philosophical speculation went hand in hand with a concentration on the empirical and historical. Even men's moral value judgments do not emerge in a vacuum but are mediated to us through our participation in a historical tradition and experience. Schleiermacher was quite correct in grounding religious faith in experience, but even he failed to see adequately that Christian experience is only appropriated through the existence of particular, objective events given in history. The new call, therefore, was not only "back to Kant" but also "back to the historical sources." The theological response to this call was the Ritschlian school of theology whose influence dominated Protestant thought in Germany from 1875 to World War I and in America from the turn of the century until as late as 1930.

The school is named after Albrecht Ritschl whose writings influenced a generation of theologians who, though independent in many respects, reflected certain common tendencies that are traceable principally to Ritschl himself. Alfred Garvie, in his study of the Ritschlian theology, summarizes the common tenets of the school as follows:

1. The exclusion of metaphysics from theology; 2. the rejection consequently of speculative theism; 3. the condemnation of ecclesiastical dogma as an illegitimate mixture of theology and metaphysics; 4. the antagonism shown to religious mysticism as a metaphysical type of piety; 5. the practical conception of religion; 6. the consequent contrast between religious and theoretical knowledge; 7. the emphasis laid on the historical revelation of God in Christ as opposed to any natural revelation; 8. the use of the idea of the kingdom of God as the regulative principle of Christian dogmatics; 9. the tendency to limit theological investigation to the contents of the religious consciousness.[1]

The skepticism concerning metaphysics, the rejection of church dogma and natural theology, the concentration on the historical Jesus and his moral teachings and the idea of the Kingdom of God as the communion of spiritually free persons has led many to consider Ritschlianism as the perfect expression of Protestant Liberal theology. The identification is accurate, although the position of the Ritschlians has often been caricatured by their conservative and neo-orthodox critics. Many of the Ritschlians were theologians and historians of great erudition, whose ideas were more subtle and complex than is generally realized.

What H. R. Mackintosh says of Ritschl is largely true of his disciples, like Harnack, as well: "Ritschl at the moment belongs, like Tennyson, to the 'middle distance,' too far for gratitude, too near for reverence."[2]

In the last decades of the nineteenth century the major theological faculties in Germany—Berlin, Marburg, Tübingen, Jena, Leipzig—were dominated by Ritschl's pupils or under the influence of his writings. The major theological journals, such as *Die christliche Welt* and *Theologische Literaturzeitung*, became organs of the Ritschlian school. Among the numerous theologians inspired by Ritschl's ideas, the most important in Germany included Wilhelm Herrmann, Julius Kaftan, Theodor Häring, and Adolf von Harnack. In America most liberal theologians in the early decades of this century, men such as Henry Churchill King, Arthur Cushman McGiffert, William Adams Brown, and Walter Rauschenbusch, acknowledged their indebtedness to the Ritschlian school. Of necessity, we will confine our discussion of Ritschlian Liberalism to three major figures: Ritschl himself, Harnack, and Rauschenbusch.

Albrecht Ritschl (1822–1889)

Ritschl was born in Berlin, the son of a prominent Lutheran preacher who became General Superintendent of the Lutheran Church of Pomerania when Albrecht was five years old. Young Ritschl grew up in Stettin amid a deep, vigorous Lutheran spirituality. When he entered the university in 1839, he was already committed to the study of theology. He attended lectures at Bonn, Halle, and Heidelberg but remained unsatisfied with the "mediating" theology he found there. At Tübingen he attached himself to the historian F. C. Baur and in his earliest work on the Gospels gave support to Baur's hypothesis concerning the origins of Christianity. A decade later in the second edition of his first important work, on the rise of the old Catholic Church, Ritschl rejected the Baurian and quasi-Hegelian theory that the early Church is a synthesis of primitive Jewish and Gentile Christianity. At this point, Ritschl began his own independent studies of the New Testament, the history of doctrine, and systematic theology.

Ritschl began his teaching career at Bonn in 1846. In 1864 he was invited to the chair at Göttingen where he taught for a quarter century. He continued to lecture on the New Testament but devoted more of his time in these later years to systematic theology. Outside of his scientific work in theology, his life, like Kant's, was uneventful. Between 1870 and 1874 he published the three volumes of his magnum opus, *The Christian Doctrine of Justification and Reconciliation*. The English translation of the important third volume appeared in 1900.

It was the publication of this great work that marks the beginning of Ritschl's wide influence which, by 1890, dominated Germany. Ritschl did not encourage the forming of a school but attacks on his writings from the orthodox, the pietists and those liberals opposed to his views soon drew men like Herrman and Harnack together in defense of his position. Ritschl was not averse, however, to theological controversy and proved an energetic and sharp disputant. The works after 1874 reflect the controversy inspired by his new ideas. Principal among these writings is *Theology and Metaphysics* (1881) and the three-volume *History of Pietism* (1880–1886). The latter, while a work of great historical learning, sought also to discredit Pietism as a malignant revival of Catholic piety within evangelical Protestantism. Ritschl's reputation as the most influential Church theologian between Schleiermacher and Barth does not rest, however, on these later works but on *The Christian Doctrine of Justification and Reconciliation*.

Ritschl's Practical View of Religion. Ritschl agreed with Schleiermacher that religion is a matter of experience and that Christian theology is a matter of Christian experience. Where the two giants of Protestant liberal theology differed was on the nature of religious experience. Ritschl considered Schleiermacher's definition of religion as "the feeling of absolute dependence" to be wrong on two counts. First of all, Schleiermacher's concentration on the "Christian consciousness" of the individual, while mediated through the Christian community, was, in Ritschl's view, dangerously close to subjectivism. Ritschl was a historian all his life, and for him the proper object of theology was not man's consciousness but the historical reality of the Gospel as given in the New Testament. Christian doctrine is to be formed solely by reference to the Gospel norm, i.e., the historical Jesus Christ. As one of Ritschl's disciples asserted, "A Ritschlian is spared the agony of self-analysis; nor is it for him by taking stock of himself to fix the factors by which he can best make clear, to himself or others, wherein the content of Christianity lies."[3] The theologian's task is simply to explicate the meaning of the content of God's *self-revelation* as historically given in the person of Jesus Christ.

Secondly, Schleiermacher's emphasis on feeling does not properly locate the essence of religious experience. For Ritschl religion is an entirely practical matter. It is neither mystical feeling nor, as with the Hegelians, metaphysical knowledge. Religion is fundamentally *the experience of moral freedom*; of being liberated from bondage to nature's blind necessity. Religious faith first emerges in relation to man's struggle with the "natural conditions of life." Man is both a creature of nature and a spiritual being who recognizes his natural limitations and his capacity to posit and strive toward the achievement of spiritual ends. Religion is the answer to this contradiction in human existence in that only God or a Supreme Power can guarantee the world of ends of the spiritual life:

In every religion what is sought, with the help of the superhuman spiritual power reverenced by man, is a solution of the contradiction in which man finds himself, as both a part of the world of nature and a spiritual personality claiming to dominate nature. For in the former *role* he is a part of nature, dependent upon her, subject to and confined by other things; but as spirit he is moved by the impulse to maintain his independence against them. In this juncture, religion springs up as faith in superhuman spiritual powers, by whose help the power which man possesses of himself is in some way supplemented, and elevated into a unity of its own kind which is a match for the pressure of the natural world.[4]

For Ritschl, God is known neither intuitively nor metaphysically but is posited as a moral need—a kind of warranty for the attainment of man's spiritual victory over the world. This does not mean that God is a "fiction" introduced to encourage man to think "as if" he had gained freedom over nature. God is experienced as that reality and power which *alone* can and does deliver man from his helplessness. It is just that such a God cannot be *known* abstractly in his metaphysical essence but only practically.

Knowledge of God can be demonstrated as *religious knowledge* only when He is conceived as securing to the believer such a position in the world as more than counterbalances its restrictions. Apart from this value-judgment of faith, there exists no knowledge of God worthy of this content.[5] (Italics added.)

The Theory of Value Judgments and the Historical Jesus Christ. The theory of "value judgments" is one of the keys to Ritschl's theology and probably his most significant contribution to religious thought. Ritschl's theory of value judgments is dependent on Lotze's modification of Kant's theory concerning how the mind receives sensations or impressions from the phenomenal world. According to Lotze, the mind receives impressions of phenomena in a twofold way. On the one hand, the mind judges sensations in respect to the causal relations in an objective system of nature. This is the method of scientific or theoretical knowledge. On the other hand, the mind receives sensations according to their worth to an ego susceptible to feelings of pleasure and pain. This is the source of the mind's knowledge of value. These two functions of the mind—making causal judgments and value judgments—go on simultaneously and both are indispensable to knowledge. In this view, no form of scientific knowledge is completely disinterested. But just because "value-judgments are determinative in the case of all connected knowledge (scientific) of the world," Ritschl went on to distinguish between what he called "concomitant" and "independent" value judgments.

The former are operative and necessary in all theoretical cognition, as in all technical observation and combination. But *independent* value judgments are all perceptions of moral ends or moral hindrances, in so far as they excite moral pleasure or pain, or, it may be, set in motion the will to appropriate what is good, or repel the opposite . . . . Religious knowledge moves in independent value-judgments, which relate to man's attitude to the world, and call forth feelings of pleasure or pain, in which man either enjoys the dominion over the world vouchsafed him by God, or feels grievously the lack of God's help to that end.[6]

It would be quite wrong to speak of these two modes of cognition as objective and subjective, if we mean by subjective value judgment a denial of the objective reality of the value. Both modes of cognition give us real, objective, though quite different, knowledge. Ritschl agrees with Kant that we cannot know things in themselves (*Ding an sich*) but, with Lotze, he asserts positively that we can know things through their qualities and effects on us and our response to them.

It is important to point out that Ritschl's discussion of the cognitive truth of value judgments is found in that section of *Justification and Reconciliation* which treats of the doctrine of God and of the failure of the Scholastic "proofs" of the existence of God. Ritschl was convinced that the critique of natural theology carried out by Hume and Kant was entirely convincing. In the case of the ontological argument, the natural theologians had failed "to prove the *objective existence* of God as contrasted with His existence in thought." In the case of the cosmological and teleological arguments, the theologians failed to prove the existence *of God*. What they proved was the necessity in thought of a first cause and last end, but these are theoretical ideas which, as Hume has shown, require none of the moral and personal attributes of the Christian God.

Now it is true that the Christian idea of God, our Father in Christ, includes in itself the ideas of a First Cause and Final End, as subordinate characteristics. But, posited as independent things, the conceptions of first cause and final end fail to transcend the conception of the world, and therefore fall short of the Christian idea of God.[7]

The fact is, according to Ritschl, that God cannot be known in himself but "only in his effects upon us," only as he reveals himself to us as the guarantor of our victory over the natural world.

Apart from this value-judgment of faith, there exists no knowledge of God worthy this content. So that we ought not to strive after a purely theoretical and "disinterested" knowledge of God, as an indispensable preliminary to the knowledge of faith. To be sure, people say that we must know the nature of God and Christ ere we can ascertain their worth for us. But Luther's insight perceived the incorrectness of such a view. The truth rather is that we know the nature of God and Christ *only in their worth for us. For God and faith are inseparable conceptions*; faith, however, confessedly does not consist in abstract knowledge or knowledge which deals with *merely* historical facts . . . . For the "goodness and power" of God, on which faith casts itself, is in Luther's view revealed *in the work of Christ alone.*[8] (Italics added.)

God can be known only in his worth for us as revealed in the work of Christ and as appropriated by faith. In Ritschl's view, "by faith" is an absolutely necessary condition for any knowledge of God, for God is not revealed *merely* in historical facts. Actually, there are no such things as neutral, disinterested, historical facts. Facts are always interpreted facts. Take, for example, the crucifixion of Jesus. Can we know that event-in-itself? Do we not appropriate the meaning of that event through the quite different responses of a dutiful but indifferent Roman soldier, a pious but doubting Pharisee, or a faithful and believing disciple who sees in it the gracious action of God? A scientific description of the crucifixion can tell us some important facts, but it cannot judge of its religious worth. And judgments of worth are fundamentally more important than mere judgments of fact, for our existential attitude toward the world and our fellows is dependent on just such judgments of value.

Ritschl would wish to add, however, that it would be quite misleading to say that while for the Christian consciousness Jesus has the value of God, for the scientific consciousness he has *only* the valua-

tion of a man. The point is that judgments of fact and judgments of value are always "mutually related" and operate simultaneously. The scientific consciousness per se can neither affirm nor deny anything about the value of Jesus, let alone about his divinity. Science simply overreaches its bounds when it attempts to make such value determinations. Therefore it cannot possibly be said that science as such gives us a "truer" picture of Jesus since it can never give us an estimate of his worth without stepping outside its limits.

The indissoluble relation between fact and value had important implications for Ritschl's whole method. It meant that we cannot know the objects of religious experience in themselves either by Hegelian ratiocination or by some special mystical sense. At the same time it implied that the norms of Christian theology are not grounded in the individual consciousness but in the concrete events of history. Yet the historical norm, i.e. the Christ, is never simply derived as an inference from the historical facts but is always a value judgment of faith. Thus Ritschl's view of the historical Jesus Christ sought to avoid the twin dangers of historical positivism and idealism. Historical positivism, as evidenced in the "back to Jesus" movement, wished to strip away the faith of the early church and get back to the "bare facts" of the original Jesus. Ritschl has often been erroneously identified with just those positivists who wished to separate the "Jesus of history" from the "Christ of faith." Nothing could have been further from Ritschl's view. For Ritschl, the historical Jesus cannot even be known in himself independent of the experience of the early Church and the effects he produces on us as members of the Christian community.

Authentic and complete knowledge of Jesus' religious significance—His significance, that is, as a Founder of religion—depends on one's reckoning oneself part of the community which he founded. . . . This religious faith does not take an unhistorical view of Jesus, and it is quite possible to reach an historical estimate of Him without first divesting oneself of this faith, this religious valuation of His Person. The opposite view is one of the characteristics which mark that great untruth which exerts a deceptive and confusing influence under the name of an historical "absence of presuppositions." *It is no mere accident that the subversion of Jesus' religious importance has been undertaken under the guise of writing His life,* for this very undertaking implies the surrender of the conviction that Jesus, as the Founder of the perfect moral and spiritual religion, belongs to a higher order than all other men. But for that reason *it is likewise vain to attempt to re-establish the importance of Christ by the same biographical expedient.* We can discover the full compass of His historical actuality solely from the faith of the Christian community.[9] (Italics added.)

Ritschl clearly had no interest in getting back to the historical Jesus in order to circumvent the risk of faith; nor was he guilty of subsuming the content or norm of the Christian religion *solely* within the subjective act of faith. Ritschl saw the hermeneutical interdependence of history *and* faith. He therefore called for the application of the most rigorous historical criticism in reconstructing the historical Jesus Christ, for he believed that only such historical honesty could save theology from subjective fancy and speculative flights from historical revelation. At the same time he saw the impossibility of getting back to the original Jesus on supposedly "objective" or "neutral" presuppositions concerning his person. Any such judgment of Jesus' person and work is a judgment of value.

Ritschl thus sought to maintain an integral connection between the *fides quae creditur* (the faith that is believed) and the *fides qua creditur* (the personal act of faith or trust).

Ritschl's insistence on beginning with the witness of the early Church concerning the historical person of Jesus Christ does not mean that he took an uncritical attitude toward the primitive traditions. Ritschl did not accept the Gospel "picture" of Jesus Christ *as such* but recognized the necessity of making historical judgments concerning the various layers of Christological tradition. He held that all the Gospel traditions must find their "criterion in the historical figure presented by his [Christ's] life." For Ritschl this meant that all speculations concerning Christ's pre-existence and post-existence must be checked by what we know concerning the historical figure. This check even extends to those "supernatural" events of the Gospels such as the Virgin birth, the miracles, and the Resurrection. For Ritschl these "historical" traditions are not integral to any estimate of the historical figure of Jesus Christ.

It is just at this point that the ambiguities of Ritschl's hermeneutic become apparent. Ritschl appears to want to say that the "back to Jesus" movement erred in seeking to derive the normative Jesus Christ solely from the historical facts and yet he himself proceeds to make judgments as to what traditions concerning Jesus Christ are normative for faith on the basis of the criterion of the "historical figure presented by His life."[10] It is clear that Ritschl wants to infer Christological normativeness only from certain strata of the historical traditions.

The Person and Work of Christ. Despite certain difficulties that one encounters in Ritschl's statements on the relation of faith and history, it is clear that he wished to begin with the historical Christ. He rejected the possibility of getting back to a Jesus behind the sources but, on the other hand, he denied the validity of the traditional Christological formulae, since they tended to be abstractions unrelated to the historical person of Christ and having no genuine bearing on experience.

For Ritschl, to know Christ's person is to know his work or, as Luther would say, his benefits. To begin with an abstract definition of Christ, such as in the Nicene and Chalcedonian formulae, is to confuse a disinterested, scientific judgment with a judgment of faith. According to Ritschl, to speak of Christ as God

is not a judgment which belongs to the sphere of disinterested scientific knowledge, like the formula of Chalcedon. When therefore, my opponents demand in this connection a judgment of the latter sort, they reveal their own inability to distinguish scientific from religious knowledge, which means that they are not really at home in the sphere of religion.[11]

To begin with a priori notions concerning God and Christ before examining historical revelation itself is a false method of theological cognition. Luther's approach to the person of Christ is, for Ritschl, the only valid one, for

while assuming the formula of the two natures, *Luther really connects the religious estimate of Christ as God with the significance which Christ's work has for the Christian community* .... According to Luther, the Godhead of Christ is not exhausted by maintaining the existence in Christ of the Divine nature; the chief point is that *in His exertions as man His Godhead is manifest and savingly effective.*[12] (Italics added.)

The attribute of *divinity* in Christ "is to be found in the service He renders, the benefit He bestows, the saving work He accomplishes."[13] For this reason Ritschl contends that it is even false to attempt to extract a doctrine of the Godhead of Christ from Christ's own words or deeds alone as in some forms of Biblicism. The reason is that

the thought of Christ's Godhead *is never other than the expression of that unique acknowledgment and appreciation which the Christian community yields to its Founder* ... apart from that relation it is inconceivable.[14] (Italics added.)

Here Ritschl's view is very similar to that of Paul Tillich. Both place great emphasis on the receiving dimension of revelation. For both theologians, Christianity begins not with the birth of Jesus but with Peter's confession, "You are the Christ."

However, Ritschl wishes to maintain that while the estimate of Christ's divinity is always made from within the community of faith, such an estimate is always based on "the greatest possible exactness to the historically certified characteristics of His active life."[15] What we see in the New Testament picture of Jesus Christ is the perfect living-out of an ethical calling or vocation, directed to the divine purpose of realizing the Kingdom of God. For Ritschl, the universal ethical Kingdom of God is the supreme end of God Himself. In Christ this idea first received shape historically and

therefore He is that Being in the world in Whose self-end God makes effective and manifest after an original manner His own eternal self-end. Whose whole activity, therefore, in discharge of His vocation, forms the material of that complete revelation of God which is present in Him, in Whom, in short, the Word of God is a human person.[16]

Such is the manner in which the Christian community joins together its *ethical* and *religious* estimate of Christ through his unique *vocation*. Ritschl prefers to use the term *personal vocation* rather than the traditional term *office* to describe Christ's work, since the former gives greater place to the personal and volitional qualities of Christ's activity and underlines Christ's continuity with the human race. Ritschl also reversed the traditional procedure by holding that the *religious* estimate of Christ (as God perfectly revealed) can only follow from, and is therefore dependent on, the *ethical* estimate of Christ's own self-realization (as man perfectly realized). According to Ritschl, Christ's work for others is necessarily related to the fulfillment of his own end.

The fundamental condition of the *ethical apprehension of Jesus* is contained in the statement, that what Jesus actually was and accomplished, that He is in the first place for Himself. Every intelligent life moves within the lines of a personal self-end. This the old theologians could not bring themselves to see, for they referred the obedience of Christ exclusively to the end of representing mankind, that is, to an end other than the personal self-end of Jesus. . . . These claim Christ so exclusively for their own salvation, that they will not concede to Him the honour of existing for Himself; although without this, how is it possible to render any real service to others?[17]

According to Ritschl, Christ is not merely the herald of the message of God's Kingdom but inaugurates or actualizes the moral will of God in his own person.

Accordingly, the permanent significance of Jesus Christ for His community is based, *first*, on the fact that He was the only one *qualified* for His special calling, the introduction of the kingdom of God; and that He devoted Himself to the exercise of this highest conceivable calling in the preaching of the truth and in loving action without break or deviation.[18] (Italics added.)

The ethical estimate of Jesus' own self-realization, nevertheless, involves the *religious* estimate of his vocation as revealer of God, since Christ clearly saw his own ethical vocation as the fulfilling of the will of God.

As the Founder of the Kingdon of God in the world, in other words, as the Bearer of God's ethical lordship over men, He occupies *a unique position* toward all who have received a like aim from Him, *therefore He is that Being in the world in whose self-end God makes effective and manifest after an original manner His own eternal self-end.*[19] (Italics added.)

Christ's continuity with his fellowmen is indicated by the fact that He is successful in reproducing His moral attributes in the lives of the members of His community, the Church. But He is also *unique* since He,

being the first to realize in His own personal life the final purpose of the kingdom of God, is therefore alone of His kind, for should any other fulfil the same task as perfectly as He, yet he would be unlike Him because dependent on Him. Therefore, as the original type of the humanity to be united into the kingdom of God, He is the original object of the love of God, so that the love of God for the members of His kingdom also is *only* mediated through Him.[20]

In what does Christ's work consist? For Ritschl, it consists in Christ's being God's instrument of redemption through the forgiveness of sins, the re-establishment of human communion with God, and the founding of a human community of reconciliation. In elucidating the nature of Christ's work, Ritschl was especially concerned to deny a purely objective conception of substitutionary atonement. For Ritschl, the ethical condition necessary for a satisfactory theory of Christ's redemptive work must be "that Christ is first of all a Priest in His own behalf before he is a priest for others." That is, "it is not the mere fate of dying that determines the value of Christ's death as a sacrifice; what renders this issue of His life significant for others is *His willing acceptance of the death inflicted upon Him by His adversaries as a dispensation of God and the highest proof of faithfulness to His vocation.*[21] (Italics added.)

Christ's fulfillment of his own *ethical vocation* leads directly to the *religious* valuation of his work for others.

In the course of His life He in the first place *demonstrated* to men His Father's love, grace, truth, by exercising His divine vocation, to found the Kingdom of God . . . . This achievement of His life is also intelligible as being not only for His own sake, but for the purpose of introducing His disciples into the same position towards God.[22]

Christ's work for others is twofold— consisting of both *justification* and *reconciliation* accomplished through his moral influence on and through His community, the Church. The first aspect of Christ's work concerns the justification (forgiveness) of those who, through sin, are alienated from God.

Their [the sinners] effective union with God is to be thought of as the forgiveness of their sins, as the ending of their separation from God, as the removal of their sense of guilt which is associated with distrust . . . . Their guilt is not taken into account in God's judgment, since they are admitted in the train of God's beloved Son to the position towards

God which was assumed and maintained by Him. The verdict of justification or forgiveness is therefore *not to be formulated in such a way that the community has its relationship to Christ imputed to it, but in such a way that the community which belongs to Christ has imputed to it His position towards the love of God, in which He maintained Himself by His obedience.*[23] (Italics added.)

In this way Ritschl relates justification integrally to *reconciliation* and again denies a purely objective idea of Christ's substitutionary atonement and formal imputation of righteousness. This is made clear in Ritschl's statement:

In so far as justification is viewed as effective, it must be conceived as reconciliation, of such a nature that while memory, indeed, preserves the pain felt at the sin which has been committed, yet at the same time the place of mistrust towards God is taken by the positive assent of the will to God and his saving purpose.[24]

In Ritschl's view, reconciliation is the affective or subjective coordinate of justification by which our adoption as unalienated sons manifests itself in the carrying out of God's will.

Thus in reconciliation the forgiveness of sins appears no longer merely as the purpose of God, but also as the result purposed. According to the conception of reconciliation with God, the individual has in faith and trust appropriated to himself the final purpose of God (the kingdom of God), and given up his enmity against God. In adoption (acceptance as children of God) the gracious purpose of the judgment of justification is carried into effect, so that God places Himself in relation of Father to the believer, and gives him the right to the full confidence of a child. *These effects of divine redemption, however, find practical application only on the condition that the believer takes at once an active part in the recognized purpose of the kingdom of God . . . .*[25]

Although Ritschl sees justification and reconciliation as inseparable, he does not confuse them. Justification or forgiveness is the necessary presupposition of reconciliation but does not insure its accomplishment. The two aspects of redemption must be held together in tension, similar to the indispensable union of faith and works in the Christian life. In Ritschl's view, orthodoxy, and even Luther, placed a one-sided emphasis on justification through Christ, to the neglect of the ethical dimension of reconciliation. According to Ritschl, the doctrine of redemption, like Christianity itself, resembles an ellipse with two foci: justification and reconciliation. In the words of a recent commentator, for Ritschl

every moment in the circumference of Christian existence is a function both of the graceful indicative and of the moral imperative. Christ restores sinners to fellowship with God, but he also enlists their discipleship for the Kingdom. The imperative defines the sin which alienates us as well as the goal which engages our no longer alienated freedom. The indicative overcomes our alienation and bestows upon us the power freely to embrace the imperative as our own.[26]

Although it is correct to speak of Ritschl's view of Christ's work as a form of moral influence, it is quite wrong to draw the inference that Ritschl's theory is purely subjective. Ritschl stresses the fact that Christ is the "first" and therefore the "unique" bearer of God's ethical lordship over men and for that reason God's justification is *only* mediated through Him. In Christ alone God's grace is fully manifest in such a way as to change objectively our own status before

God by opening the way for a changed relationship to God in us.

Ritschl's doctrine of Christ's work cannot then, without significant qualification, be labeled subjective. He was seriously concerned to avoid an individualistic conception of salvation—a doctrine he discerned as central to both Catholicism and Pietism. For Ritschl salvation is always a social fact mediated through the Church, conceived as the community of believers. It is not as if a person experienced salvation and then joined the Church; rather, it is in and through the communion of believers that the individual is made aware of his sin, hears the promise of divine forgiveness, is able to grow in grace, and is both receiver and agent of reconciliation. Ritschl, therefore, sets it down that

the Evangelical Christian's right relation to Christ is both historically and logically conditioned by the fellowship of believers; historically because a man always finds the community already existing when he arrives at faith, nor does he attain this end without the action of the community upon him; logically, because no action of Christ upon men can be conceived except in accordance with the standard of Christ's antecedent purpose to found a community.[27]

Because salvation occurs *within* the community, Christianity is at its very center a social or communal reality.

Religion is always social. Christ did not aim at any action upon men which would merely be a moral instruction of individuals. On the contrary, His purpose in the latter direction was subordinated to the creation of a new religion. The individual believer, therefore, can rightly understand his position relative to God only as meaning that he is reconciled by God through Christ *in* the community founded by Christ.[28]

One can say that Ritschl has his own conception of *Extra ecclesiam nulla salus*, except that for him the Church is marked by the communion of believers, not by a hierarchical institution, legitimized by law and dogma.

Just as Christ's redemptive work has two inseparable components, justification and reconciliation, so the redeemed life is marked by two foci. First, redeemed man is freed from bondage to nature, so that he enjoys a sense of dominion over the world. This is the religious side of reconciliation. Ritschl expounded this aspect of the redeemed life with great feeling, for he considered it to be at the heart of Luther's understanding of the "freedom of the Christian man." It is basically a serene faith in the providence of God.

In this faith, although we neither know the future nor comprehend perfectly the past, yet we judge our temporary relation to the world according to our knowledge of the love of God, and according to the assurance which this knowledge gives us of the value of every child of God in comparison with the world, which is directed by God in accordance with His final purpose, i.e., our salvation. *From this faith springs that confidence which in all its degrees is equally removed from the growing anxiety which might arise from our relation to the superior power of nature*, and from dull indifference or bold recklessness or Stoic imperturbability, because no one of these is an expression of constant spiritual freedom. In particular, faith in providence furnishes a standard by which the first impression of misfortunes as limitations of freedom or as divine punishments is transformed into a recognition of their significance as blessings, i.e., as means of education or probation. *In this judgment of evil, he who trusts in providence gives evidence of his dominion over the world . . . .*[29] (Italics added.)

Ritschl indicates that such a faith in providence represents the "personal realization of Christianity *as a religion*"

and that it guarantees "that it is not merely a doctrine of morals." Nevertheless, Ritschl sees this religious aspect of the Christian life as inseparably joined to its moral component—"labour for the Kingdom of God" in the fulfillment of one's vocation.

It is generally agreed that Ritschl, especially in his *Instruction in the Christian Religion*, gave greater place to this second, moral aspect of redemption—that is, to the Kingdom of God as "the organization of humanity through action inspired by love." According to many interpreters, the Kingdom of God is *the* regulative principle of Ritschl's theology and reveals his concentration on the social and teleological character of Christianity. For Ritschl, Christianity is not principally a good already gained for the individual, but a social ideal yet to be realized. The Kingdom of God is the highest good of the Christian community, but only insofar as "it forms at the same time the ethical ideal, for whose attainment the members of the community bind themselves together through their definite reciprocal action."[30]

The ethical realization of the Kingdom is rooted in the motive of love of God and one's neighbor. Nevertheless, it is itself *supernatural* since it is realized by men only in their union into the community of their Lord Jesus Christ who uniquely *initiated* the perfect will of God. The Kingdom of God is also *supramundane* in that it continues to exist "even when the present mundane conditions of spiritual life are changed." At the same time the Kingdom of God is radically *mundane* in the sense that it is realized concretely in the moral transformation of society through the personal vocation of selfless love as exemplified in the dutiful, virtuous lives of men.

Ritschl's emphasis on the Kingdom of God struck a true biblical theme that had long been neglected. That Ritschl's view of the Kingdom contained a strong element of late nineteenth-century moral optimism is now generally conceded, although Ritschl is frequently misread as a believer in a simple, utopian progressivism. Such a position can with greater justice be attributed to some of Ritschl's disciples, especially to those American liberals identified with the movement known as the "Social Gospel." Nevertheless, "Ritschlianism" as a *movement* means not only Ritschl but Ritschl as appropriated and interpreted by his great disciples. Chief among these was Adolf von Harnack who, through his more popular writing, gave his own peculiar stamp to Ritschlian Protestant Liberalism.

Adolf von Harnack (1851-1930)

Harnack was born in 1851 in Dorpat in Estonia. His father, Theodosius Harnack, was a professor of theology at the university and a Lutheran in the strict pietist tradition. Adolf Harnack was educated in Dorpat and Erlangen and in 1872 entered the University of Leipzig where he completed the doctorate in church history in 1873. His distinguished academic career began at Leipzig, first as a Privatdozent and in 1876 as professor-extraordinary. He held professorships at both Giessen and Marburg and in 1888 was called to a chair at the University of Berlin. His appointment to Berlin was a cause of serious controversy; it was held up for several months, and the matter was finally resolved by the Emperor William II's decision overruling the Church officials. Opposition to Harnack's appointment was based on his *History of Dogma*, the first volume of which had

appeared in 1885. The publication of the multivolume *Dogmengeschichte* introduced Harnack to a lifetime of theological controversy and led to a painful break with his father. The shadow of suspicion was never completely removed from Harnack's career as church historian and, despite his eminent position, he was never given any position of authority or honor by the Church. In spite of this fact, no man in Germany had a greater influence on Protestant Christianity at the turn of the century than Harnack. His influence was largely the result of his prolific writing which included over sixteen hundred books, monographs, and articles! The *History of Dogma*, his book on *Marcion*, and *The Mission and Expansion of Christianity* are classics in their field. Harnack's popular book *What Is Christianity?* is considered the finest and most influential statement of liberal Protestant theology.

It is difficult to believe that a man of such scholarly productivity could also be a man of action, yet Harnack held many time-consuming administrative positions during his career. In 1876 he founded the *Theologische Literaturzeitung* and for many years was its only editor. He served as Rector of the University of Berlin and his counsel was frequently sought in the Ministry of Education. In 1906, he was appointed Director General of the Royal Library and in 1911 to the position of President of the Kaiser Wilhelm Foundation, established for the creation of numerous scientific research institutes. In 1921, Harnack was offered the post of German Ambassador to the United States but declined the honor.

Of the many influences that helped to shape Harnack the historian and theologian, none was greater than that of Albrecht Ritschl. It was during his period in Leipzig that Harnack first identified himself with the Ritschlian school. A few years later Harnack acknowledged that his own *Dogmengeschichte* would not have been possible without Ritschl. What Ritschl contributed most to Harnack was a distaste for metaphysical speculation and a devotion to a historical interpretation of Christianity. It was in such a Ritschlian direction that Harnack believed "lay the future direction of Protestantism."[31] Harnack was even more rigorously historical in orientation than Ritschl, holding that Christianity could only be understood as a historical movement and by the methods of historical interpretation. He called upon each Christian to take upon himself the historical responsibility of appropriating critically his religious heritage and making it his own. To be worthy of study, history, for Harnack, must have a living relationship to the present.

> We study history in order to intervene in the course of history and we have a right and a duty to do so: for without historical insight we either permit ourselves to be mere objects put in the historical process or we shall have the tendency to lead people down the wrong way. To intervene in history—this means that we must reject the past when it reaches into the present only in order to block us.... There is no doubt that, with respect to the past, the historian assumes the royal function of a judge, for in order to decide what of the past shall continue to be in effect and what must be done away with or transformed, the historian must judge like a king. Everything must be designed to furnish a preparation for the future, for only the discipline of learning has a right to exist which lays the foundation for what is to be.[32]

Harnack agreed with the historian Ernst Troeltsch who was fond of saying that "one must overcome history by history," that is, one must come to know one's heritage, accept it, and then shape it into a living possibility in the present and for the future.

That Harnack acted on his own historical convictions is evident in his two most famous works, *The History of Dogma* and *What Is Christianity?* Harnack wrote the *History of Dogma* to show the origins and development of Christian dogma to the time of the Reformation. But, more important, Harnack produced this massive study to demonstrate historically that if the Christian gospel was to remain a living force in the modern world, it must be freed from dogma—the reason being that "as the adherents of the Christian religion had not these dogmas from the beginning . . . the business of the history of dogma is to ascertain the origin of Dogmas and then to describe their development."[33] For by delineating the process by which dogmas originate and develop, "the 'history of dogma' furnishes the most suitable means for the liberation of the Church from dogmatic Christianity"[34]—or of overcoming history by history.

According to Harnack, dogmatic Christianity is a definite step in the development of Christianity out of the Christian faith one encounters in the primitive Gospel. It is the intellectualizing or Hellenizing of the primitive faith, or, as he put it, "the work of the Greek spirit on the soil of the Gospel." Harnack did not consider the development of dogma an obviously bad thing. Understood historically, it becomes clear that dogma, like the retention of the Old Testament canon, preserved the Christian faith from powerful heresies that would have seriously distorted the Christian message. However, understood historically, it also becomes clear that dogma became embodied in an authoritarian, ecclesiastical institution which made and continues to make claims and demands very foreign to the primitive Gospel. The importance of the Reformation is to be seen in Luther's rediscovery of this Gospel freed from ecclesiastical authoritarianism. One can therefore acknowledge that the dogmatic Hellenization of the Gospel was historically necessary and at the same time recognize that those conditions no longer exist which require the retention of such an historical "form." Harnack believed that historical responsibility demanded the present liberation of Christian faith from an infallible authoritarianism that was contrary to the very spirit of the Gospel.

It is frequently commented that Harnack was a "primitivist" in that he criticized the whole history of Christianity from the normative standard of its earliest expression. Such a judgment needs rather careful qualification. Harnack the historian was very mindful of the fact that no particular historical "form" of Christianity can definitively represent its reality and, at the same time, that the reality of Christianity comes to us *only* through concrete historical traditions. However, Harnack believed that one could extract the unique essence of Christian faith from all of its historical forms which have come and gone. He saw the alternatives as follows:

Either the Gospel is . . . identical with its earliest form, in which case it came with its time and has departed with it; or else it contains something which, under differing historical forms, is of permanent validity. The latter is the true view. The history of the Church shows us in its very commencement that "primitive Christianity" had to disappear in order that "Christianity" might remain; and in the same way in later ages one metamorphosis followed upon another.[35]

The distinctive essence of Christianity, that which is of "permanent validity" within the temporal forms, is what Harnack called the *gospel of Jesus Christ*. This gospel requires no definitive historical form and has in fact outlived numerous historical traditions which must be judged by it. If such a criticism is not carried out, church dogmas and institutions will be judged by some particular historical tradition.

It is evident that the key to Harnack's reconstruction is his conception of the gospel of Jesus Christ, for he lays it down as his most fundamental rule that "that only is Christian which can be established authoritatively by the Gospel."[36] While, for Harnack, the Gospel of Jesus Christ is the normative essence of Christianity, the attempt to specify the content of this Gospel is more difficult. In Harnack's view, the Gospel is *not* an intellectual doctrine; it is a *dynamic reality*. The Gospel *is* Jesus Christ, the living person who awakens life in those who will open themselves to his reality. Harnack wished to stress the point that the Gospel was the Gospel *of* Jesus, rather than a Gospel *concerning* him. However, he made the distinction not to exclude Jesus from the Gospel (he clearly does not[37]), but because he did not want the Gospel to be confused with an intellectual dogma concerning the Person of Christ.

In *What Is Christianity?* Harnack took upon himself the historical responsibility of attempting a definition of the Gospel, the permanent essence of Christianity. According to his famous definition, set forth in that book, the Gospel as taught by Jesus embraces three themes, each being "of such a nature as to contain the whole."

Firstly, the kingdom of God and its coming.

Secondly, God the Father and the infinite value of the human soul. Thirdly, the higher righteousness and the commandment of love.[38]

The boldness of Harnack's interpretation is evident in his handling of the first theme: the difficult question of Jesus' eschatology. Harnack acknowledged that Jesus' preaching concerning the coming of the Kingdom of God was ambiguous and that Jesus shared the Jewish apocalyptical world-view of his time. Yet Harnack disagreed with those historians of religion who saw nothing in Jesus' preaching of the Kingdom but ideas already current in his time. For Harnack, the historian has the responsibility of distinguishing between the traditional "husk" and the peculiar "kernel" in Jesus' message of the Kingdom. And it is clear to Harnack that while Jesus used the vivid apocalyptical language of his day, he did so only to put in striking relief the dynamic, moral relationship between God and man. The "kernel" of Jesus' preaching of the Kingdom, Harnack claims, is

the rule of the holy God in the hearts of individuals; *it is God himself in his power.* From this point of view everything that is dramatic in the external sense has vanished; and gone, too, are all external hopes for the future . . . . It is not a question of angels and devils, thrones and principalities, but of God and the soul, the soul and its God.[39]

The second theme expresses Jesus' most persistent message and the very essence of religion itself: God the Father and the infinite value of each human being. Here it is clear that Jesus' Gospel "contains no statutory or particularistic elements." By applying the idea of Providence to the whole world Jesus shows that all life is rooted and safe in the Eternal. Such a faith is beautifully affirmed in the Lord's

Prayer and in such passages as Luke 12:6 —"Are not two sparrows sold for a farthing? and one of them shall not fall to the ground without your Father. But the very hairs of your head are all numbered." And in the verse "What shall it profit a man if he gain the whole world and lose his own soul?," it is clear that Jesus puts the very highest value on the individual person. "The man who can say 'My Father' to the Being who rules heaven and earth, is thereby raised above heaven and earth, and himself has a value which is higher than all the fabric of this world."[40]

Yet the circle of Jesus' Gospel did not include only the individual soul alone and secure with its God. It offered men this incomparable gift of assurance, but it also set them a task. The Gospel is an ethical message of "the higher righteousness and the commandment of love." What distinguishes Jesus' Gospel from other ethical thought is that Jesus severed the connection between ethics and external forms of observance. Jesus goes straight to the root of morality, to the disposition and the intention. This is what is meant by the "higher righteousness." Jesus reduced the moral life "to *one* root and to *one* motive—love."

It was in this sense that Jesus combined religion and morality, and in this sense religion may be called the soul of morality, and morality the body of religion. We can thus understand how it was that Jesus could place the love of God and the love of one's neighbor side by side; the love of one's neighbor is the only practical proof on earth of that love of God which is strong in humility.[41]

Harnack, like most Ritschlian liberals, saw the ethical task of building a community inspired by love of neighbor as an indispensable dimension of Jesus' Gospel. Despite the individualistic tenor of much of what Harnack says about "God and the soul, the soul and God," like Ritschl he saw the Christian life as essentially social or corporate in nature. Harnack, too, was committed to a "social gospel." This is made especially clear in the section of *What Is Christianity?* where he discusses "The Gospel and the poor, or the social question." There is no doubt in Harnack's mind that if Jesus were present today, he would be championing those who work to relieve the hard lot of the poor. "The fallacious principle of the free play of forces, of the 'live and let live' principle—a better name for it would be the 'live and let die'—is entirely opposed to the Gospel."[42] Harnack believed that Jesus contemplated a community of men "in which wealth, as private property in the strict sense of the word, was non-existent."

In this sense, [the Gospel] is profoundly socialistic, just as it is also profoundly individualistic, because it establishes the infinite and independent value of every human soul .... Its object is to transform the socialism which rests on the basis of conflicting interests into the socialism which rests on the consciousness of a spiritual unity.[43]

Harnack's views of the social gospel were not, however, the most provocative of his ideas. The section of *What Is Christianity?* that raised the greatest storm of protest had to do with "The Gospel and the Christological question." What alarmed many was Harnack's statement that *the Gospel, as Jesus proclaimed it, has to do with the Father only and not with the Son.* What Harnack meant to convey in this statement was his concern that the object of the Gospel not be identified with some metaphysical doctrine of the God-man unity. He did not mean to

imply that Jesus stood outside the Gospel. It is true, nevertheless, that for Harnack Jesus' Divine Sonship is conceived as residing in His *knowledge of God.*

The consciousness which he possessed of being the *Son of God* is, therefore, nothing but the practical consequence of knowing God as the Father and as his Father. Rightly understood, the name of Son means nothing but the knowledge of God.[44]

Harnack believed that this in no way detracted from the very highest view of Christ if one thing be kept in mind, namely, that

no one had ever yet known the Father in the same way in which Jesus knew Him, and to this knowledge of Him he draws other men's attention, and thereby does "the many" an incomparable service. He leads them to God, not only by what he says, but still more by what he is and does, and ultimately by what he suffers.[45]

In Harnack's view the Gospel, then, is not something taught *about* Christ, nor is Christ a mere *component* of the Gospel. Rather, "*he was its personal realization and its strength, and this he is felt to be still.*"[46] Such a living faith demands no dogmatic guarantees of Christ's uniqueness.

Fire is kindled only by fire; personal life only by personal forces. Let us rid ourselves of all dogmatic sophistry, and leave others to pass verdicts of exclusion. The Gospel nowhere says that God's mercy is limited to Jesus' mission. But history shows us that he is the one who brings the weary and heavy laden to God; and again, that he it was who raised mankind to the new level; and his teaching is still the touchstone, in that it brings men to bliss and brings them to judgment.[47]

No one who understands this can fail to affirm that here the divine appeared in as perfect a form as it can appear on this earth. And such an affirmation requires no theoretical formulation but, rather, a life lived in accordance with this message, which is "something so simple, something that speaks to us with so much power, that it cannot easily be mistaken."[48]

What Is Christianity? was originally presented as a series of public lectures at the University of Berlin during the winter semester of 1899–1900. When published that same year, the book created great excitement and in the years that followed exerted an extraordinary influence on theologians and laymen alike. The popular demand for the book is illustrated by the fact that in the year of its publication the main railway station in the city of Leipzig was blocked by freight cars in which *What Is Christianity?* was being shipped throughout the world. More than any other book it represented the spirit of Protestant Liberalism in the decades just prior to the first World War.

Walter Rauschenbusch (1861-1918)

In the quarter century before World War I, a host of young American theologians went to Germany to complete their theological studies. There they sat at the feet of many of the leaders of the Ritschlian school, men such as Herrmann, Harnack, and Kaftan. American liberal theology never became dominantly Ritschlian, but the leaders of the movement—men like William Adams Brown and Arthur C. McGiffert—were profoundly influenced by their Ritschlian mentors. This was true also of the greatest of the American liberal theologians, Walter Rauschenbusch. Like most of his American contemporaries, Rauschenbusch was theologically eclectic

—drawing upon Schleiermacher, Idealism, Ritschl, and evolutionary doctrine. Nevertheless, as in the case of Brown and McGiffert, the dominant themes in his theology have a strong Ritschlian caste.

Rauschenbusch was born in Rochester, New York, the son of a German Baptist professor of the Rochester Theological Seminary. Walter was raised in an environment of conservative German Baptist piety. He was educated both in Germany and the United States, graduating from the University of Rochester and the Rochester Seminary. After graduation, he was to take a mission post in India, but his appointment was blocked by one of his own professors who considered his views on the Old Testament too liberal. Rauschenbusch thus turned to the pastorate and accepted a call from the Second German Baptist Church in New York City. The church was located on the edge of Hell's Kitchen, one of the city's infamous slums. Here Rauschenbusch came face to face with the horrors of poverty and economic insecurity. Here he also discovered how ineffectual was pious, individualistic philanthropy in solving major social problems.

It was from his eleven years' ministry in Hell's Kitchen that Rauschenbusch emerged, as Reinhold Niebuhr has said, "the real founder of social Christianity in this country" and "its most brilliant and generally satisfying exponent." In 1897, Rauschenbusch accepted a position in the German faculty of the Rochester Theological Seminary. Five years later he became Professor of Church History in the regular faculty, a position which he held until his death. He wrote little as a church historian, and what he did write in the field was related to his first interest, the social question.

In 1907, while on leave in Germany, Rauschenbusch published *Christianity and the Social Crisis*. It was a hard-hitting, prophetic attack on the social evils of the day, advocating radical social solutions. Rauschenbusch even considered it "a dangerous book," and feared that it would cost him his teaching position. To his amazement, it awakened a wide, positive response. It was a book born at the proper moment, for large numbers of Americans were now prepared for social change and liberal theology was gaining a wider following. Rauschenbusch returned from Europe famous and cast in the role of leader of the "Social Gospel" movement. He responded with enthusiasm and gave of himself tirelessly as lecturer, preacher, and writer. In this last decade of his life he produced two other major books, which also proved popular successes: *Christianizing the Social Order* (1912) and *A Theology for the Social Gospel* (1917). The latter book is on a par with Harnack's *What Is Christianity?* as a lucid statement of liberal theology.

Rauschenbusch was not a Ritschlian in the sense that, like Hermann and Harnack, he saw himself as consciously carrying forward the program of a "school"; but the themes of his theology are extraordinarily similar to Ritschlian liberalism. Like the Ritschlians, he was disinterested in metaphysics and dogma, stressing rather the historical Jesus as the initiator of the divine community—the Kingdom of God. He saw man as caught in the struggle between his spiritual and natural impulses and conceived of salvation in ethical and social terms. However, Rauschenbusch combined with these Ritschlian themes an evolutionary theism and a social progressivism more akin to trends in American thought.

The key to Rauschenbusch's conception of Christianity is found in the words *social* or *solidaristic*. He considered the heart of Jesus' teaching to be the message of the Kingdom of God; and, as preached by Jesus, the Kingdom was never thought of as a purely internal, spiritual possession of the individual.

> The purpose of all that Jesus said and did and hoped to do was always the social redemption of the entire life of the human race on earth . . . . Christianity set out with a great social ideal. The live substance of the Christian religion was the hope of seeing a divine social order established on earth.[49]

Just as Harnack saw the Hellenization of Christianity as a defection from the Gospel, so Rauschenbusch discerned in the history of the Church a long "eclipse" of the social ideal of primitive Christianity. Only now, he believed, was it possible to see this *social* Gospel "bursting forth again with the indomitable energy of divine life." Rausbenbusch believed that the rediscovery of Jesus' message of social redemption demanded that modern theology be rewritten in accordance with this normative principle. The key to such a theological reconstruction would be the Kingdom of God. All other doctrines would then be formulated in accordance with this guiding motif. "We have a social gospel." What is needed is "a systematic theology large enough to match it and vital enough to back it."[50] This Rauschenbusch sought to provide in *A Theology for the Social Gospel*.

That Rauschenbusch did not properly understand the New Testament message concerning the Kingdom of God is today generally conceded. However, Rauschenbusch was correct in recognizing it to be one, if not *the* basic, motif of both the Old Testament and the message of

Jesus. This being so, Rauschenbusch contended, the old, individualistic conceptions of sin and salvation must be rethought and a more truly biblical and solidaristic view of man proposed. Rauschenbusch acknowledged that a frequent cause of distrust of liberal theology was its failure to appreciate the power of sin in human life. But this, too, was due to the inability of liberal theology to consider man in other than individualistic and voluntaristic terms, and, therefore, to take into consideration the complex social matrix of sin. However, a theology focused on the Kingdom of God is prepared to see these profounder social characteristics of human depravity.

The shallowness of liberal anthropology was evidenced, for example, in the eagerness of many liberal theologians to abandon the doctrine of original sin. Rauschenbusch, on the contrary, wished to defend it.

It is one of the few attempts of individualistic theology to get a solidaristic view of its field of work. This doctrine views the race as a great unity, descended from a single head, and knit together through all ages by unity of origin and blood.[51]

Science, to some extent, corroborates this ancient doctrine. "Evil does flow down the generations through the channels of biological coherence. Idiocy and feeble-mindedness, neurotic disturbances . . . and anti-social impulses in children must have their adequate biological causes . . ."[52] Where theology went wrong was in seeing sin exclusively in biological transmission rather than along the lines of social tradition.

One generation corrupts the next. The permanent vices and crimes of adults are not transmitted by heredity, but by being socialized. . . . Just as syphilitic corruption is forced on the helpless foetus in its mother's womb, so these hereditary social evils are forced on the individual embedded in the womb of society and drawing his ideas, moral standards and spiritual ideals from the general life of the social body.[53]

Rauschenbusch believed that there was general unanimity in theology that sin was essentially selfishness or egoism and that the social implication of such a definition "is proof of the unquenchable social spirit of Christianity."

Sin is essentially selfishness. That definition is more in harmony with the social gospel than any individualistic type of religion. The sinful mind, then, is the unsocial and anti-social mind. To find the climax of sin we must not linger over a man who swears, or sneers at religion, or denies the mystery of the trinity, but put our hands on social groups who have turned the patrimony of a nation into the private property of a small class, or have left the peasant labourers cowed, degraded, demoralized, and without rights in the land.[54]

When viewed in the perspective of the Kingdom of God, theology will make much less of individual sins. Rather, Christians will reserve their horror for those in high places who use powerful lobbies to defeat poverty legislation and factory laws and for nations who set the world at war because of their colonial ambitions.

Rauschenbusch saw the cause of sin as rooted in the conflict between the selfish ego and the common good of humanity, which he equated with God.[55] However, we will never be able to think of the root of sin in such social terms as long as we continue to conceive of God in feudal, monarchical categories.

The theological definitions of sin have too much the flavour of the monarchical institutions under the spiritual influence of which they were first formed. In an absolute monarchy the first duty is to bow to the royal will. A man may spear peasants or outrage their wives, but crossing the king is another matter.[56]

Sin, as taught by Jesus, is rarely depicted as a private transaction between the sinner and God. In Jesus' teaching our rebellion against God usually takes the form of profiting at the expense of our fellows. Therefore, an adequate doctrine of man and sin requires that "we democratize our conception of God."

He (God) works *through* humanity to realize his purposes, and our sins block and destroy the Reign of God in which he might fully reveal and realize himself. Therefore, our sins against the least of our fellowmen in the last resort concern God. Therefore, when we retard the progress of mankind, we retard the revelation of the glory of God. Our universe is not a despotic monarchy, with God above the starry canopy and ourselves down here; it is a spiritual commonwealth with God in the midst of us.[57]

Rauschenbusch's doctrine of God reflects the influence of the immanentism of Schleiermacher, the Hegelians, and the evolutionists, but also the insights of the Left-wing Hegelians and the *religionsgeschichtliche Schule*,* namely, that theological formulations reflect the patterns of a culture and that social change can revolutionize religious doctrines. This is not to say that Rauschenbusch believed that Christian doctrines were merely the relative products of social forces. He believed the teachings of Jesus constituted the *normative* doctrine of God. "Here",

* See Chap. Eleven.

he said, "we see one of the highest redemptive services of Jesus to the human race. When he took God by the hand and called him 'our Father,' he democratized the conception of God."[58] Nevertheless, as in the case of sin, the Christian doctrine of God has undergone periods of defection and restoration, and Rauschenbusch believed the Social Gospel was "God's predestined agent" to restore Jesus' normative vision of God. That Rauschenbusch was himself a product of the late nineteenth-century liberal, democratic spirit is nowhere more striking than in his doctrine of God. God is measured by the norms of a liberal, democratic socialism.

A theological God who has no interest in the conquest of justice and fraternity is not a Christian. It is not enough for theology to eliminate this or that autocratic trait. Its God must join the social movement. . . . The development of a Christian social order would be the highest proof of God's saving power. The failure of the social movement would impugn his existence.[59]

Like the Ritschlians, Rauschenbusch didn't concern himself with metaphysical questions of the existence and nature of God. God was the assumed ground of democratic, moral values and the supporting agent of moral redemption and progress.

Rauschenbusch's view of salvation also has affinities with Ritschlian liberalism, except that with Rauschenbusch the ethical and social dimension of salvation is given even greater place. Rauschenbusch did not overlook the importance of individual salvation but saw it as an *essential part* of a necessarily enlarged conception of salvation. It was the job of the Social Gospel to make known this wider, social nature of redemption. That is, that personal salvation itself must be affected by the biblical, "solidaristic" view of man, now rediscovered by the Social Gospel.

If our exposition of the superpersonal agents of sin and of the Kingdom of Evil is true, then evidently a salvation confined to the soul and its personal interests is an imperfect and only partly effective salvation.[60]

According to Rauschenbusch, individual salvation is inadequate on two counts. First, it tends to emphasize those qualities of personal egoism that are the antithesis of Jesus' teaching of discipleship in the Kingdom as that of servanthood and cooperation.

If sin is selfishness, salvation must be a change which turns a man from self to God and humanity. His sinfulness consisted in a selfish attitude, in which he was at the center of the universe, and God and his fellowmen were means to serve his pleasures, increase his wealth, and set off his egoisms. Complete salvation, therefore, would consist in an attitude of love in which he would freely co-ordinate his life with the life of his fellows in obedience to the loving impulses of the spirit of God . . . . Salvation is the voluntary socializing of the soul.[61]

Those persons converted by an individualistic evangelism are thus frequently "worth no more to the Kingdom of God than they were before." Their vision of salvation is selfishly focused on themselves. Therefore, we must ask ourselves the question:

If we are converted, what are we converted to? If we are regenerated, does the scope of so divine a transformation end in our "going to heaven"? The nexus between our religious experience and humanity seems gone when the Kingdom of God is not present in the idea of regeneration.[62]

Not only does an individualistic view of salvation distort Jesus' message of discipleship in the Kingdom; it also fails to consider that social institutions must be redeemed in order to create an environment in which the individual can be healed and renewed. In some environments the historical and social conditions are such as not only to weaken but also actually to thwart the possibility of reconciliation and sanctification. Rauschenbusch held it imperative, then, that not only individuals but the "superpersonal forces," the "composite personalities" such as the state and the economic institutions be converted and redeemed. These superpersonal institutions are saved when they are freed from the law of mammon and brought under the law of Christ.

The fundamental step of repentance and conversion for professions and organizations is to give up monopoly power and the incomes derived from legalized extortion, and to come under the law of service. . . . The corresponding step in the case of governments and political oligarchies . . . is to submit to real democracy. Therewith they step out of the Kingdom of Evil into the Kingdom of God.[63]

Despite his considerable grasp of the social dimensions of human sin and alienation, many of Rauschenbusch's statements, such as the above, appear today naïvely voluntaristic and utopian. Nevertheless, Rauschenbusch did not believe in an inevitable movement toward social perfection. He did believe in the possibility of "Christianizing the social order," which for him meant bringing the orders of society into harmony with the teachings and spirit of Christ. Yet even Christianizing the social order was not to be confused with perfection. "As long as men are flesh and blood, the world can be neither sinless nor painless.... If perfection were reached today, new adjustments would be demanded tomorrow by the growth of new powers."[64] There is, however, *progress toward* Christianizing men and institutions, and Rauschenbusch believed he discerned clear evidence that most of the institutions of American society had been infused with a new life reflecting the spirit of Christ.

Four great sections of our social order—the family, the organized religious life, the institutions of education, and the political organization of our nation—have passed through constitutional changes which have made them to some degree part of the organism through which the spirit of Christ can do its work in humanity.[65]

The one area of society Rauschenbusch considered still largely governed by selfish motives was the economic order. "Our business life is the seat and source of our present troubles.... Business life is the unregenerate section of our social order."[66] Yet Rauschenbusch was assured that, because "the larger part of the work of christianizing our social order is already accomplished,"[67] Christians could be confident that economic institutions would soon also come under the law of Christ. In any case, "there has been a speeding up of redemption," and every victory made progress surer.

Looking at man and society from the perspective of the past half century, the sanguine views of American liberal Protestantism appear today to be utopian, unreal, and even dangerous. However, Rauschenbusch and his followers in the Social Gospel movement should not be faulted for being men of their time. In fact, their social analyses and prescrip-

tions were often entirely relevant to the conditions of their day. Where Rauschenbusch does fall short, perhaps, is in his understanding of some basic doctrines of Christianity. His conception of sin, though far superior to that of most liberals, failed to plumb the depths of human sin as the corruption of man's spiritual freedom. His "democratized" God and his progressive conception of the Kingdom were more dependent on the ideals of a liberal culture than on the Bible and the theology of the Church. It is generally acknowledged that Rauschenbusch's theology was more subtle and profound than that of most of his liberal Protestant contemporaries. Nevertheless, those elements of his theology which most reflected his own "culture Protestantism" and were most in accord with the prevailing liberalism were what were largely appropriated and emphasized by those in the Social Gospel movement. This is well expressed in the following recent assessment of Rauschenbusch:

His keen sense of the kingdom of God as judgment, and of the deepening of the burden of guilt through the recognition of social sin; the new validity which he found in the doctrine of original sin through the recognition of the social transmission of sin; the sense of crisis in individual and social life, and the demand for repentance and rebirth; and the desperateness of the struggle against the "kingdom of evil" (the super-individual forces of evil infecting the whole social organism)— these elements of Rauschenbusch's theology were less influential than those which reinforced the characteristic liberal tenets.[68]

Protestant liberal theology reflected to a considerable degree the cultural climate of the turn of the century. Traditional metaphysics was under fire at the same time that the Bible and church dogma were undergoing rigorous historical scrutiny. There was a concern to reduce Christianity to its simplest terms, which meant for most liberal theologians a recovery of the ethical message of Jesus. Religious authority was located in the personal experience of justification and reconciliation through Jesus, rather than in the canonical Scriptures or ecclesiastical dogma. Salvation was interpreted in moral, social, and progressive terms.

If Paul Tillich is correct that a genuine theology is a "theology of correlation" between the cultural situation and the Christian message, then Ritschlian Liberalism would appear to be a near perfect theology for its time. Its formulation of the Christian message was well suited to meet the metaphysical agnosticism, historicism, and moral optimism of the pre-World War I period. But the question that must be asked is whether, in their concern to meet the cultural situation, the liberals were guilty of formulating their "answers" in such a way as to distort the Christian message? In their concern to return "to the sources," were Harnack and his fellow liberals getting back to the historical Jesus and the primitive Christian message or were they, in the words of the Jesuit Father Tyrrell,

seeing only an image of their own bourgeois Protestant faces? Did Ritschlianism involve an extensive accommodation of Christianity to the assumptions of modern culture? This was to be the judgment of two major theological movements which had their beginnings shortly after the turn of the century. Those movements were Roman Catholic Modernism and Protestant Neo-Orthodoxy. Both of these movements trace their beginnings to a repudiation of Ritschlian Liberalism. Yet, it is interesting that neither movement simply represents a reactionary tendency away from Liberalism, as was the case with American Fundamentalism. Both Catholic Modernism and Neo-Orthodoxy accepted Liberalism's openness to biblical criticism, even radicalizing it. They both focused on Jesus' message of the Kingdom of God but interpreted this biblical motif in strikingly different ways. They were also skeptical of metaphysical speculation and natural theology. Beyond this, however, the two movements have little in common other than their concern to offer a viable alternative to what they considered a reactionary Orthodoxy and an accommodating Liberalism.

NOTES

1. Garvie, Alfred, *The Ritschlian Theology* (Edinburgh, 1902), pp. 23–24.
2. Mackintosh, H. R., *Types of Modern Theology* (London, 1952), p. 141.
3. Ibid., p. 148. A quotation from F. Kattenbusch, the source not cited.
4. Albrecht Ritschl, *The Christian Doctrine of Justification and Reconciliation*, III, tr. H. R. Mackintosh and A. B. Macaulay (Edinburgh, 1900), p. 199. See also p. 17.
5. Ibid., p. 212.

6. Ibid., pp. 204–205.
7. Ibid., p. 215.
8. Ibid., p. 212.
9. Ibid., pp. 2–3.
10. Ibid., p. 406.
11. Ibid., p. 398.
12. Ibid., p. 393.
13. Ibid., pp. 396–397.
14. Ibid., pp. 400, 404.
15. Albrecht Ritschl, *Instruction in the Christian Religion*, tr. A. M. Swing, in *The*

Theology of Albrecht Ritschl (New York, 1901), p. 200.

16. *Justification and Reconciliation*, op. cit., p. 451.

17. Ibid., p. 442.

18. *Instruction*, op. cit., p. 195.

19. *Justification and Reconciliation*, op. cit., p. 451.

20. *Instruction*, op. cit., p. 197.

21. *Justification and Reconciliation*, op. cit., p. 477.

22. Ibid., p. 546.

23. Ibid., pp. 546–547.

24. Ibid., p. 85.

25. *Instruction*, op. cit., p. 214.

26. A. Durwood Foster, *A Handbook of Christian Theologians*, ed. Dean G. Peerman and Martin E. Marty (Cleveland, 1965), p. 64.

27. *Justification and Reconciliation*, op. cit., p. 549.

28. *Instruction*, op. cit., pp. 233–235.

29. Ibid., pp. 174–175.

30. Ibid., p. 179.

31. Agnes von Zahn-Harnack, *Adolf von Harnack* (Berlin, 1936), p. 91.

32. A. Harnack, "Über die Sicherheit und Grenzen geschichtlicher Erkenntnis" in *Reden und Aufsätze*, IV, 7; cited in Wilhelm Pauck, *The Heritage of the Reformation* (Glencoe, Ill., 1961). See also Pauck's "Adolf von Harnack" in D. G. Peerman and M. E. Marty, *A Handbook of Christian Theologians*, for a brief, masterful treatment of Harnack's work.

33. *History of Dogma*, I. Tr. from 3d German edition by Neil Buchanan (New York, 1958), p. 1.

34. *Grundriss der Dogmengeschichte*, 9th ed. (Berlin, 1921), p. 5; cited in W. Pauck, "Adolf von Harnack," op. cit., p. 97.

35. A. Harnack, *What Is Christianity?* tr. T. B. Saunders (New York, 1957), pp. 13–14.

36. *History of Dogma*, I, p. 13.

37. See ibid., pp. 58 ff.

38. *What Is Christianity?* p. 51.

39. Ibid., p. 56.

40. Ibid., p. 67.

41. Ibid., p. 73.

42. Ibid., p. 100.

43. Ibid., pp. 99–100.

44. Ibid., p. 128.

45. Ibid., p. 144.

46. Ibid., p. 145.

47. Ibid.

48. Ibid., p. 14.

49. Walter Rauschenbusch, *Christianizing the Social Order* (New York, 1912), pp. 67, 69.

50. Walter Rauschenbusch, *A Theology for the Social Gospel* (New York, 1917), p. 1.

51. Ibid., p. 57.

52. Ibid., p. 58.

53. Ibid., p. 60.

54. Ibid., p. 50.

55. Ibid., pp. 46–47.

56. Ibid., p. 48.

57. Ibid., p. 49.

58. Ibid., pp. 174–175.

59. Ibid., p. 178.

60. Ibid., p. 95.

61. Ibid., pp. 97–99.

62. Ibid., pp. 100–101.

63. Ibid., p. 117.

64. *Christianizing the Social Order*, op. cit., p. 126.

65. Ibid., pp. 154–155.

66. Ibid., p. 156.

67. Ibid., p. 155.

68. John Dillenberger and Claude Welch, *Protestant Christianity Interpreted Through Its Development* (New York, 1954), pp. 251–252.

SUGGESTIONS FOR FURTHER READING

RITSCHL AND RITSCHLIAN THEOLOGY

Foster, A. Durwood. "Albrecht Ritschl," in Peerman, D. G. and Marty, M. E., eds., *A Handbook of Christian Theologians* (Cleve-land: World Publishing Co., 1965). An excellent brief essay on Ritschl and his theology.

Garvie, Alfred. *The Ritschlian Theology*

(Edinburgh: T. and T. Clark, 1902). An expository and critical study of major themes in the writings of Ritschl, Herrmann, Häring, and Kaftan.

Hefner, Philip. *Faith and the Vitalities of History: A Theological Study Based on the Work of Albrecht Ritschl* (New York: Harper, 1966). A study of Ritschl which seeks to relate him to some issues central to theological discussion today. Contains an excellent bibliography of recent journal literature on Ritschl.

Mueller, David L. *An Introduction to the Theology of Albrecht Ritschl* (Philadelphia: Westminster Press, 1969).

ADOLF VON HARNACK

Glick, Wayne. *The Reality of Christianity: A Study of Adolf von Harnack as Historian and Theologian* (New York: Harper, 1967). The only extensive study of Harnack in English.

Pauck, Wilhelm. "Adolf von Harnack's Interpretation of Church History," in *The Heritage of the Reformation* (Glencoe, Ill., The Free Press, 1961).

Also see Pauck's equally fine essays on Harnack in *A Handbook of Christian Theologians*, op. cit., and *Harnack and Troeltsch: Two Historical Theologians* (New York: Oxford, 1968).

WALTER RAUSCHENBUSCH

Handy, Robert. "Walter Rauschenbusch," in *A Handbook of Christian Theologians*, op. cit.

———, ed., *The Social Gospel in America* (New York: Oxford, 1966). Selections from Rauschenbusch's writings, with introductions and bibliography.

Sharpe, Dores. *Walter Rauschenbusch* (New York: The Macmillan Co., 1942).

AMERICAN LIBERAL THEOLOGY

Cauthen, Kenneth. *The Impact of American Religious Liberalism* (New York: Harper, 1962). An excellent critical study of several American liberal theologians, including Rauschenbusch, Fosdick, and William Adams Brown.

Hopkins, C. H. *The Rise of the Social Gospel in America* (New Haven: Yale University Press, 1940).

Van Dusen, H. P. and Roberts, D. E., eds. *Liberal Theology* (New York: Charles Scribner Sons, 1942). See also Van Dusen's *The Vindication of Liberal Theology* (New York: Harper, 1963).

CHAPTER TEN

Catholicism: Modernist and Liberal

George Tyrrell

The history of Protestant thought in the nineteenth century is closely joined to the successive intellectual movements of the period—to Romanticism, Idealism, Evolution, and Neo-Kantianism. The history of Roman Catholic thought does not exhibit this same dependence on the movements of secular philosophy. Kant, Hegel, evolutionism, and vitalistic philosophy did gain the attention of, and influenced, prominent Catholic theologians, but this did not bring about the radical reconceptions of Christianity which these movements effected within Protestantism. Catholic thought evolved between 1879 and 1917, but the significant developments were dogmatic and, as such, owed little materially to intellectual movements outside the Church.

It is a fact, nevertheless, that the political and intellectual revolutions of the late eighteenth and early nineteenth centuries did present the Roman Catholic Church with a series of challenges which resulted in new, rigorous, and frequently dangerous, responses to its traditions. We have seen in Chapter Four that the Catholic revival in France after the Revolution of 1789 owed its impulse largely to Romanticism. This revival took two very different directions. First, there emerged a new form of Ultramontanism exposed by De Bonald and especially by De Maistre in *Du Pape*. As we shall see, Ultramontanism was to prove triumphant in the nineteenth century. However, the revolutions produced a second movement—what has come to be known as Liberal Catholicism. Its beginnings can be identified with the publication of Lamennais' *Des progrès de la Revolution et de la guerre contre l'Eglise* in 1829. Lamennais (1782–1854) began as an Ultramontane, for he believed that only the authority of the Pope could free the Church from its subservience to the State, as witnessed not only in the period of the Ancien Régime but during the rule of Napoleon. What differentiated Lamennais' Ultramontanism from that of De Maistre was his conviction that the Pope should not protect the interests of the Church through concordats with kings but by identifying with the liberal ideals of the people, by "baptizing" the Revolution. Through his newspaper, *L'Avenir*, Lamennais called for separation of Church and State, liberty of conscience—i.e., freedom to pick and choose one's religion—and liberty of the press. He was possessed by the liberal faith that in such a free society the Catholic Church would flourish.

Lamennais' liberal program met with no favor among the French bishops. Indeed, the hierarchy prohibited *L'Avenir*, thus provoking Lamennais and his associates to appeal to Rome. The new Pope, Gregory XVI, likewise had no sympathy with Lamennais' program of "liberal Catholicism" and responded to his appeal with the encyclical *Mirari vos* (1832). The policy of *L'Avenir* was thoroughly condemned, specific proposals being dismissed as "absurd" and "perverse."

The condemnation of *L'Avenir* was the first major defeat for the new "liberal Catholicism" and proved to be an extremely significant event in the history of the modern Roman Church. The attitude of Gregory XVI toward Lamennais' policies set a precedent for Pius IX when he issued the Syllabus of Errors in 1864 and for Pius X in his condemnation of Modernism in *Pascendi gregis* in 1907.

In its beginnings, Liberal Catholicism in France was largely political in character. In Germany and in England it was more strictly theological. In Germany two centers of liberal Catholic theology were of particular importance. The earliest was associated with the Catholic theological faculty at Tübingen, dominated in the early decades of the nineteenth century by J. A. Möhler (1796–1838). Möhler was influenced by both Schleiermacher and Hegelianism and sought to interpret dogma in more experiential and historical terms than was customary in Roman theology. After 1840 the center of German Liberal Catholicism shifted to the University of Munich and to the leadership of Dr. Ignaz Döllinger (1799–1890). Döllinger was a learned ecclesiastical historian who, early in his career, espoused a liberal Ultramontanism similar to that of Lamennais. Later, from fear of growing papal autocracy, he turned his learning to exposing what he considered the unfounded historical claims of the Church. In 1863 Döllinger organized, without ecclesiastical permission, a Congress of Catholic Scholars in Munich, the purpose of which was to explore the relationship between the scientific study of history and the Church. In his address to the Congress, Döllinger denounced Scholasticism and called for a bold and thorough use of critical tools in examining Church history and teaching, free from the ordinary magistracy of the Church and the several Roman Congregations, such as that of the Index. The Congress was hailed by liberal Catholics throughout Europe and in England, but their enthusiasm and expectations were soon to receive a severe blow.

Roman Catholic liberalism in England was identified with the figure of Sir John (later Lord) Acton (1834–1902), Regius Professor of Modern History at Cambridge. Acton had studied under Döllinger and was committed to a free, critical investigation of the Church's tradition. This policy was practiced by Acton and his circle in the pages of *The Rambler* and *The Home and Foreign Review*. When these liberal principles were condemned by the Pope in 1864 the *Review* was suspended. In an article, "Conflicts with Rome," Acton explained the reasons for the suspension.

Its (the Review's) object has been to elucidate the harmony that exists between religion and the established conclusions of secular knowledge, and to exhibit the real amity and sympathy between the methods of science and the methods employed by the Church. That amity and sympathy the enemies of the Church refuse to admit, and her friends have not learned to understand. Long disowned by a large part of our Episcopate, they are now reflected by the Holy See; and the issue is vital to a Review which, in ceasing to uphold them, would surrender the whole reason of its existence.[1]

The action of the Holy See referred to by Acton was the appearance, in December 1864, of the Encyclical *Quanta cura* and the *Syllabus Errorum*. These papal documents summed up Pius IX's condemnation of modern errors. They became, after *Mirari vos*, the second major defeat for Liberal Catholicism. Pius IX's unqualified, sweeping denunciation of almost every principle of liberal democracy was shocking to Christians and secularists throughout Europe and America. Not only did the *Syllabus* condemn atheism, rationalism, socialism, communism, and naturalism but it also condemned separation of Church and State, liberty of religion and of the press, and concluded, in Proposition 80, with the denial that "the Roman Pontiff can and should reconcile himself with, and accommodate himself to, progress, liberalism and modern civilization." Understood in its immediate historical context, it is apparent that Pius IX was directing his denunciations particularly at Italian anticlerical liberalism, which was at the time threatening the temporal power of the Papacy. Nevertheless, the harsh language and the universalizing of the condemnation not only appeared tactically inopportune but indicated the Pope's failure to discriminate between what was true and what was suspect in the new liberalism.

The majority of Catholics, including large numbers of bishops, were stupefied and at a loss as to how to interpret the *Syllabus*. It was at this point that the Bishop Dupanloup of Orléan produced an explanation that softened the unqualified tone of the literal text. Dupanloup explained the condemnations in terms of what he called "thesis" and "hypothesis." The "thesis" is what would be ideally desired in the abstract, i.e., a Catholic society. However, to claim as a result of such a "thesis" the "hypothesis" that in a present democratic society it is wrong to uphold basic religious liberties, is fallacious. Perhaps because he himself was startled at the adverse reaction produced by the *Sylla-*

bus, Pius IX did not challenge Dupanloup's ingenious distinction. The French wits, however, could not refrain from offering a current illustration of it: "The thesis is when the Church condemns the Jews; the hypothesis is when the papal Nuncio dines with the Baron de Rothschild."

The *Syllabus Errorum* halted for the time being the growing Liberal Catholic movements in France, Italy, Germany, and England. In France, Montalembert's campaign for a Catholic political liberalism was silenced; in Germany Döllinger was censured and later excommunicated for his opposition to Papal Infallibility; and in England, Acton suspended publication of the Liberal Catholic *Review*. Even so, conservative Ultramontanism had not yet achieved its greatest victory.

Shortly after the announcement of the *Syllabus* it became known that Pius IX was considering the calling of a General Council of the Church. The Council of Trent had defined the beliefs of the Church; the new Council was to define the nature of the Church itself, her authority, and her relation to the State. The Vatican Council of 1870 was not called, as is commonly believed, to define the dogma of Papal Infallibility. However, as it happened, the question was given precedence and importance above all else. The large agenda and pressure of time made it apparent to the conservative Ultramontanes that the chapters concerned with the nature and authority of the Pope might be long delayed. Their leader, the English Archbishop Manning of Westminster, with the support of two hundred prelates, appealed to the Pope to have the chapters on the papacy introduced first. Pius IX acceded to this request.

There were very few Council delegates who actually opposed infallibility. The majority were in favor of a definition. The minority party were called the "inopportunists" for they either felt that the times were not right for such a definition or feared that so subtle a concept was not capable of precise statement and would be the source of great misunderstanding. Their fears were not unfounded, since some extreme Ultramontanists spoke as if they wanted almost everything the Pope said to be considered infallible! When the moderates failed to prevent infallibility from being discussed, they turned their efforts to trying to insure that infallibility be prescribed within a very clear and limited range of pronouncements. In this they were more successful, although a large number of the minority disagreed with the final text which read that the Pope is infallible only when speaking "*ex cathedra*—i.e., when exercising the office of pastor and teacher of all Christians, he defines with his supreme Apostolic authority a doctrine concerning faith or morals to be held by the universal Church. . . ." Because they could not agree with this final wording of the decree, since it failed to say anything about the Pope's consulting the Church before defining a dogma, about sixty bishops left the Council before the final vote rather than oppose the Pope and the majority's known wishes. When on July 18, 1870, the final vote was taken, 533 voted for and only 2 voted against the decree.

Among the interesting ironies of history is the fact that, only a few weeks after this historic event, Italian armies marched into the Papal States and the city of Rome became the capital of the new Kingdom of Italy. The long history of the Pope's temporal power had come to an end. The power and prestige of the Pope outside of the Church was seldom lower than in the years following 1870. Yet, within the Church the position of the Pope after 1870 reached a height never before equaled. Conservative Ultramontanism was victorious, Pius IX had boldly denounced "modern civilization," and the prospects for a resurgent liberal Roman Catholicism appeared impossible. Yet the greatest liberal challenge to Catholic theology was only a few years off. How Modernism, "the most serious peril threatening Catholic teaching since the Protestant revolt," came into being has to do with the policies of Pius IX's successor.

Leo XIII became Pope in 1878 and reigned until 1903. He was not a liberal by conviction but, compared to his predecessor and his successor, his policies were moderate and conciliatory. Leo XIII was a gifted statesman and realized that the extreme Ultramontanism identified with Pius IX's reign had alienated the Church from the outside world. He was willing, therefore, to support republican governments, not because he cherished republican ideals, but because such policies would best serve the Church in these new democratic states. He also gave evidence of a more liberal policy in matters intellectual—e.g., by opening the Vatican Archives to Protestant scholars and by conferring a Cardinal's hat on John Henry Newman, whose *Essay on Development* and *Grammar of Assent* were deeply suspect by conservative Roman theologians. It was such policies which led a younger generation of Catholic historians and theologians to hope that a new era of scholarly freedom had come. It was in this atmosphere of new expectations that the movement known as Modernism was born.

Catholic Modernism

Like the word "liberalism," the terms "Modernism" and "Modernist" have been used in a great variety of ways in the past century. Frequently "Modernist" is used in a general sense to designate any religious idea or movement that is progressive or unorthodox. The word is often used as a synonym for Protestant liberalism, particularly Ritschlian Liberalism, while Traditionalists and Fundamentalists use the word simply as a label of abuse for all those who disagree with them. However, in its stricter and more historical sense, the term "Modernism" refers to a movement in the Roman Catholic Church which began around 1890 and lasted for a few years after its condemnation in the Papal encyclical *Pascendi gregis* in 1907.

To refer to Catholic Modernism as a *movement* also requires some clarification. *Pascendi gregis* gives the impression that there was a highly organized school of thinkers with a clear intellectual platform who cleverly sought to undermine the traditional teachings of the Church from within. In actual fact, Catholic Modernism was not a single movement but a general tendency among quite independent individuals who sought, in the words of Loisy, "to adapt the Catholic religion to the intellectual, moral and social needs of the present time." What drew the Modernists together, as happened in some cases, was a common concern to adapt the teaching of the Church to the modern age.

It is also difficult to trace the intellectual precursors of Modernism. The assumption that the Modernists stood in a discernible line of intellectual descent is not borne out by the evidence. It has been said that they were dependent on

Möhler and the Tübingen school, but this has been denied by the Modernists themselves. Newman has sometimes been called "the father of Modernism," but this claim contains only a modicum of truth. In most respects Newman was a conservative, especially in his defense of ecclesiastical authority. The views of Loisy and Tyrrell would have shocked him. Nevertheless, Newman's struggle with the problem of history and dogma and his subsequent theory, as worked out in *An Essay on the Development of Christian Doctrine* (1846), was very congenial to the Modernists. This is evident in Newman's summary of his theory, a position unacceptable to both Roman traditionalist and liberal Protestant.

It is indeed sometimes said that the stream is clearest near the spring. Whatever use may fairly be made of this image, it does not apply to the history of a philosophy or belief, which on the contrary is more equable and purer and stronger, when its bed has become deep, broad and full. . . . Its beginnings are no measure of its capabilities or scope. At first no one knows what it is or what it is worth. . . . it tries, as it were, its limbs, and proves the ground under it, and feels its way. From time to time it makes essays which fail. . . . It seems in suspense which way to go; it wavers and at length strikes out in one definite direction. In time it enters into new territory. . . . Dangers and hopes appear in new relations; and old principles appear in new forms. It changes with them in order to remain the same. In a higher world it is otherwise, but here below to live is to change and to be perfect is to have changed often.[2]

It is easy to see how Modernists like Loisy and Tyrrell, both of whom studied Newman's work, could interpret and develop such a doctrine along lines Newman never intended. In any case, Newman's *Essay* and *Grammar of Assent*

were helpful to some of the Modernists and, because of Newman's high position in the Church, were also useful. Certainly, however, the most significant influence on Loisy and Tyrrell was exposure to the new historical criticism of the Bible and tradition.

The Modernist movement began in France where it also had its greatest impact and largest following. Its beginnings can properly be associated with the Abbé Louis Duchêsne (1843–1922), for Duchêsne was the first important Catholic scholar in France in the last years of the nineteenth century to be censured for his historical-critical studies. It was he who, perhaps more than anyone else, influenced Alfred Loisy. Duchêsne had been Professor of Church History at the Catholic University of Paris since 1877. He was noted for his bold application of scientific principles to the study of ecclesiastical history and gained a wide following among the younger scholars. As a result of his criticisms, Duchêsne was suspended from the Institut Catholique for a time and was given the position of director of the Ecole Française in Rome in 1897. However, from as early as 1890 Duchêsne apparently resolved that the full acceptance by the Church of the new historiography was not possible and so removed himself from any position of leadership among the Modernists. His position was soon filled by Alfred Loisy.

Alfred Loisy (1857–1949). Alfred Loisy, referred to by a noted Catholic scholar as "one of the most dangerous adversaries whom the Church has ever encountered,"[3] was a Catholic priest until his excommunication in 1908. He is known as the intellectual leader of the Modernist movement and as one of the greatest biblical scholars of his generation. His religious vocation began when he entered the seminary at Chalons in 1874. There he distinguished himself not only by his intellectual brilliance but by his exemplary piety and was sent by his bishop to complete his training in Paris where he came under the influence of Duchêsne. Due to ill health, Loisy was forced to leave Paris but was ordained priest in 1879 and, for a brief period, served as a parish priest.

Largely because of Duchêsne's presence there, Loisy returned to the Institut Catholique in 1881 and soon after was appointed to the faculty of theology as lecturer in Hebrew. About this same time Loisy began to attend the lectures of Ernst Renan at the Collège de France. Renan, best known for his rationalistic *Vie de Jésus*, was now in his old age but at the height of his renown. Loisy's devotion to critical scholarship flowered under Renan's tutelage, although Loisy claimed to reject the great man's rationalistic conclusions. In his *Mémoires*, Loisy writes: "I instructed myself at his school in the hope of proving to him that all that was true in his science was compatible with Catholicism sanely understood."[4] There is no doubt that in those early years Loisy's resolve was to serve the Church by establishing a sounder apologetic on a solid, scientific —i.e., historical-critical—base.

In 1890 Loisy defended a thesis at the Institut Catholique on the Canon of the Old Testament. Although the thesis passed, it clearly opposed traditional teaching on the inspiration of Scripture. This victory sparked a decade of fearless critical work on the Bible marked by a series of controversies. The history of the Canon of the Old Testament was followed with one on the New Testament (1891) and the following year Loisy tackled the early chapters of Genesis, raising questions concerning their historicity. As a result, students from the Seminary of Saint-Sulpice were forbidden to attend Loisy's lectures, which caused a sensation in the Catholic intellectual world.

In 1893 Mgr. d'Hulst, rector of the Institut Catholique, published an article on *La Question biblique*, whose veiled purpose was a defense of the progressive study of the Bible and of his professor, the suspect Loisy. The result could not have been further from the intention. The article provoked a heated controversy which ended in Loisy's dismissal from his professorship and the issuance of the encyclical *Providentissimus Deus* by Leo XIII. The encyclical was addressed to the question of biblical study. It counseled against the danger of rationalism in biblical interpretation and condemned those who set aside the traditional conception of divine inspiration.

Removed from his academic post, Loisy was appointed chaplain to a girl's school at Neuilly. He submitted to the encyclical but, with less rigorous demands upon him, was able to continue his biblical studies in earnest. His catechetical duties also broadened his theological interests and made him more conscious of the apologetic task. It was during the five years at Neuilly that the groundwork was laid for his most important book, *L'Évangile et l'Église, The Gospel and the Church*. His position by this time was outside Catholic orthodoxy, although his own sense of devotion to the service of the Church remained genuine. He was sincerely committed to bringing about a union of Catholicism and modern knowledge and was still confident it could be done.

After a series of articles on the religion

of Israel were condemned by Cardinal Richard late in 1900, Loisy became lecturer at the École des hautes Études at the Sorbonne. This gave him a position of distinction in the scholarly world and greater independence from the institutional Church. In the spring of 1902 Loisy actually began the writing of *The Gospel and the Church*. He had long desired to write a modern apology for Catholicism and the popularity, in 1902, of the French translation of Adolf von Harnack's *Das Wesen des Christentums* (*What Is Christianity?*) gave him a perfect foil. Neither he nor his friends and advisers realized the sensation the book would cause—that it would be regarded as the summation of all the heresies of Modernism and would ultimately lead to Loisy's excommunication.

Because of the significance of *The Gospel and the Church* in the Modernist controversy, an analysis of its contents is the best way to gain an understanding of the Modernist doctrine and program. The book purports to be a refutation of liberal Protestantism, but this was not its principal object. The critique of Harnack's liberal Protestantism was the perfect occasion for the development of the outlines of a truly modern Catholic position. It was a shrewd stroke, but it is quite unfair to assert, as some have, that Loisy sought thereby to disguise his own unorthodox doctrines. There is no pretense in the book. The radicalness of his Catholicism is never veiled.

Each chapter begins with a statement of the liberal Protestant position as developed by Harnack in *What Is Christianity?*, and then argues for the historical and experiential validity of the Catholic view. Since we have examined Harnack's doctrine in the previous chapter, there is no need to rehearse it here. Loisy begins

his critique of Harnack's rendition of essential Christianity on the grounds laid out by Harnack himself—by appeal to the facts of history. If we take the historical view, can we derive, as Harnack has done, the complex reality of early Christianity from a single idea, such as faith in God the Father? Do the sources warrant such a judgment or, Loisy asks, is it the a priori assumption "of a theologian who takes from history as much as suits his theology"?[5] Appeal to history is not necessarily the same as what appeals to us. "The gospel has an existence independent of us," therefore, Loisy urges, let us "try to understand it in itself, before we interpret it in the light of our preferences and our needs."[6] Honest criticism forbids that we resolve as historically nonessential all that we today find unacceptable. Picking and choosing a small number of texts in support of our theories is uncritical.

Herr Harnack has not avoided this danger, for his definition of the essence of Christianity is not based on the totality of authentic texts, but rests, when analysed, on a very small number of texts, practically indeed on two passages: "No man knoweth the Son, but the Father: neither knoweth any man the Father save the Son" and "The Kingdom of God is within you," both of them passages that might well have been influenced, if not produced, by the theology of the early times.[7]

This leads Loisy to a second critical point. Literary analysis does not allow us to make the clear distinction between Jesus and the primitive tradition that Harnack appears to make. What we have in the Gospel is "but an echo, necessarily weakened and a little confused, of the words of Jesus."

Whatever we think, theologically, of tradition, whether we trust it or regard it with suspicion, we know Christ only by tradition, across the tradition, and in the tradition of the primitive Christians. This is as much as to say that Christ is inseparable from His work, and that the attempt to define the essence of Christianity according to the pure gospel of Jesus, apart from the tradition, cannot succeed, for the mere idea of the gospel without tradition is in flagrant contradiction with the facts submitted to criticism.[8]

The tradition includes the appropriation of Jesus' life and message by the Christian community and, in Loisy's opinion, no other Christ is historically available.* Nor should this be regretted. Why should the essence of a tree be identified with "but a particle of the seed from which it sprung" rather than with the complete tree? According to Loisy, Harnack has peeled away the fruit of primitive Christianity with such abandon that it is doubtful if anything will remain.

This method of dismembering a subject does not belong to history, which is a science of observation of the living not a dissection of the dead. Historical analysis . . . does not destroy what it touches nor think all movement digression, and all growth deformity.[9]

Loisy believed that if we examine the message of Jesus, freed from a priori notions and personal prejudices, we will see that it was radically eschatological, couched in the contemporary Jewish

apocalypticism of the first century.* As we have seen, Harnack was not entirely daunted by this fact. He believed that, although it was difficult, it was not impossible to distinguish what was traditional from what was new and personal, the kernel from the husk, in the preaching of Jesus concerning the kingdom of God. For Harnack the husk was, of course, traditional Jewish apocalypticism. The kernel of Jesus' own view had to do simply with faith in a merciful Father. But this, according to Loisy, was to play fast and loose with the New Testament sources.

Christ nowhere confounds the kingdom with the remission of sins. . . . Nowhere does He identify the kingdom with . . . God's power acting in the heart of the individual.[10]

The authenticity of the single text (Luke 17:20) on which Harnack most depends is, in Loisy's view, uncertain and its meaning not clearly the one Harnack gives it. In any case "to sacrifice the rest of the gospel to the doubtful interpretation of a solitary passage would be to go contrary to the most elementary principles of criticism."[11] Examined in its totality, Jesus' message is seen as an urgent and radical announcement of the approaching kingdom of God, envisioned in bold apocalyptical terms. Concern for all else, for life in this world, for law and

---

* Here Loisy was in accord with the views of the *Formgeschichte* school, soon to gain prominence through the work of the Protestant scholars Dibelius, K. L. Schmidt and R. Bultmann—viz., that the New Testament is very largely the work of the early Christian communities and that it is almost impossible to extract the history and message of Jesus from the primitive Christian traditions about him. See Chap. Eleven.

* Here again Loisy was in advance of most New Testament scholars of his time. His recognition of the centrality of apocalyptic eschatology in the message of Jesus was contemporary with that of Johannes Weiss and predated Albert Schweitzer's famous *Quest of the Historical Jesus* (1906) in which the theory of thoroughgoing eschatology is given its classic expression. Recognition of the eschatological message of Jesus did more than anything else to destroy the liberal, Ritschlian picture of the historical Jesus. See Chap. Eleven.

culture "is as though non-existent."[12] Jesus made no attempt to reconcile his radical demands to the prudential realities of life. Loisy argues that it is for this very reason that it was later absolutely necessary to detach the message from its earliest connections. The very preservation of the gospel demanded that it develop and change to meet new historical conditions.

Harnack's interpretation of Christology is open to similar criticism. His identification of Sonship with Jesus' knowledge of God is based on a single text (Matt. 11:27) which is probably not from Jesus himself but the product of the early tradition. Moreover, "the gospel conception of the Son of God is no more a psychological idea signifying a relation of the soul to God than is the gospel conception of the kingdom."[13] Jesus thought of himself as the Son of God "to the extent he avowed himself the Messiah." That is, the divine Sonship was linked to Jesus' vocation of announcing the approaching kingdom. Viewed in this perspective the gospel is not about "God and the soul, the soul and its God"; rather, at the very heart of the gospel is "the reality of the kingdom that is to come, the certainty of the gospel message concerning it, and the mission of Him who announces it."[14] Loisy readily admits that this "entire gospel" is bound up with a view of the world that is no longer ours; but at least it is the whole gospel and not some imagined essence. The very fact that the gospel detached itself, little by little, from its original form shows that that *form* was only temporary. Man changes with the ages, and it is only appropriate that the gospel "not fail to accommodate itself" to those changes.

The truly evangelical part of Christianity today is not that which has never changed . . . and has never ceased to change, but that which in spite of all external changes proceeds from the impulse given by Christ, and is inspired by His Spirit.[15]

The primitive gospel, which centered on the coming kingdom and the mission of the Messiah, was a "simple idea" for Loisy, one which the historian is now able to see as "the concrete, rudimentary, indistinct symbol of subsequent events" —e.g., the anticipation of the kingdom of God in the Church. "It was the certain presentiment of what we see today." Development, then, was not an "abasement," as Harnack claimed, for the form of the gospel necessarily had to change.

Since the Church is the historical embodiment of the gospel, it is also natural that it should grow and change and take on new forms. Struggle, movement, and modification are the very laws of life.

These struggles do not prove a diminution of life but that life is threatened: when the crisis is over, and the power of the organism is augmented, it is to be praised for its vitality, not blamed because it suffered or because it did not succumb. The Church can fairly say that, in order to be at all times what Jesus desired the society of his friends to be, it had to become what it has become: for it has become what it had to be to save the gospel by saving itself.[16]

For Loisy it is a fact that the institutional Church is as necessary to the gospel as is the gospel to the Church. The indispensability of the Church and its authority for the very preservation of the gospel does not mean, however, that Jesus consciously established the institutional Church.

It is certain that Jesus did not systematize beforehand the constitution of the Church as that of a government established on earth and destined to endure for a long series of centuries. . . . *Jesus foretold the kingdom, and it was the Church that came*; she came, enlarging the form of the gospel, which it was impossible to preserve as it was. . . . The preservation of its primitive state was impossible, its restoration now is equally out of the question, because the conditions under which the gospel was produced have disappeared forever. History shows the evolution of the elements that composed it. . . . *It is easy today to see in the Catholic Church what stands today for the idea of the heavenly kingdom, for the idea of the Messiah . . . and for the idea of the apostolate. . . .* The tradition of the Church keeps them, interpreting them and adapting them to the varying conditions of humanity.[17] (Italics added.)

The marks of the Church today are the same as those of the primitive community, only "grown and fortified." Loisy comments that the continuity of the gospel has no more need to reproduce exactly the Galilean form than a man has need to preserve, at fifty, the features and manners of life of the day he was born in order to be the same individual. Since the Church has undergone continuous change in the past, there is no reason to doubt that this process will continue in the future. Loisy even conjectures, prophetic of Vatican II, that the extreme centralization of authority in the Pope which was required by historical circumstance may have reached its limit and that a new consideration of ecclesiastical authority may bring about a reaction to the present policy. At least, "theological reflection has not yet spoken its final word on the subject."[18] And, he adds, it should not be forgotten that "the Church is an educator, rather than a dominating mistress: she instructs rather than directs, and he who obeys her only does so according to his conscience, and in order to obey God."[19]

As the institutional Church evolved and changed to meet the challenge of changing circumstances and to preserve itself, so Christian dogma constantly develops new forms to conform to the thought-patterns of contemporary knowledge and the facts of religious experience. The Hellenization of early Jewish Christianity is the most obvious illustration of this process, which continues to the present day. The doctrines of the Incarnation and Trinity are Greek dogmas, "unknown to Judaic Christianity." But they, too, can expect to undergo transformations.

Anyone who has followed the progress of Christian thought from the beginning must perceive that neither the Christological dogma nor the dogma of grace nor that of the Church is to be taken for a summit of doctrine. . . . The conceptions that the Church presents as revealed dogmas are not truths fallen from heaven and preserved by religious tradition in the precise form in which they first appeared. . . . Though the dogmas may be Divine in origin and substance, they are human in structure and composition. It is inconceivable that their future should not correspond to their past. Reason never ceases to put questions to faith, and traditional formulas are submitted to a constant work of interpretation. . . .[20]

According to Loisy, dogmatic *definitions* are always relative and variable. They are always related to the general form of human knowledge at the time of their constitution. It thus follows that a considerable revolution in knowledge renders necessary a reinterpretation of the old formula which no longer adequately expresses the original religious experience or idea. Thus a distinction should always be made between the material image of the formula and its proper religious meaning or idea. The former is relative, the latter is enduring and can be reconciled with changing knowledge. Take, for example, the statement from the Creed, "He descended into Hell, He ascended into Heaven."

These propositions have for many centuries been taken literally. Generations of Christians have followed one another believing Hell the abode of the damned to be beneath their feet, and Heaven, the abode of the elect, above their heads. Neither learned theology nor even popular preaching maintains this localization today.... May we not say, looking at the transformation that the apparent sense of the formulas has undergone, that the theology of the future will again construct a more spiritual idea of their content?[21]

The very need for ceaseless interpretation and development of dogmatic formulae makes plain the essentially spiritual character of such doctrines. They are meant to be flexible and imprecise, an aid to faith. They allow for individuality of interpretation and, contrary to Protestant opinion, do not demand a narrow subserviency.

The Church does not exact belief in its formulas as the adequate expression of absolute truth, but presents them as the least imperfect expression that is morally possible.... The ecclesiastical formula is the auxiliary of faith, the guiding line of religious thought: it cannot be the integral object of that thought, seeing that object is God Himself, Christ and His work; each man lays hold of the object as he can, with the aid of the formula. As all souls and all intelligences differ one from the other, the gradations of belief are also of infinite variety, under the sole direction of the Church and in the unity of her creed. The incessant evolution of doctrine is made by the work of individuals, as their activity reacts on the general activity, and these individuals are they who think for the Church while thinking with her.[22]

It is difficult to believe that Loisy thought his book represented a position acceptable to the ecclesiastical authorities. In fact, of course, he was quite aware that it did not. Loisy was presenting the Church with a program of modernization which, he was soon to learn, it had no intention of adopting. It has been argued by orthodox critics of Loisy that his book left no place for certain fundamental Christian beliefs, for supernaturalism, or for the historical Incarnation. A careful reading of *The Gospel and the Church* does not bear out such a claim. What the book does do is to call for a radical reform of the Church's attitude toward biblical research, the nature of its authority, and its conception of dogma. That Loisy's own theological views were later to become heterodox and skeptical is true, and perhaps it can be argued that his Modernist program was the first step in that inevitable direction. But this, too, is highly questionable since there were Catholics of liberal but orthodox faith, such as Baron von Hügel and Wilfred Ward, who considered *The Gospel and the Church* an important apology for Catholicism, and who never took the path Loisy later was to follow.

The book was enthusiastically received by many Catholic intellectuals, but within a few months of its appearance it was vigorously attacked and condemned by the Archbishop of Paris. Why was it considered dangerous, even heretical? The charges against it were numerous. Loisy had denied the Church's teaching concerning the inspiration of Scripture, he had depicted Jesus as a herald of the kingdom, as initiator of a religious spirit and movement, but not as the revealer of infallible truths. He had considered Jesus limited and fallible in his judgments, and dogma relative because conditioned by changing historical circumstances. He also viewed the bodily resurrection as mythical, and took a highly personal view of the nature and authority of the Papacy and the Church's teaching office. But, above all, what was anathema to the Church was Loisy's equivocal use of the terms *development* and *change*. The Church taught that dogma was the necessary and logical *development* of the original deposit of faith—the making explicit what was implicit in the New Testament revelation. This development was carried out on the basis of certain logical and historical principles. The doubt raised earlier by Newman's *Essay on Development* now became unmistakably clear in *The Gospel and the Church*: development involves real doctrinal change. That is, Loisy

does not treat of the New Testament as a *depositum fidei* to be explained and developed, but never *changed* by the Church, he treats it rather as something in itself subject to change, and it was in treating *development* as though it were *change* that the essence of his heresy consisted.[23]

Loisy offered a somewhat qualified "submission" to Cardinal Richard of Paris in February, 1903, but continued to pursue his historical work. Late that same year he published *Autour d'un petit livre*, a frank defense and elaboration of the principles expressed in *The Gospel and the Church*. This was a clear challenge to the authorities. They had but two alternatives: to accept Loisy's program or to condemn his views as heretical and excommunicate him from the Church.

Both of the latter steps were delayed for a few years; the first occurred with the appearance of *Lamentabili* and *Pascendi gregis* in 1907, the second a year later.

Before examining these measures taken by Pius X, the thought of two other major figures in the Modernist movement must be considered.

George Tyrrell (1861–1909) and Edouard Le Roy (1870–1954). If Loisy exemplified the scientific commitment of Modernism, Tyrrell embodied the Catholic spirit of the movement. George Tyrrell was born an Irishman and raised in the Protestant Church of Ireland. As a young man he came under the influence of High Church Anglican friends but High Anglicanism did not long satisfy him. At eighteen Tyrrell moved to London and was received into the Roman Catholic Church that same year. He had for some time held a rather idealized picture of the religious life of the Society of Jesus and, in 1880, he entered the novitiate of that order. However, from the very first there was a deep tension in Tyrrell's vocation between unselfish devotion and submission and a scrupulous independence of judgment.

During his seven years of training Tyrrell became an ardent student and disciple of St. Thomas Aquinas, opposing the more narrow scholasticism of the Jesuit Suarez (1548–1617) which was then dominant in the Society. Tyrrell was ordained priest in 1891, spent a few years in parish mission work, and then taught philosophy at the Jesuit College at Stonyhurst from 1894 to 1896. It was during these latter years that new intellectual influences began to unsettle Tyrrell's theological tranquility and he began to question the compatibility of his thought and office. The new developed friendship with the Catholic layman Baron Friedrich von Hügel was of greatest consequence, for it was largely through von Hügel that Tyrrell was introduced to the philosophical work of the liberal Catholics Maurice Blondel and Lucien Laberthonnière, and to German biblical criticism.

The first of Tyrrell's writings that clearly revealed a serious break with tradition was an article on eternal punishment entitled "A Perverted Devotion," published in 1899. Tyrrell called for an agnosticism concerning the punishment of the damned and criticized the rationalistic attitude of scholasticism toward the mysteries of the faith. In this essay the beginnings of Tyrrell's Modernist program is evident. Thereafter he was under suspicion and his priestly work was reduced. He moved to Richmond in Yorkshire where he lived from 1900 to 1905 in virtual retirement at a little Jesuit mission. During this period he continued to write articles and books, often anonymously or pseudonymously, which led inevitably to a break not only with the Society but with the Roman Church itself. Refusing to repudiate what he had written in "A Letter to a Friend," published in 1903, Tyrrell was dismissed from the Society of Jesus in February, 1906. Efforts were made to heal this breach with the Church, but these ended when Tyrrell wrote two letters to the *London Times* publicly criticizing the Encyclical *Pascendi gregis*. As a result he was deprived of the sacraments.

By this time Tyrrell saw himself as a prophet who, though never to see the Promised Land himself, was heralding a revolution in the Roman Church which would ultimately waken it from its "medieval dreams." He asked at this time:

May not Catholicism like Judaism have to die in order that it may live again in a greater and grander form? Has not every organism got its limits of development after which it must decay, and be content to survive in its progeny? Wineskins stretch, but only within measure, for there comes at last a bursting-point when new ones must be provided.[24]

From 1906 until his death in 1909 Tyrrell called for a complete revolution of Catholicism and denounced the conservatives, often in bitter, scathing language—none more so than in his attack upon Cardinal Mercier in *Medievalism* (1908). Tyrrell did not claim to have all the answers to meet the Church's need, but in his last books the general theological principles of a Modernist revolution are sketched. The most important of these books are *Lex Orandi* (1903), *A Much Abused Letter* (1906), *Through Scylla and Charybdis* (1907), *Medievalism* (1908), and *Christianity at the Cross Roads* (1910). The last book was published posthumously and, as Loisy remarked, went far beyond the "modest program of reforms" contained in *L'Évangile et l'Église*.

George Tyrrell died of Bright's disease in July, 1909. Although he received the sacraments on his deathbed, he made no retraction of his "errors" and was therefore denied a Roman Catholic burial. "When Tyrrell died," Loisy wrote, "it may be said that Modernism, considered as a movement of overt resistance to the absolutism of Rome, died with him."[25] It is significant that Tyrrell refused through the end to acknowledge he was outside the Catholic Church; rather "he died professing to defend Catholic principles against the Vatican heresies."[26] This is important in revealing Tyrrell's devotion to what he saw as Catholicism. Like Loisy, he was committed to modern critical scholarship but entirely opposed to liberal Protestantism. Unlike Loisy, Tyrrell kept his criticism and Catholic spirituality in finer balance.

In the public mind Modernism had come to mean detachment from tradition, the equivalent of Protestant Liberalism. Nothing could have been further from Tyrrell's mind. In his last book he makes this absolutely clear.

Of the avowed adherents or admirers of Modernism a large proportion understand it in this loose sense (as detachment from tradition). They believe in modernity . . . but he (the Modernist) also believes in tradition. . . . By a Modernist I mean a churchman, of any sort, who believes in the possibility of a synthesis between the essential truth of his religion and the essential truth of modernity.[27]

Whether or not such a program could have been carried out within the Roman Church at the time is doubtful, and Tyrrell's own view of Catholicism was highly personal. But it is clear that his Modernism was worlds apart from Liberal Protestantism. *Christianity at the Cross Roads* was a passionate repudiation of Protestantism.

To suppose that Modernism is a movement away from the Church and is converging towards Liberal Protestantism is to betray a complete ignorance of its meaning—as complete as that of the Encyclical *Pascendi*. With all its accretions and perversions Catholicism is for the Modernist the only authentic Christianity. Whatever Jesus was, He was in no sense a Liberal Protestant.[28]

Tyrrell accepted the apocalyptical interpretation of Jesus and his message as set forth by Loisy, Weiss, and Schweitzer and agreed that such a picture of Jesus made the Jesus of Liberalism historically untenable. In Tyrrell's classic statement, "The Christ that Harnack sees, looking back through nineteen centuries of Catholic darkness, is only the reflection of a Liberal Protestant face, seen at the bottom of a deep well."[29] But what of the Christ of Catholicism? Is He compatible with the apocalyptic visionary of the New Testament? Tyrrell believed he was—*if* we see Jesus' apocalypticism as the expression of an essential "religious idea in a certain stage of development." That religious *idea* is transcendentalism or otherworldliness. It is this idea which is so lacking in Liberal Protestantism but is the very essence both of Jesus' eschatology and Catholic spirituality.

This contempt of the world preached by Jesus was not Buddhistic in its motive. It was a contempt for a lower and transitory form of existence in favour of a higher—a proximate pessimism but an ultimate optimism. That the world was thought to be in its death-agony made it doubly contemptible. But when this thought was dropped by the Church, the world still remained contemptible. It was but a preparation and purgatory; the theatre of the great conflict between the forces of good and evil—a conflict that could be decided in favour of Good only by the Coming of the Son of Man. . . . The emphatic Persian dualism of Good and Evil, of the Kingdom of God and of Satan, is common to the idea of Jesus and the idea of Catholicism. . . . It is not between Jesus and Catholicism but between Jesus and Liberal Protestantism that no bridge, but only a great gulf, is fixed.[30]

What Jesus and Catholicism have in common, then, is the spiritual truth of his apocalyptic message. That Jesus was mistaken in his literal belief in a coming new age is not significant. Jesus was possessed by the truth of a great idea and necessarily had to embody it in the limited thought forms of his day. We, too, must interpret the transcendent and other-worldly in the thought forms of our culture, recognizing that such forms are mere human efforts to give expression to deeply felt religious truths.

The Modernism of Tyrrell, and that of Loisy, is markedly distinguished from Ritschlian Protestantism in its contention that it is the *idea* and not the historical fact that is the basis of Christianity. According to Tyrrell, religion is the embodiment of the spiritual ideal in changing historical forms; hence religious statements are always *symbolic*.

Religion, as such, deals entirely with the transcendent. Its "idea" unfolds itself and comes into clearer consciousness in an infinity of directions and degrees, dependent on its mental, moral and social environment—on the materials out of which it has to weave an embodiment for itself. But, from the nature of the case, its presentiment of the transcendent order, and of the present order in its relation to the transcendent, can never be more than symbolic . . . the transcendental can never be expressed properly. Translated into the terms of our present philosophy, the "ideal" of Jesus remains symbolic. To whatever degree we dematerialize our symbols of the spiritual, material they must remain. Our own symbolism would be as unacceptable for a later age as the apocalyptic symbolism is for us. The only remedy lies in a frank admission of the principles of symbolism. With this admission we have no need to abolish the Apocalypse, which as the form in which Jesus embodied His religious "idea" is classical and normative for all subsequent interpretations of the same. . . . What each age has to do is to interpret the apocalyptic symbolism into terms of its own symbolism.[31]

Tyrrell's doctrine of religious symbolism drove him to a revolutionary view of dogma. He made a sharp distinction between the symbolic function of Chris-

tian revelation and the science of theology which simply rationalizes and explains the original revelatory ideas.

The whole (Christian revelation) has a spiritual value as a construction of Time in relation to Eternity. It gives us the *world* of our religious life. But I do not feel bound to find an independent meaning in each element; *or to determine prematurely what elements are of literal and what of purely symbolic value—which is the core of historic fact and which idealization.*[32] (Italics added.)

Here we encounter an aspect of Modernism that was unacceptable to liberal Protestant and traditional Catholic alike. The Modernists were generally uninterested in the question of the factual bases of Christian claims, and they often were careless in distinguishing history from legend, fact from religious value. This is clear in Tyrrell's letter to von Hügel, where he summarizes his views of dogmatic formulae:

What value, then, do I attach to ecclesiastical definitions? . . . I believe the Church is precisely and only the guardian of the deposit of revelation and that she cannot add to it in any way; and that her definitions are simply safeguards and protections of revealed truths. *What* she says is often absolutely wrong, but the truth in whose defence she says it is revealed, and to that truth alone we own adhesion. . . . In affirming the philosophical concepts of transubstantiation or of the hypostatic union, she but protects the simple truths of revelation on which her affirmation *formally* falls. . . . In all controversies the Church must instinctively take the side that best protects the spiritual life. Her criticism is purely opportunist. In all her utterances she only repeats the truth revealed—their *meaning* is just the revealed truth which they protect. That a lie should be sometimes protective of truth is a consequence of the view of truth as *relative* to the mentality of a person or people. Hence, no definition of the *historicity* of the Virgin Birth could *mean* more than that the Virgin Birth was part of revelation. *Because and so long as the denial of its historicity seems to destroy its religious value, she will and must affirm its historicity in order to affirm those values.* In the implicit affirmation she is right of necessity; in the explicit protective affirmation she may be quite wrong . . . about history, she makes quite fallible affirmations protective of those implicitly affirmed revealed truths.[33] (Last italics added.)

If the truth of the "idea," the revelation, is independent *of* or at least indifferent as to, its historical or even rational verification, how does the Modernist make any distinction between religious ideas, between the revelations of one prophet and those of another? Tyrrell's answer is given most fully in *Lex Orandi*. It is essentially pragmatic.

The *religiously* important criticism to be applied to points of Christian belief, whether historical, philosophic or scientific, is not that which interests the historian, philosopher or scientist; but that which is supplied by the spirit of Christ, the *spiritus qui vivificat*: Is the belief in accord with, is it a development of, the spirit of the Gospel? What is its religious value? Does it make for the love of God and man? Does it show us the Father and reveal to us our sonship?[34]

Such a test of religious truth, however, cannot be merely private and idiosyncratic. Religious truth must possess what Tyrrell called "representative value," otherwise it is not rooted in what is universally real and fruitful. Religious truth must be in accord, then, with the very nature and laws of spiritual reality and only beliefs "that have been found by continuous and invariable experience to foster and promote the spiritual life of

the soul" can be so regarded. Tyrrell believed that Christians could be confident that their Creed bore the closest analogy to the realities of the spiritual world.

And the reason of this assurance is found in the universally proved value of the Creed as a practical guide to the eternal life of the soul— a proof which is based on the experience not of this man or that, however wise or holy, but of the whole Christian people and of the Church of the Saints in all ages and nations, on the consensus of the ethical and religious *orbis terrarum*.[35]

Tyrrell's criterion of the truth of Christian dogmas and beliefs "is simply the practical one of proved universal religious value." But what, one may ask, if the scholar demonstrates that the "faith of millions" can indeed be wrong, since what they presently believe is based on a fiction? Tyrrell answers that "in case of conflict, he (the believer) is justified in preferring to hold on to an otherwise rationally indefensible belief until its religious value is accounted for and saved in some higher truth. . . . Faith will never allow him to deny a belief of proved religious value."[36] Take, for example, the question of historical criticism.

Certain concrete historical facts enter into our creed as matters of faith. Precisely as historical facts they concern the historian and must be criticised by his methods. But as matters of faith they must be determined by the criterion of faith, i.e. by their proved religious values as universally effectual of spiritual progress. . . . The believer will desire and endeavour to play the part of historian and to harmonise every seeming discord. . . . But he will always be justified in holding to the faith-taught facts until he is convinced that their religious value is in no way imperilled by the results of historical criticism.[37]

Tyrrell was, of course, in part right. The historian is concerned with the historical and experiential consequences of "events" and ideas irrespective of the nature of their origin. Origin does not necessarily determine value or truth. Nevertheless, Tyrrell and the other Modernists, like the Idealist theologians, paid little attention to a fundamental tenet of Christian theology—i.e., that its claims are grounded in an historical revelation, in certain facts open to the scrutiny of historical investigation. For the Christian, the birth of Jesus either was or was not a Virgin birth; if that question were judicable historically (and it probably is not), the beliefs based on either claim would be substantively affected one way or another by the historical evidence. Not so for Tyrrell; for him the historical and the religious judgment each have their place but, somehow, they never can conflict.

We must see in her (the Virgin Mary) the revelation of a new aspect of the Divine Goodness.... Who can deny that the Christian spirit has been fed and fostered by this belief? ... Yet plainly, it is not the flesh but the spirit that quickeneth; it is not the physical facts that matter, but the religious values which they symbolize.... As in other matters (e.g., in His Transfiguration and Ascension) so, too, in this, the spiritual truth is given to us not in the language of parable but in that of historical fact, *which as such is subject to the criteria of history, though as the vehicle of religious value, as the earthen vessel of a heavenly treasure, it is subject only to the criterion of faith.*[38] (Italics added.)

This practical and experiential conception of dogma which characterized Modernism was most systematically formulated by the Frenchman Édouard Le Roy. Le Roy was a distinguished mathematician turned philosopher, who sought a synthesis of Catholicism, evolution, and the vitalistic philosophy of Henri Bergson. He was Bergson's successor at the Collège de France. His book *Dogme et Critique* (1907) is the clearest philosophical expression of French Catholic Modernism and a chapter of that book entitled "What is a Dogma?" is the most succinct formulation of the Modernist view on the subject.

Le Roy rejected the scholastic conception of dogma, for he believed the attempt to formulate conceptually the truth of revelation always resulted in either a crude anthropomorphism or, if we mean by the dogmatic term something incommensurate with human experience, agnosticism. But neither of these alternatives is required if we recognize the true nature and function of dogma. So considered, it will become clear that, intellectually, dogmas function in two important ways. Negatively, they serve as protections against false beliefs. Positively, the function of dogma "is, above all, the formulation of a rule of practical conduct."[39] Take, for example, the doctrines "God is personal" and the "resurrection of Christ." Consider first the negative value of these dogmas.

On the dogma: "God is personal"—I don't see any definition of the divine personality. It tells me nothing of this personality; it doesn't reveal its nature to me; it does not furnish me with a single explicit idea. But I see very well that it says to me: "God is not a simple law, a formal category, an abstract entity...." The resurrection of Christ gives rise to the same comments. At no point does the dogma inform me ... of what comprises Jesus' second life. In a word, it doesn't communicate a concept to me. But, on the contrary, it excludes certain conceptions that I would be tempted to make for myself. Death didn't put an end to Christ's activity in the things of this world; he still intervenes and lives among us. . . .[40]

These dogmas serve to exclude certain false notions but, above all, they serve to guide us in our religious life. Dogmas are essentially prescriptive, calling us to act in a certain way. For example,

"God is personal" means "Conduct yourselves in your relation to God as you do in your relations with a human being." Similarly "God is resurrected" means "Be in regard to Him as you would have been before his death, like you are now toward a contemporary.[41]

Le Roy denied that his experiential interpretation of dogmas involved theological or historical skepticism.* Nevertheless, his agnosticism concerning the actual perfections of the divine Being and his rejection of the bodily resurrection of Christ belied his denials of skepticism. In any case, his conception of dogma was a radical innovation, incompatible with the traditional view, and perilously close to subjectivism. *Dogme et Critique* was placed on the Index in the same year in which it was published.

A further characteristic of Catholic Modernism, which clearly distinguished it from Liberal Protestantism, was the great stress the Modernists placed on the Church and the social or corporate dimension of Catholic belief and practice. A true religion proved itself by its durability in time and its universality in scope. Like Newman, Tyrrell felt strongly that *quod semper, quod ubique, quod ab omnibus* was the true test of a religion and

that no religion had greater durability and scope than Catholicism. This aspect of Modernism is especially prominent in Tyrrell's "A Letter to a Friend," which was addressed to an anonymous Catholic scholar who was drifting from the faith because of intellectual doubts. It is true, Tyrrell concedes, that if adherence to Catholicism means mental assent to a system of conceptions, then his friend should separate himself from the communion of the Church. But, Tyrrell argues, Catholicism is not primarily a theological system but "a spiritual organism in whose life we participate." The essence of the Church is not doctrine or hierarchy but "the collective subconsciousness of the 'Populus Dei'." Tyrrell asks:

Is it not because you forget this that the prospect seems to you so hopeless? Is it not because you are . . . taking no account of the inscrutable voiceless life which it (Catholicism) strives feebly to formulate of the eternal truths, the Divine instincts that work themselves out irresistibly in the heart of the whole people of God?[42]

It is this subconscious spiritual *consensus gentium* that Tyrrell identifies with Catholicism—a universal spiritual society, expressing the deepest-felt religious beliefs and hopes of the race.

To belong to this world-wide authentic and original Christian society, to appropriate its universal life as far as possible, to be fired with its best enthusiasms, to devote oneself to its services and aims is to go out of one's selfish littleness and to enter into the vast collective life—the hopes and fears and joys and sorrows, failures and successes—of all those millions who have ever borne, or bear, or shall yet bear the name Catholic, and who have in any degree lived worthy of that name.

Reasons like these may hold a man fast to

---

* He was very clear in insisting that dogma interpreted as a rule of conduct involved *implicitly* the affirmation that ultimate reality is such as to justify such conduct.

the Church by a thousand ties of affection and loyalty, of moral, religious, and Christian sentiment, which can in no way be weakened by any collapse of his intellectual formulation of Catholicism.[43]

Clearly the "friend" to whom Tyrrell was addressing these sentiments was himself. And here he sums up his understanding of what constitutes genuine Catholicism and gives his own reasons for remaining in the Church despite the "Vatican heresies."

The Outcome of Catholic Modernism.

Modernism was not a single movement, as *Pascendi gregis* would lead one to believe. However, Catholics like Loisy, Tyrrell, Le Roy, and Laberthonnière held certain things in common which gave them a sense of participation in a common cause. They all felt strongly that the Roman Church had closed its mind, and even its heart, to intellectual difficulties that were besetting the Church and which were disturbing countless loyal Catholics. Most of the Modernists were critical of Scholasticism. They felt it had served Christian apologetic well in a previous age but that its categories and doctrine were foreign to a culture whose thought forms were imbued with evolution and a vitalistic life philosophy. Tyrrell also felt that the overly intellectualistic character of scholastic theology was responsible for a drying up of the spiritual life. In addition, the Modernists were all committed to historical-critical scholarship and believed the Church could and must survive such critical analysis. In this they differed from those who lost confidence in the Church's capacity to absorb the new learning. The Modernists called for a new conception

of dogma and dogmatic development. But it is significant that they wished to preserve the dogmatic tradition, while radically reconceiving its nature experientially. In this they again represented a position between Catholic traditionalism and Protestant liberalism. The Modernist program had certain affinities with the movement, a generation later, of Christian Existentialism—especially with Bultmann's program of "demythologizing" the New Testament. Bultmann has also attempted to steer a course between orthodoxy and liberalism. The common elements in these two movements are summarized as follows by B. M. S. Reardon:

Both Bultmann and the Modernists would have agreed that the proof of the Gospel rests not in historical claims likely to satisfy the requirements of the technical historian but in its capacity to act as a medium of an actual experience. . . . Both alike are at odds with liberalism no less than with conventional orthodoxy. For they deny that the Gospel can be equated with the Jesus of History, of whom historically we know very little. . . . Moreover for the representation of Christian truth which they envisage Bultmann and his predecessors alike turn to a specific philosophy. This, in the former case, is the current existentialism of Martin Heidegger. . . . (The Modernists) turned to "Activism" or personalism . . . and to the fashionable . . . pragmatism of C. S. Pierce.[44]

Modernism represented a threat to the Roman Church, as Bultmann's program has done to orthodox Protestantism, because it aimed not at a single dogma but sought to reorient the entire theological tradition. Though the Modernists were small numerically, they were to be found in all levels of the Church—laymen, priests, and prelates* and especially in places of intellectual influence. Their importance, therefore, was disproportionate to their numbers. Modernist ideas were penetrating every stratum of the Church and society. New reviews and magazines were devoted to disseminating Modernist ideas. Among these were *Demain, Revue du Clergé français*, and the highly-esteemed *Annales de philosophie chrétienne*. The issues were soon given a public airing in the popular press. Rome faced the real possibility that Modernism might spread widely and penetrate deeply into the life of the Church. While the aged Leo XIII was still Pontiff, no urgent measures were taken. This changed with the accession of Pius X to the throne in 1903. Already in the same year five works of Loisy were placed on the Index, followed shortly after by condemnations of works by Laberthonnière and Le Roy. The most decisive measures were to wait until 1907 when Pius X had two documents prepared—a catalog of errors, modeled after Pius IX's *Syllabus of Errors*, and an encyclical.

The catalog, entitled *Lamentabili sane exitu*, condemns sixty-five Modernist "errors" concerning Sacred Scripture and the doctrinal teachings of the Church. Most of the condemned propositions were extracts from the writings of Loisy, a few from Tyrrell, and at least one from Le Roy. The decree called a halt to a genuinely historical study of the Scriptures and tradition. This is evident in the

fact that it condemned such propositions as the following:

11. Divine inspiration is not to be so extended to the whole Sacred Scripture that it renders its parts, all and single, immune from all error.

18. John claims for himself the quality of a witness concerning Christ; but in reality he is only a distinguished witness of . . . the life of Christ in the Church, at the close of the first century.

34. The critic cannot ascribe to Christ a knowledge circumscribed by no limits except on a hypothesis which cannot be historically conceived and which is repugnant to the moral sense, viz., that Christ as man had the knowledge of God and yet was unwilling to communicate the knowledge of a great many things to His disciples and to posterity.

35. Christ had not always the consciousness of His Messianic dignity.

52. It was foreign to the mind of Christ to found a Church as a Society which was to last on the earth for a long course of centuries; nay in the mind of Christ the Kingdom of Heaven together with the end of the world was about to come immediately.[45]

The wording of many of the propositions was, as in some of the cases above, a curious mixture of acceptable and unacceptable notions. But acceptance of the condemnation, as such, would clearly compromise the historian's critical freedom. For example, it is legitimate to condemn the unqualified assertion that Christ did not have a Messianic consciousness or that He thought the world was about to end "immediately." But does this mean that the critic must agree that Christ "always" had a consciousness of his Messianic dignity or was minded "to found a Church which was to last for a long course of centuries"?

Two months later appeared the Encyc-

* Estimates range from forty thousand priests to a few hundred priests and laymen. Loisy's estimate of "fifteen hundred at the most" is probably a fair guess. Daniel-Rops remarks that in France, where Modernism had its widest following, the movement was lead by "no more than half a dozen men."

lical *Pascendi dominici gregis.* The encyclical letter expounds at great length the theoretical principles underlying the Modernist position, replies with a re-affirmation of the Church's traditional teaching, and concludes by enumerating certain specific steps to be taken to remedy the growing contagion. Among these practical remedies was the order that scholastic philosophy be made the basis of the sacred sciences; that anyone tainted with Modernism be excluded without compunction from teaching and administrative positions in seminaries and Catholic universities; that Bishops must hinder the publication of Modernist writings and not permit such literature to be read by seminarists and university students; and that Vigilance Committees be instituted to collect evidence of Modernist writing or teaching.[46]

Three years later, in 1910, these measures were strengthened by the imposition of the anti-Modernist oath (the *Motu Proprio Sacrarum antistitum*). This was a detailed statement which was required to be signed by all priests and is still required of all candidates for the priesthood before ordination. It includes submission to *Lamentabili* and the Encyclical *Pascendi* and acceptance of certain other theological doctrines.

With the anti-Modernist oath, Modernism came to an end within the Roman Church. By this time Loisy was excommunicated, Tyrrell was dead, and their works, as well as those of Le Roy and Laberthonnière, were on the Index. Several of the Modernist journals, by now under condemnation, ceased publishing. Most of the Modernists followed the lead of Le Roy and Laberthonnière by denouncing their errors and giving their unreserved submission to the Pope.

Only a few dozen priests left the Church. The Modernists were totally defeated, since the result of their efforts was a Church more deeply committed to entrenched positions, with strong safeguards against any differences of viewpoint. Catholic biblical scholarship was not to recover any real vitality until after World War II. Critical scholarship was severely limited.

The measures taken by Pius X were drastic, as acknowledged even by Catholic historians, and the cost of such action to the Roman Church is difficult to assess. The Modernist crisis did usher in a reaction in the Church which, in some instances, led to zealous heresy-hunting, calumny, and persecution. This movement of extreme reaction is referred to as "Integrism," due to the over-zealous efforts on the part of those involved to protect the integrity of the Catholic faith. Many innocent priests of unimpeachable orthodoxy suffered the loss of positino and reputation as a result of this new reign of fear and authoritarianism.

However, it is the view of Catholic scholars today that Pius X's action saved the Church from serious error and that, if the crushing of Modernism stifled creative, progressive thought in the Roman Catholic Church for a period of time, it certainly did not kill it. This is evident, for example, in the appearance of Karl Adam's popular *The Spirit of Catholicism* as early as 1929. In that book Adam reinterprets the decrees of Pius X in such a way as to give new scope for critical scholarship. "The Church," writes Adam,

cannot possibly be an enemy to sober criticism, least of all to the so-called historico-critical method. Even the much-attacked anti-modernist encyclical of Pope Pius X and the anti-modernist oath, do not forbid this method, but rather presuppose it. What they forbid is simply this, that men should make the affirmation of supernatural faith dependent exclusively on the results of this method.[47]

Today a great many distinguished Catholic theologians and scholars readily admit that the Modernists were right on one score at least: that there *were* serious intellectual difficulties facing the Church *and* that with the condemnation of Modernism these problems merely went underground, only to re-emerge more recently. It is also widely conceded that the Modernists were right in certain of their aims and that these can be and now are legitimately pursued. Daniel-Rops contends that the Modernist error was originally tactical, only subsequently degenerating into a doctrinal one, but that this is

no reason for rejecting what was useful and necessary in the desire to enable Christianity to resist her enemies by adopting their own weapons and methods. The condemnation fixed the limits beyond which a Catholic cannot go without falling into error; it did not forbid Catholics to tread the road along which the Modernists had gone too far. So true is this that it would be easy to show how certain currents of thought, which can be reasonably said to be more or less descended from Modernism, are today accepted by the Church.[48]

It is not quite correct, then, to say that the Modernist movement was completely killed in the Roman Church. Its aims and influence are still present and the more recent doctrines of men like Emmanuel Mounier (1905–1950) and Teilhard de Chardin (1881–1955) have some of their roots in the earlier Modern-

ism. Modernism did, however, have a more immediate influence outside Roman Catholicism, especially on the newly emerging Liberal High Anglicanism in England.

Liberal Anglo-Catholicism

Lux Mundi. Except for the biblical scholarship of the Cambridge scholars Lightfoot, Westcott, and Hort, English theology did not give evidence of much creativity in the years immediately following *Essays and Reviews* and *The Origin of Species*. With few exceptions, the mood was one of conservatism. However, there were younger men who were not satisfied with either the theological liberalism of a Jowett or the conservatism of Pusey and H. P. Liddon. These men were concerned to preserve Catholic belief and practice and yet make it consistent with modern intellectual progress. Their program was made public with the appearance of *Lux Mundi* in 1889. Like *Essays and Reviews*, this book was a collection of essays. The contributors included, among others, Charles Gore (1853–1932), Henry Scott Holland (1847–1918), J. R. Illingworth (1848–1915) and R. C. Moberly (1845–1903). These men came to be known as the *Lux Mundi* group and their particular brand of "Liberal Catholicism" continues to go by that name.

The contributors to *Lux Mundi* were all devoted High Anglicans, and several of them were close friends of older, conservative Anglo-Catholics, such as Liddon. Yet they saw the need for change, and their dual allegiance is well expressed in Gore's Preface to the book:

We have written then in this volume not as "guessers at truth" but as servants of the

Catholic Creed and Church, aiming only at interpreting the faith we have received. On the other hand, we have written with the conviction that the epoch in which we live is one of profound transformation, intellectual and social, abounding in new needs, new points of view, new questions; and certain, therefore, to involve great changes in the outlying departments of theology. . . . This is to say that theology must take a new development.[49]

What strikes the reader at once is the free and creative response of the writers to biblical criticism, evolution, and Idealism. Herein lies the "Liberal" component of their Catholicism. Idealism was dominant at Oxford in the years just before and after *Lux Mundi*, especially in the teaching of F. H. Bradley and T. H. Green. Scott Holland and Illingworth were considerably influenced by these Idealists. The use of evolutionary categories in the formulation of a new Christian apologetic is especially noticeable in the essays by Aubrey Moore ("The Christian Doctrine of God"), E. S. Talbot ("Preparation in History for Christ"), and Illingworth ("The Incarnation and Development"). Hegelian and evolutionary language is particularly striking in the latter's essay, which begins with the following acknowledgment:

The last few years have witnessed the gradual acceptance by Christian thinkers of the great scientific generalization of our age . . . the Theory of Evolution. History has repeated itself, and another of the "oppositions of science" to theology has proved upon inquiry to be no opposition at all. Such oppositions and reconciliations are older than Christianity and are part of what is often called the dialectical movement . . . out of which all progress comes. But the result of such process is something more than mere repetition of a twice-told tale. It is an advance in our theological

thinking; a definite increase of insight; a fresh and fuller appreciation of those "many ways" in which "God fulfils Himself" . . . . Evolution is in the air. It is the category of the age. . . . We cannot place ourselves outside it, or limit the scope of its operation.[50]

According to Illingworth, what evolution contributed most to theology was the rediscovery of the Divine *immanence*, the creative Logos of Greek theology. This new organic teleology

is in perfect harmony with our Christian creed, that all things were made by the Eternal Reason, but more than this, it illustrates and is illustrated by the further doctrine of His indwelling presence in the things of His creation; rendering each of them at once a revelation and a prophecy, a thing of beauty and finished workmanship, worthy to exist for its own sake, and yet a step to higher purposes, an instrument of grander work.[51]

According to Illingworth, it is in such terms that we should interpret the long, developmental preparation for the coming of the Incarnation, the divine man who has initiated a new species in the process of spiritualization.

Species once developed are seen to be persistent in proportion of their universality, their power, i.e. of adapting themselves to changes of the world around them. . . . Now in scientific language, the Incarnation may be said to have introduced a new species into the world —a Divine man transcending past humanity, as humanity transcended the rest of the animal creation, and communicating His vital energy by a spiritual process to subsequent generations of men. And thus viewed, there is nothing unreasonable in the claim of Christianity to be at least as permanent as the race which it has raised to a higher power, and endued with a novel strength.[52]

This bald use of current science and

philosophy in the defense of Christianity clearly set the *Lux Mundi* group apart from their conservative predecessors in the Anglo-Catholic movement. So also did their openness to biblical criticism. This was most evident in Gore's essay on "The Holy Spirit and Inspiration." What was significant about Gore's essay was not only what he said but the fact that *he* said it. Gore was a High Anglican and, at the time of *Lux Mundi*, the first Principal of Pusey House! It is believed that H. P. Lidden was so shocked and grieved by Gore's contribution that it hastened his death.

Accepting the idea of development, Gore acknowledged that the Old Testament contained limitations and defects. The work of the Spirit is gradual and it is therefore to be expected that there would be degrees of inspiration in the Old Testament, since it is the record of the long spiritual history of Israel; also, that not all the Old Testament narratives are historical.

Within the limits of what is substantially historical, there is still room for an admixture of what, though marked by spiritual purpose, is yet not strictly historical—for instance, for a feature which characterizes all early history, the attribution to the first founders of what is really the remoter result of their institutions.[53]

Here Gore showed that he had been influenced by the most up-to-date research on Hebrew origins. He acknowledged that the history of the Patriarchs was "idealized," that Genesis contained myth, and that the stories in Jonah and Daniel were "drama," not history.

What caused special offense was the fact that Gore questioned the historicity of narratives which were clearly considered historical by Jesus. Gore faced the problem squarely. He contended that the fact that Jesus read portions of the Old Testament as history does not require that we do the same. Jesus' view of the Old Testament does not foreclose a critical study of that literature, for "if He had intended to convey instruction to us on critical and literary questions, He would have made His purpose plainer." Jesus was clearly mistaken in certain judgments and limited in knowledge. At this point Gore introduced an idea that he was to develop at greater length later—a *kenotic* theory of the Incarnation. That is, that the knowledge possessed by Christ during His Incarnate life was limited because, in taking to Himself human nature, God actually emptied Himself of his omniscience and omnipotence. Christ revealed God, but "the Incarnation was a self-emptying (kenosis) of God to reveal himself under conditions of human nature and from the human point of view." And therefore Christ makes

His Godhead gradually manifest by His attitude towards men and things about Him, by His moral and spiritual claims . . . not by any miraculous exemptions of Himself from the conditions of natural knowledge in its own proper province.[54]

Gore's essay was distressing to many, for not only did it challenge certain claims concerning the veracity of Scripture but appeared to undermine belief in Christ's divine authority as a teacher. It forced a new consideration of the meaning of the traditional Christological formulas. For these reasons and because of the Idealism and evolutionary language of some of the essays, *Lux Mundi* was criticized, not always undeservedly. Nevertheless, *Lux Mundi* was not a radical movement within Catholicism, a was Modernism. The *Lux Mundi* group placed very real limits on their criticism. This is especially evident in Gore's attitude toward the New Testament. After acknowledging the historical difficulties encountered in certain portions of the Old Testament, Gore claims that such historical questions are not similarly met within the New Testament.

The reason is of course obvious enough why what can be admitted in the Old Testament, could not without results disastrous to the Christian Creed, be admitted in the New. It is because the Old Testament is the record of how God produced a need, or anticipation, or ideal, while the New Testament records how in fact He satisfied it. The absolute coincidence of idea and fact is vital in the realization, not in the preparation for it.[55]

If *Lux Mundi* represented a new Liberal Catholicism, it was a liberalism within what now appears to be prescribed limits. The attitude of Gore and most of his associates toward the New Testament and the Creeds was conservative. The Creeds, in the words of A. R. Vidler, were "to be accepted as statements of finally revealed truth . . . and irreformable" and it was believed that "the historical propositions in the Creed could be verified by the ordinary methods of historical inquiry."[56] Such a position could not long be maintained in light of the increasing critical work being done on the New Testament and early Christianity. At the turn of the century the work of Harnack, Schweitzer, Loisy, and other continental scholars became known in England. Gore's Liberal Catholicism soon represented an entrenched orthodoxy and Gore himself became a Bishop rather impatient of views which exceeded the critical bounds

which he himself had set thirty years earlier.

Essays Catholic and Critical. By this time a type of Liberal Catholicism was emerging in England which represented a more thorough-going reinterpretation of the Catholic tradition. This new movement was in basic sympathy with the principles of Roman Modernism, especially with the writings of Tyrrell and Le Roy. Its attitude toward New Testament criticism tended to be radical. The key to this new Anglo-Catholicism was the important place it gave to religious experience. Therefore, it has been appropriately referred to as "Empirical Catholicism." Its leader was E. G. Selwyn (1885–1959), whose editorship of *Theology* after 1920 gave the movement a public forum. Selwyn has given us his own perceptive statement of the differences between his Liberal Catholicism and that represented by Gore and *Lux Mundi*.

These two schools may be distinguished for convenience as the historical and analytical. The historical school, of which Dr. Gore is the foremost living exponent, takes its stand upon that element of simple testimony which is the original nucleus of the Gospel and which consists for the most part of historic propositions and it proceeds both to verify these facts by the recognized methods of historical inquiry and to draw out their doctrinal significance. The analytical school, on the other hand, works in to history rather than out from it. It regards the creedal statements as in the first instance as symbols of spiritual experience; and its first concern is with those *credenda* which lie closest to this experience, irrespective of whether they contain an historical element or not. Furthermore, it insists very strongly that the Creeds should not be isolated from the rest of the thought process of which they form part, as though they were *sui generis*. Symbols of equal significance and truth may be found in liturgical forms, for instance, or in beliefs which never received formal definition.[57]

This new Anglican position was worked out in a series of books by Selwyn, A. E. J. Rawlinson (1884–1960) and Will Spens (1882–1962) in the first three decades of this century. The monument of this program was the symposium *Essays Catholic and Critical* (1926), edited by Selwyn. The title sums up nicely the allegiance of the contributors and their conviction that the two components could be creatively joined together.

What distinguished this Liberal Catholicism from the Catholicism of the Tractarians and *Lux Mundi* was the significant role it gave to *religious experience* in questions of authority and dogma. This is evident, for example, in the several writings of Rawlinson on the question of religious authority.

Rawlinson acknowledged that religious belief, in the first instance, is accepted on authority and that one is always responsible to "pay reasonable deference to the wider wisdom of the community." But, at the same time, he made it clear that the older oracular conception of authority, whether of Pope, Church, Councils, or Bible, was no longer acceptable. External authority can no longer be its own guarantee. "It is doubtful," Rawlinson argues, "whether those who have accepted their beliefs on authority could continue to hold them, if the experience of life appeared flatly to contradict them". The tenacity of beliefs held originally

"merely on authority" is to be explained by the fact that the beliefs in question have mediated to those who entertain them a spiritual

experience—valuable and precious beyond everything else which life affords—of the genuineness of which they are quite certain, and with the validity of which they believe the truth of the beliefs in question to be bound up.[58]

Rawlinson essentially agrees with Tyrrell's pragmatic verification of dogma in the "faith of millions." The Modernist position

suggests that in such religious beliefs or religious practices as are discovered in experience both to exhibit "survival value" and also to be manifestly fruitful in the mediation of spiritual life of an intrinsically valuable kind, there is enshrined, at the least, some element of truth or of spiritual reality.[59]

The difficulty with Tyrrell's verification principle is that it may well show that enduring beliefs contain *some* element of truth, but it does not resolve that real modern difficulty posed by the plurality of rival claimants for a man's religious commitment. Tyrrell's stress on religious experience must be supplemented by additional tests.

The final appeal is to the spiritual, intellectual and historical content of divine revelation, *as verified at the three-fold bar of history, reason and spiritual experience.*[60]

Rawlinson returns to this same point in his otherwise appreciative analysis of Le Roy's *Dogme et Critique* in *Dogma, Fact and Experience*. Le Roy's statement that dogma, interpreted as a rule of conduct, *involves* the implicit affirmation that ultimate reality is such as to justify such conduct, is correct as far as it goes. But for Rawlinson it only raises the problem and does not resolve it. To claim that experience warrants belief that one's religion accords with objective reality may satisfy the convinced believer, but it does not constitute an effective basis for an appeal to anyone not already within the Christian fold. "We may take the efficacy of Christianity and the witness of Christian experience as our starting-point," writes Rawlinson,

but as we pursue the argument, we shall be driven either to asperse the validity of that experience, and to deny that it is what it appears and claims to be, or else to affirm the truth of the Gospel, at once historical and dogmatic, as its only sufficient ground and explanation.[61]

Experience must be put to the test of history and reason.

Since the time of *Essays Catholic and Critical*, liberal Anglican apologetic has been characterized by a strong appeal to religious experience—experience grounded in and tested by the results of a rigorous historical inquiry and rational coherence. Anglican Catholicism has taken new forms since the 1920's, but it owes considerable debt to the liberal Anglo-Catholics of that day for advancing critical freedom in the study of the

New Testament and for giving wider scope and flexibility to theological doctrine by anchoring it in an experiential base. This has freed liberal Anglicanism from both biblicism and authoritarianism. On the other hand, its Catholicism has spared Anglicanism from the reductionism so prevalent in the various forms of liberal Protestantism.

The abiding contributions of Modernist and Liberal Catholicism are many. Among the most significant are a radical freedom in biblical studies; the importance given to experience in consideration of religious truth and dogma, i.e., the role of religious devotion, the *lex orandi*, in the life of theology; a new understanding of religious authority and, perhaps above all, the profound awareness of the corporate nature and values of religion. These insights have had an influence on Christian life and thought far beyond the confines of the Roman and Anglican communions and have afforded many individuals a viable position between the alternatives of orthodox traditionalism and heterodox liberalism. A comparable alternative was offered with the emergence of Neo-Orthodoxy in the 1920's.

NOTES

1. Lord Acton, *History of Freedom and Other Essays* (1907), p. 489.
2. J. H. Newman, *The Development of Christian Doctrine* (London, 1960), p. 30.
3. Henri Daniel-Rops, *A Fight for God* (London, 1966), p. 215.
4. A Loisy, *Mémoires I* (1930), p. 118.
5. A. Loisy, *The Gospel and the Church*, tr. Christopher Home, 2d English ed. (London, 1908), p. 4.
6. Ibid., p. 8.
7. Ibid., pp. 11–12.
8. Ibid., p. 13.
9. Ibid., p. 19.
10. Ibid., p. 66.
11. Ibid., p. 72.
12. Ibid., p. 86.
13. Ibid., p. 96.
14. Ibid., p. 113.
15. Ibid., pp. 115–116.
16. Ibid., p. 150.
17. Ibid., pp. 166–167.
18. Ibid., p. 210.
19. Ibid., p. 175.

20. Ibid., pp. 210–211.
21. Ibid., pp. 216–217.
22. Ibid., pp. 224–225.
23. E. E. Y. Hales, *The Catholic Church in the Modern World* (London, 1958), p. 192.
24. *A Letter to a Friend*, *A Professor of Anthropology in a Continental University* (1903), p. 44.
25. Loisy, *Mémoires* III, p, 127.
26. See A. Vidler, *The Modernist Movement in the Roman Church* (Cambridge, 1934), pp. 179–181 for a brief comparison of the Modernism of Loisy and Tyrrell.
27. G. Tyrrell, *Christianity at the Crossroads* (London, 1963), pp. 25–26.
28. Ibid., p. 22.
29. Ibid., p. 49.
30. Ibid., pp. 63–65.
31. Ibid., pp. 80–82.
32. Letter to Baron F. von Hügel, Feb. 10, 1907, in *George Tyrrell's Letters*, ed. M. D. Petrie (London, 1920), p. 57.
33. Ibid., pp. 59–60. See *Lex Orandi*, Chap. XXIII.
34. *Lex Orandi* (London, 1903), p. 55. See *Christianity at the Crossroads*, op. cit., pp. 80–87.
35. Ibid., p. 58.
36. Ibid., pp. 167–168.
37. Ibid., pp. 169–170.
38. Ibid., pp. 175–176.
39. *Dogme et Critique* (Paris, 1907), p. 25.
40. Ibid., pp. 19–20.
41. Ibid., p. 25.

42. *A Letter to a Friend*, op. cit., p. 21.
43. Ibid., p. 25.
44. "Demythologizing and Catholic Modernism," *Theology*, Vol. LIX (Nov. 1956).
45. *Lamentabili Sane Exitu*, in Paul Sabatier, *Modernism* (London, 1908), App. III, pp. 217 ff.
46. Ibid., pp. 324 ff.
47. *The Spirit of Catholicism* (New York, 1958), pp. 231–232. I am indebted to A. Vidler's *The Modernist Movement in the Roman Church* for this reference.
48. *A Fight for God*, op. cit., p. 237.
49. *Lux Mundi*, ed. Charles Gore, 15th ed. (London, 1904), p. VIII.
50. Ibid., p. 132.
51. Ibid., p. 139.
52. Ibid., pp. 151–152.
53. Ibid., p. 259.
54. Ibid., p. 265.
55. Ibid., p. 260.
56. A. R. Vidler, *The Modernist Movement in the Roman Church*, p. 249.
57. E. G. Selwyn, *An Approach to Christianity* (London, 1925), p. 245.
58. A. E. J. Rawlinson, "Authority as a Ground of Belief" in *Essays Catholic and Critical*, ed. E. G. Selwyn (London, 1926), p. 92.
59. Ibid.
60. Ibid., p. 95.
61. *Dogma, Fact and Experience* (London, 1915), p. 52.

SUGGESTIONS FOR FURTHER READING

CATHOLIC MODERNISM

For a general survey of the history of Roman Catholicism in the nineteenth and twentieth centuries, E. E. Y. Hales, *The Catholic Church in the Modern World* (New York: Doubleday, 1960), is recommended. For brief accounts of Modernism by Catholic historians see Hales and Henri Daniel-Rops, *A Fight for God* (New York: Dutton, 1966).

Some of the best studies of Catholic Modernism are in French. These include:

Poulat, Emile. *Histoire, Dogme et Critique dans la Crise Moderniste* (Paris, 1962).

Rivière, Jean. *Le Modernisme dans l'Église* (Paris, 1929).

The following studies are especially recommended:

Petre, M. D. *Alfred Loisy: His Religious Significance* (Cambridge: Cambridge University Press, 1944).

Petre, M. D., ed. *Autobiography and Life of George Tyrrell*, 2 vols. (London, 1913).

———. *Modernism: Its Failure and Its Fruits* (London: T. C. and E. C. Jack, Ltd., 1918).

Ratté, John. *Three Modernists* (New York: Sheed and Ward, 1967). An excellent up-to-date study of Loisy, Tyrrell, and William L. Sullivan.

Vidler, A. R. *The Modernist Movement in the Roman Church* (Cambridge: Cambridge University Press, 1934).

LIBERAL ANGLO-CATHOLICISM

Carpenter, James. *Gore: A Study in Liberal Catholic Thought* (London, Faith Press, 1960).

Knox, W. L. and Vidler, A. R. *The Development of Modern Catholicism* (Cambridge: Cambridge University Press, 1923).

Mozley, J. K. *Some Tendencies in British Theology from the Publication of "Lux Mundi" to the Present Day* (London: S.P.C.K., 1951).

Ramsey, A. M. *From Gore to Temple* (London: Longmans, Green, 1960).

CHAPTER ELEVEN

Neo-Orthodoxy

Karl Barth

The greatness of Ritschlian Liberalism is in large measure traceable to its appeal to history. The Hegelians and the Catholic Modernists saw the truth of Christianity in its sublime ideas and were frequently unconcerned with whether or not these truths were anchored in concrete historical events of the past. The Ritschlians believed that the uniqueness of Christianity lay in its claim to be an historical revelation and that its truth could be shown by an appeal to the assured results of historical scholarship. The Ritschlians believed it was only by such an appeal to history itself that Christianity could be rescued from the wildest fancies of myth-makers and speculative theologians. As Harnack remarked,

"How do we gain a basis for a reliable and common knowledge of (Jesus Christ) except through a critical-historical study —in order not to exchange a dreamed-up Christ for the real one?"

As we have seen, the watchword of the Ritschlian movement was "from the Christ of dogma to the Jesus of history." Of course, not all those involved in "the quest of the historical Jesus" in the late nineteenth century were Ritschlians and many of the "Lives of Jesus" produced during this period lacked the subtle historical sense of Ritschlians like Harnack. Nevertheless, there was a common conviction that it was possible, through historical-critical research, to extract from the New Testament sources an accurate picture of the historical figure of Jesus in order to make a clear distinction between the religion of Jesus and the theology of the early Christian community. In the words of Schweitzer, the Liberals "were eager to picture Him as truly and purely human, to strip from him the robes of splendor with which he had been apparelled, and clothe him once more with the coarse garments in which he had walked in Galilee."[1]

Some of the liberal "lives of Jesus" were bald attempts to provide Christianity with an impregnable basis or proof by grounding its claims in empirical history. Most of the Ritschlians were true heirs of Luther and, therefore, recognized that such a "proof" was the very antithesis of genuine faith.* Rather, they were interested in freeing faith from the shackles of dogma and ecclesiastical tradition so that it might be encountered by its true object, the gospel of Jesus Christ. This was a noble task but, as historical-critical research was to demonstrate, the liberal quest of the historical Jesus was to prove untenable on scholarly grounds. Ironically, the demise of Ritschlian Liberalism came at the hands of historical criticism itself.

The New Historical Understanding of Christianity

In the last decades of the nineteenth century, and continuing for the first two or three decades of the twentieth century, three movements dominated biblical scholarship. These were 1. the thoroughgoing eschatological interpretation of primitive Christianity carried out by Johannes Weiss (1863–1914) and Albert

Schweitzer (1875–1965); 2. the *Religionsgeschichtliche Schule* or History of Religion School, as exemplified in the works of the biblical scholars Hermann Gunkel (1862–1932), Wilhelm Bousset (1865–1920), and the historian Ernst Troeltsch (1865–1923); and 3. *Formgeschichte* or Form Criticism which dominated the New Testament researches of K. L. Schmidt (1891–1956), Martin Dibelius (1883–1947) and Rudolf Bultmann (1884–   ). These movements played a considerable role in the decline of Ritschlian Liberalism and in preparing the way for Neo-Orthodoxy* after World War I.

The Eschatological Interpretation of Weiss and Schweitzer. There were a few theologians at the close of the nineteenth century who regarded Harnack's portrayal of Jesus as the perfect image of bourgeois moral idealism and as the embodiment of Harnack's own liberal world-view. These theologians were conscious of the great distance that separated the world-view of first-century Palestine from that of nineteenth-century Europe. As historians they were concerned to put aside their own modern preconceptions and place Jesus squarely in *his* own time and environment. They believed that when this was done Jesus and his message could be properly understood only in the context of late Jewish apocalypticism. Assuming such a perspective, the Ritschlian version of Jesus' message of the Kingdom of God was considered historically untenable. This point of view was first put forward by Johannes Weiss in a pamphlet entitled *Jesus' Preaching of the Kingdom of God* (1892). According to Weiss, there is no

---

* This was a constant theme in the writings of Wilhelm Herrmann.

* Also referred to as the Theology of Crisis, Dialectical Theology, and Theology of the Word.

evidence that Jesus conceived of the Kingdom of God as an enduring and progressively extended earthly community. Rather, Jesus looked to an imminent and catastrophic end of the present age and to the inauguration of a supernatural new creation. Jesus did not inaugurate the Kingdom but heralded its coming and finally, in desperation, gave his life to hasten its arrival in the expectation that he would return again to rule as the apocalyptical Son of Man.

Weiss' depiction of the mission and message of Jesus led to the thorough-going or "consistent eschatalogical interpretation" of the New Testament that received its classic expression in Albert Schweitzer's *The Quest of the Historical Jesus* (1906) and, more recently, in Martin Werner's *The Formation of Christian Dogma*. In the words of a contemporary New Testament scholar, Schweitzer's book proved to be both the "memorial" to the liberal lives of Jesus and their "funeral oration."[2] Noble and sincere as were the modern efforts to depict the historical Jesus, they were, nevertheless, a failure. For in each case the Jesus who emerges from the quest was portrayed largely in terms reflecting the historians' own modern philosophy of life. Each historian created Jesus in accordance with his own character. Schweitzer concludes his great work with the following pronouncement:

The Jesus of Nazareth who came forward publicly as the Messiah, who preached the ethic of the Kingdom of God, who founded the Kingdom of Heaven on earth, and died to give His work its final consecration, never had any existence. He is a figure designed by rationalism, endowed with life by liberalism, and clothed by modern theology in an historical garb.

This image has not been destroyed from without, it has fallen to pieces, cleft and disintegrated by the concrete historical problems which came to the surface one after another, and in spite of all the artifice, art, artificiality and violence which was applied to them, refused to be planed down to fit the design on which the Jesus of theology . . . had been constructed.

Whatever the ultimate solution may be, the historical Jesus of whom the criticism of the future . . . will draw the portrait can never render modern theology the services which it claimed from its own half-historical, half-modern, Jesus. . . . He will not be a Jesus Christ to whom the religion of the present can ascribe, according to its long-cherished custom, its own thoughts and ideas, as it did with the Jesus of its own making. Nor will He be a figure which can be made by a popular historical treatment so sympathetic and universally intelligible to the multitude. The historical Jesus will be to our own time a stranger and an enigma. . . . He passes by our time and returns to his own.[3]

Like Weiss, Schweitzer saw Jesus as a man of his own time, a product of Jewish apocalypticism who mistakenly conceived of the end of the world as imminent and who saw in his own death the beginning of the long-expected apocalyptical tribulations. Such a Jesus is totally foreign to our modern world, and it was the great mistake of Ritschlian theology "to suppose that Jesus could come to mean more to our time by entering into it as a man like ourselves."[4] Indeed, the whole Ritschlian appeal to the court of historical confirmation was both impossible and misguided. It was impossible because the Jesus they portrayed never existed; misguided because, in Schweitzer's opinion, the foundation of Christianity is independent of any historical warrant. According to Schweitzer, "Jesus means something to our world because a mighty spiritual force streams forth from Him and flows through our time also. This fact can neither be shaken or confirmed by an historical discovery."[5] The historical Jesus must remain for us an enigma, but his message of active love calls us, as of old it called those by the lake-side.

He speaks to us the same word: "Follow thou me!" and sets us the tasks which He has to fulfil for our time. He commands and to those who obey Him, whether they be wise or simple, He will reveal himself in the toils, the conflicts, the sufferings which they shall pass through in His fellowship, and, as an ineffable mystery, they shall learn in their own experience Who He is.[6]

Such was Schweitzer's response to the liberal quest of the historical Jesus. It was an appeal to a form of Christ-mysticism, which was freed from the outmoded apocalyptical world-view of the historical Jesus and the early Christian community.

The Religionsgeschichtliche Schule. The historians who opposed the liberal "lives of Jesus" argued that those selective reconstructions of Jesus' life were governed by presuppositions of the historian's own time and culture. A new generation of historical critics now sought to explain Jesus solely in terms of his own time. As we have seen, Weiss and Schweitzer viewed Jesus from the perspective of late Jewish apocalypticism. The historians who came to be identified with the movement known as the "History of Religions" school sought to interpret Jesus and early Christianity by reference to the beliefs and practices of late Hellenism. The Ritschlians had appealed to history but, in the judgment of men like Gunkel and

Bousset, to a very limited and provincial conception of history. Ritschl and his followers viewed Christianity as an isolated phenomenon and emphasized its historical uniqueness. For the scholars of the History of Religions school, such a conception of Christianity was extraordinarily unhistorical. In their opinion, early Christianity, when examined in the context of its environment, does not emerge as an absolutely unique reality but as a complex "syncretistic religion," the product of Late Judaism, Oriental eschatology, the Greek mysteries, Gnosticism, and Stoicism. It was Christianity's good fortune to come at a time when these Western and Oriental ideas were converging and in need of a fresh synthesis. Christianity served this purpose. In the words of Wilhelm Heitmuller:

Early Christianity lived in the atmosphere which was saturated by Mystery-bacilli and grew up in a soil which had been fertilized and broken up by the decay and syncretism of the most varied religions, a soil which was thus especially fitted to provide new life for old seeds and shoots.[7]

In his book *Kyrios Christos*, Bousset developed the thesis that Jesus came to be called *Kyrios* or Lord only when Christianity left Palestine and entered the environment of Hellenism. There Jesus was worshiped like the pagan cult dieties, fulfilling a similar function. Bousset and his colleagues concentrated on the cultic and sacramental life of early Christianity and stressed the similarities between the Christian rites and those of the Mystery religions. The result of these comparative studies was, of course, to call into question the distinctive character of Christianity and, particularly, its unique revelatory claims. Christianity was to be assigned its place in the natural evolution of man's beliefs and practices. The implication was that Christianity is a *relativistic* phenomenon in the process of historical evolution.

The theoretician of the *Religionsgeschichtliche Schule* was the brilliant historian and philosopher Ernst Troeltsch. It was Troeltsch who devoted his vast energies to the resolution of the problem of historicism (or historical relativism) and the absolute claims of Christianity. He struggled with this issue in his great work, *Der Historismus und seine Probleme* (1921), and in several important monographs but never achieved a satisfactory solution. At the close of his career he espoused a religious relativism. Troeltsch exemplifies better than anyone else the impasse reached by those who, while accepting radical historicism, attempted to develop a constructive Christian theology.

In his book *The Absoluteness of Christianity and the History of Religions* (1902), Troeltsch criticized Harnack's attempt in *What Is Christianity?* to define historically the essence of Christianity. According to Troeltsch, there is no essence of Christianity, for Christianity is an open-ended historical development and in such a historical process there is no essence. Essence implies some abstraction, but Christianity cannot be reduced to an abstracted idea.

Christianity is its history, its totality.

Thus the essence of Christianity can be understood only as the productive power of the historical Christian religion to create new interpretations and new adaptations—a power which lies deeper than any historical formulation which it may have produced. In this sense the essence of Christianity differs in different epochs, and is to be understood as something involved in the totality of its active influence.[8]

Troeltsch's historical researches had convinced him that Christianity was neither a monolithic, never-changing structure, nor did it necessarily "possess the highest claim to universality of all the religions." On the contrary, like all other movements of history, Christianity is marked by its complexity and individuality. History, like the development of Christianity,

is an immeasurable, incomparable profusion of always-new, unique, and hence individual tendencies, welling up from undiscovered depths, and coming to light in each case in unsuspected places and under different circumstances. Each process works itself out in its own way, bringing ever-new series of unique transformations in its train, until its powers are exhausted, or until it enters as component material into some new combination. Thus the universal law of history consists precisely in this, that the Divine Reason or the Divine Life, within history, constantly manifests itself in always-new and always-peculiar individualizations—and hence that its tendency is not towards unity or universality at all, but rather towards the fulfillment of the highest potentialities of each separate department of life. It is this law which beyond all else makes it quite impossible to characterize Christianity as the reconciliation and goal of all the forces of history, or indeed to regard it as anything else than a historical individuality.[9]

When seen as a purely historical, and therefore individual, phenomenon one is struck by the *relative* character of Christianity. That is, Christianity as we observe it "could only have arisen in the territory of the classical culture and among the Latin and Germanic races."[10] According to Troeltsch, Christianity is indissolubly bound up with elements of

Greco-Roman and European civilization and is not conceivable when extracted from its cultural matrix. "It stands or falls with European civilization."[11]

Troeltsch was forced by his study of history to give up his earlier contention that Christianity possessed the highest claim to universality or that it could be shown to possess "the loftiest and most spiritual revelation" of all the religions. Rather, Christianity's primary claim to validity must be seen to lie in the fact that only through it have we of the West become what we are, and that only through it can we preserve those values and forces which we require.

We cannot live without a religion, yet the only religion that we can endure is Christianity, for Christianity has grown up with us and has become a part of our very being.[12]

Of course, Christianity could not have endured if it were not possessed of great spiritual power and truth. But, Troeltsch reminds us, it is a power and a truth *for us*. Christianity

is God's countenance as revealed to us; it is the way in which being what we are, we receive, and react to, the revelation of God. It is binding upon us and brings us deliverance. It is final and unconditional for us, because we have nothing else, and because in what we have we can recognize the accents of the divine voice.

But this does not preclude the possibility that other racial groups living under entirely different cultural conditions may experience their contact with the Divine Life in quite a different way.[13]

The emphasis in the History of Religions school on the environmental factors in the development of religious beliefs and practices gave impetus to a strong element of cultural determinism in Troeltsch's historicism. He believed that the great world religions were actually "crystallizations of the thought of great races," which were themselves the product of various biological and anthropological types. As a result, Troeltsch maintained that there could be "no conversion or transformation of one into the other but only a measure of agreement and of mutual understanding"[14]

The implication of such a position for the world-wide mission of Christianity is plain, i.e., such a missionary endeavor to the non-Western peoples should be brought to an end. Troeltsch certainly failed to see the incredible possibilities of cultural adaptability and change which we have observed in more recent years and was apparently blind to the remarkable adaptive powers of Christianity in cultures outside Europe during his own lifetime. This is especially surprising in light of Troeltsch's own stress on the unpredictability of historical development, and his view that history is capable of ever new individualizations. Nevertheless, his conception of culture was consistent with his radical historicism.

Troeltsch ended his famous essay on "Christianity Among the World Religions" by denying that his views constituted a position of skepticism. "A truth which . . . is *a truth for us* does not cease, because of this, to be very Truth and Life."[15] What we must learn is that in this earthly experience "the Divine Life is not One but Many" but "to apprehend the One in the Many constitutes the special character of love."[16]

Despite Troeltsch's disclaimers, his position, if not one of skepticism, did relativize Christianity in such a way as to challenge fundamental Christian claims of uniqueness and absoluteness. Taken together with Schweitzer's *Quest of the*

Historical Jesus, the work of Troeltsch brought an end to an era of Western Christian theology. Such is the judgment, for example, of Hermann Diem:

The radical dissolution of dogmatics resulting from the challenge to theology represented by historical method was taken to its extreme conclusion by Troeltsch at the very moment when historical criticism itself was prepared to declare the bankruptcy of its own attempt to establish the historical reality of Jesus. Hence it is not astonishing that *Troeltsch marked a terminal point in the history of theology from which there could be no further progress in the same line of development.*[17] (Italics added.)

Form Criticism. Form criticism or the *Formgeschichtliche Schule* appeared in the years immediately after World War I, partly in response to the impasse of the *Religionsgeschichtliche* method of New Testament research. The History of Religions school had questioned, at least tacitly, the historicity of the Gospel accounts and had concentrated on the symbolic and cultic meaning of the New Testament traditions. Due largely to disinterest, the question of the history and reliability of the Gospel traditions concerning Jesus was not pursued. The Form critics, on the other hand, addressed themselves to the very question of the origin and historical growth of the layers of literary tradition which make up the Gospels. They were raising in a new way the question of the authenticity of the Jesus tradition.

The Form critics took their lead from the Old Testament researches of Hermann Gunkel and Hugo Gressmann. These scholars had shown that the ancient folk literature of the Hebrews had 1. originally circulated as oral traditions in certain limited fixed forms or categories, and 2. that these preliterary units of tradition were the product of the daily life of the Israelitish community. That is, they served a practical purpose in the religious life of the people, in worship, instruction, and preaching.

Since it was clear that the Gospels contained tradition that was originally oral, the Form critics sought to apply these same assumptions to the study of this literature in the hope that such a method would help answer the question of the origin and growth of the Gospel traditions. The basic tenets of the Form-critical school are nicely summarized by R. H. Lightfoot, the leading English exponent of Form criticism:

The Form critics remind us that the early Church is by no means likely to have expressed itself at once in a literary way, and they believe, first, that in the earliest years memories and traditions of the words and deeds of Jesus were only handed from mouth to mouth, and secondly, that they were valued not so much . . . in and for themselves, as for their importance in solving problems connected with the life and needs of the young churches. These needs, they think, would be chiefly concerned with mission preaching, catechetical teaching . . . and perhaps above all, worship. They believe, further, that these memories and traditions . . . would gradually assume a more or less fixed shape, through constant repetition in the churches. . . . And, finally they suggest that many of these preliterary traditions are still discernible in our written Gospels . . . and that to some extent they can be classified according to their type or form.[18]

In the brief period between 1919 and 1921, three distinguished New Testament scholars applied the Form critical method to the study of the Gospels and published their results. In 1919 K. L. Schmidt published *Der Rahmen der Geschichte Jesu* in which he demonstrated the artificial and arbitrary order of the traditions in Mark and how such details as time and place represented the later additions of the evangelist, who was himself responsible for the historical order and contexts of the separate traditions.

At approximately the same time Martin Dibelius published *Die Form-geschichte des Evangeliums* (1919; E.T. *From Tradition to Gospel*, 1934). In this important work, Dibelius attempted to trace the growth of the various oral traditions that lay behind the written Gospels and to seek out the influences which determined the different forms. Dibelius found that the *Sitz im Leben* or life situation out of which the Gospel traditions arose was principally traceable to the preaching and worship of the early Christian congregations. He divided these early units of tradition (pericopes) into five "forms": paradigm, *novelle* or tales, legend, parenesis, and myth. According to Dibelius, the most important of these forms are the paradigms or brief striking sayings or deeds attributed to Jesus. These paradigms were preserved because of their continuous use in preaching but, since they exhibit the least elaboration, are our surest source of information about the historical Jesus. The tales and legends, while not unhistorical, reflect considerable editorial addition, whereas myth shows little if any interest in history at all.

The most radical approach to Form criticism was developed by Rudolf Bultmann in *Die Geschichte der synop-tischen Tradition* (1921). Bultmann divided the forms into several classes, somewhat analogous to those of Dibelius. However, Bultmann was more hesitant than Dibelius in recognizing material that could with certainty give historical information about Jesus. This is evident, for example, in the fact that Bultmann made no dis-tinction between "legend" and "histori-cal narrative."

What was relatively new, and to many unsettling, in the work of the Form critics was their evidence that the evan-gelists were editors whose redactions were clearly discernible in the Gospels, and that these collected traditions were not meant to serve principally an histori-cal or biographical purpose; rather, that the persistence of the Jesus traditions was traceable to the ultrapractical needs of the early Church. This discovery raised the specter that even the earliest Gospel tra-ditions were rooted not in the hard rock of historical fact but on the shifting ground of religious need. That is, that the Christian community constructed a por-trait of Jesus to serve its purpose and, therefore, the figure portrayed in the Gospels is not the Jesus of history but the Christ of faith. The Gospels are not historical chronicles but religious con-fessions!

All the Form critics were agreed that the reminiscences of Jesus preserved in the Gospels were refracted through the events of the crucifixion and resurrection. The Jesus preaching in Galilee, for example, is envisioned in the tradition through the eyes of the Easter faith. Fact and faith are indissolubly joined. As the Form critics expressed it, the only Jesus to be found in the Gospels is the Jesus of the *kerygma*, of the peaching of the early community.

To the question of what we have left of the historical life of Jesus, the Form critics proffered very negative replies. This was especially true of Bultmann. In his book *Jesus* (1926), he disclaimed all interest in the *life* and *personality* of Jesus and asserted:

I do indeed think that we can now know

almost nothing concerning the life and personality of Jesus, since the early Christian sources show no interest in either, are moreover fragmentary and often legendary; and other sources about Jesus do not exist.[19]

Bultmann regarded such a state of affairs as a great boon to faith. In Bultmann's view, genuine faith cannot be dependent on the contingencies of historical-critical research. To follow such a path is to seek after a "worldly" proof and security. The only Jesus Christ found in the New Testament is the kerygmatic Christ, the proclaimed Christ.

So we may not go behind the kerygma, using it as a "source"... to reconstruct an "historical Jesus." This would be precisely the "Christ according to the flesh" who is gone. It is not the historical Jesus, but Jesus Christ, the Proclaimed One, who is the Lord.[20]

The Christ that is met in the New Testament kerygma is Christ as the living Word of God.

Christ meets us in the preaching (kerygma) as one crucified and risen. He meets us in the word of preaching and nowhere else.... It would be wrong at this point to raise again the problem of how this preaching arose historically, as though that could indicate its truth. That would be to tie our faith in the word of God to the results of historical research. The word of preaching confronts us as the word of God. It is not for us to question its credentials. It is we who are questioned, we who are asked whether we will believe the word or reject it.[21]

For Bultmann the reliability of the kerygma must not be questioned, for to try to confirm it by some historical-critical test is the very sign of unfaith. Bultmann was convinced that there was an identity between the historical Jesus and the kerygmatic Christ, but he believed that the proof of such a link was both historically impossible and theologically dubious. As we shall see, the *kerygmatic theology* of Bultmann was taken up by Neo-Orthodoxy and was to resolve for many the historical question initially raised by Schweitzer's *Quest of the Historical Jesus*. For many others, however, kerygmatic theology remained unsatisfactory, for it left unresolved the gnawing question of whether the Christ of the Church's faith rested in fact on the historical Jesus of Nazareth.

The work of historians like Schweitzer, Troeltsch, and Bultmann raised in new and radical ways the question of the historical bases of Christian faith. It is interesting to observe that the radical historical conclusions of these scholars did not lead them to a repudiation of Christian faith but to responses that tended to neutralize the historical questions which they raised in such radical fashion. Schweitzer resolved the problem with a Christ-mysticism of active love. Bultmann appealed to an existential decision of faith in response to the New Testament proclamation. The view that the historical problem, so vividly exposed, was actually irrelevant to Christian faith was the position taken up by the Neo-Orthodox theologians and is important in understanding the origin and spirit of that movement.

Sources of the Theology of Crisis

Historical criticism played a major role in the emergence of Neo-Orthodoxy in the second decade of the present century, but there were other causative factors of equal importance. Not only did liberal theology come under severe historical attack, but liberal culture as a whole appeared to be in a crisis of disintegration. This crisis was dramatically exposed with the coming of World War I and the reaction to it. The horrors of the war called into question the bourgeois optimism which had assumed progressive realization of the Kingdom of God on earth. The young men who had witnessed the devastation and terrors of battle and had themselves contributed to these horrors, returned to the universities, only to be told by their theological mentors that they had fought the good fight for Christian civilization. Many of the younger German clergy recoiled from such a facile equation of Christianity and Germanic nationalism—what Overbeck called "Bismarck-religion." Karl Barth speaks of this as decisive in his own rejection of Liberalism.

The actual end of the nineteenth century as the "good old days" falls for evangelical theology, as for other things, in the fateful year 1914. . . . For me personally one day at the beginning of August that year stamped itself as *dies ater*. It was that on which 93 German intellectuals came out with a manifesto supporting the war policy of Kaiser William II and his counsellors, and among them I found to my horror the names of nearly all my theological teachers whom up to then I had religiously honoured. Disillusioned by their conduct, I perceived that I should not be able any longer to accept their ethics and dogmatics, their biblical exegesis, their interpretation of history, that at least for me the theology of the nineteenth century had no future.[22]

The stock phrases of the time which spoke of defending Christian civilization, of making the world safe for democracy, and Christianizing the social order now sounded ambiguous, if not empty. The new mood was one of realism and even pessimism, as is reflected in the eager reception of Spengler's *Decline of the West*. The younger theologians felt that if Western civilization was corrupt and decaying, then Christianity should certainly not be reconciled with it; rather, it should stand over against it in prophetic judgment!

What was felt to be wrong with late nineteenth-century culture was its defective view of man. It did not understand either the heights or depths of human life. Its conception of man was rationalistic, moralistic, and voluntaristic. It believed that man was naturally good and would follow the right if he were instructed in the right. It lacked any sense of the profound spiritual struggle in man that was central to the Pauline and Augustinian tradition and was just now being rediscovered in the theology of Luther. Bourgeois culture lacked awareness of the power of evil and of human sin. There were a few prophetic writers, like Dostoevsky, who were repulsed by the moral optimism of their day and portrayed life in its truly ambiguous and tragic depths. In his novels Dostoevsky pictured rebellious men tortured by doubt; men who could not slake their thirst for the Eternal, but neither would they confuse the awesome belief in a loving God with the moral conventions of a liberal culture. Therefore they remained alienated outcasts of society. Henrik Ibsen, too, challenged the current bourgeosie moralism. In his great plays he dramatized the hypocrisy of conventional behavior which masked perverse and even devilish motives in seemingly noble actions. No one portrayed the demonic potential of moral idealism with more force than Ibsen in *The Wild Duck* and *The Master Builder*.

The powerful realism of Dostoevsky

and Ibsen had considerable impact on the young, disaffected liberal theologians. Karl Barth's friend Eduard Thurneysen wrote a perceptive study of Dostoevsky, the influence of which Barth acknowledged in the Preface to his book on *Romans*. What Barth and Thurneysen found in Dostoevsky especially was a profound sense of what Barth was to call the "Godness of God," the awesome otherness of the divine, the *Mysterium tremendum*. Also they found a realistic picture of man as a helpless slave to sin, whose redemption lay only in the boundless grace of God's love. Here they encountered a theme which recalled the theology of the great Reformers, Luther and Calvin.

As it happened, a rediscovery of the Reformers was already taking place in Europe in the early years of the century. The work of the historian Karl Holl and others was helping to free Luther's theology from the bondage of Lutheran scholasticism and was revealing the Reformer's radical theocentrism and his profound conception of sin, faith, and grace. The study of Dostoevsky and the Reformers drove Barth and Thurneysen back to the Bible itself and especially to Paul. There they discovered a "strange new world" which had been hidden from them by the pedantry and erudition of the biblical philologists and historians. More than any other factor, Neo-Orthodoxy grew out of a passionate engagement with the Bible itself, in the fresh expectation that the Word of God would disclose itself in new and unexpected ways.

Historicism, the crisis in bourgeois culture, World War I, the discovery of prophetic voices like Dostoevsky, the Luther renaissance, and the "new" world of the Bible all contributed to the emergence of the Neo-Orthodox movement. However, no single thinker played a greater role in determining the spirit and shaping the basic motifs of Dialectical theology than the extraordinary Danish writer Søren Kierkegaard. His influence on Karl Barth and other Neo-Orthodox theologians is so decisive in the development of their own views that an examination of his thought is indispensable to an understanding of this epochal movement in theology.

Søren Kierkegaard (1813-1855)

It would appear mistaken to discuss the thought of a man who lived in the first half of the nineteenth century in the context of the beginnings of a movement in the twentieth century. But the fact is that Kierkegaard belongs more to the twentieth century than to his own in terms of the influence of his life and writings. Kierkegaard did make a considerable impression in the Denmark of his own day, but his impact outside his own country was not to come until almost a century later. When his influence was felt in Europe after World War I it was monumental. He is known today as the "father" of Christian existentialism. While this is true, he can also be considered the spiritual founder of the Dialectical theology associated with Karl Barth. The dominant motifs in the theology of the early Barth are difficult to conceive of without Kierkergaard.

Søren Kierkegaard was born in Copenhagen, Denmark, the seventh and last child of Michael Kierkegaard and Ane Lund, a woman who before becoming Michael's second wife had served as a servant in his house. Ane bore her husband a child only four months after his first wife's death. The knowledge of this later played a decisive role in Søren's own religious pilgrimage. Though Michael Kierkegaard was a wealthy merchant, he was a melancholy man who brooded over his moral lapses. The melancholy of his elderly father had an indelible effect on the young and precocious son. As a young boy Søren compensated for a crooked back and a lack of physical robustness with vast learning and a sharp wit and, at an early age, developed a sense of his own superiority.

Kierkegaard entered the University of Copenhagen in 1830 to study theology. However, his real interests were in philosophy and literature, and he completed his masters degree with a thesis on "The Concept of Irony." He also passed his examinations in theology with honors. Nevertheless, it took him ten years to complete his university education and much of that time was spent in dilettante intellectual endeavors and as a brilliant, charming man-about-town. A series of events then brought about a spiritual crisis in Kierkegaard's life which dedicated him to the problems of religious existence, specifically to what it means *to be* a Christian.

The first event was his father's confession of his moral sin committed with his servant girl Ane. The second event was Søren's broken engagement. In 1837 he had met Regine Olsen and they had fallen in love. They were engaged, but Søren immediately felt he had done the wrong thing and broke off the engagement. His reasons were never revealed, although in his *Journals* he spoke of a "divine protest." Kierkegaard's action is partly to be explained by his feeling that his own secretiveness, his inability to communicate his innermost thoughts, was incompatible with marriage. Also his

sense of uniqueness may have caused him to believe that he was called to forego marriage in order to pursue his work.

The break with Regine began what Kierkegaard was to call his "aesthetic authorship," and the works produced during this early period included *Either-Or, Repetition, Fear and Trembling,* and *Edifying Discourses.* All these books deal with Søren's relations with Regine and were written under pseudonyms. It was during this period that another crucial event determined Kierkegaard's vocation. He had written against P. L. Moller, an esthete and editor of a scandalous paper called the *Corsair.* Kierkegaard expected his attack on this libelous publication would elicit considerable support. However, this did not occur and the *Corsair* turned on him in a series of savage articles and cartoons, holding him up to public ridicule. Kierkegaard suffered a martyrdom of laughter which resulted in isolating him further from the masses, which he came to liken to a flock of dumb geese. This experience was interpreted by Kierkegaard as providential and increased his resolve to pursue his religious authorship. From 1846 until a year before his death Kierkegaard's life was outwardly uneventful, being spent almost entirely in writing. During this period he produced his two philosophical masterpieces, *Philosophical Fragments* (1844) and the *Concluding Unscientific Postscript* (1846), and innumerable religious works, including *Purity of Heart, The Concept of Dread, Sickness Unto Death, Training in Christianity,* and *For Self-Examination.*

During the last decade of his life Kierkegaard came to a profound awareness of Christian faith and that he was called to witness to this truth as he saw it. He realized this would entail suffering for him as an individual at the hands of the majority. Such, he came to believe, was the vocation of Christian discipleship. The writings of these years all point to the difficulty of becoming a Christian and the hypocrisy of conventional Christianity and the institutional Church. When even these works failed to gain a response, Kierkegaard was moved to make a direct and unsparing attack on the state Church of Denmark. The articles and pamphlets which appeared between 1854 and 1855 are published in English as *Attack upon Christendom*. What provoked Kierkegaard's initial assault was Bishop Martensen's funeral oration for Bishop Mynster in which he referred to Mynster as "a true witness to the truth," a man of humility and suffering and poverty. For Kierkegaard such a peroration was outrageous. Bishop Mynster was a clever man, very much at home in the world— a man who, in Kierkegaard's view, had nothing in common with the early martyrs. The state Church of Denmark was itself apostate, the clergy self-satisfied functionaries of the government who spent their time baptizing, marrying, and burying people who otherwise considered the ministrations of the Church irrelevant. According to Kierkegaard, where everyone is considered Christian by the conventional act of baptism, Christianity *eo ipso* does not exist.

In the New Testament the Saviour, our Lord Jesus Christ, represents the situation thus: The way that leadeth unto life is straitened, the gate narrow—few be they that find it!—Now, on the contrary, to speak only of Denmark, we are all Christians, the way is broad as it possibly can be, the broadest in Denmark, since it is the way in which we are all walking, besides being in all respects as convenient, as comfortable as possible; and the gate is as wide as it possibly can be, wider surely a gate cannot be than through which we are all going *en masse. Ergo* the New Testament is no longer truth.[23]

In Kierkegaard's view, New Testament Christianity was so foreign to the comfortable congregations of Denmark that they weren't even capable of seeing the ludicrous disparity between the primitive Christian message and the elegant preachments of their bishops.

In the magnificent cathedral the Honorable and Right Reverend *Geheime-General-Ober-Hof-Prädikant*, the elect favorite of the fashionable world, appears before the elect company and preaches *with emotion* upon the text he himself elected: "God hath elected the base things of the world, and the things that are despised." And nobody laughs.[24]

So Kierkegaard's scathing polemic continued until, at the height of his passionate attack he was stricken down with paralysis. He spent several weeks in the hospital during which time he refused to retract what he had said about the Church and refused to receive communion from a priest. He died, however, strong in his religious convictions and in a state of great spiritual peace.

The Dialectic of Existence. Kierkegaard's writings defy easy systematization, yet they are characterized by certain prominent themes.

Hegelianism was the reigning philosophy in the Denmark of Kiekegaard's day and Kierkegaard's work must be seen in large part as an effort to overthrow the rational pretensions of Hegel's theology. In fact, Kierkegaard's work can be viewed as a sustained attack on all forms of rational theology, whether it be the moral idealism of the Kantians or the absolute idealism of the Hegelians. This becomes especially clear in Kierkegaard's own existential dialectic, which he develops in his earliest writings.

Like Hegel, Kierkegaard approaches the religious problem by means of a dialectical method. But, unlike Hegel, Kierkegaard's dialectic is existential; that is, it does not move within a closed, necessary logical system but begins with the single individual confronted with the possibilities of existence. Kierkegaard's existential dialectic moves within three chief spheres: the esthetic, the ethical, and the religious. For Kierkegaard these three existential possibilities are not to be conceived of so that the third is the logical synthesis of the first two. The triadic dialectic does not imply a necessary progression, nor does it remove the necessity of facing an ultimate "either-or" leap from one stage to another. Neither does the "leap" from the ethical to the religious stage mean that the existential choice between the esthetic and religious is forever put behind. The three spheres of existence are continually present possibilities.

Kierkegaard identified the esthetic sphere of existence with Romanticist sensibility and saw this sensibility expressed in three principal moods: sensual immediacy (Don Juan), doubt (Faust), and despair (Ahasuerus, the Wandering Jew). The chief characteristic of the esthetic sphere is the lack of involvement, the sense of detachment. It is marked by an inability to make a determined and permanent decision. The esthete lacks moral will and therefore loses power over himself. He become the drifting victim of his search for the pleasurable moment, which is never satisfied. This leads to restlessness and ennui. The futility of seeking ultimate satisfaction in the immediacy of pleasurable feeling leads to the second stage of the esthetic dialectic:

the skepticism of Faust. Faustian doubt is only a qualified form of despair, for frequently it can long remain satisfied, like Lessing, with the search for truth, though skeptical of ever finding it. Nevertheless, such doubt is frequently the covering for a deeper despair.

Recognition of despair is invoked in the figure of the Wandering Jew, in whom lurks the profounder despair which results in complete absence of hope. In *Sickness unto Death*, Kierkegaard analyses the dialectic of despair with brilliant psychological insight. Kierkegaard agrees with Hegel that despair is something a man must taste before he comes to true consciousness of life. Thus despair is dialectical and not wholly negative, for it opens up divergent possibilities of response. Despair can lead to a spiritual hardening and death; it can also serve to awaken a person to his eternal validity. But there is no salvation except in passing through despair.

I counsel you to despair . . . not as a comfort, not as a condition in which you are to remain but as a deed which requires all the power and seriousness and concentration of the soul. . . . Every man who has not tasted the bitterness of despair has missed the significance of life.[25]

To despair absolutely is to break one's bondage to the finite perspective, for "when one has willed despair (absolutely) one has chosen that which despair chooses i.e., oneself in one's eternal validity."[26] Such a change does not involve a smooth dialectical mediation. There is no rational escape from the sickness unto death. Anxiety and despair simply bring one before a decision and this decision requires a "leap" to a new stage.

The leap to the ethical stage is summed up in the imperative: "choose thyself." That is, affirm an absolute choice. For

Kierkegaard the ethical life is defined not so much by the content of one's choices as by the manner of choice. To choose ethically is to choose with passion, in an unconditional way. This is the great thesis of the *Concluding Unscientific Postscript*: "The ethical demand is that one become infinitely interested in existing."[27] The aim of the ethical life, therefore, is not simply to know the truth but to become it, not to produce objective truth but to transform one's subject self: "The real subject is not the cognitive subject since *in knowing he moves in the sphere of the possible*; the real subject is the ethically existing subject."[28] According to Kierkegaard, it is ethical decision that gives a person a sense of inner coherence, as well as a task and vocation.

Kierkegaard was not an extravagant ethical intuitionist, but he believed most ethical theories were "formalistic" and thus did not give adequate consideration to the single individual and the unique situation. Ethical judgment requires reflection, but such reflection cannot overlook the uniqueness of each person and each situation. This is exactly what is wrong with most ethical systems, such as Kant's. They are overly formal and therefore cannot take into account certain indispensable existential realities. According to Kierkegaard, a moral theology like Kant's founders on two basic issues: it tends to make evil and sin superficial rather than radical, and it fails to deal adequately with the motivation or will to carry out the moral imperative. Kant erroneously assumed that the "ought implies the can." In Kantian ethics, the ethical is situated in the *ideal* (the categorical imperative) but the *real* involves sin. As Kierkegaard observed,

An ethic that ignores sin is an altogether use-less science, but if it recognizes sin it is *eo ipso* beyond its sphere. . . . Ethics fails over repentence, for repentence is the supreme expression of ethics, but as such contains the most profound ethical contradiction.[29]

Kant's theology erroneously conceived of original sin in quantitative terms. Kierkegaard on the other hand saw sin as "total guilt"—and total guilt is not a condition that can be determined by adding up particular guilty acts.

The priority of the total guilt is not to be determined empirically, for no determination of totality ever results from numerical computation. The totality of guilt comes into being for the individual when he puts his guilt together with the relation to an eternal blessedness.[30]

That is, the person who justifies himself does so by judging himself by an all-too-human standard.

Accordingly he who turns against himself with the absolute standard will naturally not be able to live on the blissful confidence that if he keeps the Commandments . . . , if he does not die too soon, will in the course of time become all too perfect for this world—on the contrary he will again and again discover guilt and again will discover it within the total definition, as guilt.[31]

To maintain a quantitative view of guilt is in Kierkegaard's opinion, to remain religiously immature.

Childishness in relation to the consciousness of guilt assumes that today it is guilty in this or that, then a week goes by when it is innocent, but then on the eighth day something went wrong again.[32]

Kantian moral theology not only makes trivial the serious human condition of sin and guilt; it also fails to deal adequately with the question of the moral will—with the power to carry out the moral imperative. The categorical imperative convinces the individual of his duty but leaves him powerless to effect it. The idealist illicitly assumes "the ought implies the can." But that which we would do we do not; sin is a surd which proves the universal imperative an ineffectual ideal. According to Kierkegaard, only the theonomous influence of grace can resolve the ethical problem. But to speak of grace is to enter the religious stage—the stage of dogmatic parergon which Kant disallowed. Kierkegaard writes:

> With dogmatics begins the science which, in contrast to that science of ethics which can strictly be called ideal, starts with reality. . . . It does not deny the presence of sin, on the contrary, it assumes it, and explains it by assuming original sin. . . . The new science begins with dogmatics. . . . One readily sees the difference of the movement, and that the ethic of which we are now speaking belongs to another order.[33]

Kierkegaard's third criticism of the ethical stage is that its formalism leaves no place for the individual exception to the universal imperative. Kierkegaard's argument for the irreducible singularity of man's status before God is portrayed most effectively in _Fear and Trembling_. There Kierkegaard offers a sustained analysis of the story of Abraham's sacrifice of his son, Isaac. For Kierkegaard, Abraham is the prototype of the _exception_, the man called by God to perform a task which is a scandal to ethical rationalism. By means of this story, Kierkegaard asks whether there can be a "teleological suspension of the ethical." Can there be situations in which one's absolute obedience to God contravenes the categorical imperative?

The answer is "yes" because, as Kierkegaard remarks, one who knows the living God "determines his relation to the universal by his relation to the absolute, not his relation to the absolute by his relation to the universal."[34]

According to Kierkegaard, Abraham is even defendable in keeping his purpose a secret before Sarah and Isaac, for the "Knight of Faith" obeys God without seeking to be justified before men. There is something unique and ineffable about one's relation to God. Both Kant and Hegel conceived of morality as the subordination of the self to the universal—at the expense, as Kierkegaard saw it, of elements indispensable to the life of the individual.

For all the reasons we have enumerated, all "first ethics" or idealistic ethics fail and require an existential leap of faith to the religious stage of existence.

Faith and the Absolute Paradox. The religious stage itself offers two possibilities—what Kierkegaard calls "Religiousness A" and "Religiousness B." In other terms, the religion of immanence and the religion of otherness, or the religion of "Socrates" and the religion of "Jesus Christ." Kierkegaard develops the distinction between these two religious options; hence his view of Christianity in the _Philosophical Fragments_. The distinction between these two options and the problem of Christianity is posed by Kierkegaard in the title page motto of the book:

> Is an historical point of departure possible for eternal consciousness; how can such a point of departure have any other than a mere historical interest; is it possible to base an eternal happiness upon historical knowledge?[35]

Here Kierkegaard raises in the form of a question the thesis that Lessing had put to Christianity as a fact: "Incidental truths of history can never furnish the proof of necessary truths of reason."

Kierkegaard begins this "project of thought" with the Socratic problem, "How far does the Truth admit of being learned?" In answering the question, he contrasts the view of Socrates, who is Kierkegaard's symbol of all philosophical Idealism, with the Christian doctrine of revelation. Religiousness A, or the religion of Socrates, presupposes that religious Truth is present *within* every human being for, as Plato taught in the *Meno*, all true knowledge is merely recollection. All men possess Truth from eternity; what is required is a teacher or midwife who, by skillful means, can induce the student to give birth to the Truth within him. This implies that the person of the teacher and the occasion of his teaching have no special significance.

From the standpoint of the Socratic thought every point of departure in time is *eo ipso* accidental, an occasion, a vanishing moment. The teacher himself is no more than this.... In the Socratic view each individual is his own center, and the entire world centers in him, because his self-knowledge is a knowledge of God.[36]

In such a view, whether I have been instructed "by Socrates or by Prodicus or by a servant-girl" is incidental.

What, however, if the Socratic approach to Truth is wrong? What if a specific *moment* in time is of vital significance for the acquisition of the Truth? The consequence would be that the teacher ceases to be an incidental occasion in the student's own coming to the Truth but the indispensable and unique

bearer of the Truth. It follows that the student is destitute of the Truth and in a state of Error:

The seeker must be destitute of Truth up to the very moment of his learning it; he cannot even have possessed it in the form of ignorance, for in that case the moment becomes merely occasional. What is more, he cannot even be described as a seeker.... He must therefore be characterized as beyond the pale of the Truth ... or as being in Error.[37]

Now, if the learner is to acquire the Truth, the Teacher must *bring it to him and give him the condition necessary for understanding it.*

But one who gives the learner not only the Truth, but also the condition for understanding it, is more than a teacher. All instruction depends upon the presence, in the last analysis, of the requisite condition.... But this is something that no human being can do; if it is done it must be done by God himself.... The Teacher is then God himself, who in acting as an occasion prompts the learner to recall that he is in Error.[38]

A teacher who gives the learner both the requisite condition and the Truth is no ordinary teacher but should be called *Saviour* and *Redeemer*. The moment is also unique and decisive; let us call it the *Fullness of Time*. The disciple who, in a state of Error, receives the condition and the Truth "becomes another man ... a man of a different quality, or as we may call him: *a new creature*."[39]

It is clear that Kierkegaard's "project of thought" is not his own invention but takes its departure from the Christian Gospel. Accordingly, God is not *in* man, for man is separated from God by sin. Therefore, God must come to man from outside by his own grace. We start then with God, not man. But God does not need man to fulfill himself, nor is the moment of his self-revelation demanded of him. God chooses out of love to become man's teacher. Here is met what appears to be an impasse—the incommensurability between God and man.

Moved by love, God is thus eternally resolved to reveal himself. But as love is the motive so love must also be the end; for it would be a contradiction for God to have a motive and an end that did not correspond. His love is a love of the learner, and his aim is to win him. For it is only in love that the unequal can be made equal, and it is only in equality or unity that an understanding can be effected.... But this love is through and through an unhappy one, for how great is the difference between them. It may seem a small matter for God to make himself understood, but this is not so easy of accomplishment if he is to refrain from annihilating the unlikeness that exists between them.[40]

To accomplish his aim, God can neither draw man up to himself nor appear before man in all his awesome glory and majesty. The union can only be accomplished by God's descent and appearance before men, not in glory but in the form of a servant. "But," Kierkegaard reminds his reader, "the servant-form was no mere outer garment, and therefore God must suffer all things, endure all things...."[41] The Truth of Christianity comes then at a particular moment in history in which the eternal God appears in the form of a humble servant of men!

Socrates had considered human nature a great *paradox*, for when he reflected on man he could not decide whether man was a stranger monster than Typhon or a creature partaking of the divine. But, compared with the Socratic paradox, the Incarnation of the Eternal in time exceeds all the limits of human comprehension. It is, in Kierkegaard's words, the *Absolute Paradox*, the *Miracle*, the *Absurd* to which we can respond either in Faith or in Offense. The paradox of the Incarnation is doubly absurd, for it (a) claims that God has become man, that the Eternal has become temporal and (b) that man's eternal happiness can have its point of departure in an historical event the very historicity of which can only be accorded probability.

Kierkegaard recapitulates as follows:

If we do not posit the Moment we return to Socrates; but it was precisely from him that we departed, in order to discover something. If we posit the Moment the Paradox is there; for the Moment is the Paradox in its most abbreviated form. Because of the Moment the learner is in Error; and man, who had before possessed self-knowledge now becomes bewildered with respect to himself; instead of self-knowledge he receives the consciousness of sin.... (But) the reaction of the offended consciousness is to assert that the Moment is folly, and that the Paradox is folly... and what wonder, since the Paradox is the Miracle![42]

The coming of the Eternal into time is the Miracle and, as such, lies outside the realm of objective proof. The relationship between the disciple and the Paradox is always that of Faith. This is made clear by Kierkegaard in his discussion of the contemporary disciple and the disciple at second hand. It is frequently assumed that the original disciples were in a more favorable position than the believer of today. But such is not the case. It is true that a contemporary of Jesus may have been an historical eyewitness, but historical knowledge does not make the eyewitness a disciple. On the contrary, it may well make discipleship more difficult! The belief that God reveals himself in the rabbi of Nazareth is an absurdity and an offense to reason. The eyewitness has no advantage.

A contemporary may go where he can see the Teacher—and may he then believe his eyes? Why not? But may he also believe that this makes him a disciple? By no means. *If he believes his eyes he is deceived, for God is not immediately knowable.* But then perhaps he may shut his eyes. Just so; but if he does, what profit does he have from his contemporaneity?[43] (Italics added.)

How, then, does the original learner become a disciple? Kierkegaard answers:

When the Reason is set aside and he receives the condition. When does he receive the condition? In the Moment. What does this condition condition? The understanding of the eternal. ... It is in the Moment that he receives it, and from the Teacher himself. All romancing and trumpeting abroad about one's cleverness in penetrating God's incognito, though without receiving the condition from the Teacher; that one took notice of him by the impression he made, such a strange feeling coming over me in his presence; that there was something in his voice and mien, etc., etc.—all this is but silly twaddle, by which one does not become a disciple but only makes a mockery of God.[44]

According to Kierkegaard, the disciple believes *only* because he has received the condition from God. The disciple knows that he would have nothing without God's grace, for without grace he is blinded by error and cannot possibly pierce the *Absolute Paradox*, God's incognito. In that case, Faith is as paradoxical as the Paradox, for "Faith is itself a miracle, and all that holds true of the Paradox holds true of faith."[45]

It follows that there is no advantage or disadvantage to being a contemporary of Jesus or a disciple at second hand.

For whoever has what he has from God himself clearly has it at first hand; and he who does not have it from God himself is not a disciple.[46]

Two questions do remain, however. What, if anything, can the original disciple do for his successors? He can, Kierkegaard concedes, "inform him that he has himself *believed* this fact." But that is not, in the strict sense, a communication but merely affords an occasion.

For when I say that this or that has happened, I make an historical communication; but when I say: I believe and have believed that so-and-so has taken place, *although it is a folly to the understanding and an offense to the human heart*, then I have simultaneously done everything in my power *to prevent anyone else from determining his own attitude in immediate continuity with mine* ... since every individual is compelled to make up his own mind in precisely the same manner.[47] (Last italics added.)

The original disciple can relate the content of his faith, but the content exists only to be appropriated by faith. There is no short cut, no immediacy whereby the leap of faith can be removed or its indubitability assured. Likewise, the *credibility* of the contemporary witness cannot be the basis of the secondary disciple's belief. This would be the case if the *fact* referred to were a simple historical fact, but the fact in question is the *Moment*, the *absolute* or *eternal fact*. Purely historical facts are relative and so whatever can be clearly differentiated by time is *eo ipso* not the Absolute. However, if the fact referred to is an eternal fact, then every age is equally near it, for there is only one tense in relation to the eternal and that is the present. Yet, all are not equally near this unique fact "in faith; for faith and the historical are correlative concepts."[48] The sum of the matter is simply that, if the credibility of a contemporary witness is to have any interest for a successor, it must be with respect to historical fact. But if we are talking about the *Moment* we must ask, What historical fact? the historical "fact" that can become an object only for faith and which one human being cannot ever communicate immediately to another? If we are talking about this "fact," we are talking about *revelation*, which cannot be contained within the relativities and probabilities of historical research.

If the fact spoken of were a simple historical fact, the accuracy of the historical sources would be of great importance. Here this is not the case, *for faith cannot be distilled from even the nicest accuracy of detail.* The historical fact that God has existed in human form is the essence of the matter; the rest of the historical detail is not even as important as if we had to do with a human being instead of with God.[49] (Italics added.)

Kierkegaard, thus concludes his "project of thought" with one of the most discussed passages in recent theology:

If the contemporary generation had left nothing behind them but these words: "We have believed that in such and such a year God appeared among us in the humble figure of a servant, that he lived and taught in our community, and finally died," it would be more than enough. The contemporary generation would have done all that was necessary; for this little advertisement, this *nota bene* on a page of universal history, would be sufficient to afford an occasion for a successor, and the

most voluminous account can in all eternity do nothing more.[50]

The question on the title page of the *Philosophical Fragments* has now been answered. There can be an historical point of departure for an eternal consciousness which can have more than a mere historical interest—i.e., if it is a *unique* historical fact, the Paradox, the Moment of the Eternal entering into time. However, one's eternal happiness cannot be based upon historical knowledge alone, for history is the sphere of the relative and probable. Eternal Truth can be appropriated only by a Faith in the Paradox held in infinite passion. Kierkegaard's understanding of the relationship between Faith and Truth requires further analysis.

Truth Is Subjectivity. As we have seen, the theme of the Paradox is central to Kierkegaard's thought. The necessary counterpart to that theme is Kierkegaard's doctrine that *Truth is subjectivity.* Kierkegaard did not deny that there were truths independent of the knower. What he was concerned to insist on was that it is wrong to think of religious truth—i.e., faith—as acquired in the same way one obtains information. To do so is to consider the person as somehow abstracted from the truth. It does not consider the existential role of the self in the appropriation of religious truth. But this is just the problem that confronts the existing individual.

The thing is to find a truth which is true *for me, to find the idea for which I can live and die* . . . what good would it do me to be able to explain the meaning of Christianity if it had no deeper significance for me and my life.[51]

In the *Concluding Unscientific Postscript*, Kierkegaard develops the thesis that it is not the objective truth of Christianity but the relationship of the existing individual to Christianity that is the fundamental problem. In religion the truth is subjective because it is a truth that requires personal appropriation. The objective point of view overlooks this very factor.

From the objective standpoint Christianity is a *res in facto posita* whose truth it is proposed to investigate in a purely objective manner. . . . And as for the relationship of the subject to the truth when he comes to know it, the assumption is that if only the truth is brought to light, its appropriation is a relatively unimportant matter, something which follows as a matter of course. And in any case, what happens to the individual is in the last analysis a matter of indifference. Herein lies the lofty equanimity of the scholar, and the comic thoughtlessness of his parrot-like echo.[52]

The scholar misses the real point, for he confuses historical results with the appropriation of eternal truth. But history cannot produce such faith. On the contrary, scientific "results" impede faith.

Faith does not result simply from a scientific inquiry; it does not come directly at all. On the contrary, in this objectivity *one tends to lose that infinite personal interestedness in passion which is the condition of faith*.[53] (Italics added.)

Where there is undisputed evidence there is no passion, hence no faith, and therefore "while faith has hitherto had a profitable schoolmaster in the existing uncertainty, it would have in the new certainty its most dangerous enemy."[54]

In Kierkegaard's opinion, passion—or inwardness—is the very criterion of faith, for faith is by definition the appropriation of the Absolute Paradox, that which is rationally absurd and historically only probable. Only a faith which exhibits a passionate appropriation of its object is a true faith. Hence, for Kierkegaard, as for all Existentialists, the *how*, the mode of decision, takes precedence over the *what* or object of one's devotion.

If one who lives in the midst of Christianity goes into God's house—the true God's house —with the true idea of God in his mind and prays, but prays in untruth; and another who lives in a heathen country prays, but with a whole souled passion for infinity, although his eye rests upon an idol; where then is the truth ? The one prays in truth to God though he worships an idol; the other prays falsely to the true God, and hence worships in fact an idol.[55]

The inward "how" of appropriation is the passion of the infinite and the passion of the infinite is the truth. "But," adds Kierkegaard,

the passion of the infinite is precisely subjectivity, and thus subjectivity becomes the truth. . . . Only in subjectivity is there decisiveness; to seek objectivity is to be in error. It is the passion of the infinite that is the decisive factor and not its content, for its content is precisely itself. In this manner subjectivity and the subjective "how" constitute the truth.[56]

If subjectivity is the truth, then the determination of the truth must include an expression for the antithesis to objectivity and an indication of the tension and risk involved in subjective inwardness. Kierkegaard offers the following as such a definition of the truth:

An objective uncertainty held fast in an appropriation-process of the most passionate inwardness is the truth, the highest truth attainable for an *existing* individual.[57]

The truth is the existential venture which chooses an objective uncertainty with the passion of the infinite.

Here it is necessary to add a note of clarification. When Kierkegaard speaks of truth as subjectivity, as an objective uncertainty held in infinite passion, it is important to keep in mind that he is referring to a special kind of truth. It is existential truth, truth that cannot be known through a "parrot-like echo" but only through one's own activity. Such is the nature of ethical and religious truth— for the simple reason that they are incapable of being reduced to unquestioned demonstrations. In other words, when Kierkegaard speaks of the "leap of faith" he is not speaking of a method of choosing a brand of refrigerator! The "leap of faith" is a moral and religious category and has to do with what William James called "live options"— those existential decisions of life involving "limit situations" in which certainty remains impossible. This is what lies behind Kierkegaard's insistence that

the communication of results is an unnatural form of intercourse between man and man, *inasmuch as every man is a spiritual being for whom truth consists in nothing else than the self-activity of personal appropriation.*[58] (Italics added.)

A further question requires some clarification. If truth is subjectivity, does not Kierkegaard's doctrine lead to a radical subjectivism and individualism in theology? Is Kierkegaard not advocating a pure irrationalism? The question has been widely debated and the issue is a complex one. That Kierkegaard's position lends itself to subjectivism and irrationalism, there is little doubt. That he himself was guilty of such a position is

also doubtful. Book One of the *Postscript* makes it clear that the question of religious truth can be dealt with objectively but that such a stance is by itself *inadequate.* In the sphere of religion, all statements about the religious object involve the interdependence of object and subject— i.e., fact and appropriation, event and interpretation. Kierkegaard's own theology was in one sense extremely objectivist in that he accepted the biblical traditions and the Church's dogmatic formulas uncritically and was untouched by the radical historical work of men like D. F. Strauss. His almost exclusive emphasis on subjective appropriation in faith was possible, perhaps, because of his unconscious *assumption* of the tradition's reliability. Kierkegaard's disinterest in the historical bases of faith is therefore more understandable and less radical than that of Karl Barth and his followers who, while following Kierkegaard in this regard, do so in full knowledge of modern historical-critical research on the gospels and church dogma.

According to Kierkegaard, the object of religious faith is not inherently irrational or absurd. What makes it so is the "infinite qualitative distinction between time and eternity," between God and finite men. To human understanding the Incarnation will always appear absurd, but the eternal Truth of God is not itself paradoxical. As Kierkegaard says:

The eternal essential truth is by no means in itself a paradox; it becomes paradoxical by virtue of its relationship to an existing individual.[59]

The paradoxical character of this existential truth has to do in part with its objective uncertainty. "Only eternity can give an eternal certainty, while existence must rest content with a militant certainty."[60] What Kierkegaard is asserting is that for faith to be an act of existential appropriation its object cannot be certainly known. Faith involves risk.

Faith is precisely the contradiction between the infinite passion of the individual's inwardness and the objective uncertainty. If I am capable of grasping God objectively, I do not believe, but precisely because I cannot do this I must believe.[61]

The "leap of faith," however, does not imply the complete renunciation of any intelligible choice, for a thorough reflection upon the nature of human reason will lead to an understanding of its limits. The highest understanding is to know that there are things that the human understanding cannot grasp. Reason, therefore, does play a significant role in the life of faith:

It is the business of reason to eliminate everything that is only an apparent paradox and to free us once and for all from that which is *not* Absurd. Then, when *the* Absurd stands forth in all its naked clarity, then what? Why then the reason will in no wise be able to show that the Absurd is nonsense. But neither will it be able to master the Absurd, to prove its logical necessity speculatively or its incontestable actuality historically.[62]

Kierkegaard's theology was not an extreme form of irrationalism. Rather, it was based on a sophisticated awareness of the limits of human reason and the laughable pretensions of those rationalists who assumed a position *sub specie aeterni*. Nevertheless, Kierkegaard leaves one with the impression that because religion requires existential decision it does not concern itself with the objective side of knowledge. His valuable polemic against the presumptuous "immediacy" of philosophers and historians, vis-à-vis the objective uncertainty and passionate quality of the decision of faith, led Kierkegaard to exaggerate the relationship between the existential dimension of faith and the uncertainty or absence of reasons for one's existential choices. In this regard Kierkegaard has been the cause of much confusion and even nonsense in recent theological discussions. J. H. Thomas has pointed up this failure in Kierkegaard, as well as his enduring contribution.

It cannot be denied that there is a certain exaggeration here as a result of his preoccupation with the risk of faith. He failed to see that the risk is not removed if we can find some reasons, being misled by the false model of scientific reasons. What he means to say is that if there are any reasons for believing they are not reasons of the kind we have in science. The important point is that here in the religious life reasons will never amount to proof because this life is essentially one of choice and passionate commitment.[63]

As we have indicated, the immediate effect of Kierkegaard's writings outside Denmark was negligible. His works had little influence for almost a century, but when his impact was felt it was epochal. In theology Kierkegaard can rightfully be considered the father of Neo-Orthodoxy, for the themes of his major works run like a thread through the early writings of that circle of German theologians whose program came to be known as the "theology of Crisis." Like Kierkegaard, these theologians sought to divorce Christianity from a complacent, bourgeois culture and to direct men to the infinite qualitative difference between the transcendent, unknowable God and finite, sinful man. They, too, turned away from the liberal emphasis on the immanence of God and the immediacy of revelation to stress the crisis of faith and the paradoxicality and absurdity of belief. With Kierkegaard, they were to hold that faith is "objective uncertainty" and that there are no historical or natural "proofs" of Christianity. As was the case with Kierkegaard, they showed little interest in the historical Jesus and were to consider the quest of the historical Jesus a vain and faithless search for an "objective revelation" which was, by their definition, a contradiction in terms. For Kierkegaard and the Neo-Orthodox alike, there are no cogent rational defenses of Christianity outside of revelation itself, which comes to each believer as the gracious gift of the Holy Spirit. Man, in his finitude and sin, is in no position to resolve his own predicament. Salvation can come only from the Wholly Other, God Himself.

The theologian of "Crisis" whose early writings reflect most consistently the influence of Kierkegaard and whose name has become synonymous, in a very real sense, with Neo-Orthodoxy is Karl Barth. It was around Barth that the Neo-Orthodox movement took shape and it is in his early writings that the major themes of that movement are most forcefully expressed.

Karl Barth (1886–1968)

When the curtain is rung down on the twentieth century and the annals of its church history are complete, there will surely be one name that will tower above all others in the field of theology—that of Karl Barth. In him a church Father has walked among us, a theologian of such creative genius, prodigious productivity, and pervasive influence that his name is already being associated with that elite group of Christian thinkers that includes

Athanasius, Augustine, Anselm, Aquinas, Luther and Calvin.[64]

Such a judgment is not heard only from the lips of Barth's disciples, for it is widely acknowledged today that Karl Barth has been the greatest Protestant theologian of this century and, perhaps, since Schleiermacher or even the Reformers. It is not an exaggeration to say that the theological movements of the past fifty years have had to define themselves and defend themselves vis-à-vis the theology of Karl Barth. Like the Reformers and Schleiermacher, he represented a genuine watershed in the history of Christian theology. And, like them, he was extraordinarily productive. His twelve volumes of *Church Dogmatics* alone contain over six million words on seven thousand pages!

Karl Barth was born in Basel, Switzerland. His father, Fritz Barth, was a professor of church history and New Testament at Berne. At eighteen Karl began his theological studies at Berne under the direction of his father. However, following the continental custom, Barth attended several universities. He studied under many of the great liberal theologians of the turn of the century—Harnack, Reinhold Seeberg, Julius Kaftan, and Hermann Gunkel at Berlin, Theodor Häring at Tübingen, and Wilhelm Herrmann, Johannes Weiss, and Adolf Jülicher at Marburg. The most important influence of these university years was that of Hermann, the leading Neo-Kantian and Ritschlian systematic theologian. For about a decade after completing his university studies, Barth remained a faithful disciple of Herrmann's Ritschlian brand of liberalism.

In 1909 Barth entered the pastoral ministry of the Swiss Reformed Church, serving as a vicar in Geneva for two years. In 1911 he was appointed pastor of the Reformed Church at Safenwil in Aargau where he remained for ten very formative years. It was during these years that Barth broke with the liberal theology. What began to trouble Barth was preaching—which message to address to his congregation Sunday after Sunday year in, year out. The liberal message which he had learned from his professors did not provide the real resource that his people needed. This became painfully evident with the outbreak of World War I. Barth became more acutely conscious of the vacuity and hypocrisy of his task each time he mounted the pulpit. In this situation he confided in his friend and fellow pastor, Eduard Thurneysen, who was experiencing a similar crisis. The two men agreed to suspend their political and ecclesiastical busyness and begin a re-evaluation of their whole theological position. Thus began an intense period of theological study, particularly of the Bible. It was out of this that Barth discovered what he was to call "the strange new world within the Bible"—a world not opened to him by his Biblical professors Jülicher, Weiss, and Heitmuller.

In 1916 Barth began a careful reading of Paul's *Letter to the Romans*. Out of the notes compiled from this study there emerged his epoch-making commentary on *Romans*. As in the case of Luther, here also the rediscovery of *Romans* lead to a theological revolution. The first edition appeared in 1919, while the more influential second edition was published in Munich in 1922. The book was a bombshell. It soon divided the theological world of Germany into advocates and bitter detractors. Jülicher and Wernle wrote severe attacks on the book, and Harnack referred to Barth as a "despiser"

of scientific theology. Writing about the impact of the book, Barth later commented:

As I look back upon my course, I seem to myself as one who, ascending the dark staircase of a church tower and trying to steady himself reached for the banister, but got hold of the bell rope instead. To his horror, he had then to listen to what the great bell had sounded over him and not over him alone.[65]

There were numerous younger theologians who rallied to Barth's defense and saw in his *Romans* an expression of their own theological program. Among those who became identified with Barth were Emil Brunner (1889–1966), Bultmann, George Merz (1892–1959), Friedrich Gogarten (1887–1967) and Thurneysen (1888–   ). In the fall of 1922, Barth, Thurneysen, Gogarten, and Merz inaugurated a journal entitled *Zwischen den Zeiten* (Between the Times) which was to be the organ of the new "theology of crisis" or, as they preferred, the "theology of the Word of God." This little magazine played a vital role in shaping German theology for the next decade, until it was discontinued in 1933.

In 1921 Barth left Safenwil and moved to Göttingen in Germany where he had been invited to become Honorary Professor of Reformed Theology. In 1925 Barth moved on to the University of Munster as Professor of Dogmatics and New Testament Exegesis where he remained until 1930 when he became Professor of Systematic Theology at Bonn. During this decade Barth produced some of his most powerful essays and addresses which appeared in *The Word of God and the Word of Man* (1924) and *Theology and Church* (1928). In 1927 his first attempt at an independent dogmatics appeared under the title *The*

Doctrine of the Word of God, Prolegomena to a Christian Dogmatics. As Barth discovered, this was to prove a "false start." The reviews of the book made Barth aware that he was still working within a liberal, anthropocentric framework which he thought he had overcome. It also made him conscious of the serious differences between his own theological starting point and that of his friends Gogarten and Bultmann. Barth was thus forced to reconceive his whole theological method in order to avoid grounding his theology in an existential anthropology. The result was the *Church Dogmatics*, the first volume of which appeared in 1932. Between 1927 and 1932 Barth's theology developed in important new directions which represented a significant break with his earlier dialectical thinking. With this later period of the *Church Dogmatics* we are not chiefly concerned in this chapter, although something of the change in Barth's theology after 1930 will be indicated later on.

During the 1930's Barth's theological work took a very practical turn with his declaration of war against Adolf Hitler and the Nazi movement. By 1933 the German Evangelical Church had become largely a tool of the Nazi party. In April of that year the "Evangelical Church of the German Nation" was created and published the following "guiding principles":

We see in race, folk and nation, orders of existence granted and entrusted to us by God. God's law for us is that we look to the preservation of these orders. . . .

In the mission to the Jews we perceive a grave danger to our nationality. It is the entrance gate for alien blood into our body politic. . . . In particular, marriage between Germans and Jews is to be forbidden.

We want an evangelical Church that is rooted in our nationhood. We repudiate the spirit of Christian world citizenship. We want the degenerating manifestations of this spirit . . . overcome by a faith in our national mission that God has committed to us.[66]

To oppose this "German Christian" movement, Barth, along with Martin Niemoller, led in the formation of the German Confessing Church. In May of 1934 representatives of the Confessing Church met at Barmen and out of that meeting came the famous Barmen Confession which was essentially the work of Barth. It affirmed the sovereignty of the Word of God in Christ over against all idolatrous political ideologies.

In view of the errors of the "German Christians" of the present Reich Church government which are devastating the Church and are also thereby breaking up the unity of the German Evangelical Church, we confess the following evangelical truths:

Jesus Christ, as he is attested for us in Holy Scripture, is the one Word of God which we have to hear and which we have to trust and obey in life and in death.

We reject the false doctrine, as though the Church could and would have to acknowledge as a source of its proclamation, apart from and besides this one Word of God, still other events and powers, figures and truths, as God's revelation.

We reject the false doctrine, as though there were areas of our life in which we would not belong to Jesus Christ, but to other lords. . . .[67]

Barth carried further his denunciation of Nazism in a new theological journal, *Theologische Existenz heute* which he founded with Thurneysen. The publication of this journal marked the breakup of the Dialectical school. Henceforth Barth was to engage in several, often virulent, critical exchanges with Gogarten, Bultmann, and Brunner because of what he considered their willingness to acknowledge other authorities than the one Word of God in Holy Scripture.

In December of 1934 Barth was suspended from his teaching post at Bonn and that next spring was forced out of Germany by the Nazis. The Basel City Council had in the meantime elected him to the chair of theology. He therefore returned to Basel where he lived and taught from that time forward. The decades of the forties and fifties were largely occupied with lecturing and the writing of the twelve volumes of the *Church Dogmatics.* Barth retired as "Professor Ordinarius" in 1962.

Major Themes in Barth's Theology of the Word of God. *The Dialectical Method.* The theologians of *krisis* learned their method from Kierkegaard. Like the Dane, they came to recognize that the truth is not found in the smooth Hegelian transition from thesis to antithesis to synthesis but in the dialectical tension between truth and truth—a tension never fully resolved. The reason for this is that a Christian theology is grounded in revelation, i.e., in the union of the two worlds of eternity and time, for which we have no analogy. Our language about revelation consists of words which attempt to express the intersection of our horizontal line of existence by the vertical line of God's transcendence. And this relation of time and eternity can only be expressed paradoxically. Our knowledge of God is therefore never immediate. Theology has frequently attempted to get at the truth immediately, either by means of *dogmatism* or *mysticism*, but all attempts at immediacy must fail. There is, however, a third way—the way of dialectic.

It is the way of Paul and the Reformers and intrinsically it is by far the best. . . . This way from the outset undertakes seriously and positively to develop the idea of God on the one hand and the criticism of man and of all things human on the other; but they are not now considered independently but are both referred constantly to their common presupposition, to the living truth which, to be sure, may not be named, but which lies between them and gives to both their meaning and interpretation.[68]

The dialectical method never reaches a "solution," a triumphant synthesis or stable position. One who follows this method is like a bird in flight, always on the move.

On this narrow ridge of rock one can only walk; if he attempts to stand still, he will fall either to the right or to the left, but fall he must. There remains only to keep walking—an appalling performance for those who are not free from dizziness—looking *from one side to the other,* from positive to negative and from negative to positive.

Our task is to interpret the Yes and the No and the No by the Yes without delaying more than a moment in either a fixed Yes *or* a fixed No; to speak of the glory of God in creation, for example, only to pass immediately to emphasizing God's complete concealment from us in that creation; . . . of the creation of man in the image of God simply and solely to give warning once and for all that man as we know him is fallen man, whose misery we know better than his glory. . . . A Christian is the master of all things and subject to nobody—a Christian is the slave of all things and subject to everybody. I need not continue. He who hath ears to hear will understand my meaning.[69]

To the Liberal onlooker, Barth's dialectic is merely perplexing, for he is used to knowing God *immediately,* of positing a direct continuity between the divine and the human. This is exactly what Barth denies—that we can know the nature of God by starting with man's historical or psychic experience! God is not simply man writ large. Man cannot capture the Truth about the eternal God in his own finite formulas. Man can only witness to the paradoxicality of God's own self-revelation.

"How then," asks Barth, "shall the dialectician . . . meet his critic? Must he not say, in effect: 'My friend, you must understand that if you ask about *God* and if I am really to tell about *him*, dialectic is all that can be expected of *me*. I have done what I could to make you see that neither my affirmation nor my denial lays claim to being God's truth. Neither one is more than a *witness* to that truth, which stands in the center, between every Yes and No.'"[70]

The dialectical method is the only way of preserving both the truth that God is not man—that he is beyond the finite realm—and, yet, that he has revealed himself within it. It alone can maintain the "Godness of God," the Wholly Otherness of the divine self-revelation in time.

God as Wholly Other. The rediscovery of the "distance" between God and man —hence the "otherness" of God—is *the leitmotiv* of the crisis theology. It lies at the root of Barth's polemic against rationalism and mysticism, for both rely upon human resources and human experience for knowledge of God. For Barth the first task of theology is to emphasize the infinite distance between God and man. In the preface to the 1922 edition of the book on *Romans*, Barth wrote:

If I have a system, it is limited to a recognition of what Kierkegaard called the "in-

finite qualitative distinction" between time and eternity, and to my regarding this as possessing a negative as well as positive significance: "God is in heaven, and thou art on earth."[71]

God can only be known through God. The finite creation is not a direct revelation of God. On the contrary, the creation *hides* God. This, claims Barth, is the real paradoxical meaning of Romans 1:20.

What are all those enigmatic creatures of God . . . but so many problems to which we have no answer? But God only, God Himself, He is the answer. And so the boundary which bars us in and which, nevertheless, points beyond itself, can *since the creation of the world* be clearly seen *through the things that are made* by God. By calm, veritable, unprejudiced religious contemplation the divine "No" can be established and apprehended. If we do not ourselves hinder it, nothing can prevent our being translated into a most wholesome *KRISIS* by that *which may be known of God.* And indeed, we stand already in this *KRISIS* if we would but *see clearly.* And what is clearly seen to be indisputable reality is the invisibility of God, which is precisely and in strict agreement with the gospel of the resurrection—*His everlasting power and divinity.* And what does this mean but that we can know nothing of God, that we are not God, that the Lord is to be feared? Herein lies His pre-eminence over all gods; and here is that which marks Him out as God, as Creator and Redeemer.[72]

The creation, when clearly seen, will declare the divine "No," will produce that real *krisis* in which we will come to know that from our creaturely perspective God is always hidden and unknown. We will discover the Reformed principle: "*Finitum non capax infiniti*, the finite cannot contain the infinite. God is Wholly Other. He is not given directly in the heart of man or in the world of nature. "There is no way from man to God."

There is, however, the way from God to man—the way of God's gracious self-revelation. God is only known by God, by his revelation in Jesus Christ. What, then, is impossible for man has been made possible by God. In Christ, God has revealed himself, God himself speaks. But here, too, the God revealed, the *Deus revelatus*, is also the hidden God, *Deus absconditus*. We cannot say that God remains hidden until he reveals himself. In the *krisis* of faith we know that the God revealed in Jesus Christ is, indeed, the hidden God! The knowledge of God in Jesus Christ and God's hiddenness are, paradoxically, one and the same. It is especially in Jesus, as the Christ, that we see the awful hiddenness of God. For this reason, the seeing is not of the normal order of seeing—it requires the eyes of faith, which are a gift of grace. God's revelation is always indirect and veiled and thus requires grace, for it manifests itself in a world where sin and "the flesh" rule. Revelation is a mystery, for it not only signifies the hiddenness of God but his becoming manifest in a hidden or nonapparent way. God's revelation is always an "in spite of." It is never transparent. For confirmation we need only to look at the biblical picture of Jesus Christ.

He takes His place where God can be present only in questioning about Him; He takes the form of a slave; He moves to the cross and to death; His greatest achievement is a negative achievement. He is not a genius . . . he is not a hero or leader of men. He is neither poet nor thinker: *My God, my God, why hast thou for-saken me?* . . . In Jesus revelation is a paradox, however objective and universal it may be. That the promises of the faithfulness of God have been fulfilled in Jesus the Christ is not, and never will be, self-evident truth, since in Him it appears in its final hiddenness and its most profound secrecy. The truth, in fact, can never be self-evident, because it is a matter neither of historical nor of psychological experience. . . . Therefore it is not accessible to our perception. . . . In Jesus God becomes veritably a secret: He is made known as the Unknown. . . . He becomes a scandal to the Jews and to the Greeks foolishness. In Jesus the communication of God begins with a rebuff, with the exposure of a vast chasm, with the clear revelation of a great stumbling-block. . . . To believe in Jesus is the most hazardous of all hazards.[73]

In Christ, God's unveiling is also veiling, and so man's relation to God is always that of faith, never sight. The distance, the incommensurableness remains. One does *not possess* revelation as an object, but one is given the gift of faith.

In his revelation, in Jesus Christ, the hidden God has indeed made Himself apprehensible. Not directly, but indirectly. Not to sight but to faith. Not in His being, but in sign. Not, then, in the dissolution of His hiddenness—but apprehensibly. . . . For as we men view and conceive Him, so we can speak of Him. We cannot do so without the veil and therefore without the reservation of His hiddenness, or apart from His miracle of grace. It is not true that the grace of His revelation ever or in any relationship ceases to be grace and miracle.[74]

On the basis of what Barth says about revelation, it is not surprising that he has nothing but scorn for those who seek to ground faith in the Jesus "according to the flesh." The quest of the historical Jesus is both a futile historical task and a sign of unfaith. In the earthly Jesus we encounter either an apocalyptical fanatic *or* the divine incognito. In either case, God cannot be seen directly in the earthly Jesus. God is revealed in Jesus as the *Christ*, only by an event that breaks the bounds of history. The incognito is lifted by Christ's resurrection from the dead which is a scandal, for it constitutes an *eternal event*, an event that cannot be described historically.

Jesus has been . . . *declared to be the Son of God with power, according to the Holy Spirit, through his resurrection from the dead.* In this declaration and appointment—which are beyond historical definition—lies the true significance of Jesus. Jesus as the Christ, as the Messiah, is the end of History; and He can be comprehended only as Paradox (Kierkegaard), as Victor (Blumhardt), as Primal History (Overbeck). As Christ, Jesus is the plane which lies beyond our comprehension. The plane which is known to us, He intersects vertically from above. Within history, Jesus as the Christ can be understood only as Problem or Myth. As the Christ, He brings the world of the Father. But we who stand in this concrete world know nothing, and are incapable of knowing anything, of that other world. The Resurrection from the dead is, however, the transformation: the establishing or *declaration* of that point from above, and the corresponding discerning of it from below. The Resurrection is the revelation: the disclosing of Jesus as the Christ, the appearing of God, and the apprehending of God in Jesus. The Resurrection is the reckoning with what is unknown and unobservable in Jesus. In the Resurrection the new world of the Holy Spirit touches the old world of the flesh, but touches it as a tangent touches a circle, that is, without touching it. And, precisely because it does not touch it, it touches it as its frontier—as the new world. The Resurrection is therefore an occurrence in history, which took place outside the gates of Jerusalem in the year A.D. 30, inasmuch as it there "came to pass," was discovered and recognized. But inasmuch as the occurrence was conditioned by the Resur-

rection, in so far, that is, as it was not the "coming to pass," or the discovery, or the recognition, which conditioned its necessity and appearance and revelation, the Resurrection is not an event in history at all. Jesus is *declared to be the Son of God* wherever He reveals Himself and is recognized as the Messiah. This declaration of the Son of man to be the Son of God is the significance of Jesus, and, apart from this, Jesus has no more significance or insignificance than may be attached to any man or thing or period of history in itself.—*Even though we have known Christ after the flesh yet now we know him so no longer.*[75]

The hiddenness and mystery of God's revelation in Jesus Christ is further indicated in its very paradoxicality. There is no separation of grace and judgment, love and gospel, faith and works.

By being really and seriously put under the law, man comes to the gospel and by coming to the gospel through revelation and faith he is really and seriously put under the law. God's wrath and judgment is only the hard shell, the *opus alienum* of God's grace, but it is the man who knows about grace . . . who alone knows what God's wrath and judgment are.[76]

This mysterious "inner two-sidedness" of revelation in Jesus Christ is mere foolishness to the world. The gift of faith alone makes the divine transvaluation, this otherness and mystery of God's being and doing apprehensible.

The Strange World of the Bible. This strange and unexpected Word of God is what we encounter when we turn and *really* listen to the Bible. This, of course, we don't wish to do. We prefer to go to the Bible with our own presuppositions, our own world-view, which we then read out of the Bible as its own. And the Bible allows us to do this if we don't really press the question of what lies within the Bible.

The Bible gives to every man and to every era such answers to their questions as they deserve. We shall always find in it as much as we seek and no more: high and divine content if it is high and divine content that we seek; transitory and "historical" content, if it is transitory and "historical" content that we seek—nothing whatever, if it is nothing whatever that we seek.... What is within the Bible? has a mortifying way of converting itself into the opposing question, Well, what are you looking for?[77]

One can find all kinds of edifying things in the Bible—if one does not penetrate too deeply. But, on closer inspection, the Bible contains little of real value in the realm of history, morals, and religion.

The man who is looking for history or for stories will be glad after a little to turn from the Bible to the morning paper or to other books. For when we study history and amuse ourselves with stories, we are always wanting to know: How did it happen?... What are the natural causes of things? *Why* did the people speak such words and live such lives? It is just at the most decisive points of its history that the Bible gives no answer to our Why.... The Bible meets the lover of history with silences quite unparalleled.[78]

The same is true, Barth asserts, about morals. We look to the Bible for good practical wisdom and for examples of moral excellence—but again we are disappointed.

Large parts of the Bible are almost useless to the school in its moral curriculum because they are lacking in just this wisdom and just these "good examples." The heroes of the Bible are to a certain degree quite respectable,

but to serve as examples to the good, efficient, industrious, publicly educated, average citizen of Switzerland, men like Samson, David, Amos, and Peter are very ill fitted indeed. ...

The Bible is an embarrassment in the school and foreign to it. How shall we find in the life and teaching of Jesus something to "do" in "practical life" ... And in how many phases of morality the Bible is grievously wanting! How little fundamental information it offers in regard to the difficult questions of business life, marriage, civilization and statecraft, with which we have to struggle.... How unceremoniously and constantly war is waged in the Bible![79]

Frankly speaking, the Bible is of little *practical* value, and this is because it is a witness to "the 'other,' new, greater world," because it is not *of* this world.

When we come to the Bible with our questions—How shall I think of God and the universe? How arrive at the divine? How present myself?—it answers us, as it were, "My dear sir, these are *your* problems: you must not ask me! Whether it is better to hear mass or hear a sermon, whether the proper form of Christianity is to be discovered in the Salvation Army or in 'Christian Science,' whether the better belief is that of old Reverend Doctor Smith or young Reverend Mr. Jones ... you can and must decide for yourself."

It is not the right human thoughts about God which form the content of the Bible, but the right divine thoughts about men. The Bible tells us not how we should talk with God but what he says to us; not how we find the way to him, but how he has sought and found the way to us.... We have found in the Bible a new world, God, God's sovereignty, God's glory, God's incomprehensible love. Not the history of man but the history of God! Not the virtues of men but the virtues of him who hath called us out of darkness into his marvelous light! Not human standpoints but the standpoints of God.[80]

What we find in the Bible is the world of God's incomprehensible being and acting, which drives us out beyond ourselves, beyond the Bible as the mirror of our own reflection, to the world of God. It is only when we arrive at this point that we encounter the *krisis*, the awakening to the relativity of all *our* thoughts and expectations. Only then are we prepared to hear of the *last things* which make known the truth that is hidden from the wise of the world. At that point only one possibility remains, but that lies *beyond* all thinking and all things—the possibility:

> *Behold, I make all things new! The affirmation of God, man, and the world given in the New Testament based exclusively upon the possibility of a new order absolutely beyond human thought; and therefore, as prerequisite to that order, there must come a crisis that denies all human thought.*[81]

The strangeness of the Bible is connected with its very revelatory character. Revelation requires that it be received and witnessed to through the mediation of worldliness. But the fact that God chooses to so reveal himself is part of God's veiledness and mystery. That God should reveal himself in the relative and problematical literature of the Bible is comparable to the scandal and mystery of the Incarnation. The worldly character of the Bible, therefore, is no accidental condition that we could hope would some day be removed. The indirectness of its witness is integral to its revelatory character.

No one can deny the relativity or the problematical character of the Bible. And the great danger is that the elimination of the human relativity of the Bible may lead to the elimination of the very thing the Bible is intended to bear witness to: the revelation of God. For is it not the very nature of revelation that the form in which it confronts us is relative and problematical?[82]

The radically human and fallible character of the Bible is one of Barth's and Neo-Orthodoxy's most consistent themes.[83] Contrary to what liberal theology claims, the Bible does not contain universally noble and sublime truths. "The Bible," says Barth, "is the literary monument of an ancient racial religion and of a Hellenistic cultus religion of the Near East. A human document like any other."[84] This means that the biblical witnesses were fallible men whose historical and scientific judgments were often erroneous.

They shared the culture of their age and environment, whose form and content could be contested by other ages and environments. . . . In the biblical view of the world and of man we are constantly coming up against presuppositions which are not ours, and statements and judgments we cannot accept.[85]

Moreover, the vulnerability of the Bible extends to its religious or theological content.

The prophets and apostles as such . . . even in their function as witnesses, even in their act of writing down their witness, were real, historical men as we are, and therefore sinful in their acting and capable and actually guilty of error in their spoken and written word.[86]

[Finally], not a single verse of the Bible has come down to us with such absolute certainty and clarity that alternative versions cannot be suggested. We are therefore on uncertain ground.[87]

That the Bible is the word of man is plain enough. And yet, paradoxically, to say that is to speak only half the truth.

The Bible is *both* word of man and Word of God. However, the revealedness of the Bible as Word of God can be perceived, through the human limitations and barriers, only by a miracle of grace.

We have to recognize that faith as an eruption into this reality and possibility means the removing of a barrier in which we can only see and again and again see a miracle. And it is a miracle which we cannot explain apart from faith. . . . This is a miracle which we cannot presuppose. We can remember it. We can wait for it. . . . Therefore we are bound to take offence at the Bible in the light of that claim. . . . Only the miracle of faith and the Word can genuinely and seriously prevent us from taking offence at the Bible.[88]

It is evident that for Barth the Bible is not a "content" which we can control. We cannot properly even say that the Bible *is* the Word of God. Rather, we can only go to the Bible *remembering* that the Church has heard God's Word in the Bible and *expecting* that we *will also* hear God's Word—to have faith in a "divine disposing." "*The Bible is God's Word so far as God lets it be His Word.*"[89] (Italics added.) The Bible only *becomes* God's Word. To say that the Bible is the Word of God is therefore not to say that the Word of God is tied to the Bible. God's Word is nothing else than the free disposing of God's grace. "The Word of God is an act of God which happens *specialissime*, in this way and in no other, to this and that particular man."[90] Put more succinctly, for Barth knowledge of the Word of God is not an anthropological problem!

Natural Theology—Nein!. The Word of God comes to man as a gift. It is not something that man can gain independently. Barth, therefore, takes no interest in a natural theology which claims that

man in himself possesses some capacity to know God. Man cannot know God other than as God freely makes Himself known in Jesus Christ through the Holy Spirit. Revelation cannot even be prepared for. It even lies beyond all natural human comprehension.

God's revelation in its objective reality is the incarnation of His Word. . . . In other words, it becomes the object of our knowledge; it finds a way of becoming the content of our experience and our thought; it gives itself to be apprehended by our contemplation and our categories. But it does that beyond the range of what we regard as possible for our contemplation and perception, beyond the confines of our experience and our thought. It comes to us as a *Novum* which, when it becomes an object for us, we cannot incorporate in the series of our other objects, cannot compare with them, cannot deduce from their context, cannot regard as analogous with them. It comes to us as a datum with no point of connexion with any other previous datum.[91]

Barth holds that there is no point of contact, no *Anknüpfungspunkt*, between revelation and man's natural experience and knowledge. Natural theology presupposes an *analogia entis*, an analogy of being between God and man. It assumes that the being of God is similar to the being of man and that, consequently, man can gain some knowledge of God apart from God's special revelation. Barth considers the special evil of natural theology to lie in the fact that it splits up God, dividing his being from his acting in Jesus Christ. Natural theology conceives of God as a neutral being, in *abstracto*.

The intolerable and unpardonable thing in Roman Catholic theology is . . . that there is this splitting up of the concept of God and hand and hand with it the abstraction from the real work and activity of God in favour of a general being of God . . . which means the introduction of a foreign god into the sphere of the Church.[92]

The living God can be known only in his *acting*, which is the revelation of his very being. Natural theology is thereby excluded, for where do we see God's action but in his works of reconciliation in Christ, which is always a free gift of his grace. "This," Barth contends,

is the place and the only place from which as Christians we can think forwards and backwards, from which a Christian knowledge of both God and man is possible. . . . It is here that all natural theology perishes even before it has drawn its first breath. Why? Because this is the Word in which God Himself has set the beginning of knowledge in the vacuum where there is no beginning for man as estranged from God and himself.[93]

The fact is that natural man does not really want to know the true God. Because of sin, the natural man is at enmity with God. He would rather fashion idolatrous objects of worship which he can control and which can witness to his own sublime religiosity. In Barth's view, natural theology is the perfect sign that man is an estranged sinner.

Natural theology is no more and no less than the unavoidable theological expression of the fact that in the reality and possibility of man as such an openness for the grace of God and therefore a readiness for the knowability of God in his revelation is not at all evident.[94]

Natural theology issues in what Barth calls *religion*. The religious man is the man who imagines he can know God and who can justify and sanctify himself by his own efforts. Religion is the crown of

all human achievement, the sign of man's transcendence over the lesser creatures.

In religion the supreme competence of human possibility attains its consummation and final realization. . . . In the end human passion derives its living energy from that passionate desire: *Eritis sicut Deus!* In religion this final passion becomes conscious and recognizable. . . . Can there be any affirmation of passion that outstrips the passion with which Prometheus robs Zeus of his fire and uses it for his own advantage? . . . It is the crowning of all other passions with the passion of eternity, the endowment of what is finite with infinity, the most exalted consecration of the passions of men.[95]

Yet, according to Barth, religion is not only the grandeur but also the misery of man. Religion is man's misery because "it is precisely in religion that men perceive themselves to be bounded as men of the world by what is divine."[96] Like the law, religion makes man aware of the limit of human possibility, the cleavage between existence and nonexistence. Our capacity for religion directs us to that final negation—the recognition that *we must die.*

Religion, though it come disguised as the most intimate friend of men . . . is nevertheless the adversary. Religion is the most dangerous enemy a man has on this side of the grave. For religion is the human possibility of remembering that we must die: it is the place where, in the world of time and of things and of men, the intolerable question is clearly formulated—Who, then, art thou? "The Law of God brings men under condemnation; for, in so far as they are under law, they are slaves of sin, and consequently guilty of death" (Calvin).[97]

Religion ultimately exposes man's sinful condition as that of unbelief. The religious man actually wants to do what only God can do. He strives to reach God; he does not have faith. This is the spiritual rebellion of the religious man who refuses to depend on God's grace.

Sin is always unbelief. And unbelief is always man's faith in himself. And this faith invariably consists in the fact that man makes the mystery of his responsibility his own mystery, instead of accepting it as the mystery of God.[98]

This faith, which Barth calls religion, is the antithesis of the revelation of God witnessed to in the New Testament, which speaks of Jesus Christ as the one who acts for us and on us.

If the crisis of man's religion is to have a positive resolution it can only come as a breaking in upon man's religiosity from outside man. This is what happens in God's self-revelation in Jesus Christ. It is in the light of that revelation alone that man can recognize his religion as idolatry and as unbelief.

According to Barth, it is possible to speak of "true" religion but only in the same sense that we can speak of a "justified sinner," i.e., "as a creature of grace."

If by the concept of a "true religion" we mean truth which belongs to religion in itself and as such, it is just as unattainable as a "good man," if by goodness we mean something which man can achieve on his own initiative. No religion is true. It can only become true. ... And it can become true only in the way in which man is justified, from without. ... Like justified man, religion is a creature of grace.[99]

It follows that Christianity is not the true religion as such. It can only become so, by grace. "That there is a true religion is

an event in the act of the grace of God in Jesus Christ."[100] Insofar as the Christian religion is understood and lived in the light of the Christian revelation, it can rightfully be called the one and only true religion. However, it is the free grace of God as revealed in Jesus Christ and received in faith that constitutes the truth of the Christian religion—and that separates it from all human religion and natural theology.

If God has given man the decisive revelation of himself in Jesus Christ, then to seek to find God somewhere else is to fail to give God the honor. To attempt to confine or limit God to some human institution or agency, whether it be the Bible, the tradition, or the institutional church, is also to make something else more ultimate than Jesus Christ. The Bible, the Church, and the tradition— like John the Baptist in Grunewald's Isenheim altarpiece—can only point and witness to the revelation of God in Jesus Christ. To start anywhere else or to claim any other source is to go astray. In his writings Barth returns again and again to this painting by Grunewald as the final word on the issue of natural theology. Barth's description of the Isenheim Nativity is a beautiful summation of his position *in nuce.*

Over there, but quite lonely, the child Jesus lies in His mother's arms, surrounded with unmistakable signs reminding us that He is a child of earth like all the rest. Only the little child, not the mother, sees what is to be seen there, the Father. He alone, the Father, sees right into the eyes of this child. On the same side as Mary appears the Church, facing at a distance. It has open access on this side, it adores, it magnifies, it praises, therefore it sees what is indeed the glory of the only-begotten of His Father, full of grace and truth. But it sees it indirectly. What it sees directly is only the little child in His humanity; it sees the Father only in the light that falls upon the Son, and the Son only in this light from the Father. This is the way, in fact, that the Church believes in and recognizes God in Christ. It cannot run over to the right side, where the glory of God can be seen directly.... Because of this light streaming down from above, it worships before this human being as before God Himself, although to all visual appearance He is literally nothing but a human being.... It faces the mystery. It does not stand within the mystery. It can and must adore with Mary and point with the Baptist. It cannot and must not do more than this. But it can and must do this.[101]

The Later Direction of Barth's Theology.

It is not exceptional that a man with a mind and spirit as gifted and lively as Barth's should, over sixty years of publication, have set out on new and revolutionary paths. A careful study of Barth's writings reveals several such creative advances in new directions, nevertheless always within a general perspective that remained extraordinarily consistent. The most significant change evident in the later volumes of the *Church Dogmatics* after 1935 was what Hans Urs von Balthasar has called Barth's "Christological concentration." This "change" is actually only a dialectical shift of emphasis, from a theology of the Word of God to what Barth called a theology of the "Humanity of God."

In his later years Barth looked back to the book on *Romans* as a necessary "corrective" to the immanentism and humanism of liberal theology which prevailed at the turn of the century. *Romans*, with its "Wholly Other" and "infinite qualitative distinction between God and Man," had to be spoken, and, Barth believed, must still be heard. Nevertheless, it is not the whole truth of the Gospel

and needs its own dialectical corrective, which Barth sought to achieve. In a lecture delivered in 1956, Barth commented that the revolution he had forced upon theology forty years earlier was basically a rediscovery of the Godness of God, and then he asked:

But did we not largely fail to perceive that the Godness of the living God ... has its meaning and power only in the context of His history and of His dialogue with man, and therefore in His togetherness with him? Yes, indeed—and that is the point from which there must be no going back.... It is the divinity which as such has also the character of humanity. It is in this form and only in this form that the statement of the Godness of God is to be opposed to the theology of the preceding period.[102]

Barth had never conceived of God's revelation as an abstraction but instead as always present in the person of Jesus Christ. However, after 1935 Barth's whole theology became focused on Christology. Not only the doctrine of God but the doctrines of creation, election, and anthropology are now all defined christologically. This is because, for Barth, God's Godness "includes in itself His humanity." In Christ humanity is taken up into the very Godhead itself.

We must not refer to the second "person" of the Trinity, to the eternal Son or the eternal Word of God *in abstracto* .... According to the free and gracious will of God the eternal Son of God *is* Jesus Christ.... He is the decision of God in time, and yet according to what took place in time *the decision which was made from all eternity*.[103]

We cannot, then, look at Creation as the work of "the Logos in itself," of a *Deus absconditus*, but only to the work of God as it is seen in Christ. Creation must always be viewed in the light of God's *eternal covenant* in Christ. Barth thus refers to the covenant as "the internal basis of creation." Christian theology does not have the responsibility of showing

how creation promises, proclaims and prophesies the covenant, but how it prefigures and to that extent anticipates it without being identical with it; not how creation prepares the covenant, but how in so doing it is itself already a unique sign of the covenant and a true sacrament; not Jesus Christ as the goal, but Jesus Christ as the beginning of creation.[104]

According to Barth, Jesus Christ, as the only ground and goal of creation, is the clue to anthropology. If we want to understand man, we needn't construct some general anthropological model, nor should we even look to the archetypal image of fallen Adam. Christ alone is the prototype of humanity.

There in the eternity of the divine counsel which is the meaning and basis of all creation . . . the decision was made who and what true man is. There his constitution was fixed and sealed once for all. . . . No man can elude this prototype. We derive wholly from Jesus not merely our potential and actual relation to God, but even in our human nature as such. For it is He who, as the ground and goal of the covenant of grace planned for man, is also the ground and goal of man's creation.[105]

If Christ is the ground and goal of humanity, then sin and evil cannot be the last word about man.

In his relation to God a man may become a sinner and thus distort and corrupt his own nature, but he cannot revoke what was decided in Jesus apart from him concerning the true nature of man. . . . And if Jesus forgives his sins and restores his spoiled relation to God,

this means that Jesus again controls what originally belongs to Him. . . . He has the freedom and power to do this. . . . And He does just that by making Himself our Saviour.[106]

In virtue of the eternal covenant in Jesus Christ, the creation—including man—stands essentially in a *positive* relationship to God. That is the first and last word of God! Barth can therefore speak of sin and evil as "nothingness" and as the "ontological impossibility," for they are denied by the prior covenant of grace in Jesus Christ.

It (sin and evil) is that which is excluded from all present and future existence, i.e. chaos, the world fashioned otherwise than according to the divine purpose, and therefore formless and intrinsically impossible. . . . That which is ungodly and anti-godly can have reality only as that which by God's decision and operation has been rejected and disappeared and therefore only as a frontier of that which is and will be according to God's decision and action.[107]

By speaking of the "impossibility" of sin, Barth does not mean that there are no such realities as sin and evil but rather that they exist only *relatively*. Sin is an attempt to evade and escape from grace, but sin cannot finally prevent God from addressing His *Yes* to man.

Certainly even as this man he has not ceased to be the good creature and the elect of God. Even as a wrongdoer he cannot fall from the hand of God; he cannot, as it were, snatch himself out of the divine grasp.[108]

The radicalness of Barth's "Christocentric concentration" is most evident in his treatment of the doctrine of election, which he calls "the sum of the Gospel because of all words that can be said or heard it is the best."[109] It is here that Barth parts company with the Reformers most emphatically. For the Reformers, God's election—coming before Christ— is a mystery. Some men are elected to salvation and others to eternal damnation. Why some confess Christ and others remain unbelievers is part of God's inscrutable will, the work of the *Deus absconditus*. For Barth such a conception of double predestination, as a mixed message of joy and horror, is intolerable. Not because it appears unjust to our human perspective, but because it is contrary to God's eternal covenant of grace in Jesus Christ, for "before Him and without Him and beside Him God does not elect or will anything." According to Barth, Jesus Christ is both the electing God and the elected man.[110]

In Jesus Christ God in his free grace determines Himself for sinful man and sinful man for Himself. He therefore takes upon Himself the rejection of man with all its consequences, and elects man to participation in His own glory.[111]

Here Barth develops a doctrine of double predestination, but one far different from that of John Calvin. According to Barth, predestination takes place in Jesus Christ alone, but it, too, involves a twofold movement. In Jesus Christ, God elected Himself for rejection and death, but also elected sinful man for election and eternal life. Here both God's Yes and God's No are heard, but whereas the No is addressed to Christ alone as the rejected of God, the Yes is spoken to man whom God in his original covenant has elected for fellowship with Himself.

What we have to consider in the elected man Jesus is, then, the destiny of human nature, its exaltation to fellowship with

God. . . . It is in this man that the exaltation itself is revealed and proclaimed. For with His decree concerning this man, God decreed too that this man should be the cause and the instrument of our exaltation.[112]

Jesus Christ represents "the original and all-inclusive election," for of none other can it be said that "his election carries in it and with it the election of the rest." Jesus is at once the elect for all and the reprobate for all. It therefore follows that for Barth predestination is "the non-rejection of man."[113] Does this not entail a doctrine of *apokatastasis*, of universal salvation? Barth is unwilling to make such an assertion about the freedom of God's grace.

If we are to respect the freedom of the divine grace, we cannot venture the statement that it must and will finally be coincident with the . . . doctrine of the so-called *apokatastasis*. No such right or necessity can legitimately be deduced. . . . But, again, in grateful recognition of the grace of the divine freedom we cannot venture the opposite statement that there cannot and will not be this final opening up and enlargement of the circle of election.[114]

One thing is certain: man cannot place limits on the loving-kindness of God as revealed in Jesus Christ.

The fact is that God has declared himself for man, for all men. What distinction, if any, can be made between Christians and nonbelievers, if Jesus is at once elect for all? The difference, for Barth, is not that the Christian is saved and the nonbeliever damned. The Christian and nonbeliever stand together in their common need. It is God who stoops down to both.

Who is it who really has to stoop down at this point? Not one man to another, a believer to an unbeliever. . . . He who stoops down to the level of us all, both believers and un-believers, is the real God alone, in His grace and mercy. And it is only by the fact that he knows this that the believing man is distinguished from the unbeliever.[115]

The man of faith does not arrogantly glory in his election. His acknowledgement of God's grace simply makes him aware that he is called and chosen to be in Christ, to live the life of truth rather than falsehood. The Christian is called to service in response to the gift of God's grace. "This service, and therefore the blessedness of the elect, consists in gratitude for the self-offering of God."[116] If we ask what is meant by gratitude, and therefore blessedness, Barth replies that it is

participation in the life of God in a human existence and action in which there is a representation and illustration of the glory of God Himself.... The elect man is chosen in order to respond to the gracious God, to be His creaturely image, His imitator.[117]

The Christian life is marked above all else by joyful thanksgiving.

The only answer to *charis* is *eucharistia* (thanksgiving).... Grace and gratitude belong together like heaven and earth. Grace evokes gratitude like the voice an echo.[118]

It is no wonder that Barth has been called *the* theologian of the Good News. To think of Barth only as the theologian of crisis and judgment is to fail to hear the central theme of his *Church Dogmatics*, which is the gospel of God's gracious election. If anything, Barth is criticized today for his optimism! His theology has been referred to as "the triumph of grace,"[119] a triumph which, it is claimed, has relativized evil and divine judgment

and has left no place for real human freedom. It is now said that in Barth's theology man is "swamped by grace."

There is little question that Barth's theology is open to serious criticism, but it is equally clear that the old stereotype, which portrayed Barth as a gloomy, pessimistic, rather narrowly orthodox theologian who stressed the transcendent otherness of God, is now impossible for anyone who reads the *Church Dogmatics*. Barth is indeed appropriately called "God's joyful partisan."

Conclusion

The influence of Neo-Orthodoxy or the Theology of the Word of God on Christian thought since 1920 is extraordinary. Its wide appeal and considerable influence is due in large measure to the fact that it represented a rediscovery and reaffirmation of the distinctive claims of Christianity over against all other faiths and secular ideologies. It came as an authentic and unqualified word at a time of intellectual uncertainty. It called for a breaking of all alliances with philosophy, the sciences, and culture, for the simple reason that they were responsible for blunting and distorting and accommodating the Christian message in order that it might conform to the spirit of the age.

Neo-Orthodoxy should be seen essentially as a "corrective" theology which sought to disengage theology from its dependence upon a culture in crisis. It carried out its corrective task by returning to the authentic insights of classical Christianity as found in the Reformers, Augustine, the creeds of the Church and, above all, the Bible itself. The disengagement is reflected in the reaffirmation of such beliefs as *sola gratia* and *sola scriptura* which place the sovereignty of God's grace and the uniqueness of biblical authority in discontinuity with the works and traditions of men.

Neo-Orthodoxy replaced the liberal emphasis on the immanence of God in nature and human history with the transcendence of God; divine revelation now displaced religious experience as the seat of authority. Following Paul and Augustine, these theologians found the locus of sin in the corruption of human freedom and not, as did the liberals, in the natural impulses or in human ignorance, both of which could be meliorated by human effort. Nor is history to be viewed as a progressive overcoming of evil and a gradual building of the Kingdom of God. History, like nature, is a veil hiding the purposes of God. Only in faith can man discern any meaning to history and that meaning lies not in history itself but beyond history, in revelation. History is the stage where the drama of the struggle between the temporal and the eternal is played out and where man faces the ever-present eschatological "crisis" of faith.

The return to these classical Christian, and especially Reformation, themes is the reason this movement has been called Neo-*Orthodox*. However, Neo-Orthodoxy is not merely a repristination of classical Protestant Orthodoxy. To comprehend the unique character of this theology, it is just as important to understand the significance of the designation "Neo." The leaders of this movement were educated in the liberal theological tradition. Though they reacted negatively to much in that tradition, they also appropriated many principles of the liberal heritage which made a return to classical orthodoxy as such impossible.

Neo-Orthodoxy accepted the Ritschlian doctrine that theology must abjure all metaphysics. Most of the Neo-Orthodox theologians stand in the Kantian tradition and accept Kant's critique of natural theology. In their view there is no such thing as a *Christian* natural theology. Christian theology must begin with the givenness of historical revelation. Nevertheless, the historical revelation witnessed to in the Bible is not, as in Orthodoxy, infallible or inerrant. For Neo-Orthodoxy also agrees with liberalism in accepting the findings of modern scientific and historical research, even though such findings may require radical adjustments in traditional belief. Neo-Orthodoxy is, in fact, associated with some of the most radical historical conclusions concerning the biblical traditions. Like Catholic Modernism, Neo-Orthodoxy makes a sharp distinction between scientific and religious truth. The warfare between science and theology thus holds no interest for Neo-Orthodox theologians, for they see the true meaning of the biblical narratives as lying outside the province of scientific investigation. The biblical narratives depict events which contain symbolic, mythic, and parabolic truth, but not literal or scientific fact. The stories of creation, of the fall of Adam, of Christ's birth and resurrection are not properly discerned when their "truth" is put to the test of scientific evidence. Some of these events might be called "historical" but they are not simply historical in the common, empirical sense of that term.

Neo-Orthodoxy can best be understood as a creative synthesis of classical Reformation Christianity and nineteenth-century liberalism. It represents a brilliant synthesis of the old and new and, for that reason, has had wide appeal and influence. However, the union of these two very different traditions has proved to be not only creative but also problematic. In the past twenty years or so Neo-Orthodoxy has come under careful scrutiny and criticism not only from outside but from a new generation of theologians who grew up as children of the movement. The dissatisfaction felt by these critics appears to be directed at the fundamental aim of Neo-Orthodoxy, i.e., the discontinuity between Christianity and man's secular experience and norms of judgment. This criticism has focused on two principal issues: the relationship between theology and philosophy and between revelatory history and secular history.

Barth and those who have followed his lead have conceived of man's knowledge of God in terms of what we might call a radical divine "actualism." By that we mean that man remains the passive receptor of God's revelation. The question raised by such an "actualism" is whether a radically passive view of revelation is possible, considering the fact that revelation is always mediated to man by finite, human means. If revelation is a form of knowing, does this not imply that man must make some discriminating judgments between competing revelations, all of which are mediated to man through some finite channel, be it a person, a book, or an institution? And if such discriminating judgment is required, does not such reflection involve reason, hence some general philosophical presuppositions? Is not the relationship between theology, as a human science, and philosophy indispensable and more complex than Neo-Orthodoxy is willing to acknowledge?

The second issue in Neo-Orthodoxy which now appears especially problematical is the way this movement conceives of the relationship between revelation and history. These theologians frequently speak of "God acting in history," but what they mean by "history" is a *sacred* history which is veiled to the scientific historian. For revelatory history involves a transcendent dimension which cannot be contained within the categories of historiography. Such historical events are, paradoxically, *suprahistorical*. They appear to partake of two histories, ordinary empirical history—which is open to common observation—and *Heilsgeschichte*, which is only discerned by faith. But what the relationship is between these two histories and how indispensable the one is to the other is not at all clear. Revelation history appears to be neither solely in heaven nor entirely on earth but in some mysterious limbo between the two. R. R. Niebuhr has raised the question as to whether "sacred history" can properly be called history at all in Barth's theology.

When the resurrection of Christ is thought of as a "sacred event," transcending the historical continuum that conditions all experiential concepts and perception, it has in fact lost its revelatory quality. For that which is said to reveal history must participate to a significant degree in the order of reality it is supposed to illuminate.[120]

Despite the problems that Neo-Orthodoxy has bequeathed to a new generation of theologians, it remains the most formative movement in Protestant theology in the twentieth century. It achieved its greatest following in America in the 1940s and 1950's. Since the early 1960's Barth's influence on American theology has been in sharp decline. And yet it is evident that those younger theologians who are striking out in new and very different directions identify their position vis-à-vis Barth and the Dialectical theology. If there is presently emerging a new liberal theology, it will be one that will have had to learn some important lessons from the "corrective" theology of Karl Barth. Neo-Orthodoxy is one of those movements in the history of thought that can be by-passed only at great peril.

NOTES

1. Albert Schweitzer, *The Quest of the Historical Jesus* (New York, 1964), p. 4.
2. Gunther Bornkamm, *Jesus of Nazareth* (New York, 1960), p. 13.
3. Albert Schweitzer, op. cit., pp. 398–399.
4. Ibid., p. 399.
5. Ibid.
6. Ibid., p. 403.
7. W. Heitmuller, *Taufe und Abendmahl bei Paulus Darstellung und religionsgeschichtliche Beleuchtung* (Göttingen, 1903), p. 52; cited in Heinz Zahrnt, *The Historical Jesus* (New York, 1963), p. 57.
8. E. Troeltsch, "The Dogmatics of the Religionsgeschichtliche Schule," *The American Journal of Theology* (Jan. 1913), pp. 12–13.
9. E. Troeltsch, *Christian Thought: Its History and Application* (New York, 1957), pp. 44–45.
10. Ibid., p. 52.
11. Ibid., p. 54.
12. Ibid., p. 55.
13. Ibid., pp. 55–56.
14. Ibid., pp. 58–59.
15. Ibid., p. 63.
16. Ibid.
17. Hermann Diem, *Dogmatics* (Edinburgh, 1959), pp. 8–9.
18. R. H. Lightfoot, *History and Interpretation in the Gospels* (London, 1935), pp. 30–31.
19. R. Bultmann, *Jesus and the Word* (New York, 1934), p. 8.
20. R. Bultmann, *Glauben und Verstehen* I (Tübingen, 1933), p. 208; cited in Zahrnt, op. cit., pp. 84–85.
21. R. Bultmann, *Kerygma and Myth*, I, ed. H. W. Bartsch (London, 1953), p. 41.
22. Karl Barth, *God, Grace and Gospel* (Scottish Journal of Theology Occasional Papers No. 8, Edinburgh, 1959), pp. 57 f.
23. Søren Kierkegaard, *Attack Upon Christendom*, in *A. Kierkegaard Anthology*, ed. Robert Bretall (Princeton, 1946), pp. 442–443.
24. Ibid., p. 448.
25. S. Kierkegaard, *Either-Or*, II (Princeton, 1949), p. 175.
26. Ibid., p. 179.
27. S. Kierkegaard, *Concluding Unscientific Postscript* (Princeton, 1941), p. 280.
28. Ibid., p. 281.
29. S. Kierkegaard, *Fear and Trembling* (New York, 1939), p. 147.
30. *Postscript*, op. cit., p. 471.
31. Ibid., pp. 488–489.
32. Ibid., p. 473.
33. S. Kierkegaard, *The Concept of Dread* (Princeton, 1957), p. 18.
34. *Fear and Trembling* (Princeton, 1941), p. 105.
35. S. Kierkegaard, *Philosophical Fragments* (Princeton, 1952), title page.
36. Ibid., pp. 6–7.
37. Ibid., p. 9.
38. Ibid., p. 10.
39. Ibid., p. 13.
40. Ibid., p. 19.
41. Ibid., p. 25.
42. Ibid., pp. 41–42.
43. Ibid., p. 51.
44. Ibid., p. 52.
45. Ibid., p. 53.
46. Ibid., p. 84.
47. Ibid., p. 86.
48. Ibid., p. 83.
49. Ibid., p. 87.
50. Ibid.

51. S. Kierkegaard, *Journals*, 22 (IA, 75).
52. *Concluding Unscientific Postscript*, op. cit., pp. 23–24.
53. Ibid., p. 30.
54. Ibid.
55. Ibid., pp. 179–180.
56. Ibid., p. 181.
57. Ibid., p. 182.
58. Ibid., p. 217.
59. Ibid., p. 183.
60. Ibid., p. 203.
61. Ibid., p. 182.
62. S. Kierkegaard, *Papirer*, X2 A 354.
63. J. Heywood Thomas, *Subjectivity and Paradox* (New York, 1957), p. 76.
64. Karl Barth, *How I Changed My Mind*, in John Godsey, ed. (Richmond, 1966), p. 9.
65. Karl Barth, *Christliche Dogmatik* (München, 1927), p. IX; cited in Paul Lehmann, "The Changing Course of a Corrective Theology," *Theology Today* (October, 1956), p. 334.
66. Cited in Arthur C. Cochrane, *The Church's Confession Under Hitler* (Philadelphia, 1962), pp. 222–223.
67. Ibid., pp. 239–240.
68. Karl Barth, *The Word of God and the Word of Man* (New York, 1957), p. 206.
69. Ibid., pp. 207–208.
70. Ibid., p. 209.
71. Karl Barth, *The Epistle to the Romans* (New York, 1960), p. 10.
72. Ibid., pp. 46–47.
73. Ibid., pp. 97–99.
74. Karl Barth, *Church Dogmatics* II (Edinburgh, 1956), p. 199.
75. *Romans*, op. cit., pp. 29–30.
76. Karl Barth, *Church Dogmatics* I, 1 (New York, 1936), pp. 204–205.
77. Karl Barth, *The Word of God and the Word of Man*, op. cit., p. 32.
78. Ibid., pp. 35–36.
79. Ibid., pp. 38–39.
80. Ibid., pp. 42–43, 45.
81. Ibid., p. 80.
82. Karl Barth, *Against the Stream* (New York, 1954), p. 223.
83. Barth emphasized this point in strongly polemical terms in "The Strange New World of the Bible" in 1916, again throughout the *Church Dogmatics* and in his farewell lectures as Professor at Basel in 1962. See his *Evangelical Theology: An Introduction* (New York, 1963), pp. 30 ff.
84. *Word of God and Word of Man*, op. cit., p. 60.
85. *Church Dogmatics* I, 2, p. 508.
86. Ibid., p. 529.
87. *Against the Stream*, op. cit., p. 221.
88. *Church Dogmatics* I, 2, pp. 506–507.
89. *Church Dogmatics* I, 1, p. 123.
90. Ibid., p. 181.
91. *Church Dogmatics* I, 2, p. 172.
92. *Church Dogmatics* II, 1, p. 84.
93. *Church Dogmatics* IV, 1, p. 81.
94. *Church Dogmatics* II, 1, p. 135.
95. *Romans*, op. cit., p. 236.
96. Ibid., p. 242.
97. Ibid., p. 268.
98. *Church Dogmatics* I, 2, p. 314.
99. Ibid., pp. 325–326.
100. Ibid., p. 344.
101. Ibid., p. 125.
102. "The Humanity of God," in *God, Grace and Gospel*, op. cit., p. 37.
103. *Church Dogmatics* IV, 1, p. 52.
104. *Church Dogmatics* III, 1, p. 232.
105. *Church Dogmatics* III, 2, p. 50.
106. Ibid., pp. 50–51.
107. *Church Dogmatics* III, 1, p. 102.
108. *Church Dogmatics* IV, 1, p. 540.
109. *Church Dogmatics* II, 2, p. 3.
110. For a full treatment of this theme, see the *Church Dogmatics* II, 2, pp. 94–145.
111. Ibid., p. 94.
112. Ibid., p. 118.
113. Ibid., pp. 117, 167.
114. Ibid., pp. 417–418.
115. *Church Dogmatics* II, 1, p. 95.
116. *Church Dogmatics* II, 2, p. 413.
117. Ibid.
118. *Church Dogmatics* IV, 1, p. 41.
119. For a critique of Barth's theology at this point, see G. C. Berkouwer, *The Triumph of Grace in the Theology of Karl Barth* (London, 1956).
120. R. R. Niebuhr, *Resurrection and Historical*

Reason (New York, 1957), p. 87. For another very discerning critique of the problem of revelation and history in Neo-Orthodox theology, see Van Harvey, *The Historian and the Believer* (New York, 1966).

SUGGESTIONS FOR FURTHER READING

NEO-ORTHODOXY

Cobb, John B. *Living Options in Protestant Theology* (Philadelphia: Westminster Press, 1962). Part II of this book contains excellent accounts of the theologies of Emil Brunner and Karl Barth.

Robinson, James M., ed. *The Beginnings of Dialectical Theology*, Vol. I (Richmond: John Knox Press, 1968). Essays, reviews, debates having to do with the beginnings of Dialectical theology by Barth, Gogarten, Bultmann, Harnack, Tillich, and others.

SØREN KIERKEGAARD

Collins, James. *The Mind of Kierkegaard* (Chicago: Henry Regnery, 1953). An excellent survey and analysis of important themes in Kierkegaard's theology.

Diem, Hermann. *Kierkegaard's Dialectic of Existence* (Edinburgh: Oliver and Boyd, 1959).

Johnson, H. and Thulstrup, N. *A Kierkegaard Critique* (New York: Harper, 1962). A valuable collection of essays on various aspects of Kierkegaard's thought by distinguished Kierkegaard scholars.

Lowrie, Walter. *A Short Life of Kierkegaard* (Princeton: Princeton University Press, 1942). The standard, brief biography of Kierkegaard.

Thomas, J. H. *Subjectivity and Paradox* (Oxford: Blackwell and Mott, 1957). This and the Diem book are more specialized studies of Kierkegaard. Recommended to the advanced student.

KARL BARTH

Casalis, George. *Portrait of Karl Barth* (New York: Doubleday, 1963). A brief, sympathetic account of Barth's life and the development of his theology.

Come, Arnold. *An Introduction to Barth's "Dogmatics" for Preachers* (Philadelphia: Westminster Press, 1963).

Hartwell, Herbert. *The Theology of Karl Barth: An Introduction* (Philadelphia: Westminster Press, 1964). The two books above are lucid, brief surveys of the major themes of Barth's twelve-volume *Church Dogmatics*.

Torrance, T. F. *Karl Barth: An Introduction to His Early Theology, 1910–1931* (London: S.C.M. Press, 1962).

CHAPTER TWELVE

Christian Existentialism

Paul Tillich

Twentieth-century Christian Existentialism had its beginnings in many of the same movements that were discussed in our account of Neo-Orthodoxy. However, as a general philosophical stance, Existentialism can be traced back to the very beginnings of our Western heritage. Existentialism is as old as philosophy, for it represents a continuous protest against the rationalist notion that the universe and individual existence can be comprehended rationally within some logically necessary conceptual scheme. Existentialists have contended in every age that existence evades every attempt at adequate conceptualization. Existence is marked by a radical contingency and freedom which precludes any notion of a fixed human essence which determines human nature or human possibility.

Chief among the precursors of contemporary Existentialism are Pascal, Nietzsche, and Kierkegaard.* Pascal (1623–1662) lived at a time of rapid scientific advance which appeared to him to leave man in a state of frightening contingency amidst the spatial and temporal infinities of the physical universe. Pascal saw man as a grand yet pathetic creature, finding himself in a world into which he had been *cast* without his knowing why or to what end.

* For Nietzsche and Kierkegaard see Chaps. Eight and Eleven.

345

When I consider the short duration of my life, swallowed up in the eternity before and after, the little space which I fill . . . , cast into the infinite immensity of spaces of which I am ignorant and which know me not, I am frightened, and shocked at being here rather than there; for there is no reason why here rather than there, why now rather than then. Who has put me here? By whose order and direction have this place and time been allotted me? (*Pensées*, 205).

Here Pascal strikes a chord which is heard again and again in recent existentialist literature. Man finds himself alone, alienated from the physical world of nature which serves only to point up the utter contingency and apparent absurdity of his existence.

The events of two monstrous world wars and the appearance of several totalitarian powers within a period of two decades were important factors in the re-emergence of Existentialism and its predominant position in European philosophy between 1920 and 1950. Existentialism represents, in part, a response to the irrational events of those years. Nevertheless, the sources of the movement are many and stretch back to the beginnings of our history. However, there are three twentieth-century philosophers who can justly be called the creators of contemporary existentialist philosophy: Karl Jaspers (1883–1969), Martin Heidegger (1889–   ), and Jean-Paul Sartre (1905–   ). Heidegger and Jaspers were developing their philosophies independently at approximately the same time after World War I. Heidegger published his most important work, *Sein und Zeit*, in 1927; Jasper's *Philosophie* appeared in 1932. Sartre was a pupil of Heidegger and published his influential *L'Etre et le néant* in 1943.

In addition to this threesome there are numerous other philosophers and men of letters who, while perhaps not technically existentialists, have consistently expressed existentialist themes in their writings. A list of such twentieth-century figures would include Gabriel Marcel (1889–   ) and Albert Camus (1913–1960) in France, Nikolai Berdyaev (1874–1948) in Russia, the Spanish writers Miguel de Unamuno (1864–1936) and Jose Ortega y Gasset (1883–1955), and the Jewish philosopher Martin Buber (1878–1965).

It is not possible, nor is it our purpose here, to attempt a full description of the principal doctrines of any of the major existentialist philosophers. Their doctrines are complex and differ technically in important respects. Nevertheless, men like Heidegger, Jaspers, Sartre, and Marcel share several concerns in common, which place them in the same philosophical family tree. What they share are a number of themes which appear again and again in their writings. A brief analysis of these key themes will give a general picture of the movement as a whole.

Key Existentialist Themes

Existence Precedes Essence. Sartre has said that the chief doctrine of Existentialism is that existence precedes essence. This appears clear enough until one examines the term more fully. If one agrees with Kant that there is no determinate difference *in essence* between one hundred imaginary dollars and one hundred dollars in my pocket but that there is, nevertheless, all the difference in the world in my *existential* financial situation, then there are many non-existentialist philosophers who accept Sartre's doctrine.

What Sartre in fact means by this dictum is that there are no eternal essences, say in the mind of God, which precede the existence of things. For Sartre there are no such essences, for essences are determined by human, free decision. However, there are many existentialist philosophers who, though holding that "existence precedes essence," would not agree with Sartre's understanding of that phrase. What these philosophers mean by "existence precedes essence" is simply that existence must not be approached a priori but rather through immediate personal experience. One does not, for example, start with an abstract concept of man and then try to fit experience into one's concept. One begins with the concrete experience of being-in-the-world. This is not to deny that human nature and experience have some common structures or essence; however, it means that if such essences exist they must be discovered a posteriori through my experiences and my participation in the experiences of others.

This means, further, that the existentialist begins his philosophizing with problems that arise from his own personal existence as a human being. The existential thinker is not a dispassionate observer but a passionate actor whose philosophical reflection emerges from his active engagement in the world. As Feuerbach said: "Do not wish to be a philosopher in contrast to being a man ... do not think as a thinker ... think as a living, real being ... think *in* Existence."[1]

The Critique of Rational Objectivity. What the existentialists distrust about so-called objective reflection is, in the words of Kierkegaard, that it "makes the subject accidental and thereby transforms his Existence into something impersonal, and this impersonal character is precisely its objective validity...."[2] But all significant knowledge must, in the existentialist's view, pose the question "What does this knowledge mean for *me*?" There is nothing wrong with "objective" knowledge as far as it goes; where it proves dangerous is in its refusal to consider experiences that purely objective modes of judgment cannot explain or warrant. A good many issues in life can and should be settled only by objective criteria. But there are many questions (and existentially the most significant) that belie logical or empirical resolution and demand the risk of personal decision.

What is more, it is not enough that a man know the objective truth but that he make it existentially his own. A man can believe Christianity is the truth and yet remain personally aloof from it. However, "Truth," as Kierkegaard said, "consists precisely in inwardness."[3] The only reason we can observe the activities of other creatures with detached objectivity is because we are not personally touched by their lives. Place ourselves in their situation and our frame of reference would significantly alter our understanding of the situation. How, then, can a purely objective investigation ever know the truth of human existence? Is it not the case that we can only understand another way of existence by experiencing that existence existentially? Is it not true that we can only know what it means to love, trust and die by actually loving and trusting and dying? "One becomes a theologian," remarked Luther, "by living, by dying, and by being damned—not by understanding, reading, and speculating."[4]

What is further wrong with a narrowly

objective approach to life is that it denies freedom of choice and self-determination. From the scientific point of view everything can be explained deterministically within the cause-effect nexus. But when a man no longer considers himself to be self-determining in some important respects, he comes to view himself as a mere product of his environment. He loses any sense of individuality; he becomes an other-directed, inauthentic man. But deep in man's spirit is a consciousness that he is self-determining and responsible. We know that *we do make ourselves* by our own free choices. No matter how hard we try to escape, we know that we must live with this awful burden of freedom.

Authentic and Inauthentic Existence. *Being-in-the-World.* According to the existentialists, knowing or understanding is neither subjective nor objective. My being-in-the-world is not the awareness of either an empty ego or of something out there which I observe. Rather, my awareness is a *Dasein*, a "being-there" in a concrete situation. My awareness is always that of being in a situation, being confronted with possibilities. Heidegger would rephrase Descartes' *Cogito ergo sum* in terms such as "I think *something*, therefore *I am in a world*." My being-in-the-world discloses the givenness, the naked reality of a situation into which I have been thrown. Myself and the world are given together. And my immediate relation to this situation, confronting this world, is not theoretical or objective but existential.

The situation is characterized by what Heidegger calls Care (*Sorge*). For my awareness of the world is never an awareness of mere things, objects, sub-

stances in extension, but of things immediately present to my concern. They are present to me as instruments for my use, as objects of practical intention. This does not mean that things don't exist independently of me. What is is there, whether present to my awareness or not. But what is (*das Seiende*) only becomes *an intelligible world* through our human ordering or "projective understanding." Things in themselves are meaningless.

Furthermore, our relation to the world, or human awareness in its primordiality, is not characterized by rational or theoretical conceptualization but by certain moods or feelings. These feelings are not to be judged *merely* subjective. They are modes of real disclosure. Among these feelings, the most important is what Kierkegaard called "dread" and what Heidegger calls "anxiety."

Anxiety. Anxiety is a quality of human existence which the existentialists have analyzed at great length. Anxiety, first of all, should not be confused with fear. Fear, as an affective state, always has something in the world as its object. According to Heidegger, it is for this reason a disclosure of inauthentic existence because it represents a spirit of bondage to the world. Anxiety (*Angst*), on the other hand, is that which discloses to man the radicalness of his finitude and freedom. Anxiety has no specific object. It is simply the awareness or awakening to the stark reality of one's existence—one's thrown-ness into the world and one's responsibility for one's finite freedom. Dread or anxiety discloses to man that he is not at home in the world, that the world is by itself indifferent and without meaning. Genuine dread will necessarily shatter a man's contentment and his unreflective security, for it will throw him back upon his own possibilities. Kierkegaard describes dread as follows:

"One may liken dread to dizziness. He whose eye chances to look down into the yawning abyss becomes dizzy . . . . Thus dread is the dizziness of freedom, which occurs when freedom gazes down into its own possibility."

So conceived, anxiety is the necessary precondition of authentic existence, for in anxiety finite freedom becomes conscious of itself and arouses the self to decision and action. Without the experience of dread one never faces the crisis, the break with the world of the everyday. One continues to live a life of inauthenticity, of bondage through busy involvement in "worldly" concern.

Depersonalization. "Worldly" concern leads inevitably to a dehumanized world. Man's-being-in-the-world is, for the existentialists, "being-with-others" (*Mitsein*). Community belongs to being-in-the-world, for persons are not mere objects to be used as instruments of self-aggrandizement. "Worldly" care, however, transforms our relations with persons into relations with objects. An objectification involves a movement toward depersonalization and an inauthentic "being-with-others." It is what Martin Buber calls the relationship of I and It. It leads to a condition of dominance and dependence, of manipulation and alienation.

Depersonalization, when it becomes a social condition, is characterized by certain features. It is the society of "das Man" or mass man—no longer a community but what Kierkegaard calls a "public" or "crowd"—a collection of other-directed automatons. It is human life leveled down to the average, to the cliché. Life in such a society has no firm position; it is in a state of ceaseless flux, of everywhere and nowhere. The existentialists from Kierkegaard to Marcel have described the condition of mass man with great power and truth. Marcel, for example, describes the modern industrial worker as follows:

Surely everything both within him and outside him conspires to identify this man with his functions—meaning not only his functions as worker, as trade union member or as voter, but his vital functions as well. The rather horrible expression "time-table" perfectly describes his life. So many hours for each function. Sleep too is a function which must be discharged, so that the other functions may be exercised in their turn. The same with pleasure, with relaxation; it is logical that the weekly allowance of recreation should be determined by an expert on hygiene. . . . It is natural that the individual should be overhauled at regular intervals like a watch . . . . The hospital plays the part of an inspection bench or the repair shop . . . . As for death, it becomes objectively and functionally the scrapping of what has ceased to be of use and must be written off as a total loss.[5]

This mechanization of personal existence is powerfully described in Jaspers' *Man in the Modern Age.* Jaspers raises the question whether freedom is still a real possibility in our technological society.

The basic problem of our time is whether an independent, human being in his self-comprehended destiny is still possible . . . . Perhaps freedom has only existed for a real but passing moment between two immeasurably long periods of sleep, of which the first period was that of the life of nature, and the second period was that of the life of technology. If so, human existence must die out . . . in a more radical sense than ever before. . . .[6]

It is just this kind of threat which directs the existentialists' attention to what they call the limit-situations of life.

Limit-Situations. There are situations in human existence which we have not chosen and which confront us with the radical openness and alienness of being-in-the-world. These are what Jaspers has called "limit-situations." The most important of these are chance, guilt, and death. They are inescapable conditions of human life which, nevertheless, resist amelioration. They inject into our life a sickening feeling of danger and insecurity and make us conscious of our fragility and homelessness.

Rationalists have always tried to explain away these situations but evil, guilt, and death are inexplicable realities. Guilt, for example, cannot be escaped. Some try to avoid it by refraining from action. But blood on the conscience is inescapable, if blood on one's hands is not. Whether we act or not, we incur guilt. The authentic man will acknowledge his share of guilt and take responsibility for it. It will cause him suffering but he will not run away from it or try to deny it.

The same is true of death. Death is inescapable but we constantly suppress the thought of it from our conscious mind. When it is necessary to speak of it we refer to it euphemistically. We postpone facing this boundary by rationalizing that, while it is certain, it lies in the distant future. Life can proceed as usual. The truth, of course, is that death can come at any moment. Time to determine our goals and to pursue our plans is never certain.

The authentic response to the situation of death is to face the fact that our end can come at any moment and that, therefore, this fact is of momentous consequence. If faced, the fact of death can free us of all postponement; it can set before us the fullness of the present moment and the demand of giving our lives a decisiveness and significance here and now before death robs us of this most precious of gifts. To concentrate on death is not morbid. Rather, it is indispensable to achieving freedom and authenticity. It is only by meditating on such limit-situations in life that we can be awakened to decision, to freedom and, hence, to authentic existence.

It is not surprising that Existentialism has been a subject of special interest to philosophers of religion and theologians, especially Christians, for the themes of man's freedom, fallenness, evil, alienation, and authentic personal and corporate existence have been integral to the Christian vision of the human drama from St. Paul to the present.

Before exploring the thought of two of the most influential Christian existentialist theologians—Paul Tillich and Rudolf Bultmann—mention should be made of the contributions of two theistic existentialist philosophers who have had a profound impact on Christian theology in the last three or four decades. They are Martin Buber and Gabriel Marcel.

Martin Buber

Martin Buber is generally considered the most important, and certainly the most influential, Jewish religious philosopher of the twentieth century. His intellectual roots were in the German philosophic tradition and in Hasidic Judaism.* Buber spent the first half of his long teaching career in Germany, principally at the University of Frankfurt-am-Main. In 1938 he left Germany for Israel where he served as professor of social

* Hasidism was a movement of fervent Jewish mystical piety in Eastern Europe in the eighteenth century.

philosophy at the Hebrew University until his retirement in 1951.

Buber's great contribution to modern thought, and to Christian theologians such as Brunner and Tillich, was his book *I and Thou* (1923). Despite the fact the term has become a cliché, the book has had wide influence not only in theology but in the social sciences, psychotherapy, and education. "In the beginning," writes Buber, "is relation."[7] According to Buber, all real living is meeting. The "self," or the "I," of each person comes into being in one or another of two primary relations: the I-It or the I-Thou. What really determines the being of a man lies not in the objects which stand over-against him but in the way he relates himself to the beings and events in the world. It is the nature of the relation that constitutes the person.

The usual way of relating ourselves to other beings is by experiencing and using them—i.e., we observe a thing, examine it, and test it. Our relationship is essentially objective and instrumental. In its most exact operation it is what we call the experimental or scientific method, but it is the typical way we relate to things and persons in general, although in an unconscious way.

Buber acknowledges that this mode of relation is absolutely indispensable to human life and progress. Much of what we cherish in our civilization would not have been achieved without it. It is necessary in order that we understand and order our world. However, in Buber's view, the I-It relation is not the primary human relationship. That is found in the relation of I-Thou. What is wrong with the I-It relation is that it is the primary world of experiencing. But, according to Buber, experiencing takes place *within* a person and *not between*

persons. That is, experiencing is a purely subjective process—it lacks real mutuality. It is marked by the typical subject-object split. However, can we really know another person when we stand before him in such a relationship of analytical detachment? Can another man be known simply as other objects are known? Buber answers no. Man cannot truly be known as an abstraction.

Real knowledge of another person requires participation, openness, and empathy—not distance. It involves a real encounter and genuine mutuality—the primary relation of I-Thou. The knowledge of another which comes from such real meeting is never adequately expressed in speech, for speech presupposes the subject-object split. It requires the predicating of discrete qualities or characteristics, whereas the whole person always transcends the sum of his definable attributes. The person remains ineffable, and language cannot adequately convey the unique type of personal knowledge which characterizes genuine knowledge of another person. Neither can such knowledge of another be forced—it requires openness and mutuality which can be had only as a free gift, as grace. Moreover, what men learn in the I-Thou relations are the ultimate truths of man's spiritual life which are simply not accessible to man in the realm of the I-It.

Because the I-Thou relations cannot be coerced or planned, they are not relations which can simply be called forth and sustained. Rather, they are rare, intense, fleeting revelations of new depths of meaning. Hence, man cannot live continuously in the world of I-Thou's. He can live steadily and securely in the world of I-It—but, as Buber says, "he who lives with *It* alone is not a man."[8]

What has taken place in the modern

history of both the individual and the race is that the proper alternation between I-It and I-Thou has been disturbed by the increase of the I-It relation. Buber believes our culture has abdicated before the world of the It, which has made impossible a real spiritual life since man has decreased his power to enter into genuine relationships. The man who has come to terms with the world of It has divided his life into two separate provinces: one of external institutions and one of inner feelings—the It and the I. Prophetic of the dual life of contemporary suburban man, Buber wrote in 1923:

> Taking his stand in the shelter of the primary world of separation, which holds off the *I* and the *It* from one another, (man) has divided his life with his fellowmen into two tidily circled-off provinces, one of institutions and the other of feelings . . . . Institutions are "outside," where all sorts of aims are pursued, where a man works, negotiates, bears influence, undertakes, concurs, organizes, conducts business, officiates, preaches . . . . Feelings are "within," where life is lived and man recovers from institutions. Here the spectrum of the emotions dances before the interested glance. Here a man's liking and hate and pleasure are indulged and his pain if it is not too severe. Here he is at home, and stretches himself out in his rocking chair."[9]

The worlds of institutions and of feelings are both bound up with subjectivity; they both refuse real personal relation and deny the possibility of true community. Genuine community can exist only where there is mutuality. What is more, the world of It means ultimately to give life over to a fateful determinism. And this is what threatens to engulf our world. When Buber speaks of the I-Thou relation as free of such a fatalism, he doesn't mean to imply that in genuine encounter men don't act within a determinative causal nexus. Rather, he means that only out of such authentic mutual relation can man really *respond* to concrete external events. In the world of It man does not respond; he only reacts.

All that Buber has to say about the two primary relations has significance for our understanding of God. Our abdication before the world of It has meant that our normal mode of approaching God is by way of objectification, by means of proving his existence as an object among other existing things. But within the framework of I and It we can never truly know another person and, likewise, can never know God. Only when we open ourselves to God and reach out and risk commitment does God truly reveal Himself. And such a meeting with "the Thou that by its nature cannot become an It" does not require any special sacred times or places. Meeting the Eternal Thou occurs in the full acceptance and hallowing of the ordinary and everyday. "If you explore the life of things and of conditioned being you come to the unfathomable, if you deny the life of things and conditioned being you stand before nothingness, if you hallow this life you meet the living God."[10]

What this means is that

> Life cannot be divided between a real relation with God and an unreal relation of *I* and *It* with the world—you cannot both truly pray to God and profit by the world. He who knows the world as something by which he is to profit knows God also in the same way. . . . He—not the "atheist," who addresses the Nameless out of the night and yearning of his garret-window—is the godless man.[11]

The "filled present," which comes through encounter with the Eternal

Thou, is what we have traditionally called revelation. However, we receive this revelation not as a "content" but as a "Presence as power."

This presence and this power include three things, undivided, yet in such a way that we may consider them separately. First, there is the whole fullness of real mutual action, of the being raised and bound up in relation: the man can give no account at all of how the binding in relation is brought about, nor does it in any way lighten his life—it makes life heavier, but heavy with meaning. Secondly, there is the inexpressible confirmation of meaning. Meaning is assured. . . . You do not know how to exhibit and define the meaning of life, you have no formula or picture for it, and yet it has more certitude for you than the perceptions of your senses. . . . Thirdly, this meaning is not that of "another life," but that of this life of ours, not one of the world "yonder" but that of this world of ours, and it desires its confirmation in this life and in relation with this world."[12]

Revelation does not present us with a "solution" to our metaphysical conundrums. Rather, it serves as a confirmation of meaning and call to action.

We have come near to God but not nearer to unveiling being or solving its riddle. We have felt release, but not discovered a "solution." We cannot approach others with what we have received, and say, "You must know this, you must do this." We can only go, and confirm its truth. . . . All revelation is summons and sending.[13]

Martin Buber believed that the Hasidic teachings were an eloquent expression of genuine spirituality. The message of Hasidism also represents the essence of theistic existentialism.

You yourself must begin. Existence will remain meaningless for you if you yourself do not penetrate into it with active love and if you do not in your own way discover its meaning for yourself. Everything is waiting to be hallowed by you; it is waiting to be disclosed in its meeting and to be realized in it by you. . . . Meet the world with the fullness of your being and you shall meet Him.[14]

Gabriel Marcel

In Gabriel Marcel we encounter many of the same themes we have found in Buber. Nevertheless, Marcel's philosophy has very different roots from that of Buber, receiving its greatest impetus from the vitalistic philosophy of Bergson (1859–1941) and from the religious Idealism of the Americans Josiah Royce (1855–1916) and William Ernest Hocking (1873–1966).

Marcel grew up in a very proper bourgeois home and attributes his turn toward abstract and idealistic philosophy in the *lycée* and at the Sorbonne to his strict puritanical childhood. Involvement in the horrors of World War I helped free Marcel from this love of abstraction and was instrumental in turning him toward a literary career. Most of his adult life has been lived as a writer, critic, and free-lance intellectual. Marcel was converted to Roman Catholicism at the age of forty. While his new faith has had its imprint on his philosophical investigations, he does not consider himself, nor does he wish to be thought of, as a *Catholic* philosopher.

Marcel believes that both Idealism and Empiricism have led us down blind paths and have forced us into metaphysical positions which fail to take account of our true existential situation. Idealism has placed the mind in a position of an absolute, impersonal observer, but the mind cannot, actually, stand outside its own thought and treat it as an object.

Because we are engaged *in* being, no purely objective knowledge or judgment of being is possible. The empiricists have also forced us into a philosophical dead end. By dividing the mind from the external world they have left us in a continuous quandary as to the genuineness of our knowledge of the world outside the ego.

Marcel refuses to split up reality in this way. What is metaphysically indubitable is the self incarnate in a body and present *in* the world. My body is not something which I have or possess; it is not something external to me but simply my mode of presence to the world. I cannot, for instance, think of my body as nonexistent. For Marcel it is the primary given of metaphysics. All thought takes place *within* existence. Hence existence must be assumed from the start; it is the existential indubitable. The self-being-together-with-the-world is the primary datum of metaphysics. It cannot be proved but must be assumed.

It is clear that *to be*, for Marcel, means *to participate* in being. To be is to enter into some sort of commerce with the world. Our existence as given is transsubjective, which means philosophically that we should not begin our reflection with the Cartesian "I think" but with the "we are," the communion that binds me to others and in so doing gives me my real self.

Marcel acknowledges that this ontological participation can express very different modes of relation. Like Buber, Marcel sees a stage of participation which is characterized by experiencing and utilizing. This is comparable to Buber's I-It relationships. But man must be awakened out of this stage into that of authentic ontological communion or genuine personal encounter. In real communion neither the self (I) nor the other (Thou) can be reduced to mere objects, i.e., sums of certain definable characteristics. The self and the other are both irreducible mysteries. What is irreducible is primary and cannot be expressed in terms other than itself. Thus ontological communion or participation is finally nonobjectifiable; it is a mystery.

What has occurred in the modern world is a loss of communion, of participation or the sense of *presence*. Marcel calls this the loss of "ontological weight." We have reduced human relations and tasks to the status of problems to be treated and resolved as objective things. This has led to the widespread depersonalization of life with all its attendant horrors, raising the specter of a *Brave New World*.

In discussing the modes of ontological relation, Marcel distinguishes between the kind of reflection that is appropriate to the sciences and that which is appropriate to reflection on human relations. The distinction is between a problem and a mystery. According to Marcel, a problem is something which is open to solution by the application of certain techniques. It is appropriate to the sciences, since one engages in scientific study from an objective or disinterested stance and achieves a definite solution or result. However, this form of reflection is not capable of dealing with situations in which the self is inextricably involved and where the feelings or attitudes of the person toward the situation are crucial to understanding the true nature of the problem. Questions such as love, suffering, guilt, and death are examples of situations in which the individual cannot remove himself from the situation. Here we are on the threshold of what Marcel calls mystery.

A mystery is a question or situation in which the data of reflection include the self. Thus Marcel speaks of being, of ontological reflection, as a mystery, since one can never totally extract himself from his reflection on being. Mysteries are existential situations that can never be reduced to neat solutions, nor can they ever be said to be done with. They have a way of ceaselessly renewing themselves. However, what is distinctive about a mystery is not that it is insoluble. We may never discover a cure for the common cold, but that does not make the cold a mystery. It remains an unsolved problem. What characterizes a mystery is its nonobjectifiability, the fact that it points to the open, transcendent character of being with its ever-deepening implications for our existential experience. Mysteries are "metaproblematic." One approaches problems in a mood of curiosity; one faces mysteries in the spirit of wonder—what Marcel calls ontological humility or reverence.

Marcel believes that man, as a spiritual being, has an appetite or *exigence* for being, but in his reflection man's being always eludes his grasp. It must be humbly accepted as a continually bestowed gift. What is implied in such reflection is the awareness that one's being must always be a *being with*, a participation, if it is to take on authenticity and know the fullness of being. In the world of mere existence, of *having*, there is a drying up of being—a growing sense of emptiness. Thus authentic *being with* is experienced as fullness. It involves a presentiment of inexhaustibility, of transcendence, which quickens a man's spirit with joy, faith, and hope. Marcel likens this fullness to the experience of being in love.

I called the experience of fullness like that which is involved in love, when love knows that it is shared, when it experiences itself as shared. From this point of view to fulfil is not strictly speaking to accomplish, if by accomplishment we mean that something is finished or brought to a close.[15]

Our lives are lived in the ever-present possibility of fullness and hope or emptiness and despair. Despair comes when one cannot affirm being—when being is seen as fragmented and barren. Marcel believes that victory over such existential despair comes only through communion or participation in which the presence of being becomes open to the transcendent. Such communion is creative of a hope in being and a fidelity to being.

Marcel's analysis of the phenomenon of hope and fidelity are full of rich insights. Hope, according to Marcel, is not directed at some specific outcome (that is desire), nor is hope dependent on any eventual empirical success. Rather, hope is what gives life its sense of holiness; it is what keeps life open to the transcendant. Hope is expressed in what Marcel calls *disponibilité*, availability, which connotes openness, abandonment of self, welcoming. The man of hope remains open to the "absolute recourse" —he does not despair in the face of life's negativities.

Fidelity is also a fruit of genuine participation. Fidelity is a loyalty to other beings and a witness to one's trust or faith in being itself. According to Marcel, fidelity is not a virtue *possessed* by a self; rather it is through fidelity that one acquires a self, i.e., is given unity to one's disparate, immediate states of consciousness. Fidelity actually creates the self. My self is in the making, created in the present by my response to other beings.

Fidelity is not simply constancy to some principle or to one's own honor. The axis is not the self but the other person. It is, in Buber's terms, the uncoerced presence of an I to a Thou.

Marcel tells us that in every appeal from another there is, in and through it, an appeal to fidelity itself—an absolute fidelity to being. In our relationships of loyalty to other persons we come to exist in a relationship of fidelity to being itself. It is here that we enter into the region of theological reflection. Yet what underlies all theological conceptualization is this existential response of hope and fidelity.

Paul Tillich (1886-1965)

The intellectual sources of Paul Tillich's rich and monumental theological system are many. They include Platonism, the late medieval Christian mystics, such as Jacob Böhme, the German Idealist tradition, especially Schelling, as well as the existentialists from Kierkegaard to Heidegger. For this reason some have questioned whether Tillich can properly be classed as an Existentialist. However, Tillich admits to standing within the Existentialist movement and, while his theology is governed by a basic ontological structure, Tillich correlates this structure with man's existential questions and concerns. As we shall see, the existentialist stance dominates Tillich's theological method and system.

Paul Tillich was born in Starzeddel, Germany, the son of a pastor of the Lutheran Church. He attended school in the old medieval town of Königsberg-Neumark. Tillich believed that this gothic environment and his childhood summers on the Baltic sea were the principal sources of his life-long romantic sense of nature and the holy. Tillich studied at several universities, including Berlin, Tübingen, and Halle, receiving his degree of Doctor of Philosophy from Breslau in 1911, with a dissertation on Schelling. He served as an army chaplain for four years during World War I. After the war he began his teaching career at Berlin and later was Professor of Theology at Marburg, Dresden, and Leipzig. During these years he served as a colleague of Heidegger and Bultmann and began to develop his own theological system in response to the dialectical theology of the young Karl Barth.

In 1929 Tillich became Professor of Philosophy at the University of Frankfurt. At this time he was deeply involved in the Religious-Socialist movement. This political activity and his opposition to Hitler and National Socialism led to his dismissal from his university chair in 1933. As it happened, Reinhold Niebuhr was traveling in Germany that same summer and urged him to come to America. Soon after his departure from Germany, Tillich was invited to become Professor of Philosophical Theology at Union Theological Seminary in New York. He remained in that position, while also serving as a professor at Columbia University, until his retirement in 1955. He was then given the distinguished position of University Professor at Harvard. In 1962 he moved on to the University of Chicago where a special chair of theology was created for him.

Between 1951 and 1964 Tillich published the five parts (in three volumes) of his *Systematic Theology*. Along with Barth's *Church Dogmatics*, this work stands out as one of the foremost pieces of constructive theology of this century. After World War II Tillich produced several popular books including *The Courage to Be, The Shaking of the Foun-*

dations, *The New Being*, and *Dynamics of Faith*, whose influence in both the secular and religious communities was rivaled only by the writings of his colleague, Reinhold Niebuhr.

The Existential Starting Point. In an essay on "Religion as a Dimension in Man's Life," Tillich points out that the modern study of religion has been characterized by the attempt to reduce it to some other natural aspect or condition of human experience. The philosopher tends to equate religion with metaphysics, the sociologist explains religious experience on the basis of certain societal needs, and the psychologist may reduce religion to certain forms of projection and rationalization. Tillich does not deny that these analyses have a place, but he believes they do not get at the essence of religion as a dimension of the human spirit.

According to Tillich, religion is not a separate endowment of man's life which can be set side by side with man's rational, moral, and aesthetic faculties. Rather, religion is the *depth dimension* in all of man's cultural and spiritual life. What Tillich means by the use of the metaphor "depth" is that the religious dimension of life points to what is ultimate and unconditional in a man's life, i.e., what sustains one's being and gives meaning to one's life.

For Tillich, religion is a man's *ultimate concern*. Man is that curious being who has the capacity to look beyond his immediate and preliminary interests to those concerns which undergird and give meaning to his existence.

Man is ultimately concerned about his being and meaning. "To be or not to be" in *this* sense is a matter of ultimate, unconditional total and infinite concern. Man is infinitely concerned about the infinity to which he belongs, from which he is separated, and for which he is longing. . . . Man is unconditionally concerned about that which conditions his being beyond all the conditions in him and around him. Man is ultimately concerned about that which determines his ultimate destiny beyond all preliminary necessities and accidents.[16]

Like every other creature, man is concerned with those things which condition his existence, such as food and shelter. But man also has spiritual concerns which are urgent and which claim ultimacy. Such concerns can manifest themselves in any of the creative (or destructive) dimensions of life as its depth. It can express itself, for example, in the moral dimension of life as the unconditional seriousness of the demand of conscience, or in the realm of science as the passionate, unflinching search for truth.

The term "ultimate concern" is simply Tillich's abstract translation of the great commandment: "The Lord, our God, the Lord is one; and you should love the Lord your God with all your heart, and with all your soul, and with all your mind, and with all your strength" (Mark 12:29). Tillich acknowledges that not all of man's concerns which involve this kind of unconditional and total response are conscious, overt commitments. Frequently they are unconscious and hidden. But in any case, the fact of "concern" and the dimension of "ultimacy" point to the *existential* character of religious experience. The object of religious faith and loyalty is always a matter of infinite passion and interest (Kierkegaard). This existential starting point is reflected in Tillich's first formal criterion for any theology: "*The object of theology is what concerns us ultimately. Only those propositions are theological which deal with their object in so far as it can become a matter of ultimate concern for us.*"[17]

This first formal criterion makes it clear that religion and its theological formulations are confined to man's ultimate concerns. Religion is not involved in the whole range of human preliminary concerns—e.g., the buying of a television set. For that you go to *Consumer Reports.* Nevertheless, Tillich would say that man, as a spiritual creature, is an inveterate idolator and polytheist. That is, man has a proclivity for giving his unconditional trust and allegiance to very finite, limited goods. Man centers his life around a variety of idols that he worships and on which he depends for his security. Some people make social status or economic power, racial superiority or national pride objects of their ultimate concern. From his own experience with National Socialism Tillich can testify to the fact that

the extreme nationalisms of our century are laboratories for the study of what ultimate concern means in all aspects of human existence, including the smallest concern of one's daily life. Everything is centered in the only god, the nation—a god who certainly proves to be a demon, but who shows clearly the unconditional character of an ultimate concern.[18]

What do you value most in life? Tillich would say that your answer is your god. Most men offer formal worship to God but in fact worship many idols. Perhaps the greatest danger facing man as a spiritual creature is this tendency to give covert, ultimate allegiance to what deserves only preliminary commitment—to worship what is finite and ephemeral.

This leads to Tillich's second formal criterion for any theology: "*Our ultimate concern is that which determines our being or not-being. Only those statements are theological which deal with their object in so far as it can become a matter of being or not-being for us.*"[19] Here Tillich correlates his existential concern with ontology. Theology is not only limited to those unconditional, existential concerns of man but excludes from its province things which have less than the power of threatening or saving our being. At this point it should be clear that Tillich is speaking of two levels of religion and theology. On the one hand, every man is religious in that he has some object or objects of ultimate concern through which he seeks to find meaning and security in life. On the other hand, most religious commitments are idolatrous in that the object of concern is not truly ultimate and lacks the power to save our being and give a meaning to existence which neither time nor the vicissitudes of life can destroy.

The inevitable result of giving ultimate concern to what is merely temporal is what Tillich calls "existential disappointment." It is the story of "the god that failed," that leaves one empty and insecure. The loss of such meaning and security frequently leads to frantic efforts to find some new ground of assurance and purpose. In *The Courage To Be* Tillich analyzes, with considerable psychological insight, how men tend to fluctuate between fanatical commitments to mutable goods and efforts to remove themselves from freedom's demands for courage by a loss of selfhood through neurosis, drugs, intoxication, or other forms of retreat from reality.[20]

He who does not succeed in taking his anxiety

courageously upon himself can succeed in avoiding the extreme situation of despair by escaping into neurosis. He still affirms himself but on a limited scale. *Neurosis is the way of avoiding non-being by avoiding being* . . . the neurotic personality on the basis of his greater sensitivity to non-being and consequently of his profounder anxiety, has settled down to a fixed, though limited and unrealistic, self-affirmation.[21]

In Tillich's view, every genuine act of religious faith is an act of courage, for it is the free action of a finite creature affirming that which is infinite and ultimate. Hence for us finite creatures, the element of uncertainty and doubt can never be entirely removed—it must be courageously accepted. Tillich distinguishes this act of faith from the traditional notion of belief.

If faith is understood as belief that something is true, doubt is incompatible with the act of faith. If faith is understood as being ultimately concerned, doubt is a necessary element in it. It is a consequence of the risk of faith. . . . The doubt which is implicit in faith is not a doubt about facts or conclusions. . . . One could call it the existential doubt, in contrast to the methodological and the skeptical doubt. It does not question whether a special proposition is true or false. It does not reject every concrete truth, but it is aware of the element of insecurity in every existential truth. At the same time, the doubt which is implied in faith accepts this insecurity and takes it into itself in an act of courage. Faith includes courage. Therefore, it can include the doubt about itself.[22]

Every theologian is both in faith *and* in doubt, committed *and* alienated, or, as Tillich puts it, inside *and* outside the theological circle. Therefore, theology is always existential and never strictly scientific. "In every assumedly scientific theology there is a point where individual experience, traditional valuation, and personal commitment must decide the issue."[23] It is this existential dimension of theology that distinguishes it from philosophy and the stance of the philosopher of religion.

While both philosophy and theology are concerned with the question of being, the philosopher approaches being analytically. He is concerned to analyze the structures and processes of reality in itself. His cognitive attitude is objective and universal. The theologian, on the other hand, approaches being existentially. He is concerned with the meaning of being *for us*. Therefore, the theologian "must look where that which concerns him ultimately is manifest . . . that is, the *logos* manifesting itself in a particular historical event"[24] or events. Unlike the philosopher, the theologian stands within a tradition, a community of faith or theological circle whose symbols express a soteriological answer to man's existential questions. Theology follows what Tillich calls the "method of correlation," which seeks to explain the contents of faith through existential questions and theological answers in mutual interdependence. The Christian theologian thus proceeds by making an analysis of the situation out of which the human existential questions arise and then seeks to demonstrate that the symbols used in the Christian message are the answers to these questions. Tillich is emphatic that a Christian theology must be genuinely correlative. The "answers" to man's existential situation cannot be simply deduced from the "questions" which emerge from that situation. The answers are provided by the Christian message.

The Christian message provides the answers

to the questions implied in human existence. These answers are contained in the revelatory events on which Christianity is based. . . . Their content cannot be derived from the questions, that is, from an analysis of human existence. They are "spoken" *to* human existence from beyond it. Otherwise they would not be answers, for the question is human existence itself. . . . *In respect to content the Christian answers are dependent on the revelatory events in which they appear; in respect to form they are dependent on the structure of the questions which they answer.*[25] (Italics added.)

Tillich rightly holds that revelation is spoken *to* man and not by man to himself. But he is also correct in asserting that men cannot receive answers to questions they never ask. The Christian answers must therefore be couched in a form that speaks to the contemporary situation. Today, Tillich affirms, that form is what we call *existential*.

Man's Existential Situation. Tillich has said that Existentialism (as a philosophical movement) is the good luck of Christian theology. He means by this that contemporary existentialist analysis of the human situation has contributed to the rediscovery of the classical Christian interpretation of human existence: "Existentialism has analyzed the 'old eon,' namely, the predicament of man and his world in the state of estrangement."[26]

As a spiritual being man never exhausts his potentialities. To exist (from the Latin *existere*) means to "stand out" of non-being or nothingness, but for man this is never absolute, since, as a finite creature, he always remains threatened by non-being. Finite existence is marked by a sense of estrangement from one's essential being. This condition of man is characterized in the Christian tradition by the symbol of "the Fall" of Adam. In Tillich's opinion, it is imperative that theology "clearly and unambiguously represent 'the Fall' as a symbol for the human situation universally, not as the story of an event that happened 'once upon a time.'"[27] In order to make this clear, Tillich prefers to speak of "the Fall" as the "transition from essence to existence," thus underlining its universal anthropological significance. So conceived, the Fall is no longer relegated to the past, while at the same time it remains temporal and historical and not merely a speculative idea. If recognized as myth, the story of the Fall in Genesis 1–3 presents us with a rich symbolism describing the conditions and consequences of the transition from essence to existence.

According to Tillich, in *Genesis* it is man's *finite freedom* that is at the root of man's fall and estrangement. Man is free, but he is also finite and excluded from the infinity to which his spirit aspires.

Man is free, in so far as he has language. With his language, he has universals which liberate him from bondage to the concrete situation to which even the highest animals are subjected. Man is free, in so far as he is able to ask questions about the world he encounters, including himself, and to penetrate into deeper and deeper levels of reality. . . . Finally, man is free, in so far as he has the power of contradicting himself and his essential nature. Man is free even from his freedom; that is, he can surrender his humanity . . . . Symbolically speaking, it is the image of God in man which gives the possibility of the Fall. Only he who is the image of God has the power of separating himself from God.[28]

What is this essential nature from which man is fallen and estranged? Traditionally, theology conceived of this as a prehistorical time before the Fall, a kind of golden age or paradisaical existence. Tillich considers such a mythical conception of a prefallen state of perfection as fraught with difficulties. For Tillich the essential nature of man is not an actual stage of human development but is potentially "present in all stages of (man's) development, although in existential distortion."[29] Tillich prefers to speak of this state of essential being in psychological terms as *dreaming innocence*.

Both words point to something that precedes actual existence. It has potentiality, not actuality. It has no place, it is *ou topos* (utopia). It has no time; it precedes temporality. . . . Dreaming is a state of mind which is real and non-real at the same time—just as is potentiality. Dreaming anticipates the actual, just as everything actual is somehow present in the potential . . . in terms of anticipation. For these reasons the metaphor "dreaming" is adequate in describing the state of essential being.

The word "innocence" also points to non-actualized potentiality. One is innocent only with respect to something which, if actualized, would end the state of innocence. The word has three connotations. It can mean lack of actual experience, lack of personal responsibility, and lack of moral guilt. . . . It designates the state before actuality, existence and history.[30]

This state of dreaming innocence drives beyond itself and, in so doing, is experienced as temptation. Temptation is unavoidable because dreaming innocence, contrary to the older dogmatics, is not a state of perfection. Nor is it a state of sinlessness, for every life stands under the conditions of existence.

Orthodox theologians have heaped perfection after perfection upon Adam before the Fall, making him equal with the picture of the Christ. This procedure is not only absurd; it makes the Fall completely unintelligible. Mere potentiality or dreaming innocence is not perfection. *Only the conscious union of existence and essence is perfection.* . . . The symbol "Adam before the Fall" must be understood as the dreaming innocence of undecided potentialities.[31] (Italics added.)

What drives dreaming innocence beyond itself is man's unique "finite freedom." Man is conscious of the fact that his freedom is bound by his finitude. This awareness leads to anxiety, which "expresses the awareness of being finite, of being a mixture of being and non-being, or of being threatened by non-being . . . in man freedom is united with anxiety."[32] Man, therefore, sees his freedom as a "dreadful freedom" or "aroused freedom" since he is caught between the desire to actualize his freedom and the command to preserve his dreaming innocence (symbolized in the divine prohibition not to eat from the tree of knowledge).

Man experiences the anxiety of losing himself by not actualizing himself and his potentialities and the anxiety of losing himself by actualizing himself and his potentialities. He stands between the preservation of his dreaming innocence without experiencing the actuality of being and the loss of his innocence through knowledge, power, guilt. The anxiety of this situation is the state of temptation. Man decides for self-actualization, thus producing the end of dreaming innocence.[33]

For Tillich, the transition from essence to existence is "the original fact," the "universal quality of finite being" that sets the condition of spatial and temporal existence. Hidden behind the strong ethical theme which dominates the *Genesis* story of the Fall of Adam, Tillich sees elements of an older mythology of the transcendent Fall of the souls which, while clearly not biblical, does not contradict the biblical account. The myth of the transcendent Fall points to "the tragic-universal character of existence . . . that the very constitution of existence implies the transition from essence to existence."[34]

The cosmic, universal character of the Fall and estrangement raises the question of the relation between Creation and Fall. Tillich's accent on the cosmic, universal, and destined character of the Fall appears to equate the two. However, biblical theology has always held that it was the free and rebellious Fall of man that changed the universal structure of nature. Tillich rejects this as absurd for, in his view, the structures of nature, including human nature, were always what they are now. "The notion of a moment *in* time in which man and nature were changed from good to evil is absurd, and it has no foundation in experience or revelation."[35] What, then, of Creation and Fall? Do they coincide? Tillich, himself, raises the question: "The tragic universality of existence, the element of destiny in human freedom and the symbol of the 'fallen world' naturally raise the question as to whether sin is made ontologically necessary instead of a matter of personal responsibility and guilt."[36] His answer is resolute: "Actualized creation and estranged existence are identical. Only biblical literalism has the theological right to deny this assertion. He who excludes the idea of a historical stage of essential goodness should not try to escape the consequence."[37] Tillich acknowledges that creation is *good* in its essential character and, only when actualized, falls into universal estrangement. But it is imperative to remember that for Tillich, as for Hegel, essential goodness is not *perfection.** Perfection of man's essential being requires the actualization of his potentialities. Perfection involves the move from innocence through actualized but estranged existence to a condition of *non-estranged existence*. The fall is a necessary movement in this process.

According to Tillich, the state of existence *is* the state of estrangement. Man is estranged from the ground of his being, from other beings and from himself. Man, as he exists, is not what he essentially is and ought to be. Although estrangement is not a biblical term, it is implied in the mythical accounts of the beginnings and spread of sin—e.g., the expulsion from paradise, Cain and Abel, and the Tower of Babel. Tillich believes there is presently good reason to use the term estrangement rather than the word sin.

The term (sin) has been used in a way which has little to do with its genuine biblical meaning. Paul often spoke of "Sin" in the singular and without an article. He saw it as a quasi-personal power which ruled this world. But in the Christian churches, both Catholic and Protestant, sin has been used predominantly in the plural, and "sins" are deviations from moral laws. This has little to do with "sin" as the state of estrangement from that to which one belongs—God, one's self, one's world.[38]

The term "sin" must be kept, nevertheless, for it does express the personal dimension of estrangement, the willful act of turning away. Sin connotes the free dimension of tragic estrangement. "Man's predicament is estrangement but his estrangement is sin . . . a matter of both personal freedom and universal destiny."[39]

Tillich sees man's sinful estrangement

---

* To compare the above account with Hegel's doctrine of the Fall, see Chap. Six.

as characterized by *unbelief, hubris* and *concupiscence*. Unbelief is the turning away from or separation of man's will from the will of God, whereas *hubris* is the other side of unbelief, viz., the turning in on oneself and elevating the self to the center of one's world. Concupiscence is "the unlimited desire to draw the whole of reality into one's self." This is seen in all aspects of man's life. It is given classical expression in the unlimited sexual striving of a Don Juan, and in Faust's insatiable search for experience and knowledge. Nietzsche's "will to power" and Freud's "libido" are recent conceptualizations of this classical notion of concupiscence.

In his state of existential estrangement, man contradicts his essential being. "The attempt of the finite self to be the center of everything gradually has the effect of its ceasing to be the center of anything. Both self and world are threatened."[40] Estrangement means, first of all, a division within the self.

Parts of the self overtake the center and determine it without being united with other parts. A contingent motive replaces the center which is supposed to unite the motives in a centered decision; but it is unable to do so. This is the ontological character of the state described in classical theology as the "bondage of the will."[41]

This self-loss inevitably involves estrangement from other beings and being itself. Tillich describes in detail the ontological conflicts inherent in estrangement and the existential experience of guilt, loneliness, meaninglessness and, ultimately, despair which this separation creates.[42]

In the state of estrangement, man seeks salvation (*salvus* meaning "healthy" or "whole"). But because his very existence is estranged, he cannot save himself. Despite this fact, man continues to seek salvation on his own. Many approaches have been tried—legalism, asceticism, mysticism, to name only a few—but all of these attempts ultimately fail. Yet man's very search for a new being points to its presence.

The question of salvation can be asked only if salvation is already at work, no matter how fragmentarily ... the awareness of estrangement and the desire for salvation are effects of the presence of saving power, in other words, revelatory experiences.[43]

Man's situation causes him to ask for the ground and power of all being, and this very question about God implies an answer. Thus we come to the second, or answering, pole of the method of correlation.

Being-Itself, Revelation, and the New Being. Tillich considers the traditional arguments for the existence of God to have failed as proofs. Rather, they are "expressions of the *question* of God which is implied in human finitude." The continuing value of these arguments lies in the fact that they "analyze the human situation in such a way that the question of God appears possible and necessary."[44] Take, for example, the ontological argument. "It shows that an awareness of the infinite is included in man's awareness of finitude. Man knows that he is finite, that he is excluded from an infinity which nevertheless belongs to him."[45]

Tillich claims that God is the answer to the question implied in human finitude, for God is the ground of all being. *God is being-itself.* Only that which is the ultimate ground and power of all being can save our being from the forces that threaten it. In saying that God is *being-itself*, Tillich wishes to make it clear that "the being of God cannot be understood as the existence of a being alongside others or above others."[46]

If God is *a* being, he is subject to the categories of finitude, especially to space and substance. Even if he is called the "highest being" this situation has not changed. When applied to God superlatives become diminutives. They place him on the level of other beings while elevating him above all of them.[47]

Logically, God's being is "prior to" the split between essential and existential being. It is therefore a serious error, in Tillich's view, to identify God with existence. Strictly speaking *God does not exist*. In order to argue for the existence of God, Thomas Aquinas was forced to distinguish between a divine existence that is identical with essence and one that is not. But an existence of *God* which is not united with its essence makes God a being whose existence has not fulfilled his essential potentialities. Tillich believes that this is a contradiction in terms. For him "it is as atheistic to affirm the existence of God as it is to deny it. God is being-itself, not *a* being."[48]

What we as finite creatures know is known through our finitude. Hence what we can know and say about God is always symbolic, i.e., consists of statements that point beyond themselves—except, in Tillich's view, the statement that God is being-itself. Consider, for example, the statement that God lives.

Life is the actuality of being, or, more exactly, it is the process in which potential being becomes actual being. But in God as God there is no distinction between potentiality and actuality. Therefore, we cannot speak of God as living in the proper or nonsymbolic sense of the word "life." We must speak of God as living in symbolic terms. Yet

every true symbol participates in the reality which it symbolizes. *God lives in so far as he is the ground of life.*[49] (Italics added.)

The same would hold true in speaking of a God as personal.

The symbol "personal God" is absolutely fundamental because an existential relation is a person-to-person relation. Man cannot be ultimately concerned about anything that is less than personal, but since personality includes individuality, the question arises in what sense God can be called an individual.... "Personal God" does not mean that God is *a* person. It means that God is the ground of everything personal and that he carries within himself the ontological power of personality.[50]

The traditional attributes of God, such as omnipotence, eternality, and omniscience must all be seen as symbolic answers to the question posed by man's finitude—answers which serve as the basis for man's courage to be. The popular conception of omnipotence is that "God can do whatever he wants." This, of course, has lead to absurd puzzles about whether God can logically will contradictory possibilities and other similar riddles. Tillich suggests that "it is more adequate to define divine omnipotence as the power of being which resists non-being in all its expressions and which is manifest in the creative process in all its forms."[51] Faith in the power of being-itself to overcome the threat of non-being is the ground of man's courage-to-be despite the fact of finitude.

Eternity is God's omnipotence in respect to time; omnipresence is the power of being-itself in respect to space. God's omnipresence means neither that God is "endlessly extended in space nor limited to a definite space; nor is he spaceless.... God's omnipresence is his creative participation in the spatial existence of his creatures."[52] Likewise, to speak of God's omniscience should not mean that God is "all-knowing," that he knows everything past, present, and future. Rather, it is the symbolic expression of man's faith that nothing falls outside the *logos* structure of being. Chaotic non-being cannot overcome the rational character of being-itself.

However, man finds himself estranged and threatened with the loss of meaning and even the loss of his being. Because of his estrangement, he is not able to save himself, to create a new being or regain his essential manhood. The answer to man's quest for a new being can come only as an answer "spoken to" human existence from beyond it; yet it must reveal itself under the conditions of existence. Tillich points out that this quest and answer has expressed itself in the West in the expectation of a historical Messiah (Christ) who will actualize the New Being, the essential man, under the conditions of existential estrangement. It is here that the ground and power of being-itself is revealed concretely, overcoming the forces which threaten creaturely existence. Christianity is founded on the claim that Jesus the Christ is the medium of this final revelation, of the New Being present within the conditions of existential disruption. Where this claim is absent Christianity does not exist, or ceases to exist manifestly. "Christianity is what it is through the affirmation that Jesus of Nazareth, who has been called 'the Christ,' is actually the Christ, namely, he who brings the new state of things, the New Being."[53]

According to Tillich, Christianity was born not with the birth of Jesus but with the event reported to have taken place at Caesarea Philippi, where Peter was driven to confess "Thou art the Christ." The event on which Christianity is founded thus has two sides: the fact which is called "Jesus of Nazareth" and the reception of that historical person as the Christ.

One cannot speak the truth about the event on which Christianity is based without asserting both sides. . . . If theology ignores the fact to which the name of Jesus of Nazareth points, it ignores the basic Christian assertion that Essential God-Manhood has appeared within existence and subjected itself to the conditions of existence without being conquered by them. . . . Only if the existence is conquered in *one* point—a personal life, representing existence as a whole—is it conquered in principle, which means "in beginning and in power". . . . Nevertheless, the other side, the believing reception of Jesus *as* the Christ, calls for equal emphasis. Without this reception the Christ would not have been the Christ, namely, the manifestation of the New Being in time and space.[54]

The emphasis that Tillich places on the receptive side of the Christ event has required that he take a position on the relationship between Christology and historical research which reflects his continuity with such postliberal theologians as Barth and Bultmann but which also exposes a serious problem in his own Christological doctrine. Tillich agrees that the old quest of the historical Jesus has failed because it attempted to extract a minimum of reliable facts about Jesus in the Gospels from the layers of theological interpretation, thereby providing a factually certain foundation for Christian belief. Such a quest is no longer possible because, since the publication of Schweitzer's *The Quest of the Historical Jesus* and the advent of Form Criticism, it is considered impossible to separate Jesus from his reception as the Christ by the earliest Christian community.

This situation is not a matter of a preliminary shortcoming of historical research which will one day be overcome. It is caused by the nature of the sources itself. The reports about Jesus of Nazareth are those of Jesus as the Christ, given by persons who received him as the Christ.[55]

Tillich asserts that it is even inaccurate to speak of the "historical Jesus," if we mean by that term the life of a person who stands behind the Gospel message and can be extracted from it. The only historical Jesus that exists is what Tillich calls "the biblical picture of Jesus as the Christ." All that historical research can do is give us rather vague "probabilities" about the so-called historical Jesus—but a person's religious faith, his ultimate concern, cannot be based on mere historical probabilities. For this reason Tillich holds that the risk of Christian faith "lies in quite a different dimension from the risk of accepting uncertain historical facts. It is wrong, therefore, to consider the risk concerning uncertain historical facts as part of the risk of faith."[56] In what, then, does the risk of faith lie? Tillich replies that "the concrete biblical material is not guaranteed by faith in respect to empirical factuality; but it is guaranteed as an adequate expression of the transforming power of the New Being in Jesus as the Christ. Only in this sense does faith guarantee the biblical picture of Jesus."[57] Faith should concern itself only with the transforming power of the New Being for "no historical criticism can question the immediate awareness of those who find themselves transformed into the state of faith."[58]

Tillich's resolution of this modern theological problem leaves us with some serious doubts. How do we know, for example, that the Gospel picture of the New Being was, in fact, actualized in a concrete historical existence, and was not simply the figment of overly ripe imaginations? To some theologians and philosophers—for instance, D. F. Strauss and George Santayana—this historical question is really irrelevant. It is the *idea* of Christ that is important. But Tillich cannot rest in such a position as this. His doctrine *requires* that the New Being be concretely embodied in a personal historical existence, one such as supports the biblical picture. Tillich wants to reject one clearly mistaken notion: "namely, the mistake of supposing that the picture of the New Being in Jesus as the Christ is the creation of existential thought or experience."[59] The fact is, he asserts, that the biblical picture of Jesus as the Christ "*is the result of a new being; it represents the victory over existence which has taken place, and thus created the picture.*"[60] (Italics added.) Elsewhere, Tillich makes such assertions as that Jesus "surrenders himself completely" and that "a revelation is final if it has the power of negating itself without losing itself," and that "in the picture of Jesus as the Christ we have the picture of a man who possessed these qualities."[61] How does Tillich know that the biblical picture of Jesus "who possesses these qualities" corresponds to a "concrete historical actualization" without opening the theological claim to historical research?

Tillich has asserted that the foundational event of Christianity is a union of historical fact and existential participation, or faith. It is imperative to his Christology that the picture of Jesus as the Christ have been *factually, historically actualized,* and yet he wishes to insulate this picture from historical criticism. The fact is that Tillich cannot have it both ways. The problem facing Tillich here can be summarized as follows:

If Tillich insists on a correspondence between the concrete historical actualization and the kerygmatic witness, then the truth of the kerygma is conditioned by the historical claim. The saving power of the biblical picture, which is the foundation of faith, does not, then, possess its own certitude, for the saving power of the kerygma is dependent upon its having been concretely actualized. But that is, logically, at least, open to historical examination. ... Historical evidence could be relevant to the question of the truth of the kerygma. If a discrepancy could be established—Jesus did not appear "to surrender himself completely" —the claim of the kerygma would be challenged. As long as Tillich conceives the kerygma as involving Jesus' own actualization of essential God-manhood, the necessity of the correspondence, he cannot avoid a quest of the historical Jesus and the attendant historical risk that the claim of the kerygma can be disconfirmed and "faith shaken by historical research".[62]

As we have seen, in Chapter Eleven, Rudolf's Bultmann's response to the problem of the historical Jesus was similar to Tillich's, although more radical and in some ways more satisfactory, in that Bultmann sees the historical Jesus as the "bearer" of the message of the Word of God but makes no claims about Jesus' existential actualization of that message.

For Tillich Christ is the one who brings in the new eon in his own person, and "those who participate in him participate in the New Being, though under the condition of man's existential predicament and, therefore, only fragmentarily and by anticipation.[63] St. Paul spoke of Christ as the new Adam and of him who was *in* Christ as a "new creature," a "new man." The new Adam or, using

Tillich's term, the New Being in Jesus as the Christ

is essential being under the conditions of existence, conquering the gap between essence and existence. ... It is new in two respects: it is new in contrast to the merely potential character of essential being; and it is new over against the estranged character of existential being. It is actual, conquering the estrangement of actual existence.[64]

Tillich stresses the fact that in the New Being of Jesus as the Christ we see human existential estrangement conquered by one who was *fully human*—for only in personal existence, where existence *is* finite freedom, can existence be conquered. This means that Jesus as the Christ is the bearer of the New Being in the *totality* of his being and not in any single expression of it. Hence, Tillich rejects the rationalist attempt to emphasize the *words* of Jesus, the pietist the *deeds*, and the orthodox the *suffering* of Jesus, to the exclusion of all else. Jesus' whole being is an expression of the New Being, beyond the split of essential and existential being. The conflict between the unity of God and man and man's estrangement is overcome.

According to the biblical picture of Jesus as the Christ, there are, in spite of all tensions, no traces of estrangement between him and God and consequently between him and himself and him and his world (in its essential nature). The paradoxical character of his being consists in the fact that, although he has only finite freedom under the conditions of time and space, he is not estranged from the ground of his being. There are no traces of unbelief, namely, the removal of his personal center from the divine center which is the subject of his infinite concern .... In the same way the biblical picture shows no trace of *hubris* or self-elevation in spite of his awareness of his messianic vocation . . . . Nor is there any trace of concupiscence in the picture. This point is stressed in the story of the temptation in the desert.[65]

Tillich rejects the description of Jesus' conquest of estrangement as his "sinlessness," for it places Jesus above the tensions of finite freedom and thus in a position not truly comparable with our own. Tillich accentuates the seriousness of Jesus' temptations and the genuine marks of his finitude.

In relation to reality as such . . . he (Jesus) is subject to uncertainty in judgment, risks of error, the limits of power, and the vicissitudes of life. . . . Finitude implies openness to error, and error belongs to the participation of the Christ in man's existential predicament. Error is evident in his ancient conception of the universe, his judgments about men, his interpretation of the historical moment, his eschatological imagination.[66]

Jesus' being as the Christ does not remove him from the same finitude, anxiety, ambiguity, and tragedy that we all face as human beings. But the conquest of existential estrangement in Jesus as the Christ

does have the character of taking the negativities of existence into unbroken unity with God. The anxiety about having to die is not removed; it is taken into participation in the "will of God" . . . . His loneliness and his frustrated attempts in trying to be received by those to whom he came do not suddenly end in a final success; they are taken into the divine acceptance of that which rejects God . . . . Out of this unity with God he has unity with those who are separated from him and from one another . . .[67]

Tillich's creative reconception of Jesus the Christ as the New Being is carried

forward in his discussion of the Christological dogma. Tillich agrees with Luther that dogmas are "protective" doctrines which were formulated to preserve the substance of the Christian message against heretical distortions. In the case of the Christological dogma there have always been two dangers which threaten the truth about Jesus the Christ. One is the denial of the Christ-character of Jesus as the Christ and the other is the denial of the Jesus-character of Jesus as the Christ. These dangers were met in the ancient church by the formulation of the doctrine of the unity of two *natures* in Jesus Christ, his being both "fully God and fully man." Tillich believes that the two-natures doctrine was attempting to protect a genuine truth of Christian faith but was doing so with inadequate conceptual tools and therefore the traditional creedal formulation must be replaced.

The assertion that Jesus as the Christ is the personal unity of a divine and a human nature must be replaced by the assertion that in Jesus as the Christ the eternal unity of God and man has become historical reality . . . the New Being is the reestablished unity between God and man. We replace the inadequate concept "divine nature" by the concepts "eternal God-man-unity" or "Eternal God-Man-hood." Such concepts replace a static essence by a dynamic relation . . . . By eliminating the concept of "two natures," which lie beside each other like blocks and whose unity cannot be understood at all, we are open to relational concepts which make understandable the dynamic picture of Jesus as the Christ.[68]

Tillich acknowledges that his relational description does not remove the mystery of the Incarnation and that all metaphysical and psychological attempts to describe this unity must fail. "One can only say that it is a community between God and the center of a personal life which determines all utterances of this life and resists the attempts within existential estrangement to disrupt it."[69]

Tillich's restatement of Christology has certain affinities with that of Schleiermacher, the father of modern liberal theology—a point noted by Tillich:

He (Schleiermacher) replaces the two-nature doctrine by a doctrine of a divine-human relation. He speaks of a God-consciousness in Jesus, the strength of which surpasses the God-consciousness of all other men. He describes Jesus as the *Urbild* ("original image") of what man essentially is and from which he has fallen.[70]

Where Tillich believes Schleiermacher fell short was in the exclusively anthropological character of his Christological assertions. The consistently ontological nature of Tillich's Christology places him in a mediating position between the classical doctrines of the Church Fathers and those of Schleiermacher and the liberals.

The universal significance of Jesus as the Christ is expressed in the term "salvation." For Christians he is known as the Savior, the Mediator and Redeemer. Tillich points out that the Church has thought of salvation in differ-ways throughout its history, but that both in terms of its original meaning (from *salvus*, "healed") and our present situation, the most adequate meaning of salvation is "healing."

It corresponds to the state of estrangement as the main characteristic of existence. In this sense, healing means reuniting that which is estranged, giving a center to what is split, overcoming the split between God and man, man and his world, man and himself. . . .

Salvation is reclaiming from the old and transferring into the New Being.[71]

While Christianity derives salvation from the appearance of the New Being in Jesus as the Christ, it does not separate salvation in Christ from the processes of healing that are present throughout all of man's historical experience. Wherever there is a genuine revelation of the ground and power of being there is salvation, and history is filled with such authentic revelatory events. "They are saving events in which the power of the New Being is present. It is present in a preparatory way, fragmentarily, and is open to demonic distortion. But it is present and heals where it is seriously accepted. On these healing forces the life of mankind always depends."[72]

What has distorted our understanding of salvation is the belief that it is either total or nonexistent. If this were the case, only a small number of human beings would ever know salvation. "Only if salvation is understood as healing and saving power through the New Being in all history is the problem put on another level. In some degree all men participate in the healing power of the New Being. Otherwise, they would have no being."[73] Yet it is also true that "no men are totally healed, not even those who have encountered the healing power as it appears in Jesus as the Christ."[74] As men we remain finite and, to a lesser or greater extent, anxious and estranged. Hence the Christian hope for the ultimate communion of all beings in the eschatological new creation, the Kingdom of God.

What, then, is the peculiar nature of the healing which comes through participation in the New Being in Jesus as the Christ? Tillich replies that Christ is the ultimate *criterion* of every healing and saving process . . . in him the healing quality is complete and unlimited. The Christian remains in the state of relativity with respect to salvation; the New Being in the Christ transcends every relativity in its quality and power of healing. It is just this that makes him the Christ. Therefore, wherever there is saving power in mankind, it must be judged by the saving power in Jesus as the Christ.[75]

Paul Tillich's existentialist reinterpretation of the themes of classical Christian theology is one of the monumental intellectual achievements of the middle decades of this century. Nevertheless, the very scope and schematic structure of the *Systematic Theology* have raised critical questions from those who believe the concreteness and historicity of biblical faith has been distorted by Tillich's systematic penchant. Paradoxically, it is Tillich's ability to analyze the spiritual malaise of contemporary life and to serve as a guide to many of today's perplexed spirits that has won the plaudits of his theological peers.

A careful reading of Tillich's theology raises a host of questions for the theological critic—a fact evident from even this brief account. At the root of the difficulty is Tillich's use of ontological language and analysis. For example, does he not ontologize the Fall of man in such a way that finitude and sin are not properly distinguished, and sin becomes an ontological fate? What does Tillich mean when he asserts that "God is being-itself" is the only nonsymbolic statement about God? As a literal statement it is exceedingly vague—especially in view of the fact that he doesn't distinguish carefully being "being-itself," "ground of being," and "power of being," all of which mean very different things ontologically. These are just a few of the kinds of

questions that come to mind immediately when one begins to analyze Tillich's writings.

Despite these problems, Tillich's analysis of our spiritual condition and his apologetic for Christianity are not only intellectually impressive but have achieved a wide response and influence. Fundamental to Tillich's thought is the conviction that man is *homo religiosus*—i.e., a being for whom religion is the depth dimension of all creative concerns. And, further, that these ultimate concerns are a matter of being or not-being for men. At a time when there is much talk of a religionless Christianity and of a newly emerging, radically secularized man, we still have, in the words of Joseph Haroutunian,

to come to terms with (Tillich's) insight to the effect that man is a religious animal and his culture necessarily religious. . . . The religionless man may be an estranged and ill man, and he may be bent on suicide. It has to be shown that in our culture a new being has emerged who does not ask the question of being, and that he is authentically human. Until this is shown with as much intelligence as Tillich showed in refuting it, Tillich must be accepted and studied as a master theologian of our time.[76]

Rudolf Bultmann (1884-   )

Many of today's younger theologians believe that it is Rudolf Bultmann who has defined the crucial issues that will be at the center of theological discussion in the remaining decades of the twentieth century. If this is true, it is due largely to the fact that Bultmann, the historian, has bridged the gulf between historical and philosophical theology as no other theologian has succeeded in doing in this century. Troeltsch, as we have seen, was acutely conscious of this problem but failed to carry out a constructive synthesis of these two theological disciplines. Bultmann's success in joining the concerns of historical and philosophical theology does not imply that he has resolved these problems confronting Christian thought; rather, it means that he has helped to free theology from a serious case of schizophrenia and in so doing has focused on some of the germinal issues of theology for our time.

Rudolf Bultmann was born in Wiefelstede, Germany, and like many of the German thinkers we have studied, is the son of an Evangelical-Lutheran pastor. Bultmann began his theological studies at Tübingen but also attended Berlin and Marburg. In these universities, he studied under the great Ritschlian theologians, Harnack and Herrmann, and the biblical scholars Gunkel, Jülicher, and Johannes Weiss.* In 1912, Bultmann qualified as a lecturer in the New Testament at Marburg. Between 1916 and 1920, he taught at Breslau where he wrote his influential *Die Geschichte der synoptischen Tradition.* In 1921, Bultmann returned to Marburg as Professor of New Testament where he has remained, becoming professor emeritus in 1951. Few men have led a more active scholarly life after their retirement than has Bultmann. It was only about the time of his retirement from his professorship that Bultmann's program of demythologizing the Bible came to the attention of theologians outside of Germany. As the most controversial theologian of the past twenty years, Bultmann has carried on a vigorous debate with his critics and has sparked theological investigation in several important directions.

It was mentioned earlier that Bultmann,

* See Chap. Eleven.

like Tillich, represents a theological position between Ritschlian Liberalism and Neo-Orthodoxy. Bultmann places himself within the theological movements of this century in the following autobiographical reflection:

It seemed to me that in this new theological movement, as distinguished from the "liberal" theology out of which I had come, it was rightly recognized that the Christian faith is not a phenomenon of the history of religion, that it does not rest on a "religious a priori" (Troeltsch), and that therefore theology does not have to look upon Christian faith as a phenomenon of religious or cultural history. It seemed to me that, distinguished from such a view, the new theology correctly saw that Christian faith is the answer to the Word of the transcendent God which encounters man, and that theology has to deal with this Word and the man who has been encountered by it. This judgment, however, has never led me to a simple condemnation of "liberal" theology; on the contrary I have endeavored throughout my entire work to carry farther the tradition of historical-critical research as it was practiced in "liberal" theology and to make our recent theological knowledge the more fruitful as a result.

In doing so, the work of existential philosophy, which I came to know through my discussions with Martin Heidegger, became of decisive significance for me. I found here the concept through which it became possible to speak adequately of human existence and therefore also of the existence of the believer. In my efforts to make philosophy fruitful for theology, however, I have come more and more into opposition to Karl Barth. I remain grateful to him, however, for the decisive things I have learned from him.[77]

God's Action and Faith. In Chapter Eleven, we discussed briefly Bultmann's contribution to Form Criticism and the significance of that approach to the New Testament sources for our knowledge of the historical Jesus. It was pointed out there that, while Bultmann is convinced of an identity between the historical Jesus and the kerygmatic Christ, he rejects all attempts to verify such an identity by historical-critical methods. Bultmann's refusal to do this is based not only on his conviction that the very nature of these sources makes such an attempted proof impossible but, more important, that it denies the very meaning of faith. To seek such a proof is to be guilty of demanding a sign, a "worldly" security in our own works. What we need is not a proof, but to be encountered by the Word of God in our own existence and to be challenged to believe or reject that Word. What lies behind Bultmann's position at this point is his conviction that the action of God is not susceptible to objectification or empirical confirmation. God's action in the world and upon us as persons is always *existential*, hidden to every eye but the eye of faith. Here Bultmann reveals the patrimony of his Ritschlian teachers in that for them God was not known in himself or in the abstract, but only in the existential judgment of faith.

Bultmann begins his theological reflection with the Kantian doctrine that genuine knowledge is an achievement of both pure and practical reason. Authentic knowledge of the world may be approached both objectively, as is appropriate to the natural sciences, and subjectively or existentially, as is appropriate to our knowledge of persons. According to Bultmann, the objective study of the world and history does not allow for supernatural occurrences and explanations. God cannot be introduced as a factor to explain this-worldly events for modern science does not believe that the course of nature can be interrupted or, so to speak, perforated, by supernatural powers. ... The same is true of the modern study of history, which does not take into account any intervention of God or of the devil or of demons in the course of history. ... Modern men take it for granted that the course of nature and of history, like their own inner life and their practical life, is nowhere interrupted by the intervention of supernatural powers.[78]

To hold to the modern scientific view of the world does not mean, however, that God must be conceived, if at all, as deistical and unrelated to events in this world. Rather, it means that one must give up a *mythological* conception of God's action in the world. Bultmann describes the mythological view of God's action, in terms of miraculous intervention, as follows:

In mythological thinking the action of God, whether in nature, history, human fortune, or the inner life of the soul, is understood as an action that intervenes between the natural, or historical or psychological course of events; it breaks and links them at the same time. The divine causality is inserted as a link in the chain of the events which follow one another according to the causal nexus. This is meant by the popular notion that a miraculous event cannot be understood except as a miracle, that is, as the effect of a supernatural cause. In such thinking the action of God is indeed conceived in the same way as secular actions or events are conceived, for the divine power which effects miracles is considered as a natural power.[79]

The man of faith does not conceive of God's action in this mythological way, for he does not view the action of God on the level of secular, worldly events—i.e., as visible and capable of objective proof.

Rather, the man of faith thinks of God's act *not*

as an action which happens *between* the worldly actions or events, but as happening *within them*. The close connection between natural and historical events remains intact as it presents itself to the observer. The action of God is hidden from every eye except the eye of faith.[80] (Italics added.)

Bultmann is insisting that the man of faith sees all of nature and history in radical dependence on the transcendent God. Thus, events that can be fully explained in terms of natural, this-worldly causes are seen, nevertheless, as acts of God. An example would be the story of the Israelites crossing the Red (Reed) Sea. This event can be viewed mythologically as the direct, super-natural intervention of God in holding back the waters. On the other hand, the crossing can be explained naturalistically, as due to favorable winds blowing over the low, marshy route of escape and the inability of the heavy Egyptian vehicles to maneuver through the boggy terrain. The latter explanation in no way restricts one from also interpreting the event as an act of divine providence.

Stated in terms of Martin Luther and made current more recently by Kierke-gaard, Bultmann would say that God's action in the world is always *hidden* and *paradoxical*.

Faith insists not on the direct identity of God's action with worldly events, but, if I may be permitted to put it so, on the paradoxical identity which can be believed only here and now against the appearance of non-identity. In faith I can understand an accident with which I meet as a gracious gift of God or as His punishment, or as His chastisement. On the other hand, I can understand the same

accident as a link in the chain of the natural course of events. If, for example, my child has recovered from a dangerous illness, I give thanks to God because He has saved my child.[81]*

The meaning given to an event by faith cannot be translated into a general truth for others to accept. It always remains a truth *for the believer*. In Bultmann's view, this is what distinguishes Christian faith from Pantheism.

Pantheism is a conviction given in advance, a general world-view, which affirms that every event in the world is the work of God because God is immanent in the world. Christian faith, by contrast, holds that God acts on me, speaks to me here and now. The Christian believes this because he knows that he is addressed by the grace of God which meets him in the Word of God, in Jesus Christ. God's grace opens his eyes to see that "in everything God works for good with those who love him" (Rom. 8:28). This faith is not a knowledge possessed once for all; it is not a general world-view. It can be realized only here and now.[82]

The hidden and existential character of the believer's faith in God's presence in the events of history is strikingly illustrated by the story of Henning von Tresckow:

Henning von Tresckow, the man who put the bomb in Hitler's aeroplane, shot himself after the final failure of the 20 July conspiracy. His last words were, "It may be that as God once spared Sodom because there were ten right-eous men in it, so he will spare Germany because of what we have done." These words were spoken in a situation of great extremity, where evil had triumphed over

* This is a central motif in the theology of H. R. Niebuhr who makes the distinction between "Inner" and "Outer" history. See Chap. Fifteen.

good, where God seemed to have turned away His face and where for the speaker there was no way but death. These words inspire respect because they are spoken in faith in such a situation. They would not have the weight they do if they were uttered by a spectator looking at the plot from the outside. Nor, would we expect to find a historian dealing with postwar Germany to find one of the causal factors for its remarkable economic recovery in God's attitude to the 20 July conspirators.[83]

Christian faith is not faith that God is immanently present in all events and processes of this world, but, rather, faith that God has acted decisively in Jesus Christ. This faith is not grounded in empirically verified historical facts of the past but in hearing and responding to the *kerygma* ever anew.

God's word is not a general truth that can be stored in the treasure-house of human spiritual life. It remains his sovereign word, which we shall never master and which can be believed in only as an ever-living miracle, spoken by God and constantly renewed. . . . Belief in this word is the surrender of one's whole existence to it; readiness to hear it is readiness to submit one's whole life to its judgment and its grace. . . . The test of whether we have heard it aright is whether we are prepared always to hear it anew, to ask for it in every decision in life.[84]

Bultmann speaks of faith as the answer or response to the gift offered in the preaching of the *kerygma* here and now. Like Tillich, Bultmann would insist that it is the decision of faith by which the act of God in Christ is made present here and now that "guarantees the reality of the event upon which Christianity is based" (Tillich).

Bultmann's Christocentrism is reflected in his insistence that for the Christian, the New Testament *kerygma* is where God alone addresses himself decisively to man and that the *kerygma* is the source, norm, and substance of all preaching. As one writer has remarked, "what we have in Bultmann is something like a doctrine of the Real Presence in the preaching of the word."[85]

The claim that God acts in a unique and conclusively saving way in the *kerygma* of Jesus Christ is the scandal and stumbling block of Christian faith. Bultmann has no desire to remove this original stone of stumbling from the man confronted with the Christian message. However, there is another obstacle to Christian faith that most modern men regard as a serious impediment to belief in the Christian message, and that is the language and world-view in which the Christian message is presented in the New Testament. This stumbling block, Bultmann avers, must be removed so that the New Testament message can be heard for what it really is. Removal of this fortuitous scandal requires demythologization.

Demythologizing the New Testament. What modern man finds incredible in the New Testament is its pre-scientific view of the world and the attendant picture of God acting in a mythological way, i.e., as an other-worldly being intervening supernaturally in the course of worldly events. The New Testament drama of redemption is pictured in an elaborate cosmological and eschatological *mythos*:

The world is viewed as a three-storied structure, with the earth in the center, the heaven above, and the underworld beneath. Heaven is the abode of God and of celestial beings— the angels. The underworld is hell, the place of torment. . . . The earth . . . is the scene of the supernatural activity of God and his angels on the one hand, and of Satan and his daemons on the other. . . . This aeon is held in bondage by Satan, sin, and death (for "powers" is precisely what they are), and hastens toward its end. The end will come very soon, and will take the form of a cosmic catastrophe. . . . "In the fullness of time" God sent forth his Son, a pre-existent divine Being, who appears on earth as a man. He dies the death of a sinner on the cross and makes atonement for the sins of men. His resurrection marks the beginning of the cosmic catastrophe. Death, the consequence of Adam's sin, is abolished, and the daemonic forces are deprived of their power. The risen Christ is exalted to the right hand of God in heaven and made "Lord and King." He will come again on the clouds of heaven to complete the work of redemption, and the resurrection and judgment of men will follow. Sin, suffering, and death will then be finally abolished. All this is to happen very soon; indeed, St. Paul thinks that he himself will live to see it.[86]

In Bultmann's view, this mythological understanding of the world is impossible in our day and age. To call upon men to accept this form of Christian belief is to ask them to carry out a *sacrificium intellectus* and to isolate their religious beliefs from their daily experience. Bultmann believes that such a demand is neither possible or necessary. It is unnecessary because the Christian message is *not* inextricably tied to this ancient cosmic mythology. As a historian, Bultmann traces the language and world-view of New Testament mythology to the eschatology of late Jewish apocalyptic and the redemption myths of Gnosticism. He believes that a careful examination of these mythological conceptions will reveal a deeper meaning concealed under the mythological cover. Hence, what Bultmann calls for is not elimination of

the New Testament mythology, but an *interpretation* of it in terms of its underlying intention. What is this deeper meaning imbedded in the mythical imagery? Bultmann offers the following explanation:

The real purpose of myth is not to present an objective picture of the world as it is, but to express man's understanding of himself in the world in which he lives. Myth should be interpreted not cosmologically, but anthropologically, or better still, existentially. . . . Myth is an expression of man's conviction that the origin and purpose of the world in which he lives are to be sought not within it but beyond it—that is, beyond the realm of known and tangible reality—and that this realm is perpetually dominated and menaced by those mysterious powers which are its source and limit. Myth is also an expression of man's awareness that he is not lord of his own being. It expresses his sense of dependence not only within the visible world, but more especially on those forces which hold sway beyond the confines of the known. Finally, myth expresses man's belief that in this state of dependence he can be delivered from the forces within the visible world.[87]

Mythical imagery is a natural vehicle for expressing transcendent power and action in terms of this world and human life, but what is important is not the imagery but the understanding of existence that the myths enshrine.

Bultmann points out that the process of interpreting the New Testament mythology, of *demythologization*, begins in the New Testament itself, in the writings of Paul, and most decisively with John. This is especially evident in their grasp of the existential significance of the eschatological imagery.

The decisive step was taken when Paul declared that the turning point from the old world to the new was not a matter of the future but did take place in the coming of Jesus Christ. . . . To be sure, Paul still expected the end of the world as a cosmic drama, the *parousia* of Christ on the clouds of heaven, the resurrection from the dead, the final judgment, but with the resurrection of Christ the decisive event has already happened. The Church is the eschatological community of the elect, of the saints who are already justified and are alive because they are in Christ, in Christ who as the second Adam abolished death and brought life and immortality to light through the gospel. (Rom. 5:12–14; II Tim. 1:10) "Death is swallowed up in victory" (I Cor. 15:54).

After Paul, John de-mythologized the eschatology in a radical manner. For John the coming and departing of Jesus is the eschatological event. "And this is the judgment, that the light has come into the world, and men loved darkness rather than light, because their deeds were evil" (John 3:19). "Now is the judgment of this world, now shall the ruler of this world be cast out" (12:31). For John the resurrection of Jesus, Pentecost and the *parousia* of Jesus are one and the same event, and those who believe have already eternal life. . . . "He who believes in the Son has eternal life; he who does not obey the Son shall not see life, but the wrath of God rests upon him."[88]

On the basis of this New Testament precedent, Bultmann considers the contemporary task of demythologization to be entirely justified.

If such a hermeneutical procedure is justified, how is it to be carried out? As we have seen, Bultmann believes that the myths are an objectification of man's own existential self-understanding and, therefore, should be interpreted existentially. To interpret means to translate, i.e., make understandable, but this in turn presupposes some preunderstanding of the text we are interpreting. Bultmann

contends that every interpreter brings with him, consciously or not, certain conceptions and questions which he puts to the text—otherwise, the text would remain mute. In this sense there is no such thing as "presuppositionless exegesis." A *prior understanding* of the intention of the text must be assumed. Bultmann maintains that

the formulation of a question arises from an interest which is based in the life of the inquirer, and it is the presupposition of all interpretations seeking an understanding of the text, that this interest, too, is in some way or other alive in the text which is to be interpreted and forms the link between the text and its expositor.[89]

If this be the case, then the real issue in biblical hermeneutics is not whether one comes to the text with certain interpretive principles but, rather, what are the *right* presuppositions. Some types of question are more appropriate to certain types of texts than others, while other kinds of question would be entirely inappropriate to a particular text. If one were studying the evolution of the Federal Reserve System, one would not put musical questions to the documents under examination. Now, all kinds of questions can be asked of the Bible. There are, for example, books on the flora and fauna of the Bible. However, the real question at the heart of the Bible is, What is man?

Now, when we interpret the Bible, what is our interest? Certainly the Bible is an historical document and we must interpret the Bible by the methods of historical research. . . . But what is our true and real interest? Are we to read the Bible only as an historical document in order to reconstruct an epoch of past history for which the Bible serves as a "source"? Or is it more than a source? I think our interest is really to hear what the Bible has to say for our actual present, to hear what is the truth about our life and about our soul.[90]

Some theologians (Barth, for example) would deny that the Bible is about human existence; rather, they would hold that the theme of the Bible is the self-revelation of God. Bultmann, however, rejects this separation between God and man and holds that the question of man and the question of God's self-revelation are inseparable. This relationship is expressed classically in the words of Augustine: "Thou hast made us for Thyself, and our heart is restless, until it rests in Thee." Man has a relation to God in his very question about God, whether put consciously or not. Thus, Bultmann contends that "Man's life is moved by the search for God because it is always moved, consciously or unconsciously, by the question about his own personal existence. The question of God and the question of myself are identical."[91]

If the right questions to be asked of the Bible are concerned with the possibilities of authentic human existence, then it is important to discover a philosophical anthropology that will most adequately conceptualize our human situation and bring to expression the real intention of the biblical texts. Bultmann believes that existentialist philosophy provides us with just the needed conceptual framework to carry out the task of demythologization in our time. More particularly, Heidegger's existential analytic can give new significance to such time-worn terms as "sin," "faith," "spirit," "flesh," "death," and "freedom."

Bultmann's critics have claimed that this use of Heidegger's existential analysis has predetermined the Bible's message by forcing that message to conform to Heidegger's conceptual scheme. However, this criticism is mistaken, since Heidegger's existential analytic offers no normative pattern of authentic existence. Bultmann replies:

Existentialist philosophy does not say to me "in such and such a way you must exist"; it says only "you must exist"; or since even this claim may be too large, it shows me what it means to exist. . . . (Existentialism) is far from pretending that it secures for man a self-understanding of his own personal existence. For this self-understanding of my very personal existence can only be realized in the concrete moments of my "here" and "now." Existentialist philosophy, while it gives no answer to the question of my personal existence, makes personal existence my own personal responsibility, and by doing so it helps to make me open to the word of the Bible.[92]

Existential analysis can clarify man's situation in the world and even challenge man to exist authentically, but it cannot judge between rival claims to authentic existence. There is, however, a further reason why Heidegger's existentialist philosophy cannot serve as a kind of secular alternative to Christianity. Assuming that Heidegger describes authentic existence in a manner acceptable to Christians, he cannot prescribe how such an existence can be attained.

The question is whether the "nature" of man is realizable. Is it enough simply to show man what he ought to be? Can he achieve his authentic Being by a mere act of reflection? It is clear that philosophy, no less than theology, has always taken it for granted that man has to a greater or lesser degree erred and gone astray . . . . At the same time, however, these philosophers are convinced that all we need is to be told about the "nature" of man in order to realize it . . . . Is this self-confidence of the philosophers justified? Whatever the answer may be, it is at least clear that this is the point where they part company with the New Testament. For the latter affirms the total incapacity of man to release himself from his fallen state. That deliverance can come only by an act of God .... Here then is the crucial distinction between the New Testament and existentialism, between the Christian faith and the natural understanding of Being.[93]

It is at this point that Bultmann's program of demythologization has raised the most serious questions from his critics. He has called for a radical demythologizing of the New Testament and yet, as we have seen, he wishes to claim that authentic Christian existence is dependent on the unique and decisive act of God in Jesus Christ in the *kerygma*. Has not Bultmann set a definite limit to his own demythologizing in talking about an "act of God in Christ"? Does not such a limit involve a basic contradiction in his method which vitiates his program?[94] It appears clear that Bultmann wishes to carry out demythologization consistently. This involves demythologizing the event ("act of God") of Jesus Christ *insofar as that event is presented in mythical terms.* However, Bultmann does not consider the action of God in Jesus Christ to be *essentially* mythical. It is here that he parts company with those liberal theologians, such as Fritz Buri, who call for a *dekerygmatizing* of the New Testament and a transformation of New Testament theology into a philosophy of existence.[95] Bultmann underlines this difference in the conclusion of his provocative essay as follows:

We have now outlined a programme for the demythologizing of the New Testament. Are there still any surviving traces of mythology? There certainly are for those who

regard all language about an act of God or of a decisive, eschatological event as mythological. But this is not mythology in the traditional sense, not the kind of mythology that has become antiquated with the decay of the mythical world view. For the redemption of which we have spoken is not a miraculous supernatural event, but an historical event wrought out in time and space .... For the kerygma maintains that the eschatological emissary of God is a concrete figure of a particular historical past, that his eschatological activity was wrought out in a human fate, and that therefore it is an event whose eschatological character does not admit of secular proof.[96]

Bultmann insists upon the decisive action of God in the *kerygma* and that this points to the real *skandalon* of Christian faith. He also insists that the Christian self-understanding comes only by the action of God as that action is renewed in the preaching of the Word. Such a self-understanding lies outside the possibility of man to create for himself. The action of God in Christ is then a concrete, historical event but *also* an eschatological event, i.e., an event which "does not admit of secular proof" and is hidden to all but the eyes of faith. This explains why Bultmann considers the *historical* (i.e., accessible to scientific research apart from faith) Jesus irrelevant to faith and yet insists on the decisive historical action of God *in* Christ and nowhere else.

The way in which Bultmann proffers a nonmythological interpretation of the event of Jesus Christ, while holding to the historical yet eschatological character of the event, is best seen in his demythologization of the Cross and Resurrection. Bultmann admits that these events are couched in the language of the Hellenistic cult-myths, a meaningless language to modern men. But this mythical form is not required to understand the intention of this message. Bultmann asserts that "in its redemptive aspect the cross of Christ is no mere mythical event but a *permanent historical fact originating in the past historical event which is the crucifixion of Jesus*."[97] (Italics added.) What is most significant about the cross is not that it happened once but that when it did happen "it created a new and permanent situation in history." The abiding significance of the cross is that it stands for the judgment of God on man's sin and the offer of new life through God's grace. Thus—

to believe in the cross of Christ does not mean to concern ourselves with a mythical process wrought outside us and our world ... but rather to make the cross of Christ our own, to undergo crucifixion with him .... As far as its meaning—that is, its meaning for faith— is concerned, it is an ever-present reality.[98]

Bultmann frankly denies that the resurrection is an empirical fact in the realm of human history. Rather, "the cross and the resurrection form a single, indivisible cosmic event."[99] "Indeed," says Bultmann, "*faith in the resurrection is really the same thing as faith in the saving efficacy of the cross*.[100] The event of Easter *in itself* is not an event of past history. The resurrection is a historical event separable from the cross *only* in terms of the apostle's faith in the risen Christ, which became the basis of the apostolic preaching. If we ask how we can come to believe in the saving efficacy of the Christ event the answer is "faith in the word of preaching."

Once again, in everyday life the Christians participate not only in the death of Christ but also in his resurrection. In this resurrection life they enjoy a freedom, albeit a struggling freedom, from sin (Rom. 6:11 ff.). They are able to "cast off the works of darkness," so that the approaching day when the darkness shall vanish is already experienced here and now .... Through the word of preaching the cross and the resurrection are made present: the eschatological "now" is here, and the promise of Isa. 49:8 is fulfilled: "Behold, now is the acceptable time; behold, now is the day of salvation" (2 Cor. 6:2).[101]

In the existential response of faith to this message comes a new self-understanding which is distinctively Christian. It is a summons to die to the old self and all worldly security and to place one's faith in the grace of God. "It means faith that the unseen, intangible reality actually confronts us as love, opening up our future and signifying not death but life."[102]

The message of Christian faith is not principally concerned with events in the historical past, nor with a hope for some saving eschatological event in the temporal future. The Christian message is the word of God's judgment and God's grace here and now. As Bultmann concludes:

The meaning in history lies always in the present, and when the present is conceived as the eschatological present by Christian faith the meaning in history is realized .... Always in your present lies the meaning in history, and you cannot see it as a spectator, but only in your responsible decisions. In every moment slumbers the possibility of being the eschatological moment. You must awaken it.[103]

Existentialism has afforded theology a contemporary language and an analysis of the human condition that is remarkably akin to that of classical Christianity. In terms of Tillich's "method of correlation," Existentialism has posed those questions about existence that Christianity perennially has sought to answer.

More than this, it has offered theology a categorical scheme and style of doing theology which has hit a particularly responsive chord in our contemporary "age of anxiety." In stressing the irrational and absurd, in speaking of man's fallenness, depersonalization, anxiety, inauthenticity, and the demands of radical decision, Existentialism has sounded the modern temper. In using Existentialism as an interpretive tool, Christian theology has once again given evidence of its resilience and its ability to meet the challenge of modern secular culture.

However, the vitality of Christian Existentialism is seen not only in its openness to contemporary philosophy and its willingness to make use of it freely but to do so while seeking to hold to the distinctly Christian claim of God's decisive action in Jesus Christ. This we have seen emphasized in the work of both Tillich and Bultmann.

Christian Existentialism has been criticized from several directions. It has often been charged with irrationalism—but seldom has it been convicted of this charge. It would be difficult, for instance, to make this charge against the thinkers discussed in this chapter. At the other extreme there are those who claim that, through their use of Existentialism, Tillich and Bultmann have distorted the Christian message by foisting an alien philosophy upon the Bible.[104] There may be some justification in this claim but, before asserting it, the charge must be tested in specific cases. In several instances this criticism has revealed either a mistaken notion of these theologians' doctrine or a rather narrow view of Christian theology.

A criticism of theological Existentialism that is rather widely held is one mentioned earlier as directed against Neo-Orthodoxy, i.e., the conception of historical revelation. Following Barth, both Tillich and Bultmann wish to assume certain historical facts concerning God's action in Jesus but, at the same time, to insulate this history from historical-critical research. They want to claim or to assume certain things about Jesus which are immune to any historical test. This is felt by many critics not only to be unwarranted, if Christianity is to continue to claim its historical bases, but that this disinterest in the problem of the historical Jesus has tended to transform biblical revelation into an ontological abstraction in the case of Tillich and to cause Bultmann to speak of revelation as a rather contentless or formless call to decision.[105] The problem of faith and history remains one of the unresolved issues in existentialist theology and a major cause of dissatisfaction with this theology among the younger generation of theologians who were students of Barth, Tillich, and Bultmann.

Many critics also find the existentialist doctrine of God to be problematical in many respects. Buber's Eternal Thou, Tillich's Being-itself, and "God above God," and Bultmann's hidden and paradoxical God have evoked positive responses from many believers, but theologians and metaphysicians find this kind of theism experientially evocative but elusive and resistant to analysis and incommunicable to those who do not stand within the circle of faith. Some theologians believe that the present crisis of Christian belief is traceable to the failure of Ritschlianism, Neo-Orthodoxy, and Existentialism to ground faith in a reasonably convincing doctrine of God. Thus some of the younger Protestant theologians are now calling for a new Christian *natural* theology. However, natural theology has not been entirely in eclipse in this century. As we shall see, both Catholic Neo-Thomism and American naturalistic theology have sought to establish Christian belief on a common, reasonable doctrine of God.

NOTES

1. *Grundsätze der Philosophie der Zukunft* (Zurich, 1843), p. 78. Cited in Paul Tillich, *Theology of Culture* (New York, 1964), p. 89.
2. *Concluding Unscientific Postscript* (Princeton, 1941), p. 173.
3. *Training in Christianity* (Princeton, 1944), p. 87.
4. *Lecture on Psalm 5*, Weimar edition, *Luther's Works*, V, p. 183.
5. *The Philosophy of Existence* (Chicago, 1952), pp. 2–3.
6. *Man in the Modern Age* (London, 1933), p. 241.
7. *I and Thou* (Edinburgh, 1953), p. 18.
8. Ibid., p. 34.
9. Ibid., p. 43.
10. Ibid., p. 79.
11. Ibid., p. 107.
12. Ibid., p. 110.
13. Ibid., pp. 111, 115.
14. "The Silent Question," in *At the Turning* (New York, 1952), p. 44.
15. *Mystery of Being*, II (Chicago, 1960), p. 55.
16. Paul Tillich, *Systematic Theology* I (Chicago: University of Chicago Press, 1951), p. 14.
17. Ibid., p. 12.
18. Paul Tillich, *Dynamics of Faith* (New York, 1957), pp. 1–2.
19. *Systematic Theology* I, p. 14.
20. *The Courage To Be* (New Haven, 1952); see especially Chap. 3.
21. Ibid., pp. 66, 68.
22. *Dynamics of Faith*, pp. 18–20.
23. *Systematic Theology* I, p. 8.
24. Ibid., p. 23.
25. Ibid., p. 64.
26. *Systematic Theology* II (Chicago: University of Chicago Press, 1957), p. 27.
27. Ibid., p. 29.
28. Ibid., pp. 31–33.
29. Ibid., p. 33.
30. Ibid., pp. 33–34.
31. Ibid., p. 34.
32. Ibid., pp. 34–35.
33. Ibid., pp. 35–36.
34. Ibid., p. 38.
35. Ibid., p. 41.
36. Ibid., p. 43. For a critique of Tillich on this point see the remarks of Reinhold Niebuhr in "Biblical Thought and Ontological Speculation in Tillich's Theology," in *The Theology of Paul Tillich*, ed. C. W. Kegley and R. W. Bretall (New York, 1952).
37. Ibid., p. 44.
38. Ibid., p. 46.
39. Ibid.
40. Ibid., p. 62.
41. Ibid., p. 63.
42. See especially *Systematic Theology* II, pp. 59–86 and *The Courage To Be*, Chaps. 2–3.
43. *Systematic Theology* II, pp. 80, 86.
44. *Systematic Theology* I, p. 206.
45. Ibid.
46. Ibid., p. 235.
47. Ibid.
48. Ibid., p. 237.
49. Ibid., p. 242.
50. Ibid., pp. 244–245.
51. Ibid., p. 273.
52. Ibid., pp. 276–277.
53. *Systematic Theology* II, p. 97.
54. Ibid., pp. 98–99.
55. Ibid., p. 102.
56. Ibid., pp. 116–117.
57. Ibid., p. 115.
58. Ibid., p. 114.
59. "A Reinterpretation of the Doctrine of the Incarnation," *Church Quarterly Review*, CXLVII (1949), p. 145.
60. Ibid., p. 146.

61. *Systematic Theology* I, p. 133.
62. James C. Livingston, "Tillich's Christology and Historical Research," in *Paul Tillich: Retrospect and Future*, ed. T. A. Kantonen (Nashville, 1966), p. 49.
63. *Systematic Theology* II, p. 118.
64. Ibid., pp. 118–119.
65. Ibid., p. 126.
66. Ibid., p. 131.
67. Ibid., p. 134.
68. Ibid., p. 148.
69. Ibid.
70. Ibid., p. 150.
71. Ibid., p. 166.
72. Ibid., p. 167.
73. Ibid.
74. Ibid.
75. Ibid., p. 168.
76. T. A. Kantonen, ed., *Paul Tillich: Retrospect and Future* (Nashville, 1966), p. 63.
77. *The Theology of Rudolf Bultmann*, ed. Charles W. Kegley (New York, 1966), p. XXIV.
78. Rudolf Bultmann, *Jesus Christ and Mythology* (New York, 1958), pp. 15–16.
79. Ibid., p. 61.
80. Ibid., pp. 61–62.
81. Ibid., p. 62.
82. Ibid., pp. 63–64.
83. Ian Henderson, *Rudolf Bultmann* (Richmond, 1966), p. 41.
84. Rudolf Bultmann, "How Does God Speak through the Bible," in *Existence and Faith*, ed. Schubert Ogden (Cleveland, 1966), p. 169.
85. Ian Henderson, op. cit., p. 47.
86. Rudolf Bultmann, "New Testament and Mythology," in *Kerygma and Myth* I, ed. Hans Werner Bartsch (London, 1953), pp. 1–2.
87. Ibid., pp. 10–11.
88. *Jesus Christ and Mythology*, pp. 32–33.
89. *Essays Philosophical and Theological* (London, 1955), p. 240.
90. *Jesus Christ and Mythology*, pp. 51–52.

91. Ibid., p. 53.
92. Ibid., pp. 55–56.
93. *Kerygma and Myth*, op. cit., pp. 27, 33.
94. John Macquarrie argues, in *The Scope of Demythologizing*, that Bultmann imposes this limit upon demythologization and this constitutes the fundamental paradox in his thought. In *Christ Without Myth*, Schubert Ogden contends that Bultmann sets no limits to demythologizing the New Testament and that in not demythologizing the once-for-all act of God in Christ Bultmann has failed to carry out his program consistently.
95. For Buri's critique of Bultmann see "Entmythologisierung oder Entkerygmatisierung der Theologie" (*Kerygma und Mythos*, Band II) and "Theologie der Existenz" (*Kerygma und Mythos*, Band III).
96. *Kerygma and Myth*, op. cit., pp. 43–44.
97. Ibid., p. 37.
98. Ibid., p. 36.
99. Ibid., p. 38.
100. Ibid., p. 41.
101. Ibid., pp. 40, 42–43.
102. Ibid., p. 119.
103. Rudolf Bultmann, *History and Eschatology* (Edinburgh, 1957), p. 155.
104. For a critique of Tillich on this point, see Reinhold Niebuhr, "Biblical Thought and Ontological Speculation in Tillich's Theology," in *The Theology of Paul Tillich*, ed. C. W. Kegley and R. W. Bretall (New York, 1952), and Kenneth Hamilton, *The System and the Gospel* (London, 1963). For Bultmann, see volumes one and two of *Kerygma and Myth*, ed. H. W. Bartsch (London, 1953, 1962).
105. For an excellent analysis and critique of the problem of historical revelation in dialectical and existentialist theology, see Van A. Harvey, *The Historian and the Believer*, Chap. V (New York, 1966).

SUGGESTIONS FOR FURTHER READING

EXISTENTIALISM

The literature on Existentialism is immense. The following books are especially recommended:

Collins, James. *The Existentialists* (Chicago: Henry Regnery, 1952).

Heinemann, F. H. *Existentialism and the Modern Predicament* (New York: Harper, 1954).

Kuhn, Helmut. *Encounter with Nothingness: An Essay on Existentialism* (Chicago: Henry Regnery, 1949).

Wild, John. *The Challenge of Existentialism* (Bloomington: Indiana University Press, 1955).

Among the books dealing in general with Existentialism and Christian belief are:

Michalson, Carl, ed. *Christianity and the Existentialists* (New York: Scribner, 1956).

Roberts, David. *Existentialism and Religious Belief* (New York: Oxford University Press, 1959).

MARTIN BUBER

Diamond, Malcolm. *Martin Buber, Jewish Existentialist* (New York; Oxford University Press, 1960).

Friedman, Maurice. *Martin Buber: The Life of Dialogue* (New York: Harper Torchbook, 1960).

GABRIEL MARCEL

Cain, Seymour. *Gabriel Marcel* (New York: Hillary House, 1963).

Gallagher, Kenneth T. *The Philosophy of Gabriel Marcel* (New York: Fordham University Press, 1962).

PAUL TILLICH

The studies of Paul Tillich's theology are numerous. The following books represent a variety of critical positions:

Kegley, Charles W. and Robert W. Bretall, *The Theology of Paul Tillich* (New York:

Macmillan, 1952). A collection of essays by outstanding theologians and philosophers.

Kantonen, T. A., ed. *Paul Tillich Retrospect and Future* (Nashville: Abingdon Press, 1966). Essays assessing the strengths and weaknesses of Tillich's legacy to theology.

Kelsey, David H. *The Fabric of Paul Tillich's Theology* (New Haven: Yale University Press, 1967). An excellent analysis of the sources and structure of argument of Tillich's *Systematic Theology.*

McKelway, Alexander J. *The Systematic Theology of Paul Tillich* (Richmond: John Knox Press, 1964). A helpful survey of the major themes of Tillich's theology. McKelway criticizes Tillich from a Barthian perspective.

Tavard, George H. *Paul Tillich and the Christian Message* (New York: Scribner, 1962). A Roman Catholic scholar's critique of Tillich, focusing on issues of Christology.

Thomas, J. Heywood. *Paul Tillich: An Appraisal* (Philadelphia: Westminster Press, 1963). A sympathetic yet critical assessment of Tillich's doctrines using the tools of logical analysis.

RUDOLF BULTMANN

Bartsch, Hans W., ed. *Kerygma and Myth*, Vols. I and II (London: S.P.C.K., 1953 and 1962). A collection of essays on Bultmann's program of demythologization.

Kegley, Charles W., ed. *The Theology of Rudolf Bultmann* (New York: Harper and Row, 1966). Essays on the whole range of Bultmann's theology and its significance.

Macquarrie, John. *An Existentialist Theology* (New York: Macmillan, 1955). A comparison of Bultmann and Heidegger.

———. *The Scope of Demythologizing* (New York: Harper, 1960). An excellent survey of the critical responses to Bultmann's demythologizing and attempt to clarify the central issue.

Malevez, L., S.J. *The Christian Message and Myth* (London: SCM Press, 1958). A

Roman Catholic assessment, focusing on Christological issues.

Ogden, Schubert M. *Christ Without Myth* (New York: Harper, 1961). This book and those of Macquarrie represent the most incisive analysis of Bultmann's theology.

Schmithals, Walter. *An Introduction to the Theology of Rudolf Bultmann*, tr. John Bowden (Minneapolis: Augsburg Publishing House, 1968). A comprehensive study of all aspects of Bultmann's work as historian and theologian.

CHAPTER THIRTEEN

Neo-Thomism

Jacques Maritain

With the condemnation of Modernism in the encyclical *Pascendi dominici gregis*, Roman Catholic biblical and historical scholarship entered an undistinguished period which was to continue into the middle of this century. Such was not true of Catholic philosophy and theology which, partly as a result of the Modernist challenge, showed signs of a renaissance before the turn of the century. This rebirth is called Neo-Scholasticism or Neo-Thomism.*

The origins of Neo-Thomism go back to 1879 and the encyclical *Aeterni Patris* in which Pope Leo XIII called upon the bishops of the Church to "restore the golden wisdom of Thomas and to spread it far and wide for the defense and beauty of the Catholic faith." To implement the revival of scholastic studies, Leo XIII founded the Roman Academy of St. Thomas, established a commission to edit a critical text of St. Thomas, founded the Institut Supérieur de Philosophie at

* There are strong differences of opinion among leaders of this movement over the terms Neo-Thomism and Neo-Scholasticism. The historian Maurice De Wulf prefers Neo-Scholasticism, since it does not join the new philosophy exclusively to the thought of a single individual—i.e., Thomas Aquinas. Jacques Maritain dislikes the term *Neo*-Thomism for fear the *Neo* will devour the Thomism. We shall use the label Neo-Thomism to designate this movement for two simple reasons: (1) the common acceptance of the term in philosophical and theological circles and (2) the dominant influence of St. Thomas over other scholastics in the thought of the leaders of the movement.

Louvain as a center for the study and dissemination of Thomistic doctrine, and made St. Thomas the patron of all Roman Catholic colleges and schools throughout the world. On the occasion of this last action, Leo XIII expressed his conviction that "the Thomist philosophy pre-eminently possesses singular power and energy to cure the ills afflicting our time."

Among the chief goals of the restoration of scholasticism was the construction of a new scholastic synthesis which would be consistent with the progress of modern science. One of the complaints of the Modernists was that scholasticism was wedded to an outmoded world-view. Leo XIII and Pius X denied this, the latter declaring that the Modernists simply "deride and heedlessly despise scholastic philosophy and theology." As we have seen, *Lamentabili* condemned sixty-five errors of Modernism, many of which were viewed as specifically contrary to the doctrines of the new scholasticism. The Holy See and the intellectual leaders of the scholastic restoration considered the Modernists' appeal to science to be founded on superficial and erroneous notions, traceable to faulty philosophical presuppositions. The neo-scholastics called for a return to the epistemological and metaphysical realism of the *Summa theologiae* of Thomas Aquinas. In fact, Pius X insisted that he understood scholasticism to mean the teachings of Thomas Aquinas and that any previous commendation by the Holy See of other teachers was given "to the extent that it agreed with the principles of Aquinas or was in no way opposed to them." Pius X even demanded that all institutions granting pontifical degrees be required to use the *Summa theologiae* as a textbook in theology. In the Motu Proprio *Doctoris Angelici* of

1914, Pius X warned those who continued under the impression that the teachings of St. Thomas were only recommended more highly than those of other philosophers and doctors of the Church:

We therefore desired that all teachers of philosophy and sacred theology should be warned that if they deviated so much as a step, in metaphysics especially, from Aquinas, they exposed themselves to grave risk. We now go further, and solemnly declare that those who in their interpretation misrepresent or affect to despise the principles and major thesis of his philosophy are not only not following St. Thomas but are even far astray from the holy Doctor.[1]

Pronouncements and actions of pontiffs following Pius X gave increased support to the Thomistic movement. The Code of Canon Law issued under Benedict XV in 1917 required all professors of philosophy and theology to hold and teach the doctrines of St. Thomas. Pius XI, in *Studiorum Ducem* (1923), declared that "St. Thomas should be called ... the Common or Universal Doctor of the Church: for the Church has adopted his philosophy for her very own." The encyclical goes on to assert that

if we are to avoid the errors which are the source and fountainhead of all the miseries of our time, the teaching of Aquinas must be adhered to more religiously than ever. For St. Thomas refutes the theories propounded by the Modernists in every sphere ....

So we now say to all such as are desirous of the truth: *Go to Thomas*, and ask him to give you from his ample store the food of substantial doctrine wherewith to nourish your souls unto eternal life.[2]

In the light of the threat of a new

modernism after World War II in the work of men such as Teilhard de Chardin, Pius XII lamented in *Humani generis* (1950), that the teachings of Aquinas are now "scorned by some who shamelessly call it outmoded in form and rationalistic, as they say, in its method of thought." Only with the reign of John XXIII, beginning in 1958, was the rigid adherence to Thomas Aquinas relaxed and a new openness to other philosophical approaches possible in Roman Catholic theology.

Among the earliest leaders of the Thomist revival was Désiré Cardinal Mercier (1851–1926), opponent of Father Tyrrell and founder of the Institut Supérieur de Philosophie at Louvain University. Mercier's colleague at Louvain, Maurice de Wulf (1867–1947), was the greatest historian of the new scholasticism in the earlier period of the movement. His *History of Medieval Philosophy* and *Introduction to Scholastic Philosophy* are standard works in the field. Among the outstanding Neo-Thomist apologists in the early decades of this century were Ambroise Gardeil (1859–1931), Antonin Sertillanges (1863–1948), and Reginald Garrigou-Lagrange (1877–1964). It is the view of many that the two greatest and most influential Neo-Thomists of this century are Jacques Maritain (1882–   ) and Etienne Gilson (1884–   ). Gilson has taken on the mantle of de Wulf as *the* historian of the movement. He served as professor of the history of medieval philosophy at the Collège de France from 1932 to 1951, at which time he became a full-time professor at the Institute of Medieval Studies in Toronto, Canada, which he had cofounded in 1929. Among Gilson's most important works are *The Christian Philosophy of St. Thomas Aquinas*, *The Spirit of Medieval Philosophy*, *History of Christian Philosophy in the Middle Ages*, and *God and Philosophy*.

Most of the noted Neo-Thomists are Roman Catholics, but the movement is not confined to the Roman communion. Notable Neo-Thomists outside the Roman Catholic Church are the American philosopher Mortimer Adler and the Anglican theologians Austin Farrer (1904–1968) and E. L. Mascall (1905–   ).

Among the movements of modern Christian thought, Neo-Thomism has had the widest support from the institutional Church. This is evident in the encouragement and support given by the Church to the propagation of Thomist doctrine through papal pronouncements and the establishment of schools, institutes, and journals devoted to Thomistic studies. In addition to the institutes at Louvain and Toronto, a number of Catholic universities, such as Friebourg, the Pontifical Athenaeum, and the Catholic University and Georgetown University in America have been centers of Thomistic studies. Literally dozens of journals are devoted to the examination of Scholastic philosophy and theology. In America the best known are *New Scholasticism* (1927), the *Modern Schoolman* (1923), and the *Thomist* (1939).

Neo-Thomism represents, in brief, an attempt to bring the traditional teachings of Thomas Aquinas into the very different philosophical climate of the twentieth century in an effort to show that this body of doctrine is as relevant to the problems of modernity as it was to those of the thirteenth century. The theme of the movement can be stated thus: As a body of doctrine the truth of Thomism is the child of eternity, independent of time; as the elaboration of that doctrine in the course of human history, Thomism is the child of time and required to adapt to changing conditions. The theme is *continuity* and *adaptation*. This is well expressed by Maurice de Wulf:

When the new scholastic philosophy proclaims by its very name its continuity with a glorious past, it is merely recognizing this incontestable law of organic relationship between the doctrines of the centuries. It does more, however. Its endeavor to re-establish and to plant down deeply amid the controversies of the twentieth century the principles that animated the scholasticism of the thirteenth is in itself an admission that philosophy cannot *completely* change from epoch to epoch; that the truth of seven hundred years ago is still the truth of today; that down through all the oscillations of historical systems there is ever to be met with a *philosophia perennis*—a sort of atmosphere of truth, pure and undiluted, whose bright, clear rays have lighted up the centuries even through the shadows of the darkest and gloomiest clouds.

At the same time, let us hasten to add, that the new scholasticism inscribes on its programme, side by side with this respect for the fundamental doctrines of tradition, *another essential principle*, of equal importance with the first—which it supplements—and expressed with equal clearness by the name it has chosen for itself: the principle of *adaptation to modern intellectual needs and conditions.*[3]

The Thomists have sought to show that the *philosophia perennis*, as classically formulated by St. Thomas, can alone meet the crisis of modern thought which is the result of subjectivism and relativism. At the same time, these neoscholastics contend, Thomas is supple and resilient enough to incorporate those genuine truths which modern philosophers have brought to light but have either exaggerated or have failed to integrate into a larger and more adequate conceptual scheme. Thus it is that many of the Thomists have sought to show both the general inadequacies of modern philosophical positions and how the authentic truths exposed in these philosophies are consistent with and even more compatible with Thomistic realism. This procedure can be observed in the writings of Maritain on French existentialism, in the German Thomists' encounter with Heidegger and phenomenology, in the attention given to analytical philosophy by the Englishmen Farrer and Mascall, and in the American Thomist writings on naturalism and pragmatism.

Thomism, like Aristotelianism, is a system which incorporates the widest of philosophical and scientific concerns, including logic, physics, psychology, ethics, metaphysics, and aesthetics. It is not our purpose here to survey the contributions of contemporary Thomism to these diverse fields but to focus on the unique contribution of Neo-Thomism to some of the vital issues confronting modern Christian theology. In this we shall concentrate on the works of two representative figures, Jacques Maritain and E. L. Mascall. However, an understanding of these men requires some comprehension of their basic philosophical orientation. To an analysis of these principles we must first turn.

Thomistic Metaphysics

Thomism is fundamentally Aristotelian in its epistemology and metaphysics. The Thomists insist on the empirical or sensory basis of all knowledge, while rejecting both a positivist phenomenalism or Kantian idealism which would deny that science can reach through phenomena to a genuine knowledge of metaphysical reality. Nevertheless, Thomism begins with existent being, the natural world, and inquires what it is and how it exists and *from* this inquiry moves to the question of that Being which is Its own existence, whose essence is to exist. Knowledge of God can be attained only by reflection on created being. The starting point of any metaphysics then must be sense experience of material objects. However, reflection on such experience leads the mind to make certain distinctions. Objects in nature change while remaining substantially the same. Animals grow and change their shape and color. Hence a distinction must be drawn between a being's substance and its accidents. Moreover, we can even discern substantial changes in being as well as accidental ones. Material being can undergo changes which alter the substantial character of the material. When the pig eats corn the corn does not remain what it was but becomes pork. At the same time, the corn does not cease to be. It undergoes a substantial change. This observation leads to further distinctions. There appears to be an underlying material substrate of change which in itself is not any definite thing, what Thomas called "prime matter." On the other hand, matter is always determinate matter, some substantial form, corn or pork or some intermediate substance. Form is what places matter in some specific class. All material substance is thus made up of matter and form.

This analysis leads Thomas to the doctrines of potency and act as well as essence and existence. Prime matter is pure potentiality, whereas substantial form is act, i.e., that which places the material being in its specific class and determines its essence. The distinction between matter and form is that between potency and act. The potential is not yet in act but can become so. The child

has the power to become a pianist and so is potentially a pianist. Potency is to essence what act is to existence.

No finite being exists necessarily. We can conceive of a finite essence without knowing if it exists. I can conceive of a Martian, for example. Existence (esse) is the act by which an essence is or has being (ens). "Esse," says Thomas, "denotes a certain act; for a thing is not said to be (esse) by the fact that it is in potentiality, but by the fact that it is in act." (*Contra Gentiles*, I, 22). Through existence essence has being. Nevertheless, act is also determined by essence, in the sense that to be is always the existence of this or that essence. Neither essence nor existence should be conceived of as independent of the other. There is no essence without existence and no existence without essence. And yet, existence is the more fundamental, since created existence is the actualization of a potentiality. Existence is the highest perfection of any essence.

As we have observed, for Thomas no finite being exists necessarily. All finite existence is contingent. This, in Thomas' view, points to that Being which is the source of finite creatures. Such a Being cannot itself be the conjoining of essence and existence but must have existence as its essence, a Being who exists necessarily. According to Thomas, God is *Qui est*, *He who is*. Existence itself (*ipsum esse*) is the essence of God.

Thomism holds that no finite, created being is necessary nor the sufficient ground of the union of its essence and existence. Such a union must, finally, have recourse to a Being in whom essence and existence are identical. But man has no intuitive or innate a priori knowledge of God's nature or existence. That such a Being exists can be known only through demonstrations from its effects—i.e., a posteriori. While Thomists acknowledge that no perfect knowledge of God can be obtained through a purely natural knowledge of effects, proof can be given that such a cause (i.e., God as *ipsum esse*) does exist, assuming the finitude and contingency of the effects. This is possible because the human mind, while dependent upon the senses for its knowledge, can transcend sensory objects in that objects of sense bear a relation or analogy to things that transcend them. This analogy of being (*analogia entis*) is the key to Thomistic metaphysics and theology.*

In the *Summa Theologica* and the *Summa Contra Gentiles*, Thomas offered five proofs for the existence of God. Although they are not all considered equally persuasive, modern Thomists have made general use of all five. The first of the five proofs of God's existence is that from motion. We observe that things in the world are in motion, i.e., from potency to act. But a thing cannot be moved, so the argument goes, from potency to act except by something that is already in act. The latter, too, must have been moved by another agent, and so on ad infinitum. However, as an infinite regression is impossible, we must ultimately come to that mover who is unmoved, whose essence is to be in act.

The second proof is similar but focuses on the nature of efficient causation. Nothing exists of itself, or it would have to exist before itself. Since it is impossible to regress infinitely in the series of efficient causes, there must be a first cause on which the whole series of subordinated causes depends—the uncaused cause, which we call God.

The third proof is crucial and concentrates on the contingency of all things, the fact that things need not exist. We observe that things come into existence and pass away. This should make it clear that any existing being which can also cease to exist does not contain its own reason for being, is not a necessary being. Thomas argues that this fact requires that there must be a necessary being, which alone can explain why contingent beings come into existence. That anything exists implies a necessary being.

A point of clarification is needed here. The first three proofs do not, as is sometimes claimed, have to do with the possibility or impossibility of an infinite mathematical series. The order of dependence for which Thomas is arguing is not temporal but logical or ontological. The fact of a series of contingent beings without beginning still does not make them necessary. The whole series is eternally insufficient. It requires some ontological explanation—a prime, efficient, necessary cause or being.

The fourth or "henological argument"* starts with the experience of the fact that there are beings who possess varying degrees of goodness, truth, beauty, etc. and that these degrees of perfection require that there be a being who is absolutely Good and True. This

---

* Contemporary Thomists readily acknowledge that Thomas did not deal adequately with the later Humean and Kantian critiques which argue that it is illicit to draw analogies between our experience of sensible objects and an object that infinitely transcends our empirical experience. As a man of his time, Thomas, of course, could not have foreseen the critiques of the eighteenth century. For Hume's and Kant's attacks on the proofs of natural theology, see Chap. Three. Modern Thomists find it imperative to answer the Kantian critique of metaphysics, and we shall show how they attempt to do this.

* Because it argues from the many to the one.

argument is of Platonic origin and is considered by many Thomists to lack the rigor of the other arguments. It requires, for example, the assumption that there are degrees of being and perfection before the argument can move to the proof of the existence of a Perfect Being. Nevertheless, the argument is based on principles used in the earlier arguments, viz., that beings which possess certain qualities or perfections cannot account for such attributes by themselves but are dependent on some other being. Ultimately such perfections must be derived from a being which possesses the perfection in its highest degree, which *is* the perfection. Therefore, for goodness and truth to exist there must be the Goodness and Truth, just as there must be a Being who is *ipsum esse* if there is being.

The fifth way is the teleological proof. Thomas noted that we observe objects, without cognition, acting for an end. Such action must not be by chance but intentional. Since inorganic objects lack knowledge, they could not act toward their end unless directed by some being who has intelligence and knowledge. Garrigou-Lagrange states the argument in a syllogism:

A means cannot be directed towards an end except by an intelligent cause. But there exist in nature, among beings which are destitute of intelligence, means which are directed to ends. Therefore, nature is the effect of an intelligent cause.[4]

This should suffice to introduce the reader to some of the important principles of Thomistic metaphysics. We shall return to the subject of analogy and the traditional proofs of the existence of God in our analysis of the work of the contemporary Thomists, Maritain and Mascall, and indicate how they meet the modern philosophical critique of natural theology.

Jacques Maritain (1882-   )

In 1966 Jacques Maritain, then in his mid-eighties, published *The Peasant of the Garonne*, a sharp, ironic warning to post-Vatican II reformers in the Roman Church. To the uninitiated the book might well be dismissed as the work of an old traditionalist. In fact, the author was one of the intellectual leaders of what we have come to know today as the Roman Catholic renewal. In many ways this book of Maritain's old age is consistent with those of his years as a young philosopher in Paris. In all his books, spanning over half a century, one finds the same tension between tradition and openness, the same sarcastic disdain of most movements in modern philosophy and theology, and the unwavering conviction that St. Thomas was, is, and will be the supreme and common guide in man's intellectual and moral quest. He epitomizes the confident, even militant, Catholic intellectualism of the first half of this century.

Jacques Maritain was born in Paris toward the close of the nineteenth-century, when Christianity was weakened by the popularity of Comte's positive philosophy and the limpid, yet theologically corrosive, writings of Ernst Renan. Maritain's father was Catholic, but his mother, Geneviève Favre, the daughter of Jules Favre who was a founder of the Third Republic, was a Protestant, and Jacques was baptized in the French Reformed Church. He received religious instruction from the liberal Protestant theologian Jean Réville. Nevertheless, his ties to Protestantism were tenuous, and during his youth he considered himself an unbeliever.

Maritain was a student at the Sorbonne between 1899 and 1906. He found the reigning positivism and materialism stultifying and longed for philosophical certainty and spiritual purpose. It was early in this period of search that Maritain met Raissa Oumansoff, a Russian Jewish immigrant of seventeen. They were married in 1904, and for sixty years she remained not only his wife but his closest intellectual and spiritual companion. Raissa Maritain died in 1960.

Three figures stand out in the Maritains' pilgrimage to Roman Catholicism. It was Bergson's vitalistic philosophy which offered them a personalistic alternative to scientific positivism. The Maritains came from Bergson's lectures "as though vitalized by healthful air." The other crucial influences at this time were the friendships of the writers Charles Peguy and Leon Bloy. Largely through Bloy's tutorship in Catholicism, the Maritains were baptized in the Roman Church in 1906. The result was that

an immense peace descended upon us, bringing with it the treasures of Faith. There were no more questions, no more anguish, no more trials—there was only the infinite answer of God. The Church kept her promises . . . .[5]

Shortly after his conversion Maritain began studying the *Summa Theologica* and this vast treatise served as a kind of revelation in that it confirmed and illuminated the common-sense beliefs which he had long held but had found challenged by the skepticism of the universities. Thomas gave to these convictions a sound intellectual basis in philosophical realism. Maritain was now

able to say "*Vae mihi si non thomistizavero*—Woe is me if I should not Thomistize."

In 1914 Maritain was offered the chair of philosophy at the Institut Catholique of Paris and in the same year he published a major critical study of his former teacher, Bergson. In the next twenty years there were to appear several important books from Maritain's pen, including *Art and Scholasticism* (1920), *Degrees of Knowledge* (1932), *A Preface to Metaphysics* (1934), and *True Humanism* (1936).

Maritain was in the United States on a lecture tour at the time of the Nazi takeover of France in 1940. He remained in America during the war, teaching at Columbia, Princeton, and the Pontifical Institute of Medieval Studies in Toronto. In 1945, at the war's end, he was called by General de Gaulle to serve as French Ambassador to the Vatican—a difficult position to hold in the immediate postwar years. In 1948 he accepted a professorship at Princeton, where he taught philosophy until his retirement in 1953. Since then he has lived in Toulouse, France, where he is associated with the Little Brothers of Jesus. In 1965 he was given special honor by Pope Paul VI at the closing session of Vatican II.

The Disease of Anthropocentric Humanism. Maritain is at one with other Catholic intellectuals and historians, such as Christopher Dawson and Etienne Gilson, in his belief that modern society is suffering from a cultural disease which is traceable to the breakdown of the Scholastic synthesis in the Renaissance and Reformation. With that breakdown, Maritain asserts, has come a pervasive loss of unity and direction, a shallow subjectivism and relativism.

Modern positivism can trace its parentage back to the *via moderna* of William of Occam and the nominalistic repudiation of Aristotelian metaphysics. This revolution is, in Maritain's view, far more destructive than all the natural and social upheavals of the last half millennium. It is "in the first place a disease of the mind; it began in the mind, it has now attacked the roots of the mind. Is it surprising that the world should seem to us shrouded in darkness?"[6]

This intellectual revolution, which has grown since the sixteenth century, has created what Maritain calls an "anthropocentric humanism," in which the human mind and human nature are regarded as autonomous. Maritain sees this negation of a genuine Christian humanism as linked to the perverse teachings of three brilliant reformers, whose doctrines represent the anthropocentric dialectic of modern culture. These reformers are Luther, Descartes, and Rousseau. According to Maritain, Luther sought to free faith from reason and to reduce the Christian Gospel to inward experience, an effort that gave large impetus to modern anti-intellectualistic subjectivism.

Descartes, in turn, is seen as the "Father of Rationalism." Maritain sees in Cartesianism the attempt to escape from the cumulative wisdom of the past and to make thought independent of existing things, ruled only "by its own internal exigencies . . . . A world shut up, absolute—by itself alone . . . . "[7]

Such an effort to make the content of human reason the measure of reality is, in Maritain's view, "the extreme of madness, for the human reason has no content but what it has received from external objects."[8] With Descartes and his rationalist partisans human knowledge is divorced from sensory perception and considered, like that of the angels, to be intuitive and innate. Maritain refers to the sin of Cartesianism as "angelism." Descartes has not only severed reason from sense, but the body from the mind and faith from science. While Thomas distinguished in order to unite, Descartes merely separates. Thus, Maritain contends, Cartesianism is at the root of the modern malaise, and any reform of modern error must begin with a repudiation of Cartesian dualism.

Rousseau represents the third moment in the dialectic of anthropocentric humanism. As Descartes turned reason inward, so Rousseau gauges the will and the good by the inner feelings of the heart. Just as Luther erred in declaring man's nature irremediably corrupt (Christian "pessimism"), so Rousseau errs in proclaiming man's nature good and in no need of redemption (Christian "optimism"). Rousseau's

man of Natural Religion was a Christian gentleman who did not need grace, miracle or revelation, and was made virtuous and just by his own good nature. The man of Jean-Jacques Rousseau was . . . the very man of St. Paul transferred to the plane of pure nature—innocent as Adam before the fall . . . corrupted by social life and civilization as the sons of Adam by the original sin. He was to be redeemed and set free, not by Christ, but by the essential goodness of human nature, which must be restored by means of an education without constraint. . . .[9]

The philosophical revolutions inaugurated by these "three reformers" reached their culmination in the critical Idealism of Immanuel Kant. With Kant metaphysics is brought to an end and the future is turned over to scientism and positivism. Maritain writes:

We are looking on the liquidation of the modern world—of that world . . . which Luther's scission unbalanced . . . which the rationalism of Descartes and the Encyclopedists swept into an illusory optimism; which the pseudo-Christian naturalism of Jean-Jacques Rousseau led to confound the sacred aspiration of the heart of man with the expectation of a kingdom of God on earth procured by the State or by the Revolution.[10]

Maritain believes that all attempts to restore order, unity, and direction to human life by the pragmatic manipulations of political and social engineers are ephemeral and ultimately futile. The disease afflicting the modern world is ontological and metaphysical and is rooted in the mind. Thus only a healing of the mind can cure the disease—and Maritain believes that only in the Christian philosophy of St. Thomas Aquinas is the wholeness of the mind restored to its natural state of preeminence. For Maritain, Thomas'

philosophy appears as the only one with energy powerful and pure enough to influence effectively . . . the whole universe of culture; to restore the human mind to order and so, with the grace of God, to bring the world back to the paths of Truth, the loss of which may well involve the dissolution of the world.[11]

The Christian Philosophy of St. Thomas. The Neo-Thomists speak of the renewal of the Christian philosophy of St. Thomas. But is not the joining of the words *Christian* and *philosophy* a confusion of two distinct orders of knowledge and does it not destroy the essential autonomy of philosophical investigation? Is a Christian philosophy not contrary to Thomas' own distinction between philosophy and theology? Maritain's answer to these questions is helpful

in understanding his own unique calling as a philosopher—and as an introduction to an analysis of his doctrine.

The question of a "Christian philosophy" has been at the center of Thomistic discussion in recent decades. Some Neo-Thomists have denied the natural autonomy of philosophy, while others consider the notion of a Christian philosophy completely spurious. Maritain rejects both views. The solution to the question is to be found in a fine Thomistic distinction

between the *order of specification* and the *order of exercise*, or . . . between "nature" and "state." This means that we must distinguish between the *nature* of philosophy, or what it is in itself, and the *state* in which it exists in real fact, historically, in the human subject . . . .[12]

Maritain holds that philosophic truth is of its very *nature* within the reach of the natural faculties of the human mind. Therefore,

the designation *Christian* which we apply to a philosophy does not refer to that which constitutes it in its *philosophic essence*: simply as a philosophy, *reduplicative ut sic*, it is independent of the Christian faith as to its object, its principles, and its methods.[13]

Nevertheless, as soon as one no longer considers philosophy in itself but the way in which men have philosophized in the course of history, then consideration of the *essence* of philosophy no longer suffices; a consideration of its state must also be undertaken.

What are some of the components of a *Christian state* of philosophy?

First and foremost, there are those data which by their nature belong within the field of philosophy, but which in actual fact philosophers failed to recognize explicitly, and which were placed in front rank by Christian revelation. Take for example the idea of *creation*. Here also belongs the idea of a *nature* which albeit real and intrinsically consistent (this the Hindus failed to see) is not an absolute closed upon itself, and is capable (this the Greeks did not see) of being perfected by a supernatural order . . . . Then, in the moral sphere, we have the idea of sin . . . an idea of which in spite of manifold attempts Western philosophy has not managed to rid itself.[14]

Such Christian ideas as these, and there are many others, have been of cardinal importance to Western philosophy. In each case, reason has received a positive contribution from revelation, so that Gilson is correct in speaking of *revelation begetting reason*. This is not to say that these ideas were totally unknown to philosophers.

The question at issue here is rather concerned —and this is still of paramount *factual* importance—with differences of clarity that are . . . extraordinarily pronounced: what used to dwell in regions of shadow or mirage is brought forth in the full light of day . . . everything takes on a fresh hue, and every view is transfigured.[15]

The evolution of philosophy is affected then by those Christian mysteries above natural reason. For example, it is often pointed out that had it not been for the dogmatic speculations on the Trinity and Incarnation, it is unlikely that philosophers would have come to an awareness of the metaphysical problem of the person. But the contribution of Christianity to philosophy goes beyond even these historical influences, to the subjective strengthening of the philosophical activity itself. "The virtue of faith, for example, enables the philosopher, who knows of the existence of God by purely natural

means to adhere rationally to this truth with a sturdier grasp."[16]

Maritain says that the expression "Christian philosophy" does not denote a simple essence but a complex, i.e., an essence considered in a particular state. For this very reason the notion is imprecise but, nevertheless, denotes something very real. In sum it can be said that

Christian philosophy is philosophy itself in so far as it is situated in those utterly distinctive conditions of existence and excercise into which Christianity has ushered the thinking subject, and as a result of which philosophy *perceives* certain objects and *validly demonstrates* certain propositions, which in any other circumstances would to a greater or lesser extent elude it.[17]

While revelation informs and gives vitality to reason, Maritain, like Thomas, distinguishes clearly between the methods and object of theology and philosophy. Theology is rooted in faith and has as its object the data of revelation, which it seeks to elucidate rationally. What counts in philosophy is not that it is in accord with Christian revelation but that it is true. Nevertheless, once their respective natures are distinguished, nothing, in Maritain's view, is to prevent philosophy and theology from engaging in a dynamic movement which unites the lights of both without confusing them.

Thomistic Existentialism. While Maritain dislikes the term Neo-Thomist, he has been engaged in a life-long effort to demonstrate the perennial relevance of Thomism in meeting the demands of a changing philosophical scene. This is evident in his attempt to demonstrate the "authentic" existentialism of St. Thomas and in his restatement of the traditional Thomistic proofs of the existence of God.

In discussing modern Existentialism, Maritain distinguishes between what he called the "sapiential" or detached posture of the mind and the "imprecatory" bearing of man. The first attitude is "cause-seeking," i.e., philosophical; the second is the posture of "saving my all" or the dramatic struggle for the salvation of the self. This latter attitude is what we observe in the writings of Kierkegaard or Kafka. Maritain calls it *existential existentialism*. For the spiritual grandeur and power of this Existentialism Maritain has only the highest praise. "It is," he writes, "an essentially *religious* irruption and claim, an agony of faith, the cry of the subjectivity towards its God."[18] The misfortune of this Existentialism is that it developed into a religious protest *in the guise of a philosophy*. The spiritual experience of the philosopher no longer remained the nourishing soil of his reflection but became the very texture of his philosophy. The *imprecatory posture*, while stressing the singular value and primacy of the act of existing, robbed the intellect of its proper function. The error can be summarized by saying that "the nothingness *in* the existent has been replaced by the nothingness *of* the existent." But, says Maritain,

it is non-sense to think of making the bearing or posture of Jacob in the night of his combat with the angel the attitude of metaphysics, with its special way of coming to grips with the law of things . . . . We do not philosophize in the posture of dramatic singularity.[19]

In Maritain's view, academic Existentialism has confused the sapiential and imprecatory postures. The result is a philosophy of action (*praxis*) which fails

as a genuine philosophy of being and, hence, of existence.

According to Maritain, the root difficulty with modern Existentialism is that it lacks a genuine intellectual intuition of being. What does this mean? It means that the concept of existence, which is at the heart of modern existentialist analysis, cannot be cut off from the more primary concept of being (*ens*, or that which exists or whose act is to exist). "This is so because the affirmation of existence, or the judgment, which provides the content of such a concept, is itself the 'composition' of a subject with existence, i.e., the affirmation that *something exists*."[20] That is, the concept of existence cannot be isolated, cannot be visualized apart from that of being. In short,

the concept of existence cannot be detached from the concept of essence. Inseparable from each other, these two make up one and the same concept, simple although intrinsically varied; one and the same essentially analogous concept, that of being. . . . At the instant when the finger points to that which the eye sees, at the instant when sense perceives, in its blind fashion, without intellection or mental word, that *this exists*; at that instant the intellect says (in a judgment), *this being is* or *exists* and at the same time (in a concept), *being*.[21]

The genuine intuition of being, of *that which exists*, must distinguish between essence (potency) or *that which* and *existence* (act). The essence of a thing is what makes it *intelligible* as a being, what defines it insofar as it has a nature. But essence is completed or actuated by an act which adds nothing to essence as essence and yet makes it real by the act of existing. It follows, nevertheless, that to assert the primacy of existence without essence is also unthinkable. "If you abolish essence," Maritain argues, "or that which *esse* posits, by that very act you abolish existence, or *esse*. Those two notions are correlative and inseparable."[22]

Such reflection on existential or created being leads inevitably to metaphysics, i.e., to reflection on the cause of being or that being whose essence is to exist, the *Ipsum esse subsistens*. The reality of created beings consists of their essence (intelligible nature) and that act which perfects all natures by placing them in actuality. The verb *exists*, which is joined to the subject *that which*, is, according to Maritain, a super-intelligible, for created things do not place in act their own natures. Awareness of the nature of the act of existing leads directly to the ontological primacy of God.

To say *that which exists* is to join an intelligible to a super-intelligible; it is to have before our eyes an intelligible engaged in and perfected by a super-intelligibility. Why should it be astonishing that at the summit of all beings, at the point where everything is carried to pure transcendent act, the intelligibility of essence should fuse in an absolute identity with the super-intelligibility of existence . . . in the incomprehensible unity of *Him Who is*?[23]

God is the infinite act of existence itself and, therefore, as Thomas would say, "God contains within himself all the perfections of being" because He is Being itself, "the very act of existing, subsistent by itself."[24]

Authentic existentialism, as exemplified in the philosophy of Thomas, affirms the primacy of existence at the same time that it preserves the essences or natures of things, thereby safeguarding the intelligibility of being and the supremacy of the intellect. According to Maritain, it is this existentialism that alone can properly call itself a philosophy.

Maritain believes that modern atheistic existentialism also has a faulty notion of the subject or existent, despite the fact that the individual subject plays the central role in its reflection. According to Thomas, the essence and the subject of a thing must be distinguished. The essence is *that which* a thing is; a subject (*suppositum*) is *that which has* an essence, that which exercises existence. While the essence of a thing is objectifiable in thought, the subject is not. Each subject is an individual reality, an inexhaustible well of knowability. We will never know everything there is to know about a subject. What we know about subjects is through making them objects to our minds. Thus we know subjects not as subjects but as objects. The higher we progress in the scale of being, the richer is the subject in individuality and complexity. When we cross the threshold of free choice, we enter the region of personal liberty, the noblest and highest status in nature, according to Thomas.

Each personality sees itself among all the objects of its knowledge as subject, as situated at the center of the world. Such an intuition of "subjectivity as subjectivity" is inconceptualizable; it is ineffable and unknowable by the usual modes of scientific objectification. Subjectivity is intuited and felt and, therefore, is not a form of philosophic knowledge. "Subjectivity," says Maritain, "marks the frontier which separates the world of philosophy from the world of religion."[25]

The intuition of selfhood in which I regard myself as the most important person in the world is, of course, from the standpoint of common sense, foolish. I know perfectly well that I am of little consequence whatsoever to the universe as a whole. Yet these two images of myself, as subject and object, cannot be made to coincide, nor can they be given up. They can be resolved, according to Maritain, only if God exists.

If I abandon myself to the perspective of subjectivity, I absorb everything into myself, and sacrifice everything to my uniqueness, I am riveted to the absolute of selfishness and pride. If I abandon myself to the perspective of objectivity, I am absorbed into everything . . . and am false to my uniqueness . . . . It is only from above that the antinomy can be resolved. If God exists, then not I, but He is the centre; this time not in relation to a certain particular perspective, like that in which each created subjectivity is the center of the universe it knows, but speaking absolutely, as a transcendent subjectivity to which all subjectivities are referred. At such time I can know both that I am without importance and that my destiny is of the highest importance.[26]

Maritain believes that the tragedy of atheistic existentialism is found, in part, in the fact that to be known by others as an object is always to be known unjustly —to be severed from oneself and wounded. To be known by God is to be known as subject. God has no need to objectify me in order to know me. Only to God is man known as subject and not as object. The hidden recesses of one's subjectivity are obscure even to oneself. To God alone is the self uncovered. "If I were not known to God, no one would know me. No one would know me in my truth, in my own existence. No one would know me—*me*—as subject."[27]

This means that without God no one would render justice to my being—not even myself. Without justice, Maritain contends, there can be no hope for the individual. To be known by God is also to be understood, for God alone knows all the travail, the wounds and impulses of good will that mark each individual's

earthly pilgrimage. Thus the deep knowledge possessed by God is a *loving* knowledge. "To know that we are known to God is not merely to experience justice, it is also to experience mercy."[28]

Maritain further argues that while it is true that in relation to the subject's subjectivity, as that which is unique and singular, objectification is false to the subject, in relation to its *essential* structures, objectification is not only licit but philosophically necessary. Objectification alone gives us knowledge of intelligible natures. Such knowledge is never complete but ever deepening and indispensable to human existence. According to Maritain, an authentic existentialism sees the self, not as an irrational flow of sensations, a "useless passion," but as a rational soul—known in the deepest recesses of its selfhood, in its fullest actuality, by God and in its essential nature by the human intellect.

The Proofs of God's Existence. Thomistic philosophy has nowhere suffered greater rejection from moderns than in its natural theology. Since Kant the traditional proofs of the existence of God have been commonly dismissed as irretrievably discredited. Here again, Neo-Thomists like Garrigou-Lagrange, Gilson, Farrer, and Maritain have sought to restore the traditional "ways" of Thomas to their rightful place as valid arguments, both by demonstrating that Kant's critique of the cosmological argument was quite mistaken and by showing that the five ways, when properly understood, remain convincing and in keeping with developments in contemporary science.

Maritain believes that the philosophic proofs of the existence of God are, in fact, the development of a natural and primordial intuition of existence, which is simply raised to the level of scientific certitude. This prephilosophical and natural knowledge of God's existence

can be described as starting from the primordial intuition of existence and immediately perceiving that Being-with-nothingness, or things which could possibly not be—my own being which is liable to death—necessarily presuppose Being-without-nothingness, that is, absolute or self-subsisting Being, which causes and activates all beings. This pre-philosophical knowledge can also be described as a spontaneous application of the principle: no artifact is possible without a maker.[29]

It is from this natural experience that the philosophical proofs are drawn. But can they be rationally justified in the light of the modern critique of natural theology? To the Neo-Thomists the answer centers principally on the validity of Kant's assertion that the cosmological arguments imply the ontological argument, which both Kant and the Thomists reject as a genuine proof. If Kant's objection can be met, the Neo-Thomists believe the way is open to refashion the cosmological arguments in terms acceptable to modern cosmology and science.

Kant's critique of the cosmological argument was discussed earlier* but can be briefly summarized as follows: The ontological proof fails because the *concept* of an absolutely necessary being does not imply its existential reality simply because it is required by reason. It is not proper to introduce the concept of *existence* into the concept of a thing, since all existential propositions are synthetic, derived from experience alone. Moreover, according to Kant, the cos-

* See Chap. Three.

mological arguments (the first three ways of St. Thomas) depend on the ontological argument, since they argue that if anything exists an absolutely necessary being must also *exist* because the absolutely necessary being must be supremely perfect. That is, the passage from the concept of necessary being to God as *ens realissimum* requires the ontological argument that God is that being whose *existence* is logically included in the concept of its essence or perfection.

Maritain acknowledges that Kant was correct in pointing out the weakness of the ontological argument. One cannot reach existence through a purely analytical process. Where Kant erred, however, was in his belief that the notion of existence adds nothing to a subject and is not a predicate. For Kant there is nothing more in a hundred existing thalers than in a hundred possible thalers. But the biblical text is truer, for we know that a live dog is worth more than a dead lion.

The notion of existence has a content, its own intelligible value; not only is it a predicate, but a predicate which has reference to a perfection, eminent and of an order apart—actuality of every act. And if actual existence adds nothing along the line of essence and of essential predicates to the natures it actuates, it adds to them nevertheless something eminently real and intelligible, though quite outside the whole order of essence, and therefore attached to it contingently. It is not true that the concept of a hundred possible thalers is the same as that of a hundred real thalers; in the latter case there is more than in the former, although the nature or object of thought "hundred thalers" is the same in both. But in the latter there is a rational complex (the concept of thaler and the concept of real existence joined together) . . . .[30]

This joining together is what Maritain and the Thomists call *judgment*. It was this operation that Kant failed to distinguish from simple conception.

If furthermore we go on to the "second operation of the mind", to judgment, and if instead of conceiving simply *a hundred real thalers*, we affirm: *there are a hundred thalers there*, the concept of thaler and that of real existence are joined in quite another way, I mean that they are then, by an original and irreducible act which is the judgment itself, jointly referred by the mind and within the mind to the way in which things behave outside the mind, and the actual existence thus affirmed is existence in the act of effectuation or as effectively possessed (*existentia ut exercita*). When reason establishes that God exists, it does not do so by extrapolating existence *ut significata* included in a notion, in order to make of it an existence *ut exercita* affirmed in a judgment—it does so by advancing from the very outset along the line of the effectuation of existence, that is to say, by starting from certain experience data where existence is apprehended *ut exercita*, in order to compound, in this very quality of existence *ut exercita* . . . the notion of a first and supreme cause with that of existence, drawn from experience . . . .[31]

According to the above argument, when reason establishes the existence of God it does not begin with an idea but with the data of experience in which existence is apprehended and then in judgment compounds the notion of a first cause with that of existence. There is no need for the ontological argument. The ontological argument does err in proceeding from the ideal to the real by asserting that a supremely perfect being is absolutely necessary. But the cosmological argument does not simply reverse that premise. Rather it establishes that the absolutely necessary being *exists* and only then does St. Thomas conclude that such a being is pure act and infinite perfection.

St. Thomas proceeds from the real to the real—not, as Kant avers, from the ideal to the real.

Maritain has often written on the many ways men have approached God. There are as many ways "as there are wanderings on the earth or paths to his own heart." However, unlike many contemporary theologians, for whom the evidences of God are limited to man's social or private, mystical experience, Maritain considers the five ways of St. Thomas as constituting demonstrative philosophical proofs of God's existence. Nevertheless, the proofs must be restated in language which avoids the outmoded imagery and examples that were accidental to Thomas' own time and in such ways as to answer objections offered in more recent years. Take, for example, the first of Thomas' arguments from the fact of motion to a first immovable Agent.

Suppose someone were to argue that the principle of inertia, which since the time of Galileo and Newton has been regarded as a basic principle of mechanics, negates the doctrine "Everything which moves is moved by another," since uniform local motion, like rest, is assumed to be a *state* of existence. Can this objection be answered? Maritain believes that progress in physics and in the philosophy of nature may well call into question the validity of the principle of inertia. But be that as it may,

taking the principle of inertia as established . . . it suffices, in order to reply to the objection, to note that, applied to movement in space, the axiom "Everything which moves is moved by another" ought then logically, by the very fact that motion is considered a state, to be understood as meaning "Everybody which undergoes a change *in regard to its state of rest or of motion* changes under the action of another thing." And thus the axiom remains always true. According to the principle of inertia in its classic form a body once set in motion continues of itself to be moved in a uniform manner or with the same velocity. If then the velocity of its motion increases or diminishes, it will be because of an action exerted on it by another thing. We are thus confronted anew with the axiom, "Every change is produced by the agency of something *other* than the thing which changes, insofar as it changes." And we are obliged anew to ask the question: "Is that something other itself moved?" In this case it is moved, or applied to activity by another thing.[32]

Let us take as a second example Thomas' fifth way. Since Hume and Kant the teleological argument has fared little better than the cosmological arguments. The Thomists acknowledge that the argument from design does not in itself prove a Creator or any determinate idea of the "architect's" nature, e.g., his *perfect* intelligence. Nevertheless, the fifth way does demonstrate the necessity of an intelligent cause, that things act according to an intentional purpose, direction, or end and not according to chance. That the intelligent cause possesses those perfections which we attribute to God is a logical conclusion derived from the cosmological proof which, according to the Thomists, has demonstrated from experience that the absolutely self-sufficient, infinite and necessary being *exists*.

But does the teleological argument demonstrate the necessity of an intelligent purpose or end in nature? What about the assertion of mechanistic evolution that nature is the work of *chance* variations? Could the world not be the effect of chance, just as the *Iliad* could result from the merely fortuitous juxtaposition of letters thrown at random?

Maritain argues that the notion of chance is based on a sophism:

An effect can be due to chance only if some datum aside from chance is presupposed at the origin. To cast letters at random presupposes letters and presupposes the hand which casts them with this intention, or an instrument constructed for that purpose. The predictions made by the actuaries presuppose the innumerable causal lines on whose mutual interference the duration of a human organism depends. Statistical laws presuppose the existence of causal laws which can be unknown but according to which the things and energies of nature operate in certain given fields—without which, indeed, the great number of fortuitous occurences on which the certainty of statistical laws depends simply could not happen.[33]

Furthermore, Maritain argues, the very fact that one applies the calculation of chances to a case, such as the probability that a given number will be drawn from a lottery, means that one already admits the *possibility* of the event in question.

To say—and this makes sense only *on the hypothesis* in which it would be legitimate to apply the calculation of chances to the case—that, however slight the probability, there is still one chance in the incalculable myriads of myriads of chances that the world is the effect of chance, implies that one has admitted from the outset that the world *can* be the effect of chance. To attempt to demonstrate that the world can be the effect of chance by beginning with the presupposition of this very possibility is to become the victim of a potent sophism or a gross illusion. In order to have the right to apply the calculus of probabilities to the case of the formation of the world, it would be necessary first to have established that the world can be the effect of chance. And it is the same in regard to the *Iliad* . . . . Some letters cast by chance can form a group which appears to the mind as a word, but this group is not in reality a sign, a bearer of meaning. As soon as the function of signification is *real*, the assemblage *cannot* result by chance.[34]

Maritain and other Thomists are arguing that the appeal to chance is the call to abandon all explanation, an appeal to what is simply unintelligible.

For if everything is by chance and nothing by rule, there is nothing to which chance can occur. I may chance to meet my friend in the street, but only if I am walking along it in a definite way. If nothing occurs in any definite way, nothing can occur by chance or in an accidental way. It is in this sense that the "exception proves the rule." If there is no rule there can be no exception: if there is nothing essential there can be nothing accidental or by chance.[35]

Integral Humanism. The theme that dominates much of Maritain's writing is his conviction that modern Western culture is characterized by an "anthropocentric humanism" which has brought mankind to the "twilight of civilization." As we have seen, this modern image of man is traceable to Descartes, Rousseau, Kant, and the positivism which followed. Despite this trend, Maritain believes Western civilization has been able to continue until recently under the facade of Christianity—claiming human dignity, equality, fraternity, and peace while dismissing their spiritual foundations and regarding evil as only an imperfected stage of evolution. Western man is now living in a "cut-flower civilization," devoid of deep and living roots. Uprooted from his spiritual ground, secular man has inevitably sought new, idolatrous religions. In the twentieth century these have come in the form of Communism and Fascist racism.

According to Maritain, modern secularization is discernible in the fact that human reason has lost its grasp of Being. Modern man is neither "ontologic" nor

"erotic." His orientation is positivist and mechanical, and he has placed his hope in mechanism and technique "without wisdom to dominate them and put them at the service of human good and freedom. . . . The law of the machine, which is the law of matter, will apply itself to him, and enslave him."[36]

While Maritain joins Reinhold Niebuhr in taking a somber view of the follies of modern man, he too is only a "relative" pessimist. If man continues on his present apocalyptical course, there is little hope. If he does not destroy himself in a Third World War, there will be others to follow. But man can be renewed, and Maritain offers his contemporaries a scheme of recovery, his "concrete historical ideal." In a word, it is a theocentric or Christian humanism, a rediscovery of the true image of man.

After the great disillusionment of "anthropocentric humanism" and the atrocious experience of the anti-humanism of our day, what the world needs is a new humanism, a "theocentric" or integral humanism which would consider man in all his natural grandeur and weakness, in the entirety of his wounded being inhabited by God, in the full reality of nature, sin, and sainthood. Such a humanism would recognize all that is irrational in man, in order to tame it to reason, and all that is supra-rational, in order to have reason vivified by it and to open man to the descent of the divine into him. Its main work would be to cause the Gospel leaven and inspiration to penetrate the secular structures of life—a work of sanctification of the temporal order.[37]

Maritain sees hope for the world only in such a Christian regeneration. "A renewal of the social order on Christian lines will be a work of sanctity or it will not occur at all."[38] While the revival of society is a vain expectation without the work of God's grace, Maritain does not expect or desire a return to the *Medieval* notion of Christendom. The new social order will obviously have to take into account the political structures and social experience which have evolved over the past centuries. While Christianity does not change, Christendom—or the culture inspired by Christian truth—naturally changes and represents diverse types, depending on cultural conditions. And so it is that "the Christian religion is not enslaved to any temporal regime. It is compatible with all forms of legitimate government. . . . It imposes none of them upon their preference."[39]

Nevertheless, what an integral humanism and a new Christendom presuppose, and what is absent in all forms of modern Machiavellian politics, is a dynamism which is based on man's ultimate end—the vision and possession of God. Without this vertical movement toward divine union and self perfection,

the movement of civilization would lose the charge of spiritual energy, human pressure, and creative radiance which animates it toward its temporal accomplishment. For the man of Christian humanism history has a meaning and a direction. . . . The supreme ideal which the political and social work in mankind has to aim at is thus the inauguration of a brotherly city, which does not imply the hope that all men will someday be perfect on earth and love each other fraternally, but the hope that the existential *state* of human life and the structures of civilization will draw nearer to their perfection, the standard of which is justice and friendship . . . of a genuine democracy.[40]

The impulsion which directs the Christian to carry forth the redeeming work of Christ is, in Maritain's opinion,

rooted in a paradoxical understanding of the world. On the one hand, the Christian sees the world of nature as created and declared by God to be *good*. On the other hand, insofar as the world "encloses itself in the lust of the flesh, the lust of the eyes, and the pride of the spirit, it is the *adversary* of Christ and his disciples and hates them."[41] The Christian is in, but not of, the world. Maritain adds that the Christian will always be a foreigner, incomprehensible to the world. It is this paradoxical tension that Maritain believes is no longer present in the lives and preachments of the post-Vatican II Christian avant-garde.* They are guilty, Maritain says, of "kneeling and genuflecting before the world." They imagine that the first truth concerning the world (that it is created *good*) cancels the second (that the "world" is man's *adversary*), and hence that

there is no kingdom of God distinct from the world, and that the world absorbs into itself this kingdom, (that) it is the world itself which is the kingdom of God, in a state of becoming. . . . And that it hasn't the slightest need to be saved from above, nor to be assumed and finally transfigured in another world, a divine world.[42]

Maritain continues to see the Christian's stance in the world as paradoxical. He is called to struggle against the world, yet without neglecting to commit himself to the continuous battle against human suffering and injustice.

* Maritain's querulous attacks upon the secularity and optimism of the younger priests and theologians is an important indication of the hiatus that separates the Neo-Thomists of Maritain's generation from the younger theologians of the Vatican II *aggiornamento*, e.g., Hans Küng, Edward Schillebeeckx, and Johannes Metz.

Not only are the two tasks compatible, they call for one another. The temporal progress of the world requires the re-enforcement that comes from the kingdom of God elevating and enlightening souls, accordingly requires the struggle against the world insofar as it is the enemy of the kingdom. The progress of souls toward the kingdom of God requires them to love the world with that love which is charity as a creature of God on the way to its own natural ends, and therefore to cooperate in its temporal struggle against injustice and misery."[43]

E. L. Mascall

It was mentioned earlier that Neo-Thomism is not confined to contemporary Roman Catholicism. The revival of Thomistic studies has had a marked influence on Anglo-Catholic theology in the last thirty years. This is especially evident in the work of two Anglican theologians, Austin Farrer* and E. L. Mascall. While Farrer is the more original thinker, his writings are also less dependent on Thomistic philosophy. Mascall's philosophical writings draw heavily on the works of contemporary Thomists such as Garrigou-Lagrange, Gilson, Penido, and Maritain. Two of Mascall's most important books, *He Who Is* and *Existence and Analogy*, follow closely the Thomistic approach in dealing with such matters as the proofs of the existence of God, the way of analogy, and the attributes of God.

Mascall studied mathematics at Pembroke College, Cambridge, before turning to theology. His early interest in

---

* Farrer was a Fellow and Chaplain of Trinity College, Oxford, 1935–1960, and from 1960 until his death in 1968 was Warden of Keble College, Oxford. He was author of the important philosophical work *Finite and Infinite* (1943) as well as several works on theological imagery, including *The Glass of Vision* (1948).

mathematics and science has continued and is very evident in several of his writings.

Mascall is concerned to make a case for metaphysics and natural theology at a time when both Oxford analytical philosophy and revelational and secular theology have called these enterprises into serious question. This context explains, in part, the strongly apologetical and even polemical tone of much of Mascall's work, particularly in books such as *Words and Images*, *Christian Theology and Natural Science*, and *The Secularization of Christianity*. In these writings Mascall seeks to expose the assumptions and weaknesses of certain notions held by modern science, analytical philosophy, and radical theologians such as Bultmann and J. A. T. Robinson, author of *Honest to God*. In these works Mascall has established himself as the non-Roman apologist for traditional orthodoxy and a Thomistic natural theology.

Mascall was a student and tutor of Christ Church, Oxford, for many years, during which time he also served as Lecturer in the Philosophy of Religion and as priest of the Oratory of the Good Shepherd. Since 1963 he has been Professor of Historical Theology in the University of London.

Unlike some of the continental Neo-Thomists, Mascall is painfully aware of the irrelevance of natural theology for most moderns. He believes that the eclipse of natural theology is closely related to the conditions of life in modern urban, industrialized society. Such a life means that "people very rarely give themselves the leisure and the quiet necessary for the straight-forward consideration of finite being"[44]—the *sine qua non* of a natural theology. Mascall is also aware that natural theology, as we know it, shows the influence of Christian revelation, particularly the imprint of the biblical doctrines of God and creation. Despite this dependence, Mascall is convinced that a modern (i.e., Christian) natural theology can persuade rational men without recourse to special revelation—if such men can be cured of their positivistic myopia.

Mascall also regards the opposition of Liberal and Neo-Orthodox theology to natural theology to be poorly considered, for the question, How is it possible for men to talk about God? is not a problem only for natural theologians. As Austin Farrer has written:

Those who accept a revealed theology place among its articles the Creator of heaven and earth; this is the foundation upon which the rest is built. To know God as the absolute origin of all things is to know Him as God simply; the further revealed truths are concerned with what God, being such, has in particular done and said and, by these actions and words, shown or declared Himself to be. But these further revelations presuppose the first; nor is it easy to see how it itself can be a revelation in quite the same sense. What another man does and says may be his revelation of himself to me, and if he had not moved and spoken, it is very possible that I should not have noticed that he was there, or have mistaken him for a waxwork. But should I have recognized his personal self-revelation, without some knowledge of the rudiments of human personality derived from some other source, since I do not seem to introspect the other man's mind? And unless I had some mental machinery for thinking the bare notion of God, could I recognize His revelatory action as that of God? . . .

There is a superstition among revelationists, that by declaring themselves independent of any proof of God by analogy from the finite world, they have escaped the necessity of considering the analogy or relation of the finite to the infinite altogether. They are completely mistaken; for all their statements about God must be expressed and plainly are expressed in language drawn from the finite world. No revelationalist supposes these statements to be perfectly literal; God is not a man and human language requires to be read with some tacit qualification before it applies to Him. . . . This problem of analogy is in principle prior to every particular revelation.[45]

Mascall does not deny that the knowledge of God that is given by natural reason is a faint reflection of the God of revelation and "woefully insufficient to supply the religious needs of man." Nevertheless, the God of natural theology, the *ipsum esse subsistens*, when seen in the light of revelation, "is pregnant with all the fullness of Christian truth."[46] There are, of course, many Christians who would not follow Karl Barth in appealing to special revelation alone. Most Protestant Christians fall back upon their own immediate "religious experience." Mascall finds this position as problematical as that of the revelationists because this kind of experience is usually intimate and ineffable, entirely convincing to the experient and absolutely unconvincing to the outsider. Such experiences are vulnerable to the easiest kind of psychological reduction. As Gilson said after reading William James' great work on religious experience, "I still want to know if my religious experience is an experience of God, or an experience of myself."[47]

Neither revelation alone nor religious experience alone is an adequate base for belief in God. Nor is God's existence self-evident, as Anselm's ontological proof sought to demonstrate. Mascall joins his fellow Thomists in rejecting the

Anselmian proof, since "the idea of a necessarily existent being does not necessitate its existence." What grounds are there, then, for belief in God? Mascall believes that the rational grounds for theistic belief are to be found in the famous Five Ways of St. Thomas.

The Proofs of God's Existence.
Like Maritain, Mascall acknowledges that the Five Ways of Thomas need rather considerable rethinking if they are to retain their demonstrable force in the present day. The difficulties which the five proofs have encountered since the time of Hume are accountable in large measure by the fact that each proof has been isolated and then examined for its logical necessity. The highly Aristotelian form in which Thomas couched his argument is not, Mascall maintains, at all essential to it, and, in fact, distorts Thomas' real intention. According to Mascall, Thomas meant the five proofs to be but facets of one simple argument. Fr. Garrigou-Lagrange has expounded this single argument as follows:

We know beings and facts of different orders: an inanimate physical order (minerals), an order of vegetative life (plants), an order of sensitive life (animals), an order of intellectual and moral life (man). All these beings come into existence and afterwards disappear, they are born and die, their activity has a beginning and an end; thus, they do not exist of themselves. What is their cause?

If there are beings today, then there must have always been something; if for one single moment, there is nothing, then there will be nothing for evermore. . . . And it makes no difference whether the series of corruptible beings had or had not a beginning; if it is eternal, it is eternally insufficient: the corruptible beings of the past were as indigent as those of today and were no more self-sufficient

than they. How could any one of them, which cannot even explain itself, explain those that come after it? That would be to make the greater arise from the less. There must therefore be, above corruptible beings, a *First Being* which owes its existence to itself alone and which can give existence to others.[48]

In actual fact Thomas has only *one* datum for his arguments for the existence of God, viz., the existence of finite, contingent beings. For the person who cannot grasp the real fact of contingency —"and it is just this grasp that the modern mind, since the days of Hume, finds it so difficult to achieve"[49]—the five ways will indeed appear circular.

The Five Ways are not so much syllogistic *proofs* that finite being is of this type as *discussions* of finite being which may help us to apprehend that it is. Considered as proofs they may well seem to be circular. Anyone who cannot see that the essence of finite beings does not involve their existence is hardly likely to admit that they are contingent in the precise sense that the Third Way requires.[50]

Those who can grasp the reality and meaning of contingency and thereby the act by which finite existences exist "shall affirm God by recognizing him."[51]

Assuming that a person understands the reality of contingent being and the necessity of God, we have not yet solved all the thorny problems. The cosmological approach makes it clear that the First Being, the Creator, is radically different from finite beings. The very existence of finite creatures implies a Being who is self-existent, infinite, self-sufficient, unchangeable, and necessary. If this were not the case, finite creatures could do for themselves what is alleged to be done by God and the cosmological necessity of God would disappear. However, by asserting the radical difference between God and creatures, Hume's question arises all over again.

You have told us that the causality which God exerts on finite beings is altogether different from any causality which finite beings themselves can exercise; your whole argument for God's existence depends upon your assertion that there is something about finite beings, namely their existence, which no finite cause can confer. But since the only causality of which you, as a finite being, can be aware is the causality which finite beings exercise, in attributing causality to God you are using the word "causality" in a sense to which, on your own hypothesis, it is impossible to attach any meaning. You are in fact in an insoluble dilemma. If you assert existence and causality of God in the same sense in which you assert them of finite beings, you are rendering God incapable of fulfilling the very function for whose performance you alleged him to be necessary. But if you assert existence and causality of God in an altogether different sense from that in which you assert them of finite beings, you are making statements about God to which you can, *ex hypothesi*, assign no intelligible content. God therefore is either useless or unthinkable.[52]

Mascall believes that the cosmological approach remains valid and that it does *not* imply that theologians following it conceive of a being and an activity which are *ex hypothesi* inconceivable. All it asserts is

(1) that God exists, and (2) that God causes the existence of finite beings.... It may, of course, be replied that in making the judgment "God exists" we must have some sort of concept of God if this very judgment is not to be meaningless; that otherwise we are merely saying "X exists" where X has no intelligible content. But in fact neither of these

alternatives is true and they are not exhaustive. In saying "God exists" and "God causes the existence of finite beings," all that we mean by God is "that which exists self-existently." God is not defined by forming a concept of him, but by affirming his mode of existence, and existence is not conceptualizable. God is, of course, given to us in a concept, but not in a concept of God; he is given to us in the concept of finite being, which declares its dependence for existence on a transfinite cause.[53]

If we can define God only in terms of his self-existence, we still have not proceeded very far in answering Hume's question concerning the relationship of this causal explanation for the existence and intelligibility of the finite world to the God of traditional Christian belief. Mascall admits that the Five Ways do not take us as far as we would like, but asserts that (1) such knowledge as it gives us is not to be scorned, for its implications are very great indeed and (2) our rational knowledge of God need not end with the cosmological demonstration that God exists self-existently. How can we know anything else about God independent of revelation has to do with the Thomist doctrine of analogy, for analogy is concerned with the nature and not the existence of God. The doctrine of analogy thus begins where the rational demonstrations of God's existence end.

The Doctrine of Analogy. Mascall's approach to the doctrine of analogy is a somewhat mitigated one and less confident than that of some Thomists. His discussion of the subject reflects the serious criticism which has been directed at the doctrine in recent years. Mascall readily admits that the Thomistic doctrine of analogy is not without logical difficulties; however, the value of the doctrine does not, in his opinion, depend on its logical infallibility.

In the first place it must be recognized that the purpose of the doctrine of analogy and similar doctrines is not to prove that it is possible to think and speak about God, but to explain how such a prima facie unlikely activity is possible. Against the anti-metaphysical verificationists I would maintain that it is a matter of experience that some people at least sometimes make significant utterances which contain the word "God" as their subject. Whether anyone has yet produced an entirely satisfactory theory to account for this may be doubted; the classical doctrine of analogy made an attempt to do this, but opinions will no doubt vary about the extent to which it succeeded. My present point is that thought and discourse about God do not have to wait for the elaboration of a watertight explanation of their possibility and their nature. If the doctrine of analogy can provide such an explanation, so much the better for the doctrine of analogy; if it cannot, so much the worse for it, but the activity which it professed to account for will be unscathed. . . . It is very important in all these matters to keep the horse in front of the cart.[54]

What, in fact, is the doctrine of analogy, and what difficulties does one encounter in its use? The theist who wishes to say something affirmatively about God is faced with two choices. On the one hand, we can apply predicates to God in the same way we apply them to our experience of creatures. This would mean that our language as applied to God and to man is *univocal*. When we say that God is good or wise we mean that he is good or wise in the same sense as creatures. The problem with this kind of predication is that it denies that God is different in kind from his creatures. That

the very opposite is in fact the case was the principal conclusion of the cosmological arguments for the existence of God. To speak of God univocally is to fall into an *anthropomorphism* which is inimical to a genuine doctrine of God, i.e., of God as a transfinite being.

On the other hand, we can apply predicates to God in an entirely different way than we apply them to creatures in our experience. In this case our language, as applied to God and man, is *equivocal*. When we say that God is good in this equivocal sense, we mean that the term goodness does not have the same meaning as it has when applied to men. But what meaning does it have? We can't be sure, since the bond with our experience is broken. Equivocal language forces us into a position of *agnosticism* concerning God's nature. Mascall and the Thomists find neither of these alternatives acceptable or necessary. For there is a "middle" way of predication in the method of analogy. Analogical predication holds that, while two things may be different, they may have a relation of likeness or analogy of being (*analogia entis*) so that predicates applied to them, while not identical, are nonetheless analogical.

Since the time of Thomas, scholastic philosophers have employed two kinds of analogies: the analogy of *proportion* or *attribution* and the analogy of *proportionality*. The former relates two analogates that may differ widely from each other in many respects. Mascall cites the example of the adjective "healthy" as applied to both a man and a mountain resort. In this use of analogical predication, only one of the analogates (man) possesses the characteristic predicated of it in the *formal* sense and is therefore the *prime* analogate. The mountain resort is "healthy" only in the sense that it *induces* health in the man. It is therefore only "healthy" in the *relative* and *derivative* sense. In scholastic terms, the mountain resort is *virtually* not formally healthy, in that it is the cause of health in man. What this means is that we still lack knowledge of the *formal* nature of one of the analogates. Mascall sees this as posing a serious problem for theism.

Thus when we say that God and Mr. Jones are both good or that they are both beings, remembering that the content which the word "good" or "being" has for us is derived from our experience of the goodness and the being of creatures we are, so far as analogy of attribution is concerned, saying no more than that God has goodness or being in whatever way is necessary if he is to be able to produce goodness and being in his creatures. This would not seem necessarily to indicate anything more than that the perfections which are found formally in various finite modes in creatures exist *virtually* in God, that is to say, that he is able to produce them in the creatures; it does not seem to necessitate that God possesses them formally himself. Analogy of attribution certainly does not exclude the formal possession of the perfections by God, but it does not itself ascribe it to him.[55]

As the above quotation indicates, the analogy of attribution leaves us ignorant of the real nature of God. All we know is what we have already learned from the cosmological argument—viz., that God is the *cause* of life, goodness, wisdom, and so on. By itself the analogy of attribution will not fill the bill. Mascall believes that the analogy of proportionality, when taken in isolation from the analogy of attribution, fares no better. It, too, is faced with problems. An analysis of its form will make this clear.

We have seen that in the analogy of attribution the analogates are not equal, in that only one of them has qualities predicated of it in the *formal* sense.

In the strict sense, an analogy of proportionality implies that the analogue under discussion is found formally in each of the analogates but in a mode that is determined by the nature of the analogate itself.[56]

To use Mascall's example, if we take the term "life" as an analogous concept we can assert that cabbages, elephants, men, and God each possess life formally or literally but in a mode appropriate to each thing's distinctive nature. This can be expressed in the following manner:

$$\frac{\text{life of cabbage}}{\text{essence of cabbage}} = \frac{\text{life of elephant}}{\text{essence of elephant}}$$

$$\frac{\text{life of man}}{\text{essence of man}} = \frac{\text{life of God}}{\text{essence of God}}$$

When applied to theological language, such an analogy would mean that a term predicated of God would belong formally to his nature in a way *proportionate* to his nature. Thus God's "goodness" or "love" is not unrelated to man's goodness and love, nor is it identical. Analogy of proportionality would appear to avoid both equivocal and univocal terms and steer a "middle way" between agnosticism and anthropomorphism. However, Mascall finds at least two serious flaws in this second form of analogy.

First of all, if we assume (as we must in this form of analogy) that the term "life" is not univocal, then the equal sign used in the above diagram cannot be taken too literally.

For the point is not that the life of the cabbage is determined by the essence of the cabbage in the *same* way as that in which the life of the man is determined by the essence of man, but that the way in which cabbage essence determines cabbage life is proper to cabbagehood, while the way in which the human essence determines human life is proper to mankind.[57]

Once this is recognized we are involved in an infinite regress in which the supposed bond of equality can never be brought back together. We are left with the recognition that cabbages and men have nothing in common except "that men have described them both as being alive."

Mascall believes that an even more serious objection can be raised against the analogy of proportionality when used in discourse about God. If we refer back to the diagram above, we note that it is claimed that life is to man's nature in man in the same way as life is to God's nature in God. We can readily agree on what we mean by man's nature but

our formula will not in fact tell us in what sense life is to be predicated of God. For the essence of God is as little known to us as is his life; indeed his life is, formally considered, identical with it. Our equation has therefore two unknowns and cannot be solved.... Sheer agnosticism seems to be the outcome.[58]

In theological discourse the analogy breaks down, since both terms on the right side of the formula are unknown.

Several contemporary Thomists have sought to meet this objection by arguing that either the third[59] or fourth[60] term of the formula *is* in fact known. Many Thomists, including Mascall, acknowledge that in any case the two types of analogy, when taken separately, are insufficient. Only in combination or "mixed" can they do what is required, i.e., allow one to speak of God meaningfully and formally.

The conclusion would thus seem to be that, in order to make the doctrine of analogy really satisfactory, we must see the analogical relation between God and the world as combining in a tightly interlocked union both analogy of attribution and analogy of proportionality."[61]

According to Mascall, it is only in the "mixed" use of analogy that it is clear that our thoughts about God go beyond the level of concepts to the level of existential judgment. If we remember, following the cosmological arguments, that by God we mean "that which exists self-existently" and that God is defined not by a concept but by affirming in judgment his mode of existence, then it is clear that it is in this existential character of our affirmations about God that analogical discourse is made possible. Mascall describes how this existential judgment operates in the "mixed" use of analogy when we consider, for example, God's "goodness."

We can see how we must interpret the formula

$$\frac{\text{goodness of finite being}}{\text{finite being}} = \frac{\text{goodness of God}}{\text{God}}$$

as holding not merely in the order of essence but in that of existence, as expressing not a comparison of concepts but an existential judgment. The second term on the left-hand side of our formula ("finite being") expresses precisely that contingency of existence which arises from the fact that in finite beings essence and existence are really distinct; the second term on the right-hand side ("God") expresses that necessity of existence which arises from the fact that in God essence and existence are really identical. *And the two sides of the formula are held together by that analogy of attribution which asserts, not merely in the conceptual but in the existential order, that finite being can exist only in dependence upon God.* (Italics added.) The goodness of God is thus declared to be self-existent goodness and, as such, identical not merely with God's essence but with the act by which God exists. Analogy does not enable us to *conceive* God's goodness as identical with his essence but to *affirm* it as identical with his existence. Hence all our assertions about God are grossly inadequate in so far as they apply concepts to him, but they are thoroughly adequate in so far as they affirm perfections of him.[62]

Before leaving the question of analogy it is important to recall exactly what the doctrine is and does. It does *not* furnish us with knowledge of God; rather it *explains how* we can have knowledge of God. "The knowledge itself," Mascall underscores, "rests upon our apprehension of finite being in the cosmological relation."[63] And when we reflect on the contingency and finitude of created being we can come to know certain things about God and his relation to the world, such as his unity, infinity, immutability, and impassibility. To these questions we must now turn briefly.

The Nature of God: The Doctrine of Divine Impassibility. To apprehend God as the cause of finite beings is not simply to apprehend his existence, but to affirm important perfections of his nature. Reflection on finite being implies God's self-existence and that God as self-existent is wholly other than finite creatures. God's independence of his creation is an important and, Mascall would argue, necessary doctrine of orthodox Christian theism.

The very essence of our argument has been that the only hope of explaining the existence of finite beings at all is to postulate the existence of a Being who is *self*-existent. A first cause who was himself in even the very least degree involved in the mutability, contingency, or insufficiency of the universe would provide no more in the way of an explanation of the existence of the universe than it could provide itself. . . . Unless we are prepared to accept the God of classical theism, we may as well be content to do without a God at all. If we admit any dependence of God upon the world, the very basis of the arguments by which we have been led to him is destroyed; a "first cause" who is not self-sufficient explains nothing.[64]

Thomists have consistently argued that only a doctrine of God's entire independence of creation—his aseity and impassibility—is consistent with orthodox Christian belief and natural theology. It is this very doctrine of divine independence and impassibility that has been vigorously challenged since the beginning of the nineteenth century. In Germany these traditional notions of God were rejected by both Schelling and Hegel. In England John Stuart Mill (1806–1873) and later the Cairds and F. R. Tennant (1866–1957) proposed theistic doctrines which stressed the interdependence of God and the world. More recently Process philosophers such as A. N. Whitehead (1861–1947) and Charles Hartshorne (1897–   ) have maintained that, while God is in some respects free from contingency and change, God also is enriched by his experience of the world and is in a process of change.*

Mascall believes that theology must altogether reject "the assertion of Hegel that 'God without the world is not God,' or of Whitehead, that 'God is completed by the individual, fluent satisfactions of finite fact,' or of Tennant that 'God

---

* For an account of contemporary Process theology and its critique of classical Christian theism, see Chap. Sixteen.

without a world or a Real other is not God but an abstraction.'"[65] The relation that exists between God and the finite world is, Mascall argues, absolutely unique. Christian theology calls this unique relation *creation*, which, according to the scholastic definition, is

the production of the whole substance of a thing in the previous absence both of itself and of any other subject.

The fundamental affirmation of traditional Christian theism can thus be stated in the following highly remarkable form: the existence of the world implies the existence of a God, and moreover the existence of a God whose existence does *not* imply the existence of a world.[66]

Mascall acknowledges that if theology rejects the notion of the interdependence of God and the world, certain questions beg to be answered. If God possesses the perfections of aseity and impassibility, so that his being is neither increased nor diminished by the creation and the events of the created world, must we not ask (1) How can there by anything else that is possible of existence if God is himself fullness of being? (2) Why should God decide to create a world? and (3) How does a doctrine of entire independence and impassibility avoid a deistical view of God as totally unconcerned with the lives of his creatures? The latter question has to do with how God's self-sufficiency is compatible with his love. All of these questions are based on the fundamental question of how you can have a being related to another without conceiving of the relation as reciprocal. Mascall believes that all of these questions can, with the help of some scholastic distinctions, be answered and the necessity of the tra-

ditional perfections of aseity and impassibility affirmed.

The first issue can be restated as follows: God *and* the world are something more than God alone. Since creation has increased the sum-total of existence, God without the world must be less than the fullness of being and in some respects deficient. Mascall's reply to this is that

the statement, "God *plus* the world is more than God," is not true of a God who is the unique self-existent and infinite Being, in the sense in which we have attributed those terms to him. Of any merely finite God, however great he might be, the objection would hold. The sum of any two finite beings is always greater than either of them taken separately. But if God is literally infinite this simply does not hold. God and the World being of radically different orders of reality cannot be added together.

To add beings together we must add them in respect of their common qualities. . . . But when it is a question of adding finite beings to God, the sum simply cannot be made. In Thomist terminology God is not in any genus and any argument that treats him as if he were is illicit at the start.[67]

Assuming that creation adds nothing to the being of God, why then should God decide to create a world at all? Mascall admits that the answer to this question is shrouded in mystery, but he maintains that the very impossibility of giving an answer is a consequence of the position which is being upheld, viz., that the basis of the argument

for the existence of God is that no reason can be assigned why the world should exist; hence we have been led to postulate a God who by a sheer and unconditioned act of will has given it existence.[68]

The only being that God wills necessarily is himself.

Whether the act by which God wills himself includes the willing of this world or of some other world or of no world at all, in every case no difference is made to that supreme act. For God and the world simply do not add up.[69]

Many Christians will feel that the notion that the creation is unnecessary to God is not consistent with the biblical teaching of God's loving-kindness and long-suffering. Do not God's judgment, forgiveness, and love mean that God is genuinely affected by the events in the world and that he is not impassible but gains something from the interaction with his creatures? Mascall believes that the notion that God's love of the world involves the fulfillment of his own being is not only unnecessary but debases the divine being by maintaining, in anthropomorphic fashion, that God's love cannot be disinterested.

So far from diminishing the love shown by God in creation, the doctrine that creation is unnecesssary to God enhances it. It is precisely because creation can give nothing whatever to God which in any way enhances his beatitude, that creation is an act of entire giving on the part of God. God would not be lonely or bored or idle if we did not exist. . . . In creating the world he gains nothing for himself; that is why creation is an act of supreme love.[70]

To argue that this kind of disinterested, unreciprocal love is not love as we know it is, of course, true. But then we must not attribute love to God univocally but analogically. God's compassion and intimate concern for his creatures is in no way incompatible with his impassibility.

While the notion of divine impassibility may appear to some to be emotionally unsatisfying, the doctrine of a finite God is, in Mascall's view, destructive of a genuine theistic faith.

When we reflect upon the fragility and tenuosity of the beings that compose this finite world of ours and upon the ephemerality of all in it that we hold most dear, we shall see that the God who can meet our deepest needs will not be one who is himself entangled in its contingencies—not merely "the great companion—the fellow sufferer who understands"—but one who, while his loving care extends even to the least of his creatures and while he knows them in their weakness and need better than they know themselves, is himself unchanged and unchangeable, the strength and stay upholding all creation who ever doth himself unmoved abide, a God in whom compassion and impassibility are reconciled in the union of omnipotence and love. "I the Lord change not; therefore ye, O sons of Jacob, are not consumed" (Mal. 3:6).[71]

The modern Thomist revival has now been in existence for a century. As one might expect, its progress has not been steady or marked by uniform success. Neo-Thomism has had its share of unimaginative scholastics who reflect the mentality of the older Aristotelian manualists. However, our study of Maritain and Mascall makes it clear that Neo-Thomism, while standing in opposition to much of modern philosophy, is able to enter into creative discussion and debate with contemporary thought. Yet, like Neo-Orthodoxy, Neo-Thomism has come in for severe criticism in recent years, both outside and within the Catholic Church. In fact, there is rather considerable "anti-Thomism" sentiment among Catholic philosophers and theologians today. It is odd, but not unexpected, that at just the time when Catholics are finding Thomism too rationalistic, Protestants are turning from revelational and experiential theology and exploring anew the possibility of a contemporary Christian natural theology.

Despite *Humani generis*, issued by Pope Pius XII in 1950, there has been a growing chorus of anti-Thomist criticism since World War II. The complaint continues to be heard that Thomism is out of touch and unable to understand and address itself relevantly to the contemporary situation because of its highly intellectualist and essentialist approach to problems. Some Catholic critics go so far as to claim that modern Thomism has given considerable impetus to contemporary atheism by upholding an outmoded hellenic metaphysics—and that the obsolescence of Thomism is inevitable with the shedding of Christianity's hellenic cultural form.[72] Leslie Dewart thus suggests that a new Catholic theology "should begin with a consideration of the needs of the Christian faith, not those of Greek metaphysics."[73]

Many Catholic philosophers now contend that while Thomism is an important tool in the reconstruction of a modern theology, it is not the only philosophic source that can be called upon for this task. Thomism, they contend, need not be adhered to rigidly, and other philosophies might legitimately supplement or even be substituted for it. These Catholics are calling for a philosophical pluralism which is anathema to the traditionalists.

For other Catholic intellectuals Thomism no longer remains an adequate guide because it is so lacking in historical-critical methods which are essential to modern theological work. Such a complaint is made by the Jesuit biblical scholar, J. L. McKenzie:

> What I find lacking in the Thomistic synthesis . . . and in speculative theology as a whole—are historical and critical methods and approach. In modern education and in the modern intellectual world these have a place in the training of the educated man which they did not have in the thirteenth century. . . . The historical and critical attitude exhibited by St. Thomas . . . does not meet the standards of modern historians and critics. . . . For this a theology . . . different from the scholastic synthesis as it is currently taught in seminaries, seems necessary.[74]

While much of this kind of criticism is warranted, there is no reason to believe that Thomism will retreat into an obsolete Medievalism. Rather, its creative adherents will continue to remain loyal to the tradition while attempting to discover and seeking to incorporate the truths of modern thought and experience into the Thomistic synthesis. Of course, there will remain those both in and outside the Church who will find Thomistic natural theology fundamentally unacceptable. There will be those who remain convinced of the Humean and Kantian critique of natural theology and continue to hold that a natural knowledge of God is incompatible with the theistic claim that God is infinite. For these people the way of analogy fails despite the efforts of Mascall and others.

On the other hand, there are the Barthians and biblicists who will continue to assert that man can have no knowledge of God apart from special revelation. Finally there are those who are committed to a natural theology, but one which is freed from the assumptions of Aristotelian metaphysics—particularly the notion of the impassible, self-sufficient prime mover. For all of these critics Thomism is dangerous and anachronistic. Can Thomism serve as the foundation for a theology of the future? The answer will depend in large measure on whether Scholasticism can be radically restructured so that it can continue to appropriate and integrate into its synthesis the genuine experience of contemporary man. The breadth and genius of Thomas' philosophic vision is such that he should remain the surest guide for the future of Christian theology, according to Pope Paul VI, as expressed in an allocution delivered to the Pontifical Gregorian University of Studies in 1964:

Let teachers reverently pay heed to the voice of the Doctors of the Church, among whom St. Thomas holds the principal place; for the Angelic Doctor's force of genius is so great, his love of truth so sincere, and his wisdom in investigating, illustrating, and collecting the highest truths in a most apt bond of unity so great, that his teaching is a most efficacious instrument not only in safeguarding the foundations of the faith, but also in profitably and surely reaping the fruits of its sane progress.[75]

NOTES

1. *Doctoris Angelici*, cited in full in Jacques Maritain, *St. Thomas Aquinas* (London, 1946), pp. 155 ff.
2. *Studiorum Ducem*, Ibid., pp. 160 ff.
3. Maurice de Wulf, *An Introduction to Scholastic Philosophy* (New York, 1956), pp. 161, 163.
4. R. Garrigou-Lagrange, *Dieu* (Paris, 1928), p. 315.
5. Raissa Maritain, *We Have Been Friends Together* (New York, 1941), p. 178.
6. *St. Thomas Aquinas*, op. cit., p. 56.
7. J. Maritain, *The Dream of Descartes* (New York, 1944), p. 171.
8. J. Maritain, *Three Reformers* (New York, 1929), p. 85.
9. J. Maritain, *The Range of Reason* (New York, 1942), p. 185.
10. J. Maritain, *Christianity and Democracy* (New York, 1944), p. 21.
11. *St. Thomas Aquinas*, op. cit., p. 56.
12. J. Maritain, *An Essay on Christian Philosophy* (New York, 1955), p. 11.
13. Ibid., p. 15.
14. Ibid., pp. 18–19.
15. Ibid., p. 21.
16. Ibid., p. 26.
17. Ibid., p. 30.
18. J. Maritain, *Existence and the Existent* (New York, 1966), p. 125.
19. Ibid.
20. Ibid., p. 24.
21. Ibid., pp. 24–25.
22. Ibid., pp. 3–4.
23. Ibid., pp. 34–35.
24. *Summa theologica*, I, 4, 2; c.
25. *Existence and the Existent*, p. 72.
26. Ibid., pp. 75–76.
27. Ibid., p. 77.
28. Ibid., p. 79.
29. Jacques Maritain, *On the Uses of Philosophy* (New York, 1965), p. 60.
30. Jacques Maritain, *The Dream of Descartes*, op. cit., p. 136.
31. Ibid., p. 137.
32. Jacques Maritain, *Approaches to God* (New York, 1954), pp. 32–33.
33. Ibid., p. 63.
34. Ibid., pp. 64–65.
35. R. P. Phillips, *Modern Thomistic Philosophy*, Vol. II (Westminster, Md., 1964), p. 291.
36. Jacques Maritain, "Christian Humanism," in *The Range of Reason* (New York, 1952), p. 187.
37. Ibid., p. 194.

38. Jacques Maritain, *Freedom in the Modern World* (New York, 1936), p. 147.
39. Jacques Maritain, *Scholasticism and Politics* (New York, 1940), p. 85.
40. Jacques Maritain, *The Range of Reason*, op. cit., p. 198.
41. Jacques Maritain, *The Peasant of the Garonne* (New York, 1968), p. 60.
42. Ibid.
43. Ibid., pp. 61–62.
44. E. L. Mascall, *He Who Is* (London, 1945), p. 80.
45. Austin Farrer, *Finite and Infinite* (Dacre Press, 1943), p. 2.
46. Mascall, *He Who Is*, op. cit., pp. 81–82.
47. Etienne Gilson, *Reason and Revelation in the Middle Ages* (New York, 1938), p. 97.
48. R. Garrigou-Lagrange, *God, His Existence and Nature* (St. Louis, 1934), I, pp.252 f.
49. E. L. Mascall, *Existence and Analogy* (London, 1949), p. 67.
50. Ibid., p. 78.
51. Ibid., p. 79.
52. Ibid., pp. 86–87.
53. Ibid., pp. 87–88.
54. E. L. Mascall, *Words and Images* (London, 1957), pp. 102–103.
55. *Existence and Analogy*, op. cit., p. 102.
56. Ibid., p. 104.
57. Ibid., p. 104.
58. Ibid., p. 110.
59. R. Garrigou-Lagrange, *God: His Existence and Nature*, op. cit.
60. T.-L. Pénido, *Le rôle de l'analogie en theologie dogmatique* (Paris, 1931).
61. *Existence and Analogy*, op. cit., p. 113.
62. Ibid., p. 120.
63. Ibid., p. 124.
64. Mascall, *He Who Is*, op. cit., p. 96.
65. Ibid., p. 97.
66. Mascall, *Existence and Analogy*, p. 125.
67. Mascall, *He Who Is*, op. cit., pp. 102–103
68. Ibid., p. 103.
69. Ibid., p. 104.
70. Ibid., pp. 108–109.
71. *Existence and Analogy*, op. cit., pp. 142–143.
72. This view is expressed by the Catholic philosopher Leslie Dewart in *The Future of Belief* (New York, 1966), pp. 152 ff. (Adolf von Harnack took a similar view of the hellenization of Christianity but did not attempt to suggest a new metaphysics which might replace it.)
73. Ibid., p. 165.
74. J. L. McKenzie, S.J., "Theology in Jesuit Education," *Thought* (Autumn, 1959), pp. 353–354.
75. *Acta Apostolicae Sedis* 56 (1964), p. 365; cited in *The Documents of Vatican II*, ed. Walter Abbott, S.J. (London, 1967), p. 452.

SUGGESTIONS FOR FURTHER READING

THE NEO-THOMIST MOVEMENT AND PHILOSOPHY

De Wulf, Maurice. *An Introduction to Scholastic Philosophy* (New York: Dover Publications, 1956).
Garrigou-Lagrange, Reginald, *God, His Existence and Nature*, 2 vols. (St. Louis, Mo.: Herder, 1934).
Gilson, Etienne. *The Christian Philosophy of St. Thomas Aquinas*, tr. L. K. Shook (New York: Random House, Inc., 1956).
———. *Elements of Christian Philosophy* (New York: Doubleday and Co., 1960).
Phillips, R. P. *Modern Thomistic Philosophy*, 2 vols. (Westminster, Md.: The Newman Press, 1964).

JACQUES MARITAIN

There are no up-to-date, thorough studies of Maritain's philosophy as a whole. The following works will be of some help:

Evans, Joseph W., ed. *Jacques Maritain: The Man and His Achievement* (New York: Sheed and Ward, 1963). Thirteen essays on Maritain's thought.
Fecher, Charles A. *The Philosophy of Jacques Maritain* (Westminster, Md.: The Newman

Press, 1953). The only work in English that attempts to deal with Maritain's life and thought as a whole. Uncritical.

Gallagher, Donald and Idella. *The Achievement of Jacques and Raissa Maritain* (Garden City, N.Y.: Doubleday and Co., 1962). An extensive bibliography of the works by and about Maritain.

The Maritain Volume of the Thomist (New York: Sheed and Ward, 1943). Essays on the life and thought of Maritain.

E. L. MASCALL

There are no extensive studies of Mascall's work. For a critical analysis of his doctrine of God and use of analogy see:

Cobb, John B., Jr. *Living Options in Protestant Theology* (Philadelphia: Westminster Press, 1962). Part I, Chap. 2.

Ferre, Frederick. *Language, Logic and God* (New York: Harper & Row, 1961).

CHAPTER FOURTEEN

American Empirical and Naturalistic Theology

Henry Nelson Wieman

Liberal Protestantism is a complex development of the modern period which finds its unity in a common temper or spirit. As we have seen, that spirit includes an appeal to reason and experience, freedom and tentativeness in the sphere of doctrinal belief, stress on the divine immanence and on the ethical imperative of the gospel. On these points, all liberal theologians could agree. In Germany, Protestant Liberalism was predominantly Ritschlian,* while liberal theology in Great Britain was either Ritschlian or Modernist.† We have noted that Ritschlians and Modernists were strikingly different in many respects, but they were agreed in their desire to reconceive the essential elements of the historic faith and thereby make Christian belief intelligible and relevant to modern culture. In this they were thoroughly evangelical.

In America, Liberal Protestantism between 1900 and 1940 took two rather different directions. One was what has been called *Evangelical Liberalism*. While

* See Chap. Nine.

† See Chap. Ten.

it was made up of many influences, it was predominantly Ritschlian in its method and major themes. Kenneth Cauthen has aptly described this school of American liberal theologians:

The evangelical liberals can appropriately be thought of as "serious Christians" who were searching for a theology which could be believed by "intelligent moderns." They stood squarely within the Christian tradition and accepted as normative for their thinking what they understood to be the essence of historical Christianity. These men had a deep consciousness of their continuity with the main line of Christian orthodoxy and felt that they were preserving its essential features in terms which were suitable to the modern world. One of the evidences of the loyalty of the evangelical liberals to the historic faith is the place they gave to Jesus. Through his person and work, there is mediated to men both knowledge of God and saving power. He is the source and norm of the Christian's experience of God. In short, evangelical liberalism is Christocentric.[1]

Included among the evangelical liberals were such figures as Henry Churchill King (1858–1934), Walter Rauschenbusch,* William Adams Brown (1865–1943), and Harry Emerson Fosdick (1878–1969).

Theological liberalism in America between 1910 and 1940 was characterized, however, by a movement in a more radical direction. This movement is associated with the "Chicago School" of empirical and naturalistic theology. It has been termed *Liberal Modernism*, an appropriate label if this uniquely American theology is not confused with either Catholic or Anglo-Catholic Modernism. Cauthen gives us an excellent précis of the spirit of this movement as well.

* See Chap. Nine.

The modernistic liberals can best be thought of as "intelligent moderns" who, nevertheless, wished to be thought of as "serious Christians" in some real sense. They are called "modernistic" because they were basically determined in their thinking by a twentieth-century outlook. They had no real sense of continuing in the line of the historic faith. Rather, they were conscious that they were introducing something new. Nevertheless, they believed that there were elements of permanent significance in the Christian tradition which ought to be retained. However, the standard by which the abiding values of the Christianity of the past were to be measured was derived from the presuppositions of modern science, philosophy, psychology, and social thought. Nothing was to be believed because it was to be found in the Bible or Christian tradition. . . . The thinking of these men was not Christocentric. Jesus was important—and even unique—because he illustrated truths and values which are universally relevant. However, these truths and values can be validated and even discovered apart from Jesus.[2]

American modernism is frequently referred to as the "Chicago School" because, with very few exceptions, it was made up of men associated with the Divinity School and other faculties of the University of Chicago. Among those identified with this school are Gerald Birney Smith (1868–1929), Shailer Mathews (1863–1941) and, somewhat later, Henry Nelson Wieman (1884–). Douglas Clyde Macintosh (1877–1948) is also associated with this group. Macintosh did his graduate work in both philosophy and theology at Chicago, but taught at Yale from 1909 until 1942.

As in the case of the Evangelical Liberals, the American Modernists do not represent a simple uniformity. They exhibited important differences, especially in their basic methods of approaching theology. G. B. Smith was greatly influenced by John Dewey's instrumentalism and by the pragmatism of William James. Mathews and his colleague, Shirley Jackson Case, developed a functional and sociohistorical approach to the study of Christianity. Wieman's philosophical theology was shaped through the impact of Dewey although he eschewed theological pragmatism. What all of these men did have in common was their claim to a scientific approach to the study of Christianity and their desire to develop a theology as an empirical science.

In our study of Ritschlianism, we have touched on the spirit and controlling ideas of evangelical liberalism. In this chapter, we shall examine the more radical liberalism of twentieth-century American empirical and naturalistic theology, as illustrated in the thought of D. C. Macintosh and H. N. Wieman.

American Empirical Theology: Douglas Clyde Macintosh

Like Wieman, D. C. Macintosh spent his career attempting to bring together the new perspective of American philosophical realism and Christian theology. In this effort, he was absorbed with the question of religious knowledge. He was convinced that Christian theology must be grounded in an adequate philosophical foundation. Such a framework he found in critical realism.

Macintosh was born in Breadalbane, Ontario, in 1877, and graduated from McMaster University in Toronto. He did graduate work in philosophy and theology at the University of Chicago where he came under the influence of the "Chicago School" in the persons of Edward Scribner Ames, Shailer Mathews,

G. B. Foster, and G. B. Smith. Foster and Smith weaned Macintosh away from his youthful idealism and toward Ritschlianism and pragmatism. However, he was never entirely comfortable in that theological position, for he felt it imperative that theology take up the metaphysical task. It was only after moving to Yale in 1909 that Macintosh began developing in earnest his own realistic empirical theology. In 1916 he became Dwight Professor of Theology, and in 1933 Professor of Theology and Philosophy of Religion. He also served as Chairman of the Department of Religion in the Yale Graduate School from 1920 to 1938. Macintosh's most important theological works include *Theology as an Empirical Science* (1919), *The Reasonableness of Christianity* (1925), *The Pilgrimage of Faith* (1931), "Experimental Realism in Religion," in *Religious Realism* (1931), and *The Problem of Religious Knowledge* (1940).

Macintosh's Method. In 1909, William James remarked: "Let empiricism become associated with religion, as hitherto, through some strange misunderstanding, it has been associated with irreligion, and I believe that a new era of religion, as well as philosophy, will be ready to begin."[3] Macintosh took James' counsel as a challenge and made it the motto of his first theological work, *Theology as an Empirical Science*. In this book Macintosh reflects his radical liberalism in offering experience, rather than the Bible or church doctrine, as the criterion of religious truth. Theology, Macintosh asserts, can be divided into two main types of methodology, the *conservative* and the *radical*.

The conservative method is dependent upon

external authority. Beginning with the teachings of its recognized traditional authority, whether it be Church or Bible or individual Teacher, its aim is to conserve as fully as possible the whole of the doctrinal content received.[4]

Macintosh contends that such a method is perilous, for if

on grounds of reason or experience it becomes impossible for him to retain all of this traditional content, the method comes to be one of progressive subtraction from the originally accepted content.[5]

The radical theologian begins quite otherwise and may well end up with orthodox doctrines, more reasonably and thus more firmly held.

The radical theologian, interested primarily in religious and theological certainty, refuses to begin with a docile acceptance of any doctrinal content solely upon the basis of its having been taught by some recognized institution or book or person, no matter how great the prestige of that authority. On the contrary, he adopts some criterion which he can apply as an independent thinker and investigator and accepts only such doctrines as can be built from the ground up by this radical method. Unlike the conservative's theology, his theological system will, at first, be poor in content; but if it contains less truth, it also contains less error, and it has the advantage of having from the first been more careful than the other to make provision for certainty. Moreover, if the radical method has been happily chosen, it may lead in the end to a system containing all the vital truths to which the traditionalist clings so tenaciously, but often with so little final certainty.[6]

Empirical theology begins with man's religious experience but, unlike the psychology of religion, it is not interested in the subjective states of personal consciousness but, rather, in that which is experienced, in *knowledge of God*. Therefore, an empirical theology presupposes some type of realistic epistemology which can overcome the subjectivism which has plagued modern theology, since Schleiermacher and Feuerbach, without at the same time falling into the dogmatic objectivism of a Barth or Brunner. Macintosh devoted much of his effort to developing and defending just such an epistemology, which he called a "critical monistic realism." Critical monistic realism recognizes that the character of human knowledge conditions the nature of the object as known, and yet affirms that

there may still be such an existential unity or identity between them as to enable one to say with truth that an object which is real independently of our conscious experience has been presented in experience and directly known, even though not all the qualities of the independent reality have been directly presented, and even though not all of the qualities of the object as presented need be thought of as belonging to it in its independent existence.[7]

Among the basic assumptions of an empirical or scientific theology, then, is the claim to a genuine knowledge of reality in general—an assumption common to all science. Such a theology also presupposes

the laws of thought and such assumptions with regard to method and principles as are common to all scientific investigation of an empirical sort. The scientific theologian . . . ought to presuppose all pertinent and well-established results of the other empirical sciences . . . including the results of scientific, historical, and literary criticism of sacred books, and the essential facts about great religious personalities, such as the historic Jesus.[8]

One presupposition unique to empirical theology is the reality of God. Just as in the physical sciences, one does not assume the physical world and then become sure of it, so in theology it may be expected that the theologian

will posit the existence of God—defined, to be sure, in preliminary fashion—because he is already practically sure, on the basis of religious experience, that God really exists. . . . On the basis of knowledge of God through religious experience, one can scientifically assume *that* God is, although he may have as yet very little knowledge as to *what* God is. It is just this latter, viz., what God is, that is to be investigated through scientific theological observation and experiment under the guidance of definite working hypotheses.[9]

It should be emphasized again that theology is no different from other sciences in making this basic assumption.

Having established the presuppositions of a scientific theological inquiry, Macintosh proceeds to set apart the religious data with which an empirical theology must work. These data are *revelation* or "facts of the recognizable presence of the divine within the field of human experience." The criterion for discerning the factual presence of the divine reality, i.e., revelation, is fundamentally "the value-producing factor and behavior in the universe driving toward right adjustments on man's part." Revelation is thus the perception of religious value by the human spirit issuing in the right adjustment to the religious object or Divine Reality. "It is in this ethically holy human spirit, and in the process of making it more so, that we find the presence, or revelation, of the divine."[10]

It is clear that Macintosh simply assumes certain absolute and universal values and that men can know them. As an ethical intuitionist, he holds that such values as rationality, righteousness, and unselfish love are "intuitively appreciable as intrinsic, ultimate, and universally valid, whether universally appreciated or not."[11] It would follow that revelation, or the perception of religious value, is not restricted to Christian sources or experience, a point which Macintosh readily acknowledges.

In a scientific theology, naturally, other religions besides the Christian may present whatever universally valid empirical revelation they possess, and their contributions will be welcomed. Revelation is presumably as universal as experimental religion of any spiritual value.[12]

We are, therefore, surprised to hear Macintosh continue that, despite his analysis of revelation, "our attention will be directed chiefly to the data made available in the Christian religion" for "within the limits of experimental religion the most normative revelation of the divine is to be found, apparently, in the personal life and character of Jesus" and because in the Bible we encounter "the most original available record of what seems undoubtedly to be the most significant progressive revelation in the history of experimental religion."[13] These criteria of normativeness are set forth without any substantiation. Here, we encounter a curious blindspot in Macintosh's empirical method. He simply assumes the Christian system of values to be universally normative in the examination of man's religious experience. In fact, what Macintosh's empirical theology amounts to is a defense of the Christian religion on radically empirical grounds.

From an analysis of the distinctive data of an empirical theology, Macintosh next turns to the formulation of a body of empirically verified laws based on these data. As in the formulation of any scientific laws, certain constants and variables must be recognized before such laws can be established. The constants in theology include the uniformity of nature, certain aspects of the social environment and of human nature in general, but most important "the being and character of God. This is *the Constant* of empirical theological laws."[14] Theology assumes the dependability of God to respond to the right religious adjustment by man.

The variables in the formulation of theological laws include certain aspects of the social environment and of individual training and capacity and especially "the quality and degree of responsiveness of nature or constitution and the particular religious adjustment adopted."[15] In the light of the many unknown factors involved, theology can never claim to be an *exact* science. Nevertheless, Macintosh is assured that "the quality and direction characteristic of the Constant's action may be learned through empirical investigation."[16]

It should be evident that Macintosh is quite opposed to those traditional theologies which give little or no place to man in the divine action. For Macintosh, God's positive action is contingent upon the right religious adjustment of men. Such adjustment includes (1) concentration of attention on God as the object of religious dependence and on those moral ends of which He is the source; (2) a whole-hearted self-surrender to God and consecration of one's self to be worked

upon and through by the divine power in the fulfillment of those morally desired ends; (3) a willed responsiveness to the divine guidance; (4) a steady persistence in this religious attitude.

On the basis of such a religious adjustment, certain theological laws can be discovered. Macintosh divides the laws of empirical theology into primary and secondary laws, the primary laws having to do with the volitional experiences of men while the secondary laws are concerned with man's emotional, intellectual and psychological experiences. Macintosh subdivides the primary laws into those having to do with certain *elemental* religious experiences and those laws of certain *composite* experiences. The laws of elemental religious experience include the receiving of moral aspiration, for self-control and courage, and for victory over temptation. The laws of such elemental experiences may be stated in abbreviated form as follows:

"On condition of the right religious adjustment with reference to desired truly moral states of the will . . . God the Holy Spirit produces the specific moral results desired."[17]

Laws concerning what Macintosh calls "composite experiences" cover such traditional Christian experiences as "regeneration," "perseverence," "fullness of the Spirit," and "sanctification." Macintosh states the laws of regeneration and sanctification as follows:

The theological law of regeneration, or of the genesis of the new or essentially Christian life may be formulated thus: On condition of the right religious adjustment with a view to being turned permanently from sin and to God and the Christian way of life, God the Holy Spirit works primarily in the will and ultimately in the nature more generally the definite and manifest beginning of a new and specifically Christian spiritual life.

The law of the development of essentially Christian character . . . of what has been called "sanctification" and "growth in grace," is as follows: On condition of continued cultivation of the right religious adjustment, especially when it is so constant and wholehearted as to lead to the permanent health and healthful activity of the Christian life, and when the individual has adequate information for right conduct, God the Holy Spirit produces in him the Christ-like or Christian character, with its habitual readiness and equipment for right action.[18]

The laws having to do with man's emotional, intellectual, physiological, and social experiences follow essentially this same pattern. The question that begs to be answered at this point, of course, is how does Macintosh know that these laws refer to the working of an external Reality—i.e., God—and are not merely a description of the inner workings of the human psyche? James Bissett Pratt raised just this question about Macintosh's theology:

It is probably a verifiable fact that when persons of a certain disposition and temperament and with proper training enter into and persist in a certain describable attitude toward a religious object regarded as real, differences of a certain describable sort in their spiritual experience may be depended upon to follow. This is probably a fact and a scientific fact—scientific because repeatable and verifiable. But it is a fact not of theology but of the psychology of religion.[19]

Macintosh's not very satisfactory reply to this kind of criticism is simply that, while such laws can be formulated as psychological laws, they are also justifiable evidences of the existence of God.

If it is a verifiable fact that certain results dependably follow a certain religious adjustment (psychology of religion), it is also a verifiable fact that Reality, or a dependable factor in Reality is the cause of these dependable results, and since this dependable factor, whether we can say anything more about it or not, is the real God of experimental religion, the fact, thus stated is a fact of empirical theology.[20]

On the basis of the scientific laws of empirical theology, Macintosh believed we could claim scientific knowledge about God as the Divinely Functioning Reality, that is, about what God *does.*

We may say that the Divine Reality is a reality that dependably responds to the right religious adjustment, that answers true prayer, that regenerates the human spirit, that maintains the regenerate life, that promotes the health of the spiritual life and develops essentially Christian ethico-religious character. Furthermore, this same Divine Reality convicts of sin, gives peace and joy, and "sheds abroad the love of God," in human hearts . . . .[21]

Normative Theology and Christian Belief. In Macintosh's view, all this can be known about God's action in the world as strict scientific fact. However, scientific empirical theology is not the whole of theology and knowing what God *does* is not to know fully what God *is.* There are questions—for example, the oneness or unity of God—which lie outside the province of empirical theology. Scientific theology alone gives us *knowledge,* but it cannot answer all the legitimate questions of the theologians. In addition to scientific theology, there is a place for what Macintosh calls *normative theology.* Whereas scientific theology is based on perceptual intuitions, normative theology is grounded in "imaginal" intuition. Such intuitions are strong subjective convictions concerning the nature of God which, however, transcend our empirical experience. Macintosh believed it was entirely legitimate to hold beliefs which are in accord with and support the realization of our highest ideals. Therefore, he was willing to accept a critical pragmatic criterion of belief similar to that of William James. Macintosh formulated this criterion as follows:

"We have the right to believe that those theological doctrines are true which are necessary for . . . the maintenance of the morality which is necessary for the maintainance of the highest well-being of humanity."[22]

A theological belief is permissible if it accords with our scientific knowledge, does not contradict our empirical religious experience, appears at the same time practically necessary for the realization of our purposes or, in other words, appears to us as "reasonable." Macintosh was insistent that there was a vast difference betwcen a crude utilitarian test and a reasonable will to believe. Special care must be taken to guard against any easy but false "rationalization" of one's own religious beliefs. To avoid such "rationalizations" of Christian belief, for example, certain procedures must be followed:

First of all we shall ask what fundamental attitudes and beliefs, uncontradicted by known fact, are so bound up with critically examined values that they must be regarded as essential to religion at its best, whether that religion should turn out to be Christian or not. We shall then raise the question as to whether this universal essence of valid religion is or is not also Christian. Then, in the event of an affirmative answer, in order to make sure of including the whole vital essence of Christianity, we shall ask what additional content of historic Christianity seems essential, either because of its value in facilitating the realization of the true ideal of humanity or for any other reason, and we shall finally inquire whether this further content is reasonable and therefore presumably true.[23]

It is quite obvious that Macintosh, the ethical intuitionist, has set up his own criteria of "religion at its best" and will test Christian belief by that norm. If Karl Barth was scornful of Schleiermacher's serene confidence in judging Christianity from a position above it, what must he have thought of Macintosh's theology!

On the basis of "imaginative intuition" and a critical pragmatic criterion, certain moral and metaphysical attributes of God can be affirmed which do lie beyond a purely scientific theology—e.g., the belief that God is one, that he is personal, conscious, and purposeful and "supremely trustworthy and worshipful." Such doctrines as immortality and human freedom are, likewise, reasonably believed, as is any doctrine of arbitrary divine predestination or election to be rejected, since we cannot reasonably hold that a morally perfect God would arbitrarily choose one individual and reject another.

All that has been established so far about the action and being of God in empirical and normative theology has been accomplished without any reference to the person or work of Jesus Christ—despite the fact that Macintosh spoke of himself as a Christian theologian and thought of Christ as theologically "normative" in important ways. And this is perfectly consistent with Macintosh's intention, for with him *God* and *not* Christ is the final criterion of any theology. Our knowledge of God is fundamentally scientific (i.e., universal) and must not be tied to the contingencies of a particular historical revelation. In fact, Macintosh believes that apologetically there is considerable advantage in showing how much can be established theologically as consistent with positive Christianity, thereby demonstrating Christian belief to be both scientifically verifiable and rationally justifiable without reference to past historical authority:

We escape the danger of infecting the entire content of essential Christian belief with the necessary incertitude of historical opinion. All that has been said of the reasonableness and truth of Christianity is demonstrably valid, whether we have any Christology or not, and whatever we may or may not believe about the historic Jesus. It would still be valid if it should turn out that Jesus was essentially different from what has been commonly believed, or even that he was not truly historical at all.[24]

The reason for this is that

it should be clear that the Christian moral ideal is valid, apart altogether from the question as to how far it was historically realized or even taught by the historic Jesus; and similarly it should be clear that Christian optimism and faith in God are reasonably believable and progressively verifiable in human experience today, whether they were believed and verified by the historic Jesus or not. If one can believe in an essentially Christian morality and Christian optimism, with what the latter involves for belief in God and a future life, he can logically believe enough to enable him to become a Christian and experience the revelation of God in moral salvation.[25]

All this is not to say that Jesus is unimportant. First of all, belief in the historical Jesus has proven psychologically valuable in the Christian nurture of countless millions, and appeal to the historic Jesus Christ has had tremendous pedagogical value, the moral example of Jesus being the pivotal influence in the lives of many in the experience of redemption and reconciliation. All Macintosh wants to assert is that belief in the historicity of Jesus is not *logically* indispensable to the exercise of an essentially Christian faith. Nevertheless, while not indispensable, the logical value of the historic Jesus is very great indeed. For if we acknowledge the distinction between historical and scientific fact and can *assume* the historical fact of Jesus, "we can point to a more impressive instance of individual verification of the Christian type of faith in his experience than is to be found anywhere else . . . . In his experience the reality of an uplifting power, able to deliver from evil on condition of the right religious adjustment, was amply demonstrated."[26]

According to Macintosh, Jesus Christ is a reasonable norm for judging revelation because in Jesus we find the supreme example in history of the right religious adjustment to God. It is on the basis of Jesus' moral and religious example that the traditional doctrines of his person and work are to be first understood. "We could say that we have in the religious experience of Jesus our best illustration . . . of what God, in the sense of a divinely functioning Reality and Cause, can do."[27] It is reasonable to believe that in Jesus Christ we have the fullest revelation of God. Take first the doctrine of Christ's person:

If through his dependence upon and responsiveness to God a truly moral life in exceptional measure was achieved in him, this is reasonably interpreted as a divine work in his life. . . . The quality of his life would thus represent the ideal toward which the divine activity was and always is directed. This amounts to saying that the quality of Jesus' life was first the quality of the divine will itself. And if the quality of Jesus' life and character revealed the quality of God's life and character, Jesus may be said to have been *divine in the quality or value of his personality*.[28]

What is involved in the view that Christ's life was divine in quality is simply that "God must be Christlike; and if God is Christlike, he must have done and be doing a Christlike work for the salvation of men."[29]

To speak of Christ's divineness or to refer to him as *the* Divine Man is to emphasize the special Christian doctrine of divine immanence. However, it must be stressed that such a doctrine does not require the denial of the divine immanence elsewhere. Quite the contrary. The Christian doctrines of Christ and the Holy Spirit

taken with the evolutionary concept, suggest once more a wider divine immanence as the necessary precondition of the specialized immanence in Christ and the Christlike. But the acme of immanence is incarnation. God was in Christ, and it is there that we most surely and satisfactorily find him.[30]

As in the case of the person of Christ, so in our understanding of Christ's work: we begin first with his example and proceed to a deeper conception.

In so far as man is led by this inspiring moral *example* to adopt Jesus' principle and imitate from the heart his way of life, he is *at one* with God.

But the moral example of Jesus brings to sinful man a feeling of self-condemnation, and not inspiration alone. When Jesus is viewed not as human simply but as divine, when the cross of Christ is taken as revealing "the cross eternally in the heart of God" on account of the sin of man whom God loves, when the pure

self-giving love of Christ is taken as *revelation* of the love and grace of God, then sinful man is impelled to come to God in repentence and trust, in self-surrender and love. Thus, through responding to the love and grace of God, man becomes reconciled to God at heart and fulfils, in sincere repentence, the necessary moral condition of forgiveness, or what is called in less personal terms justification.[31]

Macintosh was at one with the liberal theologians in rejecting a purely objective view of substitutionary atonement. He held that the only satisfaction of the Christ-like God was in the destruction of sin and evil which, in the light of present historical experience, must lie in the future and not in the past. With the Ritschlians, Macintosh viewed redemption in essentially social terms: "Full atonement is impossible without the at-one-ment, or unification of man with man in a universal brotherhood. Full atonement is thus not a fact of past history, but an ideal for the future."[32]

From this analysis of Macintosh's theology it can be seen that while Macintosh's *method* is radically different from that of the Ritschlians, the *content* of his theology is at many points hardly distinguishable from that of evangelical liberalism. His concentration on Jesus as moral exemplar, as having the value of God, his conception of Christ's person as being different from that of other men in degree only, and his conception of the work of Christ are in all essentials consistent with Ritschlian theology. Where Macintosh's radical modernism is most evident is in his commitment to a strictly scientific method and his assurance that the essentials of Christian belief could be established quite independently of any appeal to special revelation. The latter, especially, separated Macintosh from the Ritschlians, all of whom *began* with the Christocentric principle and held firmly to the interdependence of Christian experience *and* positive historical revelation. The evangelical liberals were fundamentally opposed to Macintosh's logical separation of Christian belief from knowledge of the historical Jesus Christ.

One reads Macintosh with considerable uneasiness for it is impossible to shake the conviction that, despite his scientific and empirical pretensions, his theology is built on a basically specious circular argument. Macintosh begins by claiming that our knowledge of God is derived from "universal" religious experience of the "right religious adjustment." But how does one judge a "right religious adjustment"? How does one make a proper selection from the vast data of religious experience? Macintosh blithely informs us that such a selection "presupposes sufficient progress in religious discrimination to be able to distinguish the distinctly divine elements within the human experience" and then, presumably on the basis of his own intuitions, sets it down that

within the limits of experimental religion the most normative revelation of the divine is to be found, apparently, in the personal life and character of Jesus, the "Christ," in his "atoning" work, in the resultant Christian experience of "salvation," and in the developing "Kingdom of God".[33]

Why Macintosh accepts Jesus' "religious adjustment" as normative is never clarified. On the one hand, Jesus gives us the supreme example of the "right religious adjustment"; on the other hand, Jesus' adjustment is "right" because it encourages those values which Christians "perceive" to be divine.

The circularity of Macintosh's procedure is evident. What he sets out to prove experimentally is predetermined by his commitment to a given religious tradition. The difficulty inherent in Macintosh's method is aptly summarized in the following critique:

Do the findings of empirical theology as understood by (Macintosh) mean more than that, if one "intuits," "apperceives," "perceives," or chooses "on faith" to act upon certain value hypotheses, then certain results follow? Are the hypotheses themselves thereby proved valid or invalid, since the worth of the results is itself to be decided in terms of value-judgements? The "right" religious adjustment surely cannot itself establish the validity of the criteria in terms of which its own "rightness" is delineated.[34]

Macintosh considered his theology to be radically modern and untraditional in its commitment to a scientific method. As we have seen, in content his language and doctrine, though liberal, were strikingly evangelical. However, Macintosh's empirical theology lacks conviction because his Christian commitments put very obvious limits on what he claims are the "universal" and "objective" standards of his "scientific" theology. More radically freed from traditional Christian doctrine than Macintosh is Henry Nelson Wieman whose efforts to formulate an empirical Christian theology, although not without serious difficulties, have been on the whole more rigorously logical and adequate.

American Theological Naturalism: Henry Nelson Wieman

Wieman represents the farthest extreme of Christian modernism. For him, the Christian theological tradition is not an adequate guide for men. He maintains that scientific inquiry and not tradition is the guiding principle and power that will shape our lives in this modern technological age. "The bomb that fell on Hiroshima," writes Wieman, "cut history in two like a knife. Before and after are two different worlds. That cut is more abrupt, decisive, and revolutionary than the cut made by the star over Bethlehem."[35] Many critics have held that Wieman's relationship to the Christian tradition is so tenuous that referring to him as a *Christian* theologian is confusing in the extreme. Wieman is constantly questioned as to whether he considers himself a Christian theologian or a philosophical theist freed from the perspective of any special tradition. Wieman has little patience with this kind of query and has no desire to appropriate for himself the name of Christian if anyone is eager to question his right to such a classification. The ambivalent answer which he gave to the philosopher Edwin A. Burtt perhaps expresses most accurately Wieman's views of his vocation as a theologian:

I find it difficult to answer this question without causing misunderstanding. Certainly I am shaped and biased by the tradition in which I was reared. *The Christian tradition with its error, its evil and its truth, is my chief source. Yet I strongly resent the current practice of appealing to the Christian and Jewish tradition as being the guide to life and identifying this tradition with God rather than seeking what operates in all human life to create, save, and transform.*[36]

Henry Nelson Wieman is a native of Missouri and graduated from Park College in 1907. Three years later he completed his seminary course at San Francisco Theological Seminary. This was followed by two years of study in Germany at Jena and Heidelberg under Windelband and Troeltsch. Neither Harnack nor Troeltsch awakened any interest in Wieman, who remarked at the time that "history cannot tell us how to live." Like John Dewey, Wieman felt we were living in a new period and that the past could help us very little. This bias against history has remained with Wieman and has cut his theology loose from any historical tradition. If anything, his language is reminiscent of the now-quaint psychological terminology of the 1920's and 1930's.

Upon his return to this country, Wieman served four years in a Presbyterian pastorate in California. In 1915, he moved to Harvard to work toward the doctorate in the Department of Philosophy. William Ernest Hocking and Ralph Barton Perry had considerable influence on Wieman at this time, Perry's concern with the problem of value remaining a life-long interest of Wieman's.

While at Harvard, Wieman became acquainted with the work of John Dewey and it was Dewey who forced Wieman to see something which he has ever since steadfastly maintained, viz.,

Inquiry concerning what makes for the good and evil of human life must be directed to what actually and observably operates in human life. Otherwise, the inquiry will produce misleading illusions. . . . The transcendent, the supernatural, the ineffable, the infinite, the absolute being itself, and other such ideas inevitably lead inquiry astray unless they can be identified with something which observably operates in human life.[37]

Bergson's and Whitehead's concern with process and creativity had a formative influence on Wieman and these interests also have remained to the present.

However, through the years, Wieman has become less and less interested in process metaphysics and has shown an ever-increasing affinity with Dewey's experimentalism and instrumentalism in his delineation of the creative process.

Wieman began his teaching career at Occidental College. In 1927, he moved to the Divinity School of the University of Chicago where he remained as Professor of the Philosophy of Religion until his retirement in 1949. Since then, he has taught philosophy at several American universities. Among his most important theological writings are *Religious Experience and Scientific Method* (1926), *The Wrestle of Religion with Truth* (1927), *The Source of Human Good* (1946), *The Directive in History* (1949), and *Man's Ultimate Commitment* (1958).

When Wieman came to Chicago in 1929, Ritschlian theology was in decline in America and Neo-Orthodoxy had not yet made its impact on this side of the Atlantic. The disaster of World War I had called into question the social idealism of Rauschenbusch and the Social Gospel. The Christocentric emphasis in Ritschlianism had long left unanswered many searching questions about the reality of God. Protestant liberalism in the 1920's was marked by a subjectivism that was hardly distinguishable from religious humanism. Wieman wanted to break through this subjectivism and humanism and restore the objective reference (i.e., God) within religious experience. It was during this period that Wieman gave a distinctly American theistic answer to a burgeoning humanism. Thus, Wieman was to do for a modernist Christian theology in America what Barth was doing for Continental theology, i.e., directing the attention of the theologians from subjective religious feelings to the sovereign objectivity of God. Speaking of Wieman's place in the religious history of our time, a student and colleague of Wieman's has written:

He spoke out of the American experience at a specific time in our history when the fate of the liberal era hung in the balance. In many respects, he bypassed the main concerns of liberal theology; yet at a time when liberalism in America was being threatened by its own logic—a logic which led to humanism— Wieman proved a formidable antagonist to religious humanism. For many American liberals during the 1920's, particularly in the Middle West and Southwest, he reopened the way to a theistic faith.[38]

Wieman's Radical Modernism. Wieman wanted to get beyond man to God, to insist on the absolute priority of God, but he refused to do so by turning back to the theological tradition, to the Bible, the Fathers, or the Reformers, as was done by Karl Barth. For Wieman, these old traditions were no longer adequate. In his view, tradition is the repository of evocative words and symbols that have lead to the confusing of desires and sentiments with reality. For Wieman, there is only one kind of knowledge which can free us from subjective illusion and that is the knowledge of scientific method, of experience and testing.

As scientific method serves to save Christianity from sentimentality, so also it may deliver religion from the bondage of tradition.... Tradition perverts religion unless the critical mind is turned upon it; and the critical mind is science. As Francis Bacon so clearly announced, the first task of science is to turn upon tradition with criticism.[39]

Here Wieman reflects his radical

modernism. He believed the old traditions were of little or no help in the present and called for a complete reconstruction in approaching our experience of nature, man, and God on the model of John Dewey's *Reconstruction in Philosophy*. For Wieman, our only access to theological knowledge is the empirical, i.e., knowledge arrived at by observation, experimental testing, and rational inference. No special appeal can be made to revelation or some special religious faculty.

Two views have been held concerning the way we know God. One has asserted that we must know God just as we know any other object; that there are no other powers or faculties of knowledge except those by which we know ordinary objects; and that we must know God as we know trees and houses and men or else not know Him at all. The other view has tried to show that knowledge of God is a special kind of knowledge; that there is a certain feeling, inner sense ... instinct or intuition, faith, spiritual organ, moral will or what not, which has God as its special object .... We hold this view wrong ... because it resorts to a peculiar and mysterious faculty .... These mysterious faculties of discernment have long since been regarded as mythical by psychology and epistemology .... To cling still to such a view with respect to discernment of God is to put the knowledge of God outside the field of scientific knowledge, where it can be neither examined or tested.[40]

According to Wieman, all *knowledge* must depend ultimately upon science, which is simply the process of knowing. The knowledge of God must then be subjected to the scientific method of experiment. This means that God, like any other being, must be perceptible in experience. God is an object to be perceived through sense experience.

Surely any object that sustains human life must effect our senses. Since God is that something that sustains human life he sustains the senses and hence affects the senses. For who will deny that the senses are a part of human life? But anything that affects the senses is an object that may be perceived when men learn to note and interpret its sensuous effect. Hence God is an object to be perceived through sense experience. We do not mean that he must necessarily have a certain spatial magnitude. We do not mean that we must be able to rub our hands against him any more than we can rub our hands against an atom .... But we do mean that there must be ways of apprehending sense experience which would reveal to a competent observer the presence and character of that Something upon which human life is ultimately dependent for its maximum security and abundance. When this way of apprehending becomes established as a form of habitual reaction rendered accurate through experimental tests, we perceive God.[41]

In the above statement, and elsewhere in his writings, Wieman makes it clear that an empirical knowledge of God includes two factors. First of all, all perceptual knowledge involves certain requisite habits. We have developed those habits necessary to perceive trees and houses. The trained scientist is disciplined to perceive things not observed by the untrained layman. And so it is with our knowledge of God. Such knowledge comes only through the development of certain habits such as worship, prayer, the cultivation of certain values and openness to new values. Through these habits new awareness and new visions of possible good can be opened up. But the rich increment of these data of religious experience does not give us knowledge by itself. Secondly, it must be tested by critical analysis and shown to be consistent with the whole range of scientifically verified knowledge and then further tested in on-going experience. Knowledge of God requires an alternation between creative, new experience and critical test.

Human creativity consists in bringing together these two sides of discovery, open awareness on the one hand, and theorizing on the other—with its analysis, discrimination, definition and experimentation. When these two are united and rightly balanced, human life leaps forward like an open spillway.... But wide open mystic awareness flounders helplessly and blindly when unassisted by scientific method. And scientific method becomes barren definition of concepts without yielding anything to enrich life when not supported by open awareness.[42]

Unlike Macintosh's theology, Wieman's empirical theism demands a thoroughgoing naturalistic world-view. This means there can be no ultimate separation of God from nature. God, however finally defined, must be a natural process or structure which can be known like any other natural entity. Wieman speaks of his doctrine as the "newer naturalism" to distinguish it not only from supernaturalism but also from the older naturalism which tended toward a reductionistic materialism. While the newer naturalism holds that all reality consists basically of spatiotemporal events, it does not deny that this reality includes qualities and values which make life infinitely rich. What naturalism does assert is

that there is nothing in reality accessible to the human mind more basic than events and their qualities and relations. ("Relations" is another word for structure.) No knowable cause or explanation for anything that happens can reach deeper than events and their structure and qualities.[43]

This is to demand that an empirical theology have no recourse to any "transcendental grounds, orders, causes or purposes" beyond events, their qualities, and relations.

We ignore the transcendental affirmation in the Jewish Christian tradition of a creative God who not only works in history but resides beyond history. The only creative God we recognize is the creative event itself. So also we ignore the transcendental affirmation in the Greek Christian tradition of the reality of Forms of value, uncreated and eternal.... The only forms of value we recognize are produced by the creative event.... The form of the creative event itself at our higher levels of existence is determined by the creative process at more elementary levels....

These claims rest upon an analysis of our experience, revealing that no transcendental reality could ever *do* anything. It could not make the slightest difference in our lives except in the form of something happening, some event.... But when the transcendental becomes an event it is no longer transcendental.[44]

Wieman is convinced that of all the factors presently obstructing the creative advance of human life, theologies based on faith in a transcendent, supernatural God are among the most dangerous to man's future. Among the theological obstacles to the triumph of creative good that Wieman identifies with twentieth-century supernaturalism and Neo-orthodoxy are the two following:

The first is the illusion that everything will come out all right "beyond history." This illusion will be fatal if not corrected, because it blinds men to the fateful decision which must be made when man's power becomes great enough to control the conditions of his existence.

The second theological obstacle standing in

the way of this triumph is the exclusion of scientific inquiry from the religious context .... Present-day theology interprets faith in such a way that scientific inquiry is irrelevant .... This excludes science from that kind of religious responsibility which it must assume in the hour of decision, when it holds the power which will be used either to meet the demands of creativity by providing the required conditions, or to ignore these demands with fatal consequence.[45]

There are two types of theological transcendence that Wieman has consistently rejected as imperiling the salvation of men. One is a theology transcendent of time; the other is a theology transcendent of reason. Of the former he has written:

To set up any eternal, superhistorical, time-transcending reality as the ground and goal of our existence, the meaning and purpose of all we do, the recipient and fulfiller of our sacrifice, is to throw us back helplessly into the temporal process, for there alone can any difference be made. It throws us back *helplessly* because, having put all our faith and hope upon the eternal, we are incapacitated for seeking out and finding in the temporal world that creative event which does, in fact, find progressive fulfilment in and through our lives when we meet the conditions demanded.[46]

Wieman believes that contemporary existentialist and Neo-orthodox theologies, seen for example in the work of Tillich and Barth, are especially pernicious because of their stress on a theism which transcends human reason. Tillich speaks of God as "Being-itself" or "the power of being," transcending all cognitive symbols and structures. God, therefore, does not exist, since existence presupposes some definite, limiting structure or form. Wieman asserts that such

talk of God's mystery and nonexistence courts harmful illusions and opens the way for the helpless play of the emotions.

What commands our faith has a structure by which it can be known and distinguished from other kinds of being. To know this structure we must have cognitive symbols. In opposition to Tillich, I contend that God is not the unknowable mystery.[47]

In a different fashion, Barth places our knowledge of God beyond any empirical or rational test.

The truth about God no man can believe, says Barth, unless a special gift from God enables him to believe. The truth about God as set forth by Barth is beyond the reach of all the powers of human knowledge. Only by a special gift of God can one believe and know it. This truth cannot be found in holy scriptures unless God has given you the freedom to know and believe. Since the ordinary tests distinguishing true and false do not apply, the only way to know if one has the truth given of God is to find out if one agrees with Karl Barth. And yet, Barth admits that dogmatics is liable to error. But how can anyone detect what is error and what is truth if all the ordinary tests are repudiated save only the freedom to believe given by God?[48]

The Doctrine of God. If Wieman rejects any notion of God as independent of temporal events, and thus from human experience and reason, how does he conceive of the reality of God? Does God's radical immanence in nature mean that God lacks transcendence and sovereignty over man? What of the traditional attributes of God, what of God's self-relevation in Christ?

To understand Wieman's doctrine of God, it is imperative that we recognize his basic ontological assumptions. With the process philosophers (e.g., Bergson and Whitehead), Wieman holds that ultimate reality does not consist of levels or orders of disconnected atomic agents or beings but, rather, of the organic *process of events and their qualities.*

Every event accessible to human experience is a quality or a complex of qualities. . . . Quality, then, is the ultimate substance of the world out of which all else is made. . . . Diversity of kinds and nuances of change in quality of events as they occur are infinite in their complexity. . . . "Structure" is the name we give to the demarcation and interrelations of events whereby we can apprehend them as different events and yet in meaningful relation to one another. One structure is better than another if it enables us to experience more of the qualities of the events by way of unifying contrasts and meaningful relations.

Quality is always intrinsic to the total situation. It does not characterize merely one object in the situation. . . . The quality is not in the organism or in the mind or in the air or in any one of the single components necessary to yield the quality. . . . The quality is these components in their total operative togetherness as one single inclusive event with its components immediately experienced; and beyond such experience we cannot go.[49]

Wieman begins with the immediacy of events, their felt qualities, and their relations or conjunctions. On this fundamental ontology, Wieman builds his theory of value and doctrine of God. In analyzing the qualities, events, and processes that make up reality, what is the absolute good—i.e., that factor that is the source of creative human good—that produces and sustains value? According to Wieman, quality is the root of any value theory. Value grows through increasing the extent to which a life is able to experience the manifold qualities of the world. The more qualities we take in, the more worth our lives take on.

However, the felt quality of life is enhanced by meaning. Meaning joins or relates the parts of experience so that something experienced in the present can convey qualities of past events and potential values. The world takes on more qualitative meaning. It is this qualitative meaning that Wieman identifies with the *created good* of life. Qualitative meaning or created good is *intrinsic good,* for it is not simply instrumental to the achievement of some other good.

Is there any good that is greater than the created good of qualitative meaning? There is, says Wieman, and it is that which produces qualitative meaning. It is *creative good* or the *creative event.* If there is anything better than created good it is the process, the event, which continues, through all frustrations and destructive conflicts, to produce qualitative meaning. *God is this creative event.*

Here again, we see Wieman's break with the theological tradition. The tradition conceived of God as a being transcendent of the world. But, if reality consists of events and their qualities then God must be that process or event which is the source of all our created good. God must be thought of functionally, not substantially. And, to ask what produces human good or how the growth of qualitative meaning occurs is to ask an empirical question which can be answered only by experience that is open to all who would take the proper care. What we can thereby know about God may not encompass his reality but it will be genuine knowledge.

Wieman has described the working of God or the creative event in slightly different ways,[50] but his fullest analysis is given in *The Source of Human Good* in terms of a fourfold event.[51] The four subevents are described as follows:

(1) *The emerging awareness of qualitative meaning derived from other persons through communication;* (2) *integrating these new meanings with others previously acquired;* (3) *expanding the richness of quality in the appreciable world by enlarging its meaning.* This third subevent leads to the increase and variety of qualities of experience, including new reaches of ideal possibility that were never before perceived. Such an expansion of one's appreciable world may, however, make a man more unhappy and unsatisfied than he was before. He now knows there are possibilities of good that might be achieved though they are not yet actualized. It is such an expansion of consciousness and craving for genuine community among men that "would drive a man to that desperate madness in which he dreamed that by dying on a cross he could somehow bring this kingdom of love into existence."[52] The *fourth* subevent involves "*deepening the community among those who participate in this total creative event of intercommunication.*"[53] (Italics added.) As in the case of the third subevent, so is it true of the fourth that creative interaction and the deepening of community do not imply all sweetness and light.

Increase in genuine community, which is not mere increase in backslapping geniality, will include all this discernment of illness and evil in one another. Increase in community is not necessarily pleasant; the good produced by the creative event brings increase in suffering as well as increase in joy; community brings a burden as well as a release. Those who cannot endure suffering cannot endure the increase of human good.[54]

Wieman points out that the creative event is constituted by the four subevents working together and that the fourfold distinction is made solely for the purpose of analysis. Each event may occur separately, but in that case it is not creative. The unitary fourfold combination is necessary to the creativity.[55]

It might appear from Wieman's description of the creative event that this most worthful event (i.e., God) is so identified with human interaction as to be indistinguishable from human creativity itself. Is not Wieman's doctrine a form of religious humanism? Wieman's reply is an unqualified no! First of all, it must be kept in mind that Wieman has quite intentionally limited himself to a description of God at the level of human experience and not at other levels of existence. But even on the plane of human existence *man cannot do what the creative event does.* Wieman analyses why this is so:

Human effort cannot accomplish anything which the human mind cannot imagine. If something results from human effort which was not intended and which the human mind could not imagine prior to its occurrence, it is an accident relative to human effort. It is not, of course, an accident in the absolute sense of being without cause. But, even though the existence and labors of men are part of the many causes issuing in this consequence, the consequence is not the work of man if the human intent sought a result different from this consequence. . . . The structure of value produced by the creative event cannot be caused by human intention and effort, because it can be produced only by a transformation of human intention and effort . . . . Man's creative ability is something produced in him as a consequence of the prior working of the creative event . . . . The creative event is suprahuman, not in the sense that it works outside of human life, but in the sense that it creates the good of the world in a way that man cannot do . . . . The work of the creative event is different in kind from the work of man.[56]

Man does not create his own good. Rather, man is called upon to commit himself to this process of continuous creative transformation.

Here, then, we have the one master reality which will always be beyond man's control and yet which determines a destiny more glorious than anything else in the universe. If this be true, man's greatness is attained not by devoting himself to the exercise of control over what commands his ultimate commitment but to the very opposite. His greatness is attained by giving himself over to be controlled, shaped, and progressively created by it.[57]

Devotion to the creative event implies a trustful openness to continuous renewal and a surrender of all past attainments or final achievements.

Man is made not for human life as it is but for the creativity which transforms life.... No Utopia can ever satisfy the individual in the wholeness of his being ... the greatest good for the human being is not any state of existence whatsoever. Neither is it any possibility in the form of an end result. Neither is it any realm beyond the existing world. Rather this greatest good is the creativity which everlastingly transforms every state of existence toward more richness of felt quality, more comprehensive knowledge and power of control, more appreciative understanding between individuals, and more mutual control.[58]

If man's highest devotion is to the creative event, evil and sin are that which obstruct the process of creative growth. For Wieman evasion, inertia, and complacency are the great evils, since they block the creative event. When man becomes satisfied with things as they are, he is in danger of committing the greatest sin for "sin is any resistance to creativity for which man is responsible."[59] Sin is rebellion against the will of God, the creature turning away from the creator. This sin often manifests itself in the form of idolatry, of giving to some created good our absolute commitment. All created goods can turn demonic: patriotism, education, democracy, technology.

The gravest peril that men have to face resides in the way qualitative meaning, created good, can arouse an absoluteness and supremacy of loyalty which only its source, creative good, really commands.... Every value pursued in modern life can become demonic—beauty, truth, morality alike—if and when it excludes the demands of creative good in the name of the false finality of what has been created.[60]

Like so many of the early Christian symbols, the "devil" is illuminating if properly demythologized. Wieman's devil is that which tempts us to the beatific vision.

The devil is the most glorious vision of good that our minds can achieve at any one time when *that vision refuses to hold itself subject to creativity*. This is the most subtle and dangerous and obstructive sin that man can sin.[61]

Similarly, the notion of "original sin' is meaningful if properly interpreted. Original sin is not a condition of the newborn infant, but rather "the inability of men to give themselves completely to what saves and transforms."[62]

The religious problem of man is to be saved from that sin which obstructs commitment to the creative event. But men cannot be freed from the evil which vitiates human life until they acknowledge that they cannot commit themselves perfectly to creative interchange and cannot free themselves from their personal resistance to such a commitment. Before salvation can come men must, in Wieman's view, despair of finding any hope in any created good. "If one clings to something as though it were the source of all good when it is not, then the true source cannot dominate and penetrate and so cannot do what is called the 'forgiving of sin.'"[63]

Wieman's conception of the forgiveness of sin and spiritual growth in grace are traditionally orthodox on at least two points. Wieman recognizes that the total eradication of sin from human life is impossible—man remains a sinner despite the fact that the absolute grip of sin can be broken. Wieman also maintains that the forgiveness of sins cannot be brought about by human effort alone. Wieman describes, as follows, the process of overcoming those barriers to what can save:

The forgiveness of sin refers to what causes that change in the sinner which enables him to confess freely and fully his guilt and unfaithfulness, condemning them as evil, and doing it in such a way that this repentance intensifies his devotion and the completeness of his commitment. His unfaithfulness and his sin continue; but his confession of it and his condemnation of it serve to make his commitment more complete. . . . In this manner his unfaithfulness ceases to be a barrier between himself and what commands his ultimate commitment. By the ardor and sincerity of his confession and repentance he has nullified its power to separate him from what saves.[64]

The question of what causes this change in the sinner can, in Wieman's view, be found only by empirical inquiry. Therefore, he rejects many traditional theological answers, especially

the claim that a declaration of forgiveness by a supernatural person can bring about such a change, whether that declaration is granted freely or must be purchased by the blood and suffering and death of Christ or by any other kind of sacrifice practiced in the various religions.[65]

Clinical studies in psychology and reports of cases of religious conversion give evidence that the change which enables an individual to recognize and repent of his guilt and unfaithfulness is what Wieman calls *creative interchange* between individuals in openness and acceptance.

When members of the Salvation Army or of a church receive a sinner with this appreciative recognition of his individuality, not condoning the evil in him, rather recognizing it in its true character, but accepting him nevertheless and giving him that kind of esteem which goes by the name of respect, this change can occur enabling the individual to confess, repent, and repudiate his sin.[66]

The process of creative interchange which leads to forgiveness of sins and spiritual growth is an entirely natural process, but the cause of this change is not within the individuals themselves.

This cause rendering sin no longer an insuperable barrier does not reside in the participant individuals who engage in creative interchange. Rather, it resides in the creativity of this interchange. . . . the forgiveness of sins is the work of God and not of man.[67]

At this point, it should be clear that Wieman's naturalistic theism differs in marked ways from traditional Christianity. This becomes even more evident in Wieman's rejection of such doctrines as the personality and omnipotence of God and his conception of God's transcendence.

As we have seen, Wieman prefers not

to think of God as a being, but as an event or process which reveals a certain structure or pattern. According to Wieman's ontology, persons are not the most basic reality; persons are abstracted from events. Creativity is ontologically prior to personality and it should be evident that our devotion must be directed to the creator and not the creatures. Wieman believes that it can be clearly shown that God is not a personality.

A personality can only exist in a society. Personality is generated by interaction between individuals. We do not mean that we first had this interaction, and out of it personalities arose. We mean, rather, that this kind of interaction develops concomitantly with personality. This kind of interaction is communication. It is the sharing of experience. Personalities are developed just in so far as individuals develop a common body of experience which each can share with the others.
 Now if personality is thus absolutely dependent upon such social interaction, if it is generated, sustained, enriched, enobled by social interaction, and is degraded, impoverished and perverted when social interaction goes wrong, it is plain that God cannot be a personality.[68]

Wieman believes the tradition has held to the doctrine of God as a person for purely anthropocentric reasons. For instance, we argue that God must be a person because personality is the highest form of existence *we* know, or because man cannot commune with God if God is not a person. This, says Wieman, is anthropocentric religion with a vengeance! The creative event creates, sustains, and transforms as no mere person could ever do. Of course, we can say that God is a person or mind unlike any person or mind that we know, but then we might as well be saying that a circle is a square.

If we resort to empirical inquiry there is also no clear evidence that God is omnipotent. Wieman's view of the universe is pluralistic. The creative event is one event or process among many and we cannot be certain that it is the most powerful. The creative event, like all other processes, is characterized by a distinctive pattern. Among all the innumerable, diverse, and interacting processes of existence is this one which works to save man from evil and to make for the greater good. But God is not absolute in power, and evil may well become regnant. In Wieman's view, God is absolute only in the sense that creative good is trustworthy under all conditions and circumstances.

We can be sure that the outcome of its working will always be the best possible under the conditions. . . . We can also be sure creative good will always be with us. When all other good is destroyed, it springs anew; it will keep going when all else fails.[69]

 What cannot be claimed is that "absolute good means all-powerful good," that is, that the creative event

overrules all evil so that in the end everything will come out all right, no matter how long and how great the intervening evils may be . . . (that) nothing can prevent ultimate, absolute, and complete regnancy of supreme value, somehow, sometime, somewhere, although the human mind cannot know how this may be.[70]

 From Wieman's perspective such a claim cannot be defended. To those who would hold to a belief in a coercive supernatural omnipotence, in face of the possibility that man might destroy this world by atomic warfare, Wieman simply replies that

No religion with any realism in it has ever said that God would save unless men meet certain required conditions. So here, men must meet the required conditions. This is man's responsibility. If God's salvation comes by way of coercion ... it would be a self-contradiction to call it salvation because it would provide safety without that creature transformation of man which alone can make life worth living.[71]

Furthermore, we should keep in mind that man's ultimate faith is not in this earth or even in the continuance of the human species—at least as we know it. Man's ultimate commitment is to creative good.

With this commitment, he does not depend ultimately upon any known structure of the universe nor any known structure of human personality or society, because he is committed to a creativity transforming all of these. The structures now in existence may destroy his body, but they cannot destroy his faith and his hope, because he looks beyond this universe to other universes to be brought forth by creativity if required conditions are provided for its effective operation.[72]

We have already emphasized Wieman's rejection of any theism which posits a God wholly transcendent of space and time. However, it must be stressed that despite his radical rejection of several traditional attributes of God, Wieman insists on God's transcendence. It is true that God does not transcend nature, or his own activity which is constitutive of his reality. Rather, for Wieman, God's transcendence must be viewed axiologically and functionally. The creative event is axiologically transcendent in that this event has an *absolute* goodness, irrespective of time or place, which is not possible with the created good of man. For Wieman, the contrast between "creative good" and "created good" is the same as that between God and man in the Bible. The creative event is also functionally suprahuman: "The creative event is supra-human, not in the sense that it works outside of human life, but in the sense that it creates the good of the world in a way that man cannot do."[73] God works in ways that men cannot foresee, ahead of and often contrary to human desires and purposes. This means moreover, that God is "transcendent" in the sense that the creative event is beyond or more than our knowledge can comprehend.

Jesus and the Creative Event. All that we have said so far about God and his saving activity has been free of any mention of the person or work of Jesus Christ. In one sense this is perfectly logical, for Wieman's theism is not dependent on special biblical revelation. Yet, it is also unquestionable that central to Wieman's discussion of the creative event and creative interchange are the events surrounding Jesus and the birth of the primitive Christian community. What then is the place of Jesus Christ in Wieman's theology?

First of all, Wieman repudiates any notion that the man Jesus was God. The revelation of God in Christ should not be identified with the man Jesus.[74] In Wieman's opinion, we do not know enough about the facts of Jesus' life and personality to make such a judgment about his person but, even if we did, "we still do not have that supernatural knowledge of God which would be required to say that any feature pertaining to Jesus exemplifies a feature essential to the being of God."[75]

Nevertheless, the events surrounding the life and ministry of Jesus constitute one of the unique creative thrusts in the history of life as we know it. The Christ event marks a breakthrough in creative interchange. "This reversal in the direction of human devotion is not new," says Wieman. "It is, we believe, the very substance of the original Christian faith."[76]

What Wieman finds significant about Jesus is not his person but the fact that in the events of his life, death, and resurrection, the work of the creative event was *definitely* present in history. Wieman describes the "work" of Christ in the following way:

Jesus engaged in intercommunication with a little group of disciples with such depth and potency that the organization of their several personalities was broken down and they were remade. They became new men, and the thought and feelings of each got across to the others. . . . *It was not something Jesus did.* It was something that happened when he was present like a catalytic agent. . . . Something about this man Jesus broke the atomic exclusiveness of those individuals so that they were deeply and freely receptive and responsive each to the other. . . . Thus, each was transformed, lifted to a higher level of human fulfilment. Each became more of a mind and a person, with more capacity to understand, to appreciate, to act with power and insight. . . . The appreciable world expanded round about those men . . . the world was more rich and ample with meaning and quality. . . . The disciples found themselves living in a community of men vastly deeper and wider than any before accessible to them.[77]

Wieman is here describing the fourfold creative event as occurring in the interchange between Jesus and his disciples. He sees the crucifixion and resurrection of Jesus as essential to this creative event, for in these occasions the creative interchange broke the narrow bounds of established

Jewish expectations and universalized its scope.

What happened after the death of Jesus was the release of this creative power from the constraints and limitations previously confining it; also, the formation of a fellowship with an organization, ritual, symbols, and documents by which this dominance of the creative event over human concern might be perpetuated through history. . . . When Jesus was crucified, his followers saw that he could never carry to fulfilment the mission of the Jewish people as they conceived it. . . . They reached that depth of despair which comes when all that seems to give hope to human existence is seen to be illusion. . . . After about the third day, however, when the numbness of the shock had worn away, something happened. The life-transforming creativity previously known only in fellowship with Jesus began again to work in the fellowship of the disciples. It was risen from the dead. . . . What rose from the dead was not the man Jesus; it was creative power. It was the living God that works in time. It was the Second Person of the Trinity. It was Christ the God, not Jesus the man.[78]

It is important to recognize that for Wieman the creative event is not confined to Jesus' person, for the creative event involves human interaction. Jesus is a *participant* (albeit the catalyst) in the event.

The creative transformative power was not in the man Jesus. . . . Rather he was in it. It required many other things besides his own solitary self. It required the Hebrew heritage, the disciples . . . and doubtless much else of which we have little knowledge.[79]

What the Christ event did was to reverse "the order of domination in the life of man *from* domination of human concern by created good *over to* domination by creative good."[80] The event included the establishment of a community, which has continued down through the centuries, dedicated to this creative interchange. For this reason, Wieman believes the Christ event can be considered "ultimate" or "final." The winning of the victory for the creative good in the lives of men would often appear doubtful.

But it is won in the sense that World War II was won at Stalingrad. The strategic victory determining the outcome of history occurred not on the Volga but on the Jordan, and the most critical turning-points in this battle were the life of Jesus, his death and the Resurrection.[81]

Because of this battle and this victory, we can have hope that the gates of hell will not prevail against the advance of creative good.

Wieman is loath to claim that it is in the Christ event that the redemptive creative event is "uniquely" or most fully revealed. It is unjustifiably dogmatic to make such a claim. Whether or not it is true would have to be discovered by empirical inquiry, but it is extremely difficult to judge such things in traditions alien to one's own. Like Troeltsch, Wieman believes it is enough to say that "for us, in our tradition, Christ alone is our salvation."[82]

Christianity is final if through it man attains to the last freedom and the unconquerable hope through ultimate commitment to creative good. If other religions also open the way to this salvation, it should be cause for great rejoicing.[83]

Wieman's modernism is once again clearly evident in his Christology. While his theology gives a significant place to Jesus Christ, that significance is found in the fact that the Christ event *illustrates* or *exemplifies* the creative interchange which is the cardinal doctrine of Wieman's religious philosophy. What is revealed in Jesus may have reached a peak or dominance in his life not observable elsewhere in our history, but that creative transformation is not unique in kind in the Christ event nor is it limited to that event. It is universal in its work whereever the proper conditions are met. Jesus Christ is not the necessary source of salvation, although for Western man he has served that revelatory function. Had Jesus not lived, the creative event would have been redemptively at work, creating the greatest good possible and, at other times and in other worlds, has and will continue to do so.

Despite its severe reduction of traditional Christian substance, Wieman's radical reconception of Christian theology is rich in provocative insights that should be explored more carefully by Christian thinkers than has been the case. The reason for this failure is due, in part, to the difficulty one encounters in attempting to relate Wieman's doctrine to the mainstream of the Christian theological tradition. Many would say that Wieman's theology stands as a bold alternate to that tradition. To underscore the issue, only a few of the difficulties encountered in Wieman's thought by the Christian theologian need be mentioned.

First of all, there are several problems that emerge in reflecting on Wieman's doctrine of God. Is Wieman's God one? Is the creative event always the same event? Isn't it difficult for an empiricist to claim that all the creative events are one metaphysically? For Wieman, God's unity is a unity of structure, not of mind or substance. All creative events exemplify a single structure. But is this an empirical judgment or a metaphysical intuition? And, if *all* creative events exemplify a particular structure then is there not one structure that is primordial and eternal through and in time? Doesn't the First Person of the traditional Trinity have to be examined more carefully by Wieman?

Wieman says that human beings do not produce emerging good since they do not foresee or intend the good that is created. Good is the work of God. Yet, Wieman says that God is not a person, is not conscious, does not have memory or purpose. God does not foresee value, nor appreciate and enjoy it. Only man can do this and, apparently, make the judgment that God is infinitely greater than man for not being able to do so! On the other hand, the Christian tradition has held that God is personal and conscious, God's redemptive love revealed in Christ being a *conscious* act of will.

Wieman's view of history appears to be tragic, for in Wieman's doctrine of creativity there is little interest in the preservation of the past or in cumulative historical achievement of value. The future is radically open and evil might win out. In any case, there is no hope for any redemption "beyond history" in any eschatological new creation or Kingdom of God. Wieman's realism wisely repudiates any simple perfectionism or notion of historical progress, but it also negates the Christian hope as it is expressed in the eschatological symbols of the New Testament. For Wieman, our hope should not go beyond the evidence, i.e., the present innovating activity of creative interchange, if it is to avoid illusion.

Finally, Wieman's picture of Jesus and the primitive Christian community would raise serious questions for many biblical scholars and theologians. Is Wieman's demythologization of the Christ event tenable or is it a simple fitting of his own scheme onto the rich complexity of the New Testament? Was the creative event at work among Jesus and his disciples as Wieman describes it? Did not the disciples fight among themselves, did not Judas betray, Peter deny, and James reflect a narrow parochialism? The Christian community of which Wieman speaks was not so much a reality as a possibility from which both we and the disciples are estranged and whose realization we all—then, as now—block.

Despite the several problems raised by Wieman's theology, it must be kept in mind that he speaks from within the Christian community and tradition and has always seen his radical reinterpretation of Christian belief as central to his philosophical work and desperately needed in these days of magnified technological power and social revolution. The scope and earnestness of Wieman's vision is not only impressive, but his doctrine demands serious consideration in this post-existentialist and post-Neo-Orthodox period. Like Barth, Wieman has freed theology from the worship of human ideals and subjective values but, unlike Barth, Wieman's theocentric faith makes its appeal to those moderns whose scientific outlook and empirical temper make it difficult, if not impossible, for them to find meaning in the hoary language of biblical theology and church dogmatics. At a time when the highly evocative "God language" is under severe logical scrutiny perhaps Wieman's new language can add needed clarity to theological analysis.

While theologians like Barth, Tillich, and Bultmann have done much to revitalize the existential dimension of personal faith, they have given us little help in understanding how God does in fact act in nature and history. It is doubtful that a sense of God's objective reality can long be sustained when men remain ignorant of how God works in and through the events of historical experience. Here, perhaps more than anywhere else, empirical theology can contribute to a reconstructed Christian theology in the last decades of this century.

NOTES

1. Kenneth Cauthen, *The Impact of American Religious Liberalism* (New York, 1962), pp. 27–28.
2. Ibid., p. 29.
3. William James, *A Pluralistic Universe* (New York, 1909), p. 314.
4. D. C. Macintosh, *Theology as an Empirical Science* (New York, 1919), p. 7.
5. Ibid., p. 8.
6. Ibid., pp. 8–9.
7. D. C. Macintosh, *The Reasonableness of Christianity* (New York, 1925), p. 198.
8. *Theology as an Empirical Science*, p. 28.
9. Ibid., p. 29.
10. Ibid., p. 108.
11. D. C. Macintosh, *The Problem of Religious Knowledge* (New York, 1940), p. 374.
12. *Theology as an Empirical Science*, p. 109.
13. Ibid.
14. Ibid., p. 140.
15. Ibid., p. 141.
16. Ibid.
17. Ibid., p. 148.
18. Ibid., pp. 148–150.
19. *American Journal of Theology*, XXIV (1920), p. 185; cited in *The Problem of Religious Knowledge*, op. cit., p. 198.
20. *The Problem of Religious Knowledge*, p. 198.
21. Ibid., p. 209.
22. *Theology as an Empirical Science*, p. 22.
23. *The Reasonableness of Christianity*, pp. 24–25.
24. Ibid., pp. 135–136.
25. Ibid., p. 138.
26. Ibid., pp. 140–141.
27. D. C. Macintosh, *Personal Religion* (New York, 1942), p. 217.
28. *The Reasonableness of Christianity*, p. 150.
29. Ibid., p. 152.
30. Ibid., p. 154.
31. Ibid., pp. 157–158.
32. Ibid., p. 159.
33. *Theology as an Empirical Science*, p. 109.
34. James Alfred Martin, Jr., *Empirical Philosophies of Religion* (New York, 1945), p. 81.
35. *The Source of Human Good* (Chicago, 1946), p. 37.
36. H. N. Wieman, "Reply to Burtt," in *The Empirical Theology of Henry Nelson Wieman*, ed. Robert W. Bretall (New York, 1963), p. 388.
37. H. N. Wieman, "Intellectual Autobiography," in Bretall, op. cit., p. 9.
38. Bernard E. Meland, "The Root and Form of Wieman's Thought," in Bretall, op. cit., p. 45.
39. H. N. Wieman, *Religious Experience and Scientific Method* (New York, 1927), p. 59.
40. Ibid., pp. 21–22.
41. H. N. Wieman, *The Wrestle of Religion With Truth* (New York, 1929), pp. 94–95.
42. *Religious Experience and Scientific Method*, op. cit., p. 197.
43. H. N. Wieman, *The Source of Human Good* (Chicago, 1946), p. 6.
44. Ibid., pp. 7–8.
45. H. N. Wieman, in Bretall, op. cit., pp. 105–106.
46. *The Source of Human Good*, p. 36.
47. H. N. Wieman, "Intellectual Autobiography," in Bretall, op. cit., p. 14.
48. Ibid., pp. 16–17.
49. *The Source of Human Good*, pp. 301–303.
50. See *Intellectual Foundation of Faith* (New York, 1961), pp. 125–126 and *The Source of Human Good*, pp. 58–65.

51. *Source of Human Good*, pp. 58–65.
52. Ibid., p. 63.
53. Ibid., p. 58.
54. Ibid., p. 65.
55. Ibid., p. 58.
56. Ibid., pp. 75–76.
57. H. N. Wieman, *Man's Ultimate Commitment* (Carbondale, Ill., 1958), p. 77.
58. Ibid., p. 73.
59. *Source of Human Good*, p. 126.
60. Ibid., pp. 24–25.
61. Ibid., pp. 128–129.
62. *Man's Ultimate Commitment*, p. 133. Wieman's most concise reinterpretation of many of the traditional Christian symbols is found in Chap. 1 of the above book.
63. *Source of Human Good*, pp. 278–279.
64. *Man's Ultimate Commitment*, pp. 15–16.
65. Ibid., p. 16.
66. Ibid., p. 17.
67. Ibid.
68. "Theocentric Religion," in *Contemporary American Theology*, ed., Vergilius Ferm (New York, 1932), pp. 349–350.
69. *Source of Human Good*, p. 81.
70. Ibid., pp. 81–82.
71. *Intellectual Foundation of Faith*, p. 79.

72. Ibid.
73. *Source of Human Good*, p. 76.
74. *The Empirical Theology of Henry Nelson Wieman*, pp. 191, 365, 373.
75. Ibid., p. 365.
76. *Source of Human Good*, p. 39.
77. Ibid., pp. 39–41.
78. Ibid., pp. 41–44.
79. Ibid., p. 41.
80. Ibid., p. 269.
81. Ibid., pp. 271–272.
82. Ibid., p. 287.
83. Ibid. In *Man's Ultimate Commitment* Wieman indicates that "whatever has come from Jesus Christ and the early Christians did not complete the work of establishing the conditions which must be present for creativity to operate widely and securely throughout human life" (p. 303). A creative modern technology and the change of institutions and individuals to the dominance of creativity are also required if man's salvation is to be achieved. In Wieman's writings since *The Source of Human Good*, less attention is given to the ultimate victory achieved in the Christ event.

SUGGESTIONS FOR FURTHER READING

The Empirical Movement in American Theology

Martin, James Alfred, Jr. *Empirical Philosophies of Religion* (New York: Kings Crown Press, 1945).

Meland, Bernard E. ed. *The Future of Empirical Theology* (Chicago: University of Chicago Press, 1969).

Wieman, Henry N., and Meland, Bernard E. *American Philosophies of Religion* (Chicago: Willett, Clark, and Co., 1936).

Bixler, J. S., Calhoun, R. L., and Niebuhr, H. R. eds. *The Nature of Religious Experience* (New York: Harper and Brothers, 1937).

Macintosh, D. C., ed. *Religious Realism* (New York: The Macmillan Co., 1931). This book and Bixler, Calhoun, and Niebuhr contain essays expounding, defending, and criticizing empirical theology.

Douglas Clyde Macintosh

There are no extensive studies of Macintosh's theology available. In addition to the Martin book cited above, the following books contain helpful brief studies of Macintosh's thought:

Cauthen, Kenneth. *The Impact of American Religious Liberalism* (New York: Harper and Row, 1962).

Peerman, Dean and Marty, Martin E., eds. *A Handbook of Christian Theologians* (Cleveland: The World Publishing Co., 1965).

Henry Nelson Wieman

In addition to the Cauthen and Martin

books cited above, the following studies are recommended:

Bretall, Robert W., ed. *The Empirical Theology of Henry Nelson Wieman* (New York: The Macmillan Co., 1963). This work contains a wide range of interpretations and criticisms of Wieman's thought by outstanding theologians and philosophers.

Cobb, John B., Jr. *Living Options in Protestant Theology: A Survey of Methods* (Philadelphia: The Westminster Press, 1962).

CHAPTER FIFTEEN

Christian Realism:
Post-Liberal
American Theology

Reinhold Niebuhr

Liberal theology in Europe was in sharp decline between the two world wars. In America, theological liberalism maintained an important though vulnerable position during the 1920's and 1930's. It was attacked on the right by a vocal and well-organized Fundamentalism and on the left by a naturalistic humanism critical of the exclusive claims of Christian theism but responsive to religious values. Except for a few theologians, notably Henry Nelson Wieman, Protestant Liberal theology was fast losing its credibility.

Out of this situation emerged a new theological movement which, though superficially comparable to European Neo-Orthodoxy in both thought and influence, could embrace neither the older liberalism (whether Ritschlian or modernist) nor Barthianism. Instead it sought to formulate a new liberal theology on a more *realistic* basis. The beginnings of what came to be called "American

Realistic" theology is frequently associated with the publication of Reinhold Niebuhr's *Moral Man and Immoral Society* in 1932. It was this book, more than any other, which launched the American attack upon the premises of liberalism.

Though Niebuhr was the dominant voice, there were others—some independent of his influence—who were raising serious questions in the early years of the 1930's about the viability of liberal Christianity to meet the intellectual and social realities of the day. In 1931, Henry P. Van Dusen, a young teacher at Union Theological Seminary, was writing about "The Sickness of Liberal Religion."[1] In 1933 an article by John C. Bennett entitled "After Liberalism— What?"[2] appeared in *The Christian Century* and a few years later, in that same journal, the great defender of liberalism Harry Emerson Fosdick published his famous article "Beyond Modernism."[3] Liberalism and Modernism were now under attack by some of their most illustrious younger spokesmen. The spirit of the new movement was summarized in Walter Marshall Horton's book *Realistic Theology* (1934). A few years earlier, Horton had been an eager apologist for a scientific liberal theology and was closely allied with the modernism of H. N. Wieman. Now he found liberalism defunct, its doctrines

as dead as the shibboleths of the Gnostics and the Arians though they have only just died and their flesh is still warm. They have not died as a result of any concerted, effective attack upon their validity, but simply as a result of a general change in the intellectual climate.[4]

The root weakness of liberalism, as viewed by the realists, was centered in their doctrine of man and their naïvely voluntaristic vision of the amelioration of evil. Horton now had to confess that orthodoxy spoke the truth about man.

I believe orthodox Christianity represents a profound insight into the whole human predicament. I believe that the basic human difficulty *is* that perversion of the will, that betrayal of divine trust, which is called sin; and I believe that sin *is* in a sense a racial disease, transmissible from generation to generation. In affirming these things, the Christian fathers and the Protestant Reformers spoke as realists, and could have assembled masses of empirical evidence to support their views.[5]

In his article "After Liberalism— What?" John C. Bennett pointed to the extraordinary theological implications of the liberal confidence in man.

The premise of liberalism is faith in man and his highest values as the clue to the nature of God. This faith in man makes possible confidence in human reason and insight as the basis of authority in religion. It makes possible the emphasis upon the immanence of God. It makes possible the identification of the divinity of Christ with his ideal humanity. It makes possible the optimistic faith in progress which is now under such a cloud. . . . I think that *the best short-cut to an understanding of the present theological situation is to realize that liberalism diverges from orthodoxy and neo-orthodoxy in its various forms in its doctrine of man, and that other differences follow from that.*[6]

As we have shown in Chapter Eleven, Neo-Orthodoxy did not represent a complete break with the liberal tradition in theology. However, the American Realists represent much closer ties with liberalism than does Continental Neo-Orthodoxy, despite the Realists' rejection of the more extreme liberal doctrines.

Reinhold Niebuhr may appear to contradict this claim, but a careful reading of Niebuhr shows that he was carrying on his battle on two fronts, against the older liberalism on the one side and the orthodox and Barthians on the other. What the Realists sought was a new, chastened liberalism, corrected by the stubborn realism about man and history which was the heritage of classical Christianity and the Reformers.

The American Realists* saw themselves as continuing the liberal tradition in theology "with a view," in Horton's words, "to carrying over and incorporating into our realistic theology whatever genuine values may be rescued from the wreck," for liberalism "still stands for precious truths and values which must not be allowed to die."[7] The spirit of the movement is expressed in Bennett's characterization of himself as "a changed liberal—but still a liberal."[8]

Among those identified with the

* Because of the many associations of the word "realism" in twentieth-century philosophy and theology, some clarification of the term "Realistic theology" is perhaps in order. Realistic theology is not to be confused with either the slightly older "religious realism" associated with D. C. Macintosh and H. N. Wieman (see Chap. Fourteen) or with the metaphysical realism of Samuel Alexander, A. N. Whitehead, and Charles Hartshorne (see Chap. Sixteen) or with Catholic Neo-Thomist realism (see Chap. Thirteen). Religious realism was realistic in its epistemology and in its view of God (following the empirical, scientific method), as against idealism and moral subjectivism. Realist metaphysics rejected the idealist conception of mind and idealism's dismissal of the spatiotemporal world as merely the phenomenal appearance of a timeless reality. Some of the realist theologians, notably Horton, Calhoun, and H. R. Niebuhr were influenced by the new realism in epistemology and metaphysics, but the distinctive mark of Realistic theology was neither its theory of knowledge nor its metaphysics. What chiefly characterized this theology was its realism concerning the nature of man and human history.

movement were Walter Marshall Horton (1895–1966), John C. Bennett (1902–), Robert L. Calhoun (1896–), H. Richard Niebuhr (1894–1962), and Reinhold Niebuhr (1892–). All of these men had distinguished careers as professors of theology and as leaders in the ecumenical movement. They have left an indelible impress on a whole generation of churchmen and teachers now in the forefront of American Protestantism. Here we will exemplify Realistic Theology in the thought of its two most notable representatives: Reinhold and H. Richard Niebuhr.

H. Richard Niebuhr

Like so many of the thinkers we have studied, Reinhold and H. Richard Niebuhr were sons of the manse. Their father, Gustav Niebuhr, was a pastor of the German Evangelical and Reformed Church in Wright City, Missouri, where the two brothers were born. Both boys attended their small denominational schools, Elmhurst College, and Eden Theological Seminary.

After graduation from seminary, H. Richard Niebuhr served as pastor of a church in St. Louis from 1916 to 1918, during which time he received an M.A. from Washington University. He returned to Eden Seminary as a teacher between 1919 and 1922 but interrupted more than a decade of service to his college and seminary to complete his graduate studies at Yale. Niebuhr received the B.D. degree from Yale in 1923 and the Ph.D., with a dissertation on Ernst Troeltsch, in 1924. Between 1924 and 1927 Niebuhr served as President of Elmhurst College and from 1927 to 1931 as Professor of Theology at Eden Seminary. In 1931 he returned to Yale to teach in the Divinity School. At the time of his death in 1962 he was Sterling Professor of Theology and Christian Ethics at Yale.

We have underlined the fact that Christian Realism represents an effort to formulate a new liberal theology on a *realistic* basis. In that effort it remained open to the best in the liberal heritage *and* the classical Christian tradition, while appropriating some of the more radical insights of the new Continental theology, represented by Kierkegaard and Karl Barth. The complexity of influences which make up Christian Realism is exemplified in the development of H. Richard Niebuhr's theology.

Niebuhr remained profoundly committed to the nineteenth-century tradition which ran from Schleiermacher through Ritschl to Troeltsch. With Schleiermacher and Ritschl he stressed the experiential root of theological reflection—that God cannot be known outside of the response of man in faith. From Troeltsch he gained a radically historical and social orientation toward theology. But there were other, newer influences that began to take hold of Niebuhr in the Thirties. Chief among these was the rediscovery of Jonathan Edwards and the European theologians of "crisis"—particularly Tillich, Kierkegaard, and Barth. What Niebuhr found in these writers was a radical monotheism which stressed the priority of God's being and action over against man and a devastating attack on liberal "anthropomorphism." The influence of the new Continental theology is evident in Niebuhr's contribution to D. C. Macintosh's book, *Religious Realism*, published in 1931. There he wrote:

The anthropocratic and anthropocentric spirit

of the nineteenth century is by no means exhausted. But a varied revolt against its dominance has arisen and despite the variety this revolt has a common realistic character. . . . All of these movements of religious realism are united by a common interest in maintaining the independent reality of the religious object. Hence they represent a movement distinctly different from nineteenth century liberal theology which found its center of gravity in the idea of the ethical value of religion. Though realism shares this ethical interest and accepts many of the critical results of liberalism, it has shifted the center of interest from the subject to the object, from man to God, from that which is purely immanent in religious experience to that which is also transcendent.[9]

Niebuhr's first book, *The Social Sources of Denominationalism* (1929), exposed those anthropocentric factors which fragment the Christian churches, binding them to narrow ideological commitments and blinding them to some obvious facts. Nevertheless, the book reveals an ambivalent attitude toward the older liberalism, as did Reinhold Niebuhr's books during the same period. Theologically the book represented "a late-flowering of the older Social Gospel in its Christian Socialist aspect."[10]

The new realism and radical monotheism make their appearance in Niebuhr's second book, *The Kingdom of God in America* (1937). It is here that Niebuhr's break with the older liberalism is made clear, most powerfully in his oft-quoted judgment on the Social Gospel: "A God without wrath brought men without sin into a kingdom without judgment through the ministrations of a Christ without a cross."[11] From this point on a single dominant chord runs through Niebuhr's works, viz., the shift from man to the sovereignty of God. Along with the other realists, Niebuhr finds the root failure of liberalism in its superficial doctrine of man. It is to this defect that liberalism's inadequate notion of God and salvation are traceable.

For Niebuhr, a realistic doctrine of man must include recognition of the fact of sin as *disloyalty*—i.e., the failure of man to worship the true God, but also the giving of one's ultimate loyalty to something other than God. Positively considered, the essence of such sin is *idolatry*, and it is this idolatrous predilection that Niebuhr discovers in liberal anthropocentrism. The theme of radical monotheism—which remains the dominant motif in Niebuhr's strictly theological writings between 1940 and 1960—is what marks him off with the other realists as a post-liberal theologian.

During this same period, Niebuhr was consumed with another problem which reveals his dependence on and continuity with the nineteenth-century liberal tradition. That problem has to do with how divine revelation—i.e., knowledge of God—is communicated and validated. In seeking an answer to this fundamental theological question, Niebuhr had recourse to Kant, Schleiermacher, and Troeltsch.[12] Hence, Niebuhr's theology can be viewed as a sophisticated effort to mediate the concerns of Ernst Troeltsch and Karl Barth—a fact which sets his theology apart from both the older liberalism and Neo-Orthodoxy and makes it an important contemporary alternative. To see how Niebuhr attempts such a mediation requires an examination of the central themes of his major works.

Faith in Gods and in God. Niebuhr begins his theological work with an acknowledgment of his indebtedness to Kant. We do not know things as they exist in themselves. Our knowledge is always conditioned by the point of view which we occupy in space and time. For Niebuhr, awareness of our historical relativity is one of the germinal notions affecting our present way of thinking. Theology, too, has had to confess its limitations, i.e., that theology cannot describe God in himself but only as He is known in human experience. Christian faith, then, begins with a revelation which has been mediated through an historical community, the Church. Here Niebuhr joins Schleiermacher and Barth. Theology begins with the faith of the Church, with what men believe and what men see from the standpoint of the Christian community.

Such a stance is not unique to the Christian vision, for all men stand within some social and cultural matrix which gives orientation and meaning to their experience. Hence, every man should recognize the relativity of his apprehension of the truth or the absolute and that his understanding involves an existential factor. Expressed in another way, men should acknowledge that they live by faith. For Niebuhr, such a faith is not to be construed as intellectual assent to the truth of certain propositions but seen as an original, practical relationship of trust, reliance, or confidence. Such a faith is evident in the scientist's trust in the intelligibility of things and in the daily confidence which we have in one another as persons. This kind of faith is universal and can rightly be called religious.

This is the faith that life is worth living, or better, the reliance on certain centers of value as able to bestow significance and worth on our existence. It is a curious and inescapable fact about our lives, of which I think we all become aware at some time or another, that we cannot live without a cause, without some object of devotion, some center of worth, something on which we rely for our meaning. In this sense all men have faith because they are men and cannot help themselves, just as they must and do have some knowledge of their world, though their knowledge be erroneous.[13]

All men rely or trust in something, have some object of commitment and loyalty. According to Niebuhr, to have such a faith and to have a god are one and the same thing.

We arrive, then, at the problem of deity by setting out from the universal human experience of faith, of reliance or trust in something. Luther expressed this idea long ago when he asked, "What does it mean to have a god, or what is God?" and answered his question by saying, "Trust and faith of the heart alone make both God and idol. . . . For the two, faith and God, hold close together. Whatever then thy heart clings to . . . and relies upon, that is properly thy God."[14]

The object of our faith can be almost anything. Some people place their faith in a political ideal, in their nation, in themselves, or in a particular religion. Most men are divided and have many competing sources of faith and loyalty. Hence, polytheism is actually the dominant religion of most men. But men recognize, unconsciously at least, that such gods are finite, that

none of these beings on which we rely to give content and meaning to our lives is able to supply continuous meaning and value. The causes for which we live all die. . . . The ideals we fashion are revealed by time to be relative. . . . At the end nothing is left to defend us against the void of meaninglessness. We try to evade this knowledge, but it is ever in the background of our minds. . . . We know

that "on us and all our race the slow, sure doom falls pitiless and dark."[15]

Because men are torn by competing loyalties, they are divided selves; they lack any unified inner history. But even a single, unifying loyalty may prove to be the source of anxiety and disappointment if one's faith is placed in some god whose power, goodness, and absoluteness are uncertain. Such doubt often leads to the worst kind of fanaticism. Faith can be both integrating and liberating only when it is faith in that reality which is the absolute and eternal ground of being—that which will abide when all else passes. Such faith drives us away from reliance on all finite values and expectations and even enables us to say to this reality, "Though it slay us yet will we trust it." "And insofar as our faith . . . has been attached to this source and enemy of all our gods, we have been enabled to call this reality God."[16]

Now, Being or Being-itself which the man of faith addresses as God can be encountered in other ways as well. Men may respond to Being authentically but negatively or cynically. An example of a genuinely religious yet profoundly negative response to Being is that of Bertrand Russell in *"A Free Man's Worship."*[17] The important point here is that there is no final, objective way of deciding which apprehensions and response to Being is true. Hence, one must begin with revelation, with the way Being has been revealed in personal, existential encounter. Every man begins with faith in the way Being reveals itself to him and, according to Niebuhr, one person's response (e.g., the atheist's) cannot simply assume to be based on more objective information than another's. All such commitments reach beyond the limits of our scientific experience and therefore are personal, existential, and relativistic.

Despite the relativity of all revelation, Niebuhr is concerned to distinguish his view from subjectivism.

Relativism does not imply subjectivism and scepticism. It is not evident that the man who is forced to confess that his view of things is conditioned by the standpoint he occupies must doubt the reality of what he sees. It is not apparent that one who knows that his concepts are not universal must also doubt that they are concepts of the universal, or that one who understands how all his experience is historically mediated must believe that nothing is mediated through history.[18]

The principal reason why revelation is not to be considered subjective is that it is not an individualistic affair. Our apprehension of Being, the way God reveals Himself, is always to persons in history, i.e., to persons in a social, communal context. Revelation is never given in a vacuum; it is mediated to us through a community which has largely shaped our angle of vision. Thus "every view of the universal from the finite standpoint of the individual in such a society is subject to the test of experience on the part of companions who look from the same standpoint in the same direction."[19] Our faith is not without social corroboration but, Niebuhr argues, "it is not to be gained either from consultation with those who, occupying a different point of view, look in a different direction and toward other realities than we do."[20]

Inner and Outer History. Another way of speaking of revelation as personal and communal is to see revelation as "the story of our life," as the existential appropriation of the personal memory of a community. The locus of revelation is in what Niebuhr calls "inner history"— that history in which selves are revealed to one another. Inner history is to be distinguished from "outer history." Outer or external history is impersonal history; it treats its data as objects. "Even when such history deals with human individuals it seeks to reduce them to impersonal parts."[21] In the terms of a Kantian critical idealism, Niebuhr would distinguish external history as the sphere of pure reason from internal history as the sphere of practical reason, or, in Martin Buber's formulation, the relations between the "I" and the "It" from relations between the "I" and the "Thou."

In external history value means a valency or measurable strength which can be reached impartially and objectively by any trained person who has access to the data.

In internal history, however, value means worth for selves; whatever cannot be so valued is unimportant and may be dropped from memory. Here the death of Socrates, the birth of Lincoln, Peter's martyrdom, Luther's reform . . . the granting of the Magna Carta are events to be celebrated . . . . Value here means quality, not power; but the quality of valued things is one which only selves can apprehend.[22]

Revelation is that history which makes life intelligible by giving a key or pattern to one's personal life and to history. The difference between history as lived and history as observed can perhaps best be seen in their different attitudes toward time.

In our internal history time has a different feel and quality from that of the external time with which we deal as exoteric historians. The latter time resembles that of physics .... All these time-concepts have one thing in common—they are all quantitative; all these times are numbered. Such time is always serial. In the series past events are gone and future happenings are not yet. In internal history, on the other hand, our time is our duration. What is past is not gone; it abides in us as our memory; what is future is not non-existent but present in us as our potentiality. Time here is organic or it is social .... We are not in this time but it is in us.[23]

There are, then, two ways of viewing the same historical event. Take, for example, the accounts of a blind man restored to sight.

Of a man who has been blind and who has come to see, two histories can be written. A scientific case history will describe what happened to his optic nerve or to the crystalline lens, what technique the surgeon used or by what medicines a physician wrought the cure, through what stages of recovery the patient passed. An autobiography, on the other hand, may barely mention these things but it will tell what happened to a self that had lived in darkness and now saw again trees and the sunrise, children's faces and the eyes of a friend.[24]

The difference between these two historical accounts is not at all one of truth and falsehood; it is, rather, a difference of perspective. What is of the utmost importance to one individual may be common or even unobservable to another. This dual nature of history should make it clear that neither external nor internal history is itself superior or inferior. The two perspectives are indispensable and interdependent. Inner history is necessary as long as men seek the meaning of their lives. On the other hand, external history can serve as a needed corrective of internal histories. In the case of the inner history of the Christian community, Niebuhr sees external history as providing two important functions.

In the first place ... we have found it necessary in the Christian church to accept the external views of ourselves which others have set forth and to make these external histories events of spiritual significance .... Such external histories have helped to keep the church from exalting itself as though its inner life rather than the God of that inner life were the center of its attention and the ground of its faith.

Secondly, just because the Christian community remembers the revelatory moment in its own history it is required to regard all events, even though it can see most of them only from an external point of view, as workings of the God who reveals himself and so to trace with piety and disinterestedness, so far as its own fate is concerned, the ways of God in the lives of men.[25]

Revelation is that part of our inner history that illuminates and gives form to the flux of experience. Niebuhr compares revelation to hitting upon a luminous sentence in a complicated book. That one sentence can make sense out of all that came before and will come after. Similarly, Whitehead has written that "rational religion appeals to the direct intuition of special occasions, and to the elucidatory power of its concepts for all occasions."[26] Christianity appeals to just such an occasion.

The special occasion to which we appeal in the Christian church is called Jesus Christ, in whom we see the righteousness of God, his power and wisdom. But from that special occasion we also derive the concepts which make possible the elucidation of all the events in our history. Revelation means this intelligible event which makes all other events intelligible. . . . Such a revelation, rather than being contrary to reason in our life, is the discovery of rational pattern in it.[27]

Revelatory occasions not only give intelligibility to our experiences but give to the mind the "impulsion" it requires to do its work. Here Niebuhr stresses the Augustinian priority of the heart and the will in the act of knowing.

What the revelatory occasion does, first of all, is make the past intelligible. "Through it we understand what we remember, remember what we have forgotten and appropriate as our own past much that seemed alien to us."[28] The elucidatory power of the Christ event involves awareness of one's community with mankind, the breaking down of all barriers of alienation. Hence, while one begins with the particularity of a revelatory occasion, that occasion breaks the bounds of the isolated or tribal self. One begins confessionally but ends with universal identification or brotherhood.

Secondly, the revelatory event gives us a new standpoint by which to view the present. By using the Christ event as parable and analogy

we gain a new understanding of the present scene; we note relations previously ignored; find explanations of our actions hitherto undreamed of . . . . Not with complete clarity, to be sure, yet as in a glass darkly, we can discern in the contemporary confusion of our lives the evidence of a pattern in which, by great travail of men and God, a work of redemption goes on which is like the work of Christ.[29]

If properly understood, it is essential, in Niebuhr's opinion, to speak of revelation as *progressive.* Just as in our conceptual knowledge we move back and forth from reason to experience and back to reason, so it is with revelation and experience.

By moving back from experience to the categories in our mind we find out more clearly what was in our mind. The reason of the heart engages in a similar dialectic, and it does not really know what is in the revelation, in the illuminating moment, save as it proceeds from it to present experience and back again from experience to revelation. In that process the meaning of the revelation, its richness and power, grow clearer. This progressive understanding of revelation is an infinite process.[30]

Niebuhr contends that it is this capacity of revelation to cast light on the whole range of man's experience that validates its claim upon men's minds and hearts. The truth of a revelation depends upon its *adequacy,* i.e., its ability to illuminate the widest possible range of experience and to bring this whole range of experience into a meaningful whole. Thus a revelation is validated by its success in overcoming what Niebuhr calls "the evil imaginations of the heart." Evil imagination is characterized by an egoism or isolated subjectivity which cannot transcend its narrow vision. It is the tribal and scapegoat mentality which is unable to see others as real persons.

So all nations tend to regard themselves as chosen peoples. Defeated or victorious they only become more aware of themselves, using both pain and pleasure to fortify themselves in the conviction that all the world is centered in their destiny. Such imagination can never enter into the knowledge of another self; it is always the "I" that is known and never the "Thou" . . . . Evil and selfhood are left as mysteries. Solipsism in thought and action or irrational pluralism in theory and practice are the consequences. The impoverishment and alienation of the self, as well as the destruction of others, issues from a reasoning of the heart that uses evil imaginations.[31]

Niebuhr believes that the Christian revelation enables men to escape both tribalism and the impersonalism of the modern scientific outlook by offering a personalistic vision of man's relation to his fellowman that is universal in scope because it stands in judgment on all egocentric and subjective interpretations of experience.

The moral consequence of this faith is that it makes relative all those values which polytheism makes absolute, and so puts an end to the strife of the gods. But it does not relativize them as self-love does. A new sacredness attaches to the relative goods. Whatever is, is now known to be good, to have value, though its value be still hidden to us. The moral consequence of faith in God is the universal love of all being in him . . . . So faith in God involves us in a permanent revolution of the mind and of the heart, a continuous life which opens out infinitely into ever new possibilities. It does not, therefore, afford grounds for boasting but only for simple thankfulness. It is a gift of God.[32]

Niebuhr rejects the notion that the criteria used by the Christian to validate his revelation can also be used as a means of *proving* Christianity and *disproving* other revelatory claims. The theological task of the Christian community is confessional, not apologetic. That is, "it must ask what revelation means for Christians rather than what it ought to mean for all men, everywhere and at all times."[33]

It is this idea of revelation and the task of theology that raises a number of questions in the minds of critics. Niebuhr asserts that the Christian theologian's task is confessional, that he is called to analyze "what Christians see from their limited point of view in history and faith." Yet Niebuhr also insists that the relativity of faith does not imply subjectivism for "it is not apparent that one who knows that his concepts are not universal must also doubt that they are concepts of the universal."[34] But if we are willing to acknowledge that what we see from our relative point of view is also true beyond the limits of our community, then we have moved beyond the circle of confessional theology into philosophical or apologetical theology. This raises the question of whether such a Christian theology can finally avoid engaging in the metaphysical discussion.[35] The alternative would appear to be a theological positivism which Niebuhr would disavow.

Related to the above question is another concerning the adequacy of Niebuhr's fundamental distinction between external and internal history. The problem lies in Niebuhr's ambiguous use of the notion of external history. He often means by the term simply disinterested, value-free history. However, he also includes in this notion all *alien* internal histories that are not disinterested or objective. The fact is that most "external" histories are not disinterested but inner histories of other, alien communities, e.g., the positivist, the Marxist, etc. This being the case, how can Christians "accept the external views of ourselves which others have set forth and make these external histories events of spiritual significance" when Niebuhr has just told us that it is impossible to penetrate into the inner histories of other communities "without abandoning ourselves and our community?"[36]

The point is that Niebuhr's sharp division between external (i.e., alien) and internal history and his consequent relativistic perspectivism is not really the situation in which the modern believer finds himself. In the words of Van Harvey, Niebuhr's

division of history into internal and external history obscures the fact that there are not just two possible perspectives on any given event . . . but a plurality of them. There is a multiplicity of possible inner histories just as there are a number of possible external histories. . . . It is misleading, then, to place the Christian perspective over against any given other one as if they were necessarily mutually exclusive. Any modern Christian perspective will contain much that is not specifically Christian. . . . The Christian's mind is informed by the physical science, sociology, economics, and psychology of his time, as well as by his own Christian convictions.[37]

The very multiplicity of our perspectives and inner histories makes it possible to distinguish the kind of judgments compatible with certain types of events or questions. It is perfectly possible both to understand another perspective or judgment and to disagree with it or consider it vacuous. Therefore many critics would argue that the theologian is not bound by Niebuhr's historical dualism. This in turn would suggest that Christian theology is not confined to a confessional role. As will become clear, what distinguishes Reinhold Niebuhr's theological method, in part, from that of his brother is his willingness to engage in the apologetic task.

Reinhold Niebuhr

Reinhold Niebuhr preceded his younger brother through Elmhurst College and Eden Theological Seminary and then entered Yale University. He completed his B.D. degree at Yale in 1914 and remained there to work for the M.A. degree the following year. At first Niebuhr was excited by D. C. Macintosh's lectures in philosophical theology, but in time he became bored with the abstract problems of religious epistemology. This disenchantment and family needs, occasioned by his father's death, prompted Niebuhr to quit graduate study and accept a parish. In 1915, his Home Mission Board assigned him to a small, newly organized church in industrial Detroit.

Niebuhr's thirteen years at Bethel Church in Detroit had the same resolute influence on him as Rauschenbusch's experience in the slums of New York. However, in Niebuhr's case the social realities of industrialism produced a more decisive break with his youthful liberal optimism. What struck Niebuhr with particular force was the moral pretension of the automobile industrialists, particularly Henry Ford whose five-dollar-a-day wage was widely viewed as a sign of the generosity of the new industrial managers. Few realized that Ford's policy of shortened weeks and enforced vacations through prolonged layoffs led to grossly inadequate annual wages. In 1927 Niebuhr wrote:

I have been doing a little arithmetic and have come to the conclusion that the car cost Ford workers at least fifty million in lost wages during the past year. No one knows how many hundreds lost their homes in the period of unemployment, and how many children were taken out of school to help fill the depleted family exchequer.

What a civilization this is! Naïve gentlemen with a genius for mechanics suddenly become the arbiters over the lives and fortunes of hundreds of thousands. Their moral pretensions are credulously accepted at full value. No one bothers to ask whether an industry which can maintain a cash reserve of a quarter of a billion ought not to make some provision for its unemployed. . . . The cry of the hungry is drowned in the song, "Henry has made a lady out of Lizzy."[38]

During his Detroit years Niebuhr gained a national reputation as a "radical" and his close association with secular labor and socialist leaders resulted in reproach from many within the Church. During this period, Niebuhr's thought was still largely in tune with the liberal ethos. He joined and became national head of the pacifist Fellowship of Reconciliation. He played a dominant role in organizing the Fellowship of Socialist Christians which, in its beginnings, was tentatively Marxist in its orientation. It was not until the Thirties that Niebuhr became more critical of the liberal premises that undergirded his own Christian radicalism.

In 1928, Niebuhr became Professor of Applied Christianity at Union Theological Seminary in New York, where he remained until his retirement in 1960. In the Thirties and Forties, Niebuhr was engaged in an astonishing variety of activities that would have taxed ten ordinary men. He not only taught at the Seminary but was ceaselessly active in public affairs, helping to found political organizations such as the Liberal Party and Americans for Democratic Action. He also helped found publications like *Radical Religion* and *The World Tomorrow*, as well as *Christianity and Crisis* which he also served as Editor. His name appeared on the masthead of several journals for which he wrote hundreds of editorials and articles. At the same time he kept up a demanding schedule of public speaking before political groups and university audiences and, almost every weekend, preached in a college chapel.

Intellectually Niebuhr often found himself at considerable odds with his colleagues in the Church, in politics, and in the university. However, this did not embitter him or turn him away from active involvement in organizations and causes devoted to defending human rights and welfare. As John C. Bennett, his friend and colleague of many years, has written:

Niebuhr, after excoriating the illusions of many a liberal rationalist, will be found the next day sitting with these victims of illusion on a committee drafting a political manifesto or planning to rescue someone, perhaps some poor Utopian, from jail.[39]

In 1939, Niebuhr was invited to give the prestigious Gifford Lectures at the University of Edinburgh (only the fourth American to be so honored). The product of those lectures was Niebuhr's magnum opus, *The Nature and Destiny of Man*, which became one of the influential books of the first half of this century and changed the whole climate of theology in America. In the years following, Niebuhr has written close to a dozen important works, including *Faith and History*, *Christian Realism and Political Problems*, *The Self and the Dramas of History*, and *The Structure of Nations and Empires*.

In all of these books Niebuhr has shown himself to be *the* contemporary apologist for Christianity by demonstrating the relevance of biblical faith for understanding the hard realities of our human nature and history. Niebuhr's apologetic does not follow a clearly spelled-out methodology, although his writings reveal a consistent pattern. First of all, his writing is polemical. In seeking to refute alternative secular views of man and history, Niebuhr tends to cite the more extreme and less subtle positions of his antagonists. Moreover, he frequently exaggerates even these extravagant views, which on occasion has led his critics to complain that he is attacking straw men. Secondly, Niebuhr's apologetic is *dialectical* and open-ended. In showing the weaknesses and limits of alternative doctrines (e.g., idealism and naturalism or rationalism and romanticism) he points to those facets of biblical faith which take into account truths of the human condition either exaggerated or ignored by either alternative doctrine. Niebuhr *points* to the truth of biblical faith without attempting to reduce these often-paradoxical truths to some rationally coherent synthesis. Nevertheless, while remaining irreducible to some simple logic, the interpretation of life which Niebuhr finds in the Bible is not, in his opinion, irrational. It is truer to the *facts of experience* than any alternative analysis.

A third characteristic of Niebuhr's method is his constant joining together of biblical faith and the contemporary situation. Karl Barth has said that theologians should read the Bible and the morning newspaper with the same conscientious regularity. Niebuhr has developed this precept into a methodological program. He shows how the Bible illuminates the actual events and moral ambiguities of our present historical experience—from the larger issues of international conflict to relatively smaller issues as diverse as the Kinsey Report, price fixing, and White House religious services.

The closest that Niebuhr has come to a statement of his method is in an essay entitled "Coherence, Incoherence, and Christian Faith"—in which all three characteristics of his method are evident. Niebuhr begins by attacking those theories which seek to force a simple rational coherence upon experience, thereby distorting some of the facts of human life in order to establish their doctrine. Niebuhr believes there are four basic perils in any system which attempts to press some rational coherence upon experience:

1. Things and events may be too unique to fit into any system of meaning; and their uniqueness is destroyed by a premature coordination to a system of meaning, particularly a system which identifies meaning with rationality.... There are unique moral situations which do not simply fit into some general rule of natural law....

2. Realms of coherence and meaning may stand in rational contradiction to each other. ... Thus the classical metaphysics of being could not appreciate the realities of growth and becoming....

3. There are configurations and structures which stand athwart every rationally conceived system of meaning and cannot be appreciated in terms of the alternative efforts to bring the structure completely into one system or the other. The primary example is man himself, who is both in nature and above nature and who has been alternatively misunderstood by naturalistic and idealistic philosophies....

4. Genuine freedom, with the implied possibility of violating the natural and rational structures of the world, cannot be conceived in any natural or rational scheme of coherence. ... The whole realm of genuine selfhood, of sin and of grace, is beyond the comprehension of various systems of philosophy.[40]

According to Niebuhr, the Christian vision of man and history doesn't allow for such rational schemes of coherence. Rather,

the situation is that the ultrarational pinnacles of Christian truth, embodying paradox and contradiction and straining at the limits of rationality, are made plausible when understood as the keys which make the drama of human life and history comprehensible and without which it is either given a too simple meaning or falls into meaninglessness.[41]

Niebuhr's critique of rationalism makes him no less aware of the dangers of the opposite tendency—particularly among theologians—of reveling in the incoherences and irrationalities of Christian belief. Christian faith is not without its own wisdom and persuasive realism. However, this cannot be seen nor can it persuade unless the exposition of Christain faith is made vis-à-vis its commerce with culture. Otherwise, Christian belief becomes an esoteric system itself, unrelated to common experience.

There is, in short, no possibility of fully validating the truth in the foolishness of the Gospel if every cultural discipline is not taken seriously up to the point where it becomes conscious of its own limits and the point where the insights of various disciplines stand in contradiction to each other, signifying that the total of reality is more complex than any scheme of rational meaning which may be invented to comprehend it.[42]

Niebuhr believes that it is only in terms of its dialectical relationship to the doctrines and events of secular culture that the truth of Christian faith can be shown with any force or relevance. To scorn the apologetic task is to court a prideful irrelevance.

The Nature of Man. With some notion of Niebuhr's way of proceeding, we can now examine how he applies this methodology to specific issues—first of all, to the question of human selfhood.

Niebuhr's doctrine of man emerged out of his own struggle with the social issues of twentieth-century industrial society and his efforts to find some realistic guidance in facing these complex problems. His search convinced him that most analyses of man, both past and present, were tragically in error in their estimates of human nature. Man and history were viewed either pessimistically, as in Hobbes and Schopenhauer, or optimistically, as in liberal Christianity and Marxism. In our own day the failure of liberal optimism has turned many to a new historical despair and to a search for solace in some form of mysticism. The extremes are portrayed in Arthur Koestler's *The Yogi and the Commissar*.

Niebuhr rejects all dualistic doctrines of man which would interpret man as either a natural object or pure mind or spirit. Man is a union of both nature and spirit, and it is in the tension between his natural creatureliness and his self-transcendence that man's uniqueness is discovered.

If man insists that he is a child of nature and that he ought not to pretend to be more than an animal, which he obviously is, he tacitly admits that he is, at any rate, a curious kind of animal who has both the inclination and the capacity to make such pretensions. If on the other hand he insists upon his unique and distinctive place in nature and points to his rational faculties as proof of his special eminence, there is usually an anxious note in his avowals of uniqueness which betrays his unconscious sense of kinship with the brutes.[43]

To consider man either idealistically or from the perspective of a naturalistic behaviorism is to distort his uniqueness. The attempt to reduce man to a purely natural object is the danger of *scientism**

* Niebuhr has no quarrel with science; what he attacks is scientism, i.e., the metaphysical pretensions of some scientists in claiming to have the key solution to all human problems.

and is especially evident in the pretensions of modern social science. There is a naïve yet dangerous confusion between descriptive and normative judgments in the work of some scientists—for example, in the Kinsey Report on the sexual behavior of American males and females. The naturalist and materialist have an inadequate doctrine of man for the simple reason that the unique self-transcendence of human personality remains a surd to naturalistic determinism and, therefore, cannot be seriously taken into account.

However, neither can a rationalistic idealism do justice to the uniqueness and freedom of the self.

The self of idealistic rationalism is both less and more than the real self. It is less in the sense explained by Kierkegaard: "The paradox of faith is this . . . that the individual determines his relation to the universal by his relation to the absolute, not his relation to the absolute by his relation to the universal." In idealism the true self is that reason which relates the self to the universal. But since the true self in idealistic thought is neither more nor less than this universal reason, the actual self is really absorbed in the universal. The actual self is, however, less, as well as more, than reason; because every self is a unity of thought and life in which thought remains in organic unity with all the organic processes of finite existence.[44]

Niebuhr believes that the Christian view of man allows for a unitary conception of human personality which takes into account both his creatureliness and his capacity for self-transcendence. It is in man's self-transcendence that the Christian tradition has located the *imago Dei* in man. Self-transcendence is the dimension of the eternal in the human spirit which is reflected in the ability of the self to transcend both the processes of nature and its own rationality.

The human spirit has the special capacity of standing continually outside itself in terms of indefinite regression. Consciousness is a capacity for surveying the world and determining action from a governing center. Self-consciousness represents a further degree of transcendence in which the self makes itself its own object in such a way that the ego is finally always subject and not object. The rational capacity of surveying the world, of forming general concepts and analyzing the order of the world is thus but one aspect of what Christianity knows as "spirit." The self knows the world, in so far as it knows the world, because it stands outside both itself and the world, which means that it cannot understand itself except as it is understood from beyond itself and the world.[45]

Self-transcendence is the key to human freedom and hence to genuine selfhood. Nevertheless, man's capacity for infinite self-transcendence must be kept in tension with man's awareness of his creaturely finitude. It is this tension which points to both the grandeur and the misery of man, for man can direct his radical freedom toward both creative and destructive ends. Niebuhr thus rejects any simple identification of man's self-transcendence and his virtue. It is this unique spiritual capacity which is at the root of Christianity's paradoxically high and low estimate of human nature.

Indeed, it is man's radical and boundless freedom which is the basis of the self-destructive as well as creative powers; and there is no simple possibility of making nice distinctions between human destructiveness and creativity. In the words of Pascal, the "dignity of man and his misery" have the same source. Man stands perpetually outside and beyond every social, natural, communal, and rational cohesion. He is not bound by any of them, which makes for his creativity. He is tempted to make use of all of them for his own ends; that is the basis of his destructiveness.[46]

Man is that ambiguous creature who finds himself at the juncture of nature and spirit and whose predicament lies in the fact that his self-transcendence makes him a finite being encompassed by natural limitations but with infinite expectations and pretensions. It is this equivocal situation which makes man conscious of his insecurity—what Niebuhr calls *anxiety*.

Man, being both free and bound, both limited and limitless, is anxious . . . . Anxiety is the internal precondition of sin. It is the inevitable spiritual state of man, standing in the paradoxical situation of freedom and finiteness.[47]

Anxiety is the precondition of sin in that it is the internal description of the temptation which leads to sinful self-assertion. However it must not be identified with sin, since there is always the possibility that faith can purge man of his insecurity and anxiety and serve as the spur to further creativity rather than destructiveness. Yet Niebuhr believes that man's insecurity invariably leads him to seek to overcome it—to gain some basis of security for the self at the expense of others. Sin emerges out of the self's efforts to secure its safety and enhance its well-being.

Niebuhr is fond of saying that sin is not necessary but it is inevitable. What he means is that sin does not follow from the natural conditions of human life as such (finitude) but that we can point to no human life that is completely free of destructive, egoistic anxiety. It is not

man's finitude but his efforts to deny or overcome his finitude that is the source of human sin. Sin, then, is not of the flesh but of the will and is manifest in man's unwillingness to acknowledge his creatureliness and dependence. This egocentricity is expressed in man's idolatrous proclivity, i.e., his absolutizing of the relative.

Niebuhr's analysis of the phenomena of human temptation and sin is probably his greatest contribution to anthropology. Even his most severe critics have had to acknowledge that Niebuhr's description of the subtle workings of human pride and sensuality is compelling. Sin, according to Niebuhr, "resides in the inclination of man, either to deny the contingent character of his existence (in pride and self-love) or to escape from his freedom (in sensuality)."[48] For Niebuhr the sin of pride is more basic than sensuality, in part because the latter is a derivative of the former. The sin of pride has many faces, but it shows itself most clearly in man's pride of power, of knowledge, and of virtue. Both Nietzsche and Freud have made us more conscious of the fact that the will-to-power is, perhaps, man's most powerful drive. Niebuhr sees this rudimentary desire as prompted by two very different responses.

There is a pride of power in which the human ego assumes its self-sufficiency and self-mastery and imagines itself secure against all vicissitudes. It does not recognize the contingent and dependent character of its life and believes itself to be the author of its own existence, the judge of its own values and the master of its own destiny. This proud pretension is present in an inchoate form in all human life but it rises to greater heights among those individuals and classes who have a more than ordinary degree of social power. Closely related to the pride which seems to rest upon the possession of either the ordinary or some extraordinary measure of human freedom and self-mastery, is the lust for power which has pride as its end. The ego does not feel secure and therefore grasps for more power in order to make itself secure. It does not regard itself as sufficiently significant or respected or feared and therefore seeks to enhance its position in nature and society. . . . In the one case the ego seems unconscious of the finite and determinate character of its existence. In the other case the lust for power is prompted by a darkly conscious realization of its insecurity.[49]

It is at the higher and more established levels of human life and history that the sin of pride is most dangerous and just because of the mixture of self-sufficiency and insecurity.

The more man establishes himself in power and glory, the greater is the fear of tumbling from his eminence, or losing his treasure, or being discovered in his pretension. Poverty is a peril to the wealthy but not to the poor. Obscurity is feared not by those who are habituated to its twilight but by those who have become accustomed to public acclaim. . . . The powerful nation, secure against its individual foes, must fear the possibility that its power may challenge its various foes to make common cause against it . . . . Thus man seeks to make himself God because he is betrayed by both his greatness and his weakness; and there is no level of greatness and power in which the lash of fear is not at least one strand in the whip of ambition.[50]

Man's intellectual pride is closely related to his pride of power. Intellectual pride is rooted in man's unwillingness to acknowledge that all knowledge is infected with an "ideological" taint, that it is *finite* knowledge, gained from a particular perspective and therefore cannot claim finality or infallibility. Intellectual pride usually involves the inability

to recognize the limited character of one's own doctrines at the very time that one is excoriating others for their ideological bias. Moral pride, likewise, is revealed in man's self-righteousness which condemns others for failing to live up to one's own standards. But, as Niebuhr remarks,

since the self judges itself by its own standards it finds itself good. It judges others by its own standards and finds them evil, when their standards fail to conform to its own . . . . Moral pride is the pretension of finite man that his highly conditioned virtue is the final righteousness and that his very relative moral standards are absolute.[51]

Niebuhr agrees with Luther's insistence that the unwillingness of the sinner to acknowledge himself as sinner is the final form of sin. The man who can justify himself neither knows God as judge nor needs God as Saviour.[52]

While pride blinds man to the contingent character of his existence, that other form of sin, i.e., sensuality, reveals both man's inordinate self-love *and* his anxious awareness of and efforts to escape from his limitation.

Sensuality represents an effort to escape from the freedom and the infinite possibilities of spirit by becoming lost in the detailed processes, activities and interests of existence, an effort which results inevitably in unlimited devotion to limited values. Sensuality is man "turning inordinately to mutable good" (Aquinas).[53]

The sensualist often exhibits an unlimited self-love in his search for gratification but, as Niebuhr observes, this inordinate drive may well reveal a desperate effort to escape an insecure and even despised self. Take the example of drunkenness:

The drunkard sometimes seeks the abnormal stimulus of intoxicating drink in order to experience a sense of power and importance which normal life denies him .... But drunkenness may have a quite different purpose. It may be desired not in order to enhance the ego but to escape from it.[54]

According to Niebuhr, man's sin is "original" in that no man can claim to be freed from the taint of egoism. Yet sin is not necessary in the sense that it is an ontologically essential ingredient in human nature. Man's essence is in his self-transcendence or freedom. "Sin," says Niebuhr, "is committed in that freedom .... It can only be understood as a self-contradiction, made possible by the fact of his freedom but not following necessarily from it."[55] Man and man alone is responsible for his sin through the misuse of his freedom. Christianity is therefore justly considered "the religious expression of an uneasy conscience."

What Niebuhr sees as one of the marks of modern culture is its denial of man as sinner and its accompanying "easy conscience." In this denial modern man has sought all kinds of scapegoats for the evils experienced in history. He finds evil everywhere but in himself. As Adam blamed Eve and Eve blamed the serpent, so men continue to excuse themselves by pointing the finger elsewhere. The evils of life are blamed on social forces, cultural lags, poor environments, institutional rigidity, and faulty education.

No cumulation of contradictory evidence seems to disturb modern man's good opinion of himself. He considers himself the victim of corrupting institutions which he is about to destroy or reconstruct, or of the confusions of ignorance which an adequate education is about to overcome. Yet he continues to consider himself as essentially harmless and virtuous.[56]

Christianity, on the other hand, sees sin as resident in the human will, a condition which all the programs of social meliorism will fail to exorcize. Nor can the self restore the self, for it is the will itself that is bound. And when we are the judges of our own actions we are always finally righteous. For Niebuhr the solution to the human problem is to be found only in religious contrition:

The prayer of the Psalmist: "Search me, O God, and know my heart: try me and know my thoughts: and see if there be any wicked way in me, and lead me in the way everlasting" measures the dimension in which our self judgments must take place. We must recognize that only a divine judgment, more final than our own, can complete the whole structure of meaning in which we are involved.[57]

Only when the self knows itself to be under such a divine ultimate judgment will it no longer be confident and righteous in its own self-esteem. The fruit of such humility is a faith that the redemption of our personal and corporate lives is ultimately a gift of grace and not the consequence of our own clever schemes. For the Christian both divine judgment and grace are discerned in the figure of the Cross. To understand Niebuhr's doctrine of Christ and the Cross we must turn to the question of human destiny and history, for it is in man's search for meaning in his history that the Christ event is especially luminous.

The Dramas of History. Just as the self is found at the juncture of nature and spirit, so is human history a curious mixture of natural coherences and radical freedom. Man is both a creature of and creator of history in that history is the realm of both destiny and freedom. When men have ignored either of these factors they have been led all too frequently to a historical pessimism or utopianism. There is an irrevocableness about the events of history that should (but, alas! does not) chasten zealous social planners who would reverse social patterns by some simple manipulations.

Actually the past is present to us not only in our memory of its events but in the immediacy of the accomplished events which it places upon our door steps. . . . We do not merely remember that our fathers brought slaves to this country from Africa. We are reminded of their action by our colored fellow-citizens. The problems which arise from the actions of our fathers remind us that past actions are not simply revocable. We can not simply undo what our fathers have done, even though our fathers might have had the freedom to take another course of action.[58]

But man is not only a creature of history. He is also the creator of history because through memory he can freely act upon the historical past and bring about new configurations of events in the present and historical future. This freedom should save men from a too-easy acquiescence to "inevitable" social structures and authorities. However, Niebuhr believes it is man's radical freedom as creator of history that has led him to make erroneous estimates of his capacity to bend human destiny to his own will. Niebuhr gives as an example the words of the religious humanist, Eustace Hayden:

The world today knows nothing more familiar than man's success in imposing his will on the flow of events. No time is wasted by the man of affairs in anxious speculation about the supposed metaphysical controls and rigidities of the universe or human nature. He changes the face of the earth and alters the habits of men.[59]

Niebuhr comments on this kind of voluntarism:

This optimistic creed contains the modern error in baldest form. The optimism is based on the erroneous assumption that the "habits of men" are in the same category of conquerable territory as the "face of the earth" and that there is therefore no difference between the conquest of nature by technical power and the management of historical destiny by the social wisdom which must deal with the "habits of men." It also assumes that the knowledge of nature and self-knowledge belong in the same category of wisdom.[60]

History is not subject to the causal analysis or prediction that is possible in natural science because of the freedom of the human agents in history which creates causalities of endless complexity. To fully understand the forces at work in any complex of events would require knowledge of the hidden motives of the agents involved. Therefore, the meaning of history is not susceptible to a strictly scientific interpretation. Furthermore, no interpretation of history can escape the fact that the interpreter views history from his own particular finite locus in history. Every historian has his implicit or explicit framework of meaning through which he observes and makes judgments of value and meaning.

When we weigh not the actions and reactions of the atoms of nature, but the ambitions and purposes of our competitors and comrades, we are never disinterested observers. . . . Our judgments of others are mixed with emotions prompted by our strength or our weakness in relation to them. . . . We are involved as total personalities in the affairs of history. Our mind is never a pure and abstract intelligence when it functions amidst the complexities of human relations.[61]

The question of the meaning of the past and the future is always related to the question of the meaning of life itself. There is, then, no widely agreed upon rational solution to the meaning of history. The study of history poses the question of its meaning but does not yield its own meaning.

History in its totality and unity is given a meaning by some kind of religious faith in the sense that the concept of meaning is derived from ultimate presuppositions about the character of time and eternity, which are not the fruit of detailed analyses of historical events.[62]

In the history of Western civilization Niebuhr discerns three dominant approaches to the question of the nature of human history: Greek classicism, the Biblical-Christian vision, and the modern view. Niebuhr believes that both the classical and modern views of history are blind to some obvious facts of human experience and that the Biblical-Christian view gives meaning to the ambiguities of man's historicity.

The classical Greeks held an essentially negative view of history in that they conceived of history after the cyclical model of nature. History followed the cyclical pattern of "coming to be" and "passing away." For the Greeks there was "nothing new under the Sun." The world of history, like nature, was considered an inferior realm of ceaseless change and flux. History itself did not offer the Greeks any hope for meaning. Meaning and fulfillment were possible

only through emancipation from the natural-historical cycle of occurrences. This otherworldly, ahistorical form of spirituality is founded on the assumption that there is that divine and rational element in human nature which can be purged of the corruptions of finitude and can raise man to the contemplation of that which is timeless and universal. The unique mixture of nature and spirit in man is obscured by the Greeks, who are therefore prone to view man either too pessimistically or too optimistically.

The only alternatives are either to reduce the meaning of life to the comparative meaninglessness of the natural order, or to emancipate life from this meaninglessness by translating it into the dimension of pure reason, which is to say, pure eternity.[63]

While classical philosophy was radically pessimistic about finding any meaning *in* history, modern culture is at one in its common faith in historical development as a redemptive process. As Diderot remarked, for modern man posterity has become the object of hope that the other world was for the man of the Middle Ages. The idea of historical progress is a pervasive modern dogma. Niebuhr traces this modern belief to the Renaissance where there was a convergence of classical and biblical worldviews:

The Renaissance as a spiritual movement is best understood as a tremendous affirmation of *the limitless possibilities of human existence, and to a rediscovery of the sense of a meaningful history.* This affirmation takes many forms, not all of which are equally consistent with the fundamental impulse of the movement. But there is enough consistency in the movement as a whole to justify the historian in placing in one historical category such diverse philosophical, religious and social movements as the early Italian Renaissance, Cartesian rationalism and the French enlightenment; as the liberal idea of progress and Marxist catastrophism; as sectarian perfectionism and secular utopianism. In all of these multifarious expressions there is a unifying principle. It is the impulse towards the fulfillment of life in history. The idea that life can be fulfilled without those reservations and qualifications which Biblical and Reformation thought make is derived from two different sources; from the classical confidence in human capacities and from the Biblical-Christian impulse towards sanctification and the fulfillment of life, more particularly the Biblical-eschatological hope of the fulfillment of history itself.[64]

There are elements in this modern view of history that are salutary when compared with the ahistorical pessimism of classical culture. There is a dynamism, a sense of novelty and indeterminate possibility in the modern view which does justice to man's experience as a creator of history. Nevertheless, modern man's vision of redemption in history is fraught with dangerous illusions. First of all, modern man has an unrealistic notion of his freedom and power over history—due to the illusory notion that he can manipulate the conditions of existence. Niebuhr gives the example of Alexis Carrel:

Alexis Carrel in *Man The Unknown* comes to the conclusion that the management of human affairs requires a thorough knowledge of "anatomy and physics, physiology and metaphysics, pathology, chemistry, psychology, medicine, and also a thorough knowledge of genetics, nutrition, pedagogy, aesthetics, ethics, religion, sociology and economics." He estimates that about 25 years would be required to master all these disciplines so "that at the age of 50 those who

have submitted themselves to these disciplines could effectively direct *the reconstruction of human beings.*"

This vision of world salvation through the ministrations of an elite of encyclopedists is a nice symbol of the inanity to which the modern interpretation of life may sink.[65]

What is basically wrong with this kind of social utopianism is the erroneous identification of man's freedom and reason with virtue—the failure to take seriously man's sinful predilections. Niebuhr sees this error in the utopian scheme of the well-known psychologist, B. F. Skinner, as set forth in his book *Walden II*. Niebuhr comments that Skinner

admits that he has "managed" the development of the individual components of the harmonious community and that there are, therefore, similarities between him and the notorious dictators of our day. But he feels that there is a great distinction between him and them because he has done what he has done for the good of the community.[66]

This total lack of awareness of one's own limited and egoistic perspective on what is "good" for whole societies of other human beings would be comical if it weren't so common and so dangerous.* Modern man will, in Niebuhr's view, go to any extreme to locate the source of evil outside himself.

The modern liberal creed of progress has issued in two major forms of utopianism that imperil the world today.

* The humorous aspect of this pretension is illustrated by a straight-faced observation from a medical journal cited in *The New Yorker*: "'Men and women are becoming increasingly equal but there are unfortunately some anatomical differences between them which can never be eliminated.'" The magazine greeted this bit of wisdom with the words: "Goody. Goody."[67]

Niebuhr refers to them as "hard" and "soft" utopianism.

Hard utopianism might be defined as the creed of those who claim to embody the perfect community and who therefore feel themselves morally justified in using every instrument of guile or force against those who oppose their assumed perfection. *Soft utopianism* is the creed of those who do not claim to embody perfection, but expect perfection to emerge out of the ongoing process of history.[68]

Hard utopianism is seen most clearly in Marxism where the messianic pretensions of a party have allowed it to identify its purposes so completely "with the very purposes of history that every weapon became morally permissible ... and every vicissitude of history was expected to contribute to the inevitability of their victory."[69] Its zealous messianism imbues Marxism with an unbridled sense of its own sanctity and righteousness, while its liberal perversion of Christian eschatology enforces its illusion of the coming of a kingdom of perfect righteousness in history. Soft utopianism escapes the self-righteous fanaticism which justifies the use of any means to achieve its ends. But the soft utopians assume that men are progressing toward higher and more inclusive forms of social life. It is apparent that soft utopianism has infected much of modern liberal Christianity which has accepted the notion of the progressive triumph of pure love. Liberal Christianity is usually pacifistic,

holding to the conviction that if only all Christians did live perfectly by the law of love, all strife and contention would be progressively eliminated and a universal kingdom of love established. ... In the words of a typical exponent of the American "social gospel," "The

new social order will be based not on fighting but on fraternity. ... not simply because the cooperative fraternal life is the highest ideal of human living but because the spirit and method of cooperation is the scientific law of human progress.[70]

In Niebuhr's opinion, liberal Christianity, like secular liberalism, suffers from a romantic evasion of the hard, tragic realities of human life. Such sentimentality can lead to fatal consequences when, for example, the soft utopians are prepared "to meet malignant evil with nonresistance, hoping that kindness would convert the hearts of tyrants."[71] In fact, the greatest peril results when a hard utopianism is met by the illusions of a soft utopianism, as in the case of Russia and American democratic idealism. Nevertheless, these bitter enemies share a common faith in historical development as a redemptive process. According to Niebuhr, this "ultimate similarity between Marxist and bourgeois optimism ... is, in fact, the most telling proof of the unity of modern culture."[72]

Niebuhr has exposed the errors and failures of secular and sectarian Christian philosophies of history with remarkable perception. What is it that he finds in the Biblical-Christian faith that gives meaning to history while taking account of the mysteries and realities of our historical experience?

First of all, Niebuhr finds in the biblical concept of the sovereignty of God a number of important corollaries. Faith in God's sovereignty points to the unity and universality of history under God's rule. History has meaning and purpose, but this meaning is not one that can be discerned by reason—as in Hegel or Marx or Toynbee. It is perceived by faith.

(The) Biblical conception which establishes the unity of history by faith, rather than by sight, is a guard against all premature efforts to correlate the facts of history into a pattern of too simple meaning. It is indeed one of the proofs of the ambiguity of man . . . that he cannot construct systems of meaning for the facts of history, whether of a particular story in it or of the story of mankind as a whole, without making the temporal locus of his observation into a false absolute vantage point.[73]

In the biblical vision, the meaning disclosed in history is set in a mystery— that is, the meaning disclosed is not reducible to a simple rational intelligibility, nor is that meaning fully proven or vindicated in the events of our history. While faith discerns meaning, history remains ambiguous. Meaning is disclosed but not fulfilled.

Biblical faith must be distinguished on the one hand from the cultures which negate the meaning of history in the rigor of their effort to find a transcendent ground of truth; and on the other hand from both ancient and modern affirmations of the meaning of life and history, which end by giving history an idolatrous center of meaning.[74]

Another corollary of belief in the unity of history under the sovereignty of God is the reality of sin and idolatry in human history.

The second contribution of the Biblical idea of divine transcendence to the concept of universal history is contained in the rigor with which the inclination of every human collective, whether tribe, nation, or empire, to make itself the center of universal history is overcome in principle. The God who has chosen Israel promises peril, rather than security, as the concomitant of this eminence. The God who is revealed in Christ brings all nations under his judgment. . . . The scandal that the idea of universal history should be the fruit of a particular revelation of the divine, to a particular people, and finally in a particular drama and person, ceases to be scandalous when it is recognized that the divine Majesty, apprehended in these particular revelations, is less bound to the pride of civilizations . . . than supposedly more universal concepts of life and history by which cultures seek to extricate themselves from the historical contingencies and to establish universally valid " values."[75]

By faith in God's revelation man can discern a meaning in history which both breaks the sinful pretension of man's own little systems and points to the fulfillment of that disclosure of meaning "beyond" history. That is, the fulfillment of our history will also represent a transfiguration of history or a new creation. The historical process will not in itself solve the enigmas of history—and this is what distinguishes Christian hope from all utopianism.

Niebuhr holds that the Christian sees history as an *interim*. In Christ the Christian affirms that the Messiah has come and the meaning of life is assured, and yet Christ is crucified in history.

The idea that history is an "interim" between the first and second coming of Christ has a meaning which illumines all the facts of human existence. History, after Christ's first coming, has the quality of partly knowing its true meaning. In so far as man can never be completely in contradiction to his own true nature, history also reveals significant realizations of that meaning. Nevertheless history continues to stand in real contradiction to its true meaning, so that pure love in history must always be a suffering love. But the contradictions of history cannot become man's norms, if history is viewed from the perspective of Christ.[76]

Niebuhr sees in the Cross of Christ meanings which illumine many of the enigmas of our human experience. First of all, as we have seen, the Cross makes clear the seriousness of human sin. Christ was crucified by the "good" men and institutions of his day, not by criminals—which points to the fact that even the best in human history is tainted by sin. The Cross also clarifies the character of God and his will for men. In Christ we see the love of God which goes beyond his transcendent judgment of all human life by taking the consequences of his divine judgment upon Himself. Niebuhr sums up the wisdom of the Cross in these words:

The climax of the Biblical revelation of the divine sovereignty over history is in the self-disclosure of a divine-love, which on the one hand is able to overcome the evil inclination to self-worship in the human heart and which on the other hand takes the evil of history into and upon itself. These two facets of the divine love establish the two most important aspects of the Biblical interpretation of history. On the one hand there is the possibility of the renewal of life and the destruction of evil, whenever men and nations see themselves as they truly are under a divine judgment, which is as merciful as it is terrible. On the other hand, the life of each individual as well as the total human enterprise remains in contradiction to God; and the final resolution of this contradiction is by God's mercy. From the one standpoint human history is a series of new beginnings. These new beginnings are not the inevitable springtime which follows the death of winter in nature. . . . Life may be reborn, if, under the divine judgment and mercy, the old self or the old culture or civilization is shattered. From the other standpoint human life and human history remain a permanent enigma which only the divine mercy can overcome. . . . Human powers and capacities may continue to develop indeter-

minately. But a "last judgement" stands at the end of all human achievements; and the "Anti-Christ" manifests himself at the end of history.[77]

The eschatological symbols of the Bible point to the inconclusive nature of history itself and to the fact that the finite mind cannot conceive of the fulfillment of history except in terms of symbols and myths. Nevertheless, if not taken literally the biblical symbols of the end of history can teach us important truths of our historical life. The symbols of a "last judgement" and "Anti-Christ" signify the rejection of all utopian notions of moral progress in history and the idea that history is its own redeemer. Evil is joined with the good until the end of human history. In the light of God's transcendent wisdom and love, all human achievements stand to be finally judged.

Niebuhr believes that despite literalistic interpretations of the "second coming of Christ," the biblical imagery conveys profound truths of the Christian faith. The symbol points to the fact that meaning is fulfilled at the *end* of history and not in some otherworldly realm *above* history. At the same time, it affirms that fulfillment will not come *within* the historical process itself. The symbol affirms that Christian hope is neither ahistorical nor utopian. In similar fashion, the hope of the "general resurrection" points to the uniquely Christian attitude toward history.

On the one hand it implies that eternity will fulfill and not annul the richness and variety which the temporal process has elaborated. On the other it implies that the condition of finiteness and freedom, which lies at the basis of historical existence, is a problem for which there is no solution by any human power. Only God can solve this problem.[78]

The wisdom that is in Christ is a wisdom that comes by faith and not by reason. It is not, says Niebuhr, "a truth which could have been anticipated in human culture and it is not the culmination of human wisdom. The true Christ is not expected."[79] Niebuhr insists that the "wisdom" of God is also the "power" or grace of God in and over us. By this he means that the wisdom of the Cross is not the product of our autonomous reason but a gift of grace. It can be accepted only by those who have come to a realization of the limits of all human systems of meaning, whose self-sufficiency is broken and who, in humility and contrition, are aware that the wisdom of God is not an achievement but the wisdom of "being completely known and forgiven."

While the wisdom revealed in Christ is no human achievement, it does become the basis of a new wisdom. The truth of the Gospel does not, therefore, stand in perpetual contradiction to experience. "On the contrary it illumines experience and is in turn validated by experience."[80]

Reinhold Niebuhr has often disclaimed the title of theologian. He thinks of himself as a social critic and moralist. Niebuhr's natural milieu is theological ethics and, therefore any attempt to grasp his apologetic for Christian faith requires some understanding of his contribution to this area of contemporary thought.

Love, Justice, and Power. According to Niebuhr, the Cross reveals not only the wisdom of God but the norm and law of human life. For in the Cross we discern that perfect, heedless, suffering love (agape) of Christ. This pure, heedless love is, in Niebuhr's judgment, the pinnacle of the moral life.

The Christian faith affirms that the same Christ who discloses the sovereignty of God over history is also the perfect norm of human nature. . . . This perfection is not so much a sum total of various virtues or an absence of transgression of various laws; it is the perfection of sacrificial love.[81]

Niebuhr's pragmatism and realism could easily disguise the radical perfectionism of his ethical norm. Against those theologians who would appeal to other less rigorous norms, such as mutual love or natural law, Niebuhr holds to the perfect love of Christ as the ethical norm. The severity which Niebuhr discerns in Christ's love ethic is brought into sharp focus in passages such as the following:

The ethic of Jesus which is founded upon this love is an absolute and uncompromising ethic. . . . The injunctions "resist not evil," "love your enemies," "if ye love them that love you what thanks have you?" "be not anxious for your life," and "be ye therefore perfect even as your father in heaven is perfect," all are of one piece, and they are all uncompromising and absolute.[82]

The absolutism and perfectionism of Jesus' love ethic sets itself uncompromisingly not only against the natural self-regarding impulses, but against the necessary prudent defenses of the self, required because of the egoism of others. It does not establish a connection with the horizontal points of a political or social ethic, or with the diagonals which a prudential individual ethic draws between the moral ideal and the facts of a given situation. It has only a vertical dimension between the loving will of God and the will of man.[83]

If there are any doubts about the predominant vertical religious reference of Jesus' ethic they ought to be completely laid by a consideration of his attitude on the ethical problem of rewards. Here the full rigorism and the non-prudential character of Jesus' ethic are completely revealed . . . . The service of God is to be performed not only without hope of any concrete or obvious reward, but at the price of sacrifice, abnegation, and loss . . . . The sovereignty of God is pictured as a pearl of great price or like a treasure hid in a field which to buy men sell all they have. If any natural gift or privilege should become a hindrance to the spirit of perfect obedience to God it must be rigorously denied: "If thine eye offend thee, pluck it out, and cast it from thee: it is better for thee to enter into life with one eye, rather than, having two eyes, to be cast into hell fire." In all of these emphases the immediate and concrete advantages which may flow from right conduct are either not considered at all or their consideration is definitely excluded. The ethic demands an absolute obedience to the will of God without consideration of those consequences of moral action which must be the concern of any prudential ethic.[84]

Niebuhr believes that the transcendent norm of divine *agape* stands in judgment on all our moral pretensions. Yet this heedless form of love is not totally transcendent of human possibility. In fact the love discerned in Christ clarifies a truth about our human condition and finds validation in our common experience. That truth is that egoism is self-defeating and that giving egocentrism the appearance of normality merely betrays the desperation of an uneasy human conscience.

The law of love is the final law for man in his condition of finiteness and freedom because man in his freedom is unable to make himself in his finiteness his own end. The self is too great to be contained within itself in its smallness. The Gospel observation that "whosoever seeketh to gain his life will lose it" is thus not some impossible rule imposed upon life by Scriptural fiat. It describes the actual

situation of the self which destroys itself by seeking itself too immediately.[85]

Niebuhr has been criticized for holding the divine *agape* as his ethical norm since the very radicalness of its disinterestedness raises a question of its moral relevance. Some of these critics would thus prefer to substitute a norm of mutual love. Niebuhr rejects mutual love as a norm because it lends itself to hypocritical forms of ego justification in the guise of unselfish affirmations of the other. *Agape*, he affirms, serves as a check on the subtle forms of egoism in all mutual relations. Niebuhr further argues that mutual love is itself dependent on disinterested love.

Love, heedless of the self, must be the initiator of any reciprocal love. Otherwise the calculation of mutual advantages makes love impossible. But heedless love usually wins a response of love. That is a symbol of the moral content of history. But this response cannot be guaranteed. . . . That is symbolic of the "tragic" dimension of history and a proof that the meaning of life always transcends the fulfillments of meaning in history.[86]

When not replenished with heedless love, mutual love easily degenerates into cool calculation of personal advantage and then into resentment over the failure of genuine reciprocity.

Niebuhr holds that *agape* is the Christian's ethical norm and that it *is* relevant to our history—though not directly as an historical strategy. Rather, its relevance is to be seen in its function as a limit-concept which points to the bounds of what is possible in human experience. Sacrificial love is no simple possibility for man, but neither is it a human impossibility. It is, says Niebuhr, the "impossible-possibility."

The radicalness of the *agape* norm has

led other critics to complain that, while Niebuhr theoretically holds *agape* as his norm, in actual practice his social realism makes constant appeal to such other norms as mutual love and justice. This, too, is to misunderstand Niebuhr's position, for it fails to recognize the *dialectical* relationship between Niebuhr's norm and historical action. This is made clear in his view of the relationship between love and justice.

According to Niebuhr, love and justice are neither to be confused nor torn asunder. Justice is only an approximation of heedless love, but it is also the *relative* embodiment of love in our social existence. Their relationship is dialectical. On the one hand, love is the *negation* of justice in that

love makes an end of the nicely calculated less and more of structures of justice. It does not carefully arbitrate between the needs of the self and of the other, since it meets the needs of the other without concern for the self.[87]

Justice is not finally normative because of the indeterminate possibilities of unconditional love.

On the other hand, the absolute norm of *agape*—if maintained as an ideal severed from the proximate goals of mutuality, justice, and equality—degenerates into sentimentality and an ineffectual moralism. Justice, says Niebuhr, is love making its way in the world, it is the concrete embodiment of love. Structures of justice are the expression of a love which does not trust its own moral intentions.

A simple Christian moralism counsels men to be unselfish. A profounder Christian faith must encourage men to create systems of justice which will save society and themselves from their own selfishness.[88]

To deny the need for more inclusive structures of justice is to deny the norm of love. Yet, for the Christian justice is not the end of ethical action because, as Niebuhr remarks, "without the 'grace' of love, justice always degenerates into something less than justice"[89] "Justice without love is merely the balance of power."[90] Justice sets limits upon each man's interests and thereby achieves a harmony in social affairs. But the balance achieved by justice is only an approximation of genuine brotherhood and needs to be *fulfilled* by love. Love and justice, then, must be kept in a dialectical relationship, for the norm of love can always raise systems of justice to new heights and wider vistas, but justice can keep love practical, concrete, and unsentimental.

Niebuhr's concern with justice as the embodiment of love in a sinful world led him, during the Thirties, to a more realistic and positive attitude toward the uses of power and coercion in ethical strategies and action than was characteristic of the Protestant Liberalism ascendant at the time. It was this issue that caused Niebuhr to break with the pacifists and to maintain that America should enter the war against the Nazi menace. Niebuhr recognized that the achievement of justice was not a simple matter of reason and moral persuasion. Because of the persistence of sinful pride and self-deception, every struggle for justice involves efforts to secure a more equal distribution of power in society. In fact, justice is dependent on a contest and balance of power which can be achieved only by political means. Niebuhr maintains that disproportionate power is always irresponsible power and a cause of injustice. Exponents of Liberal Christianity have generally rejected coercive measures in their ethical strategies and have appealed to various forms of rational and ethical persuasion to change existing injustices. But Niebuhr believes the appeal to moral sentiments, such as good will and philanthropy, reveals the self-deception and ineffectiveness of this form of Christian action to achieve real justice. Philanthropy, for example,

does not touch the equilibrium of social power and it is therefore something less than justice. It becomes corrupted into the enemy of justice as soon as the next step is taken and it is used by the powerful to beguile the weak from challenging the basic equilibrium of justice.[91]

Liberal Christianity has erroneously equated power as such with evil when, in fact, power can serve the cause of both good and evil. To reject the use of power is to be blind to the power inherent in one's own idealistic notion of what constitutes the common good and in one's own status or interests. The failure to maintain an equilibrium of power through the use of power also supports injustice by leaving power in the hands of a particular group or class. A persistent human sin is man's failure to recognize his own will to power and to work for structures of justice which would set limits on his own egoism as an approximation of heedless love of neighbor. Niebuhr sums up his understanding of the interdependence of love, justice, and power in the following passage.

For to understand the law of love as a final imperative, but not to know about the persistence of the power of self-love in all of life . . . results in an idealistic ethic with no relevance to the hard realities of life . . . . To know both the law of love as the final standard and the law of self-love as a persistent force is to enable Christians to have a foundation for a pragmatic ethic in which power and self-

interest are used, beguiled, harnessed and deflected for the ultimate end of establishing the highest and most inclusive possible community of justice and order. This is the very heart of the problem of Christian politics: the readiness to use power and interest in the service of an end dictated by love and yet an absence of complacency about the evil inherent in them.[92]

Such an ethic demands the most searching awareness of one's own limits and the fragmentary and tainted character of one's judgments and virtue. Such an awareness can issue in a sense of humility and repentance without disabling a man from engaging in resolute action. However, it does make a man aware that his actions always stand under a divine judgment and that he is justified not by his works but by grace through faith. Such a faith can save a man from both self-righteousness and despair. The spirit of such a faith has seldom been expressed more eloquently than by Niebuhr:

Nothing that is worth doing can be achieved in our lifetime; therefore we must be saved by hope. Nothing which is true or beautiful or good makes complete sense in any immediate context of history; therefore we must be saved by faith. Nothing we do, however virtuous, can be accomplished alone; therefore we are saved by love. No virtuous act is quite as virtuous from the standpoint of our friend or foe as it is from our standpoint. Therefore we must be saved by the final form of love which is forgiveness.[93]

Perhaps no theologian in this century (with the possible exception of Karl Barth) has raised more of a furor and has more opponents both within and outside the Christian community than Reinhold Niebuhr. But it is also true that few theologians in our time have had a greater positive influence within the Church and in the secular world. Humanists and religious naturalists, like Henry Nelson Wieman, chide Niebuhr for his appeal to a transcendent being and realm of meaning beyond the natural processes and structures of life. Conservative evangelicals criticize him for his critical approach to the Bible. But the largest chorus of criticism has come from religious liberals, both old and new, who censure Niebuhr for what they call his pessimistic view of man and his suspicion of all redemptive schemes in history. According to these critics, Niebuhr's doctrine of original sin does not allow for a break with sin *in fact* but only as a mere possibility. This relates in turn, to his understanding of Christian love. Niebuhr's critics assert that his doctrine of man and God contributes to a "we must live with ourselves as we are" sort of attitude, since the pride of man and the judgment of God make all human efforts equally suspect.

We have already said that most critics of Niebuhr's ethical norm fail to understand its dialectical relation and relevance to history. The charge of pessimism is also suspect. Niebuhr can be interpreted as a pessimist if one is selective in his reading of Niebuhr, but then one must overlook all those passages that speak of man's self-transcendence and his "indeterminate possibilities" in history.* Niebuhr has admitted that, in terms of the apologetic task, his stress on original sin may have been self-defeating, but he does not reject his realistic analysis of the stubbornness of human sin. In 1965 Niebuhr wrote:

I still think the "London Times Literary

Supplement" was substantially correct when it wrote some years ago: "The doctrine of original sin is the only empirically verifiable doctrine of the Christian faith."[95]

Among the younger theologians of the Sixties there has emerged a new spirit that exudes a confidence in man and an optimism about the redemptive possibilities in history. These men wish to return to some of the themes of the Enlightenment and of the older Protestant Liberalism and even recapture the element of utopianism in the radical Reformation. Harvey Cox reflects this mood when he writes that he

would begin any Christian anthropology with an affirmation of man's possibilities within history, despite all the evidence to the contrary. I would bring in sin as a minor rather than a major motif.[96]

There is need to redress the balance when either the sin or virtue of man is stressed to the point that the other facts of human life are disregarded. The record does not indicate that Niebuhr was guilty of such an imbalance; and most of the younger neo-liberals are chastened in their optimism. Nevertheless, there are men and movements within the Church today which appear either not to have learned or to have forgotten the lessons taught by Reinhold Niebuhr. In the words of another Christian realist, Niebuhr remains an indispensible guide for those

who are tempted to relate the Kingdom of God very closely to the secular city; (for) those who are inclined to accept the new ideologies of revolution without understanding the warnings against revolutionary utopianism; (for) those who project once again upon the world an American democratic ideology; and

---

* For instance: "There are no limits to be set in history for the achievement of more universal brotherhood, for the development of more perfect and more inclusive human relations."[94]

(for) those who partake to some extent of the illusion of American omnipotence and are untroubled by the American arrogance of power. Niebuhr's Christian realism needs to be applied to all sides in present conflicts, but it is a part of the Christian meaning of such realism that we should apply it first of all to ourselves.[97]

NOTES

1. *The World Tomorrow*, XIV (August, 1931), pp. 256–259.
2. *The Christian Century*, L (Nov. 8, 1933), p. 1403.
3. Ibid., Dec. 4, 1935.
4. W. M. Horton, *Realistic Theology* (New York, 1934), p. 8.
5. Ibid., p. 56.
6. *The Christian Century*, L (Nov. 8, 1933), p. 1403.
7. *Realistic Theology*, p. 15.
8. John C. Bennett, "A Changed Liberal—But Still a Liberal," *The Christian Century*, LVI (Feb. 8, 1939), pp. 179–181.
9. "Religious Realism in the Twentieth Century," in D. C. Macintosh, ed., *Religious Realism* (New York, 1931), pp. 416, 419.
10. Sidney E. Ahlstrom, "H. Richard Niebuhr's Place in American Thought," *Christianity and Crisis*, XXIII, 20 (Nov. 25, 1963), p. 214.
11. *The Kingdom of God in America* (Chicago, 1937), p. 193.
12. For such an interpretation of Niebuhr see the essay by Hans Frei, "Niebuhr's Theological Background," in *Faith and Ethics*, ed. Paul Ramsey (New York, 1957).
13. H. R. Niebuhr, *Radical Monotheism and Western Culture* (New York, 1960), p. 118.
14. Ibid., p. 119.
15. Ibid., pp. 121–122.
16. Ibid., p. 123.
17. This is Niebuhr's own illustration, given to John B. Cobb in a personal conversation. See Cobb, *Living Options in Protestant Theology* (Philadelphia, 1962), p. 289.
18. *The Meaning of Revelation* (New York, 1959), pp. 18–19.
19. Ibid., pp. 20–21.
20. Ibid., p. 141.
21. Ibid., p. 64.
22. Ibid., p. 68.
23. Ibid., pp. 68–69.
24. Ibid., pp. 59–60.
25. Ibid., pp. 84–86.
26. A. N. Whitehead, *Religion in the Making*. Cited in *The Meaning of Revelation*, p. 93.
27. *The Meaning of Revelation*, pp. 93–94.
28. Ibid., p. 110.
29. Ibid., pp. 123–125.
30. Ibid., p. 136.
31. Ibid., pp. 101–102.
32. *Radical Monotheism and Western Culture*, p. 126.
33. *The Meaning of Revelation*, p. 42.
34. Ibid., p. 18.
35. See John Cobb's perceptive criticism of Niebuhr on this point in *Living Options in Protestant Theology*, pp. 296 ff.
36. *The Meaning of Revelation*, p. 82. For this line of argument and what follows, the writer is dependent on Van Harvey, *The Historian and the Believer* (New York, 1966), pp. 234 ff.
37. *The Historian and the Believer*, pp. 239–242.
38. Reinhold Niebuhr, *Leaves from the Notebook of a Tamed Cynic* (Cleveland: World Publishing Co., 1957), pp. 180–181.
39. *Reinhold Niebuhr: A Prophetic Voice in Our Time*, ed., Harold R. Landon (Greenwich, Conn., 1962), p. 58.
40. *Christian Realism and Political Problems* (New York, 1953), Chap. 11.
41. Ibid.
42. Ibid.
43. Reinhold Niebuhr, *The Nature and Destiny of Man* (New York, 1951), Vol. I, p. 1.
44. Ibid., p. 75.

45. Ibid., pp. 13–14.
46. Reinhold Niebuhr, *Christian Realism and Political Problems* (New York, 1953), p. 6.
47. *Nature and Destiny of Man*, I, p. 182.
48. Ibid., p. 185.
49. Ibid., pp. 188–189.
50. Ibid., pp. 193–194.
51. Ibid., p. 199.
52. Ibid., p. 200.
53. Ibid., p. 185.
54. Ibid., p. 234.
55. Ibid., p. 17.
56. Ibid., pp. 94–95.
57. R. Niebuhr, *Discerning the Signs of the Times* (New York, 1946), p. 14.
58. R. Niebuhr, *Faith and History* (New York, 1949), pp. 19–20. In this section, the author is especially indebted to Gordon Harland's excellent systematic presentation of the complexities of Niebuhr's doctrine of history in *The Thought of Reinhold Niebuhr*, New York, 1960.
59. *Quest of the Ages*, p. 210, as cited in *Faith and History*, p. 80.
60. *Faith and History*, p. 80.
61. *Discerning the Signs of the Times*, pp. 7–8.
62. *Faith and History*, p. 118.
63. *Nature and Destiny of Man*, II, p. 15.
64. Ibid., p. 160.
65. *Faith and History*, p. 90.
66. *The Irony of American History* (New York, 1952), pp. 84–85.
67. *Faith and History*, p. 76.
68. Reinhold Niebuhr, "Two Forms of Utopianism," *Christianity and Society*, Vol. 12 (Autumn, 1947), p. 7.
69. *Faith and History*, pp. 209–210.
70. Ibid., p. 207; Niebuhr is quoting from Harry F. Ward, *The New Social Order*, p. 104.
71. Ibid., p. 208.
72. Ibid., p. 4.
73. Ibid., p. 112.
74. Ibid., p. 114.
75. Ibid., pp. 113–114.
76. *Nature and Destiny of Man*, II, p. 51.
77. *Faith and History*, pp. 125–126.
78. *Nature and Destiny of Man*, II, p. 295.
79. Ibid., p. 62.
80. Ibid., p. 63.
81. Ibid., p. 68.
82. *Christianity and Power Politics* (New Yok, 1940), p. 8.
83. *An Interpretation of Christian Ethics* (New York, 1956), p. 45.
84. Ibid., pp. 55–56.
85. *Faith and History*, p. 174.
86. Charles W. Kegley and Robert W. Bretall, eds., *Reinhold Niebuhr: His Religious, Social and Political Thought* (New York, 1956), p. 424.
87. *Nature and Destiny of Man*, I, p. 295.
88. "Justice and Love," *Christianity and Society*, Vol. 15 (Autumn, 1950), pp. 6–7.
89. Ibid., p. 7.
90. "Moralists and Politics," *The Christian Century* (July 6, 1932), p. 858.
91. *Beyond Tragedy*, p. 186.
92. "Christian Faith and Social Action," in J. A. Hutchison, ed., *Christian Faith and Social Action* (New York, 1953), p. 241.
93. *The Irony of American History* (New York, 1952), p. 63.
94. *The Nature and Destiny of Man*, II, p. 85.
95. *Man's Nature and His Communities* (New York, 1965), p. 24.
96. "Christian Realism: Retrospect and Prospect," *Christianity and Crisis*, XXVIII, 14 (August 5, 1968), p. 180.
97. John C. Bennett, "The Contribution of Reinhold Niebuhr," *Union Seminary Quarterly Review*, XXIV, 1 (Fall, 1968), p. 16.

SUGGESTIONS FOR FURTHER READING

CHRISTIAN REALISM

Bennett, John C. *Christian Realism* (New York: Scribner, 1941).

Horton, Walter M. *Realistic Theology* (New York: Harper, 1934).

Thelen, Mary Frances. *Man as Sinner in Con-*

temporary American Realistic Theology (New York: King's Crown Press, 1951).

H. RICHARD NIEBUHR

Ramsey, Paul, ed. *Faith and Ethics: The Theology of H. Richard Niebuhr* (New York: Harper, 1957).

REINHOLD NIEBUHR

Bingham, June. *Courage to Change: An Introduction to the Life and Thought of Reinhold Niebuhr* (New York: Scribner, 1961). An examination of Niebuhr's thought in the context of a study of his life.

Carnell, John E. *The Theology of Reinhold Niebuhr* (Grand Rapids, Mich., Eerdmans Publishing Co., 1960). A study and critique of Niebuhr's theology from the perspective of conservative Evangelicism.

Harland, Gordon. *The Thought of Reinhold Niebuhr* (New York: Oxford University Press, 1960). The best systematic exposition of Niebuhr's thought to date. A sympathetic and uncritical study.

Hoffmann, Hans. *The Theology of Reinhold Niebuhr* (New York: Scribner, 1956). A study of the major themes of Niebuhr's theology, focusing on the doctrine of sin.

Kegley, Charles W. and Bretall, Robert W. *Reinhold Niebuhr: His Religious, Social and Political Thought* (New York: The Macmillan Co., 1956). This work includes a wide range of interpretations and criticisms of Niebuhr's thought by theologians, philosophers, and historians.

CHAPTER SIXTEEN

Some Contemporary Trends

Dietrich Bonhoeffer

The movements that dominated theology in the years immediately following World War II—Neo-Orthodoxy, Existentialism, Neo-Thomism, and Christian Realism—all represented a reaction to the liberalism and optimism of the earlier prewar era. These movements were often militant in their attack upon secularism and modernity. They were also resourceful in their appropriation and reinterpretation of the doctrines of an older, more orthodox theological tradition. During the first postwar decade Christian theology was self-confident and on the offensive. These were the years during which Kierkegaard, Tillich, Maritain, Niebuhr and—in the English-speaking world—Karl Barth reached the height of their influence. And then at the end of the 1950's something happened. The voices of these giants became stilled. The great themes of anxiety and sin, of despair and faith, of the wholly otherness and transcendence of God no longer seemed to speak to the situation of a new generation of Christians. This change is described by one of the younger theologians who abruptly found himself in a newer situation and without any solid footing.

No more than five years ago the "younger theologians" seemed to have a comfortable basis for their task, fashioned by the great theologians of the 20's, 30's, and 40's.... We saw ourselves as a generation of "scholastics" whose function would be to work out in greater detail the firm theological principles already forged for us. We knew from our teachers what theology was, what its principles and starting points were, how to go about it and above all we were confident about its universal value and truth.

The most significant recent theological development has been the steady dissolution of all these certainties, the washing away of the firm ground on which our generation believed we were safely standing. What we thought was solid earth has turned out to be shifting ice—and in recent years, as the weather has grown steadily warmer, some of us have in horror found ourselves staring down into rushing depths of dark water.[1]

What caused this unexpected shift in the theological situation is not entirely clear at this point. However, two factors are decisive. One is the fact that many of the problems raised by nineteenth-century liberal theology were simply circumvented by theologians writing in the "crisis" years between the two world wars. This is especially true of problems relating to the doctrine of God. Concentration on man's plight and on the transcendence of God left many theological questions begging. A second factor, while momentous, is less easily understood. It is the resurgence of a secular, this-worldly spirit—but *within the Christian community itself*. The younger generation of Christians no longer see themselves as polarized against the world and secular culture, but as suffering the same doubts and celebrating the same joys and hopes as their unbelieving companions. The cultural factors effecting this change are complex, but some of the theological influences are evident enough.[2] What has emerged in the 1960's is a new radical, secular Christian theology. While having certain affinities with the older liberalism, it represents a genuinely new movement that is widespread and quite heterogeneous.

Radical Secular Theology

At the center of the new radical theology is a concern for and a new appreciation of the secular mode of contemporary life. What distinguishes this theology from that of the immediate past is its optimism and its positive evaluation of human culture and historical possibilities. Almost all of the younger theologians look favorably upon the increasing secularity* of contemporary life and are agreed that a viable Christian theology must view this secular spirit positively. Indeed, a number of the radical theologians argue that modern secularity is rooted in and dependent upon biblical faith, which represents man's break with a mythically conceived cosmos.[3] The theologian upon whom many of the younger thinkers are dependent for this notion is Friedrich Gogarten, who early in his career was associated with Karl Barth and the "theology of crisis." Gogarten has written extensively on the secularization or historicization of human existence, and it is his contention that with Israel the "sacralizing" of nature and the social orders was broken and man's radical historicity first affirmed. With this new consciousness came a sense of freedom, of newness and creative

---

* Meaning a this-worldly, empirical, responsible attitude toward history and society. *Secularity* is to be distinguished from *secularism*, which these theologians identify with an antireligious, scientifically positivist ideology.

responsibility for history and society. This historical consciousness was lost in the Middle Ages, during which time a static metaphysical conception of nature and history was dominant. However, modern man has returned to a thorough-going secular outlook in which he "is able to envisage history only from the point of view of his own responsibility for it."[4] Reality is now understood only in this-worldly, historical terms and, according to Gogarten,

this means that metaphysical thinking has lost its position of dominance. History is now no longer, as it was, for the medieval theology of history, "a process within a stationary—that is to say a metaphysically conceived—world." "On the contrary, the world and the entire relation of man to it have now become part of history. It is not the world which is the all-embracing problem, but history."[5]

The theme of secularization and its rootedness in biblical faith has been popularized in Harvey Cox's *The Secular City*. Cox relates these themes to contemporary urbanism, technology, and life style in an interesting and provocative way. According to Cox, the biblical world-view marks a "disenchantment" with the world of nature, a "desacralization" of politics and a "deconsecration" of values. The idolatrous worship of natural powers and social orders and ideologies is broken in the biblical doctrine of creation and history, and man is free to harness nature and to develop provisional and utilitarian social policies and programs. The biblical neutralizing of nature and history finds its fruits in the utterly secular, pragmatic, and tentative posture of contemporary urban man.

Life for him is a set of problems, not an unfathomable mystery. He brackets off the things that cannot be dealt with and deals with those that can. He wastes little time thinking about "ultimate" or "religious" questions. And he can live with highly provisional solutions.

It is characteristic of urban-secular man that he perceives himself as the source of whatever significance the human enterprise holds. . . . Symbol systems, the constellations of meaning by which human life is given value and direction, are seen as projections of a given society. . . . There is nothing timeless or divine about them.[6]

According to the secular theologians, contemporary man is neither religious nor antireligious; he is simply unreligious or secular. This lack of religiosity is not to be lamented but seen as man's coming of age, his putting aside of an animistic, mythological, and even metaphysical world-view. On the theme of man's coming of age, the secular theologians have also drawn heavily on the late writings of Dietrich Bonhoeffer and his notion of a "religionless" Christianity. Bonhoeffer's *Letters and Papers from Prison* (1951; American ed., *Prisoner of God*, 1954), more than any other single factor, was the spark that ignited the radical secular movement of the early 1960's.

Dietrich Bonhoeffer (1906–1945) is now viewed as the harbinger of a newly emerging form of Christianity which he saw and enigmatically sketched while imprisoned and awaiting execution by the Nazis for participation in the plot on Hitler's life. The key to Bonhoeffer's discovery was his positive assessment of secularization as a sign of man's emergence from a self-inflicted, immature dependency on religion. Like Kant a century and a half earlier, Bonhoeffer called upon Christian believers to come of age. In the last period of his life,

Bonhoeffer came to believe that the time for religion was over.

> We are proceeding towards a time of no religion at all: men as they now are simply cannot be religious any more . . . . Our whole nineteen-hundred-year-old Christian preaching and theology rests upon the "religious premise" of man. . . . But if one day it becomes apparent that this *a priori* premise simply does not exist, but was an historical and temporary form of human self-expression, i.e. if we reach the stage of being radically without religion—and I think this is more or less the case already . . . what does that mean for Christianity?[7]

As the frontiers of knowledge are pushed back, the God of traditional religion has continued to lose more and more ground.

> Religious people speak of God when human perception is (often just from laziness) at an end, or human resources fail: it is really always the *deus ex machina* they call to their aid, either for the so-called solving of insoluble problems or as support in human failure—always that is to say, helping out human weakness or on the borders of human existence. Of necessity that can only go on until men can, by their own strength, push those borders back a little further, so that God becomes superfluous as a *deus ex machina*. Is even death today, since men are scarcely afraid of it any more, and sin, which they scarcely understand any more, still a genuine borderline? It always seems to me that in talking thus we are only seeking frantically to make room for God.[8]

God has become a kind of stopgap to explain those infrequent limit-situations of life or some of our metaphysical puzzles. But this is to appeal to God only in our human weakness and bewilderment. Bonhoeffer wishes, rather,

to speak of God not on the borders of life but at its center, not in weakness but in strength, not, therefore, in man's suffering and death but in his life and prosperity. On the borders it seems to me better to hold our peace and leave the problem unsolved.[9]

According to Bonhoeffer, man's coming of age means "the linchpin is removed from the whole structure of our Christianity to date." He sees secularization as, in part, God's chastisement of the Church for its unfaithfulness and misrepresentation of the Gospel—just as God has used Assyria against the Israelites of old. However, secularization represents more than divine judgment; it signals the "golden age" of the Church which lies in the future. It heralds the beginnings of a religionless Christianity, freed from an individualistic piety and a metaphysical supernaturalism, both of which abandon this world.

Bonhoeffer's prison papers do not develop systematically his notion of a secular Christianity. However, the God of such a faith will not be conceived of either as our metaphysical or personal problem solver.

> Our coming of age forces us to a true recognition of our situation vis-à-vis God. God is teaching us that we must live as men who can get along very well without him. The God who is with us is the God who forsakes us (Mark 15:34). The God who makes us live in this world without using him as a working hypothesis is the God before whom we are ever standing. Before God and with him we live without God. God allows himself to be edged out of the world and on to the cross.[10]

In Bonhoeffer's view, the only conception of God appropriate to a religionless Christian faith is that of God in his powerlessness and suffering for others, viz. the Crucified.

Our relation to God is not a religious relationship to a supreme Being, absolute in power and goodness, which is a spurious conception of transcendence, but a new life for others, through participation in the Being of God. The transcendence consists not in tasks beyond our scope and power, but in the nearest thing to hand. God in human form . . . man existing for others, and hence the Crucified.[11]

God's transcendence must be seen as a *this-worldly transcendence* in that God is known neither by abstract reasoning nor by mystical contemplation but in concrete living for others. The Christian's life is a "worldly" life in that Christians are called to "range themselves with God in his suffering" at the hands of a godless world. And thus the vocation of the Church is that of servant.

The Church is her true self only when she exists for humanity. . . . She must take part in the social life of the world, not lording over men, but helping and serving them. . . . It is not abstract argument, but concrete example which gives her word emphasis and power.[12]

It is this vision of a this-worldly, secular Christianity which is shared by a large number of younger Christian theologians and laymen today. For these people the prison papers are a kind of manifesto of a new Christian life-style. The radical movement of the 1960's ranges across a wide spectrum of theological positions from the somewhat milder radicalism of Harvey Cox, Gabriel Vahanian,[13] and Bishop J. A. T. Robinson[14] to the so-called "Death of God" theologians Thomas J. J. Altizer,[15] William Hamilton,[16] and Paul Van Buren.[17] Despite fundamental differences in their positions, these men and countless others of like mind share a spirit and certain convictions in common.

These convictions are strikingly reminiscent of the ideas that dominated the Enlightenment.

1. First of all, these theologians affirm this "world," the secular culture in which we carry out our daily tasks, as the only legitimate concern of Christians. They are uninterested in, or regard as meaningless, any concern for an "other world" or "the life of the world to come." Similarly, they are opposed to setting apart so-called "religious" activities— i.e., prayer, church-going, etc.—from the everyday activities of earning a living or engaging in politics. In fact, activities such as civil rights, war resistance, and the war on poverty have become for many the only possible way of expressing their faith and worship. Like Matthew Tindal in the eighteenth century, they "place the whole of their religion in benevolent actions," believing that everything "religious" is superstitious and dangerous if not directly conducive of the amelioration of social problems.

2. Since a secular this-worldly existence is the only proper concern of man, it follows that our knowledge and norms of judgment must be derived from our empirical experience in this world and not from some heteronomous authority such as biblical revelation or the Church. If the Bible and Church tradition are accepted as normative authorities, they are so through the exercise of the individual's autonomous reason and experience. In any case, theological beliefs are to be restricted to what a man can personally believe, and this usually means what is consistent with an empirical, scientific world-view.

3. The secular theology discloses a new interest in the historical Jesus as the paradigm of "this-worldly transcendence." The radical theologians show

little interest in the classical Christological doctrines but see in the historical Jesus a man who was authentically open, who lived for others, who was free from anxiety and fear, and most important, radically free for his neighbor. William Hamilton speaks of our "becoming Jesus" by which he means an imitation of Christ in terms of our identification with the problems and sufferings of our neighbor.

4. At the center of the radical theology is a deeply felt experience of the unreality of God in our time. It is this rather pervasive experience that has led to the various assertions of the "eclipse" and the "death" of God. As a result of its publicity in the mass media, the meaning of the "death of God" is largely confused. The label is applied rather indiscriminately to a number of very different theological positions. There are, however, several important meanings of the term—all of which reflect one or another of the problems facing contemporary theism.

(a) The most prevalent meaning of the death of God is that God is "absent," "silent," or in "eclipse." This notion was suggested by Martin Buber and has been used and developed by others. What Buber means by the "silence" or "eclipse" of God is that man, largely through the development of a modern technocracy, has diminished the possibilities of genuine I–Thou relationships through which alone God can speak or be present. Man has silenced God by his very techniques and life-style.

(b) Some radical theologians, particularly Gabriel Vahanian, speak of God's death in terms of our acculturation or domestication of God. Christendom has made God into a cultural idol—and it is this ersatz God that is dead or dying.

Hence Vahanian sees hope that men may again be encountered by the transcendent, living God of biblical faith. The time may not yet be ripe for such an encounter and, therefore, we must wait without idols.

(c) A number of radical theologians, including William Hamilton, Bishop Robinson, and Harvey Cox, have followed Bonhoeffer's lead in announcing the death of God as father-image—the God whom Freud saw as the projection of human weakness and dependency: The God to whom we pray to insure Junior's success in school or our safety as we take off in a jet; the God who gives us pat answers to the problems of suffering and evil, this God is dead. According to these theologians, we must learn to live without such a God as human problem solver. God has given man freedom and dominion over the earth, and we are called to exercise our freedom and maturity in accepting responsibility for our lives and our world.

(d) According to Paul Van Buren and others, the *word* God no longer has any clear or meaningful referent. God is a vacuous utterance. And this is because the word is connected with an outmoded, metaphysical view of the world in which God is conceived as a transcendent Being or ultimate ground of the natural world. According to Van Buren, our empirical age regards metaphysical statements about God as either confused (i.e., with statements about human ideals or policies of action) or meaningless. While many lay Christians would not comprehend Van Buren's critique of metaphysics, they would no doubt acknowledge, with Bonhoeffer, that it is difficult—if not impossible—to speak of God authentically in our modern idiom. The word has become overladen with abstract metaphysical and pietistic connotations that do not ring true today.

The radical theologians have caught the mood and unarticulated convictions of large numbers of Christians who find their allegiance to the Church disturbing because they discern a hiatus between what the Church teaches and what they honestly believe. Many theologians, on the other hand, while to a greater or lesser degree sympathetic with the radicals, find numerous deficiencies in their secular proposals. A common complaint is the naïve optimism which they discern in writings such as Cox's *The Secular City*. Europeans and Americans raised on a heavy diet of Niebuhrian realism are especially critical of this new optimism over secularization and life in the technopolis. Related to this is an often uncritical accommodation to an empirical and positivistic scientific world-view, without consideration of current alternatives, including alternative metaphysical models such as those proposed in current process or neo-classical metaphysics.

The new interest in the historical Jesus may be a salutary corrective to kerygmatic theology, except that what the radical theologians say about Jesus appears to blatantly ignore the lessons of the nineteenth-century "quest of the historical Jesus" and Form-criticism. There also appears to be a conflict in the secular theologians' loyalties in that they wish to be loyal both to a secular life-style and to the pattern of Jesus. However, a reading of the Gospels indicates that Jesus' eschatology and ethics are expressive of a spiritual world radically alien to modern secular optimism. The secular theologians, like the older liberals, tend to see Jesus in their own mirror-image.

Finally, there are numerous critics who assert that it is foolish and contradictory

to speak of Christianity without speaking about God. The word God may be elusive and theology may be in need of a radical reconstruction, but Christian faith is bound up with belief in God. The difficulty facing the secular theologian is indicated in Schubert Ogden's distinction between faith as theoretical assent and faith as existential assent.[18] The secularist has accepted the classical description of God and then, in the light of philosophical criticism, has denied intellectually that such a being exists. Yet these same secularists respond to and make claims about Jesus as their ultimate concern. But does not such an ultimate concern imply certain metaphysical notions or claims—or else why Jesus? In other words, isn't the problem one of finding a more adequate metaphysical model with which to develop a theology consonant with Christian faith and modern experience? This is the assertion of those who now are seeking to develop a Christian natural theology in terms of contemporary evolutionary and process metaphysics.

Process Thought: A New Christian Natural Theology?

Process metaphysics is not new in philosophy, but its adoption by a growing number of Christian theologians is a fairly recent phenomenon. The beginnings of process thought can be traced to two dominant movements of the nineteenth century: the German romantic evolutionism of Herder, Schelling, and Hegel and to Darwinism. The notion that evolution, development, and process constitutes the essential nature of reality is the key to this school of thought. We have seen how Hegelianism* and Dar-

* See Chap. Six.

winism* effected important changes in Christian theism. Nevertheless, while making dominant the idea of evolution, Hegelianism and Darwinism do not constitute the principal sources of contemporary process *philosophy*. The origins of current process thought can be traced principally to two major philosophers of the early decades of this century: Henri Bergson [19] (1859–1941) and Alfred North Whitehead[20] (1861–1947). Other significant influences include C. Lloyd Morgan's *Emergent Evolution* (1923) and Samuel Alexander's *Space, Time and Deity* (1920). While differing widely, the two contemporary philosopher-theologians who have carried on this tradition and have profoundly influenced several of today's younger theologians are Charles Hartshorne[21] (1897–   ) and Père Pierre Teilhard de Chardin[22] (1881–1955).

Process thought begins with the conviction that time and process are constitutive of all reality.[23] Experience shows us that reality is not made up of static, discrete entities—what Whitehead calls the "fallacy of simple location"—but is dynamic, organic, and social. The world is a creative process. Moreover, this process is a movement of interrelated and interdependent societies. The world process is an interlocked society of societies, giving and receiving from one another. This world process is what Whitehead calls *concrescence*, or a growing together of many entities and events into a complex unity.

According to Whitehead's metaphysical scheme, the most generalized analysis of the actual, temporal world shows the presence of four factors. The first is *creativity*, whereby the world advances

toward novelty or new modes of being. Creativity is not an entity, however, and is real only through the second factor: those *actual entities* which exemplify it. Actual entities are the final real things of which the world is made. Nothing is more real. Nevertheless, actual entities are complex and interdependent. They appropriate or prehend the past, realize their own peculiar, subjective form and eventually perish and become an objective datum for some other entity. To account for the determinate and orderly process of the temporal world, Whitehead posits a third factor: *eternal objects* or pure potentials. An example would be a color which comes and goes but does not perish. Wherever it comes it is the same color. Eternal objects are the real potentialities, patterns, structures, and grades of relevance and value which are revealed in our world. They are entities but in the mode of potentiality. Actual entities incorporate creativity and these eternal potentials in ways which lead to full actualization.

According to Whitehead, the cosmic process requires a fourth component—an everlasting actual entity—*God*. "God," says Whitehead, "is an actual entity, and so is the most trivial puff of existence in far-off empty space." However, unlike other entities, God is everlasting and does not perish. Creativity itself cannot account for the actual course of becoming, and the eternal objects, being in the mode of potentiality, lack causal efficacy. According to Whitehead, it is God who grounds the eternal objects in actuality and makes possible their ingression into the ordered process of becoming. God also supplies each entity with its initial aim and serves as the principle of relevance, i.e., as the source of ideal grades of relevance among the eternal

* See Chap. Eight.

objects as they ingress in the order of nature.

While it is true that God is unique in these respects, he is also the chief exemplification of the metaphysical scheme—not its foremost exception. This means that God is *not* independent, immutable, impassable but rather is to be conceived, like other entities, as dependent, changing, and thus in some respects temporal and in process. Unless we hold to the analogy of being, i.e., that God is in some sense like the creatures, he is, in Whitehead's view, simply unknown.

But how do we account for the fact that God is both unique in his causal efficacy as the principle of limitation, concretion, and relevance, and the chief metaphysical exemplification of that process that is constitutive of reality? Whitehead's answer, and that of all process theologians, is that God, like other entities, is *di-polar*. Corresponding to the "mental pole" of finite entities is what Whitehead calls God's *primordial nature*. This is the conceptual structure of Deity which orders, grades, and adjusts the eternal objects and makes them accessible for ingression in the temporal world. This primordial nature of God is the original fact in the universe. However, God in his primordial nature is an abstraction, lacking or deficient in actuality. As such, the primordial nature of God is unconscious and impersonal.

The other pole of God's being is his *consequent nature*. This corresponds to the "physical pole" of other entities. God as an actual entity prehends, takes in, and in turn is affected by the concrete entities of the world. God is always receiving new data from the temporal entities, hence is always in a process of becoming. God and the world thus constitute a society of interdependent entities

God, as well as being primordial, is also consequent. He is the beginning and the end. . . . Thus, by reason of the relativity of all things, there is a reaction of the world on God. The completion of God's nature into a fullness of physical feeling is derived from the objectification of the world in God. He shares with every new creation its actual world; and the concrescent creature is objectified in God as a novel element in God's objectification of that actual world. . . . God's conceptual nature is unchanged, by reason of its final completeness. But his derivative nature is consequent upon the creative advance of the world.[24]

In Whitehead's panentheism, God is not the only entity involved in creation. Creative advance requires the interdependence of God and the world. For Whitehead, God is better conceived of as the "savior" of the world than as its Creator. While all finite entities perish, they do furnish God with new experience for his prehension and incorporation into his consequent nature. Whatever God receives from actual entities never fades away. Hence all perishing entities achieve a kind of objective immortality in God. In turn, God seeks to pour back into the world what is worth saving, to afford entities a new ideal vision of the possibilities of creative advance. However, God is not omnipotent in the traditional theistic sense. His relation to the world is persuasive, not coercive. Finite creatures are free to reject God's ideal envisagement and lure. There is, then, real loss and tragedy in the world and in God.

In Whitehead's opinion, Christian theism went astray when it joined its vision of God to Aristotle's Unmovedmover. The Christian God thereafter became the cosmic monarch with no checks on his power and impassive in his relations. It was, Whitehead asserts, "the fashioning of God in the image of the

Egyptian, Persian, and Roman imperial rulers . . . . The Church gave unto God the attributes which belonged exclusively to Caesar.''[25] It was especially the positing of absolute omnipotence in God—which made him responsible for everything that happens—that made theology such an easy prey of the likes of David Hume. According to Whitehead, if God remains the cosmic monarch, Hume's argument is unanswerable. Furthermore, absolute omnipotence makes no sense of love. Genuine love requires a *free* response, not coercion. Since Christianity affirms the reality of human freedom, God's action in history must thus be understood to be the persuasion of love and not the coercion of power.

Among contemporary philosophers, Charles Hartshorne has devoted himself single-mindedly to the formulation of a natural theology on the foundations of Whitehead's metaphysics. Hartshorne has also addressed himself to theological questions more central to Christian reflection—e.g., Christology, ethics, and the doctrine of love. Like the radical theologians, Hartshorne believes that traditional supernaturalism is no longer tenable but that atheism is not the obvious alternative. For Hartshorne the alternative to classical theism is *panentheism*. He outlines the three possibilities as follows:

I. There is a being in *all* respects absolutely perfect or unsurpassable, in no way and in no respect surpassable or perfectible. (Theism of the First Type, absolutism, Thomism, most European theology prior to 1880.)

II. There is no being in all respects absolutely perfect; but there is a being in *some* respect or respects thus perfect, and in some respect or respects not so, in some respects surpassable, whether by self or others being left open. Thus it is not excluded that the being may be relatively perfect in all the re-spects in which it is not absolutely perfect. (Theism of the Second Type; much contemporary Protestant theology, doctrines of a "finite-infinite" or perfect-perfectible God.)

III. There is no being in *any* respect absolutely perfect; all beings are in all respects surpassable by something conceivable, perhaps by others or perhaps by themselves in another state. (Doctrines of a merely finite God, polytheism in some forms, atheism.)[26]

Hartshorne believes that the second type of theism has only recently been considered—and only in order to limit the notion of omnipotence in order to preserve human freedom and spare God responsibility for evil. But the traditional notions of omnipotence and impassability must be rejected for a more basic reason than these.

It has become customary to say that we must limit divine power to save human freedom and to avoid making deity responsible for evil. But to speak of limiting a concept seems to imply that the concept, without limitation, makes sense. The notion of a cosmic power that determines all decisions fails to make sense. For its decisions could refer to nothing but themselves. They could result in no world; for a world must consist of local agents making their own decisions. Instead of saying that God's power is limited, suggesting that it is less than some conceivable power, we should rather say: his power is absolutely maximal, the greatest possible, but even the greatest possible power is still one power among others, is not the only power. God can do everything that a God can do, everything that could be done by "a being with no possible superior."[27]

According to Hartshorne's panentheism, God and the world are interdependent. The world is in God, although not coincident with him, since he exceeds the world in certain respects.

Nevertheless, God is relative to what happens in the world in that he changes when the world changes. Thus God is not absolutely perfect in *every* respect but is absolutely perfect in *some* respects and *relatively* perfect in others. God's relative perfection (e.g., his power) means that he is unsurpassable by anything but himself. There is nothing illogical, Hartshorne argues, about a being who cannot be surpassed but who can grow in experience.

Hartshorne believes that only a panentheistic doctrine can make genuine sense of the Christian notion of God's love, since love is a social category and is meaningless apart from a real relationship of giving and receiving. This notion of divine love is exactly what the orthodox tradition has denied, for it maintains that God's perfection and aseity preclude his receiving or gaining anything from the world. But love as we know it, Hartshorne argues, is a "*participation* in the good of others, so that some sort of value accrues to the self through the very fact that value accrues to another self."[28] It is this idea of God's love as including desire that is rejected by traditional theism.*

They sought to maintain a distinction between love as desire, with an element of possible gain or loss to the self, and love as purely altruistic benevolence; or again between sensuous and spiritual love, *eros* and *agape*. But the distinction between lower and higher forms of love which is alone given meaning by experience—that is, which alone has meaning—is not of this character. Benevolence *is* desire for the welfare of others . . . of course it must be a superrationally enlightened, an all-comprehending, never

* Compare Mascall's discussion of impassibility in Chapter Thirteen.

wearying desire for others' good, that is attributed to God. But still desire, so far as that means partial dependence for extent of happiness upon the happiness of others . . . that is, a wish, *capable of being painfully disappointed or happily fulfilled.*[29]

Hartshorne believes that the older view of God's love also implies a purely egoistic human response to God. "You cannot be motivated by consideration of the value you contribute to another, if that other is so constituted that he can receive no value from any source."[30] Religion has always assumed that man can give to God, but classical theism has denied it.

Is not the noblest aspect of religious aspiration the wish to have a cause to serve, some value to enrich by our contributions, which is more satisfying as an object of service than mere men? Men die, the race seems destined to die, taking all our contributions back into the nothingness of blind matter again. Besides we often try to help men and fail, with none perhaps ever to know of our attempt, never any to fully understand and appreciate it— none except mayhap God. But now we are told, directly or in effect, that we can do nothing for God, that he certainly will gain nothing from our actions . . . . The whole point of religion is destroyed.[31]

Hartshorne believes that Jesus is the matchless historical symbol of the panentheistic doctrine. In Jesus our abstract, metaphysical knowledge of God is made concrete and empirical. Hartshorne suggests that

Jesus appears to be the supreme symbol furnished to us by history of the notion of a God genuinely and literally sympathetic (incomparably more literally than any man ever is), receiving into his experience the suffering as well as the joys of the world.[32]

If Jesus is literally divine, as orthodoxy teaches, then the panentheist case must be acknowledged by the theologians.

I can only say that if it is Jesus as literally divine who loves men, really loves them, then my point, so far as I can see, is granted. . . . Instead of simply *adding Jesus to an unreconstructed idea of a non-loving God*, should we not take him as proof that God really *is love*—just that, without equivocation?[33]

Jesus' suffering and love means not that he is like God but that he *is* God, suffering and loving, in that he points to the very reality of God. Jesus' life can also reveal other truths about God and the world. For example, Jesus' suffering with and for men and them with and for him, expresses the social interrelatedness of all life. Jesus' relations with men also reveal the genuine freedom of human response, in that Jesus does not coerce but seeks only to persuade. But, above all, Jesus' suffering love teaches us what God's love really is.

The increased interest in process theology over the past twenty years has been confined very largely to Protestantism. Among those contemporary theologians who are presently seeking to develop a natural theology along the lines set out by Whitehead and Hartshorne are Norman Pittenger,[34] Daniel Day Williams,[35] John B. Cobb, Jr.,[36] and Schubert Ogden.[37] While there is an indication of a growing interest in process thought among contemporary Roman Catholic theologians, this concern appears to have little or no connection with Whitehead and Hartshorne but finds its impetus in the recent, mercurial popularity of Pierre Teilhard de Chardin. Some attention to the thought of this Jesuit scientist-theologian is, therefore, in order.

Père Teilhard was a palaeontologist of distinction who sought to relate the Christian vision of God and the world to a scheme of evolutionary process. In his many books which have appeared since his death in 1955, Teilhard has portrayed the cosmos as constituted by a kind of fundamental energy in the process of development. What we can observe of this process is an evolutionary movement toward greater complexity of energy systems, from elemental particles into atoms and on until we reach complex multicellular organisms. While this process is a continuous, uninterrupted flow, it does reveal three stages or "critical points" in which nature has been marked by profound changes.

In every domain, when anything exceeds a certain measurement, it suddenly changes its aspect, condition, or nature. The curve doubles back, the surface contracts to a point, the solid disintegrates, the liquid boils, the germ cell divides, intuition suddenly bursts on the piled-up facts. Critical points have been reached, rungs on the ladder involving a change of state.[38]

Teilhard relates that the first of these critical thresholds was the emergence of inorganic matter when the earth's crust solidified after a long process of cooling. The second stage was the emergence of life which, after a long process, encircled the earth's surface with a covering or "biosphere." Only five or six hundred thousand years ago did a new phenomenon occur which has radically changed the earth. This was the appearance of mind, or the "noosphere," which involved the critical movement from instinct to thought, the "hominization" of life or emergence of man. Teilhard speaks of this as "a mutation from zero to everything."[39] With man the universe becomes "personalistic." Man is the crown of the present evolutionary process, and his emergence marks a crucial turning point, for henceforth evolution need not proceed blindly but can follow a conscious direction.

This sudden deluge of cerebralization, this biological invasion of a new animal type which gradually eliminates or subjects all forms of life that are not human . . . this immense and growing edifice of matter and ideas . . . seems to proclaim that there has been a change on the earth and a change of planetary magnitude. . . . The greatest revelation open to science today is to perceive that everything precious, active and progressive originally contained in the cosmic fragment from which our world emerged is now concentrated in and crowned by the noosphere.[40]

For Teilhard, the evolutionary pattern has moved inexorably toward man or the noosphere and will in the future exhibit an extension of this process in the direction of a higher consciousness. This is what Teilhard calls "noogenesis," or the growth process of mind or reflective consciousness. He sees human life moving toward greater interpersonal communion which will lead to the emergence of a new level of complexity-consciousness. The first phase of noogenesis involved a kind of centrifugal force which exhibited an increase in individuality and personal freedom but a rather slow advance of socialization. Teilhard sees the next phase as centripetal, constituting greater intercommunion and socialization on a planetary scale. This process of unification lies in the future, but Teilhard believes we can know the general direction of the future as extending along lines similar to the past development of complexity-consciousness. Thus it appears quite certain to Teilhard that the "planetization" of mankind will advance toward a new convergence. Teilhard calls this point of convergence the *Omega*, since it constitutes the end of the evolutionary process. At the Omega-point all things will reach a suprapersonal unity in God in which agape, or self-transcending love, will reign.

It is not entirely clear whether Teilhard considers the Omega-point *as* God or the point at which all things are brought into perfect unity with God. If the former were the case, Teilhard, like Hegel and other process philosophers, would uphold the notion of God's actual growth and dependence on the world. Teilhard's position appears, however, to be more orthodox. The Omega is not only the end point of natural evolution but the divine *Logos* or Word which governs the whole process of cosmic evolution and the power of attraction which drives the process toward its *telos* or end. For example, Teilhard writes:

To satisfy the ultimate requirements of our action, Omega must be independent of the collapse of forces with which evolution is woven. . . . While being the last term of (evolution's) series, it is also outside all series. . . . If by its very nature it did not escape from time and space which it gathers together, it would not be Omega."[41]

Here the Omega is seen by the Christian as given in foretaste in the person of Christ as the divine *Logos* incarnate. For the Christian

in place of the vague focus of convergence demanded as a terminus for evolution, we now have the well-defined personal reality of the Incarnate Word in whom all things hold together.[42]

However, a certain ambiguity remains in Teilhard's view of the terminus of the evolutionary process and God's relation to it. Teilhard believes that there are "rational invitations to an act of faith," that the cosmos is moving toward the Omega point. Still he agrees with other process theologians that the future is open and that the direction of the evolutionary process is not divinely determined but is to a great extent dependent on man himself. He speaks, for instance, of the superpersonal level of consciousness, by which he means the

superior state which humanity appears destined to achieve *if* it succeeds in totalizing itself completely upon itself, body and soul, by pushing to the end the movement of which it is the historical culmination.[43]

In passages such as these Teilhard appears, like Whitehead, to conceive of God as offering to man the attraction and lure of creative advance, but only as a persuasive agency. God and the creatures are interdependent, and the future remains genuinely open.

There are two aspects of process thought that are especially important in our present context. One is the effort on the part of theologians to open up the possibility of a theology which claims a naturalistic starting point and a familiarity with and complete openness toward scientific investigation. The second factor of special significance is the attempt to develop a new natural theology or doctrine of God which takes into account the fact of evolution and process as constitutive of reality. The problems which process thought poses for Chris-

tian theology are many. Basic, of course, is the question of whether the notion of God's temporality and interdependence with the world is actually compatible with Christian belief. Related to this is the question of whether God's persuasion is an adequate conception of how God acts in the world. While process philosophy has advanced our understanding of human freedom and genuine love as involving real relationships of giving and receiving, the problem of evil remains. Some will look with dismay upon the notion that God is impotent to put down evil; that he can only offer the world new possibilities of creativity. That the world can actually impede or ultimately frustrate God's creative will, so that there is real loss and real tragedy not only in the world but in God, is an idea not easily integrated into Christian theism. Nevertheless, there is evidence that process thought is presently looked to by a growing number of Christian thinkers as the only metaphysical scheme within which to develop a viable theology for our scientific age.

The Impact of Vatican II

Among all the events and movements within Christianity in the past few decades, perhaps in this century, the directives set forth by the Second Vatican Council are by far the most significant for the possible future of Christianity. The road taken by the Roman Catholic Church after the Vatican Council of 1870 and the condemnation of Modernism at the beginning of this century had left other Christians, as well as non-Christians, alarmed and totally estranged by Rome's apparent papal monarchism and disdain of those communities and problems outside its own spiritual orbit. The entire modern period has been characterized by tragic distrust and alienation between Protestants and Catholics, based frequently on incredible ignorance, prejudice, and fear.

With the coming of Pope John XXIII to the papal throne, a new era was inaugurated not only within the Roman Catholic Church but also in her relations with other Christians, the non-Christian religious traditions, and the secular world itself. Pope John's short reign (October 1958–June 1963) was marked by such important but controversial encyclicals as *Mater et Magistra* (1961) and *Pacem in Terris* (1963) and the calling of the Second Vatican Council. It is often remarked that with these actions Pope John ushered the Roman Catholic Church into the actual world of the twentieth century.

On January 25, 1959, John XXIII announced his intention to summon an Ecumenical Council of the Church, and on October 11, 1962, the first session of the Second Vatican Council was opened in St. Peter's in Rome. In the following passage, Robert McAfee Brown illustrates symbolically the distance that many consider that the Roman Catholic Church has traveled in less than a century:

The first Vatican Council (1869–1870) ended inside St. Peter's during a fearful thunderstorm, in the midst of which was promulgated the dogma of papal infallibility —the dogma that has most separated Roman Catholicism from the rest of Christendom.

The second Vatican Council (1962–1965) ended outside St. Peter's on a beautifully sunny day, with the Church offering itself as the servant of the world—a theme that will increasingly unite Roman Catholicism not only with the rest of Christendom but with all men of good will.[44]

The concern that was to mark the deliberations of Vatican II was not the definition of new doctrine but *aggiornamento*, or "a bringing up to date." The position taken by all to many of John's predecessors on the papal throne was essentially backward-looking. Not infrequently they viewed the present with pessimism and were prone to compare it most unfavorably with the Christendom of medieval times. The spirit of Pope John's opening speech to the Council was pitched in a very different key. It radiated a hopeful, even joyful optimism about the future, much in the spirit of Teilhard de Chardin.

In the daily exercise of our pastoral office, we sometimes have to listen, much to our regret, to voices of persons who, though burning with zeal . . . say that our era, in comparison with past eras, is getting worse. . . . We feel we must disagree with those prophets of gloom, who are always forecasting disaster, as though the end of the world was at hand. . . . Divine Providence is leading us to a new order of human relations which by men's own efforts, even beyond their very expectations, are directed towards the fulfillment of God's superior and inscrutable design. Everything, even human differences, leads to the greater good of the Church.[45]

Most Catholics, excluding the archconservatives, see the decisions of Vatican II as only a pointer and beginning of the *aggiornamento*. Vatican II is viewed as the sign suggesting the direction of renewal of the Church and its relation to the modern world. Thus, while the Council itself represents a new "breakthrough," its real achievements will depend on whether its decisions are put into effect in the actual day-to-day life of the Church —whether, that is, the Council is seen as a terminus or as only a new beginning.

What kind of decisions were made at the Council, and what is their status and eventual effect? The distinction to be drawn between the constitutions, decrees, and declarations issued by the Council fathers is not entirely clear, but is apparently not to be taken too precisely. All of the documents published by the Council were determined by conciliar decision and received papal approval. Sixteen documents were finally accepted. Not all of these are of equal importance to the future life of the Church, but several do represent crucial new directions. Chief among these is the *Dogmatic Constitution on the Church* ("Lumen Gentium"). Here is set forth a new ecclesiology markedly different from the image of the Church which had dominated Roman theology since the Council of Trent in the sixteenth century. The older, Tridentine conception of the Church stressed the perfection and indefectibility of the Church, its visible, militant, and monarchical character. The image of the Church in "Lumen Gentium" is very different. Here the emphasis is placed on the ancient image of the Church as the *people of God*, rather than on ecclesiastical hierarchy and authority. The Church's spiritual and invisible character is stressed, rather than its visible and governmental structure. Most important, the role of the laity is given a central place.

Of special significance for dogmatic theology and ecumenical relations is Chapter 3 on the hierarchical organization of the Church. As we noted in Chapter Ten, Vatican I spoke only of the authority of the papacy—although this was not its original intention. The new Constitution on the Church, passed by a vote of 2151 to 5 on November 21, 1964, sought to balance the action of Vatican I, whose deliberations were halted by political events. This corrective is affirmed in the doctrine of the "collegiality of the bishops." The text of Chapter 3 reads:

The order of bishops is the successor to the college of the apostles in teaching authority and pastoral rule; or, rather, in the episcopal order the apostolic body continues without a break. *Together with its head, the Roman Pontiff, and never without this head, the episcopal order is the subject of supreme and full power over the universal Church. . . . The supreme authority with which this college is empowered over the whole Church is exercised in a solemn way through an ecumenical council.* A council is never ecumenical unless it is confirmed or at least accepted as such by the successor of Peter. It is the prerogative of the Roman Pontiff to convoke these councils, to preside over them, and to confirm them. *The same collegiate power can be exercised in union with the Pope by the bishops, living in all parts of the world, provided that the head of the College calls them to collegiate action, or at least so approves or freely accepts the unified action of the dispersed bishops,* that it is made a true collegiate act.[46] (Italics added.)

While the text affirms the special prerogatives of the Roman Pontiff, it nevertheless stresses the supreme power of the college of bishops meeting in ecumenical council. The Pope and other bishops together constitute the episcopal authority of the Church. While this represents a public declaration of a long-muted teaching of the Church, in no way does it diminish the Church's earlier declaration of papal power. This is made clear in an explanatory note appended to the Constitution which affirms that the Council does not recognize an *equality* between the head and the members of the college of bishops and that "the Sovereign Pontiff can always exercise his authority as he chooses." Also, the college of bishops, while always existent, does not for that reason permanently operate through *strictly* collegial action. . . . In other words, it is not always "in full act"; indeed, it operates through collegial actions only at intervals and only *with the consent of its head.*[47]

It is apparent that very different emphases can be placed on certain statements from the text on collegiality. However, what is also certain is that the Council affirmed the bishops' collegiality but not that of the Pope. While this might appear to change very little, it marks the possibility of a decided shift in the modern Roman Catholic doctrine of authority. As the progressive theologian Edward Schillebeeckx, O.P., has remarked:

> If, in spite of everything, the affirmation of papal collegiality had been won from a minority, the pope would have been placed in a position, after the Council, where he was compelled to give constant proof to the minority that papal primacy has in no way suffered from the new definition. Now on the contrary, his position is that he must constantly prove that his papal authority does not harm the bishops' collegiality.[48]

The collegiality of bishops is a theological fact, accepted by the Church. Whether it actually becomes a reality in the governance of the Church depends largely on the actions of the present and future Popes. The active implementation of collegiality would involve a genuine reformation of the church and open the way for a deepening ecumenical dialogue with other Christian churches.

Another proclamation of the Council which marks an important shift from the post-Tridentine theology is the *Constitution on Divine Revelation* ("Dei Verbum"). Since the Council of Trent, the Roman Catholic Church has generally taught that there are two separate and distinct sources of divine revelation: Scripture and tradition. It was in line with this convention that the conservative preparatory commission produced its Council report, *De Fontibus Revelationis*, upholding the two-sources doctrine. In addition, this first draft, in the spirit of the anti-Modernist struggle, was negative, scholastic, and lacking in an awareness and use of modern biblical scholarship and theology. The final draft which was passed by 2,344 votes to 6, reversed all of this, including the long-standing two-sources doctrine. In its place the Council affirmed that there are not two but only one source of revelation, viz., God. God's revelation is his Word to man in Christ. The transmission of this Word is through preaching and the written Scriptures as interpreted by the Church. While there are not two sources of revelation, nevertheless, the primitive kerygma and written Bible cannot stand alone without the Church's guidance and interpretation, i.e., tradition. As the text states it:

> Sacred tradition and sacred Scripture form one sacred deposit of the word of God, which is committed to the Church. . . . The task of authentically interpreting the word of God, whether written or handed on, has been entrusted exclusively to the living teaching office of the Church, whose authority is exercised in the name of Jesus Christ. This teaching office is not above the word of God, but serves it, teaching only what has been handed on, listening to it devoutly, guarding it scrupulously and explaining it faithfully by divine commission and with the help of the Holy Spirit. . . . It is clear, therefore, that sacred tradition, sacred Scripture, and the teaching authority of the Church . . . are so linked and joined together that one cannot stand without the others. . . .[49]

While the position taken here leaves many problems unresolved for the Protestant, it does, nevertheless, break with the two-sources theory and recognizes (as many Protestants do not) the integral and necessary relationship between the Word of God, the written Scriptures, and the teaching office and authority of the Church. In this it opens up new possibilities of overcoming a major obstacle in a Catholic-Protestant *rapprochement*. It is now up to the Protestants to move beyond their uncritical notion of *sola Scriptura*.

"Dei Verbum" not only broke with the notion of Scripture *and* tradition as independent sources of revelation but positively affirmed the centrality of the Bible in the life and preaching of the Church. It speaks of the study of Scripture as "the soul of sacred theology" and calls for the Church "to move ahead daily toward a deeper understanding of the sacred Scriptures" and for "the sons of the Church who are biblical scholars to continue energetically with the work they have so well begun." Finally, it reminds the Church that "this sacred Synod earnestly and specifically urges all the Christian faithful . . . to learn by frequent reading of the divine Scriptures the 'excelling knowledge of Jesus Christ' (Phil. 3:8)."[50]

For many persons the most revolutionary breakthrough occasioned by Pope John and Vatican II is in the area of ecumenical relations. The new spirit of ecumenism was signaled by Pope John on January 30, 1959, when he said:

We do not intend to set up a tribunal to judge the past. We do not want to prove who was right and who was wrong. Responsibility was divided. All we want to say is: "Let us come together. Let us make an end to our divisions."[51]

This call found its response in the Council's "Decree on Ecumenism." Of paramount significance is the fact that in this decree the Council recognized, for the first time since the Reformation, that the non-Roman Catholic Christian communities are also *churches* or ecclesial communities. What this means is that non-Roman communions are viewed as having genuine ecclesial marks and significance. The ecumenical faith is thus not only constituted by the Roman Church and individual believers separated from Rome but also by those identified "as members of the corporate groups in which they have heard the gospel, and which each regards as his Church and, indeed, God's."[52]

The first chapter of the decree affirms that the Roman Church not only looks with "respect and affection" upon separated brethren but acknowledges that such men

who believe in Christ and have been properly baptized are brought into a certain, though imperfect, communion with the Catholic Church. . . .

Moreover some, even very many, of the most significant elements or endowments which together go to build up and give life to the Church herself can exist outside the visible boundaries of the Catholic Church: the written word of God; the life of grace; faith, hope and charity, along with other interior gifts of the Holy Spirit and visible elements. . . .

The degree goes on to affirm:

The brethren divided from us also carry out many of the sacred actions of the Christian religion. Undoubtedly, in ways that vary according to the condition of each Church or

Community, these actions can truly engender a life of grace, and can be rightly described as capable of providing access to the community of salvation.[53]

What this means is that Catholic ecumenism is no longer predicated on the notion of a wholesale "return" of the separated churches but now sees genuine gifts within these communions which can "contribute to an even more perfect penetration of the mystery of Christ and of the Church." Edward Schillebeeckx, O.P. writes:

Without abandoning her religious conviction that Christ's Church as the apostolic fullness is essential for salvation, the Roman Catholic Church in this Council has officially given up her monopoly of the Christian religion or of Christianity.[54]

In the long run the passage in the "Decree on Ecumenism" which may prove to be of greatest importance is that concerning the recognition of a "hierarchy of truths." The decree advises Catholic theologians engaged in ecumenical dialogue to remember "that in Catholic teaching, there exists an order or 'hierarchy' of truths, since they vary in their relationship to the foundation of the Christian faith."[55] For a long time Protestants have been convinced, and not without warrant,* that all Catholic doctrines were on the same level of theological significance. The "Decree on Ecumenism" appears to officially reject such an assumption. If this is true, the way is indeed opened for theological dialogue with other Christians.

* Pope Pius XII, for example, stated in 1950, at the time of the promulgation of the bull on the Assumption of the Virgin, that one who denies the dogma "has cut himself off entirely from the divine and Catholic faith."

Closely related to the new ecumenism is the radically new turn of the Roman Catholic Church on such matters as the Church's relations with non-Christian religions and religious freedom. The "Declaration on the Non-Christian Religions" is marked by two very noteworthy advances in the Roman Catholic attitude toward other religious traditions. First of all, the declaration states positively the Church's recognition of the common religious experiences and problems which all faiths share in terms of their co-humanity. Secondly, the Church repudiates anti-Semitism and the representation of the Jews as deicides, declaring that "what happened in His (Christ's) passion cannot be blamed upon all the Jews then living, without distinction, nor upon the Jews of today."[56]

The "Declaration on Religious Liberty" reflects a similar new attitude toward those outside the Roman communion. John XXIII had prepared the way for the Council declaration in *Pacem in Terris*. There he had stated:

Every human being has the right to honor God according to the dictates of an upright conscience and therefore the right to worship God privately and publicly.[57]

The Church had long recognized the rights of individual conscience but had not given its approval of the free, *public* expression of religious doctrine or practice thought dangerous or contrary to Catholic teaching. With *Pacem in Terris* and Vatican II, religious liberty is now affirmed in the Roman Catholic Church, assuring immunity from coercion and the positive freedom of public worship and expression. In declaring that "truth cannot impose itself except by virtue of its own truth," the Vatican fathers place themselves in the tradition of toleration espoused by the likes of Pierre Bayle and John Locke at the beginning of our modern era.

The whole spirit of *aggiornamento*, which is manifest in the documents selected for discussion, is epitomized in the "Pastoral Constitution on the Church in the World Today," debated and passed at the last session of the Council in December, 1965. The Constitution breaks radically with what is now disparagingly called the "syllabus mentality" of Rome and focuses on the positive advances of human culture. "The triumphs of the human race," reads the document, "are a sign of God's greatness and the flowering of his mysterious design."[58] The Church is called to acknowledge the legitimate autonomy of human affairs and to throw itself into its "earthly mission" of building the earthly city. In words similar to those used by the proponents of a "secular Christianity," the Constitution declares that the duty of Christians

in no way decreases, but rather increases, the weight of their obligation to work with all men in constructing a more human world. . . . For when, by the work of his hands or with the aid of technology, man develops the earth so that it can bear fruit and become a dwelling worthy of the whole human family, and when he consciously takes part in the life of social groups, he carries out the design of God.[59]

The Second Vatican Council calls for nothing less than a new beginning for the Church. The Council's decisions will, of course, be only what the Church makes of them. But it appears clear that the Council has laid to rest the image of the aloof and triumphal Church of the Counter Reformation. The new Church is an open Church, a Church with the courage to change. Reflecting on the future of Christianity in the postconciliar period, Karl Rahner, one of the architects of Catholic renewal, expresses the sentiments of the faithful and most hopeful Christians not only of the present but in every age:

The Church is always in the flux of history, not on the motionless bank, but in this movement God's eternity is present with it, his life, his truth, his fidelity. Consequently the Church has less reason than any other historical reality to fear its historical character. For the current of history does not carry it to the shore of death but to eternal life. The Church can and must, therefore, have the courage to change by adapting the eternal which it possesses ever anew and more and more to its needs.

Consequently, the individual Christian himself must bear the courage and patience of the Church. . . . He will make the experience that what endures is alive, and the ultimate depth of what is changing is the eternal, that what endures has the strength to change. The Church is something enduring of just that kind. We grasp what is enduring in it if we trust to the changes which its own Spirit gives to the Church throughout history by leading it more and more into all truth and into the plentitude of God's life.[60]

NOTES

1. Langdon Gilkey, "Dissolution and Reconstruction in Theology," *Christian Century*, February 3, 1965.

2. On the cultural and theological background of contemporary radical theology, consult the excellent discussion by

Langdon Gilkey, *Naming the Whirlwind: The Renewal of God-Language* (Indianapolis, 1969).

3. For the development of this theme, see Friedrich Gogarten, *Demythologizing and History* (New York, 1955); Arend van Leeuwen, *Christianity in World History* (New York, 1965); and Harvey Cox, *The Secular City* (New York, 1965).

4. Friedrich Gogarten, op. cit., p. 19.

5. Ibid., p. 26.

6. Harvey Cox, op. cit., pp. 63, 72.

7. Dietrich Bonhoeffer, *Prisoner of God* (New York, 1954), pp. 122–123.

8. Ibid., pp. 123 ff.

9. Ibid., p. 124.

10. Ibid., p. 163 f.

11. Ibid., p. 179.

12. Ibid., p. 180 f.

13. Author of *The Death of God* (1961), *Wait Without Idols* (1964), and *No Other God* (1966).

14. Author of *Honest to God* (1963) and *The New Reformation* (1965).

15. Author of *Mircea Eliade and the Dialectic of the Sacred* (1963), *The Gospel of Christian Atheism*, and, with William Hamilton, *Radical Theology and the Death of God* (1966).

16. Author of *The New Essence of Christianity* (1961) and *Radical Theology and the Death of God* (1966).

17. Author of *The Secular Meaning of the Gospel* (1963) and *Theological Explorations* (1968).

18. Schubert Ogden, "The Christian Proclamation of God to Men of the So-called Atheistic Age" (*Concilium*, June, 1966).

19. Author of *Introduction to Metaphysics* (E.T., 1913), *Matter and Memory* (E.T., 1911), and *Creative Evolution* (E.T., 1911).

20. Author of *Religion in the Making* (1926), *Process and Reality* (1927), *Science and the Modern World* (1926), and *Adventures of Ideas* (1933).

21. Author of *The Divine Relativity* (1948), *Reality As Social Process* (1953), *The Logic of Perfection* (1962), and *A Natural Theology for Our Time* (1967).

22. Author of *The Phenomenon of Man* (E.T., 1959), *The Divine Milieu* (E.T., 1960), *The Future of Man* (E.T., 1964).

23. The following discussion of Whiteheadian metaphysics will, of necessity, be a mere sketch and will not develop the complexities or problematics of the scheme. For a helpful guide to Whitehead's process philosophy, see I. Leclerc, *Whitehead's Metaphysics* (New York, 1958) and D. W. Sherburne, *A Key to Whitehead's "Process and Reality,"* (New York, 1966).

24. A. N. Whitehead, *Process and Reality* (New York, 1929), pp. 523–524.

25. Ibid., p. 520.

26. Charles Hartshorne, *Man's Vision of God* (Chicago, 1941), pp. 11–12.

27. Charles Hartshorne, *The Divine Relativity* (New Haven, 1964), p. 138.

28. Charles Hartshorne, *Man's Vision of God*, p. 115.

29. Ibid., p. 116.

30. Ibid., p. 117.

31. Ibid.

32. Charles Hartshorne, *Reality as Social Process* (Boston, 1953), p. 24.

33. Charles Hartshorne, *Man's Vision of God*, p. 165.

34. See his *The Word Incarnate* (1959) and *Process-Thought and Christian Faith* (1968).

35. See *The Spirit and Forms of Love* (1968).

36. See *A Christian Natural Theology* (1965).

37. See *The Reality of God* (1966).

38. Pierre Teilhard de Chardin, *The Phenomenon of Man* (New York, 1965), p. 78.

39. Ibid., p. 171.

40. Ibid., pp. 183–184.

41. Ibid., pp. 270–271.

42. Pierre Teilhard de Chardin, *The Future of Man* (New York, 1964), p. 34.

43. Pierre Teilhard de Chardin, *Oeuvres* VI (Paris, 1962), p. 50; cited in Christopher F. Mooney, *Teilhard de Chardin and the Mystery of Christ* (New York, 1968).

44. Robert McAfee Brown, *The Ecumenical Revolution* (New York, 1967), p. 155.

45. John XXIII, in Walter M. Abbott, S.J., ed., *The Documents of Vatican II* (New York, 1967), pp. 712–713.

46. "Dogmatic Constitution on the Church," III, 22; in W. M. Abbott, S.J., op. cit., pp. 43–44.
47. Ibid., p. 100.
48. E. Schillebeeckx, O.P., *Vatican II: The Real Achievement* (London, 1967), p. 18.
49. "Dogmatic Constitution on Divine Revelation," II, 10; in W. M. Abbott, S.J., op. cit., pp. 117–118.
50. Ibid., VI, 23–25; Abbott, pp. 126–127.
51. Cited in Adrian Hastings, *A Concise Guide to the Documents of the Second Vatican Council*, I (London, 1968), p. 180.
52. "Decree on Ecumenism," Introduction; in W. M. Abbott, S.J., op. cit., p. 342.
53. Ibid., I, 2; Abbott, p. 345–346.
54. Schillebeeckx, op. cit., pp. 66–67.
55. "Decree on Ecumenism," II, 11; Abbott, op. cit., p. 354.
56. "Declaration on the Relationship of the Church to Non-Christian Religions," 4; in W. M. Abbott, S.J., op. cit., p. 666.
57. *Pacem in Terris*, par. 14.
58. "Pastoral Constitution on the Church in the World Today," 34; in W. M. Abbott, S.J., op. cit., p. 232.
59. Ibid., 57; Abbott, p. 262.
60. Karl Rahner, *The Christian of the Future* (London, 1967), pp. 35–38.

SUGGESTIONS FOR FURTHER READING

DIETRICH BONHOEFFER

Bethge, Eberhard. *Dietrich Bonhoeffer* (New York: Harper and Row, 1970). The standard biography of Bonhoeffer.

Bosanquet, Mary. *The Life and Death of Dietrich Bonhoeffer* (New York: Harper and Row, 1968).

Godsey, John D. *The Theology of Dietrich Bonhoeffer* (Philadelphia: Westminster Press, 1960). An extensive précis of the major themes of Bonhoeffer's theology integrated into an account of his life.

Marty, Martin E., ed. *The Place of Bonhoeffer* (New York: Association Press, 1962). An important collection of essays on the problems and possibilities of Bonhoeffer's theology from a variety of perspectives.

Phillips, John A. "*Christ for Us*," in the *Theology of Dietrich Bonhoeffer* (New York: Harper and Row, 1967). An important study which focuses on the centrality of Christology in Bonhoeffer's theology.

For excellent bibliographies on the vast Bonhoeffer literature, see John Deschner, "Bonhoeffer Studies in English," *The Perkins School of Theology Journal*, Spring, 1969, and Peter Vorkink II, ed., *Bonhoeffer in a World Come of Age* (Philadelphia: Fortress Press, 1968), pp. 133–140.

THE RADICAL AND SECULAR MOVEMENTS IN THEOLOGY

Altizer, Thomas J. J. and Hamilton, William. *Radical Theology and the Death of God* (Indianapolis: Bobbs Merrill Co., 1966). Essays by Altizer and Hamilton and an excellent bibliography of background materials.

Gilkey, Langdon. *Naming the Whirlwind: The Renewal of God-Language* (Indianapolis: Bobbs Merrill Co., 1969). Part I of this book is an excellent study of the background and analysis and critique of the new secular theology.

Ogletree, Thomas W. *The Death of God Controversy* (Nashville: Abingdon Press, 1966). A lucid, brief analysis and critique of the work of Altizer, Hamilton, and Van Buren. Includes a good bibliography of books and journal literature.

Smith, Ronald Gregor, *Secular Christianity* (New York: Harper and Row, 1966). Smith's view of secular Christianity has more affinity with the radical historicity of Gogarten, Bultmann, and Bonhoeffer.

PROCESS THOUGHT

Alfred North Whitehead

Leclerc, Ivor. *Whitehead's Metaphysics* (New York: The Macmillan Co., 1958).

Sherburne, D. W. *A Key to Whitehead's "Process and Reality"* (New York: The Macmillan Co., 1966).

Charles Hartshorne

James, Ralph E. *The Concrete God: A New Beginning for Theology—The Thought of Charles Hartshorne* (Indianapolis: The Bobbs Merrill Co., 1967).

Peters, Eugene H. *The Creative Advance: An Introduction to Process Philosophy as a Context for Christian Faith* (St. Louis: The Bethany Press, 1966). See especially Chaps. VI and VII.

Pierre Teilhard de Chardin

de Lubac, Henri. *The Religion of Teilhard de Chardin* (New York: Doubleday, Image Book, 1968).

Mooney, Christopher F. *Teilhard de Chardin and the Mystery of Christ* (New York: Doubleday, Image Book, 1968).

Wildiers, N. M. *An Introduction to Teilhard de Chardin* (London: Collins, 1968).

Some Contemporary Efforts to Employ Process Thought in Theology

Cobb, John B., Jr. *A Christian Natural Theology* (Philadelphia: The Westminster Press, 1965).

Hamilton, P. N. *The Living God and the Modern World* (Philadelphia: The United Church Press, 1968).

Ogden, Schubert. *The Reality of God* (New York: Harper and Row, 1966).

Pittenger, W. Norman. *The Word Incarnate* (New York: Harper and Row, 1959).

———. *Process Thought and Christian Faith* (New York: The Macmillan Co., 1968).

Williams, D. D. *The Spirit and Forms of Love* (New York: Harper and Row, 1968).

THE SECOND VATICAN COUNCIL

Commentaries

Abbott, Walter M., S.J., ed. *The Documents of Vatican II* (New York: Herder and Herder and Association Press, 1966).

Hastings, Adrian. *A Concise Guide to the Documents of the Second Vatican Council*, 2 vols (London, Darton, Longman and Todd, 1968).

Interpretations and Appraisals

Rynne, Xavier. *Letters from Vatican City* (1963), *The Second Session* (1964), *The Third Session* (1965), *The Fourth Session* (1966) (New York: Farrar, Straus and Giroux, 1963–66). These pseudonomous volumes constitute the fullest and most important Roman Catholic account and interpretation to date.

Lindbeck, George A., ed. *Dialogue on the Way* (Minneapolis: Augsburg Publishing House, 1965).

———. *The Future of Roman Catholic Theology* (Philadelphia: Fortress Press, 1970).

Quanbeck, W. A., ed. *Challenge and Response* (Minneapolis: Augsburg Publishing House, 1966).

These three books are among the best theological assessments of Vatican II by Protestant scholars.

Miller, John H., C.S.C., ed. *Vatican II: An Interfaith Appraisal* (New York and South Bend: Association Press and University of Notre Dame Press, 1966). Appraisals of all aspects of the Council by world-renowned theologians.

Contemporary Catholic Theology

For a sampling of contemporary progressive Roman Catholic theology, the following are recommended:

Küng, Hans. *The Council, Reform and Reunion* (New York: Sheed and Ward, 1961).

———. *The Church* (New York: Sheed and Ward, 1968).

———. *Truthfulness: The Future of the Church* (New York: Sheed and Ward, 1968).

Metz, Johannes B. *Theology of the World* (New York: Herder and Herder, 1969).

Rahner, Karl. *Theological Investigations*, 6 vols. (Baltimore: Helicon Press, 1961–).

Schillebeeckx, Edward. *Revelation and Theology*, 2 vols. (New York: Sheed and Ward, 1967).

———. *God: The Future of Man* (New York: Sheed and Ward, 1968).

Epilogue

In 1875 Matthew Arnold wrote: "At the present moment two things about the Christian religion must surely be clear to anybody with eyes in his head. One is that men cannot do without it; the other, that they cannot do with it as it is." Arnold's observation about the status of Christianity in late Victorian England could appropriately be extended to characterize the whole of our modern epoch. Modern Western culture has been marked by exactly this kind of ambivalence toward the Christian faith. This tension, with its attendant challenges and responses, has been one of the major themes of this book.

For the past three hundred years, despite a continuous and growing secularizing trend, Christianity has shown remarkable resilience and creativity. It has fallen upon dark days of defeat and of abject capitulation to secularism, but such periods have been countered with vigorous theological responses which have refused merely to close ranks and hold fast to ancient positions.

We are frequently told that we are fast moving into a post-Modern, even post-Christian period, marked by an increasingly secularist or "sensate" way of life. What distinguishes us from Arnold's late Victorians, as well as most moderns until fairly recently, is that while we cannot do with Christianity as it is, greater numbers find it quite possible to do without it entirely. Our present post-Modern ethos reflects a newly emerging consciousness, characterized by a sense of pluralism and relativism, which is

fundamentally non-ideological and pragmatic, and by a rather romantic hedonism.

Whether the new consciousness is post-Christian is a moot point. What is certain is that the older, modern Christian theology and apologetic, which we have traced to the beginnings of our Modern era, do not strike the newer consciousness with any sense of authenticity or relevance. The older metaphysical and historical questions which engaged Christian thought from the Enlightenment until very recently appear to the post-Modern mind as pseudo-problems. Whether or how long this will continue is impossible to foretell. There is reason to believe that theological work in the near future may be unrecognizable when compared to the models and languages of Classical and Modern theology.

There will be those who will shrink back in horror at these bold new efforts and will seek refuge in a repetition of the past. Others, in their anxiety, will stridently dismiss the past and uncritically "baptize" every novel perspective that the purveyors of popular culture can promote. It is to be hoped that there will be those who will neither repeat the past nor embrace every new cultural fad but who will meet the creative uncertainties of their time with courage and the nonchalance of faith.

Christianity is not a metaphysics; nor is it tied to any world-view or cultural pattern. Christianity is a community of faith and a way of life in search of a metaphysics or coherent philosophical perspective. That search has involved Christian thinkers in a continuous dialogue with secular culture, involving ever new reconceptions of the form and symbols of Christian faith and vision. That dynamic process of reconception will continue, perhaps at a terrifying and confusing pace. How future Christians respond to this process will depend on whether or not they see the movements of history into an uncertain future as a sign of promise and hope.

As Karl Rahner has written, the Christian community has less reason to fear the flux of history than any other community, for Christians believe that the ultimate depth of all that changes is the eternal and that what is enduring has the strength to change to meet new conditions. To live by that faith is to live in confidence that radical secularization itself can become the occasion of unexpected revelations of transcendence and divine grace.

INDEX

Only those works are cited which are quoted or discussed significantly in the text.